WILLIAM NEISH
GEORGE KAHWATI

WWW.MHHE.COM/AU/MYOB19

14TH EDITION

COMPUTER ACCOUNTING USING

MYOB

BUSINESS
SOFTWARE

VERSION 19.10

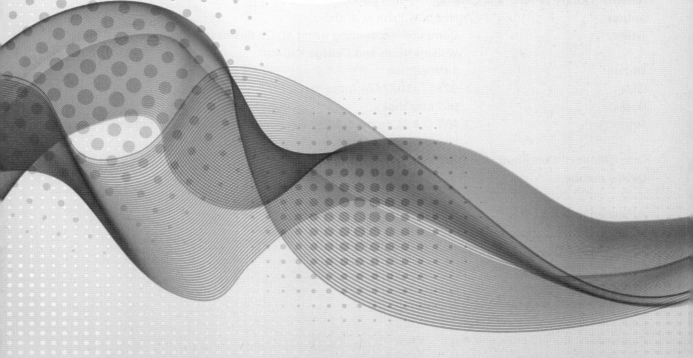

Mc
Graw
Hill
Education

MYOB ACCOUNTRIGHT PLUS v19.10
MYOB ACCOUNTRIGHT ENTERPRISE v19.10
MYOB ACCOUNTEDGE v13

MYOB
Publishing Partner

Reprinted 2015, 2017

Screen captures from MYOB accounting software reproduced with permission. Every effort has been made to trace and acknowledge copyrighted material. The authors and publishers tender their apologies should any infringement have occurred.

National Library of Australia Cataloguing-in-Publication Data

Author:	Neish, William J., author
Title:	Computer accounting using MYOB business software version 19.10/ William Neish and George Kahwati.
Edition:	14th edition
ISBN:	9781743077474 (paperback)
Notes:	Includes index.
Subjects:	M.Y.O.B. (Computer file)—Accounting—Computer programs—Handbooks, manuals, etc.
Other Authors/Contributors:	Kahwati, George, author.
Dewey number:	657.0285536

Published in Australia by

McGraw-Hill Education (Australia) Pty Ltd

Level 33, 680 George Street, Sydney NSW 2000

Publisher: Norma Angeloni Tomaras

Product developer: Alex Payne

Editorial coordinator: Genevieve MacDermott

Cover design: Dominic Giustarini

Proofreader: Ronald Buck and Anne Savage

Indexer: Helen Kahwati

DVD preparation: William Neish

Printed in China on 80 gsm matt art by 1010 Printing International Ltd

Contents

Acknowledgments

The authors wish to acknowledge the input from students and teachers at many colleges and universities. The list of contributors is now so long that we cannot print all of the individual names. The feedback from users, both criticism and praise, is highly appreciated. Changes to the current edition are due mainly to the excellent suggestions for making the book more user friendly. We hope that it will continue. All errors of commission and omission remain our sole responsibility.

The staff at McGraw-Hill Education (Australia) Pty Ltd deserve commendation for their vision in accepting and producing a book using a specific accounting package. Special thanks to Norma Angeloni Tomaras and Alex Payne for their continued professional and friendly support.

We would like to give a very special thanks to Helen Kahwati for her assistance in testing the data files, and for her welcome advice on changes to the text.

Finally, a very special mention to those who over the years have forfeited much family time because of the authors' involvement in this project. Special thanks to Helen, Mary Ann and Susie Kahwati, and to Helen Neish.

Bill Neish

George Kahwati

Preface

The accounting package *MYOB Accounting Plus* makes bookkeeping easy! First-time users of an accounting package vary, from people with little or no accounting knowledge to qualified accountants. This book should prove useful to all levels of users.

All new concepts are introduced in the same structured way. A generic "How to ..." instruction list is followed by a specific example using *MYOB Accounting Plus* files, which are supplied on disk. Most examples are then followed by an on-screen video demonstrating the actions for the example. A self-test exercise follows immediately, and answers to these self-test exercises are included at the end of each chapter. The unique "How to ..." index at the front of the book and the corresponding instruction lists are invaluable to both users and students alike.

For providers of accredited courses, assessment material is provided at the end of each chapter. Some assessment material is cumulative to allow for module integration and re-enforcement of material covered in previous chapters. Lecturers and trainers will have access to additional solutions and figures at www.mhhe.com/au/myob19.

Notes for the 14th edition

The fourteenth edition is written for *MYOB AccountRight Plus v19.10*. The *AssetManager* program is no longer supported by MYOB and references to this program have been removed from the book. The files for *MYOB AccountRight Plus v19.*10 can also be used with *MYOB AccountRight Enterprise v19.10*. Files for Apple MacIntosh users of *MYOB AccountEdge Prov13* are also included on the DVD and can be used with this text.

A DVD containing student editions of MYOB software is included with the book. The DVD contains a menu program allowing the user to download the demonstration and assessment data files and to run the videos using a Windows PC.

> **If you encounter difficulties with the software for *MYOB AccountRight Plus v19.10*, *MYOB AccountEdge Pro v13*, *MYOB AccountRight Enterprise* (or *Premier*) *v19.10*, you will need to contact the suppliers of the software (http://www.myob.com.au). McGraw-Hill Education (Australia) Pty Ltd will not be able to answer queries on the software. If there are any problems with the data files supplied with this book, please contact McGraw-Hill Education (Australia) Pty Ltd.**

How to ... index by chapter

How to ... index by function

Accounts – maintenance and display:

Transactions:

***NOTE**: Chapters 10 and 11 are located on the accompanying DVD and can be viewed through the DVD menu.*

Installation of files from the DVD

To complete exercises and assessments in this book you will need two things:

1. Access to the MYOB Program version 19.10:
   Either *AccountRight Plus* or *AccountRight Enterprise*; *and*
2. The data files.

Student editions (test drives) for *MYOB AccountRight Plus*, *MYOB AccountRight Enterprise* and *MYOB AccountEdge Pro* are included on the DVD packaged with this textbook. You will need to install these programs on your hard drive (if not already installed) and copy the data files from the DVD to your hard drive or USB before you can use them.

If the DVD starts to run automatically on a Windows PC

The DVD contains an "AutorunPro" command and should start automatically when you put the DVD in the drive of a Windows PC. (Apple MacIntosh systems cannot run the "Autorun Pro" Windows program and Mac users should look at page xxiv later for using the files on the DVD.)

Make a selection by clicking on any of the eight options.

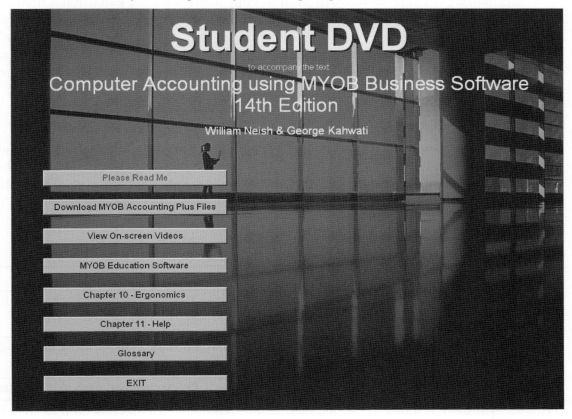

If the DVD does not run automatically or manually

If the DVD does not automatically or manually display the above menu, you will need to use the following instructions.

If your DVD fails to start – you can start the above menu manually

If the menu does not start, wait for about 30 seconds, then eject the DVD and insert it again. Usually that solves the problem. However, you can also *manually* start the menu by double clicking on the *application* file "MYOB_CD" or "MYOB_CD.exe", which is located on your DVD (usually drive **D:**). You can access the DVD drive through the *My Computer* or *Computer* button on your desktop, or on the *Start* menu.

Copying the data files – Windows PC

It is worth remembering that the DVD supplied with this textbook is a READ-ONLY DVD. Basically, that means: *All the files on the DVD are read-only. MYOB data files cannot be opened if they are read-only.* Therefore, you need to copy the files <u>first</u> to your hard drive or onto removable disks (e.g. USB flash disks).

Once you copy a file, you need to check and, if necessary, change the *read only* attributes. You will then be able to use it and save your work to it. All required data files are on the DVD (except for those that are required to be created by the user). These files end with the extensions ".myo", ".box" or ".qif". For a *MYOB AccountRight* exercise you will need to copy a file with the extension ".myo". When you open the file for the first time the program will create (if it does not already exist) an accompanying file with the same name, but with the extension ".box". For example, for the first demonstration exercise in Chapter 1, the instructions will require the use of a file called "dem11.myo". To copy the file manually you will need to copy the file "dem11.myo", which is located on the DVD, to your nominated disk. Once you open the file, *MYOB AccountRight* will create a secondary file called "dem11.box".

The data files for a Windows PC are located on the DVD in a folder called "Student Files – Windows". You can copy the data files from the DVD to your hard drive. The next step is to cancel the "read-only" attribute on these copied files in order to use them.

How to cancel the read-only attribute on a data file – Windows PC

Step	Instruction
1	Open ***My Computer***, ***Computer*** or ***Windows Explorer*** and locate the data files on your disk (but **not** on the DVD drive).
2	Highlight the data file or files (to select all data files, click on the ***Edit*** pull-down menu and click on the ***Select All*** option).
3	Click on the ***File*** pull-down menu and select ***Properties*** (or press Alt + Enter).
4	If there is a tick in the box next to the "read-only" field, click on it to clear it (not ticked).
5	Click ***OK***.

Installing the Test Drive programs

▶**Important**: You **only** need to do the following if your DVD <u>does not start</u> (automatically or manually) and does not display the menu.

How to install a test drive program on your hard disk – Windows PC

Step	Instruction
1	Place the DVD that came with the textbook in the computer.
2	Double click on *My Computer* on the computer desktop and double click on the DVD drive (usually D:) to open it.
3	Double click on the folder called "**MYOBED**" to open it.
4	Double click on the appropriate file to start installation. Follow the instructions to install. **For this MYOB software:** **Double click this file:** *AccountRight Plus* "MYOB_AccountRight_Plus_v19.10_ED" *AccountRight Enterprise* "MYOB_AccountRight_Enterprise_v19.10_ED"

 Videos on the DVD

You should use the menu on the DVD to run the videos on a Windows PC (preferred option). However, if you have a problem starting the menu or you are using an Apple MacIntosh computer you can follow these steps:

1) Access the DVD as demonstrated earlier above.
2) Change to the folder called "**Videos**".
3) There are two types of files "*.swf" and "*.htm" – you can use either type.
4) Check the name of the file to find the required video. The first part of the name refers to the chapter number (for example "1-01 OpenMyobFile.swf" refers to a video from Chapter 1 on opening MYOB files). Common videos (not specific to a particular chapter) have no chapter number (e.g. Backup.htm) is a general video on creating (and restoring) MYOB backup files.
5) Double click on the selected file to view the video.

Note for users of
MYOB Premier and *Enterprise*

Although the references to data files in this book are for *MYOB AccountRight Plus* business software, you can start and use *MYOB AccountRight Premier* or *MYOB AccountRight Enterprise* instead to complete all the examples and exercises.

MYOB AccountRight Enterprise (or *Premier*) *v19.10* business software can read and use *MYOB AccountRight Plus v19.10* data files – they are compatible. If you are using *MYOB AccountRight (Premier* or *Enterprise) v19.10*, you can open data files created by *MYOB AccountRight Plus v19.10* and use them in your exercises.

The <u>main</u> difference between *MYOB AccountRight Plus* and *MYOB AccountRight Enterprise* (or *Premier*) is that the latter is a multi-user and multi-currency program. Users of *Enterprise* can also manage inventory in more than one location.

MYOB AccountRight Enterprise v19.10 can be installed from the accompanying DVD.

Logging on for *MYOB AccountRight Enterprise* users

For "User ID:" sign on as the "Administrator", unless otherwise instructed, and (if requested) select "Single-User Access". All other steps and instructions in the book will be the same for both programs. However, some dialogue boxes of the *Enterprise* version might have one or two extra options that are not relevant to the exercises in this textbook.

Note for users of Apple MacIntosh and *MYOB AccountEdge Pro v13*

The notes and screen images in this book have been prepared using *MYOB AccountRight Plus* business software running on a Windows PC. Apple MacIntosh computer users can use this text with the *MYOB AccountEdge Pro v13* software education version. While the windows screen images look different, the selections and options are the same. Logging in looks different and this procedure is shown on the next page.

You can install the education version of *MYOB AccountEdge Pro v13* from the DVD supplied with this book.

Installing *MYOB AccountEdge Pro V13* program

 How to install a test drive program on your hard disk – Apple MacIntosh

Step	Instruction
1	Place the DVD that came with the textbook in your Mac.
2	In *Finder*, locate and expand the folder called *Apple MacIntosh*. Double click on the file called *AccountEdge Pro v13.dmg*
3	Double click on the Setup icon: MYOB AccountEdge Pro V13 — 2 items AccountEdge Pro® v13.5 — Education Edition Double click → Setup Resources © 2014 MYOB Technology Pty Ltd **MYOB**
4	Follow the usual MacIntosh on-screen instructions for installing software.

The files for *MYOB AccountEdge Pro v13* will not open in *MYOB AccountRight Plus v19.10*. A separate set of files for *MYOB AccountEdge Pro v13* is included on the DVD that comes with this text.

How to obtain the MYOB AccountEdge Pro v13 *data files*

Step	Instruction
1	Place the DVD that came with the textbook in your Mac.
2	In *Finder*, locate and expand the folder called *Apple MacIntosh*.
3	Drag and drop the folder called *Student Files - MYOB AccountEdge* into your *Documents* folder and use these files for exercises and assessments.

Starting a file using *MYOB AccountEdge Pro v13* on an Apple MacIntosh computer

How to open an AccountEdge *data file*

Step	Instruction
1	Start *MYOB AccountEdge Pro v13*
2	At the *Welcome* window, click on the *Browse* button to search for the file that you want to open.

○○○   Welcome to AccountEdge Pro

Welcome to

AccountEdge·Pro

Looking to go Mobile?

AccountEdge Mobile is a companion app to AccountEdge on your Mac. Sync customers and items, etc. Create and sync orders, quotes, and expense transactions all with this free app.

◀ ▶   Read More

MYOB

Open
ass11

Browse
Find and open your company file

Sample Company
Explore our Clearwater company file

Support
FAQ's, discussions, guides, and email support

Go Mobile
Get the free AccountEdge Mobile app for iOS.

Company File Maintenance ▼

Step	Instruction
3	Log on as the *Administrator* without a password.

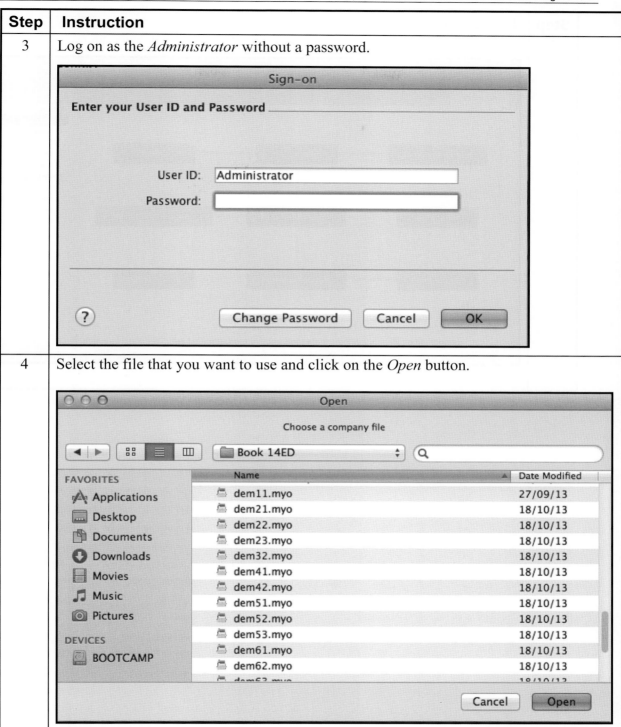

Step	Instruction
4	Select the file that you want to use and click on the *Open* button.

Step	Instruction
5	The *Command Centre* window will show: 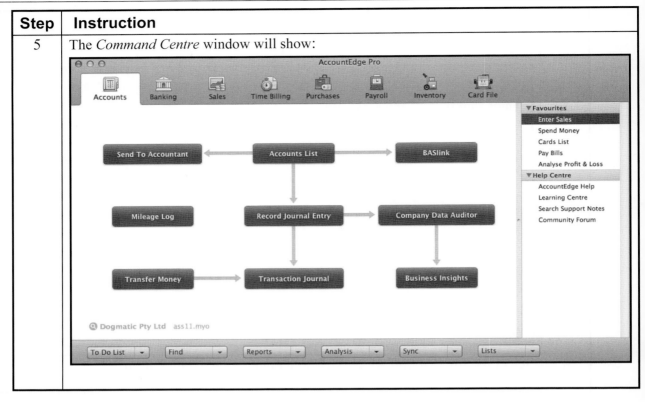

Introduction to *MYOB AccountRight Plus*

1

An introduction to the basic operations of a computer-based accounting system using *MYOB AccountRight Plus*.

After completing this chapter you will be able to:

1. Select a Command Centre and options within that centre.
2. Open an existing *MYOB AccountRight Plus* data file.
3. Carry out *MYOB AccountRight Plus* essential operations.
4. Use the keyboard and mouse of your computer to enter some everyday transactions using *MYOB AccountRight Plus*.
5. Record transactions and exit a file correctly.
6. Backup a file.
7. Display financial reports on the screen.
8. Print a balance sheet and a profit and loss statement.

Introduction

The aim of this book is to help people learn the accounting process using a modern integrated accounting package. People in education and those small businesses contemplating *MYOB AccountRight Plus* should find it a useful addition to the manual and tutorial supplied by the distributors of *MYOB AccountRight Plus*. The exercises are designed to reinforce the *MYOB AccountRight Plus* tutorial as well as helping with –

- the design of the accounting system
- accounting for transactions not covered in the tutorial
- accounting for different types of businesses.

  To cater for training courses requiring assessment (usually part of an accounting course) there are assessment exercises or tests. The format of this book is therefore –

- notes, 'How to …' lists followed by examples and screen layouts solutions
- self-test problems with solutions at the end of each chapter
- assessment exercises at the end of each chapter which can be marked by course leaders.

It is not necessary to go through the chapters in any particular order as each will commence as a separate module – for example, the chapter on cash book will start by learning how to process transactions through a cash book where the accounting system is already set up. A simple set-up of accounts will then be undertaken so that any person may use the cash book 'stand-alone'. Later chapters will integrate the cash book with other modules (called command centres in *MYOB AccountRight Plus*).

Included in this edition is a chapter on *MYOB AssetManager Pro* v3.6, a stand-alone package for keeping track of assets.

Conventions used in this book

In this book, the following conventions will apply (usually to avoid repetition):

- ↵   This symbol will indicate that you should tap the ENTER or RETURN key. For example, an instruction to "Enter Account Number 4-1100" ↵ tells you to type in the account number 4-1100 and tap the Enter key to complete.

- *Command centre*   The command centre to be selected will be in italics – For example, select *Accounts* will mean pointing to the *Accounts* command centre icon and click. Selections within the command centres will also be stated with italics – For example, select *Accounts List* will mean point to the *Accounts List* option in the *Accounts* command centre and click.

- ***"Text and numbers"***   Text and numbers to be entered will be enclosed in double quotes – do **NOT** type these quotes in! – For example, an instruction to enter "2778" in the debit column will mean that you would type in 2778 when the cursor is blinking in the space under the column headed debit.

- **'Field label'**   A field for the purpose of this book will be any entry required on a screen. Each field has a label describing the entry required. Examples of fields are customer name, address, account number, amount, quantity, etc. Fields will be indicated by <u>single</u> quotes. For example, with the cursor on 'Supplier:' field type "D" ↵ will mean that you type D (or d) when the cursor is blinking on the screen in the field next to the label Supplier: and then tap the Enter key.

- ***Buttons***   Rectangular buttons to be selected (point and click) will be in italics. These buttons include *OK*, *Record*, *Use Account*, and *Close*.

  Square buttons containing icons will also be in italics. The first time a button is used it is sometimes shown in the text like the following instruction to click the *Print* button –

- ***Windows***   Windows used will be noted in italics. For example, an instruction to "Close the *Sales – New Item* window" will require you to use the windows close button, or click on the *Close* button at the foot of the *Sales – New Item* window.

Using the 'How to ...' lists

Throughout this book, instructions are given in generic lists that always start with the words 'How to'. The word "generic" means that the list can be applied to any situation requiring the particular action. For example, a list of instructions on "How to open an existing file" means that these instructions can be followed to open <u>any</u> *MYOB AccountRight Plus* data file.

To use these lists effectively, you should read them as you go through each chapter. The 'How to ...' list is followed by an example and often a self-test exercise. When you cannot remember how to carry out a task that was demonstrated in an earlier chapter, you can look up the 'How to ...' index at the front of the book. This index is shown by chapter, and by function. For example, if you are using the payroll chapter and you are asked to "Open the file dem81.myo" and you cannot remember how to open an existing file, you can look up the instruction in the list by chapters or in the list by function. This will give you the page in the book that has the step-by-step instructions to open an existing file.

MYOB AccountRight Plus and the GST

The Goods and Services Tax (GST) applies to most goods and services sold in Australia. It is not the purpose of this book to instruct people in the legal aspects of the GST. However, all of the demonstrations, self-test exercises and assignment material include the GST where necessary. You will not be required to determine the GST status of any particular transaction, as the instructions will make this clear. A very brief introduction to the GST, setting up additional tax codes and using/printing the Business Activity Statement (BAS) is shown in Chapter 2.

Opening an existing file

The authors have already set up the files for demonstrations and most exercises in this book. If you are using *MYOB AccountRight Plus* on your own computer, you should download the files from the CD provided with the text. Make an extra copy of any file you are using so that they can be re-installed if you save changes to them when practising. If you are using *MYOB AccountRight Plus* in a classroom, make sure that you are using copies of the demonstration files on your own data disk (do **NOT** experiment with the demonstration file on the classroom files!).

The following instructions are used to open an existing file.

How to open an existing file in MYOB AccountRight Plus

Step	Instruction
1	Click on the *Start* button and select the *MYOB AccountRight Plus* program or double-click on the MYOB icon on the desktop.
2	Click on the button to *Open your company file.*
	Click → Open your company file / Create a new company file / Explore the sample company / What's New in this version / Exit AccountRight Plus — Welcome to AccountRight Plus — Payroll — AccountRight Plus v19 — MYOB
	(continued on the next page)

Step	Instruction
3	From the list of files on your disk, highlight the file required and click the *Open* button (or double click on the file name). The following picture shows the file called dem11.myo in a folder called MYOBDATA on the hard disk selected: 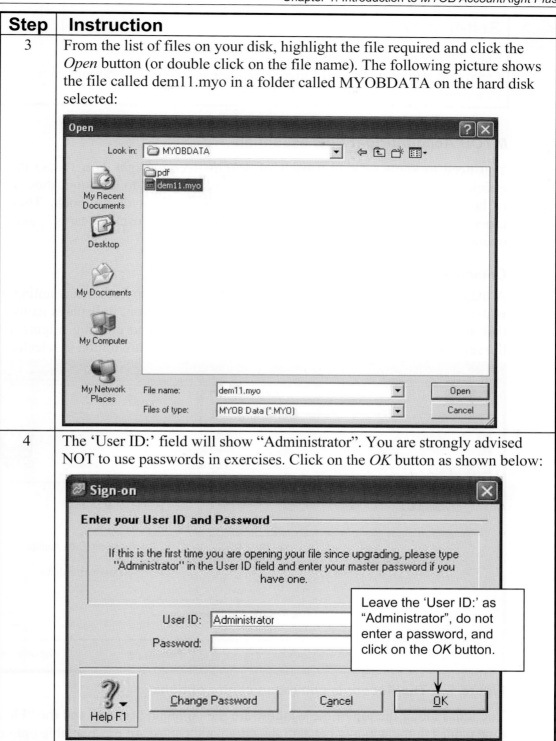
4	The 'User ID:' field will show "Administrator". You are strongly advised NOT to use passwords in exercises. Click on the *OK* button as shown below:

Video: A video showing you how to open an existing file is on the DVD

Self-test exercise 1.1

Start *MYOB AccountRight Plus*.
Open the file called dem11.myo and sign on as the "Administrator" without a password. What is the name of the business?

MYOB AccountRight Plus essentials

You need to know general aspects of *MYOB AccountRight Plus* to use the package efficiently. Later chapters will expect you to know how to carry out these operations or how to look up the 'How to ...' index at the front of the book. These general aspects cover file operations, setting preferences, using "cards" and printing operations.

Command centres

A major difference between *MYOB AccountRight Plus* and other accounting packages is its menu system. Rather than produce a list for selection, it displays icons or names that are selected by pointing to them with the mouse and clicking. Figure 1.1 shows the selections available when the *Accounts* command centre button is selected:

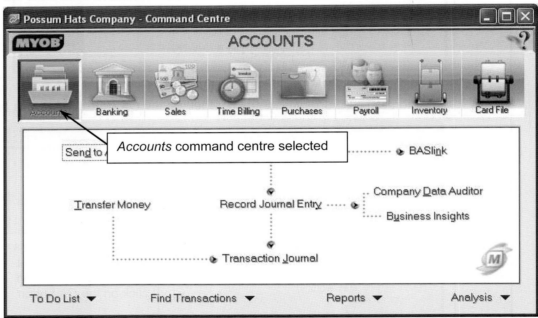

Figure 1.1: The *Accounts* command centre options

The icons along the top of the window are the command centres and the "Flow-chart" type names in the window beneath the command centre are the available options.

Every command centre window has four other options with drop-down selections at the bottom of the window. These are the *To Do List*, *Find Transactions*, *Reports* and *Analysis*. Figure 1.2 on the next page shows the *To Do List* window as at 15 August 2011 with the *A/P* (accounts payable) tab chosen (overdue days will depend on your system date):

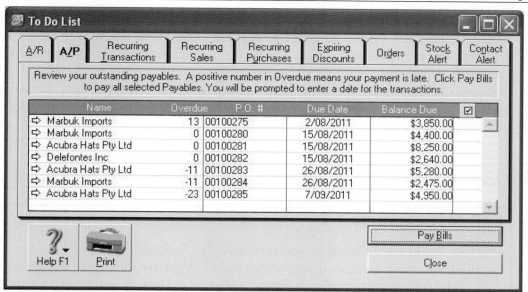

Figure 1.2: An example of a *To Do List* for accounts payable

Figure 1.3 shows the result of using *Find Transactions* in an account:

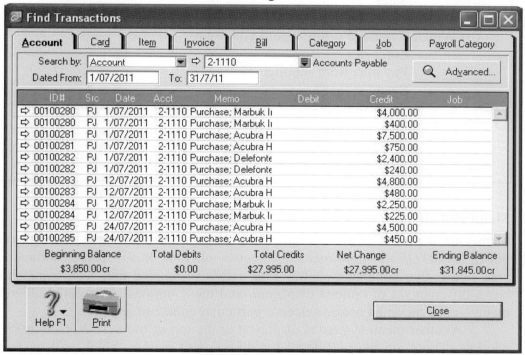

Figure 1.3: An example of using *Find Transactions* on a general ledger account

MYOB AccountRight Plus command centres also have an option to use the *M-Powered Services Centre* – this enables a business to connect electronically to banks, suppliers and superannuation funds. A business needs to subscribe (pay) for this additional service.

To select a command centre (or an option within a command centre) you use the mouse to move the on-screen arrow so that the point of the arrow is in the object being selected. The mouse button is then "clicked" – a quick press of the left-hand button. This process is called "point and click". An instruction in these notes to "Select ..." will mean that you use the mouse to move the on-screen pointer (arrow) so that the point of the arrow is on the item to be selected and you tap (click) the mouse button – do not hold your finger down on the button, but give it a quick press.

Video: A video about command centres is on the DVD

Self-test exercise 1.2

The file dem11.myo should be open. Answer the following:
(a) How many command centres are there? What are the principal functions of the following command centres? (Hint: Use Help as outlined in Chapter 12 on the CD)

        Banking
        Sales
        Card File.

(b) Which command centre would you use to:

        Enter sales?
        Pay bills from suppliers?
        Spend money?
        Set item prices?
        Print Payment Summaries?
        Prepare time billing invoice?
        Reconcile accounts?

Menu system

Menus allow you to select from displayed alternatives. You have already been using one of the *MYOB AccountRight Plus* menus – clicking on a displayed command centre area selects that command centre. You will have noticed that each command centre has a different set of options displayed, and these options represent another level of menu – clicking on an option selects a particular course of action.

Another menu system is displayed at the top of the *MYOB AccountRight Plus* window. These are the pull-down (or drop-down) menus, which will be familiar to anyone who has used any Windows based program. In Windows XP, the title bar and menu bar with the *Setup* pull-down menu selected will look like Figure 1.4 on the next page.

A drop-down menu item may have a small arrow at the right-hand side and this indicates that a sub-menu exists. Click on the small arrow to display a sub-menu: Figure 1.5 on the next page shows a sub-menu for the *Payroll Categories* item in the *Lists* menu.

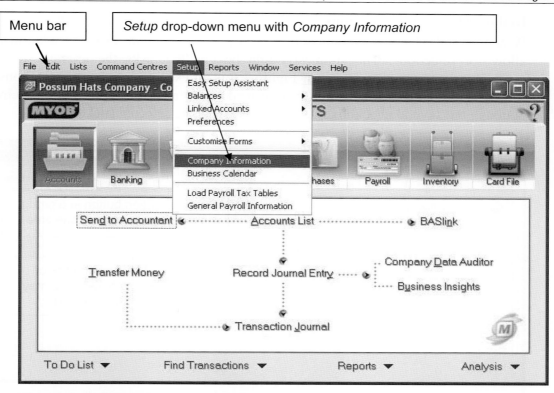

Figure 1.4: *Setup* **drop-down menu**

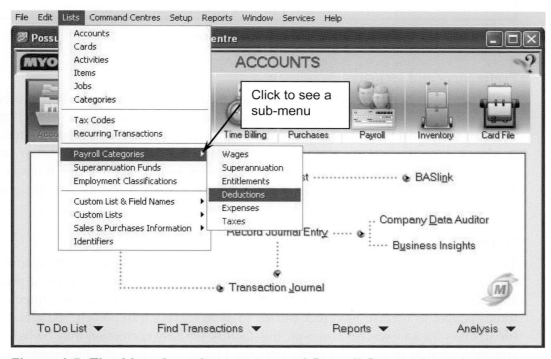

Figure 1.5: The *Lists* drop-down menu and *Payroll Categories* sub-menu

 Video: A video on using menus is on the DVD

Dialogue boxes and selections

Windows and Macintosh applications make use of *dialogue boxes* – windows that allow for selections. The simplest might be one that asks the operator to either continue an operation or cancel it. Figure 1.6 is an example of typical selections that can be made. Only one selection can be made from a set of option buttons (circular buttons), but several checkboxes (square boxes) can be selected (ticked).

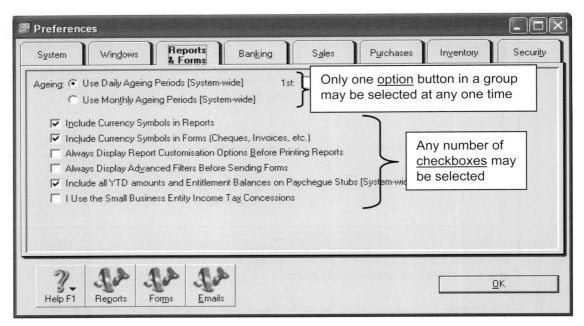

Figure 1.6: Options and checkboxes in a dialogue box

Preferences and security

Under the *Setup* pull-down menu is an option for preferences. The preferences window has tabs for some command centres, under which there are several options. Some of these will be looked at when examining the particular command centre. There is also a tab for system preferences, windows, reports and forms setup and for security. For the purpose of class work, preferences will be set to make it easier to use *MYOB AccountRight Plus*. Some of the preferences will probably not mean a great deal at the moment, but the following notes are appropriate at this stage.

Security

The files provided with this book have been set up so that changes can be readily made and errors corrected easily. This is not necessarily the best internal control procedure and in practice the first security option should be turned on and password protected. This forces people to reverse incorrect entries so as to leave a trail. When you create a new file in class for an exercise however, this facility for easy correction may be barred, and you may need to re-set the security options. Figure 1.7 shows the preferences window with the security selections.

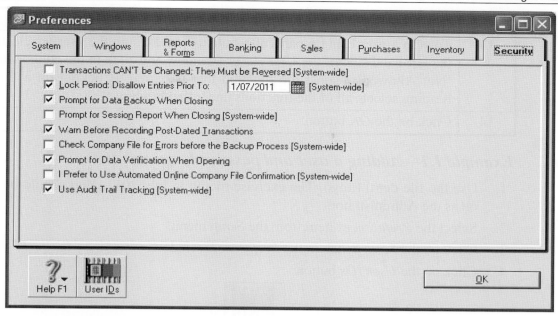

Figure 1.7: *Security* **preferences**

How to set the security preferences and add users with passwords

Step	Instruction
1	Select the *Setup* pull-down menu.
2	Select the *Preferences* item from the menu.
3	Click on the tab for *Security*.
4	There are several items which can be turned on or off by clicking in the appropriate selection checkbox. For ease of correcting errors or cancelling a transaction, the first checkbox should be turned off (no tick in the box). If you do not want a backup message to appear when you exit *MYOB AccountRight Plus*, turn the third checkbox off.
5	The second item has a drop-down selection list. Tick this preference and point to the white box and drag down to make your selection.
6	To add users and set passwords, click on the *User IDs* button at the foot of the security window.
7	Only the person logged in as the Administrator with the master password can add or edit users and their passwords. To add a user click on the *New* button.
8	Enter a 'User ID:' and TAB to the 'Password' field.
9	Type in a Password and TAB.
10	Type in the password again to confirm.
11	You can copy a set of restrictions from another user by selecting the other user from the drop-down list in the 'Copy Restrictions' field.
12	Click on the *OK* button.
	(continued on the next page)

Step	Instruction
13	To stop a user using a particular function, make sure the user is selected on the left-hand side of the *User Access* window and click in the column headed 'Not Allowed' against the function that is barred. (Clicking on a function heading selects all of the functions under that heading.)
14	Click on the *OK* button.

Example 1.1—Adding a user and password

1. Use the file dem11.myo. The exercise month is July 2011. You should be signed on as the Administrator.

2. Select the *Preferences* item from the *Setup* menu.

3. Click on the *Security* tab in the *Preferences* window.

4. Click on the *User IDs* button.

5. Click on the *New* button to add a user.

6. Type in "OZZIE" as the 'User ID' and use the TAB key.

7. Type in the 'Password' as "HATARI" (all in capital letters) and use the TAB key.

8. Repeat the password "HATARI" in the 'Confirm Password' field and click on the *OK* button if your *New User Details* window looks like Figure 1.8:

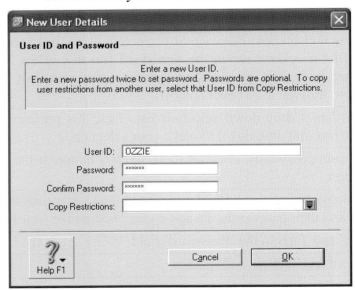

Figure 1.8: User ID and password set up

Note: You can use the drop-down list at the end of the 'Copy Restrictions:' field if you already have another user set up with the same restrictions as this new user.

9. In this example, the user "OZZIE" is not allowed to access any Banking functions. In the right-hand side of the *User Access* window, scroll down and click against the *Banking* function as shown in Figure 1.9:

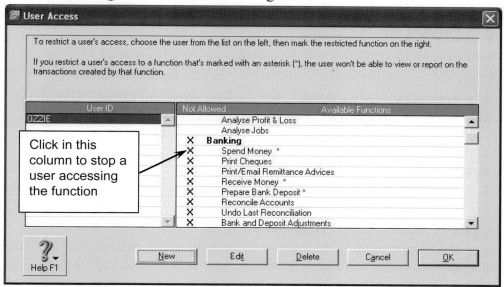

Figure 1.9: User "OZZIE" not allowed to access Banking functions

10. Click on the *OK* button.

Video: A video on how to add a new user is on the DVD

System preferences

The preferences are set and removed by clicking in the checkbox next to the preference. A checkbox with a tick in it means that the preference is "on". The system preferences that may be selected are shown in Figure 1.10:

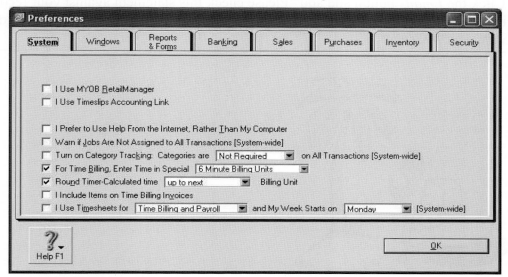

Figure 1.10: *System* preferences

Self-test exercise 1.3

Start *MYOB AccountRight Plus.*

If the file dem11.myo is not open, open this file and sign on as the "Administrator" without a password.

Change the security preferences so that they are as per Figure 1.7.

Change the system preferences so that they appear as in Figure 1.10.

Add a 'User ID' of "MKUBWA". Set a master password called "DIMBULA". This user is not allowed to use the *Banking, Payroll* or *Setup* functions.

Reports and Forms

In the *Reports and Forms* preferences you select the option button for the method of ageing to be used: daily ageing periods or monthly ageing periods. Turn the checkboxes on (ticked) for the preferences required.

The *Reports and Forms* buttons in the bottom left-hand corner are clicked to set font styles for reports and forms. In the *Reports* preferences, each section of the report can be set up for fonts and colours. You use the *Email* button to set up the default message and subjects for emailing invoices and purchase orders.

Self-test exercise 1.4

Open the file called dem11.myo and sign on as the "Administrator" without a password. Select the *Setup* pull-down menu *Preferences* item and click on the *Reports & Forms* <u>tab</u> at the top of the *Preferences* window. Edit the preferences so that they agree with those shown in Figure 1.11 on the next page.

Click on the *Reports* button at the foot of the *Reports & Forms* window and change the font for the main body of a report to Times New Roman 12 point.

Click the *Emails* button and add "Please check this statement against your records and report any differences to our accountant (bill.kahwati@possum.com.au)" to the *Statement Message.*

How do I send an email complaining about my statement?

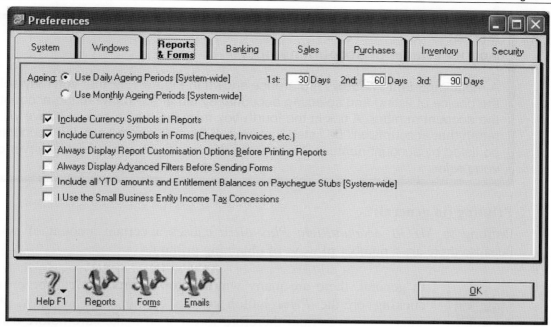

Figure 1.11: Preferences for *Reports & Forms*

Windows

The *Windows* preferences determine how the windows will look and act when entering or selecting fields. Figure 1.12 shows the setup for the file dem11.myo.

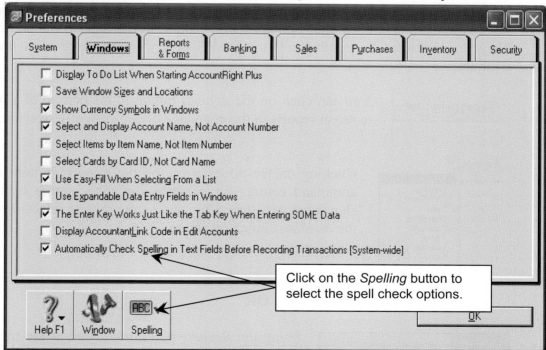

> Click on the *Spelling* button to select the spell check options.

Figure 1.12: *Windows* preferences

Video: A video on selecting preferences is on the DVD

Memo:
Account name or account number?

A most important *Windows* preference shown in Figure 1.12 that you may select is
the choice of listing and selecting accounts by either the name of the account or
the account number. A tick in the fourth box from the top as shown above will
mean that accounts will be listed by name. If the tick is removed, the accounts will
be listed by account number. Throughout this book, you may use whichever option
you prefer.

Printing (in general)

Printing in *MYOB AccountRight Plus* often causes a certain amount of confusion
because there are a number of ways of obtaining printouts.

In general, there are many windows or reports that can be printed by
clicking on the *Print* button in the bottom of a window. Printing
consumes paper (and therefore forests), so make sure before using this
button that the report is what you <u>really</u> want!

Options for printing documents are available directly from the command centre
menus. For example, the three options shown above are directly available from the
Sales command centre. Similar options will be found in the other command centres.
They are restricted to printing all or a "run" of <u>documents</u> each with the same
attribute.

You can click on the *Reports* button in the bottom of a window
to select reports in the command centre currently selected.

Clicking on the down arrow on the *Reports* button lists the
command centres for pre-selection. The picture on the left
shows the *Accounts* command centre reports selected while in
the *Banking* command centre.

OR

Using the *Reports* pull-down menu at the top of the
screen and selecting *Index to Reports* as shown here
accesses all reports. If you are not in the correct
command centre, click on the tab in the reports
window and select the report required.

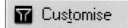

Select the *Customise* button to change the report's features – for example, you may or may not want accounts with zero balances shown in a balance sheet printout, or you may want to specify the amount of detail shown on any report by selecting the report level. Note that if you set the preferences as per Figure 1.11, a customise window will be displayed automatically when you print a report.

Before sending the report to the printer it is a good idea to look at it on the screen by clicking on the *Display* button, which is found in the bottom right-hand corner.

The *Format* button in a display window allows you to customise the colours and fonts for sections of the particular report to be printed. Unlike the *Reports* button in Figure 1.10, this customisation only covers the current report to be printed.

The *Send To* button allows you to export the report instead of printing. The report can be exported to an Excel spreadsheet, emailed, set as a "PDF" or an "HTML" file or a simple text file. You must have the requisite programs installed on your computer for all of these to work.

"Zoom" or "Detail" Arrows ⇨

Throughout *MYOB AccountRight Plus* you will notice small arrows to the left of certain items or fields. Clicking on these will reveal details about that particular item or field. Depending on the preferences set up earlier, some of these detail arrows may be shaded, and this indicates that the details cannot be altered.

Example 1.2—Using zoom (or detail) arrows

1. Use the file dem11.myo. You should be signed on as the Administrator.

2. Select the *Purchases* command centre and the *Transaction Journal* item.

3. Make sure dates stated at the top of the window are from 1/7/2011 to 31/7/2011.

4. Click on the detail arrow ⇨ next to the transaction on 1/7/2011 with ID# 100282 as shown in Figure 1.13 on the next page.

5. In the *Purchases – Edit Item* window, click on the detail arrow ⇨ next to the item number "D-118".

6. Click on the *Selling Details* tab at the top of the *Item Information* window.

7. Check that the 'Base Selling Price' of this item is $48.00 each, the 'Tax Code When Sold:' field is 'GST', and that sales prices are tax exclusive (checkbox not ticked).

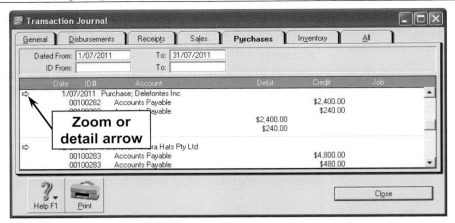

Figure 1.13: Selecting a purchase invoice from the *Transaction Journal*

8. Close back to the *Purchases* command centre window. Click the *Cancel* button for the spell check on the item name – you should turn the spell checking off by deselecting this preference as shown in Figure 1.12 if you do not want this message.

Video: A video showing you how to use "detail arrows" is on the DVD

Self-test exercise 1.5

Use the file dem11.myo. You should be signed on as the Administrator.

Select the *Sales* command centre *Transaction Journal* item.

Select the detail arrow for Invoice #8301. What is the description of the item sold?

Registers

The *Registers* are journal search and edit facilities for banking, purchases, sales and inventory transactions. For example, in the *Purchases* command centre there is an option called *Purchases Register*. This option is used to search for purchase quotes, orders, open bills (unpaid supplier invoices), closed bills (paid supplier invoices), debit notes and recurring purchase templates. Similar registers are found in the *Sales*, *Banking* and *Inventory* command centres.

How to use the Purchases Register to search

Step	Instruction
1	Select the *Purchases* command centre.
2	Select the *Purchases Register* option.
3	If necessary, use a tab at the top of the *Purchases Register* window to narrow the search to the type of purchase required.
4	Set the search criteria and the dates if necessary.
5	Click on a detail (zoom) arrow next to the document required.

Example 1.3—Using the purchases register

In this example, a quote received from Marbuk Imports is looked up.

1. Use the file dem11.myo. You should be signed on as the Administrator.

2. Select the *Purchases* command centre and the *Purchases Register* option.

3. Click on the *Quotes* tab at the top of the *Purchases Register* window. Make sure dates stated at the top of the window are from 1/7/2011 to 31/7/2011. There is only one quote and it should be highlighted as shown in Figure 1.14:

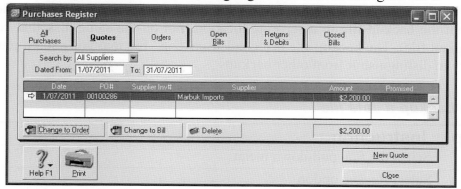

Figure 1.14: List of Quotes in the *Purchases Register*

4. Click on the detail (zoom) arrow for the quote from Marbuk Imports dated 1 July 2011. The quote shown in the *Purchases – Edit Item* window is for 100 of item I444 "Golf Caps" at $22 (including GST). This quote is shown in Figure 1.15:

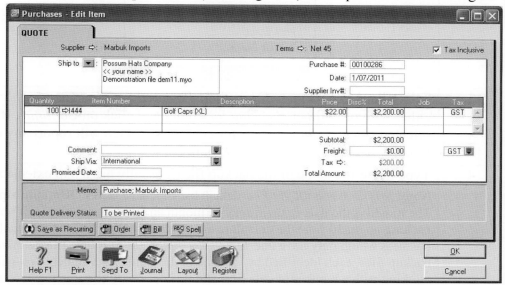

Figure 1.15: Quote received from Marbuk Imports

5. Click *OK* to close the *Purchases – Edit Item* window and close the *Purchases Register*.

Video: A video on registers is on the DVD

Self-test exercise 1.6

Use the file dem11.myo. You should be signed on as the Administrator.

Use the *Sales Register* option in the *Sales* command centre and look up an *Open Invoice* number 8302 for Macho Menswear. What is sold on this invoice?

Backing up a file

You will see reminders throughout this book to back up the MYOB data file. You should put the backup file in a separate location (not on the same disk that contains your original file). The backup file is a condensed "zip" file that you should rename if necessary to distinguish it from other backups.

How to backup a data file

Step	Instruction
1	Select the *File* pull-down menu.
2	Select *Backup* option. File Edit Lists Command Centres New Ctrl+N Open... Ctrl+O Close Window Esc Print... Ctrl+P Print Setup... Default Fonts... Backup...
3	Select *Backup Company File and M-Powered Services Centre only* and either with or without *checking for errors* and click on *Continue.* If you selected *Check Company File for errors* a message will report any errors found. Check it and click the *OK* button.
4	Type in the file name of the backup file (it usually has a .zip extension). **Note:** *MYOB AccountRight Plus* default backup name is **MYOBmmdd.zip** The mmdd is the date in the format of **m**onth and **d**ay. For example, if you are backing up on 30 June the default name would be MYOB0630.zip. Usually a business would only have one *MYOB AccountRight Plus* data file but numerous backup files, each identified by the date in the name. As a student you will be working with a number of data files and it is necessary to name the backup files differently (i.e. use the <u>original file name</u> but with the .zip extension).
5	Change Drive and Folder if necessary (the default is a folder called Backup in the directory containing the main file).
6	Click the *OK* button.

Note: *MYOB AccountRight Plus* will **NOT** save a backup file to a floppy disk if the original (source) file is also located on the floppy.

Example 1.4—Backing-up a data file

1. If not already open, open the file called dem11.myo.
2. Select the *File* pull-down menu.
3. Click on the menu item called *Backup*.
4. Select the two options:

   Backup Company File and M-Powered Services Centre only **and**
   Check Company File for errors.

5. Click on the *Continue* button.
6. Check the message for any errors and click the *OK* button.
7. Type the file name as: dem11.zip, change the Drive to drive C: and the Folder to TEMP i.e. C:\TEMP. (**Note** if the folder c:\Temp does not exist, select another suitable folder.)
8. Click on the *Save* button to create the backup file.

Video: A video on making a backup is on the DVD

How to exit MYOB AccountRight Plus

Step	Instruction
1	Select the *File* pull-down menu.
2	Select the *Exit* menu item (click on it).
3	Answer any notices. The notices will depend on the preferences set (see Figure 1.7 on page 1-11 for preferences on closing).
4	Select *Yes* if you want to make a backup of your file, and select the backup file name and destination (see example 1.4 above).

Self-test exercise 1.7

Exit the file dem11.myo and *MYOB AccountRight Plus* without a backup.

Sample operations

All of the operations in this part will be covered in detail in later chapters. The purpose here is to let you see how *MYOB AccountRight Plus* works when it has already been set up. Later lessons will show you how to set up the business and the command centres so that everyday transactions are automatically entered correctly in the accounts. Some people will have to get used to the mouse while others will have to get used to window operations. The style of future exercises and notes will also be the same.

> **Note:** All of the sample transactions are entered using the file **dem11.myo**

Example 1.5—Sample transactions

This example is of a business that is a wholesale distributor of a limited line of hats. It has already been set up and most of the July transactions have been entered. The following notes will go through the start-up procedures and some typical transactions. Follow these notes carefully but do not be concerned if you make errors – part of the learning process is to see where errors can occur. In later chapters you will learn of "recovery" procedures from errors. As stated above, these transactions will be examined in detail in later chapters and the purpose here is to become aware of *MYOB AccountRight Plus* procedures and screens. For these exercises, turn the spell checking off by deselecting this preference as shown in Figure 1.12 on page 1-15.

1. The exercise month is July 2011. You do not have to change the computer's system date.
2. Start *MYOB AccountRight Plus*.
3. Open the file called dem11.myo and sign on as the Administrator.
4. If you are doing a formal course your printouts will need to include your name. The way to do this is to include your name in the company information. The files provided allow you to enter your name in the *Address* section. The following 'How to ...' instructions are used to change the business address, and other information.

How to change the existing business address

Step	Instruction
1	Select the *Setup* pull-down menu at the top of the screen.
2	Select the *Company Information* menu item (click on it). The window should look like Figure 1.16 on the next page.
3	Type in any changes required to the company information. Use the TAB key to exit the address field.
4	Change a field by selecting it and editing the contents. To select a field, point to it and click. Normal windows editing applies.

Self-test exercise 1.8

Change the business address in the *Company Information* window by inserting your own name where it shows << your name >>.

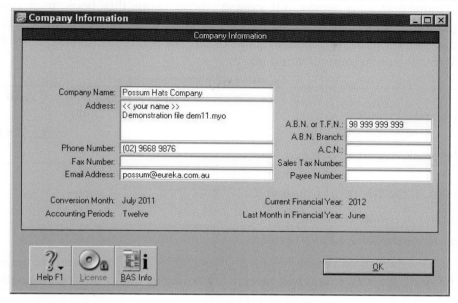

Figure 1.16: *Company Information* **window**

Try your first self-assessment!

Before continuing, check that you can now confidently do the following:

	I can now do the following:	√
1	Start *MYOB AccountRight Plus*	
2	Open an existing *MYOB AccountRight Plus* file	
3	Select a command centre	
4	Use a pull-down menu	
5	Access and change the business information	
6	Use the *MYOB AccountRight Plus* zoom arrows	
7	Exit *MYOB AccountRight Plus*	
8	Smile	

General journal entry

The first entry to try is a general journal entry to reverse accrued wages on 1 July 2011. General journal entries are usually the domain of accountants. Don't worry if you do not understand all of this section – just see if you can follow the instructions to see how *MYOB AccountRight Plus* works. Of course, those using this book in a computer accounting subject will need to know how to enter general journal entries. At 1 July 2011 there is a credit of $2,778 in an account called 'Accruals'. A reversal entry for this in a hand-written general journal would be –

	Debit	Credit
Accruals	$2,778.00	
Salaries and wages		$2,778.00
Reversal of accrued wages		

To record this in the file dem11.myo you –

1. Select the *Accounts* command centre.

2. Select *Record Journal Entry* option.

3. The system date should be highlighted – type "1/07/2011" ↵. If you are entering this before 1 July 2011, you will receive a warning as this is the security option selected as per Figure 1.7 on page 1-11.

4. An explanation of the entry is entered in the 'Memo' field (equivalent to a "narration" in hand written records). Type in the Memo as "Reversal of accrued wages" ↵.

5. If you have not changed the *Windows* preference from that shown in Figure 1.12 (see page 1-15 where the preference is set to list accounts by name), the cursor should be on the first line of the journal 'voucher' under the column headed 'Account'. To enter an account name you may:

   Tap the Enter key and select the account from the resulting list; or

   Use the selection list icon ▼ at the end of the field and select from the list; or

   Type in the first letter, or some of the first few letters, of the name and ↵; or

   Type in the full name and ↵.

   If you are using account numbers in a form you may either type it in (including the mandatory prefix), or tap the enter key for a selection list. You can then select the correct account from the list.

   For this demonstration, type in the first few letters of "Accruals" until the full account name is shown and then use TAB to go to the 'Debit' column.

6. Enter "2778" in the Debit column and ↵.
   Unlike many other accounting packages, *MYOB AccountRight Plus* will not object to the dollar sign or commas in the entry of dollar amounts, but you need not type them if you set the preferences to include them.

7. You could also allocate the amount to a particular job by entering in a job reference in the 'Job' column. An additional Memo may also be entered for each line of the journal entry in the 'Memo' column. The first line of the journal entry should show a default tax code of "N-T". This tax code is used for any entry that has no effect on GST collected or paid. For tax codes and their meaning look at Chapter 2.

8. Type "Sa" to select the "Salaries and Wages" account or type the account number for "Salaries & Wages".

9. TAB to the 'Credit' column and enter "2778" and ↵ (**Note**: The TAB key is used extensively in *MYOB AccountRight Plus* whenever a line of a journal or document is being entered).

10. Make sure that at the bottom of the window the totals of the Debits and Credits agree and that the 'Out of Balance' field is $0.00. Your *Record Journal Entry* window should look like Figure 1.17.

11. If you have made a mistake, point to the field, click and correct the error. If you want to cancel the whole entry, use the *EDIT* pull-down menu and select *Erase General Journal Transaction*.

12. Before you record any transaction you can use the *EDIT* pull-down menu at the top of the screen and select the *Recap Transaction* menu item. This will give you a preview of how the transaction will affect the accounts in the general ledger. Figure 1.18 on the next page is the *Recap Transaction* window for the journal entry shown in Figure 1.17.

13.

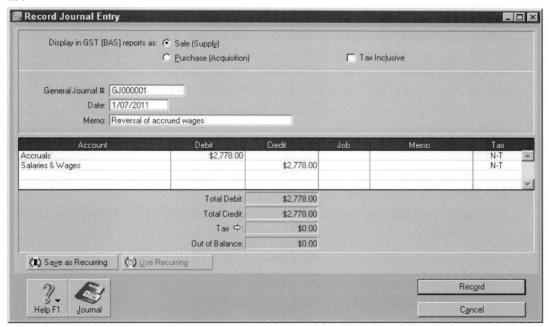

Figure 1.17: A general journal entry in the *Record Journal Entry* window

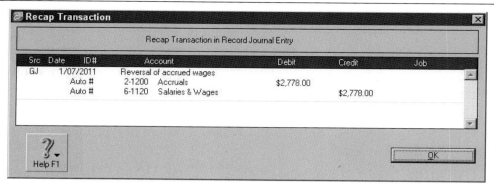

Figure 1.18: *Recap Transaction* **for a general journal entry**

14. Click the *OK* button to close the *Recap Transaction* window.

15. Click on the *Record* button.

16. Click on the *Journal* button at the bottom of the *Record Journal Entry* window. The beginning and ending dates at the top of the *Transaction Journal* window should be set from 1/07/2011 to 31/7/2011. The entry just recorded should appear as an entry.

17. Click on the *Close* button to close the *Transaction Journal* window.

18. Close the *Record Journal Entry* window by clicking the *Cancel* button.

Video: A video on recording a general journal entry is on the DVD

Purchase of an inventory item on credit

This transaction will be for the purchase of 100 hats (Item # D-113) from a supplier called Delefontes Inc. on the 28 July 2011. The purchase base price is $18 each (excluding the GST) and the tax code is GST. The *Purchases* command centre and inventory item has been set up to automatically increase inventory, increase accounts payable and record the GST input tax credit when this purchase is recorded.

In Chapter 6 the purchasing procedure of obtaining quotations, ordering the goods and receiving a supplier invoice (a bill) will be examined. For this introductory example, a bill will be recorded for goods received.

1. Select the *Purchases* command centre.

2. Select the *Enter Purchases* option.

3. Make sure that the document selected is a *Bill* (top of the *Purchases – New Item* window).

4. In this example, the window should be headed *Purchases – New Item*. In other cases, this can be changed to a *services* purchase by selecting the *Layout* button at the foot of the window. A purchase order may be for an item of inventory or for a service (e.g. repairs to a fork lift).

5. Make sure that the 'Tax Inclusive' box at the top of the *Purchases – New Item* window is ticked (that is, the purchase price on this purchase includes GST).

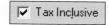

6. With the cursor on the 'Supplier:' field, enter the supplier's name – you may:

   Tap the Enter key and select the supplier from the resulting list; or

   Use the *Selection List* icon ▼ to the right of the field and select from the list; or

   Type in the first, or some of the first few letters, of the name and ↵; or

   Type in the full name and ↵.

   For this exercise, type "D" for the supplier and ↵. The full name "Delefontes Inc" should appear in the 'Supplier:' field. Your business name should appear in the 'Ship to:' field. If you want to leave the field as is, you use the TAB key.

7. TAB through to the 'Purchase #' field and enter "100287" ↵.

8. In the 'Date' field, change the date to "28/07/2011" ↵.

9. Enter the 'Supplier Inv#' as "4890" ↵.

10. The cursor will now be on the first line item under the column headed 'Bill'. Enter "100" for the quantity on the Bill and press the TAB key. If you press the Enter key you will jump down to the next line item! If you accidentally do this, use the up-arrow key – the cursor should move to the previous line. You will find that the TAB key must be used in any window to enter information <u>across</u> a line.

11. Use TAB to leave the 'Backorder' field blank.

12. Enter the inventory 'Item #'. Use the same technique as before – i.e. use the Enter key for a selection list and select the item from this list, click on the *Selection List* button ▼ or type in the item number and TAB. Select the item number by tapping the Enter key and select item D-113 from the list as shown in Figure 1.19:

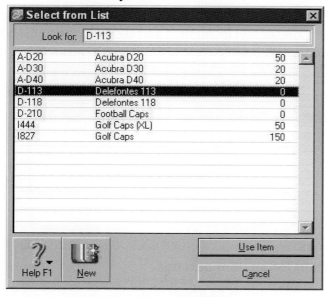

Figure 1.19: Item selected from the list

13. TAB across to the 'Price' column and type in "19.8" ↵.

14. The *Purchase – New Item* window should look like Figure 1.20:

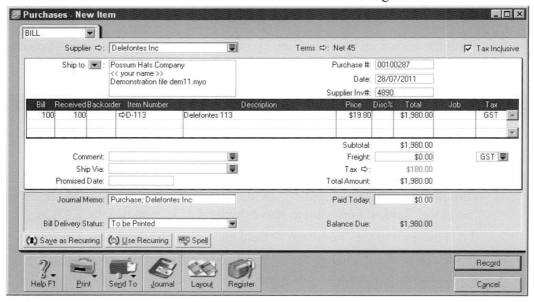

Figure 1.20: A *Bill* for the purchase of items on credit

15. The *Total* column should show the extension of $1,980.00. The code 'GST' should also appear in the *Tax* column. The summary at the bottom of the invoice should also show that $1,980.00 is the total amount and the balance on this invoice due ($1,800.00 plus GST of $180.00). You could change the 'Journal Memo' and other fields by pointing to them, clicking and entering in different data. You can also add comments to the Purchase Order. This will be covered in Chapter 6.

16. If your screen is not as per Figure 1.20 you may point to any incorrect field, click, and re-enter the correct data. You may also abandon this purchase by selecting *Erase Purchase* from the *Edit* pull-down menu and re-do the entry

17. Use the *Edit* menu, *Recap Transaction* menu item and compare the transaction with Figure 1.21. Click on the *OK* button to close the *Recap Transaction* window.

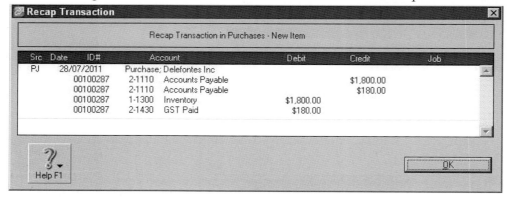

Figure 1.21: *Recap Transaction* for an item purchase

18. Select the *Record* button to enter this as an actual purchase.

19. Click on the *Cancel* button to close the *Purchases – New Item* window. You will return to the *Purchases* command centre window.

20. Click on the *Transaction Journal* option. Set the dates from 1/7/2011 to 31/7/2011.

21. Use the scroll bar to go to the end of the journal display and you should see your entry for the $1,800 plus $180 GST for goods purchased from Delefontes Inc.

22. Close the *Transaction Journal* window.

Video: A video on recording a bill for purchasing an item is on the DVD

Sale of inventory items on credit

This transaction will be for the sale of 60 D-113 hats and 100 I827 Golf Hats to Macho Menswear on Invoice Number 8303. The sale date is 29 July 2011. The *Sales* command centre and inventory items have been set up to automatically record a sale as an increase in the amount owing by a customer and increase the sales income account. It will decrease the inventory for the cost of the goods sold, increase the account for Cost of Goods Sold (this is explained in detail later in Chapter 7) and record the GST liability on the sale.

In Chapter 5 the full sales procedure of giving quotations, receiving an order for the goods or services and issuing an invoice to the customer will be examined. For this introductory example, an invoice will be recorded for goods sold without recording a quote and an order.

1. Select the *Sales* command centre.

2. Select the *Enter Sales* option.

3. The window title should be *Sales – New Item*. This can be changed to a services sale by selecting the *Layout* button at the foot of the window. A sales invoice may be for an item of inventory or for a service (e.g. software support).

4. Make sure that the document selected is an *Invoice* (top of the *Sales – New Item* window).

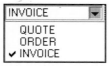

5. Make sure that the 'Tax Inclusive' box at the top of the *Sales – New Item* window is ticked (that is, the sales price on this sales invoice includes GST).

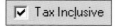

6. With the cursor on the 'Customer:' field, enter the customer name – you may

    Tap the Enter key and select the customer from the resulting list; or

    Use the *Selection List* icon to the right of the field and select from the list; or

    Type in the first letter, or some of the first few letters, of the name and ↵; or

    Type in the full name and ↵.

For this exercise, type "m" for the customer and ↵. There are two customers with names beginning with "M", but 'Macho Menswear' is the first name in alphabetical order and is displayed in the field. The full delivery address for Macho Menswear should appear in the 'Ship to:' field.

7. TAB through to the 'Date' field and enter the date "29/07/2011" and ↵.

8. Enter "3686" as the 'Customer PO #:' (purchase order number) and ↵.

9. Enter "60" for the quantity under the 'Ship' field and use the TAB key.

10. TAB to leave the 'Backorder' field blank.

11. Enter the 'Item Number'. Use the same technique as before – i.e. tap the Enter key for a selection list and select the item from this list, or type in the item number and ↵, or use the *Selection List* button 📋. Select the item number "D-113". Tap the Enter key to go to the next line of the invoice.

12. Enter "100" for the quantity to ship and TAB to the 'Item Number' field.

13. Select "I827" as the 'Item Number' and ↵. The sales invoice should appear as in Figure 1.22:

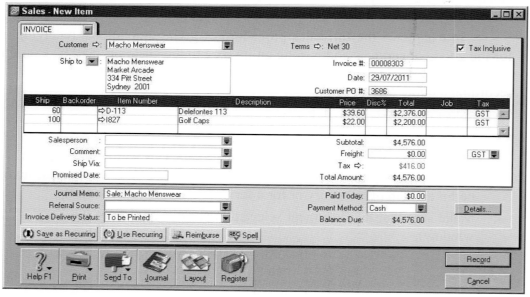

Figure 1.22: A *new sale invoice* for items sold on credit

14. If your screen is not as per Figure 1.22 you may point to any incorrect field, click, and re-enter the correct data. You may also abandon this sale by selecting *Erase Sale* from the *Edit* pull-down menu and re-do the entry.

15. Use the *Edit* menu, *Recap Transaction* menu item and compare the transaction with Figure 1.23 on the next page. As a perpetual inventory system is used with items of inventory, the entry combines the sale to a customer and the transfer of cost from inventory to the cost of goods sold account. Click on the *OK* button to close the *Recap Transaction* window.

16. Select the *Record* button to enter this as an actual sale.

17. Click on the *Cancel* button to close the *Sales – New Item* window.

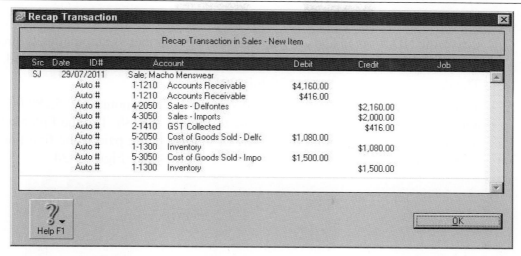

Figure 1.23: Recap Transaction journal for sale of inventory items

18. Click on the *Transaction Journal* option. Set the dates at the top of the window from 1/7/2011 to 31/7/2011.

19. Use the scroll bar to go to the end of the journal display and you should see your entry for the sale to Macho Menswear on the 29 July 2011.

20. Close the *Transaction Journal* window.

Video: A video on recording an inventory sale on credit is on the DVD

Receipt of money from a customer (accounts receivable)

This transaction will record the receipt of $5,280 from an account receivable called "Jag Gear Pty Ltd". This amount is paying Invoice # 8288 and is received on 30 July 2011. The file has been set up to automatically record this money in an account called "Undeposited Funds" and to decrease the amount owing by the debtor. The next section will show how to deposit this receipt into the bank.

1. Select the *Sales* command centre.

2. Select the *Receive Payments* option.

3. With the cursor on the 'Customer:' field, enter the customer name – you may:

> Tap the Enter key and select the customer from the resulting list; or

> Use the *Selection List* icon ▼ to the right of the field and select from the list; or

> Type in the first letter, or some of the first few letters, of the name and ↵ ; or

> Type in the full name and ↵.

For this exercise, enter "j" for Jag Gear Pty Ltd and ↵ ↵.

4. Enter "5280" as the amount received ↵.

5. Jag Gear has paid by cheque. Use the *Selection List* icon ▼ in the 'Payment Method:' field and select "Cheque" from the list of methods. You can also type "ch" for a cheque.

6.   TAB or ENTER to the 'Memo:' field and accept the default ⏎.

7.   Leave the 'ID #' as is and ⏎. This cash receipt number is automatically produced in numerical sequence and only needs to be changed if a receipt is cancelled.

8.   The date of this transaction is "30 July 2011" ⏎.

9.   <u>TAB</u> to the column headed 'Amount Applied'. The amount of $5,280.00 should appear in this column and should relate to Invoice # 8288. Tap the Enter key. You may use the mouse to point to the line of invoice being paid if the first line is not correct. The *Receive Payments* window should look like Figure 1.24:

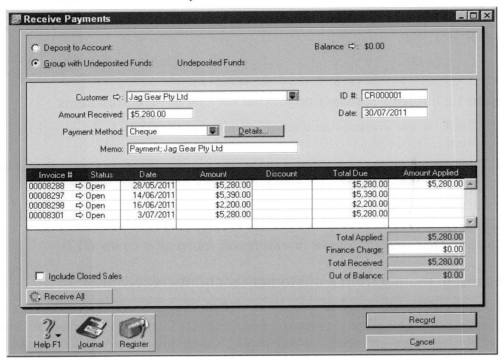

Figure 1.24: Payment received from a customer

10. If your *Receive Payments* window is not as per Figure 1.24 you may point to any incorrect field, click and re-enter the correct data. You may also abandon this receipt by selecting *Erase Payment* from the *Edit* pull-down menu and re-do the entry.

11. Use the *Edit* menu, *Recap Transaction* menu item and you should see that the account "Undeposited Funds" has been debited, with a credit to "Accounts Receivable" account. Click on the *OK* button to close the *Recap Transaction* window.

12. Click on the *Record* button.

13. Click on the *Cancel* button to close the *Receive Payments* window.

14. Click on the *Transaction Journal* option and the *Receipts* tab. If necessary, set the dates at the top of the window for July 2011.

15. You should see your entry for the receipt of $5,280.00 from Jag Gear Pty Ltd on 30 July 2011.

16. Close the *Transaction Journal* window.

Video: A video on recording a receipt from a customer is on the DVD

Make a deposit

The previous section showed the receipt of a cheque from an account receivable. There could be several cheques received in any one day in addition to other methods of payment. You will see in Figure 1.24 that the money received has been debited to an account called "Undeposited Funds", and this must now be deposited at the bank. The *Prepare Bank Deposit* option is used to bank these payments in a single deposit to the bank.

1. Select the *Banking* command centre.

2. Click on the *Prepare Bank Deposit* option.

3. Enter the date as "30/07/2011" ↵.

4. Leave the 'Select Receipts by:' field as "All Methods" and the 'Memo:' as "Bank Deposit".

5. In the 'Deposit' column, click against the cheque that is going to be deposited and a "√" should show. The total deposit should show $5,280.00 as in Figure 1.25:

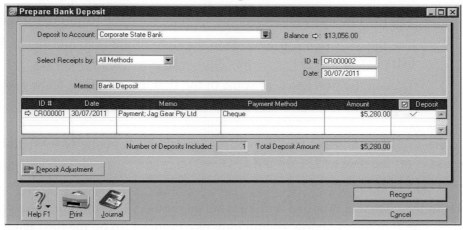

Figure 1.25: Cheque received now deposited at bank

6. Click on the *Record* button.

7. Click on the *Cancel* button to close the *Prepare Bank Deposit* window.

8. Click on the *Transaction Journal* option and the *Receipts* tab. Set the dates from 1/7/2011 to 31/7/2011.

9. You should now see that the receipt of $5,280.00 from Jag Gear Pty Ltd recorded earlier into "Undeposited Funds" has now been deposited at the bank.

10. Close the *Transaction Journal* window.

Video: A video on making a deposit is on the DVD

> **Memo:** If you only have a single receipt in a day, you can override the default setup in this file and record the receipt directly to the bank account. At the top of the *Receive Payments* window in Figure 1.24 you will see that the receipt from Jag Gear was debited to "Undeposited Funds". If you select the option button for *Deposit to Account,* the receipt is debited to the account for "Corporate State Bank" and you would not use *Prepare Bank Deposit.*

Payment of money to an account payable

This transaction will record the payment of $3,850 to an account payable called "Marbuk Imports". This amount pays Purchase # 100280 and is paid on 31 July 2011. The file has been set up to automatically decrease the amount in the bank account and to decrease the amount owing to the creditor.

1.   Select the *Purchases* command centre.

2.   Select the *Pay Bills* option.

3.   With the cursor on the 'Supplier:' field, enter the account payable name – you may:

> Tap the Enter key and select the supplier from the resulting list; or
>
> Use the *Selection List* icon ▼ to the right of the field and select from the list; or
>
> Type in the first letter, or some of the first letters, of the name and ↵ ; or
>
> Type in the full name and ↵.

For this exercise, type "m" for Marbuk Imports ↵.

4.   Use the TAB key to leave the 'Payee:', 'Memo:' and 'Cheque No.:' fields as they are and enter the date as "31/07/2011" ↵.

5.   Enter "3850" as the amount ↵.

6.   TAB to the 'Amount Applied' column and apply the $3,850 to Purchase # 100275 and ↵. The *Pay Bills* window should look like Figure 1.26 on the next page.

7.   If your *Pay Bills* window is not as per Figure 1.26 you may point to any incorrect field, click, and re-enter the correct data. You may also abandon this receipt by selecting *Erase Payment* from the *Edit* pull-down menu and re-do the entry.

8.   Use the *Edit* menu, *Recap Transaction* menu item and you should see that "Accounts Payable" account has been debited, with a credit to the bank account "Corporate State Bank". Click on the *OK* button to close the *Recap Transaction* window.

9.   Click on the *Record* button.

10.   Click on the *Cancel* button to close the *Pay Bills* window.

11.   Click on the *Transaction Journal* option and the *Disbursements* tab. Set the dates from 1/7/2011 to 31/7/2011.

12.   You should see your entry for the payment to Marbuk Imports on 31 July 2011 (Cheque ID# 250161).

13.   Close the *Transaction Journal* window.

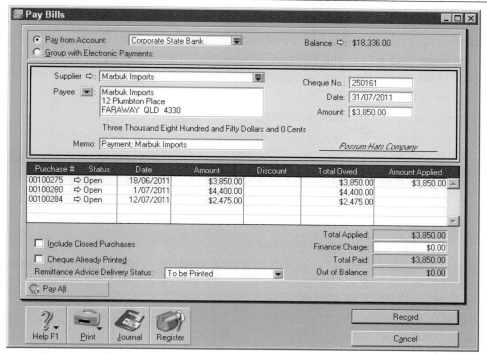

Figure 1.26: Payment made to a supplier

Video: A video on recording a payment to an account payable is on the DVD

Payment of money for a service

This transaction will record the payment of $462 (including $42 GST) to the Prospero County Council for electricity. This has not previously been recorded as owing. The payment is made on 31 July 2011. The *Banking* command centre automatically reduces the amount of money in the nominated bank account, but the account to be debited (charged) in the General Ledger must be entered by the operator – in this case it will be an expense account for electricity. The account name is the preferred method of showing the accounts list in this chapter.

1. Select the *Banking* command centre.

2. Select the *Spend Money* option.

3. Make sure that the 'Tax Inclusive' box at the top of the *Spend Money* window is ticked (that is, the amount we will record on this cheque includes the GST).

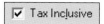

4. Type in the date, which is "31 July 2011" ↵.

5. Enter "462" as the amount ↵.

6. At the 'Card:' field use the TAB key to move through to the 'Payee' field (the use of Cards will be explained in detail later).

7. In the 'Payee:' field type in "Prospero County Council" and use the TAB key to move to the 'Memo:' field. (If you use the Enter key in the 'Payee:' field it will only move down one line in that field because you can enter a multi-line address).

8. Enter a 'Memo' – for example, "Electricity account paid" ↵.

9. If you have not changed the *Windows* preference from that shown in Figure 1.12 (see page 1-15 where the preference is set to list accounts by name), the cursor should be on the first line of the journal "voucher" under the column headed 'Account Name'.

   To enter an account name you may:

   > Tap the Enter key and select the account from the resulting list; or

   > Use the *Selection List* icon ▼ at the end of the field and select from the list; or

   > Type in the first letter, or some of the first few letters, of the name and ↵; or

   > Type in the full name and ↵.

   If you are using account numbers in a form you may either type it in (including the mandatory prefix), or tap the enter key for a selection list. You can then select the correct account from the list.

   For this demonstration, type in the first few letters of "Electricity" and TAB across to the 'Amount' column.

10. $462.00 should appear in the 'Amount' column, as this is the tax-inclusive amount. The tax included is shown in grey as $42.00. The 'Tax' column should have "GST" as the tax code ↵. Your *Spend Money* window should appear as in Figure 1.27:

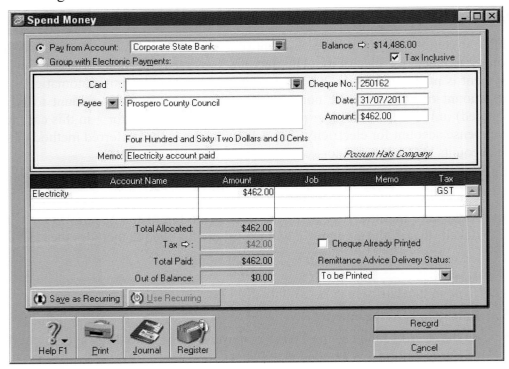

Figure 1.27: Cheque used to pay electricity account

11. If your *Spend Money* window is not as per Figure 1.27 you may point to any incorrect field, click, and re-enter the correct data. You may also abandon this receipt by selecting *Erase Cheque Transaction* from the *Edit* pull-down menu.

12. Use the *Edit* menu, *Recap Transaction* menu item and you should see that account number 6-1050 "Electricity" has been debited with $420 (the expense excluding the GST), account number 2-1430 "GST Paid" has been debited with $42, and the bank account number 1-1120 "Corporate State Bank" has been credited with $462. Click on the *OK* button to close the *Recap Transaction* window.

13. Click on the *Record* button.

14. Click on the *Cancel* button to close the *Spend Money* window.

15. Click on the *Transaction Journal* option. If your system date has been set correctly you will see the journal entries for all the payments in July 2011 (if not, set the beginning and ending dates at the top of the window).

16. You should see your entry for the payment of $462.00 to Prospero County Council on 31 July 2011 ($420.00 for electricity and $42.00 for the GST paid).

17. Close the *Transaction Journal* window.

 Video: *A video on recording a cheque for an expense is on the DVD*

 ### How to recall, edit or delete a transaction

Step	Instruction
1	Select the transaction journal concerned.
2	Use the scroll bar to locate the transaction required.
3	To Recall the transaction, click on the detail arrow ⇨ to open it. Go to step 5. To Edit the transaction do steps 4 & 5. To Delete the transaction go to step 6.
4	Edit the transaction if necessary (and if allowed).
5	Click on the *OK* button to record any changes or click on the *Cancel* button to exit without changes.
6	To delete, select *Delete 'Transaction'* menu item from the *Edit* pull down menu.

 IMPORTANT: Transactions cannot be modified and/or deleted if the first box in the *Security* tab of the *Preferences* is ticked on: 'Transactions CAN'T be Changed ...' See Figure 1.7 on page 1-11.

Video: A video on editing and deleting transactions is on the DVD

Self-test exercise 1.9

Using the file dem11.myo, recall sales invoice #8301 made out to Jag Gear Pty Ltd on 3 July 2011. The transaction journal is for sales. Answer the following:

(a) What is the description of the item that was sold on this invoice?

(b) How many hats were sold on this invoice?

(c) Who was the salesperson?

(d) Use the 🖳 *Selection List* icon at the 'Salesperson' field and write down the <u>number</u> of employees. Click the *Cancel* button to return to the invoice.

(e) Which carrier was used to transport the goods?

(f) What is the <u>full</u> comment on this invoice? Write it down.

(g) What was the promised delivery date?

(h) What is Jag Gear's 'Ship To' address?

Print financial statements

Printing in general was looked at earlier. The example has been set up to produce a Balance Sheet and an Income Statement in a particular format. Follow the 'How to ...' instructions below and complete self-test exercises 1.10 and 1.11.

How to print general ledger reports

Step	Instruction
1	Select the *Accounts* command centre and click on the *Reports* button. Click ⟶ Reports ▼
OR	Click on the down arrow on the *Reports* button while in any command centre and select *Accounts*. Reports ▼ ◀— Click Accounts Banking GST/Sales Tax Sales Time Billing Purchases Payroll Inventory Card File Custom Drag down and select from drop-down list
2	To select a report, click on its name. Select *Standard Balance Sheet* in the *Index to Reports* window. Your screen should be similar to Figure 1.28 on the next page, which shows the *Standard Balance Sheet* report selected.
	(continued on the next page)

Step	Instruction
3	Click on the *Display* button to review the report on screen. Display If you set up preferences to always show *Customise* options (as per Figure 1.11 on page 1-15 earlier), the *Report Customisation* window will be displayed.
4	To change print options before displaying the report you can click on the *Customise* button. ▼ Customise
5	Make selections from the resulting *Report Customisation* window under the *Advanced Filters* tab – report level, selected period, date, and financial year etc. This is shown in Figure 1.29 on the next page.
6	Click on the *Finishing* tab in the *Report Customisation* window and click on the checkboxes for report preferences. Figure 1.30 on page 1-40 shows selections for a balance sheet with zero balances included. **Note:** If you want to save the particular customisation set up for the report, click on the last checkbox for 'Add Reports to Menu'.
7	Select the *Display* button to review the report on screen. Check for all possible errors of fact or formatting (this is important to avoid unnecessary printing of incorrect reports).
8	Click on the *Print* icon at the bottom left of the screen to obtain a printout.

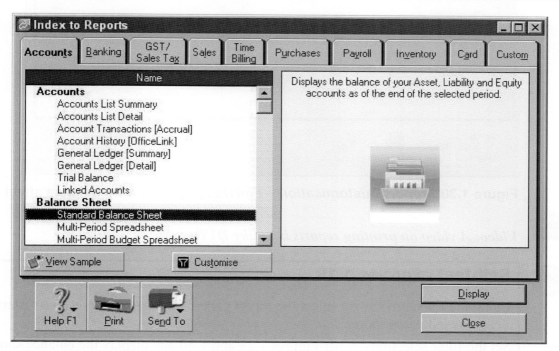

Figure 1.28: *Standard Balance Sheet* **selected as the report to print**

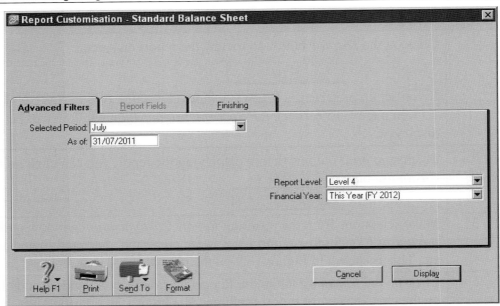

Figure 1.29: *Report Customisation – Advanced Filters* for a balance sheet

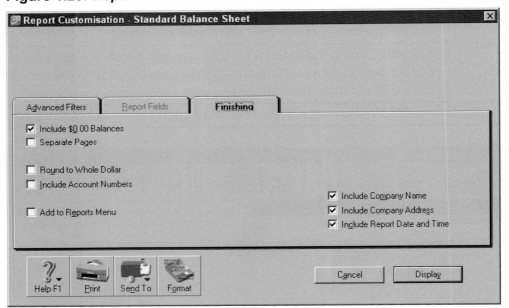

Figure 1.30: *Report Customisation – Finishing* options for a balance sheet

Video: A video on printing reports is on the DVD

Self-test exercise 1.10

Using the file dem11.myo, select the report called *Standard Balance Sheet* from the *Accounts* index to reports.

Set the filter selections as per Figures 1.29 and 1.30 and display the balance sheet on the screen (expand the window to see more of it at one time).

Print the balance sheet. Compare your printout with the answer to this exercise.

Self-test exercise 1.11

Using the file dem11.myo, select the report called *Profit & Loss [Accrual]* from the *Accounts* index to reports.

Set the filter selections to include zero balances and with dates from 1/7/2011 to 31/7/2011.

Display the profit & loss statement on the screen.

Print the profit & loss statement and check against the answer.

How to close a MYOB AccountRight Plus *session*

Step	Instruction
1	Close any window back to the *Command Centre* window.
2	Select *Exit* from the *File* pull-down menu.

Self-test exercise 1.12

Exit *MYOB AccountRight Plus*.

Try self-test exercise 1.13. Remember that the purpose in this introduction is to become familiar with *MYOB AccountRight Plus*, the mouse and Windows. If you look back at pages 1-22 to 1-39 for examples, the following transactions will follow the order given on those pages.

Self-test exercise 1.13

Use the file dem11.myo. This self-test problem follows on from the Hat business example above.

All of the following entries are at 31 July 2011.

Record a general journal entry to accrue $2,438 salaries and wages at the end of the month. This entry is –

	Debit	Credit
Salaries and Wages	$2,438.00	
Accruals		$2,438.00

Accrued salaries and wages at 31/7/2011

(see page 1-24 for example)

Record a bill for the purchase of 60 A-D40 hats from Acubra Hats Pty Ltd on credit at $49.50 each (including GST). Supplier invoice number is 8948. Select the comment "We appreciate your business" and the Ship Via is Best Way Transport **(see page 1-26 for example)**.

Record an invoice for the sale of 40 Golf Caps (Item # I827) on credit to Jag Gear Pty Ltd at $22.00 each (including GST) – (their PO #482). Ship via Hills Transport **(see page 1-29 for example)**.

(continued on the next page)

Self-test exercise 1.13 *(continued)*

Use *Prepare Bank Deposit* and bank the $5,390.00 received from Jag Gear Pty Ltd **(see page 1-33 for example)**.

Paid $8,250.00 to Acubra Hats Pty Ltd on PO #100281 **(see page 1-34 for example)**.

Paid $50.60 ($46 plus GST) to Norman's Newsagency for newspapers supplied in July. Charge this to the account called "Office Expenses" **(see page 1-35 for example)**.

Print a Standard Balance Sheet as at 31 July 2011 and a Profit & Loss [Accrual] for July 2011. This time do **NOT** include zero balances **(see page 1-38 for instructions)**.

Complete the final competency checklist.

Competency checklist

	I can now do the following:	✓
1	Start *MYOB AccountRight Plus*	
2	Open an existing *MYOB AccountRight Plus* file	
3	Use a pull-down menu	
4	Access and change the business information	
5	Select a Command Centre	
6	Select an option in a Command Centre	
7	Exit *MYOB AccountRight Plus*	
8	Use the TAB key correctly in document entry	
9	Use the *Selection List* icon ▼ to produce a selection list	
10	Use the detail arrow ⇨ to examine the detail for an item	
11	Select and print a financial statement report	
12	Use the Customise windows to set required output in a report	
13	Display a general ledger report on the screen	

End

You should now have a general idea of how *MYOB AccountRight Plus* works. Do not worry if you are not fully conversant with how to enter some of the transactions. You are not yet expected to be able to repeat the entries shown in this chapter as an assessment exercise. In later chapters you will learn to set up *MYOB AccountRight Plus* correctly and learn in greater detail the various options available. You will also get plenty of practice in transaction entry!

Chapter 1: Assessment exercises

1.1   The month for this exercise is July 2011.

Start *MYOB AccountRight Plus*.

Open the existing file ass11.myo. Sign on as the Administrator without a password.

Change the company information so that your name appears in the address field.

Write down answers to the following:

- What is the company name?
- Display the Accounts List on screen. What is the balance of the National Bank account?
- Display the sales transaction journal for July 2011. Use the 'zoom' arrow next to invoice # 1027 on 18 July and write down the items that were sold, and the salesperson.
- Select the *Card File* command centre, *Cards List* option and click on the *Supplier* tab. Use the 'zoom' arrow next to "Mwangi Mills" and write down the phone number and contact name.

Print a balance sheet as at 31 July 2011 (include zero balances).

How much is the liability for the Goods and Services Tax (GST)?

Exit *MYOB AccountRight Plus*.

1.2   The month for this exercise is July 2011.

Start *MYOB AccountRight Plus*.

Open the existing file ass12.myo. Sign on as the Administrator without a password.

Change the company information so that your name appears in the address field.

Write down answers to the following:

- What is the company name?
- Display the Accounts List on screen. What is the balance of the Colonial State Bank (Account 1-1100)? How much is the GST liability (Account 2-1200)?
- Display the sales transaction journal for July 2011. Use the 'zoom' arrow next to Invoice ID# 1333 and write down the items that were sold, the amount of GST on the invoice, the salesperson and the transport company.
- Select the *Card File* command centre, the *Cards List* option and *Employee* tab. Use the 'zoom' arrow and write down Peter Kosiak's salutation and email address.

Print the accounts list summary (include zero balances).

Exit *MYOB AccountRight Plus*.

1.3   Using the abbreviations given, indicate the classification of the accounts listed:

CA	–	Current Assets
NCA	–	Non-Current Assets
CL	–	Current Liabilities
NCL	–	Non-Current Liabilities
P	–	Equity (Proprietorship)
I	–	Income
E	–	Expense

Plant & Equipment
Accumulated Depreciation – Plant & Equipment
Cash at Bank – Commonwealth Bank
Cash at Bank – Westpac
Accounts Payable
Bills Receivable
Inventory
Sales
Commission Received
Salaries & Wages

Prepayments
Advertising
Bad Debts
Depreciation – Plant & Equipment
Depreciation – Motor Vehicles
Bank Overdraft – Commonwealth Bank
Bank Interest Paid
Loan From Finance Co (Repayable in 3 years)
General Expenses
Staff Amenities Expense
Group Tax Deductions
GST Collected
Rates
Accrued Expenses
Petty Cash
Provision for Doubtful Debts
Doubtful Debts

Discount Received
Discount Allowed
Insurance
Printing and Stationery
Bank Charges
Accounts Receivable
Capital
Motor Vehicle Running Costs
Motor Vehicles
Acc. Depreciation – Motor Vehicles
Cost of Goods Sold
Postage
Telephone & Fax Expense
Cartage Inwards
Customs Duty
Bad Debts Recovered
Payroll Tax
Fines (Non-deductible)
Legal Expenses
Travel
Entertainment
GST Paid
Repairs and Maintenance
Electricity
Fringe Benefits Tax
Accounting
Audit Fees

1.4   Using the information in Question 1.3 (and your answer), prepare a draft balance sheet. Use group headings, indent account names for items that will be totalled, and indicate where totals will appear. Here is a start –

Assets
    Current Assets
        Cash
            Commonwealth Bank
            Westpac
            Petty Cash
        Total Cash
        Accounts Receivable
            Accounts Receivable
            Provision For Doubtful Debts
        Net Accounts Receivable
        Bills Receivable
        Inventory
        Prepayments
    Total Current Assets

    Non-Current Assets
        etc.

> **Note:** In the example above, there are four indents (or margins). From left to right they go from the most general heading to the most specific posting account. This four-level layout, and the difference between headings and posting accounts is most important in designing a Chart of Accounts in *MYOB AccountRight Plus*.

1.5   List the advantages of using a computerised bookkeeping system rather than a manual system. Are there any disadvantages?

Chapter 1: Answers to self-test exercises (where applicable)

1.1   The business name for the dem11.myo file is "Possum Hats Company".

1.2   **(a)** There are 8 Command Centres. The Banking Command Centre contains options for receiving and paying money. This includes electronic payments and bank deposits. The other principal option in this Command Centre is "Reconcile Accounts" and this is used mainly for bank reconciliations.

The Sales Command Centre is used to record invoices for goods and services sold to customers on credit and to record payments received from them. There are also options for printing or emailing documents.

The Card File Command Centre is used to maintain (add/edit/delete) information about customers, suppliers, employees and personal contacts. Options are also available to use the card information for labels and form letters.

(b)
Enter sales – Sales Command Centre
Pay bills from suppliers – Purchases Command Centre
Spend money – Banking Command Centre
Set item prices – Inventory Command Centre
Print Payment Summaries – Payroll Command Centre
Prepare time billing invoice – Time Billing Command Centre
Reconcile accounts – Banking Command Centre

1.3   The preferences are shown in Figures 1.9 and 1.10. Part of the *User Access* window for the user called "MKUBWA" is:

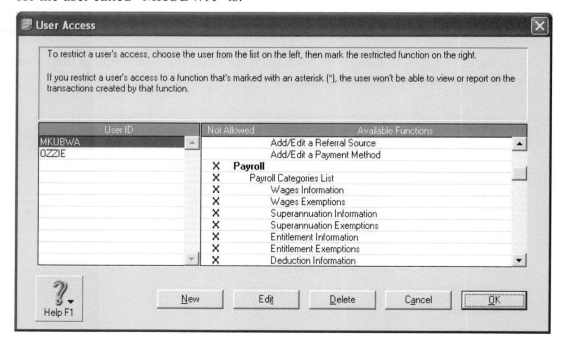

1.4 The window for the reports and forms preferences is already shown in Figure 1.11.

The *Report Format* window showing the new font for the report line:

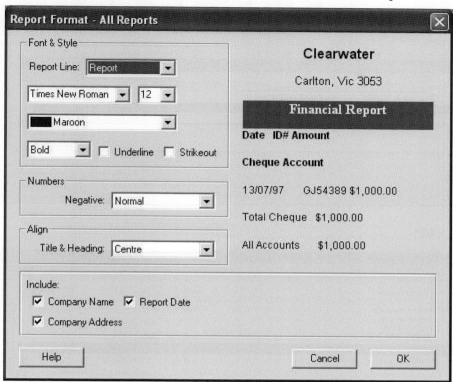

The message to be shown on all statements sent to customers:

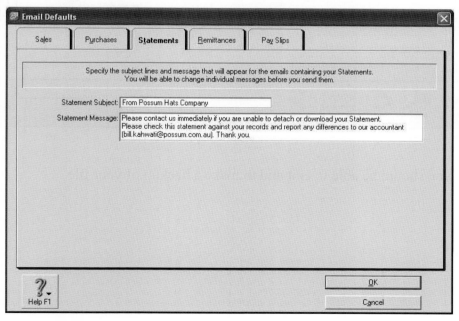

1.5   The description of the item sold is "Delefontes 118".

1.6 *Sales Register* window – Open Invoices

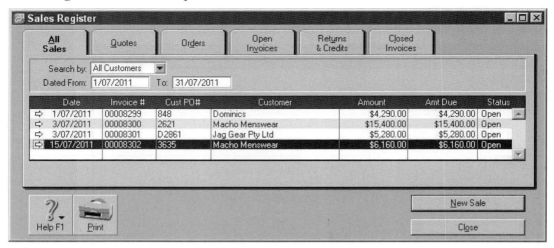

Open Invoice 8302

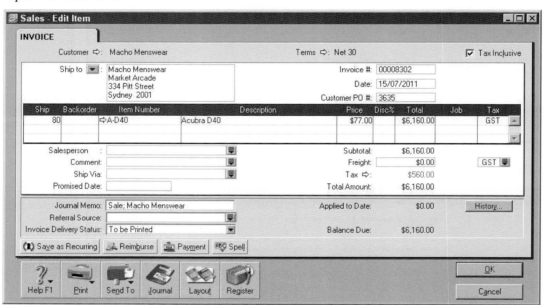

1.7 No answer – you should be able to exit and to make a backup of your file.

1.8

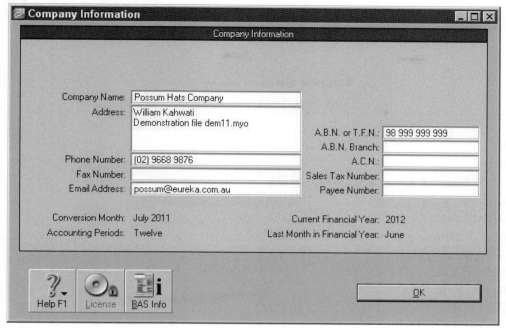

1.9   The details on Invoice #8301 made out to Jag Gear on 3 July are:

(a)   The description of the item sold was "Delefontes 118"

(b)   100 hats were sold on this invoice

(c)   The salesperson was Aravinda Wickeramasinge

(d)   There are two employee cards

(e)   The carrier as per the 'Ship To:' field was "Hills Transport"

(f)   The full comment is "Call Steven on 0457 893 456 for next month's specials"

(g)   The promised delivery date was 15/7/2011

(h)   The delivery address for Jag Gear is 44A Silvertail Drive, Manly, NSW 2095

1.10

Possum Hats Company
Answer to self-test exercise 1.10

Balance Sheet
As of July 2011

Assets
  Current Assets
    Cash and Bank

Corporate State Bank	$14,024.00		
Petty Cash	$500.00		
Undeposited Funds	$0.00		
Electronic Clearing	$0.00		
Payroll Cheque Account	$0.00		
Total Cash and Bank		$14,524.00	
Accounts Receivable			
Accounts Receivable	$43,296.00		
Provision for Doubtful Debts	($500.00)		
Total Accounts Receivable		$42,796.00	
Inventory		$14,440.00	
Deposits		$0.00	
Prepayments		$2,100.00	
Total Current Assets			$73,860.00
Non-Current Assets			
Furniture & Fixtures			
Furn. & Fittings – at cost	$11,800.00		
Acc. Depreciation – F&F	($2,360.00)		
Total Furniture & Fixtures		$9,440.00	
Office Equipment			
Office Equipment – at cost	$26,000.00		
Acc. Depreciation – Off.Equip.	($8,400.00)		
Total Office Equipment		$17,600.00	
Motor Vehicles			
Motor Vehicles – at cost	$88,000.00		
Acc. Depreciation – Motor Veh.	($18,200.00)		
Total Motor Vehicles		$69,800.00	
Deposits Paid		$0.00	
Total Non-Current Assets			$96,840.00
Total Assets			$170,700.00

Liabilities
  Current Liabilities

Accounts Payable	$29,975.00	
Sundry Creditors	$0.00	
Accruals	$0.00	

1.10 *(continued)*

PAYG Withholding Payable		$1,664.00
Payroll Liabilities		$0.00
GST Control		
GST Collected	$18,426.00	
GST Paid	($20,079.71)	
Total GST Control		($1,653.71)
Customer Deposits		$0.00
Unearned Service Contracts		$0.00
Total Current Liabilities		$29,985.29
Non-Current Liabilities		
Loan – D. Doubleday & Crap	$5,000.00	
Loan – A.G.C. Finance	$15,000.00	
Total Non-Current Liabilities		$20,000.00
Total Liabilities		$49,985.29
Net Assets		$120,714.71
Equity		
Capital – P. Doubleday		$92,931.15
Drawings		$0.00
Retained Earnings		$0.00
Current Year Earnings		$3,004.91
Reserves		$24,778.65
Historical Balancing		$0.00
Total Proprietorship		$120,714.71

1.11

Possum Hats Company
Answer to self-test exercise 1.11
Profit & Loss Statement
July 2011

Income		
Sales – Acubras	$19,600.00	
Sales – Delefontes	$6,960.00	
Sales – Imports	$5,900.00	
Total Income		$32,460.00
Cost of Sales		
Cost of Goods Sold – Acubras	$12,440.00	
Cost of Goods Sold – Delefontes	$3,480.00	
Cost of Goods Sold – Imports	$4,500.00	
Total Cost of Sales		$20,420.00
Gross Profit		$12,040.00

1.11 *(continued)*

Expenses		
Advertising	$413.23	
Bank Charges	$56.00	
Depreciation	$0.00	
Discount Allowed	$0.00	
Electricity	$420.00	
Employer Expenses	$0.00	
Insurance	$661.15	
Interest	$28.00	
Motor Vehicle	$401.66	
Office Expenses	$206.61	
Postage	$71.07	
Professional Fees	$0.00	
Rent	$1,652.89	
Repairs & Maintenance	$56.20	
Salaries & Wages	$4,222.00	
Telephone	$347.11	
Travel	$499.17	
Payroll Tax	$0.00	
Workers Compensation	$0.00	
Penalties (non-deductible)	$0.00	
Entertainment (non-deductible)	$0.00	
Total Expenses		$9,035.09
Operating Profit		$3,004.91
Other Income		
Interest Received	$0.00	
Commission Received	$0.00	
Total Other Income		$0.00
Net Profit/(Loss)		$3,004.91

1.12   No answer – you should be able to exit an MYOB file.

1.13

Possum Hats Company
Answer to self-test exercise 1.13
Balance Sheet As of July 2011

Assets
  Current Assets
    Cash and Bank

Corporate State Bank	$11,113.40		
Petty Cash	$500.00		
Total Cash and Bank		$11,613.40	
Accounts Receivable			
Accounts Receivable	$38,786.00		
Provision for Doubtful Debts	($500.00)		
Total Accounts Receivable		$38,286.00	
Inventory		$16,540.00	
Prepayments		$2,100.00	
Total Current Assets			$68,539.40
Non-Current Assets			
Furniture & Fixtures			
Furn. & Fittings – at cost	$11,800.00		
Acc. Depreciation – F&F	($2,360.00)		
Total Furniture & Fixtures		$9,440.00	
Office Equipment			
Office Equipment – at cost	$26,000.00		
Acc. Depreciation – Off.Equip.	($8,400.00)		
Total Office Equipment		$17,600.00	
Motor Vehicles			
Motor Vehicles – at cost	$88,000.00		
Acc. Depreciation – Motor Veh.	($18,200.00)		
Total Motor Vehicles		$69,800.00	
Total Non-Current Assets			$96,840.00
Total Assets			$165,379.40

Liabilities
  Current Liabilities

Accounts Payable		$24,695.00	
Accruals		$2,438.00	
PAYG Withholding Payable		$1,664.00	
GST Control			
GST Collected	$18,506.00		
GST Paid	($20,354.31)		
Total GST Control		($1,848.31)	
Total Current Liabilities			$26,948.69
Non-Current Liabilities			
Loan – D. Doubleday & Crap		$5,000.00	
Loan – A.G.C. Finance		$15,000.00	

1.13 *(continued)*

Total Non-Current Liabilities	$20,000.00	
Total Liabilities		$46,948.69
Net Assets		$118,430.71

Proprietorship

Capital – P. Doubleday	$92,931.15	
Current Year Earnings	$720.91	
Reserves	$24,778.65	
Total Proprietorship		$118,430.71

Profit & Loss Statement
July 2011

Income		
Sales – Acubras	$19,600.00	
Sales – Delefontes	$6,960.00	
Sales – Imports	$6,700.00	
Total Income		$33,260.00
Cost of Sales		
Cost of Goods Sold – Acubras	$12,440.00	
Cost of Goods Sold – Delefontes	$3,480.00	
Cost of Goods Sold – Imports	$5,100.00	
Total Cost of Sales		$21,020.00
Gross Profit		$12,240.00
Expenses		
Advertising	$413.23	
Bank Charges	$56.00	
Electricity	$420.00	
Insurance	$661.15	
Interest	$28.00	
Motor Vehicle	$401.66	
Office Expenses	$252.61	
Postage	$71.07	
Rent	$1,652.89	
Repairs & Maintenance	$56.20	
Salaries & Wages	$6,660.00	
Telephone	$347.11	
Travel	$499.17	
Total Expenses		$11,519.09
Operating Profit		$720.91
Other Income		
Net Profit/(Loss)		$720.91

GST basics

2

An introduction to the basic operations of a computer-based accounting system using *MYOB AccountRight Plus*.

After completing this chapter you will be able to:

1   Explain key concepts of the *Goods and Services Tax (GST)*.

2   Create and edit Tax codes in *MYOB AccountRight Plus*.

3   Produce accrual and cash GST reports.

4   Prepare the Business Activity Statement Option 1 manually.

Introduction

The aim of this chapter is to help people learn about GST basics and how tax codes are used in *MYOB AccountRight Plus*. In particular, the set up and recording must be done correctly so that a business will comply fully with the GST legislation and rulings. A report called the "Business Activity Statement" (BAS for short) must be prepared each tax period by businesses registered for the GST. The usefulness of reports from *MYOB AccountRight Plus* for preparing the Business Activity Statement will depend on how *MYOB AccountRight Plus* has been set up.

This chapter, and the rest of this book, is <u>NOT</u> intended as a book on the GST. Only very basic knowledge about the GST-status of normal business transactions required for set-up and recording is touched on. The legislation, rulings and legal arguments about specialised areas are not covered.

Most goods and services sold will be subject to the GST. A very brief introduction to the GST system is necessary so that you know why some transactions are treated differently.

Basic GST concepts

In theory, the GST is simple. It is a value-added, or consumption tax that has been adopted by many countries. The concept is that businesses will charge tax on their outputs but receive credits for tax paid on inputs. The net tax paid by the business is therefore only on the value it has added – sales value less cost.

Value-added tax in the supply chain

Goods sold and services rendered will have a 10% goods and services tax added to them. Most businesses must be registered for the GST, and these registered businesses will add the GST when making supplies of goods or services. Customers will then pay that business the GST. The business supplier of the goods and services must send the GST collected from customers to the Australian Taxation Office (ATO).

If another registered business receives the supply of goods or services that includes a charge for the GST, that business will be entitled to a credit for the GST from the ATO. If, however, the recipient of the goods or services is an unregistered consumer, no credit is available for the GST paid.

For example, a manufacturer sells a motorcar to a car dealer for $25,000 plus $2,500 GST. The manufacturer is required to send the $2,500 GST to the Australian Taxation Office (ATO) and will collect this when the car dealer pays for the motorcar. The car dealer sells the motorcar to an individual (the final consumer) for $35,000 plus $3,500 GST. The car dealer will send only $1,000 to the ATO, being the $3,500 received from the individual, less the $2,500 paid to the manufacturer. The individual is the final consumer and has paid the full GST on the motorcar. For this transaction alone the manufacturer and the retailer have not paid any GST. Of course, the supply chain goes back further – the manufacturer will have paid GST on raw materials, component parts and other manufacturing overheads which will be claimed back from the ATO. Figure 2.1 on the next page is a diagrammatic representation of the collection and payment of the GST for this supply. Notice that the total GST collected by the ATO equals the total payment of GST by the final consumer who buys the car.

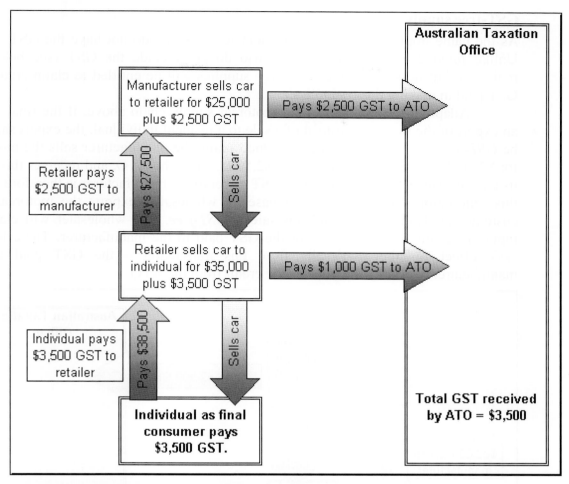

Figure 2.1: Example of value-added supply chain

While the GST should be a relatively simple system, it is complicated by different "rules" for some goods and services. This has been complicated further by political considerations, especially arguments about food, health and education. There are therefore some other concepts that need to be considered.

Taxable supply

A *taxable supply* is a good or service that is subject to the 10% GST. The motor car in the previous example is an example of a *taxable supply*. All supplies of goods and services that are not **GST-free** or **Input Taxed** are taxable supplies and subject to the GST. *GST-free* and *Input Taxed* goods and services are discussed below. There are many examples of *taxable supplies* because most goods and services are subject to the GST. Some other examples of *taxable supplies* are:

Accounting or legal advice	Stationery
Motor vehicles	Meals in a restaurant
Computers	Hot take-away meals
Cosmetics	Books
Air fares	Motor car repairs

GST-free supply

As the name implies, these are goods and services that do not have the GST added. Unlike *Input Taxed* supplies, which also do not include the GST (see below), a registered business that makes *GST-free* supplies will be entitled to claim credits for GST paid in making those supplies.

Adapting the example of the motorcar supply chain above, if the final sale is an export of the motorcar instead of a sale to a resident individual, the export sale will be *GST-free* as shown in Figure 2.2. Once again, the manufacturer sells the motorcar for $25,000 plus $2,500 GST. It pays $2,500 GST to the ATO, and receives this when its customer pays their account. The GST effect to the manufacturer is therefore nil for this transaction. This time the purchaser, a wholesaler, exports the motorcar to a customer in Saudi Arabia, and this sale is *GST-free*. The wholesaler will claim an input tax credit from the ATO for the GST paid to the manufacturer. There is a nil GST effect for the wholesaler from this transaction – the GST paid to the manufacturer is exactly the same as the credit from the ATO.

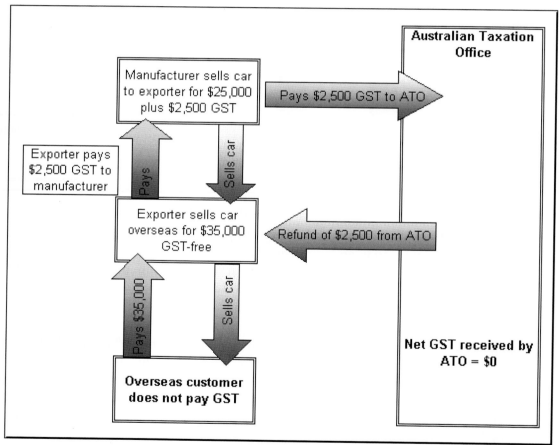

Figure 2.2: Example of GST-free export

Input Taxed supply

Input Taxed supplies have no GST added to the price of a supply by the seller. In some of the GST systems overseas, these supplies are called "exempt". The customer receiving such a supply does not pay GST and therefore has no input tax credit. The supplier may pay GST on its own acquisitions but cannot claim an input tax credit for any GST paid. Some expenses incurred by a supplier of financial services, an *Input Taxed* supply, may be subject to a reduced input tax credit that is currently 75%.

Residential rent is an *Input Taxed* supply. In the example shown in Figure 2.3, the landlord pays a decorator for painting a flat he lets as residential property. The decorator charges the landlord $6,000 plus $600 GST. The decorator sends the $600 GST received from the landlord to the ATO. The landlord cannot claim an input tax credit for the $600 of GST paid, because this was incurred in order to receive an *Input Taxed* supply (residential rent).

The landlord collects rents of $450 per week, but as this is an *Input Taxed* supply, no GST is added to the rent. Financial supplies and residential rent are the two main *Input Taxed* supplies. Financial supplies include services by banks, credit unions and other financial institutions for account keeping, interest, issuing shares etc.

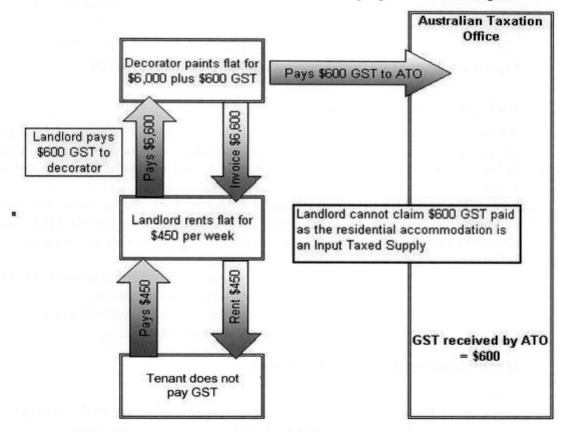

Figure 2.3: Residential rent as an Input Taxed supply

With *Input Taxed* supplies the seller (the supplier) cannot claim credits for the GST paid on acquisitions relating to that supply. On the other hand, the seller of *GST-free* goods and services can claim credits for GST paid on acquisitions. *GST-free* supplies are like *taxable supplies* with a 0% GST tax rate!

Simplified GST Accounting Methods

As this text is about accounting, the method used to report GST will be based on recording the tax on each transaction. However, you should be aware that some small businesses do not have to record the GST on every sale and purchase of trade goods.

Where a small retailer sells both taxable and GST-free goods they may be able to use one of the five simplified accounting methods to split their sales and/or purchases into taxable or GST-free for reporting purposes. The method used for this allocation and the percentages are outlined in various publications available on the ATO website (see end of this chapter for useful web sites). It is not the purpose of this text to examine GST in detail and a very brief overview of the methods from one of these publications is shown in Figure 2.4:

Method	Business norms	Stock purchases	Snapshot	Sales percentage	Purchases snapshot
Turnover threshold	SAM turnover of $2 million or less	SAM turnover of $2 million or less	SAM turnover of $2 million or less	GST turnover of $2 million or less	GST turnover of $2 million or less
How you estimate your GST-free sales and/or purchases	You apply standard percentages to your sales and purchases.	You take a sample of purchases and use this sample.	You take a snapshot of your sales and purchases and use this.	You work out what percentage of GST-free sales you made in a tax period and apply this to your purchases.	You take a snapshot of your purchases and use this to calculate your GST credits.

Figure 2.4: Simplified GST Accounting Methods (source ATO)

GST general ledger accounts

When a new *MYOB AccountRight Plus* file is created, GST accounts will already be set up. You cannot delete accounts that are linked and the GST accounts may be linked to GST codes. See Chapter 3 on how to add or edit accounts in the general ledger.

The usual accounts in a general ledger will be shown under the liabilities, although this can be changed by creating new accounts, re-linking the GST codes and removing the old accounts. The usual accounts are (the names are suggested only – call them what you want):

"GST Collected"	an account for the amount of GST collected on income
"GST Paid"	an account to record GST paid on acquisitions

MYOB AccountRight Plus tax codes

A tax code is used in a transaction to:

- Calculate, add and show the correct amount of tax on the document evidencing the transaction; and
- Accumulate transactions according to type for tax reporting.

A tax code can be set up for entries required on the Business Activity Statement. For example, the BAS requires a separate figure for Export income to be reported and if a business exports goods, an *MYOB AccountRight Plus* tax code can be set up so that the tax report will show the amount to enter on the form.

Many businesses will not require codes for every item on the Business Activity Statement. When you purchase *MYOB AccountRight Plus*, many codes are already set up. You may enter as many three-character codes as you want, but the code used should reflect the tax group involved.

How to add/edit a tax code

Step	Instruction
1	Select the *Lists* pull-down menu at the top of the window.
2	Select the *Tax Codes* menu item.
3	To edit a code, click on the detail arrow ⇨ next to the code required, click on the field required and edit it.
OR	To add a new code, click on the *New* button.
4	Enter a tax code (up to three characters) ↵.
5	Type in a description of the tax involved ↵.
6	Click on the 'Tax Type:' selection box and select the type from the resulting drop-down box.
7	Enter a tax rate. For GST tax codes this will be 0% or 10% ↵.
8	If the tax type selected was ***Input Taxed*** there will be no more fields to fill in. Click the *OK* button in this case.
9	Select a linked account to which tax amounts collected (and due to the ATO) will be posted when a transaction is entered. Hit the Enter key and select from the list of accounts, or click the *List* button 🔽 and select from the list of accounts. For GST codes, the account for GST to be credited might be called "GST Collected".
10	Select a linked account to which tax amounts paid will be posted when a transaction is entered. Hit the Enter key and select from the list of accounts, or click the *List* button 🔽 and select from the list of accounts. For GST codes, the account for GST to be debited might be called "GST Paid".
11	Enter or select a card for the ATO if this has been set up (or is to be set up). This entry is optional.
12	Click on the *OK* button.

> **Memo:** Even when the tax rate is 0%, if the 'Tax Type' selected is anything other than *Input Taxed* the accounts for tax collected and tax paid need to be entered. For example, recording GST-free export goods will have a tax type of "Goods and Services Tax" and a rate of 0%. This will require linked account numbers even though no GST is collected.

Example 2.1—Entering a tax code for export supplies

1. Open the file dem21.myo. Sign on as the Administrator without a password.
2. Change the *Company Information* by entering your name in the address field.
3. Select the *Lists* pull-down menu.
4. Select the *Tax Codes* menu item.
5. Click on the *New* button.

6. Enter the three character tax code as "EXP" ↵.
7. Type in the description as "Export Sales" ↵.
8. The type of tax is "Goods and Services Tax" ↵.
9. The tax rate is 0% (export sales are *GST-free*) ↵.
10. Enter the linked account for tax collected by the business from customers as "GST Collected" (type the number in or use the *List* button 🔽 and select from the accounts list). If you are using account numbers to display accounts (see Chapter 1), select account number 2-1210 "GST Collected" as the linked account.
11. Select the account "GST Paid" (account number 2-1230) as the linked account for GST paid by the business to suppliers of goods and services.
12. Select the "Australian Taxation Office" as the linked tax authority that is to be paid (type "au" or use the *List* button 🔽 and select from the accounts list).
13. The *Tax Code Information* window should look like Figure 2.5 on the next page (using the account name to list accounts). Edit any incorrect part and click the *OK* button to finish.

Self-test exercise 2.1

The file is dem21.myo.

Enter the following new GST codes. TAX type: "Goods & Services Tax":

Code	Description	Rate %	GST Received Account	GST Paid Account
ITS	Input Taxed Supply	0%	GST Collected	GST Paid
NON	Non-deductible/ Private Use	0%	GST Collected	GST Paid

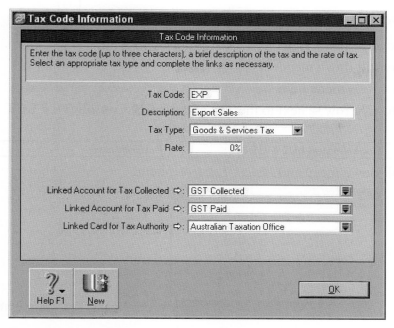

Figure 2.5: A new tax code for export sales

As well as the codes entered in the previous exercise, there should already be a number of codes including those called:

"GST"   this is for the 10% GST on taxable supplies and acquisitions;

"FRE"   this is the code used for GST-free purchases other than export sales; and

"INP"   the 10% GST included in acquisitions for which there is no input tax credit.

If you are using tax codes to assist in preparation of the Business Activity Statement, you should enter a tax code for all income and for all acquisitions except salaries and gift deductible donations.

Deleting tax codes

There are several tax codes already set up when *MYOB AccountRight Plus* is purchased. Some of these may not be necessary and can be deleted to "tidy up" the tax list. A consolidated tax code must be deleted before the individual codes can be deleted. (A consolidated code is used to group together more than one code.)

How to delete a tax code

Step	Instruction
1	Select the *Lists* pull-down menu at the top of the window.
2	Select the *Tax Codes* menu item.
3	To delete a code, click on the detail arrow ⇨ next to the code required; select the *Edit* pull-down menu and click on *Delete Tax Code* item.

Example 2.2—Deleting the tax codes for luxury car tax

1. Open the file dem21.myo. Sign on as the Administrator without a password.
2. Select the *Lists* pull-down menu.
3. Select the *Tax Codes* menu item.
4. Click on the detail arrow ⇨ next to the Tax code "**LCG Consolidated LCT & GST**".

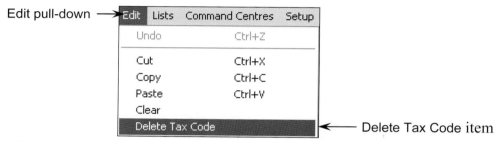

Click ⟶ ⇨ LCG Consolidated LCT & GST | Consolidated | 43%

5. Select *Edit* pull-down menu and *Delete Tax Code* item.

Edit pull-down ⟶

| Edit | Lists | Command Centres | Setup |

Undo	Ctrl+Z
Cut	Ctrl+X
Copy	Ctrl+C
Paste	Ctrl+V
Clear	
Delete Tax Code		⟵ Delete Tax Code item

6. Click *OK* to exit the *Tax Code Information* window.
7. Click on the detail arrow ⇨ next to the Tax code "LCT Luxury Car Tax".

Click ⟶

⇨ LCT Luxury Car Tax | Luxury Car Tax | 33%

8. Select *Edit* pull-down menu and *Delete Tax Code* item.
9. Click *OK* to exit the *Tax Code Information* window.

Self-test exercise 2.2

The file is dem21.myo and you should be signed on as the Administrator.

This business does not deal in wines so the tax codes relating to tax on wines can be deleted. Delete the Tax Code "**GW Consolidated WEG and WET**". Then delete the tax codes "WEG" and "WET".

Delete the tax code "WST" as this no longer applies to this business.

After you have deleted these codes, compare your *Tax Code List* with the solution at the end of this chapter.

GST codes for items

If the business buys and sells items and uses the *Inventory* features of *MYOB AccountRight Plus*, the default GST code for each item can be set up. This means that when an item is purchased or sold, the GST code will be inserted automatically, and the amount of GST will be calculated and shown on the purchase order or sales invoice. Setting up an inventory item including its default tax codes is covered in Chapter 7 "Inventory and Integration".

GST codes for customers

The same item can have a different tax code depending on the customer. For example, an item that is set up with a tax code of "GST" when it is sold in Australia would need to have the tax code changed to "EXP" on an export invoice (exports of goods from Australia are **GST-*free***). However, the default terms for an overseas customer can be set up so that the tax code for all items sold to that customer will be GST-free and override the item's GST code. This customer setup is covered in Chapter 5 of this book.

Tax-inclusive and tax-exclusive transactions

A tax-inclusive transaction means that the price, or amount, shown on the document includes the GST. In a tax-exclusive transaction, GST is added afterwards to the amount that excludes the GST.

In *MYOB AccountRight Plus* there is an option for recording transactions as either tax-inclusive or tax-exclusive. To see how a transaction may be recorded using these options, a cheque payment for the purchase of stationery for $80 (excluding the GST) will be demonstrated. **DO NOT RECORD THIS TRANSACTION** – it is only a demonstration of the difference between tax-inclusive and tax-exclusive transactions.

Figure 2.6 shows a **Tax Inclusive** cheque for the purchase of stationery:

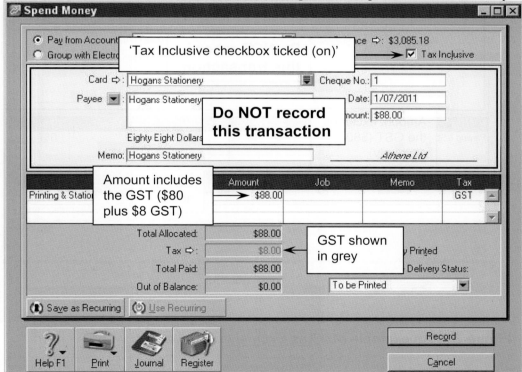

Figure 2.6: An example of a <u>Tax Inclusive</u> cheque

Before recording a transaction, you can examine the accounting entry by selecting the *Edit* pull-down menu and the *Recap Transaction* item. Figure 2.7 on the next page shows the *Recap Transaction* window for the above cheque.

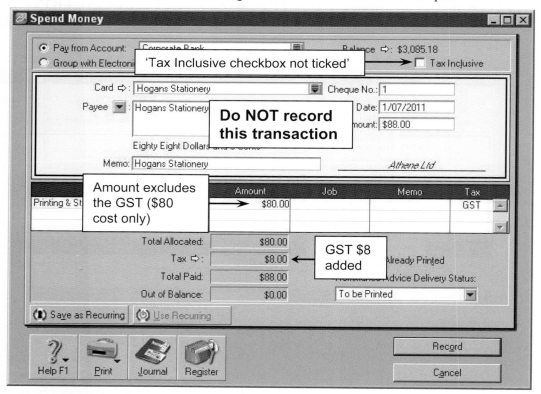

Figure 2.7: *Recap Transaction* **window for a cheque**

Figure 2.8 shows the <u>same</u> cheque payment but recording it as the GST-exclusive amount and adding GST to the total. **DO NOT RECORD THIS CHEQUE** – it is only shown to contrast the difference between tax-inclusive and tax-exclusive transactions. The *Recap Transaction* window for the tax-exclusive payment will look exactly the same as that shown in Figure 2.7 for a tax-inclusive cheque.

Figure 2.8: An example of a <u>Tax Exclusive</u> cheque

Printing GST reports

The *MYOB AccountRight Plus* package produces GST reports that assist with the preparation of the Business Activity Statement. A separate tab, **GST/Sales Tax** at the top of the *Reports* window, is available and this is where all GST reports are located.

How to print a GST report (for cash basis or accrual basis)

Step	Instruction
1	From any command centre, click on the arrow at the end of the *Reports* button and select *GST/Sales Tax*. Reports ▼ Accounts Banking GST/Sales Tax Sales Time Billing Purchases Payroll Inventory Card File Custom
2	For Cash Basis: Select either the *GST [Summary – Cash]* report or the *GST [Detail – Cash]* report. For Accrual Basis: Select either the *GST [Summary – Accrual]* report or the *GST [Detail – Accrual]* report.
3	Click on the *Customise* button to filter the report's options.
4	Click in the 'Tax Codes:' field to select either "All" or specific tax codes that you select for the report.
5	As all taxes for the GST are paid to ATO leave the 'Cards' field as "All".
6	In the *Advanced Filters* tab, click on the date fields and enter the <u>starting</u> and <u>ending dates</u> for the report. (**Note:** It is very important that these are entered accurately.)
7	If necessary, click on the field 'Collected/Paid:' to change the selection.
8	Complete any other details in this view as necessary.
9	The sales and purchases values in the report can be printed either 'Tax inclusive' or 'Tax exclusive'. In the *Finishing* tab change the fields 'Display Sales Values:' and 'Display Purchase Values:' as necessary. (**Note:** Since most fields in BAS require tax inclusive values it might be advisable to select 'Tax inclusive' for both.)
10	In the *Reports Fields* tab select or deselect the fields to be printed.
11	Click on the *Display* button to see the report on screen (you may need to maximise the window to get a better view of the report).
12	Click on the *Print* button to send the report to the printer.

Example 2.3—Printing the GST report

1. Use the file **dem22.myo**. You should be signed on as the Administrator without a password.
2. Click on the *Reports* button at the bottom of any command centre window.
3. Select the *GST/Sales Tax* item or tab.
4. Select the *GST [Detail – Accrual]* report as shown in Figure 2.9:

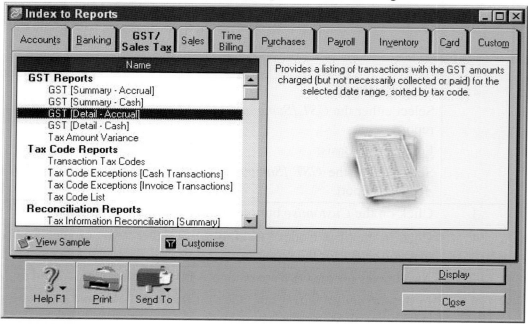

Figure 2.9: GST report selected from list

5. Click on the *Customise* button and select the dates from **1/07/2011 to 31/07/2011**.
6. Select "Both Collected and Paid". The *Report Customisation* window under the *Advanced Filters* tab should look like Figure 2.10 on the next page.
7. Click on the *Finishing* tab. The 'Display Sales Values' and the 'Display Purchases Values' should both be "Tax Inclusive". The *Report Customisation – GST [Detail – Accrual]* window under the *Finishing* tab should look like Figure 2.11 on the next page.
8. Click the *Display* button to accept the customisation.
9. Click on the *Print* button. Check your report against the report shown in Figure 2.12 on page 2.16.

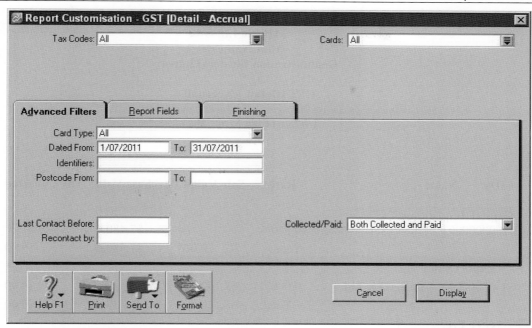

Figure 2.10: *Report Customisation* window under the *Advanced Filters* tab

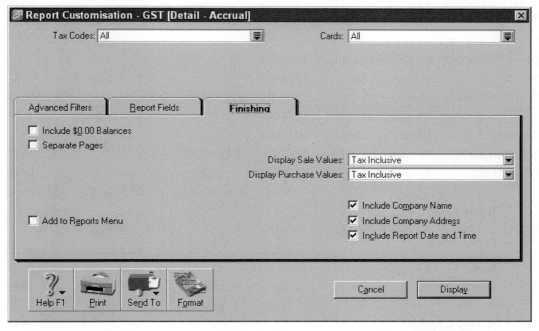

Figure 2.11: *Report Customisation* window under the *Finishing* tab

Self-test exercise 2.3

The file is dem22.myo

Print a *GST [Summary – Accrual]* report for the quarter 1/7/11 to 30/9/11. Select a report for both tax collected and paid. Also, select *Tax Inclusive* values for sales and purchases.

Athene Ltd
<<your Name>>
Demonstration file dem22.myo

GST [Detail – Accrual]

1/07/2011 To 31/07/2011

Page 1

Date	ID#	Name	Rate	Sale Value	Purchase Value	Tax Collected	Tax Paid
CAP	**Capital Acquisitions**						
25/07/2011	00000003	Blue Leaf Computers	10.000%		$7,480.00		$680.00
			Total:	$0.00	$7,480.00	$0.00	$680.00
EXP	**Export Sales**						
24/07/2011	00000002	Abnego Pty Ltd	0.000%	$68,160.00		$0.00	
			Total:	$68,160.00	$0.00	$0.00	$0.00
FRE	**GST Free**						
24/07/2011	00000002	Abnego Pty Ltd	0.000%	$195.60		$0.00	
31/07/2011	00000003	Pharmaceutical Distri	0.000%	$5,280.00		$0.00	
			Total:	$5,475.60	$0.00	$0.00	$0.00
GST	**Goods & Services Tax**						
4/07/2011	00000001	Davis Manufacturing	10.000%		$47,300.00		$4,300.00
11/07/2011	1	J. Leung & Co	10.000%		$1,815.00		$165.00
16/07/2011	00000001	Colzmier Pty Ltd	10.000%	$32,340.00		$2,940.00	
18/07/2011	00000002	Skincare Labs Pty Ltd	10.000%		$43,758.00		$3,978.00
23/07/2011	2	Glass Fixers Pty Ltd	10.000%		$505.78		$45.98
31/07/2011	00000003	Pharmaceutical Distr	10.000%	$23,760.00		$2,160.00	
31/07/2011	CR000002	Cash sale of obsolete	10.000%	$88.00		$8.00	
			Total:	$56,188.00	$93,378.78	$5,108.00	$8,488.98
INP	**Input Taxed**						
30/07/2011	4	G. Hubris Pty Ltd	0.000%		$2,310.00		$0.00
			Total:	$0.00	$2,310.00	$0.00	$0.00
ITS	**Input Taxed Supply**						
30/07/2011	CR000001	Rent of premises to	0.000%	$1,200.00		$0.00	
			Total:	$1,200.00	$0.00	$0.00	$0.00
N-T	**Not Reportable**						
25/07/2011	3	Aust. Taxation Office	0.000%		$21,456.39		$0.00
			Total:	$0.00	$21,456.39	$0.00	$0.00
			Grand Total:			$5,108.00	$9,168.98

Figure 2.12: GST Detail report

The Business Activity Statement

Entities that are registered for the GST must nominate a tax period. The tax period will generally be a quarter, but businesses with a turnover of $20 million or more must have a monthly tax period and pay the ATO electronically. The GST collected by a business must be paid to the ATO each tax period, and must be accompanied by a Business Activity Statement. A business with turnover of less than $20 million may elect to submit its Business Activity Statement monthly. Businesses that expect to receive a refund (input tax credits exceed the GST payable for the period) would most likely have a cash flow benefit from lodging monthly returns.

The Business Activity Statement is a return for all of the business obligations under the new tax system. In addition to the GST, a business will report and pay its income tax instalment for the quarter, Fringe Benefits Tax instalment, its monthly Pay-As-You-Go (PAYG) tax withholdings, Wine Equalisation Tax and Luxury Car Tax.

MYOB BAS information setup

The *BAS Information* window is used to set up the main options for reporting. This requires selecting a number of options for the GST, PAYG Withholdings and PAYG Income Tax instalments. The *BAS Information* set up is accessed using the *Setup* menu, *Company Information* menu item and clicking on the *BAS Info* button.

How to set up the BAS Information for GST

Step	Instruction
1	Select the *Setup* pull-down menu at the top of the window.
2	Select the *Company Information* menu item.
3	Click on the *BAS Info* button at the foot of the window. BAS Info
4	In the Goods and Services Tax (GST) section, select the reporting frequency (monthly or quarterly), the accounting basis (cash or accrual), the calculation method (using accounts or the Calculation Worksheet), and the GST reporting option (1, 2 or 3).
5	The PAYG Instalments and PAYG Withholdings are not covered in this chapter but you should look at the possible selections to get some idea of what might be required in the work place.

Figure 2.13 on the next page is the GST section where Option 1 is chosen (see later about options), the reporting frequency is Quarterly, and the calculation method is by using the calculation worksheet. Change these selections and see additional fields required for other choices.

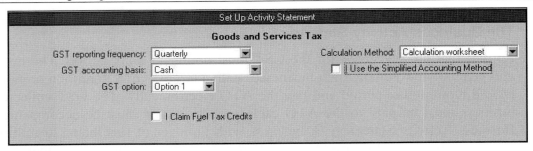

Figure 2.13: GST section of the BAS Information set up

There are a number of options in the BAS Information set up and these are selected using the drop-down arrows at the end of each selection field.

GST reporting frequency

Large businesses with turnovers of greater than $20 million per annum are required to report monthly. In this case, the business does not have any options. Other registered businesses may report quarterly but may select to report monthly, especially if the business has net amounts of GST to collect from the Australian Taxation Office (ATO).

GST accounting basis

The Non-Cash (Accrual) basis is usual except for some small businesses and non-profit organisations. This means that GST is calculated at the time you make a purchase or sale regardless of the time when payment occurs. The cash basis determines GST at the time money changes hands and will be used in Chapter 4. You may use the cash basis if your turnover is less than $1 million and under certain other circumstances.

Calculation method

A calculation worksheet may be used to determine tax. This must be used when using the "Simplified Accounting Method" (not covered in this book). An alternative is to derive the GST direct from the accounts (using *MYOB AccountRight Plus*, for example).

GST reporting options for small business

The GST regime and the BAS have gone through several changes since their introduction. At the time of producing this book, most businesses that do not report monthly have three options for reporting the GST on their BAS:

Option 1: Calculate the GST and report quarterly on the BAS. The report for Self-test exercise 2.3 is reproduced on the next page as Figure 2.14 and will be used to demonstrate the entries in the boxes for Option 1 on the BAS. The box references have been added to the report so that you can see which items are included in each box. For example, the figure to be entered at G1 "Total Sales" will be the addition of all items labelled "G1" on the report in Figure 2.14. There are only 5 items to report for the GST and the amounts shown in the table in Figure 2.15 on the next page is the completed Option 1 section of the BAS taken from the report.

Athene Ltd
GST [Summary – Accrual]
1/07/2011 To 30/09/2011

Code	Description	Rate	Sale Value	Purchase Value	Tax Collected	Tax Paid
CAP	Capital Acquisitions	10.000%		$7,480.00		$680.00
				G10		
EXP	Export Sales	0.000%	$68,160.00			
			G1 & G2			
FRE	GST Free	0.000%	$5,475.60			
			G1 & G3			
GST	Goods & Services	10.000%	$56,188.00	$93,378.78	$5,108.00	$8,488.98
			G1	**G11**		
INP	Input Taxed	0.000%		$2,310.00		
				G11 & G13		
ITS	Input Taxed Sales	0.000%	$1,200.00			
			G1			
N-T	No Tax			$21,456.39		
				Total:	$5,108.00	$9,168.98

Figure 2.14: GST Summary report for a quarter

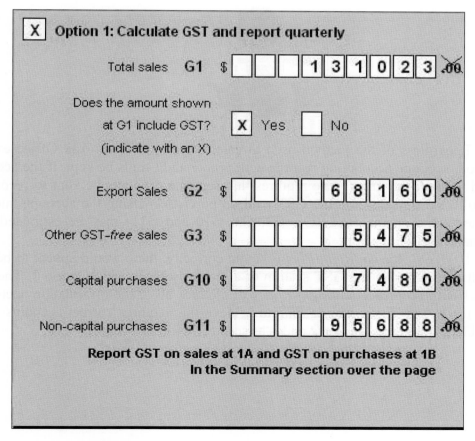

Figure 2.15: Option 1 on front page of the BAS

Option 2: Calculate the GST and report annually. The <u>annual</u> report will be for items G2, G3, G10 and G11 as shown in Figure 2.15 above. Item G1 is still reported quarterly.

Option 3: The third option is available to businesses with an annual turnover of less than $2 million. In this option, the business pays an amount that is calculated by the Tax Office and then completes an annual return. The amount to be paid is printed on the BAS received by the business, as shown in Figure 2.16:

Figure 2.16: Paying an instalment amount calculated by the Tax Office

The GST recorded in one of the tables shown above is entered in the summary on the second page of the return.

Half past five! Time to go home?

Regardless of the method used to calculate the GST, the Tax Office expects that good, accurate accounting records with proper audit trails be kept. If the accounts method is used, the Tax Office requires that separate accounts be kept to record the GST collected on sales and the GST paid on purchases. Using the accounts method, the other items on the BAS (G1, G2, G3, G10 and G11) may be estimated on a "reasonable basis".

If *MYOB AccountRight Plus* is set up correctly, there would appear to be little difficulty in preparing the GST section of a quarterly BAS using Option 1. The GST reports from *MYOB AccountRight Plus* will produce all of the information necessary. To set up *MYOB AccountRight Plus* to achieve this requires correct accounts in the general ledger and the use of tax codes as seen earlier in this chapter.

Self-test exercise 2.4

Open the file dem23.myo and enter your name in the address field for company information. For the period 1 July 2011 to 30 September 2011:

(a)   Print a *GST [Summary – Accrual]* report. Select Customise to report for both tax collected and paid. Also, select *tax inclusive* values for sales and purchases.

(b)   Prepare entries in Option 1 of the BAS.

Useful sources of Information on BAS and the GST (Internet addresses)

You can contact any of these Internet addresses for up-to-date information on the *New Tax System* including GST and BAS:

www.ato.gov.au   The Australian Taxation Office
www.myob.com.au   MYOB Limited
www.business.gov.au   Business Section of ATO
www.reinsw.com.au   The Real Estate Institute of NSW.

Each one of these addresses can direct you to other Internet locations for further information.

Competency checklist

	I can now do the following:	✔
1	Start *MYOB AccountRight Plus*	
2	Describe the GST system	
3	Add and Edit GST codes	
4	Delete GST codes	
5	Set the default GST code for inventory items	
6	Set GST codes for customers	
7	Describe the difference between "Tax-Inclusive" and "Tax-Exclusive"	
8	Select and print GST Reports	
9	Prepare the Option 1 Section of a quarterly Business Activity Statement	

Chapter 2: Assessment exercises

2.1   The following exercise requires you to add and delete some GST codes, record two transactions and to print a GST report.

- Open the file ass21.myo and sign on as the Administrator without a password.
- Change the company address field in *Company Information* (found in the Setup menu) so that your own name is included where indicated.
- Delete the tax codes LCT, WEG, WET and WST.
- Add the following GST type tax codes:

Code	Description	Rate %	GST Received Account	GST Paid Account
EXP	Export Sales	0%	GST Collected	GST Paid
ITS	Input Taxed Supply	0%	GST Collected	GST Paid
NON	Non-deductible/ Private Use	0%	GST Collected	GST Paid

- Record the receipt of a cheque on 29 July 2011 of $2,000 from Andy Warburton for the monthly rent of a flat attached to the business premises. This is an input taxed supply and the tax code is "ITS".

- Record a cheque on 28 July 2011 for the payment of the June petrol account to Mobil Castle Hill. The total of this cheque is $636.11 and it is to be split as follows:

Account	Amount (incl. GST)	Tax Code
Motor Vehicle Running (6-1065)	533.50	GST
Drawings (3-2000)	102.61	NON

- Print a tax-inclusive GST [Summary Report – Accrual] report for the period 1 July 2011 to 31 July 2011. This report should include both tax received and tax paid and should include zero balances.

2.2 Prepare the Option 1 section of a BAS for the quarter ended 30 September 2011 from the following GST report. The report is GST-inclusive for both sales and purchases.

Doonuthing Pty Ltd

GST [Summary – Cash]

1/07/11 To 30/09/11

Code	Description	Rate	Sale Value	Purchase Value	Tax Collected	Tax Paid
EXP	Export Sales	0.000%	$13,985.60			
FRE	GST Free	0.000%	$15,526.40	$248.50		
CAP	Capital Asset Purchase	10.000%		$6,479.00		$589.00
GST	Goods & Services Tax	10.000%	$70,015.00	$57,337.50	$6,365.00	$5,212.50
INP	Input Taxed	0.000%		$4,562.00		
ITS	Input Taxed Sales	0.000%	$2,400.50			
				Total:	$6,365.00	$5,801.50

2.3 Prepare the Option 1 section of a BAS for the month of August 2011 from the following GST report. The report is GST-inclusive for both sales and purchases.

Disparate Pty Ltd

GST [Summary – Cash]

1/08/11 To 31/08/11

Code	Description	Rate	Sale Value	Purchase Value	Tax Collected	Tax Paid
EXP	Export Sales	0.000%	$18,985.75			
FRE	GST Free	0.000%	$6,423.00	$156.65		
CAP	Capital Asset Purchase	10.000%		$17,380.00		$1,580.00
GST	Goods & Services Tax	10.000%	$53,416.00	$68,640.00	$4,856.00	$6,240.00
INP	Input Taxed	0.000%		$1865.00		
ITS	Input Taxed Sales	0.000%	$1,896.30			
				Total:	$4,856.00	$7,820.00

Chapter 2: Answers to self-test exercises

2.1

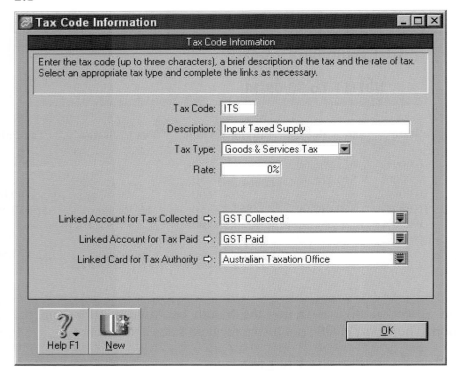

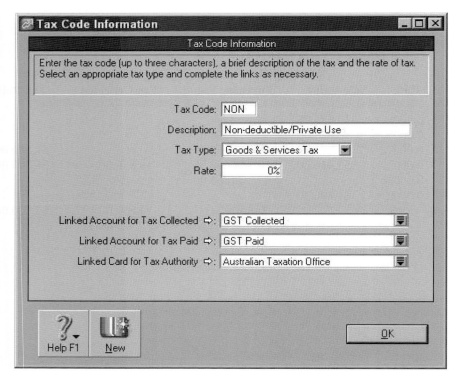

2.2 Tax Code list after additions and deletions

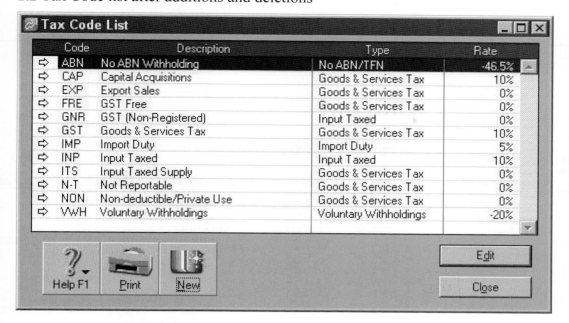

	Code	Description	Type	Rate
⇨	ABN	No ABN Withholding	No ABN/TFN	-46.5%
⇨	CAP	Capital Acquisitions	Goods & Services Tax	10%
⇨	EXP	Export Sales	Goods & Services Tax	0%
⇨	FRE	GST Free	Goods & Services Tax	0%
⇨	GNR	GST (Non-Registered)	Input Taxed	0%
⇨	GST	Goods & Services Tax	Goods & Services Tax	10%
⇨	IMP	Import Duty	Import Duty	5%
⇨	INP	Input Taxed	Input Taxed	10%
⇨	ITS	Input Taxed Supply	Goods & Services Tax	0%
⇨	N-T	Not Reportable	Goods & Services Tax	0%
⇨	NON	Non-deductible/Private Use	Goods & Services Tax	0%
⇨	VWH	Voluntary Withholdings	Voluntary Withholdings	-20%

Help F1   Print   New   Edit   Close

2.3

Athene Ltd
<< your name >>
demonstration file dem22.myo

GST [Summary - Accrual]

1/07/2011 To 31/07/2011

29/06/2010
3:27:53 PM
Page 1

Code	Description	Rate	Sale Value	Purchase Value	Tax Collected	Tax Paid
CAP	Capital Acquisitions	10.000%		$7,480.00		$680.00
EXP	Export Sales	0.000%	$68,160.00			
FRE	GST Free	0.000%	$5,475.60			
GST	Goods & Services Tax	10.000%	$56,188.00	$93,378.78	$5,108.00	$8,488.98
INP	Input Taxed	0.000%		$2,310.00		
ITS	Input Taxed Supply	0.000%	$1,200.00			
N-T	Not Reportable	0.000%		$21,456.39		
				Total:	$5,108.00	$9,168.98

2.4

(a)

Uhuru Company
<<your Name>>
Demonstration File dem23.myo

GST [Summary - Accrual]

1/07/2011 To 30/09/2011

29/06/2010
3:58:28 PM
Page 1

Code	Description	Rate	Sale Value	Purchase Value	Tax Collected	Tax Paid
CAP	Capital Acquisitions	10.000%		$63,261.00		$5,751.00
EXP	Export Sales	0.000%	$101,600.00			
FRE	GST Free	0.000%	$56,910.00	$48,510.00		
GST	Goods & Services Tax	10.000%	$119,817.50	$189,354.00	$10,892.50	$17,214.00
INP	Input Taxed	0.000%		$6,540.00		
ITS	Input Taxed Supply	0.000%	$6,000.00			
N-T	Not Reportable	0.000%		$10,153.13		
NON	Non-deductible/Private U	0.000%		$190.00		
				Total:	$10,892.50	$22,965.00

(b)

X	**Option 1: Calculate GST and report quarterly**

Total sales   **G1** $ [ ][ ][ ][2][8][4][3][2][7].00

Does the amount shown
at G1 include GST?   [X] Yes   [ ] No
(indicate with an X)

Export Sales   **G2** $ [ ][ ][ ][1][0][1][6][0][0].00

Other GST-*free* sales   **G3** $ [ ][ ][ ][ ][5][6][9][1][0].00

Capital purchases   **G10** $ [ ][ ][ ][ ][6][3][2][6][1].00

Non-capital purchases   **G11** $ [ ][ ][ ][2][4][4][5][9][4].00

**Report GST on sales at 1A and GST on purchases at 1B
In the Summary section over the page**

General ledger 3

Setting up a new company file and editing the accounts list. Preparing general journal entries and printing financial reports.

After completing this chapter you will be able to:

1 Start a new file in *MYOB AccountRight*.

2 Enter the business name, address, ABN, ACN etc. and set the financial year.

3 Maintain an Accounts List (Chart of Accounts) – add, edit, delete and combine accounts.

4 Enter in the opening general ledger balances.

5 Print "pro-forma" financial statements to verify correct set-up for the general ledger.

6 Record special transactions using the general journal.

7 Prepare end-of-year entries.

8 Start a new financial year.

9 Print an accounts list, trial balance and financial statements.

Introduction

People without accounting knowledge who only want to use *MYOB AccountRight* as set up by an accountant should treat this chapter as background knowledge to an understanding of how the package works. This chapter is <u>very</u> important for those attending formal courses who are required to set up the whole accounting system. The lesson is in two parts:

- Setting up a general ledger for the first time
- Entering transactions using the general journal.

A Chart of Accounts is an index of account numbers and corresponding account names for the general ledger. In *MYOB AccountRight*, the Chart of Accounts is called an Accounts List. In the MYOB *AccountRight* computerised general ledger, 'account' numbers are also assigned to headings that will appear in reports. The numbering system in *MYOB AccountRight* has an automatic prefix denoting the type of account (asset, liability, income etc.), with the user supplying a unique 4-digit account code.

The production of meaningful financial statements depends on the correct design of the Chart of Accounts. In practice it also depends on sound internal controls over the whole of the office procedures and the entry of data into the computer. Some of the bookkeeping errors in a hand-written system, such as entry, transcription and calculation errors, are eliminated by using *MYOB AccountRight* provided it has been set up correctly. Other internal controls that relate to <u>all</u> computer accounting systems are only dealt with briefly in this book (e.g. authorisations, security, validations etc.). A person considering the installation of a computerised accounting package without this knowledge is advised to consult an accountant.

> You should have completed Chapters 1 and 2 before starting this chapter. It is expected that you can:
> - Start *MYOB AccountRight*
> - Change the business name and/or address
> - Select *Command Centres* and options
> - Recognise the conventions used in this book (for example, the sign ⏎ is an instruction to tap the *Enter* key).
>
> **You may need to refer back to Chapter 1 to do these tasks. A quick way of finding the place for instructions is to use the 'How to ...' index at the front of the book. You can also look at the videos from the CD.**

Creating a new file

In *MYOB AccountRight*, all information and data are kept in a single physical file on the disk. When a new set of accounts is to be opened, a new file is created. The name of the file is <u>not</u> necessarily the name of the business – you need to keep the file name as compact as possible. Do **not** type in an extension, as an extension of **.myo** will be automatically added to the file name.

MYOB AccountRight comes with a number of account lists already prepared for different types of businesses. These will usually require modification to adapt to any particular business. In this chapter, an account list supplied with the *MYOB AccountRight* software will be adapted by editing the accounts list.

There is a "user friendly" Wizard for starting a new set of accounts. The whole setup can be done using this wizard, including chart of accounts maintenance and preferences. However, in this chapter only the creation of a new file using an accounts list template will be covered.

How to start a new set of accounts in MYOB AccountRight

> **Note:** The Wizard has navigation buttons at the bottom of each window. To move onwards through the steps click on the *Next* button or use the *Enter* key. Use the *Back* button to return to the previous window, the *Quit* button to abandon the process, and the *Finish* button to complete the setup.

Step	Instruction
1	Start *MYOB AccountRight* and click on the **Create** *a new company file* icon. Create a new company file
2	Read the *Welcome* window and click on the *Next* button or ↵.
3	If you are a registered user, type your serial number in the 'Serial Number' field. If you are not a registered user, leave this field blank.
4	TAB to the 'A.B.N.' field and enter the business ABN. Using the TAB key to move through the fields, enter the business name as the "Company Name", the business office address, phone, fax and Email address. Click *Next* or ↵.
5	Change the accounting year details if necessary. Use the TAB key between fields and enter the year, final month in that year, the month during the financial year in which figures are first entered into *MYOB AccountRight* (the Conversion Month) and the number of accounting periods in the year. Click *Next* or ↵.
6	Check the confirmation details carefully and click *Next* or ↵.
7	Select how you are going to enter a new account list. You may use a list provided by the *MYOB* program, import an external list or build your own. Make a selection and click *Next* or ↵.
8	Accept the file location and name or click on the *Change* button and complete the New file save window. Click on the *Next* button to create the file.
9	Click on either the *Setup Assistant* button to continue with a full setup, or on the *Command Centre* button to complete the basic setup.

Example 3.1—Creating a new file using New Company File Assistant

1. Start *MYOB AccountRight* and click on the *Create new company file* icon.
2. Click on the *Next* button after reading the welcome message.

3. There is no Serial Number in the Education version. TAB and type in "Ecstatic Company" as the company name. TAB to the 'ABN' field (if you use the Enter key, you will go to the next window – if you do this, use the *Back* button to return).

4. Type in an ABN (Australian Business Number). In this example, type in "98999999999" as the ABN.

5. TAB to the 'Address' field and type your name in the address field. Tab and enter your phone number. Click the *Next* button.

6. Enter the current financial year as "2012". The other options in the accounting year screen should show that June is the last month in the financial year, the conversion month is July (2011) and that this business uses 12 accounting periods in a year. Click on the *Next* button.

7. Confirm that your accounting information is correct and agrees with Figure 3.1:

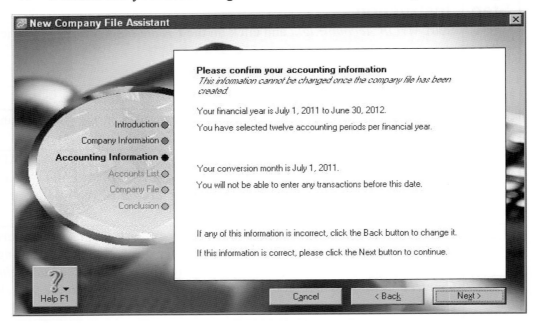

Figure 3.1: Confirm important setup details

8. Click on the *Next* button.

9. For this exercise, select the first account list option so that an accounts list provided with *MYOB AccountRight* will be used (this option should already be selected as the default). Click on the *Next* button.

10. This business wholesales computers and peripherals. Use the drop-down list arrow for 'Industry Classification' and select "Other" ("Wholesale" is not given as an option).

11. Use the drop-down list for 'Type of Business' and select "Wholesale Business". You could click on the *Print* button to print the suggested accounts list but this list is going to be modified and printed later in this chapter. If your selection window looks like Figure 3.2 on the next page, click on the *Next* button.

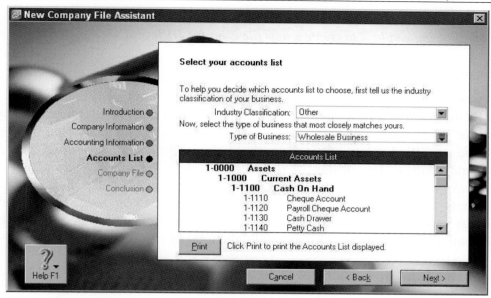

Figure 3.2: Industry classification and type of business selected

12.   The file location and name suggested by *MYOB AccountRight* might look like "C:\Plus 19ED\Ecstatic Company.myo". For this exercise, this is to be changed so click on the *Change* button.

13.   Select the location for the file and change the file name to "dem31.myo". Figure 3.3 shows this file is to be saved to a directory called "MYOB Data Files" on the hard disk. Click on the *Save* button.

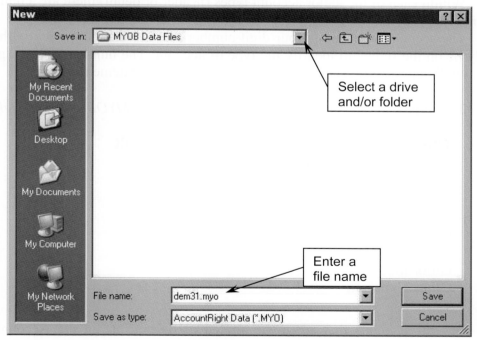

Figure 3.3: New file name and location

14.   Click on the *Next* button to save the file.

15.   In this chapter the remainder of the set up is not used, so click on the *Command Centre* button to start using the new file in *MYOB AccountRight*.

A video showing you how to create a new file is on the DVD

Accounts List maintenance

The word "maintenance" is used wherever relatively permanent data is to be added, deleted or edited in a computer file. The *Accounts List* must be set up before any other "module" or command centre can be used. The list will contain account numbers that must be specified when setting up the *Sales*, *Purchases*, *Inventory* and *Payroll* command centres. The design of the *Accounts List* (Chart of Accounts) in *MYOB AccountRight* must take into account how you want the balance sheet and revenue statements to appear. Unlike hand-written records, the *Accounts List* includes the headings required in financial statements – for example, Current Assets in a balance sheet, and totals for groups – for example, the total of current assets.

There are two major types of accounts possible in an *Accounts List*:

- **Header Account** – used to enter headings (for example, Current Assets). A section header <u>must</u> be used if a total is required for a group of accounts. Non-postable means that this account number will not accept figures.

- **Detail Account** – a normal account in which bookkeeping entries are to be made (posted).

Within each of the major account types (header or detail) there are a number of account types that may be nominated.

The account number is a four-digit number that is added to the prefix that will already be on the screen to identify the type of account. The number that you give an account will determine its order and grouping in financial statements.

The types of account and their prefix used in *MYOB AccountRight* are:

TYPE	PREFIX
Asset	1
Liability	2
Equity (Proprietorship)	3
Income	4
Cost of Sales	5
Expense	6
Other Income	8
Other Expense	9

Several accounts that are to be altered or deleted are in the Accounts List supplied by *MYOB AccountRight*. The first step is to edit these account numbers so that they will fit into the chart of accounts required by this business.

How to edit or delete an account in the Accounts List

Step	Instruction
1	Select the *Accounts* command centre.
2	Select the *Accounts List* option.
3	Select the account type file tab at the top of the window. These appear as: [All Accounts] [Asset] [Liability] [Equity] [Income] [Cost of Sales] [Expense] [Other Income] [Other Expense]
4	Click on the detail arrow ⇨ next to the required account. The *Edit Accounts* window will open with the *Profile* tab selected. Tabs in the *Edit Accounts* window. **Edit Accounts** [Profile] [Details] [Banking] [History]
5	To change a main option button, click on the one required. ○ Header Account ⦿ Detail Account
6	To change a *Detail Account* type, select from the drop-down arrow at the end of the 'Account Type' field. Account Type: Bank ▼ ← Click to select
7	For a *Header Account*, you can edit the 'Account Name' field. For a *Detail Account*, you can edit the 'Account Number', 'Account Name' and 'Opening Balance' fields. To edit, click in the field and use normal editing procedures.
8	To turn the totalling on or off for a <u>header</u>, click on the *Details* tab at the top of the *Edit Accounts* window and select the tick box. ☑ When Reporting, Generate a Subtotal for This Section
9	For a Detail account, click on the *Details* tab at the top of the *Edit Accounts* window and select the tax code using the *List* button ▼ at the end of the 'Tax Code' field.
10	For a "Bank" type *Detail Account*, bank details can be entered by selecting the *Banking* tab at the top of the *Edit Accounts* window.
11	To delete an account, use the *Edit* pull-down menu at the top of the screen while in the *Edit Accounts* window and select the *Delete Account* item.
12	To change the level of an account, click once on the account name in the *Account List* and use one of the *Up* or *Down* buttons. ⬆ Up ⬇ Down

Example 3.2—Editing existing accounts in the Accounts List

1. Start *MYOB AccountRight*.

2. If you have previously closed the dem31.myo file, open it. (If you are not sure how to open an existing file, find the 'How to …' instruction for opening an existing file in Chapter 1 – use the index at the front of the book). Sign on as the Administrator without a password.

3. Select the *Accounts* command centre and the *Accounts List* option.

4. If you are not in the *Asset* section, click on the tab for *Asset* at the top of the window. The top part of the *Accounts List* window should look like Figure 3.4:

Figure 3.4: The assets shown in the *Accounts List* window at the start

5. Click on the detail (or zoom) arrow ⇨ for account 1-1110 "Cheque Account".

6. TAB to the 'Account Name' field. The account name should be highlighted. Type in "Commonwealth Bank". Leave the 'Account Type' as "Bank". The opening balance could be entered here but all opening balances will be entered later. Your *Edit Accounts* window should look like Figure 3.5 on the next page.

7. Click the *OK* button.

8. Click on the detail arrow next to account 1-1210 "Less Prov'n for Doubtful Debts".

9. Change the account number to 1-1220 ↵. Click the *OK* button.

10. Click on the detail arrow next to account 1-1200 "Trade Debtors".

11. Change the account number to 1-1210 ↵, and type in the name as "Accounts Receivable". Click the *OK* button.

12. If the top part of your assets section in the *Accounts List* looks like Figure 3.6 on the next page click on the *Close* button.

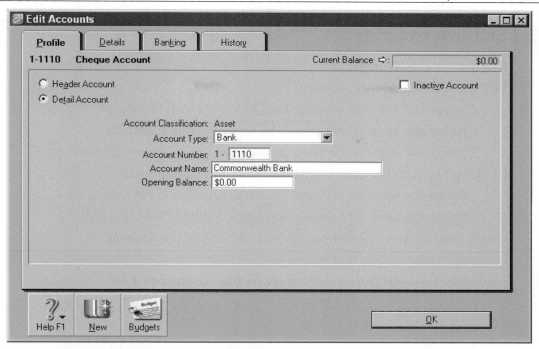

Figure 3.5: Detail bank type account for "Commonwealth Bank"

Figure 3.6: Assets section of the *Accounts List* window with some changes

Video: A video on how to edit the Accounts List is on the DVD

Self-test exercise 3.1

Use the file dem31.myo.

Edit the following asset accounts:

    Change the name of account 1-1120 to "Payroll Clearing"

    Change the name of account 1-1400 to "Prepaid Expenses"

    Change the name of heading account 1-2000 to "Non-Current Assets"

Click on the *Liability* tab and change the following accounts:

    Change the name of account 2-1200 to "Accounts Payable".

    Change the name of heading account 2-1300 to "GST Control".

Check your answers with those given at the end of this chapter.

Example 3.3—Deleting accounts in the Accounts List

1. If not already open, open the file dem31.myo and sign on as the Administrator without a password.
2. Select the *Accounts* command centre and the *Accounts List* option.
3. Select the *Asset* tab at the top of the *Accounts List* window.
4. Click on the detail (or zoom) arrow ⇨ for account 1-1150 "Cash Drawer".
5. From the *Edit* menu at the top of the screen, select the *Delete Account* menu item.

Video: A video on how to delete accounts from the list is on the DVD

Self-test exercise 3.2

Open the file dem31.myo.

Delete the following asset accounts:

    1-1500 "Prepaid Interest"

    1-1600 "Prepaid Taxes"

    All of the accounts for "Lease Improvements".

I knew I shouldn't have deleted that account!

Accounts now need to be added for both headings and other posting accounts.

Note: There are no "accounts" for totals in the *MYOB AccountRight* package and totals are generated by indicating this in the heading for a section.

How to enter a heading in the Accounts List

Step	Instruction
1	Select the *Accounts* command centre.
2	Select the *Accounts List* option.
3	Select the account type file tab at the top of the window. These appear as: All Accounts | Asset | Liability | Equity | Income | Cost of Sales | Expense | Other Income | Other Expense
4	Click on the *New* button at the foot of the window. New
5	Type in the account number and ↵.
6	Make sure that "New Account" appears as the account name. Type in the correct account name and ↵.
7	Click on the option button for *Header Account*. ⦿ Header Account ◯ Detail Account
8	To generate a sub-total under this heading when a report is produced, select the *Details* tab and click the tick box provided. ☑ When Reporting, Generate a Subtotal for This Section

Example 3.4—Creating headers in the Accounts List

1. Open the file called dem31.myo.
2. Select the *Accounts* command centre.
3. Select the *Accounts List* option.
4. Select the *Asset* tab.
5. Click on the *New* button.

6. Enter the account number "1200" and ↵.
7. Check that the highlighted account name is "New Account" and type in the account name as "Trade Debtors & Receivables" and ↵.
8. Select the option button for *Header Account*.
9. Your *Edit Accounts* window under the *Profile* tab should look like Figure 3.7 on the next page.

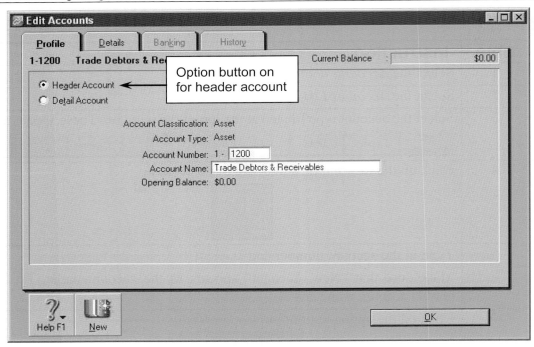

Figure 3.7: A new header account in the *Edit Accounts Profile* window

10.   Click on the *Details* tab at the top of the *Edit Accounts* window. Click on the tick
       box to generate a sub-total for this heading. This is shown in Figure 3.8:

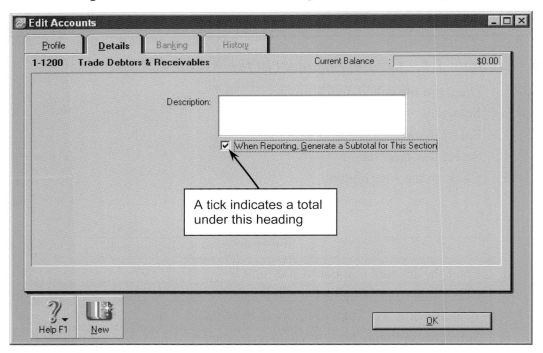

Figure 3.8: Tickbox selected to show a total under this header account

11.   Click the *OK* button. Click on the <u>name</u> for account number 1-1210 "Accounts
       Receivable" and click on the *Down* button to shift this account to the right under
       the heading (refer to Step 12 on page 3-7 for use of the *Up* or *Down* button).
       Repeat this for account 1-1220 "Less Prov'n for Doubtful Debts".

12. Your *Accounts List* should now show the header for "Accounts Receivable" and the two accounts under this heading will be down one level as shown in Figure 3.9:

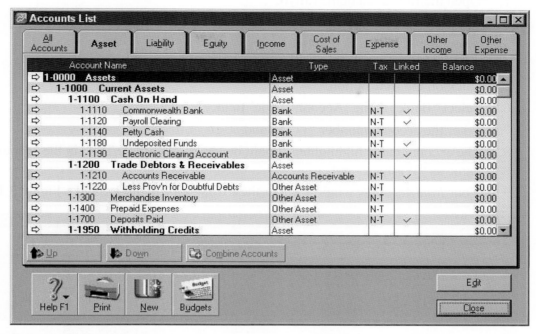

Figure 3.9: Header for current assets and accounts moved down

Video: A video on how to add a header account is on the DVD

Self-test exercise 3.3

The file is dem31.myo.
Add **header** accounts called "Computer System" (account number 1-2800) and "Goodwill" (account number 1-2900) to the assets in the *Accounts List*.

How to enter a detail bank type account in the Accounts List

Step	Instruction
1	Select the *Accounts* command centre.
2	Select the *Accounts List* option.
3	Select the account classification tab at the top of the *Accounts List* window.
4	Click on the *New* button at the foot of the window.
5	Use the drop-down arrow at the end of the 'Account Type' field and select "Bank" as the type.
6	Type in the account number and ↵.
7	Type in the account name and ↵.
8	Click on the *Banking* tab at the top of the *Edit Accounts* window and enter in bank details.

Example 3.5—Adding a detail bank type account to the Accounts List

1. Open the file called dem31.myo.
2. Select the *Accounts* command centre.
3. Select the *Accounts List* option.
4. Select the *Asset* tab at the top of the *Accounts List* window.
5. Click on the *New* button.
6. Select "Bank" in the 'Account Type' field.
7. Enter the account number "1115" and ⏎.
8. The account name highlighted should be "New Account". Type in the account name as "Westpac" and ⏎.
9. Your *Edit Accounts* window under the *Profile* tab should look like Figure 3.10:

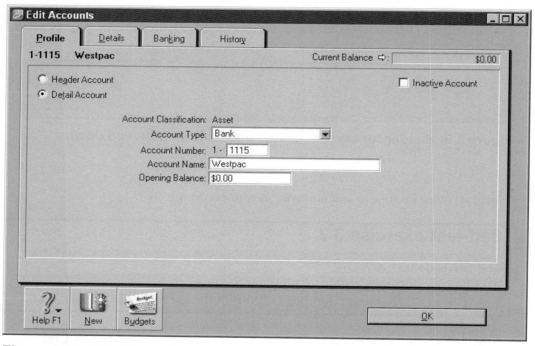

Figure 3.10: Detail bank type account profile

10. Click on the *Banking* tab at the top of the *Edit Accounts* window and enter bank details: 'BSB' is "068-333"; 'Bank Account Number' is "12345678"; 'Bank Account Name' is "ECSTATIC COMPANY"; and the 'Company Trading Name' is "ECSTATIC COMPANY".
11. Click on the 'Electronic Payment Type' tick box. Enter in the details required for preparing electronic payments: 'Bank Code' is "WEP"; 'Direct Entry User ID' is "3386". The tick box for 'Direct Entry File' should be selected (ticked).
12. If your *Edit Accounts* window under the *Banking* tab looks like Figure 3.11 on the next page, click on the *OK* button.

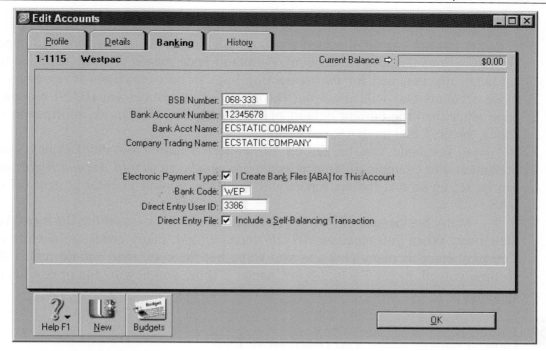

Figure 3.11: Detail bank type account banking details

Your *Accounts List* window for *Assets* should now show the detailed cheque account for "Westpac" as shown in Figure 3.12:

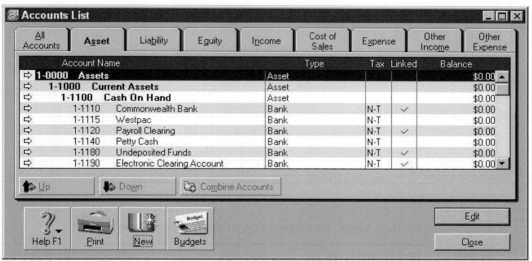

Figure 3.12: *Accounts List* window showing detail bank type accounts

Video: A video on adding bank type accounts to the Accounts List *is on the DVD*

Self-test exercise 3.4

The file is dem31.myo.

Add a detail bank type account number 1-1117 called "National Bank Deposit" to the *Accounts List*. No bank details are to be entered for this account.

Default GST codes for accounts

A detail account can be allocated a default GST code. A default code will appear on all transactions that use the account. A default code means that this tax code will be automatically assumed for the transaction but can be overwritten if necessary. Only those accounts that will affect the Business Activity Statement (BAS) require a tax code other than the current default of "N-T" (no tax). For more information on tax codes, the GST and the BAS, see Chapter 2.

A tax code can be set up for entries required on the Business Activity Statement. For example, if a business exports goods, an *MYOB AccountRight* tax code can be set up so that the tax report will show the amount to enter at item G2 on the BAS.

Many businesses will not require codes for every item on the Business Activity Statement. When you purchase *MYOB AccountRight*, many codes are already set up. You may enter as many codes as you want, but the code used should reflect the tax group involved. Pages 2-6 to 2-8 in Chapter 2 show you how to add or edit tax codes, and page 2-9 in Chapter 2 shows how to delete a tax code.

Video: A video on adding a tax code is on the DVD

Self-test exercise 3.5

The file is dem31.myo.

Enter the following new tax codes. (Refer to pages 2-6 to 2-9 if you cannot remember how to do this.)

Code	Description	Rate %	GST Received Account	GST Paid Account
EXP	Export Sales	0%	GST Collected Code 2-1310	GST Paid 2-1330
PRI	GST on Private Use	0%	GST Collected Code 2-1310	GST Paid 2-1330

How to add a non-bank detail account to the Accounts List

Step	Instruction
1	Select the *Accounts* command centre.
2	Select the *Accounts List* option.
3	Select the *Account Classification* tab at the top of the window.
4	Click on the *New* button at the foot of the window.
5	Select an appropriate account type from the drop-down arrow at the end of the 'Account Type' field.
6	Type in the account number and ↵.
	(continued on the next page)

Step	Instruction
7	Make sure that the default name is "New Account" and type in the account name ↵.
8	Click on the *Details* tab at the top of the *Edit Accounts* window and select the appropriate default tax code. Use the *List* button ▼ and select from the list of tax codes.
9	The option button for *Detail Account* should already be selected as the default. Click on the *OK* button.

Example 3.6—Adding a non-bank detail account to the Accounts List

1. If it is not already open, open the file called dem31.myo.
2. Select the *Accounts* command centre.
3. Select the *Accounts List* option.
4. Select the *Asset* tab at the top of the *Accounts List* window.
5. Click on the *New* button.
6. Use the drop-down arrow for 'Account Type' and select "Fixed Asset".
7. Enter the account number "2810" and ↵.
8. Make sure that the default name is "New Account". Type in the account name as "Computer System at Cost". Your *Edit Accounts* window under the *Profile* tab should look like Figure 3.13:

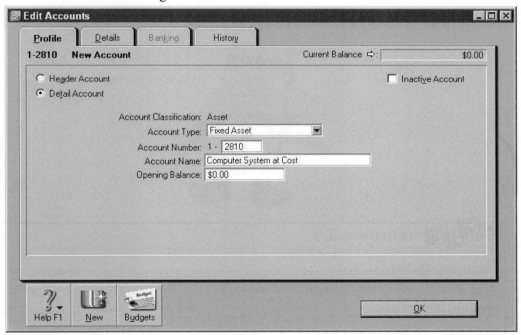

Figure 3.13: A new detail account added

9. Click on the *Details* tab at the top of the *Edit Accounts* window. In the 'Description' field, type in "New CRM System". Select "CAP" as the tax code and leave the cash flow classification as "Investing".

3-17

10.   If your *Edit Accounts* window looks file Figure 3.14, click on the *OK* button.

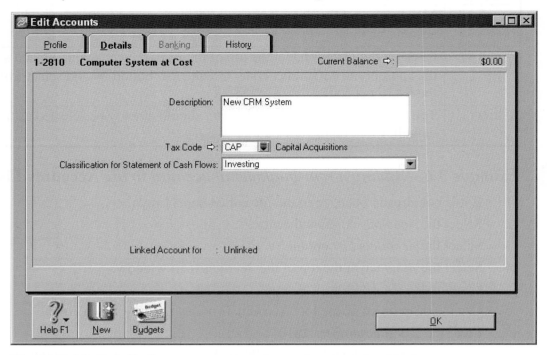

Figure 3.14: Details for a non-current asset account added

Video: A video on adding a non-bank detail account to the list is on the DVD

Do **you** understand all this?

Self-test exercise 3.6

Open the file dem31.myo.

Add the following detail asset accounts to the *Accounts List*:

Number	Type	Name	Tax Code
1-2820	Fixed Asset	Computer System Accum Dep	N-T
1-2910	Fixed Asset	Goodwill at Cost/Impairment	CAP

Check the non-current assets section of your *Accounts List* window for *Assets* against the answer.

Self-test exercise 3.7

Have the file dem31.myo open.

Click on the appropriate tab in the *Accounts List* window and:

Delete the following accounts (not required in this business):

Number	Name
2-1110	Bankcard
2-1120	Diners Club
2-1350	Fuel Tax Accrued
2-2200	Other Long Term Liabilities
4-8000	Miscellaneous Income
4-9000	Fuel Tax Credits
6-3120	Cooperative Adv Allowance
6-4800	Shrinkage/Spoilage

Edit the following accounts:

2-1210	Change the account number to 2-1220
2-1200	Change the account number to 2-1210
3-1000	Change the name to "Owner's Equity"
3-1100	Change the name to "Capital <<your name>>"
3-1200	Change the name to "Less: Drawings"
4-1000	Change the account number to 4-1100, the name to "Sales – Hardware" and the tax code to "GST"
5-1000	Change the account number to 5-1120 and the tax code to "GST"
8-1000	Change the account number to 8-4000 and the name to "Interest Received". The tax code should be "FRE".

Add the accounts shown below to the *Accounts List*. If you are not sure of the levels and how the financial reports are to appear, look at the solutions to this self-test exercise. Don't forget that you can use the *Up* and *Down* buttons to change the margin (or level) of an account, and <u>all</u> of the Header Accounts have a total reported. **Header Accounts** are shown in **bold.**

Classification Account Number	Account Name	Account Type	Header Tax Code
Liability			
2-1200	**Trade Creditors & Accruals**	**Liability**	**Header**
2-1230	Accrued Expenses	Other Current Liability	N-T
2-2200	Loan from Finance Company	Long Term Liability	N-T
Equity			
3-2000	**Retained Profits**	**Equity**	**Header**
Income			
4-1000	**Sales**	**Income**	**Header**
4-1200	Sales – Software	Income	GST

(continued on the next page)

Self-test exercise 3.7 *(continued)*

Cost of Sales

5-1000	**Cost of Goods Sold**	**Cost of Sales**	**Header**
5-1100	**Cost of Goods Available**	**Cost of Sales**	**Header**
5-1110	Opening Inventory	Cost of Sales	N-T
5-1130	Cartage Inwards	Cost of Sales	GST
5-1200	Less: Closing Inventory	Cost of Sales	N-T

Expense

6-2000	**Financial Expenses**	**Expense**	**Header**
6-2010	Bad Debts	Expense	GST
6-2020	Bank Interest Paid	Expense	FRE
6-2030	Discount Allowed	Expense	GST
6-2040	Doubtful Debts	Expense	N-T
6-4150	Electricity	Expense	GST
6-5107	Sales Commissions	Expense	N-T

Other Income

8-1000	Bad Debts Recovered	Other Income	GST
8-2000	Commission Received	Other Income	GST
8-3000	Discount Received	Other Income	GST

Memo: Several income and expense accounts in the *Accounts List* provided by *MYOB AccountRight* do not have the correct tax codes. In practice, these accounts may be edited and the tax code inserted.

Using account names

When setting up new accounts, account numbers are used. If you prefer to use account names, select this option in the *Windows* preferences (select *Preferences* from the *Setup* menu at the top of the screen and under the *Windows* tab, tick the checkbox for 'Select and Display Account Name, Not Account Number').

For the remainder of this chapter, account names will be used.

Editing linked accounts

Linked accounts are used to provide some automatic entry into the accounts and into some setups. For example, the debits and credits to various expense and liability accounts from the payroll can be set up so that these postings are completed each time you pay someone (see Chapter 8 for Payroll setup). Linked accounts will be used in all the following chapters. Linked accounts are looked at now only for the purpose of changing account numbers and names. In the 'Linked' column of the *Accounts List*, a tick mark indicates that an account is linked. If you want to delete a linked account you first have to remove the link.

How to edit linked accounts

Step	Instruction
1	Select the *Setup* pull-down menu.
2	Select the *Linked Accounts* menu item.
3	Select the group of linked accounts to edit.
4	Click on a tick box to select or de-select an optional linked account.
5	Enter account name or number in box for tick box selected.
6	Click the *OK* button to close.
7	To delete an account, click on its detailed arrow ⇨ next to its name in the *Accounts List*, select the *Edit* pull-down menu and *Delete Account* menu item.

(Step 3 illustration shows the Setup menu with "Easy Setup Assistant", "Balances", "Linked Accounts", "Preferences", "Customise Forms", "Company Information", "Business Calendar", "Load Payroll Tax Tables", "General Payroll Information". The Linked Accounts sub-menu shows "Accounts & Banking Accounts", "Sales Accounts", "Purchases Accounts", "Payroll Accounts". Note: Linked Sales Accounts shown as an example.)

(Step 4 illustration shows: Selected — ☑ I charge freight on sales; Income Account for Freight ⇨: Freight Charged; Not Selected — ☐ I track deposits collected from customers.)

Example 3.7—Editing linked accounts

1. If not already open, open the file called dem31.myo.

2. Select the *Setup* pull-down menu and *Linked Accounts* item.

3. Select *Sales Accounts* from the sub-menu of linked accounts.

4. All of the checkboxes are selected in the file created by *MYOB AccountRight*. For the option 'I give discounts for early payment', change the account from "Discounts Given" (income account number 5-3000) to "Discount Allowed" (an expense account number 6-2030).

5. Click on the last checkbox to de-select the option for 'I assess charges for late payment'. Your *Sales Linked Accounts* window should look like Figure 3.15 on the next page.

6. Delete the accounts "Discounts Given" (5-3000) and "Late Fees Collected" (4-6000) from the *Accounts List*.

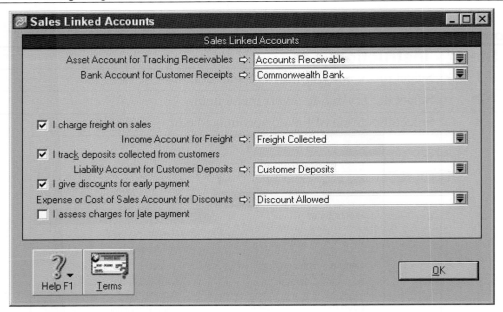

Figure 3.15: *Sales Linked Accounts* **window after editing some options**

Video: A video about editing linked accounts is on the DVD

Self-test exercise 3.8

Have the file dem31.myo open and change the *Purchases Linked Accounts* as follows:

Set the linked account for 'I take discounts for early payments' to "Discount Received" – account number 8-3000. (Ignore the warning that discount received is usually an expense account as we are treating it as income in this exercise – click the *OK* button.)

As no charges are to be paid on late payments, de-select this option.

Delete the accounts "Discounts Taken" (6-1600) and "Late Fees Paid" (6-1800) from the *Accounts List*.

Printing financial reports to check design

The best way of determining whether or not your design is correct and that you have not forgotten to set the headings, totals and levels correctly is to print financial statements with zero account balances. The instructions for printing financial reports are on pages 1-38 to 1-40 in Chapter 1.

Self-test exercise 3.9

Print a *Standard Balance Sheet* as at 31 July 2011 and a *Profit & Loss [Accrual]* for July 2011 including accounts with zero balances (In the *Report Customisation* window click on the *Finishing* tab and select the checkbox for 'Include $0.00 Balances').

Entering existing balances

The existing opening balances for the general ledger accounts are not entered using the general journal. The general journal is used to enter assets and liabilities for a brand new business (the opening entry). You may have noticed that when adding new accounts to the *Accounts List* that there was a field for balances. Existing balances can be entered when setting up the *Accounts List*. However, it is probably better to concentrate on correct design when setting up the *Accounts List*, and using the other method to enter opening balances. The other method uses a specific option for entering account balances. The balances are entered through the *Setup* pull-down menu at the top of the screen and using the *Balances – Account Opening Balances* option.

MYOB *AccountRight* is designed to recognise the sign of account types. An account that has been entered in the *Accounts List* under the 'Assets' category with a prefix of "1" is expected to be a debit. Accounts such as "Accumulated depreciation" and "Allowance for doubtful debts" are included under assets but are in fact credits (deductions from the relevant assets). **You must therefore enter these in the opening balances as minuses (type the minus sign before typing in the figures).** Do not put the minus sign before an amount for say a liability account – *MYOB AccountRight* expects accounts with the prefix "2" to be credits as they are liabilities. If you have an account with a prefix of "2" but with a debit balance (as for example, "GST Paid"), this would need to be entered with the minus sign.

How to enter existing historical balances into general ledger using Setup

Step	Instruction
1	Click on the *Setup* pull-down menu at the top of the screen.
2	Click on the *Balances* item in the pull-down menu.
3	Click on the *Account Opening Balances* item from the sub-menu.
4	Enter the opening balances, making sure that the resulting *Historical balance* account is zero (remember to enter accumulated depreciation, Prov'n for Doubtful Debts, Drawings and perhaps GST Paid as negative amounts).
5	Click on the *OK* button.

Example 3.8—Entering existing balances

1. The balances are as at 1 July 2011. If not already open, open the file called dem31.myo.
2. Select the *Setup* pull-down menu.
3. Click on the menu item called *Balances* and select *Account Opening Balances*.
4. Type in the opening balances listed below. Enter the two accumulated depreciation figures, the Provision for doubtful debts and GST Paid as minus figures – see Figure 3.16 on page 3-25. Enter all other figures as positive numbers.

	Debit $	Credit $
Commonwealth Bank	4,380	
Westpac	880	
Petty Cash	500	
Accounts Receivable	17,217	
Less prov'n for Doubtful Debts		1,327
Merchandise Inventory	7,600	
Furniture & Fixtures at Cost	60,100	
Furniture & Fixtures Accum Dep		18,010
Office Equip at Cost	34,950	
Office Equip Accum Dep		18,860
Warehouse Equip at Cost	44,250	
Warehouse Equip Accum Dep		26,405
Motor Vehicles – at cost	108,500	
Accum Dep'n – Motor Vehicles		56,200
MasterCard		345
Accounts Payable		3,420
Accrued Expenses		240
GST Collected		3,810
GST Paid	2,630	
Payroll Accruals Payable		780
PAYG Withholding Payable		3,500
Loan from Finance Company		20,000
Capital – <<your name>>		128,110

5. Make sure that the *Historical balancing* account shows a zero balance and the amount shown as still to be allocated is zero (see Figure 3.16 on the next page). Do not record these opening balances until this account is zero (make corrections!).

6. Click on the *OK* button when complete.

Video: A video about entering opening account balances is on the DVD

Self-test exercise 3.10

Have the file dem31.myo open.
Print a Standard Balance Sheet at 31 July 2011 without zero balance accounts. Display this on the screen for checking before printing. Save the file and exit *MYOB AccountRight*.

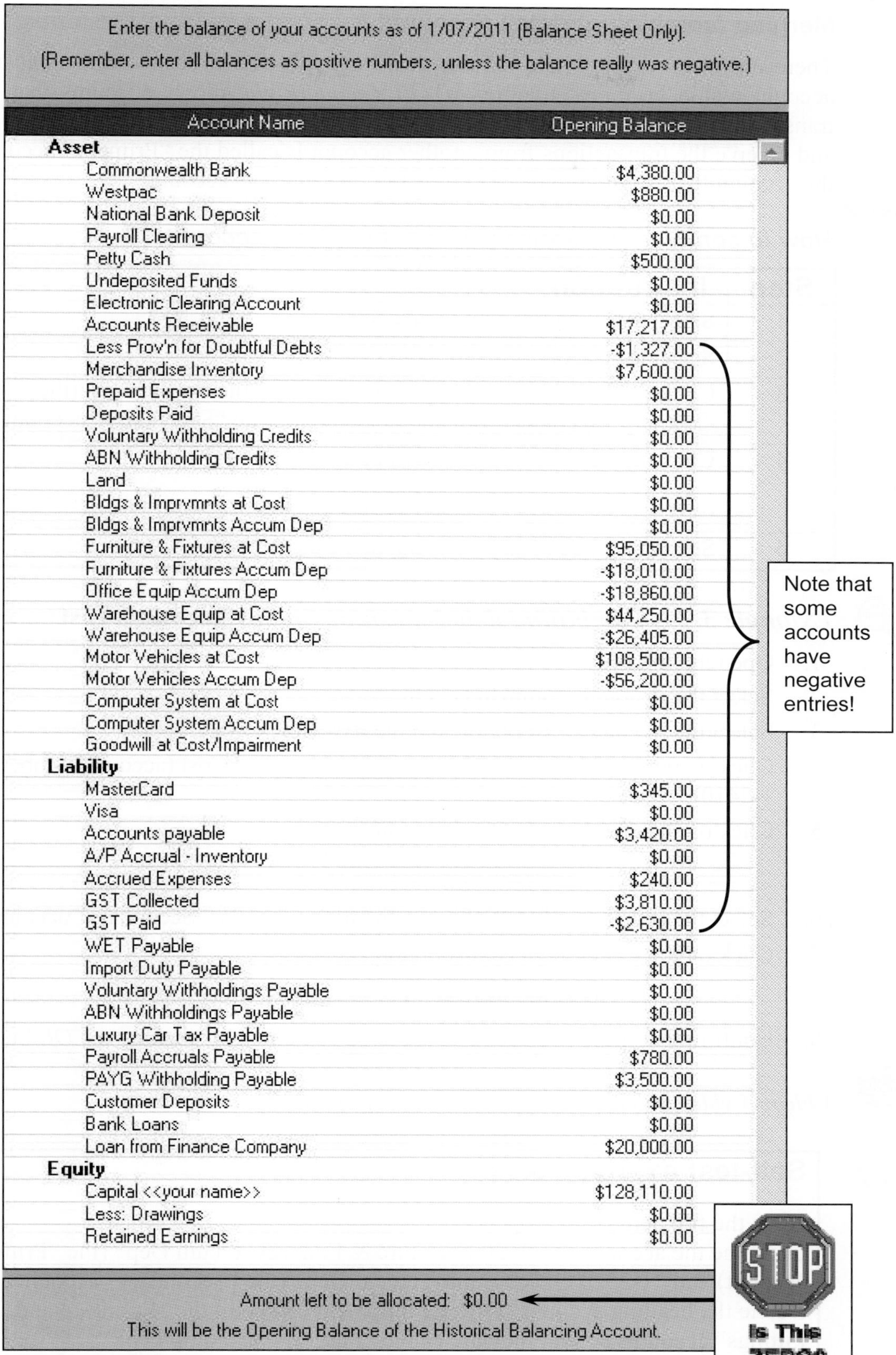

Enter the balance of your accounts as of 1/07/2011 (Balance Sheet Only).

(Remember, enter all balances as positive numbers, unless the balance really was negative.)

Account Name	Opening Balance
Asset	
Commonwealth Bank	$4,380.00
Westpac	$880.00
National Bank Deposit	$0.00
Payroll Clearing	$0.00
Petty Cash	$500.00
Undeposited Funds	$0.00
Electronic Clearing Account	$0.00
Accounts Receivable	$17,217.00
Less Prov'n for Doubtful Debts	-$1,327.00
Merchandise Inventory	$7,600.00
Prepaid Expenses	$0.00
Deposits Paid	$0.00
Voluntary Withholding Credits	$0.00
ABN Withholding Credits	$0.00
Land	$0.00
Bldgs & Imprvmnts at Cost	$0.00
Bldgs & Imprvmnts Accum Dep	$0.00
Furniture & Fixtures at Cost	$95,050.00
Furniture & Fixtures Accum Dep	-$18,010.00
Office Equip Accum Dep	-$18,860.00
Warehouse Equip at Cost	$44,250.00
Warehouse Equip Accum Dep	-$26,405.00
Motor Vehicles at Cost	$108,500.00
Motor Vehicles Accum Dep	-$56,200.00
Computer System at Cost	$0.00
Computer System Accum Dep	$0.00
Goodwill at Cost/Impairment	$0.00
Liability	
MasterCard	$345.00
Visa	$0.00
Accounts payable	$3,420.00
A/P Accrual - Inventory	$0.00
Accrued Expenses	$240.00
GST Collected	$3,810.00
GST Paid	-$2,630.00
WET Payable	$0.00
Import Duty Payable	$0.00
Voluntary Withholdings Payable	$0.00
ABN Withholdings Payable	$0.00
Luxury Car Tax Payable	$0.00
Payroll Accruals Payable	$780.00
PAYG Withholding Payable	$3,500.00
Customer Deposits	$0.00
Bank Loans	$0.00
Loan from Finance Company	$20,000.00
Equity	
Capital <<your name>>	$128,110.00
Less: Drawings	$0.00
Retained Earnings	$0.00

Note that some accounts have negative entries!

Amount left to be allocated: $0.00

This will be the Opening Balance of the Historical Balancing Account.

STOP Is This ZERO?

Figure 3.16: *Account Opening Balances* **window**

Merging (combining) detail accounts

There are often cases where similar detail accounts have been created but a single account would be more suitable. *MYOB AccountRight* allows accounts that contain transactions to be merged without losing historical data. The account that is to remain and receive the transactions from another account is called the "Primary" account, and the account that is going to be deleted is the "Secondary" account.

How to combine the transactions of two detail accounts

Step	Instruction
1	Select the *Accounts* command centre.
2	Select the *Accounts List* option.
3	Click on the detail account that is to receive the transactions (the "Primary" account) from another account (the "Secondary" account).
4	Click on the *Combine Accounts* button. 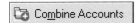
5	Select the "Secondary" account name or number.

Example 3.9—Combining detail accounts in the Accounts List

1. Open the file called dem31.myo.
2. Select the *Accounts* command centre.
3. Select the *Accounts List* option and the *Asset* tab.
4. Click on the account called "Furniture & Fittings" at Cost (account number 1-2410).
5. Click on the *Combine Accounts* button.

6. Select the account called "Office Equip at Cost" as the "Secondary" account.
7. Click on the *Combine Accounts* button.

8. Confirm that these two accounts are to be combined by clicking the *OK* button.

Video: A video about merging accounts is on the DVD

Self-test exercise 3.11

Have the file dem31.myo open.
Combine the accounts "1-2420 Furniture & Fixtures Accum Dep" (the "Primary" account) and "1-2520 Office Equip Accum Dep" (the "Secondary" account).
Delete the heading account "Office Equipment" and edit the "Furniture and Fittings" accounts so that they are called "Furniture & Equipment".

Adding budget data to accounts

A budget is a planned estimate of results for forthcoming accounting periods. Budgeted data can be entered into accounts so that reports can be printed that will compare actual results with the expected budget.

How to enter budgeted data into the accounts in the Accounts List

Step	Instruction
1	Select the *Accounts* command centre.
2	Select the *Accounts List* option.
3	Click on the *Budgets* button at the foot of the *Accounts List* window. 
4	Select either 'Profit and Loss' or 'Balance Sheet' from the drop down list at the top of the *Prepare Budgets* window.
5	Enter the budget amounts in the column for the first month of the financial year.
6	If the amounts are going to be the same for the succeeding months, click on the *Copy Amounts to Following Months* button.

Example 3.10—Entering budget data for income and expenses

1. Open the file **dem32.myo** and sign on as the administrator. This is a new file.   **◁ NEW FILE**

2. Use the *Setup* pull-down menu, *Company Information* item and enter your name in the address field.

3. Select the *Accounts* command centre.

4. Select the *Accounts List* option.

5. Click on the *Budgets* button.

6. Make sure that the 'Account Type' at the top of the *Prepare Budgets* window is for "Profit and Loss" and that the 'Financial Year' is the year ended 30 June 2012.

7. In the July column for "4-1100 Sales – Hardware" type in a budget of "20000". Before you use the Enter key, click on the *Copy Amount to Following Months* button and ↲. Totals for 'Sales' and 'Income' are calculated by the program.

8. Type in "25000" in the July column for "4-1200 Sales – Software" and copy the amounts across the following months ↲.

9. Your *Prepare Budgets* window should look like Figure 3.17 on the next page.

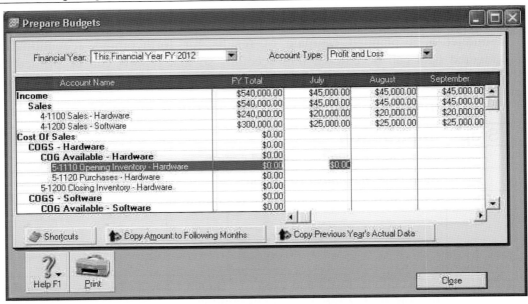

Figure 3.17: Sales budget data entered for current financial year.

 Video: A video about adding budget data is on the DVD

Self-test exercise 3.12

Start *MYOB AccountRight*.

Open the file dem32.myo if it is not already open.

Use the *Setup* pull-down menu, *Company Information* item and enter your name in the address field.

Add the following budget cost of goods sold data in all months of the current financial year (FY 2012). All months have the same budgeted amount.

Account	Amount
5-1110 Opening Inventory – Hardware	$15,000.00
5-1120 Purchases – Hardware	$15,000.00
5-1200 Closing Inventory – Hardware	$15,000.00
5-2110 Opening Inventory – Software	$15,920.00
5-2120 Purchases – Software	$18,000.00
5-2200 Closing Inventory – Software	$15,920.00

Memo: Budgeted expenses would be entered in the same way as above. If the amount budgeted in following months is expected to change (for example, a sales price increase will occur from 1 January), click on the month concerned and enter a new budget figure. Then click on the *Copy Amounts to Following Months* button so that the new amount will be entered from then on.

Recording general journal entries

The general journal is used to record transactions, events or adjustments that cannot be recorded using the other command centres. The entries that will be made in the general journal include:

- Acquisition (purchase) of another business as a going concern.
- Recording the depreciation of non-current assets.
- Correcting errors made in previous entries.
- Recording balance day adjustments (principally accrued or prepaid expenses).
- Recording inventory when the business does not use item inventories and the inventory command centre.
- Writing off assets.

The demonstration file to be used for the journal entries is dem32.myo and your name needs to be entered in the company information.

 How to record a general journal entry

Step	Instruction
1	Select the *Accounts* command centre.
2	Select the *Record Journal Entry* option.
3	Set the "Tax Inclusive" box on or off depending on the transaction.
4	Enter the date and ↵.
5	Type in a memo – this is a short "narration" explaining the entry and ↵.
6	Enter an account name or number and TAB. (Type in the first few letters of the account name or use the Enter key and select from the list if you do not know the account number.)
7	Enter an amount in the debit column, or TAB and enter in the credit column.
8	TAB and enter a Job number if these are being used.
9	TAB and enter any note that may be required about this line of the journal in the 'Memo' column.
10	TAB and edit the tax code if necessary and ↵.
11	Enter all the other lines until the totals of the debits agree with the total of the credits.
12	If a tax code has been entered, select the option button for 'Display in GST [BAS] report as:' either a Sale or a Purchase. Where the code is "N-T" this selection is not important, as this is not recorded on the Business Activity Statement (BAS). In the following example and exercises, "N-T" is the tax code used.

You may also need to add accounts while you are preparing an entry. Use the following instructions for adding an account while in the middle of a journal entry.

How to add an account while entering a transaction

Step	Instruction
1	When asked for an account name or number, use the Enter key to bring up the list of accounts.
2	To add an account to the Chart, click on the *New* button at the bottom of the *Selection List* window.
3	Enter the new account and click the *OK* button (see the 'How to …' list for this chapter if you cannot remember).
4	Re-select the account for the journal entry.

Example 3.11—An example of a general journal entry – purchase of a business as a going concern

1. Open the file dem32.myo if it is not already open.

2. Select the *Accounts* command centre.

3. Select the *Record Journal Entry* option.

4. In this example the amounts will not include any GST so the 'Tax Inclusive' tick-box can be either on or off. For some entries you may need to select or de-select this tick box.

5. On 28 July 2011, the business of Jeremy Fisher was acquired as a going concern. The hand-written journal entry for this is:

	Debit	Credit
Motor Vehicles	24,800.00	
Inventories	12,200.00	
Goodwill	13,000.00	
Jeremy Fisher – Vendor		50,000.00

Acquisition of business from Jeremy Fisher.

6. Enter the date as 28/7/2011 ↵.

7. Type in the 'Memo' as "Acquisition of Jeremy Fisher's business" ↵.

8. The cursor should be on the first line of the journal "voucher" under the column headed "Account". The preferences for this file have been set to show and list accounts by name. You may change this if you want to select by account numbers (see the 'How to …' instruction in Chapter 1). Enter the account name (or number) for "Motor Vehicles – at cost" (account number 1-2210) and TAB. You

may use the *List* button 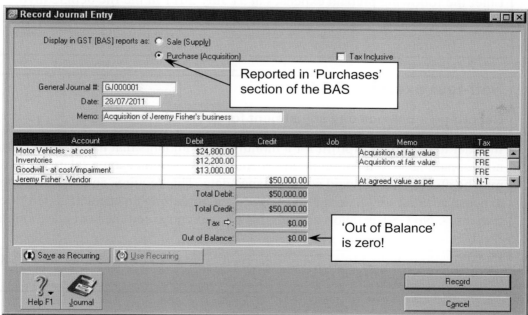 at the end of the field and select from the list or type the details in.

9. In the 'Debit' column, type in the amount "$24,800.00" and TAB.

10. There is no Job involved so TAB to the 'Memo' column.

11. Type in a short note "Acquired at fair value" and TAB to the 'Tax' column.

12. Change the Tax code from "CAP" to "FRE" (the purchase of a business as a going concern is GST-free) ↵.

13. Enter the other two assets, inventories and goodwill, in the same way as Motor Vehicles (the line memo for inventories will be "Acquired at fair value" and leave the memo for 'Goodwill' as a blank. The tax codes for all assets will be "FRE").

14. For the credit to Jeremy Fisher, create and use a liability account with type "Other Current Liability" called "Jeremy Fisher – Vendor" that has an account number of 2-1990. This account will have a tax code of "N-T".

15. Enter "$50,000.00" in the 'Credit' column and TAB to the line 'Memo' column. Enter a memo for this line as "At agreed value as per contract" and leave the default tax code of "N-T".

16. Make sure that there is no "out of balance" figure and that the *Purchase* option button is on for the 'Display in GST [BAS] reports as:' selection. If your *Record Journal Entry* window looks like Figure 3.18, click on the *Record* button. If you do not balance, click on any incorrect field and correct it.

Figure 3.18: A journal entry for the acquisition of a business

You should now be able to enter journal entries for a number of different transactions using your knowledge of debits and credits. Do not worry if mistakes are made – one of the best features of *MYOB AccountRight* is the ease with which corrections can be made. Check your answers for self-test exercises as you go with the suggested solutions at the end of this chapter.

Video: A video on how to record a journal entry is on the DVD

Balance day adjustments

In order to determine a profit for a month, some payments that have been made for a year need adjusting – for example, Advertising and Insurance entered for 12 months may be prepaid (paid for in advance) at the end of the accounting period. In addition, some expense may have been incurred but not yet paid for by the end of the accounting period. In an accrual accounting system, these are recorded using entries known as "balance day adjustments".

Self-test exercise 3.13

Recording a balance day adjustment for prepaid expense

Amounts might need to be paid in advance. Some of the expense to be incurred in future accounting periods needs to be carried forward into these future periods. The entry is to debit the account called "Prepayments" and to credit the accounts for advertising and insurance. No GST is involved with this journal entry, and the tax codes should be "N-T". Type in suitable memos (refer to the answer at the end of this chapter before recording).

Enter the following prepaid expenses at 31 July 2011 in the file dem32.myo:

      Advertising – half the amount paid in July – $600 (1/2 of $1,200)

      Insurance – 11 months prepaid – $4,400 (11/12th of $4,800).

Self-test exercise 3.14

Recording a balance day adjustment for accrued expense

In order to determine a profit for a month, some amounts that have been incurred but not yet paid need to be brought into account. For example, some salaries and wages may be due but not yet paid at the balance date. This requires an entry debiting the expense account for "Salaries and Wages" and crediting an account called "Accrued Expense". No GST is involved with this journal entry, and the tax codes should be "N-T".

Enter an amount of $440 as 1 day's accrued salaries and wages at 31 July 2011 in the file dem32.myo.

Are you checking your answers with those at the end of this chapter before recording?

Self-test exercise 3.15

Correcting an error using the general journal

There are lots of possible errors requiring correcting entries. This requires good accounting skills. The objective obviously is to reverse the effect of the incorrect entry and enter the correct one. Try and do this in a single entry.

Suppose that in July, a repair to a motor vehicle costing $280 (excluding GST) has been entered as "Printing & Stationery". Prepare a correcting entry as at 31 July 2011. It will require a debit to "Motor vehicle running" expense (6-2035) and a credit to "Printing & Stationery" (6-2040) of $280. Record this correction. Change the tax codes for both accounts to "N-T" because the GST paid has already been recorded in the original incorrect entry.

Providing for doubtful debts

Unlike a hand-written bookkeeping system, bad debts are not recorded in *MYOB AccountRight* using the general journal. Any event or transaction that will affect the account of an accounts receivable must be entered using the *Sales* command centre. In fact, it requires an adjustment note (a negative invoice) using the *Sales* command centre to write a debtor's account off as bad, and this is covered in Chapter 5 of this book.

However, a business might record an amount reducing profits by expected but unknown doubtful debts. There are a number of ways to determine an adequate provision for doubtful debts, but these are beyond the scope of this book. The following exercise requires an entry to create a provision for doubtful debts using the general journal.

Self-test exercise 3.16

Creating a provision for doubtful debts

Management would like to create a provision for doubtful debts of $2,000.00 on 31 July 2011. This requires a debit to an expense account called "Doubtful Debts" (account number 6-3030) and a credit to the balance sheet account called "Provision for Doubtful Debts" (account number 1-1220). Use "N-T" as the tax codes.

Depreciation

The cost of a non-current asset is written off over the asset's useful life. The amount to be written off (expensed) in each accounting period can be calculated using a number of different methods. The general journal entry for the amount to be expensed is always debited to an expense account called "Depreciation" and it is credited to an account called "Accumulated depreciation". The "Accumulated depreciation" account, as its name implies, accumulates all of the depreciation written off an asset until it is eliminated when the asset is sold.

Assets such as leases and patents are written off over a definite time period. The expense is called "amortisation" instead of "depreciation" because the asset is not depreciating due to wear and tear.

Where a business wants regular profit reporting (say monthly), depreciation entries can be set up as recurring entries. These recurring entries can be recalled and posted each month without having to set the journal up each time.

Example 3.12—Recording depreciation and creating a recurring entry

1. Open the file dem32.myo.

2. Select the *Accounts* command centre.

3. Select the *Record Journal Entry* option.

4. Depreciation on Furniture and equipment of $118.00 for July is to be recorded on 31 July 2011. It will also be set as a monthly recurring entry.

5. Enter the date as "31/7/2011" ↵.

6. Type in the Memo as "Depreciation of furniture and equipment for the month" ↵.

7. The cursor should be on the first line of the journal "voucher" under the column headed "Account". Enter the account name (or number) for "Depreciation – Furn. & Equip't" (account number 6-2008) and TAB. You may use the *List* button ▼ at the end of the field and select from the list or type the details in.

8. Type in the amount "$118.00" in the 'Debit' column and TAB to the 'Memo' column.

9. Enter "As per depreciation schedule" as the line memo and ↵ (the tax code of "N-T" is correct).

10. Enter the account "Accum. Depr. – Furn & Equipt" (account number 1-2120) and TAB.

11. TAB to the 'Credit' column and enter "$118.00". Enter "As per depreciation schedule" as the line memo and ↵ (the tax code of "N-T" is correct).

12. If your journal entry looks like Figure 3.19, click on the *Save as Recurring* button.

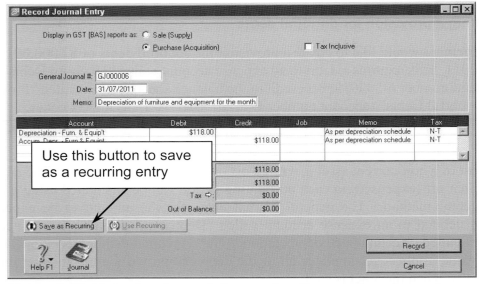

Figure 3.19: Entry for depreciation on furniture and equipment

13. In the *Edit Recurring Schedule* window, change the name of the recurring entry to "Depreciation of Furn & Equip". Leave the 'Frequency' as "Monthly" and the

'Starting on:' date as the system date (in practice this date will be the next date that this entry will be made, but *MYOB* will not allow a date before the current system date). Leave the other options for this example and click on the *Save* button if the *Edit Recurring Schedule* window looks like Figure 3.20:

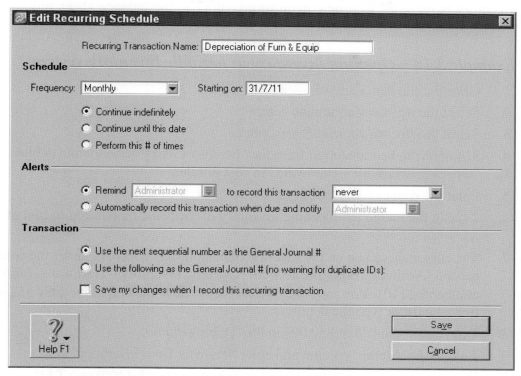

Figure 3.20: Recurring transaction saved for future use

14. Click the *Record* button in the *Record Journal Entry* window to record the entry for July.

Self-test exercise 3.17

On 31 July 2011, prepare a single journal entry for July depreciation on motor vehicles ($1,555.00) and computers ($390.00). Save this as a recurring entry before recording it. Select the option to notify the administrator on its due date. Leave the default "N-T" as the tax code in all lines.

Periodic inventory entries

Where a business has items set up using the *Inventory* command centre in *MYOB AccountRight* and uses *Item* type purchases and sales (see Chapter 7), the accounts will be set up to record inventory increases and decreases through the inventory account (perpetual inventory system). When a sale is made using a perpetual inventory system, an entry will be created reducing the inventory and debiting a "Cost of Goods Sold" account.

The file dem32.myo is set up using a periodic inventory system. This means that purchases are debited to an account in the Cost of Sales section of the Accounts List. The cost of goods sold is determined by transferring the opening and closing inventories that are "periodically" calculated (counted and costed) to the cost of sales section.

The opening inventory for the period is transferred from the balance sheet inventory account to the debit of opening inventory in cost of sales. The closing inventory is recorded as a new debit to inventory in the balance sheet and a credit to closing inventory in cost of sales.

Example 3.13—Opening inventory in periodic inventory system

1. Open the file dem32.myo.
2. Select the *Accounts* command centre.
3. Select the *Record Journal Entry* option.
4. $24,850 is to be transferred from the "Inventory asset" account and debited to "Opening Inventory – Hardware" in cost of sales.
5. Enter the date as "31/7/2011" ↵.
6. Type in the memo as "Opening inventory of hardware transferred to cost of sales" ↵.
7. The cursor should be on the first line of the journal "voucher" under the column headed 'Account'. Enter the account "Opening Inventory – Hardware" (account number 5-1110). You may use the *List* button ⊟ at the end of the field and select from the list or type the details in.
8. Type the amount "$24,850.00" in the 'Debit' column.
9. TAB to the 'Memo' column and enter "Transfer from inventory" and ↵.
10. Enter the account for "Inventories" (account number 1-1400) and TAB.
11. TAB to the 'Credit' column and enter "$24,850.00".
12. TAB to the 'Memo' column and enter "Transfers to cost of sales" and ↵.
13. If your journal entry looks like Figure 3.21 on the next page, click the *Record* button. Click on any incorrect part and edit before recording.

Self-test exercise 3.18

On 31 July 2011, record the transfer of $18,270 opening inventory from the "Inventories" account to the debit of "Opening Inventory – Software" in cost of sales. Leave "N-T" as the tax code for each line.

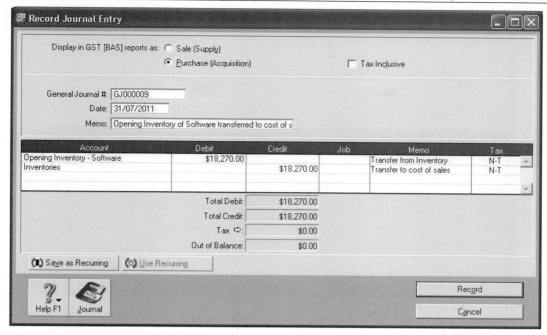

Figure 3.21: Opening inventory transfer in a periodic inventory system

Example 3.14—Closing inventory in periodic inventory system

1. Open the file dem32.myo.
2. Select the *Accounts* command centre.
3. Select the *Record Journal Entry* item.
4. $12,043 of hardware inventory on hand at 31 July is to be brought to account.
5. Enter the date as "31/7/2011" ↵.
6. Type in the memo as "Closing inventory of hardware brought to account" ↵.
7. Enter the account name for "Inventories" (account number 1-1400) and TAB.
8. Type in the amount "$12,043.00" and TAB to the 'Memo' column.
9. Type in the memo "As per physical stocktake records at 31 July" TAB and ↵.
10. Enter the account for "Closing Inventory – Hardware" (account number 5-1200) and TAB.
11. TAB to the 'Credit' column, enter "$12,043.00". Use the same line memo and ↵.
12. If your journal entry looks like Figure 3.22 on the next page, click the *Record* button. Click on any incorrect part and edit before recording.

Self-test exercise 3.19

On 31 July 2011, record the closing inventory of Software valued at $18,120.00 (debit "Inventories" account 1-1400 and credit "Closing Inventory – Software" account 5-2200).

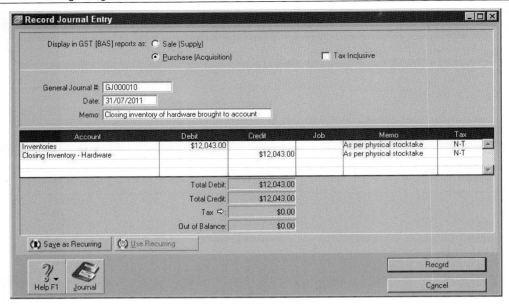

Figure 3.22: Closing inventory in periodic inventory system

Writing off an asset

A non-current asset that is sold will usually be recorded using either the *Banking* command centre (sold for cash), or through the *Sales* command centre (sold on credit or using an invoice). However, when an asset is written off, or written down in value, an entry will be made in the general journal.

Example 3.15—Writing off a depreciated asset

1. Open the file dem32.myo.
2. Select the *Accounts* command centre.
3. Select the *Record Journal Entry* option.
4. An old accounting machine with a book value of $750.00 (original cost $8,900.00 less accumulated depreciation of $8,150.00) – often called the "written-down value" – is scrapped on 31 July 2011.
5. Enter the date as "31/7/2011" ↵.
6. Type in the memo as "Old accounting machine scrapped" ↵.
7. The cursor should be on the first line under the column headed "Account". Enter the account for "Accum. Depr. – Furn & Equipt" (account number 1-2120) and TAB.
8. In the 'Debit' column, type in the amount "$8,150.00" being the accumulated depreciation.
9. TAB to the 'Memo' column and enter a suitable memo. (The tax code is "N-T".)
10. Enter the account for "Furniture & Equip't – at cost" (account number 1-2110) and TAB.
11. TAB to the 'Credit' column and enter "$8,900.00" being the original cost of the machine.

12. TAB to the 'Memo' column and enter a suitable memo.

13. TAB to the 'Tax' column and change the tax code from "CAP" to "N-T" ↲.

14. Enter the account for "Loss on Disposal of Assets" (account number 9-1000) and TAB.

15. The amount of "$750.00" is entered in the debit column, being the book value of the machine (and the "book" loss as it is being scrapped). The tax code should be "N-T" ↲.

16. TAB to the 'Memo' column and enter a suitable memo. (The tax code is "N-T".)

17. If your journal entry looks like Figure 3.23, click the *Record* button. Click on any incorrect part and edit before recording.

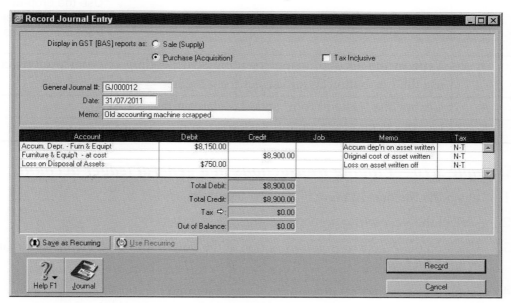

Figure 3.23: Non-current depreciated asset written off

Self-test exercise 3.20

On 31 July 2011, prepare a journal entry to write off some old furniture. The original cost of this furniture was $1,480.00 and accumulated depreciation on it to date is $1,200.00. Debit the loss to the "Loss on Disposal of Assets" account 9-1000 and the tax code on each line is "N-T".

There are many other general journal entries that accountants will have to make. Some of these are:

- Writing off obsolete inventory
- Revaluing assets upward (for example, freehold land)
- Recording various transactions involving company share capital
- Adjustments between partners in the books of a partnership
- Adjustments in livestock trading accounts
- Providing for company income tax
- Providing for dividends payable by a company
- Transferring profits to reserve accounts.

Making an account inquiry

It is sometimes very useful to look at the details of an account. From this inquiry you can click on the "detail" arrow and examine (and edit) any transaction in the account.

How to make an account inquiry

Step	Instruction
1	Select the *Accounts* command centre.
2	Click the *Find Transactions* option at the foot of the command centre window. Click ⟶ Find Transactions ▼ ◄—— Use the drop-down arrow to list other transaction types
3	Type in the account name (or number depending on your preferences) or use the *List* button ▦ and select from the list.
4	Change the 'Dated From' and 'To' dates if necessary.
5	Use the *Print* icon button if a printout of the account is required.

Example 3.16—Finding transactions in a general ledger account

1. Open the file dem32.myo.

2. Select the *Accounts* command centre.

3. Click on the *Find Transactions* option at the bottom of the *Accounts* command centre window.

4. Enter the account for "Inventories" – account number 1-1400 ↵.

5. Make sure that the 'Dated From' date is 01/07/2011 and the 'To' date is 31/07/2011. The *Find Transactions* window should be as in Figure 3.24 on the next page.

6. Note that you can click on a tab at the top of the *Find Transactions* window to select another type of transaction.

7. Also note that there is a button called *Advanced* that allows for further refining (filtering and/or sorting) of the inquiry request – click it to see the possibilities.

8. Click the *Print* button at the foot of the *Find Transactions* window to get a printout of the inquiry details (very useful if you need to check the details with documents – or exercises!).

9. Click on the *Close* button to finish with the *Find Transactions* window.

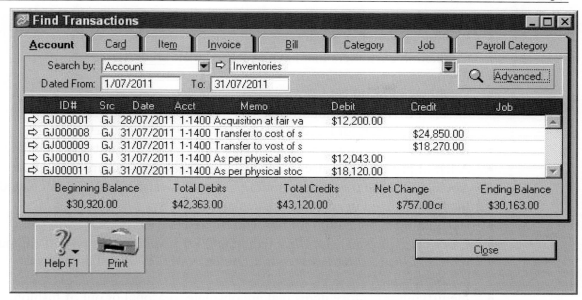

Figure 3.24: *Find Transactions* **window showing details for an account**

Self-test exercise 3.21

Display an account inquiry

In the file dem32.myo, use *Find Transactions* and *Account* type and display on screen the details for the "Furniture & Equip't – at cost" account for the month of July 2011. Check with the answer at the end of this chapter.

Video: A video on using the Find Transactions option is on the DVD

End of financial year

This chapter concludes with the *End of Year* procedures. *MYOB AccountRight* has two end-of-year procedures – *Start a New Financial Year* and *Start a new Payroll Year*. Payroll end of year procedures will be covered in Chapter 8, 'Payroll'.

During the last month of the financial year (usually June), preparations are carried out, reports are printed and reviewed, and decisions are made by management or the proprietors before closing the books at the end of one year and starting the next.

The following are some of the reports that are printed and reviewed:
- Trial balance, Profit & Loss and Balance Sheet
- Customer reports, e.g. customer aged report
- Supplier reports, e.g. supplier aged report
- Inventory list report.

The following preparations and actions are taken (assuming *June* is the last month in the financial year then all calculations are made to or as at the 30 June):
- Reversal of errors detected from reports
- Reconciling customers' and suppliers' accounts

- Creating adjustment transactions (e.g. Credit Notes)
- Settling outstanding accounts
- Contacting customers that have exceeded their credit terms
- Recognising and writing off bad debts
- Establishing or reviewing provisions, such as:
  - o Provision for doubtful debts
  - o Provision for holiday leave, sick leave and long service leave
- A list of outstanding expenses is made and accrual amounts are calculated
- A list of pre-paid expenses is made and prepaid amounts are calculated
- Accrued income (other than trading income) is established and calculated
- Income received in advance is calculated
- Calculating depreciation for non-current assets
- Carry out a physical *stocktake* (count and list inventory items) and compare it with *MYOB AccountRight* records (Actual v *MYOB's*) and do necessary adjustments
- Identifying inventory items that are obsolete, seasonal or out of fashion, damaged or to be discontinued with a view to writing these off prior to end of year
- Identifying capital items that have passed their useful life with a view to disposing of or updating these with newer models
- Reconcile all bank accounts
- If the business is a company, determine the Income Tax liability and provide for this
- Prepare and complete the Business Activity Statement (GST and PAYG)
- Compare actual figures with budgets and prepare new budgets
- Backing up all files
- Purge files and
- Carry out *MYOB* Accounting *Start a New Year* procedure ...

Some of the above procedures are managerial rather than accounting. Nevertheless, as accounting is an integral part of the management information system (MIS), the accounts will be affected by most managerial decisions.

In the examples that follow, use a file called **dem33.myo** that should be on your working disk. It relates to a business called *Bee-n-Gee Sports* that specialises in selling sporting gear and shoes. It has been in operation for a few years and started using *MYOB AccountRight* (converted to this software) as from 1 May 2012.

The transactions up to 30 June 2012 are already entered. Adjustments relating to accounts receivable and payable (debit and credit notes) will be covered in Chapters 5, 6 and 7. For the purpose of this exercise these adjustments, which include writing off bad debts, reversing errors, entering returns and allowances from suppliers and to customers, have already been entered. Similarly a bank reconciliation that will be covered in Chapter 4 has already been performed. Payment Summaries and end of Payroll year are covered in Chapter 8.

In this exercise the end-of-year ***General Ledger*** adjustments will be made.

Note: if you attempt to date a transaction with a date prior to the conversion date (e.g. 1/4/2012), you will receive the following message. ⟶

Make sure all transactions in this exercise are recorded as at **30/6/2012**.

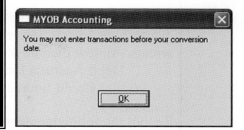

Self-test exercise 3.22

The exercise date is **30 June 2012**.
Open the file **dem33.myo** and change the business address to include your name. Record the following at 30 June 2012 using "N-T" as the tax code in **all** cases, and ignoring jobs and line memos:

NEW FILE

$650 recorded as Purchases (5-1100) in error should be recorded as Store Equipment (1-2110):

Debit Store Equip. – at cost (1-2110)	$650.00	
Credit Purchases (5-1100)		$650.00

Increase the provision for doubtful debts to $1,200.00. The current balance of the allowance is $900.00:

Debit Doubtful debts (6-2200)	$300.00	
Credit Provision for doubtful debts (1-1210)		$300.00

Shop rent expense is paid on the 15th of each month. The rent is currently paid to 15/6/2012. We need to record the accrued expense for period 15/6/12 to 30/6/12 (i.e. half a month). The monthly rent is $1,000 excluding GST:

Debit Rent (6-0410)	$500.00	
Credit Accrued Expenses (2-1200)		$500.00

The business leases an office to a third party for $275 per week including GST. The tenant has paid rent to 7/7/2012. Income received in advance is $250 ($275 ÷ 1.1) excluding GST:

Debit Rent Received (Commercial) (8-5000)	$250.00	
Credit Income Rec'd in Advance (2-1250)		$250.00

Annual insurance premium $1,200.00 excluding GST was recorded in February 2012 for the period 1/3/2012 to 28/2/2013. Four months premium is for this financial year (March to June) and eight months is prepaid (8/12 of $1,200 = $800.00):

Debit Prepayments (1-1400)	$800.00	
Credit Insurance expenses (6-0345)		$800.00

(continued on the next page)

Self-test exercise 3.22 *(continued)*

$60,000 is invested with ANZ Bank (short term deposit) @ 4%p.a. Interest is paid quarterly in arrears. Interest received is currently paid to 1/4/2012 i.e. 3 months in arrears. Annual income 4% × 60,000 = 2,400 and 3/12 of 2,400 = $600).

Debit Accrued Income (1-1420)	$600.00	
Credit Interest Income (8-3000)		$600.00

Record the following depreciation expenses:
$100 for Store equipment and $750 for Motor vehicle:

Debit Depreciation expense (6-0330)	$850.00	
Credit Store Equip. – Accum Dep'n (1-2120)		$100.00
Credit Motor Vehicle – Accum.Dep'n (1-2220)		$750.00

Transfer the opening inventory and enter $29,615.00 as the closing inventory at 30/6/2012:

Debit Opening Inventory (5-1050)	$26,750.00	
Credit Inventory (1-1300)		$26,750.00
Debit Inventory (1-1300)	$29,615.00	
Credit Less: Closing Inventory (5-2000)		$29,615.00

Print a Standard Balance Sheet as at 30/6/2012. Do not include zero balance accounts.

Print a Profit & Loss [Accrual] for the period 1/7/2011 to 30/6/2012. Do not include accounts that have zero balances.

Before starting a new year, you should back up the data file. Use the *File* menu and select the *Backup* menu item. Full instructions for making a backup file in *MYOB AccountRight* are shown in Chapter 1.

How to start a new financial year

> **Note:** This procedure must **NOT** be carried out until **ALL** transactions relating to the current year are entered, reports are printed and checked and finally, a backup copy has been made.

Step	Instruction
1	Select the *File* pull-down menu.
2	Click on the *Start a New Year* menu item and then select *Start a New Financial Year* option. File Edit Lists Command Centres Setup Reports Window Help New Ctrl+N Open... Ctrl+O Close Window Esc Print... Ctrl+P Print Setup... Default Fonts... Backup... Restore... Verify Company File... Optimise Company File Purge Journal Entries Start a New Year ▶ Start a New Financial Year Start a New Payroll Year Import Data ▶ Export Data ▶ AccountantLink ▶ Exit
3	A warning is displayed with a message to do a backup first before proceeding. Refer back to Chapter 1 for instructions on backing up a file. If a backup has already been done, click on *Continue*.
4	*MYOB AccountRight* lists the actions that will take place next – namely: Historical Balances are updated. Transactions are purged, except those dated after end of financial year, pending, outstanding, unpresented or open. All income and expense accounts are zeroed and net profit or loss is calculated and transferred to "*Retained earnings account*". Read this important message and click *Continue*.
5	The new year, the last month in fiscal year and the number of periods are already entered – review and change as necessary and click *Continue*.
	(continued on the next page)

Step	Instruction
6	If you have any receipts not yet banked and included in the account "Undeposited Funds", any electronic payments not yet processed and included in the account "Electronic Payments", or any payroll liability accruals, tick the boxes so that these receipts, payments and accruals will not be erased. Click on *Continue*.
7	The 'Audit Trail Entries' should be purged. Click on *Continue*.
8	If the closed transactions are to be kept, turn the checkbox for this on and select the year from which these transactions should be kept. Click on *Continue*.
9	A list of all of the general ledger accounts is displayed. Mark any account you do not want *MYOB AccountRight* to purge. Click on *Continue*.
10	Click on *Start a New Financial Year*.

Example 3.17—Start a new financial year

1. Make a copy or backup the file dem33.myo.
2. If not already open, open the file called dem33.myo completed earlier in self-test 3.22 above.
3. Select the *File* pull-down menu.
4. Click on the *Start a New Year* menu item and then select *Start a New Financial Year* option.
5. If a backup file has not been made, back up the file (click on the *Back Up* button and follow the instructions provided in Chapter 1). When a backup file has been created click on the *Continue* button.
6. Read about the procedures and click on the *Continue* button.
7. The new financial year should be "2013", the last month "June" and number of periods remaining "12". Click on the *Continue* button.
8. Leave the checkboxes for 'Undeposited funds', 'Electronic Payments' and 'Payroll Liability Accruals' selected (ticked) and click on the *Continue* button.
9. The 'Audit Trail Entries' should be purged (a tick should be in the checkbox). Click on the *Continue* button.
10. The closed transactions for the previous year are to be kept so tick the checkbox and accept "2012" as the year. Click on the *Continue* button.
11. Click against the account "ANZ Bank" (account number 1-1110) in the left-hand column if not already ticked. This will retain any outstanding deposits and unpresented cheques from a bank reconciliation. Click on the *Continue* button.
12. Click on the *Start a New Financial Year* button.

The reversals

The first transactions in the new year would be general journal entries reversing some balance day adjustments such as accruals and prepayments made at the end of the previous year.

Self-test exercise 3.23

The exercise date is **1 July 2012**.

Open the file dem33.myo and enter the following in the general journal at 1 July 2012. The tax code in all cases is "N-T" and there is no need for line memos:

Reverse the accrued expenses adjustment

Debit Accrued expenses	$500.00	
Credit Rent		$500.00

Reverse Income received in advance adjustment

Debit Income Rec'd in Advance	$250.00	
Credit Rent received (Commercial)		$250.00

Reverse prepaid expenses adjustment

Debit Insurance expense	$800.00	
Credit Prepayments		$800.00

Reverse Accrued income adjustment

Debit Interest Income	$600.00	
Credit Accrued Income		$600.00

Print the General Journal for July 2012.

Competency checklist

	I can now do the following:	✔
1	Switch the computer and screen on	
2	Adjust chair and equipment to suit ergonomic requirements	
3	Sit correctly at the computer terminal	
4	Use rest periods and appropriate exercises regularly	
5	Access information from manuals and/or on-line help	
6	Solve operational problems	
7	Select and open *MYOB AccountRight* files	
8	Create and maintain a Chart of Accounts (*Accounts List*)	
9	Prepare and record general journal entries for transactions and closing inventories	
10	Use the general ledger inquiry option and examine the details of an account. Print these details	
11	Prepare and record general journal entries to correct errors	
12	Use the *Reports* pull-down menu and print various reports including *Accounts List* (summary or detail), Trial balance, Balance sheet and Profit & Loss	
13	Apply techniques to minimise paper wastage such as using screen inquiries and recycling paper from printouts	

Chapter 3: Assessment exercises

<u>Note:</u> Throughout the following practical exercises you should continually observe relevant Occupational Health and Safety practices and apply recycling techniques to minimise paper wastage. In addition, you should use the on-line help facilities (the F1 key and/or Windows *Help* menu) and the notes to solve any problems you encounter.

3.1   *Create a new file and maintain the Accounts List – Retail Industry*

(a) Start *MYOB AccountRight*.

(b) Create a new file using the following data:

Company name	Qian Enterprises
ABN	98 999 999 999
Address	<< your own name >>
Accounting year	Current 2012, Last month June, Conversion month July, 12 accounting periods
Account list	Supplied by *AccountRight Plus*, industry classification is Retail and type of business is Furniture Dealer
File name	ass31.myo and save this to a suitable location

(c) Edit the following accounts in the accounts list. If the number remains the same, no new account number is shown.

Present Number	Present Name	New Number	New Name
1-1110	Cheque Account		Banque Nord
1-1210	Less Prov'n for Doubtful Debts	1-1220	Less Prov'n for Doubtful Debts
1-1200	Trade Debtors	1-1210	Accounts Receivable
1-2000	Fixed Assets		Non-Current Assets
2-1210	A/P Accrual – Inventory	2-1220	A/P Accrual – Inventory
2-1200	Trade Creditors	2-1210	Accounts Payable
2-1300	GST Liabilities		GST Control
2-2000	Long Term Liabilities		Non-Current Liabilities
3-1000	Owner/Shareholder Equity		Owner's Equity
3-1100	Owner/Sharehldr Capital		Owner's Capital
3-1200	Owner/Sharehldr Drawings		Less: Drawings

(d) In the tax codes list, delete the tax codes GW, IMP, LCG, LCT, WEG, WET and WST.

(e) Delete the following accounts from the accounts list:

Number	Name
1-1130	Cash Drawer
1-2300	Buildings and Improvements
1-2310	Bldgs & Imprvmnts at Cost
1-2320	Bldgs & Imprvmnts Accum Dep
1-2700	Delivery Trucks

(continued on the next page)

1-2710	Delivery Trucks at Cost
1-2720	Delivery Trucks Accum Dep
2-1110	Bankcard
2-1120	Diners Club
2-1350	Fuel Tax Credits Accrued
2-1355	WET Payable
2-1360	Import Duty Payable
2-1390	Luxury Car Tax Payable

(f) Add the following accounts to the *Accounts List*. Use the *Up* and *Down* buttons if necessary to put accounts under headings. All accounts under a "Header" account will have totals.

Number	Name	Type	
1-1200	Trade Debtors & Receivables	Asset	Header
2-1200	Trade Creditors & Accruals	Liability	Header
2-1250	Accrued Expenses	Other Current Liability	Detail
3-2000	Reserves	Equity	Header

(g) Enter opening balances from the Trial Balance at 1 July 2011:

Account	Debit	Credit
Banque Nord	3,789.60	
Petty Cash	500.00	
Accounts Receivable	23,456.95	
Less Prov'n for Doubtful Debts		3,000.00
Merchandise Inventory	22,146.75	
Furniture & Fixtures at Cost	14,883.20	
Furniture & Fixtures Accum Dep		3,460.00
Office Equip at Cost	19,775.00	
Office Equip Accum Dep		5,446.00
Motor Vehicles at Cost	79,550.00	
Motor Vehicles Accum Dep		22,100.00
MasterCard		456.35
Accounts Payable		16,875.00
GST Collected		2,456.85
GST Paid	1,865.40	
PAYG Withholding Payable		1,875.00
Bank Loans		20,000.00
Owner's Capital		?

(h) Print a Balance Sheet as at 1 July 2011. Include accounts that have zero balances.

3.2 *Create a new file and maintain the* **Accounts List – Consulting Business**

(a) Start *MYOB AccountRight*.

(b) Create a new file using the following data:

Company name	G & B Business Services
ABN	98 999 999 999
Address	<< your own name >>
Accounting year	Current 2012, Last month June, Conversion month July, 12 accounting periods
Account list	Supplied by *AccountRight Plus*, industry classification is Service and type of business is Consulting Firm
File name	ass32.myo and save this to a suitable location

(c) Edit the following accounts in the accounts list. If the number remains the same, no new account number is shown.

Present Number	Present Name	New Number	New Name
1-1110	Cheque Account		Bank of Id
1-1210	Less Prov'n for Doubtful Debts	1-1220	Less Prov'n for Doubtful Debts
1-1200	Trade Debtors	1-1210	Accounts Receivable
1-1400	Prepaid Insurance		Prepaid Expenses
1-2000	Fixed Assets		Non-Current Assets
1-2700	Furniture and Fixtures		Furniture and Equipment
1-2710	Furniture & Fixtures Orig Co		Furniture & Equip at Cost
1-2720	Furniture & Fixt. Accum Dep		Furniture & Equip Accum Dep
2-1210	A/P Accrual – Inventory	2-1220	A/P Accrual – Inventory
2-1200	Trade Creditors	2-1210	Accounts Payable
2-1300	GST Liabilities		GST Control
2-1500	Accrued Expenses	2-1230	Accrued Expenses
2-2000	Long Term Liabilities		Non-Current Liabilities
2-2100	Bank Loans		Loan – Due 31/3/2016
3-1000	Owner's/Shareholder Equity		Owner's Equity
3-1100	Owner's/Sharehldr Capital		<< your name >> – Capital
3-1200	Owner's/Sharehldr Drawings		Less: Drawings
4-1000	Consulting Fees	4-1100	Consulting Fees
4-2000	Other Service Fees	4-1200	Training Fees

(d) In the tax codes list, delete the tax codes GW, IMP, LCG, LCT, WEG, WET and WST.

(e) In the linked Sales Accounts (look under *Setup* menu, linked accounts menus item), de-select all of the optional linked accounts. The only linked accounts for sales should be links to "Accounts Receivable" (1-1210) and "Bank of Id" (1-1110).

(f) In the linked Purchases Accounts, de-select all of the optional linked accounts. The only linked accounts for purchases should be links to "Accounts Payable" (2-1210) and "Bank of Id" (1-1110).

(g) Delete the following accounts from the *Accounts List*:

Number	Name
1-1130	Cash Drawer
1-1500	Prepaid Interest
1-1700	Other Prepayments
1-2200	Leasehold Improvements
1-2210	Improvements at Cost
1-2220	Improvements Amortisation
1-2300	Buildings & Improvements
1-2310	Bldgs. & Imprv at Cost
1-2320	Bldgs & Imprv Accum Dep
2-1110	Bankcard
2-1120	Diners Club
2-1130	MasterCard
2-1220	A/P Accrual - Inventory
2-1350	Fuel Tax Credits Accrued
2-1355	WET Payable
2-1360	Import Duty Payable
2-1390	Luxury Car Tax Payable
4-5000	Freight Collected
4-6000	Late Fees Collected
4-8000	Miscellaneous Income
4-9000	Fuel Tax Credits
5-1000	Discounts Given
6-1040	Amortisation
6-1600	Discounts Taken
6-1700	Freight Paid
6-1900	Company Taxes
6-4000	Shrinkage/Spoilage
6-6020	Rates

(h) Add the following accounts to the *Accounts List*. Use the *Up* and *Down* buttons if necessary to put accounts under headings. All accounts under a "Header" account will have totals.

Number	Name	Type	
1-1200	Trade Debtors & Receivables	Asset	Header
2-1200	Trade Creditors & Accruals	Liability	Header
3-2000	Reserves	Equity	Header
4-1000	Fee Income	Income	Header
4-1300	Secretarial Fees	Income	Detail

(i) Enter opening balances from the Trial Balance at 1 July 2011:

Account	Debit	Credit
Bank of Id	8,873.25	
Petty Cash	300.00	
Accounts Receivable	12,556.35	
Less Prov'n for Doubtful Debts		1,000.00
Prepaid Expenses	486.00	
Vehicles at Cost	89,060.00	
Vehicles Accum Dep		8,550.00
Furniture & Equip at Cost	12,574.00	
Furniture & Equip Accum Dep		4,860.00
Accounts Payable		11,456.35
Accrued Expenses		2,854.05
GST Collected		2,975.40
GST Paid	2,006.30	
PAYG Withholding Payable		1,086.50
Loan – Due 31/3/2016		25,000.00
<< your name >> - Capital		?

(j) Enter the following monthly income and expense budgets. The same amount is to be shown for all months in the current financial year.

Number	Name	Amount
4-1100	Consulting Fees	32,000
4-1200	Training Fees	15,600
4-1300	Secretarial Fees	8,000
6-1005	Accounting Fees	500
6-1020	Bank Charges	50
6-1030	Depreciation	1,500
6-1050	Postage	150
6-1060	Office Supplies	200
6-1070	Dues and Subscriptions	150
6-1080	Telephone	300
6-1110	Advertising	500
6-1140	Repairs & Maintenance	150
6-5110	Staff Amenities	150
6-5120	Superannuation	2,200
6-5130	Wages and Salaries	18,000
6-5140	Workers' Compensation	360
6-6010	Rent	3,000
6-6060	Electricity	140
6-6090	Water	50
9-1000	Interest Expense	160
9-2000	Income Tax Expense	6,000

(k) Print a Balance Sheet (Standard) as at 1 July 2011 and a Profit & Loss (Budget Analysis) for July 2011. Include accounts that have zero balances.

3.3   Start a file, maintain a Chart of Accounts, display and print reports

Start *MYOB AccountRight* and open an existing file called ass33.myo.

The exercise month is July 2011.

Put your name in the address for company information.

Classify the following accounts by hand. In the *Accounts List*, enter necessary headers, change account numbers and/or names and levels as necessary and add accounts to end up with <u>at least</u> the following accounts in a sensible order and format.

Unless you are familiar with the GST, you may ignore entering tax codes.

Commonwealth Bank	Undeposited Funds
Payroll Clearing	Electronic Clearing Account
Petty Cash	Accounts Receivable
Inventories on Hand	Prepaid Expenses
Motor Vehicles – at Cost	Accumulated Depreciation – Motor Vehicles
Office Furniture – at Cost	Accumulated Depreciation – Office Furniture
Office Equipment – at Cost	Accumulated Depreciation – Office Equipment
Goodwill – at Cost	MasterCard
Accounts Payable	Accrued Expenses
GST Collected	GST Paid
Import Duty Payable	PAYG Withholding
Shark Finance – Due 30/3/2012	Bank Loan – Due 31/10/2015
Capital <<your name>>	Less: Drawings
Sales	Purchases
Advertising	Bad Debts
Bank Charges	Depreciation – Motor Vehicles
Depreciation – Office Furniture	Depreciation – Office Equipment
Electricity	General Expenses
Insurance	Motor Vehicle Running
Postage	Printing and Stationery
Rent	Salaries and Wages
Telephone and Fax Expense	Travel

Print a Standard Balance Sheet as at 1 July 2011 and a Profit and Loss [Accrual] for the month of July 2011. Make sure that before printing, you click on the *Customise* button and turn the zero balance option on. You should display the reports on the screen first to ensure that they look sensible.

Your answer to this question is used in assessment 3.4.

3.4   A challenging exercise in headings and levels for Cost of Sales section

Start *MYOB AccountRight* and open the existing file ass33.myo completed in assessment exercise 3.3.

Set up the *Cost of Sales section* so that it is in the format shown at the top of the next page (you should already have the account for "Purchases", but you may need to change its number to fit the two lines above it in the correct order).

Cost of Goods Available

Opening Inventory	$xx.oo
Purchases	$xx.oo
Cartage Inwards	$xx.oo
Customs Duty	$xx.oo
Total Cost of Goods Available	$xx.oo
Less: Closing Inventory	$xx.oo
Total Cost of Sales	$xx.oo

Print a Profit & Loss [Accrual] report for the month of July 2011, including all zero balance accounts.

Your answer to this question is used in the next assessment 3.5.

3.5   *Opening balances, journal entries and reports*

The exercise month is July 2011.

Start *MYOB AccountRight* and open the existing file ass33.myo completed in assessment exercise 3.4.

Record the following opening balances and general journal entries; print the transaction journal (General Journal) for July and a standard balance sheet. You may need to add accounts to the General Ledger as you go. Tax codes are "N-T" unless otherwise stated.

(**Note**: Click *OK* when warned about using the linked accounts for "Accounts Receivable" and "Accounts Payable" – *MYOB AccountRight* expects these accounts to be used in the *Sales* and *Purchases* command centres and not in the General Journal.)

(a)   Record the following opening assets, liabilities, and capital at 1 July 2011:

	$	$
Commonwealth Bank	8,000.00	
Accounts receivable	11,521.00	
Inventories on hand	4,879.00	
Motor vehicles at cost	28,000.00	
Accumulated Depreciation – Motor Vehicles		5,900.00
Office furniture at cost	18,450.00	
Accumulated Depreciation – Office furniture		6,650.00
Office equipment at cost	17,635.00	
Accumulated Depreciation – Office equipment		4,980.00
Accounts payable		8,448.00
Shark Finance – Due 31/3/2012		20,000.00
Bank Loan – Due 31/10/2015		10,000.00
Capital		32,507.00
	$88,485.00	$88,485.00

(b)   The business of Jaques Villain is acquired as a going concern for $50,000 cash on 10 July 2011. Assets acquired at fair values were:

	$
Accounts receivable (tax code "FRE")	4,800.00
Office Equipment (tax code "FRE")	18,560.00
Office furniture (tax code "FRE")	12,640.00
Goodwill (tax code "FRE")	14,000.00

(c) Office Furniture with a book value of $340.80 (cost $2,980.00 less accumulated depreciation of $2,639.20) is written off on 29 July 2011. Debit the loss to an account "Loss on Disposal of Assets" – account number 9-1000.

(d) $3,800 recorded as Office furniture is to be transferred to Office equipment on 31 July 2011 (no depreciation has been recorded on this asset).

(e) At 31 July 2011, transfer the balance in the inventory account to cost of sales and bring to account inventory valued at $19,540.50.

(f) Record depreciation for July 2011:

Motor Vehicles	$580.00
Office Furniture	$115.00
Office Equipment	$110.00

3.6 *Opening balances, journal entries and reports*

Start *MYOB AccountRight*.

Open the existing file ass36.myo and put your name in the company information address.

Record the following opening balances and general journal entries. Print the transaction journal (General Journal) for July and a standard balance sheet as at 31 July 2011. You may need to add accounts to the General Ledger as you go. Tax codes for journal entries are "N-T" unless otherwise stated and line memos may be ignored.

(**Note**: Click *OK* when warned about using linked accounts for "Accounts Receivable" and "Accounts Payable" – these accounts are not usually used in the General Journal.)

(a) Enter the opening balances at 1 July 2011:

	$	$
Gnome bank	5,680.00	
Accounts receivable	8,786.00	
Inventory	5,540.00	
Petty cash float	500.00	
Plant & machinery	24,000.00	
Accumulated Depreciation – Plant & Machinery		2,980.00
Office furniture	9,470.00	
Accumulated Depreciation – Office furniture		2,765.00
Computer system	13,465.00	
Accumulated Depreciation – Computer system		7,548.00
Accounts payable		3,540.00
PAYG Withholding		1,546.00
GST Collected		4,261.00
GST Paid	3,315.00	
ANZ Bank Loan – Due 31/3/12		5,000.00
ANZ Bank Loan – Due 31/3/14		5,000.00
Capital		38,116.00
	$70,756.00	$70,756.00

(b)   The business of Caramel Miranda is acquired as a going concern for $30,000 on 8 July 2011. Payment is deferred until September 2011. The book value of assets acquired were:

	$
Accounts receivable (Tax code "FRE")	2,870.00
Plant and Machinery (Tax code "FRE")	13,130.00
Office furniture (Tax code "FRE")	10,000.00

(c)   Office furniture, which originally cost $2,490 and now has a book value of $300.00, is scrapped on 31 July 2011.

(d) $3,800 recorded as Office furniture is to be transferred to Patents on 31 July 2011.

(e)   At 31 July 2011, transfer the balance in the "Inventory" account to "Cost of Sales" (hardware $3,320.00 and software $2,220.00). Bring to account inventory valued at $12,100.00 (hardware $8,824.00 and software $3,276.00). You will have to set up the "Cost of Sales" accounts similar to those in Exercise 3.4 above for these entries.

(f)   Record depreciation for July 2011:

Plant & Machinery	$120.00
Office Furniture	$60.00
Computers	$110.00

3.7   *Chart of accounts, opening balances, journal entries and reports*

The exercise month is July 2011.
Start *MYOB AccountRight* and open the existing file ass37.myo.
Put your name in the address for company information.

(a)   Classify the following accounts by hand and add to the *Accounts List*. Enter necessary headers, change account numbers and/or names and levels as necessary to end up with <u>at least</u> these accounts in a sensible order and format.

Colonial State Bank	Undeposited Funds
Payroll Clearing Account	Electronic Clearing Account
Petty Cash	Accounts Receivable
Prepaid Expense	Inventories
Motor Vehicles at cost	Motor Vehicles Accum Dep
Computers at cost	Computers Accum Dep
Office Furn & Equip at cost	Office Furn & Equip Accum Dep
Goodwill	Visa
Accounts Payable	Accrued Expense
GST Collected	GST Paid
Import Duty Payable	PAYG Withholding
XYZ Loan – Due 31/3/2012	XYZ Loan – Due 31/3/2013
Capital	Drawings
Sales	Commission Received
Interest Received	Freight Recovered

Opening Inventory	Purchases
Cartage Inwards	Closing Inventory
Advertising	Bad Debts
Bank Charges	Electricity
General Expenses	Insurance
Motor Vehicle Running	Postage
Printing & Stationery	Rent
Salaries and Wages	Telephone & Fax Expense

(b)   Enter the following opening balances at 1 July 2011:

	$
Colonial State Bank	18,478.00
Accounts receivable	18,256.00
Inventories	11,780.00
Petty cash float	500.00
Motor Vehicles	68,980.00
Motor Vehicles Accum Dep	22,980.00
Computers	18,000.00
Computers Accum Dep	5,430.00
Office Furniture & Equipment	11,546.00
Office Furn & Equip Accum Dep	4,320.00
Goodwill	20,000.00
Visa	250.00
Accounts payable	8,540.00
GST Collected	2,486.00
GST Paid	1,425.00
PAYG Withholding	1,546.00
Payroll Deductions Payable	466.00
XYZ Loan – due 31/3/2012	10,000.00
XYZ Loan – due 31/3/2013	10,000.00
Capital	?

(c)   Record the following general journal entries: (**Note**: Click *OK* when warned about using the linked accounts for "Accounts Receivable" and "Accounts Payable" – these accounts are not usually used in the General Journal). Tax codes are "N-T" unless otherwise stated.

    (i)   The business of Descartes Pty Ltd is acquired as a going concern for $40,000 on 7 July 2011, payable in September 2011. The book value of the assets acquired were:

	$
Accounts receivable (Tax code "FRE")	3,548.00
Computers (Tax code "FRE")	12,150.00
Office furniture (Tax code "FRE")	14,302.00

    (ii)   Office furniture costing $1,400 and with accumulated depreciation to date of $1,250 is scrapped on 31 July 2011.

(iii) $1,800 recorded as Computers is to be transferred to Office Furniture & Equipment on 31 July 2011.

(iv) At 31 July 2011, transfer the balance in the inventory account to cost of sales and bring to account inventory valued at $10,775.00.

(v) Record depreciation for July 2011:

Motor Vehicles	$1,440.00
Computers	$495.00
Office Furniture and Equipment	$72.00

(vi) On 31 July 2011, create a provision for doubtful debts of $1,000.

(d) Print a Standard Balance Sheet at 31 July 2011 and the general journal transactions for July 2011. Make sure that before printing, you click on the *Customise* button and turn the zero balance option on. You should display the reports on the screen first to ensure that they look sensible.

3.8 *Chart of accounts, opening balances, journal entries and reports*

The exercise month is July 2011.
Start *MYOB AccountRight* and open the existing file ass38.myo.
Put your name in the address for company information.

(a) Classify the following accounts by hand and add to the *Accounts List*. Enter necessary headers, change account numbers and/or names and levels as necessary to end up with at least these accounts in a sensible order and format. Ignore Tax Codes in this exercise.

National Bank	Undeposited Funds
Payroll Clearing Account	Electronic Clearing Account
Petty Cash	Accounts Receivable
Prepaid Insurance	Inventories On Hand
Motor Vehicles at Cost	Motor Vehicles Accum Dep
Office Furniture at Cost	Office Furniture Accum Dep
Office Equipment at Cost	Office Equipment Accum Dep
Goodwill	MasterCard
Accounts Payable	Accrued Expenses
GST Collected	GST Paid
PAYG Withholding	Mako Finance Loan – Due 31/7/14
Capital	Drawings
Sales	Rent Received
Purchases	Cartage Inwards
Advertising	Bad Debts
Bank Charges	Donations
Electricity	Fines
General Expenses	Insurance
Motor Vehicle Running	Postage
Printing & Stationery	Rent
Repairs & Maintenance	Salaries and Wages
Telephone & Faxes	Travel

(b) Enter the following opening balances at 1 July 2011:

	$
National Bank	16,960.20
Petty Cash	400.00
Accounts Receivable	10,154.60
Prepaid Insurance	1,100.00
Inventories	5,480.50
Motor Vehicles at Cost	51,258.00
Motor Vehicles Accum Dep	19,768.00
Office Furniture at Cost	11,580.00
Office Furniture Accum Dep	5,897.00
Office Equipment at Cost	19,875.00
Office Equipment Accum Dep	6,875.00
Accounts Payable	8,448.00
Accrued Expenses	1,880.00
GST Collected	3,564.30
GST Paid	2,054.00
PAYG Withholding	2,130.00
Mako Finance Loan – Due 31/7/14	20,000.00

(c) Prepare journal entries for the following in July (use the tax code "N-T" except for the assets acquired as a going concern where the code will be "FRE". (**Note**: Click *OK* when warned about using the linked accounts for "Accounts Receivable" and "Accounts Payable" – these accounts are not usually used in the General Journal.)

(i) The business of Peter Pan is acquired as a going concern for $40,000 on 11 July 2011, payable in October 2011. Assets acquired were:

	$
Accounts Receivable	9,850.00
Motor Vehicle	13,550.00
Office Furniture	9,600.00

(ii) Office equipment costing $2,346.00 and with a book value of $246.00 is scrapped on 31 July 2011.

(iii) $2,900 recorded as Office Furniture is to be transferred to Office Equipment on 31 July 2011.

(iv) At 31 July 2011, transfer the balance in the inventory account to cost of sales and bring to account closing inventory valued at $6,138.00.

(v) Record depreciation for July 2011:

Motor Vehicles	$1,070.00
Office Furniture	$109.00
Office Equipment	$345.00

(vi) On 31 July 2011, create an allowance for doubtful debts of $500.

(d)   Print a Standard Balance Sheet at 31 July 2011 and the general journal transactions for July 2011. Make sure that before printing, you click on the *Customise* button and turn the zero balance option on. Display the reports on the screen first to ensure that they look sensible.

3.9   Nancy Nugan has been trading for a number of years wholesaling palm trees and exotic ferns. Due to expansion she has computerised the business using a simple integrated accounting system.

Required:

(a)   The exercise month is October 2011. Start *MYOB AccountRight*.

(b)   Open the file ass39.myo. Change the company information to show your name in the address field for company information.

(c)   Create an *Accounts List* for the general ledger. Some necessary accounts are already in this chart, but you may change these account numbers and names if necessary. Print your *Accounts List* in summary form.

(d)   Record the opening balances as at 1 October 2011.

(e)   Record the October general journal entries only. Click *OK* at warning messages about linked accounts for accounts receivable and accounts payable.

(f)   From the *Accounts* command centre use the *Reports* option and print at 31 October:

(i)   A trial balance at 31 October
(ii)   The general journal transactions for October
(iii)   A Standard Balance Sheet at 31 October (including zero balances).

On 30 September 2011, a trial balance from the manual general ledger shows:

	$	$
Inventory (trees and ferns)	12,480	
Accounts receivable	18,690	
R & M Bank	8,456	
Petty cash	500	
Freehold Land at Cost	200,000	
Buildings at Cost	198,780	
Accumulated Depreciation – Buildings		11,927
Motor Vehicles at Cost	48,480	
Accumulated depreciation – Motor Vehicles		12,980
Equipment at Cost	24,900	
Accumulated Depreciation – Equipment		9,450
Accounts Payable		13,785
GST Collected		9,850
GST Paid	2,332	
PAYG Withholding		3,500
Payroll Accruals Payable		504

Mortgage on Freehold		98,000
Capital		330,000
Retained Earnings		34,150
Drawings	16,000	
Sales		98,458
Purchases	44,306	
Advertising	1,850	
Bank Fees	280	
Cleaning	1,580	
Depreciation	3,879	
Employment Expenses	1,512	
General office Expense	6,452	
Insurance	2,780	
Motor Vehicle Running	4,880	
Printing & Stationery	3,889	
Telephone and Fax	1,458	
Wages & Salaries	16,800	
Mortgage Interest	2,320	
	422,604	422,604

Record the following general journal entries in October 2011:

(i)   Nancy Nugan acquires the potting mix business of Graham Potter as a going concern for $60,000 on 24 October 2011, payable in December 2011. Assets acquired were:

	$
Accounts Receivable	3,890.00
Motor Vehicle	13,550.00
Equipment	29,600.00

(ii)   Some old equipment that originally cost $4,880.00 and with a current WDV of $780.00 is scrapped on 31 October 2011.

(iii)   A debit of $2,400 to printing and stationery in September should have been debited to Equipment. Prepare a correcting entry on 31 October 2011.

(iv)   At 31 October 2011, transfer the balance in the inventory account to cost of sales and bring to account stock of trees and ferns at 31 October 2011 that is valued at $17,500.

(v)   Record depreciation for October 2011:

Freehold Buildings	$330.00
Motor Vehicle	$808.00
Equipment	$155.00

(vi)   On 31 October 2011, create a provision for doubtful debts of $1,000.

Chapter 3: Answers to self-test exercises

3.1

	Account Name		Type	Tax	Linked	Balance
⇨	1-1120	Payroll Clearing	Bank	N-T	✓	$0.00
⇨	1-1130	Cash Drawer	Other Asset	N-T		$0.00
⇨	1-1140	Petty Cash	Bank	N-T		$0.00
⇨	1-1180	Undeposited Funds	Bank	N-T	✓	$0.00
⇨	1-1190	Electronic Clearing Account	Bank	N-T	✓	$0.00
⇨	1-1210	Accounts Receivable	Accounts Receivable	N-T	✓	$0.00
⇨	1-1220	Less Prov'n for Doubtful Debts	Other Asset	N-T		$0.00
⇨	1-1300	Merchandise Inventory	Other Asset	N-T		$0.00
⇨	1-1400	Prepaid Expenses	Other Asset	N-T		$0.00
⇨	1-1500	Prepaid Interest	Other Asset	N-T		$0.00
⇨	1-1600	Prepaid Taxes	Other Asset	N-T		$0.00
⇨	1-1700	Deposits Paid	Other Asset	N-T	✓	$0.00
⇨	**1-1950**	**Withholding Credits**	Asset			$0.00
⇨	1-1960	Voluntary Withholding Credits	Other Asset	N-T		$0.00
⇨	1-1970	ABN Withholding Credits	Other Asset	N-T		$0.00
⇨	**1-2000**	**Non-Current Assets**	Asset			$0.00

	Account Name		Type	Tax	Linked	Balance
⇨	2-1120	Diners Club	Credit Card	N-T		$0.00
⇨	2-1130	MasterCard	Credit Card	N-T		$0.00
⇨	2-1140	Visa	Credit Card	N-T		$0.00
⇨	2-1200	Accounts payable	Accounts Payable	N-T	✓	$0.00
⇨	2-1210	A/P Accrual - Inventory	Other Liability	N-T	✓	$0.00
⇨	**2-1300**	**GST Control**	Liability			$0.00
⇨	2-1310	GST Collected	Other Liability	N-T		$0.00
⇨	2-1330	GST Paid	Other Liability	N-T		$0.00

3.2

	Account Name		Type	Tax	Linked	Balance
⇨	**1-0000**	**Assets**	Asset			$0.00
⇨	**1-1000**	**Current Assets**	Asset			$0.00
⇨	**1-1100**	**Cash On Hand**	Asset			$0.00
⇨	1-1110	Commonwealth Bank	Bank	N-T	✓	$0.00
⇨	1-1120	Payroll Clearing	Bank	N-T	✓	$0.00
⇨	1-1140	Petty Cash	Bank	N-T		$0.00
⇨	1-1180	Undeposited Funds	Bank	N-T	✓	$0.00
⇨	1-1190	Electronic Clearing Account	Bank	N-T	✓	$0.00
⇨	1-1210	Accounts Receivable	Accounts Receivable	N-T	✓	$0.00
⇨	1-1220	Less Prov'n for Doubtful Debts	Other Asset	N-T		$0.00
⇨	1-1300	Merchandise Inventory	Other Asset	N-T		$0.00
⇨	1-1400	Prepaid Expense	Other Asset	N-T		$0.00
⇨	1-1700	Deposits Paid	Other Asset	N-T	✓	$0.00
⇨	**1-1950**	**Withholding Credits**	Asset			$0.00
⇨	1-1960	Voluntary Withholding Credits	Other Asset	N-T		$0.00
⇨	1-1970	ABN Withholding Credits	Other Asset	N-T		$0.00
⇨	**1-2000**	**Non-Current Assets**	Asset			$0.00
⇨	1-2100	Land	Other Asset	N-T		$0.00
⇨	**1-2300**	**Buildings and Improvements**	Asset			$0.00
⇨	1-2310	Bldgs & Imprvmnts at Cost	Other Asset	N-T		$0.00
⇨	1-2320	Bldgs & Imprvmnts Accum Dep	Other Asset	N-T		$0.00
⇨	**1-2400**	**Furniture and Fixtures**	Asset			$0.00

3.3 *Accounts List* with non-current asset headers for Computer System and Goodwill added

Account Name		Type	Tax	Linked	Balance
⇨	1-1970 ABN Withholding Credits	Other Asset	N-T		$0.00
⇨	**1-2000 Non-Current Assets**	Asset			$0.00
⇨	1-2100 Land	Other Asset	N-T		$0.00
⇨	**1-2300 Buildings and Improvements**	Asset			$0.00
⇨	1-2310 Bldgs & Imprvmnts at Cost	Other Asset	N-T		$0.00
⇨	1-2320 Bldgs & Imprvmnts Accum Dep	Other Asset	N-T		$0.00
⇨	**1-2400 Furniture and Fixtures**	Asset			$0.00
⇨	1-2410 Furniture & Fixtures at Cost	Other Asset	N-T		$0.00
⇨	1-2420 Furniture & Fixtures Accum Dep	Other Asset	N-T		$0.00
⇨	**1-2500 Office Equipment**	Asset			$0.00
⇨	1-2510 Office Equip at Cost	Other Asset	N-T		$0.00
⇨	1-2520 Office Equip Accum Dep	Other Asset	N-T		$0.00
⇨	**1-2600 Warehouse Equipment**	Asset			$0.00
⇨	1-2610 Warehouse Equip at Cost	Other Asset	N-T		$0.00
⇨	1-2620 Warehouse Equip Accum Dep	Other Asset	N-T		$0.00
⇨	**1-2700 Motor Vehicles**	Asset			$0.00
⇨	1-2710 Motor Vehicles at Cost	Other Asset	N-T		$0.00
⇨	1-2720 Motor Vehicles Accum Dep	Other Asset	N-T		$0.00
⇨	**1-2800 Computer System**	Asset			$0.00
⇨	**1-2900 Goodwill**	Asset			$0.00

3.4

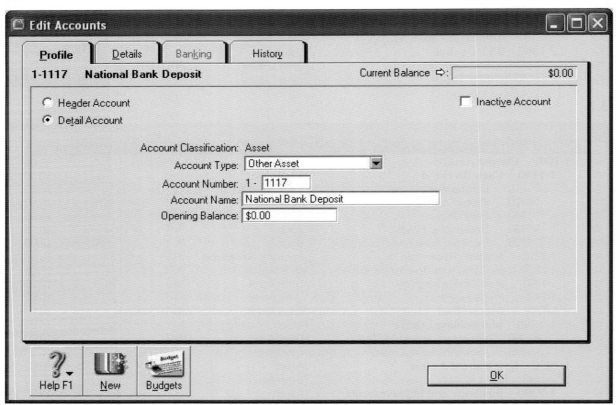

3.5 The tax code list after adding "EXP" and "PRI"

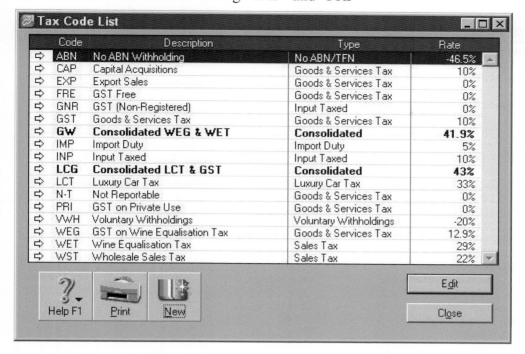

3.6 Non-current assets section of the *Accounts List*

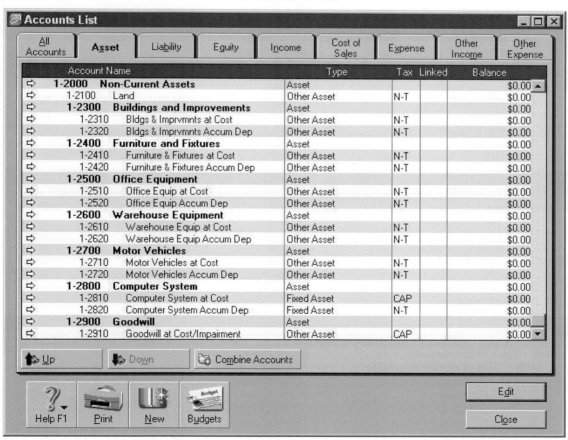

3.7 "Liability" accounts

Account Name			Type	Tax	Linked	Balance
⇨ **2-0000 Liabilities**			Liability			$0.00
⇨	**2-1000 Current Liabilities**		Liability			$0.00
⇨	**2-1100 Credit Cards**		Liability			$0.00
⇨	2-1130	MasterCard	Credit Card	N-T		$0.00
⇨	2-1140	Visa	Credit Card	N-T		$0.00
⇨	**2-1200 Trade Creditors & Accruals**		Liability			$0.00
⇨	2-1210	Accounts payable	Accounts Payable	N-T	✓	$0.00
⇨	2-1220	A/P Accrual - Inventory	Other Liability	N-T	✓	$0.00
⇨	2-1230	Accrued Expenses	Other Current Liability	N-T		$0.00
⇨	**2-1300 GST Control**		Liability			$0.00
⇨	2-1310	GST Collected	Other Liability	N-T		$0.00
⇨	2-1330	GST Paid	Other Liability	N-T		$0.00
⇨	2-1355	WET Payable	Other Liability	N-T		$0.00
⇨	2-1360	Import Duty Payable	Other Liability	N-T		$0.00
⇨	2-1370	Voluntary Withholdings Payable	Other Liability	N-T		$0.00
⇨	2-1380	ABN Withholdings Payable	Other Liability	N-T		$0.00
⇨	2-1390	Luxury Car Tax Payable	Other Liability	N-T		$0.00
⇨	**2-1400 Payroll Liabilities**		Liability			$0.00
⇨	2-1410	Payroll Accruals Payable	Other Liability	N-T	✓	$0.00
⇨	2-1420	PAYG Withholding Payable	Other Liability	N-T		$0.00
⇨	2-1600	Customer Deposits	Other Liability	N-T	✓	$0.00
⇨	**2-2000 Long Term Liabilities**		Liability			$0.00
⇨	2-2100	Bank Loans	Other Liability	N-T		$0.00
⇨	2-2200	Loan from Finance Company	Long Term Liability	N-T		$0.00

"Equity" accounts

Account Name			Type	Tax	Linked	Balance
⇨ **3-0000 Equity**			Equity			$0.00
⇨	**3-1000 Owner's Equity**		Equity			$0.00
⇨	3-1100	Capital <<your name>>	Equity	N-T		$0.00
⇨	3-1200	Less: Drawings	Equity	N-T		$0.00
⇨	**3-3200 Retained Profits**		Equity			$0.00
⇨	3-8000	Retained Earnings	Equity	N-T	✓	$0.00
⇨	3-9000	Current Year Earnings	Equity	N-T	✓	$0.00
⇨	3-9999	Historical Balancing	Equity	N-T	✓	$0.00

"Income" accounts

Account Name			Type	Tax	Linked	Balance
⇨ **4-0000 Income**			Income			$0.00
⇨	**4-1000 Sales**		Income			$0.00
⇨	4-1100	Sales - Hardware	Income	GST		$0.00
⇨	4-1200	Sales - Software	Income	GST		$0.00
⇨	4-2000	Returns and Allowances	Income	N-T		$0.00
⇨	4-5000	Freight Collected	Income	N-T	✓	$0.00
⇨	4-6000	Late Fees Collected	Income	N-T	✓	$0.00

"Cost of sales" accounts

Account Name			Type	Tax	Linked	Balance
⇨ **5-0000 Cost of Sales**			Cost of Sales			$0.00
⇨	**5-1000 Cost of Goods Sold**		Cost of Sales			$0.00
⇨	**5-1100 Cost of Goods Available**		Cost of Sales			$0.00
⇨	5-1110	Opening Inventory	Cost of Sales	N-T		$0.00
⇨	5-1120	Purchases	Cost of Sales	GST		$0.00
⇨	5-1130	Cartage Inwards	Cost of Sales	GST		$0.00
⇨	5-1200	Less: Closing Inventory	Cost of Sales	N-T		$0.00
⇨	5-3000	Discounts Given	Cost of Sales	N-T	✓	$0.00

3.7 *(continued)*

"Expense accounts"

Account Name		Type	Tax	Linked	Balance
⇨ **6-0000 Expenses**		Expense			$0.00
⇨	**6-1000 General & Administrative Exp**	Expense			$0.00
⇨	6-1050 Accounting Fees	Expense	N-T		$0.00
⇨	6-1100 Legal Fees	Expense	N-T		$0.00
⇨	6-1200 Bank Charges	Expense	N-T		$0.00
⇨	6-1300 Depreciation	Expense	N-T		$0.00
⇨	6-1400 Subscriptions	Expense	N-T		$0.00
⇨	6-1500 Office Supplies	Expense	N-T		$0.00
⇨	6-1600 Discounts Taken	Expense	N-T	✓	$0.00
⇨	6-1700 Freight Paid	Expense	N-T	✓	$0.00
⇨	6-1800 Late Fees Paid	Expense	N-T	✓	$0.00
⇨	**6-2000 Financial Expenses**	Expense			$0.00
⇨	6-2010 Bad Debts	Expense	GST		$0.00
⇨	6-2020 Bank Interest Paid	Expense	FRE		$0.00
⇨	6-2030 Discount Allowed	Expense	GST		$0.00
⇨	6-2040 Doubtful Debts	Expense	N-T		$0.00
⇨	**6-3000 Advertising & Promotion Exp**	Expense			$0.00
⇨	6-3100 Advertising	Expense	N-T		$0.00
⇨	6-3110 In-store Promotions	Expense	N-T		$0.00
⇨	**6-4000 Operating Expenses**	Expense			$0.00
⇨	6-4100 Cleaning	Expense	N-T		$0.00
⇨	6-4150 Electricity	Expense	GST		$0.00
⇨	6-4200 Postage	Expense	N-T		$0.00
⇨	6-4300 Printing	Expense	N-T		$0.00
⇨	6-4400 Rent	Expense	N-T		$0.00
⇨	6-4500 Store Supplies	Expense	N-T		$0.00
⇨	6-4600 Telephone	Expense	N-T		$0.00
⇨	6-4700 Water	Expense	N-T		$0.00
⇨	**6-5100 Employment Expenses**	Expense			$0.00
⇨	6-5105 Fringe Benefits Tax	Expense	N-T		$0.00
⇨	6-5107 Sales Commissions	Expense	N-T		$0.00
⇨	6-5110 Staff Amenities	Expense	N-T		$0.00
⇨	6-5120 Superannuation	Expense	N-T		$0.00
⇨	6-5130 Wages & Salaries	Expense	N-T	✓	$0.00
⇨	6-5140 Workers' Compensation	Expense	N-T		$0.00
⇨	6-5150 Other Employer Expenses	Expense	N-T	✓	$0.00

"Other income" accounts

Account Name		Type	Tax	Linked	Balance
⇨ **8-0000 Other Income**		Other Income			$0.00
⇨	8-1000 Bad Debts Recovered	Other Income	GST		$0.00
⇨	8-2000 Commission Received	Other Income	GST		$0.00
⇨	8-3000 Discount Received	Other Income	GST		$0.00
⇨	8-4000 Interest Received	Other Income	FRE		$0.00

3.8

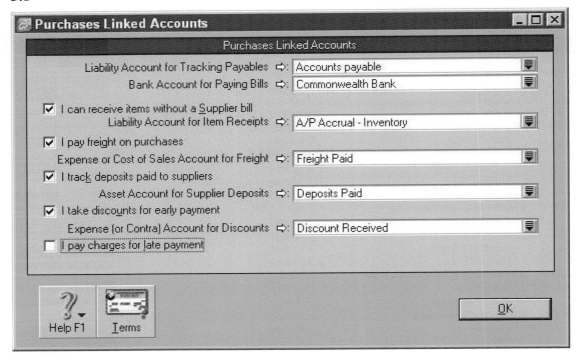

3.9

Ecstatic Company

Answer to self-test exercise 3.9

Balance Sheet

As of July 2011

Assets			
Current Assets			
Cash On Hand			
Commonwealth Bank	$0.00		
Westpac	$0.00		
National Bank Deposit	$0.00		
Payroll Clearing	$0.00		
Petty Cash	$0.00		
Undeposited Funds	$0.00		
Electronic Clearing	$0.00		
Total Cash On Hand		$0.00	
Trade Debtors & Receivables			
Accounts Receivable	$0.00		
Less Prov'n for Doubtful Debts	$0.00		
Total Accounts Receivable		$0.00	
Merchandise Inventory		$0.00	
Prepaid Expense		$0.00	
Deposits Paid		$0.00	
Withholding Credits			
Voluntary Withholding Credits	$0.00		
ABN Withholding Credits	$0.00		
Total Withholding Credits		$0.00	
Total Current Assets			$0.00

3.9 *(continued)*

Non-Current Assets				
Land		$0.00		
Buildings and Improvements				
Bldgs & Imprvmnts at Cost	$0.00			
Bldgs & Imprvmnts Accum Dep'n	$0.00			
Total Buildings and Improvements		$0.00		
Furniture and Fixtures				
Furniture & Fixtures at Cost	$0.00			
Furniture & Fixtures Accum Dep	$0.00			
Total Furniture and Fixtures		$0.00		
Office Equipment				
Office Equip at Cost	$0.00			
Office Equip Accum Dep	$0.00			
Total Office Equipment		$0.00		
Warehouse Equipment				
Warehouse Equip at Cost	$0.00			
Warehouse Equip Accum Dep	$0.00			
Total Warehouse Equipment		$0.00		
Motor Vehicles				
Motor Vehicles at Cost	$0.00			
Motor Vehicles Accum Dep	$0.00			
Total Motor Vehicles		$0.00		
Computer System				
Computer System at Cost	$0.00			
Computer System Accum Dep	$0.00			
Total Computer System		$0.00		
Goodwill				
Goodwill at Cost/Impairment	$0.00			
Total Goodwill		$0.00		
Total Non-Current Assets			$0.00	
Total Assets				$0.00
Liabilities				
Current Liabilities				
Credit Cards				
MasterCard	$0.00			
Visa	$0.00			
Total Credit Cards		$0.00		
Trade Creditors & Accruals				
Accounts Payable	$0.00			
A/P Accrual – Inventory	$0.00			
Accrued Expenses	$0.00			
Total Accounts Payable & Accruals		$0.00		
GST Control				
GST Collected	$0.00			
GST Paid	$0.00			
Total GST Control		$0.00		
WET Payable		$0.00		
Import Duty Payable		$0.00		
Voluntary Withholdings Payable		$0.00		
ABN Withholding Payable		$0.00		

3.9 *(continued)*

Luxury Car Tax Payable		$0.00		
Payroll Liabilities				
Payroll Accruals Payable	$0.00			
PAYG Withholding Payable	$0.00			
Total Payroll Liabilities		$0.00		
Customer Deposits		$0.00		
Other Current Liabilities		$0.00		
Total Current Liabilities			$0.00	
Long Term Liabilities				
Bank Loan		$0.00		
Loan from Finance Company		$0.00		
Total Non-Current Liabilities			$0.00	
Total Liabilities				$0.00
Net Assets				$0.00
Equity				
Owner's Equity				
Capital <<your name>>		$0.00		
Less: Drawings		$0.00		
Total Owner's Equity			$0.00	
Retained Profits				
Retained Earnings		$0.00		
Current Earnings		$0.00		
Total Retained Profits			$0.00	
Historical Balancing			$0.00	
Total Equity				$0.00

Ecstatic Company
Answer to self-test exercise 3.9
Profit & Loss Statement
As of July 2011

Income			
Sales			
Sales – Hardware	$0.00		
Sales – Software	$0.00		
Total Sales		$0.00	
Returns and Allowances		$0.00	
Freight Collected		$0.00	
Total Income			$0.00
Cost of Sales			
Cost of Goods Sold			
Cost of Goods Available			
Opening Inventory	$0.00		
Purchases	$0.00		
Cartage Inwards	$0.00		
Total Cost of Goods Available		$0.00	
Less: Closing Inventory		$0.00	

3.9 *(continued)*

Total Cost of Goods Sold	$0.00	
Total Cost of Sales		$0.00
Gross Profit		$0.00
Expenses		
General & Administrative Exp		
Accounting Fees	$0.00	
Legal Fees	$0.00	
Bank Charges	$0.00	
Depreciation	$0.00	
Subscriptions	$0.00	
Office Supplies	$0.00	
Employment Expenses	$0.00	
Freight Paid	$0.00	
Total General & Administrative Exp		$0.00
Financial Expenses		
Bad Debts	$0.00	
Bank Interest Paid	$0.00	
Discount Allowed	$0.00	
Doubtful Debts	$0.00	
Total Financial Expenses		$0.00
Advertising & Promotion Exp		
Advertising	$0.00	
In-store Promotions	$0.00	
Total Advertising & Promotion Exp		$0.00
Operating Expenses	$0.00	
Cleaning	$0.00	
Electricity	$0.00	
Postage	$0.00	
Printing	$0.00	
Rent	$0.00	
Store Supplies	$0.00	
Telephone	$0.00	
Water	$0.00	
Total Operating Expenses		$0.00
Employment Expenses		
Fringe Benefits Tax	$0.00	
Sales Commissions	$0.00	
Staff Amenities	$0.00	
Superannuation	$0.00	
Wages & Salaries	$0.00	
Workers' Compensation	$0.00	
Other Employer Expenses	$0.00	
Total Employment Expenses		$0.00
Total Expenses		$0.00
Operating Profit		$0.00

3.9 *(continued)*

Other Income		
Bad Debts Recovered	$0.00	
Commission Received	$0.00	
Discount Received	$0.00	
Interest Received	$0.00	
Total Other Income		$0.00

Other Expenses		
Interest Expense	$0.00	
Income Tax Expense	$0.00	
Total Other Expenses		$0.00

Net Profit / (Loss)		$0.00

3.10

Ecstatic Company
Answer to self-test exercise 3.10
Balance Sheet
As of July 2011

Assets		
Current Assets		
Cash Accounts		
Commonwealth Bank	$4,380.00	
Westpac	$880.00	
Petty cash	$500.00	
Total Cash Accounts		$5,760.00
Trade Debtors & Receivables		
Accounts Receivable	$17,217.00	
Less: Prov'n for Doubtful Debts	($1,327.00)	
Total Accounts Receivable		$15,890.00
Inventory		$7,600.00
Total Current Assets		$29,250.00
Non-Current Assets		
Furniture and Fixtures		
Furniture & Fixtures at Cost	$60,100.00	
Furniture & Fixtures Accum Dep	($18,010.00)	
Total Furniture and Fixtures		$42,090.00
Office Equipment		
Office Equip at Cost	$34,950.00	
Office Equip Accum Dep	($18,860.00)	
Total Office Equipment		$16,090.00
Warehouse Equipment		
Warehouse Equip at Cost	$44,250.00	
Warehouse Equip Accum Dep	($26,405.00)	
Total Warehouse Equipment		$17,845.00

3.10 *(continued)*

Motor Vehicles			
Motor Vehicles at Cost	$108,500.00		
Motor Vehicles Accum Dep	($56,200.00)		
Total Motor Vehicles		$52,300.00	
Total Non-Current Assets			$128,325.00
Total Assets				$157,575.00
Liabilities			
Current Liabilities			
Credit Cards			
MasterCard	$345.00		
Total Credit Cards		$345.00	
Trade Creditors & Accruals			
Accounts Payable	$3,420.00		
Accrued Expenses	$240.00		
Total Accounts Payable & Accruals		$3,660.00	
GST Control			
GST Collected	$3,810.00		
GST Paid	($2,630.00)		
Total GST Liabilities		$1,180.00	
Payroll Liabilities			
Payroll Accruals Payable	$780.00		
PAYG Withholding Payable	$3,500.00		
Total Payroll Liabilities		$4,280.00	
Total Current Liabilities			$9,465.00
Non-Current Liabilities			
Loan from Finance Company		$20,000.00	
Total Non-Current Liabilities			$20,000.00
Total Liabilities			$29,465.00
Net Assets			$128,110.00
Equity			
Owner's Equity			
Capital – (your name)		$128,110.00	
Total Owner's Equity			$128,110.00
Total Equity			$128,110.00

3.11

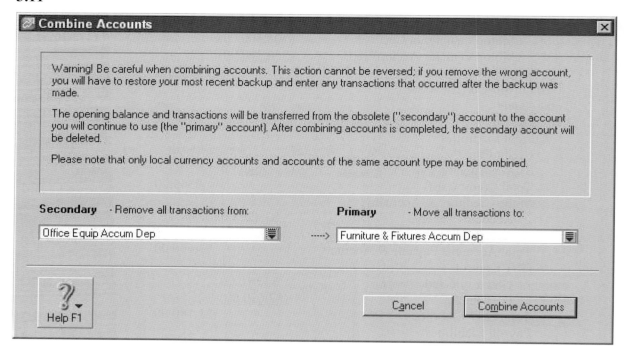

Section of accounts list after combining non-current asset detail accounts.

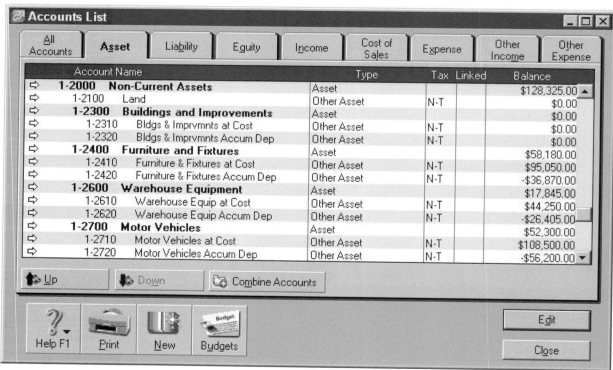

3.12

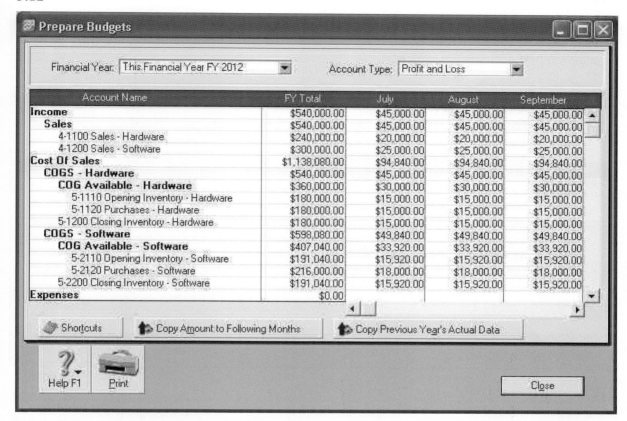

3.13

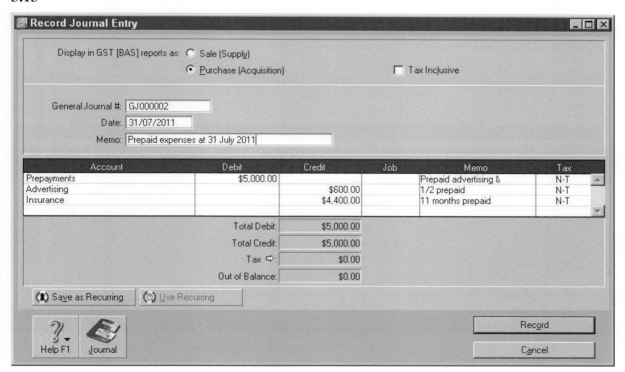

3.14

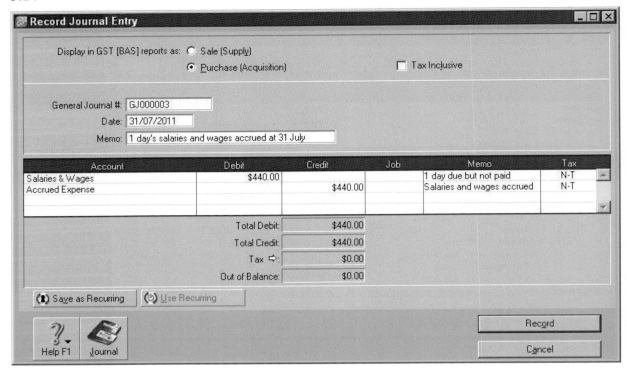

3.15

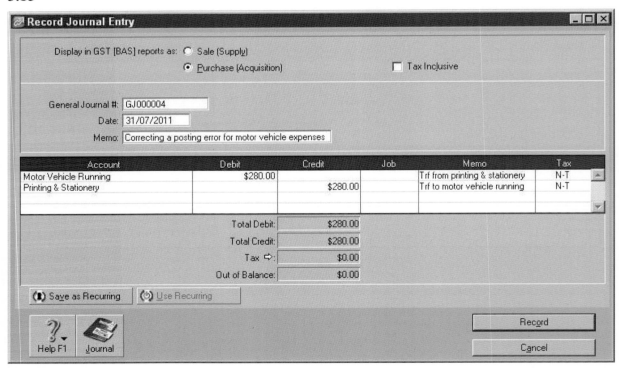

3.16

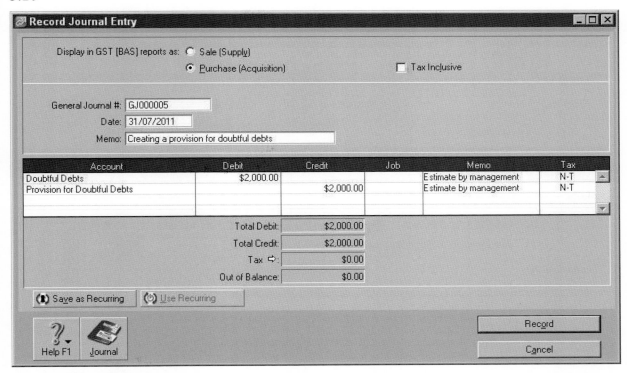

3.17

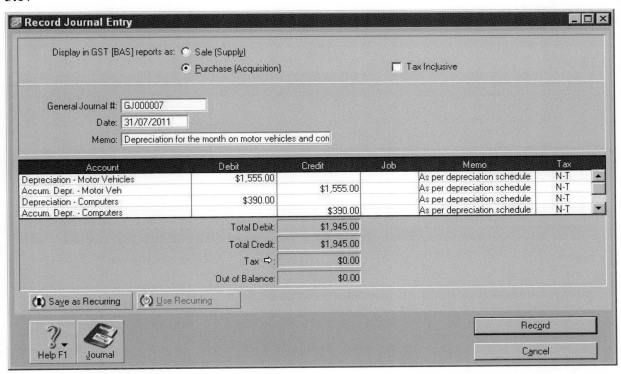

3.17 *(continued)*

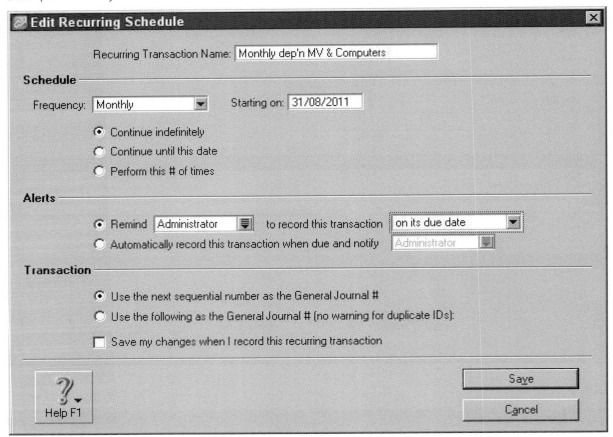

3.18

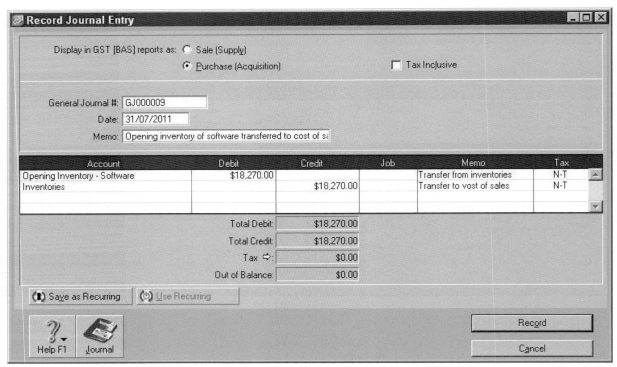

3.19

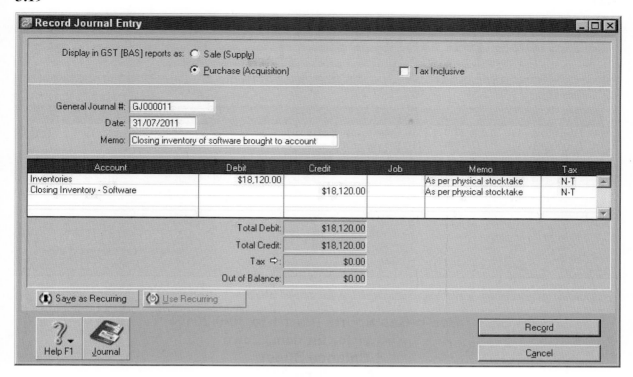

3.20

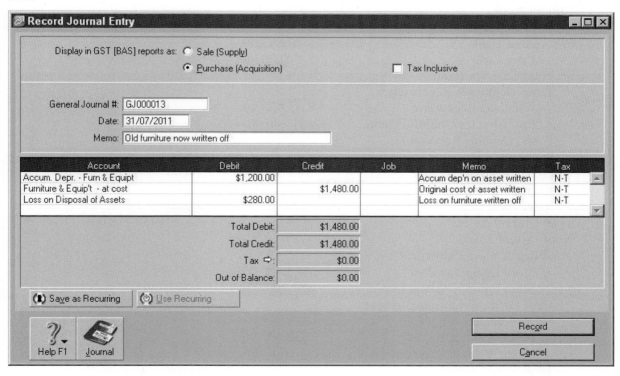

3.21

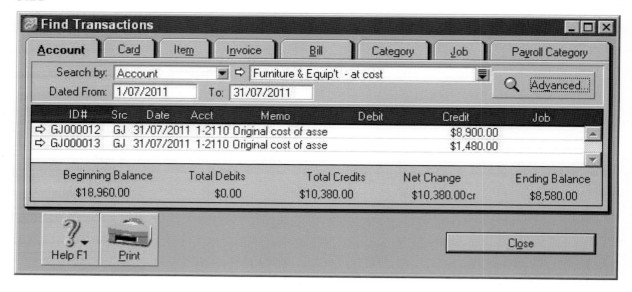

3.22

Bee-n-Gee Sports (Part 1 to 30/6/2012)
Answer for file dem33.myo
Balance Sheet
As of June 2012

Assets
   Current Assets
      Cash On Hand

ANZ Bank	$24,893.00	
Petty Cash	$500.00	
Total Cash On Hand		$25,393.00
Trade Debtors & Receivables		
Accounts Receivable	$243,070.00	
Provision for Doubtful Debts	($1,200.00)	
Total Accounts Receivable		$241,870.00
Inventory		$129,615.00
Prepayments		$800.00
Accrued Income		$600.00
ANZ Term Dep		$60,000.00
Total Current Assets		$458,278.00

Non-Current Assets
   Office & Store Equipment

Store Equip – at Cost	$25,800.00	
Store Equip – Accum Dep'n	($2,700.00)	
Total Office & Store Equipment		$23,100.00
Motor Vehicle		
Motor Vehicle at cost	$35,500.00	
Motor Vehicle – Accum. Dep'n	($10,600.00)	
Total Motor Vehicle		$24,900.00
Total Non-Current Assets		$48,000.00
Total Assets		
$506,278.00		

3.22 *(continued)*

Liabilities
 Current Liabilities
  Accounts Payable $15,000.00
  Accrued Expenses $500.00
  Income Rec'd in Advance $250.00
  GST Control
   GST Collected $35,698.18
   GST Paid   ($4,890.89)
  Total GST Liabilities $30,807.29
  PAYG Liabilities
   Salary PAYG Deductions $3,815.00
   Payroll Deductions Payable $100.00
  Total PAYG Liabilities $3,915.00
 Total Current Liabilities $43,400.92
 Non-Current Liabilities
  ANZ Bank Loans – Due 3/2010 $100,000.00
 Total Non-Current Liabilities $100,000.00
Total Liabilities $150,472.29

Net Assets $355,805.71

Equity
 Capital
  Capital $28,415.00
  Drawings   ($10,500.00)
 Total Capital $17,915.00
 Retained Profits
  Retained Earnings $7,500.00
  Net Profit (Loss) $330,390.71
 Total Retained Profits $337,890.71
Total Equity $355,805.71

Bee-n-Gee Sports (Part 1 to 30/6/2012)
Answer for file dem33.myo
Profit & Loss Statement
July 2011 through June 2012

Income
 Sales & Services
  Sales $465,003.09
  Mending & Adjustments $3,678.73
 Total Sales & Services $468,681.82
Total Income $468681.82

Cost of Sales
 Goods available for Sale
  Opening Inventory $26,750.00
  Purchases $100,494.11
  Cartage Inwards $215.00
 Total Goods available for Sale $127,459.11
 less Closing Inventory   ($29,615.00)
Total Cost of Sales $97,844.11
Gross Profit $370,837.71

3.22 *(continued)*

Expenses			
Sales & Marketing Expenses			
Advertising	$350.00		
Cartage Outwards	$1,005.00		
Total Sales & Marketing Expenses		$1,355.00	
General & Administrative Exp			
Bank Charges	$95.00		
Depreciation Expense	$10,200.00		
Insurance	$1,200.00		
Office Supplies	$219.00		
Postage	$42.00		
Printing & Stationery	$190.00		
Rent	$12,000.00		
Telephone & Fax Expense	$748.00		
Total General & Administrative Exp		$24,694.00	
Employment Expenses			
Wages & Salaries	$19,129.00		
Staff Amenities	$32.00		
Superannuation	$890.00		
Workers' Compensation	$640.00		
Total Employment Expenses		$20,691.00	
Financial Expenses			
Doubtful Debts	$300.00		
Interest Expense	$5,700.00		
Total Financial Expenses		$6,000.00	
Total Expenses			$52,740.00
Operating Profit			$318,097.71
Other Income			
Interest Income		$2,400.00	
Rent Received (Commercial)		$13,000.00	
Total Other Income			$15,400.00
Other Expenses			
Income Tax Expense			
PAYG Instalment	$3,107.00		
Total Income Tax Expense		$3,107.00	
Total Other Expenses			$3,107.00
Net Profit / (Loss)			$330,390.71

3.23

Bee-n-Gee Sports (Part 2 Year 2012)
Answer for file dem33.myo
General Journal
1/07/2012 To 31/07/2012

	ID#	Acct#	Name	Debit	Credit
GJ	1/07/2012	End of Year Adjustment			
	GJ000000	3-2200	Net Profit (Loss)	$330,390.71	
	GJ000000	3-2100	Retained Earnings		$330,390.71
GJ	1/07/2012	Reversal of accrued expenses			
	GJ000009	2-1200	Accrued Expenses	$500.00	
	GJ000009	6-0410	Rent		$500.00
GJ	1/07/2012	Reversing income received in advance			
	GJ000010	2-1250	Income Rec'd in Adv	$250.00	
	GJ000010	8-5000	Rent Received (Commercial)		$250.00
GJ	1/07/2012	Reversing prepaid expense			
	GJ000011	6-0345	Insurance	$800.00	
	GJ000011	1-1400	Prepayments		$800.00
GJ	1/07/2012	Reversing accrued income			
	GJ000012	8-3000	Interest Income	$600.00	
	GJ000012	1-1420	Accrued Income		$600.00
			Grand Total:	$332,540.71	$332,540.71

Cash transactions 4

Record the receipt of money and payment of cheques. Prepare a bank reconciliation and print reports.

After completing this chapter you will be able to:

1 Enter receipts of money and deposit daily cash into a bank account.

2 Prepare cheques for payments and record into a cash disbursements journal.

3 Maintain a Petty Cash record.

4 Use the Card File for Payee names.

5 Set up and use periodical payments.

6 Reconcile the bank account in the general ledger with the details received from the bank.

7 Record data from bank statement into ledger accounts.

8 Print a bank reconciliation statement.

9 Print GST Cash Reports for preparation of the Business Activity Statements.

10 Print financial statements.

Introduction

A small business may only want to record cash received and paid throughout an accounting period. *MYOB AccountRight* has a *Banking* command centre that allows this, provided an *Accounts List* already exists and there is at least one "Detail Cheque" account. The resulting general ledger accounts can then be adjusted by an accountant or tax agent to produce final financial statements. This chapter uses the *Banking* command centre to enter cash received and cash paid. The entries in the general ledger bank account will then be reconciled to information received from the bank (a bank statement).

Under the Goods and Services Tax (GST), a business is required to prepare a Business Activity Statement (BAS) each tax period (monthly or quarterly depending on turnover or elections made). Part of the BAS relates to the GST. *MYOB AccountRight* has tax codes that keep track of GST transactions, and the final task in this chapter is the production of a GST report that will help in preparing the BAS on a cash basis.

You should have completed Chapters 1 and 2 before starting this chapter. It is expected that you can:

- Start *MYOB AccountRight*.
- Change the business name and/or address.
- Select *command centres* and options.
- Recognise the conventions used in this book (for example, the sign ↵ is an instruction to tap the *Enter* key).

You may need to refer back to Chapter 1 to do these tasks. A quick way of finding the place for instructions is to use the 'How to ...' index at the front of the book.

The Goods and Services Tax (GST)

A Goods and Services tax of 10% is applied in Australia on most goods and services. The demonstration, exercises and assessments in this chapter will include the GST where necessary. The *Accounts List* for each file includes the necessary accounts for recording the GST. A business with a turnover of less than $2,000,000 per annum may account for the GST on a cash basis (provided some other criteria are also met). You are not required to know the legal aspects of the GST, but you will be required to record the GST included in cash received and cash paid.

Where a business accounts on a cash basis, the GST received in a payment is credited to an account usually called "GST Collected". This account will accumulate the GST collected that will be paid to the Australian Taxation Office (ATO). The GST paid by a business for purchases (trade goods, most expenses and purchases of assets) is debited to an account usually called "GST Paid". The balance of this account at the end of a tax period is deducted from the balance in "GST Collected" account to arrive at the net GST to be paid to the ATO (or a refund to be received from the ATO where the GST Paid exceeds the GST Collected).

The payment to the ATO (or refund from the ATO) will be either monthly or quarterly depending on the tax period of the taxpayer, and is paid in the month following the end of the tax period.

The *Banking* command centre

A file called dem41.myo will be used to demonstrate the options in the *Banking* command centre. The month for entering examples and self-test exercises throughout this chapter is July 2011. Whenever you start a file, you should sign on with the User ID "Administrator" and you should avoid using a password. Use the self-test exercise 4.1 to start this file and enter your name in the address field.

Self-test exercise 4.1

If you are not sure how to start *MYOB AccountRight* and open an existing file, refer to the 'How to ...' instructions for Chapter 1 (look in the index of 'How to ...' instructions at the front of this book) or look at a video on this on the CD.

Start *MYOB AccountRight*.

Open the file dem41.myo (remember to sign on as the Administrator <u>without</u> a password).

Change the 'Company Information' by entering your name in the address field. Refer to Chapter 1 if you are not sure how to do this.

Print the *Accounts List* [Summary]. Refer to the 'How to ...' index for Chapter 1 or Chapter 3 if you are not sure how to do this.

The business in this exercise started on 1 October 1994. It sells craft material and craft books. Most of the transactions are for cash but some credit transactions do occur. The owner is going to use *MYOB AccountRight* from 1 July 2011 to record the cash transactions only and will employ an accountant to produce monthly financial reports and year-end reports. The business uses a cash basis to account for the GST and the BAS (Business Activity Statement) information has already been set up.

Select the *Banking* command centre. Figure 4.1 on the next page shows its main features. *Spend Money* is used to enter all cash payments. Payments not involving an actual cheque can also be entered using this option (for example, a bill of exchange paid). *Receive Money* is used to enter cash received. *Prepare Bank Deposit* is used when several receipts in a day are taken to the bank and deposited in a single deposit. *Reconcile Accounts* is used to reconcile the balance of the bank account in the general ledger with a statement received from the bank. *Prepare Electronic Payments* allows you to pay accounts payable and expenses electronically through the bank.

Account name or account number?

When you record a payment or a receipt using the *Banking* command centre, the program automatically records one side of the transaction in the nominated bank account or "Undeposited Funds". You will have to nominate the account(s) involved in the other side of the transaction. For example, if you record a receipt of money for a cash sale using the *Receive Money* option, you will need to tell *MYOB AccountRight* to credit the account for "Sales".

You can list and enter accounts either by account code (number) or by account name. If you use the name you can type in the first few letters and if you use account numbers you may type in the number. You can also use the *List* button 🔽 to list the accounts either by number or by name. You select your preference for either using account names or account numbers in the *Window Preferences* (*Setup* menu, *Preferences*, *Windows*).

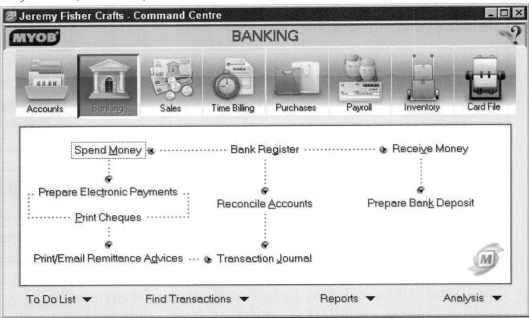

Figure 4.1: The *Banking* command centre options

Figure 4.2 shows preferences used in this chapter – accounts will be selected and listed by account name as indicated by the fourth checkbox. If you prefer to use account numbers, deselect this checkbox. Throughout this book, you may use whichever option you prefer.

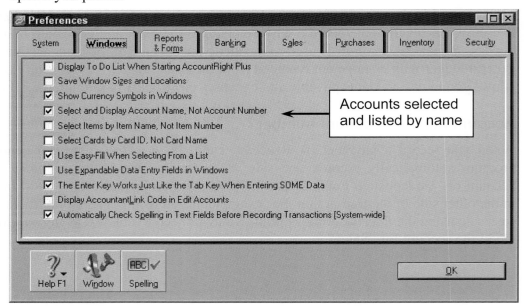

Figure 4.2: Preference for selecting and displaying accounts by name

Recording money received

There are two methods of recording money received by the business. Money received from accounts receivable must be entered using the *Receive Payments* option in the *Sales* command centre, and this is covered in the following chapter. The *Receive Money* option in the *Banking* command centre is used for all cash received other than money received from customers who were invoiced using the *Sales* command centre.

If a business normally records several receipts in any one day, from both accounts receivable and from other sources, these should be recorded in a temporary "Undeposited Funds" account. The money in the "Undeposited Funds" account can then be banked using the *Prepare Bank Deposit* option. This means that there will be one entry in the general ledger bank account that will correspond to the amount of the deposit shown on the bank statement. This makes the task of reconciling the bank account in the general ledger with the statement received from the bank a lot easier (see later). If there is only one receipt in a day, the amount can be entered directly into the general ledger bank account without going through "Undeposited Funds".

How to record money received and deposited in a bank account

Step	Instruction
1	Select the *Banking* command centre.
2	Select the *Receive Money* option.
3	If not already selected, the option button for deposit to a bank account should be selected. Change the bank account <u>if necessary</u> by using the selection *List* button ▤ at the end of the 'Deposit to Account' field and select a bank account from the list.
4	Look at the 'Tax Inclusive' checkbox and change if necessary.
5	Leave the ID #. This is automatically incremented by one for each new deposit.
6	Type in the date ↵. If the month and year are already correct, only type in the day of the month.
7	If a card exists for this payor (see later), type in the first few letters of the payor's name and ↵. If several receipts are being deposited, a card for "Daily Banking" or "Daily Deposit" might be used ↵.
8	Enter the total amount of the deposit and ↵.
9	Select a payment method. You may type this in or use the selection *List* button ▤ at the end of the 'Payment Method' field and select from the list ↵. You may also enter details of cheques or credit cards by clicking on the *Details* button. Details ...
10	Enter a memo for this transaction and ↵. This might appear on transaction listings, so it should describe the transaction fully.
	(continued on the next page)

Step	Instruction
11	Enter the account name (or number) for the account to be credited for the first receipt being deposited and use the TAB key.
12	Enter the amount of the first receipt. TAB to the 'Job' column and enter a job number if you are using jobs.
13	TAB to the column headed 'Memo' and enter any line memo if necessary.
14	TAB to the 'Tax' column and enter the three-character code for the GST tax involved ↵.
15	Continue entering any other line items making up this deposit.
16	Click the *Record* button.

Example 4.1—Recording a single receipt and depositing to a bank account

1. Make sure that you have the file dem41.myo open. A cash sale of books amounting to $3,212.00 (including the GST) is to be recorded.

2. Select the *Banking* command centre.

3. Click on the *Receive Money* button.

4. At the top left-hand corner of the *Receive Money* window a choice can be made to record the receipt directly to a bank account or to *Group with Undeposited Funds*. As this is a single receipt to be deposited into the Standard Bank, leave this selection as shown here:

5. Check that the checkbox for 'Tax Inclusive' at the top of the *Receive Money* window is on – that is, there is a tick in the box as shown above.

6. Leave the ID # as "CR000001". This is a computer-generated number to identify the receipt (or in this case a deposit).

7. Enter the date as "1/07/2011". You can press the space bar to activate the calendar and click on the date or if the month and year are already correct (July 11), type 1 ↵.

8. The 'Payor' field is used to enter the name of the person or business making the payment. In *MYOB AccountRight* "cards" can be created for names, addresses and other permanent information for customers, suppliers (vendors), employees and contacts. The information on a card can be entered into various forms by selecting the card from a card file, and this saves a great deal of typing. Type in "d" to select "Daily Banking" ↵ ↵.

9. Enter the total amount of the deposit as "3212" and ↵ (note that the dollar sign, the comma separating thousands, the decimal point and zero decimals are not required, and the resulting figure will be shown as $3,212.00).

10. This payment is made in cash. Type "Cash" in the 'Payment Method' field or use the *List* button ▣ and select "Cash" from the list. There are no details required for cash.

11. TAB through to the 'Memo' field. Leave the memo as "Daily Banking" and ↵.

12. The account to credit is "Sales – Books", account number "4-1200". If you are using account names, type in the first few letters "sa" and TAB twice. If you are using account numbers, type in the account number as 4-1200 and use TAB. Remember that a slower method is to use the *List* button 🔳 or hit Enter (↵), search for the account and use it. If the account number is known, it is far quicker to type in the known account number.

13. The amount $3,212.00 should be showing in the 'Amount' field (the GST-inclusive amount). TAB through to the 'Memo' column, leaving the 'Job' column blank.

14. Type in additional (optional) information about this line item in the 'Memo' column – enter "Cash sale of books for the day" as the line memo and TAB.

15. Check that "GST" is the tax code (this account has been set up with a default tax code of GST).

16. Your *Receive Money* window should look like Figure 4.3:

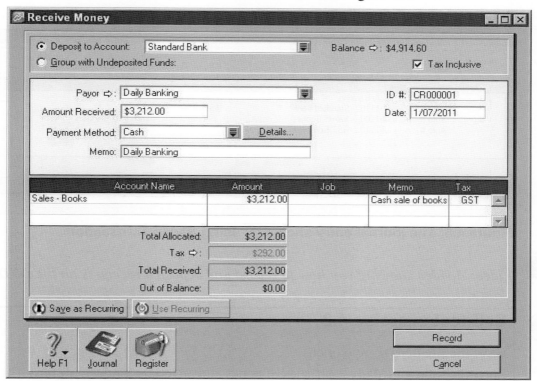

Figure 4.3: Daily banking deposit

17. If there are any errors click in the incorrect field and edit it.

18. Before recording the deposit, you can examine how the amounts will be recorded in the general ledger. Select the *Edit* pull-down menu at the top of the screen and then select the *Recap Transaction* item as shown in Figure 4.4 on the next page.

19. The *Recap Transaction* window for the deposit should look like Figure 4.5 on the next page.

20. Click on the *OK* button to close the *Recap Transaction* window.

21. Click on the *Record* button to record the deposit.

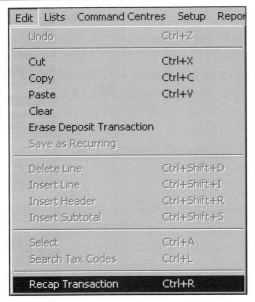

Figure 4.4: The *Edit* pull-down with *Recap Transaction* selected

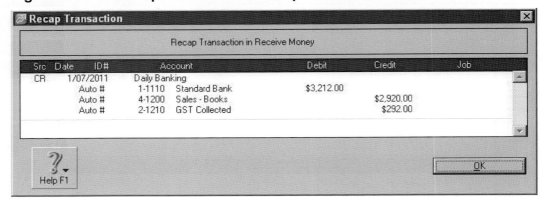

Figure 4.5: The journal entry shown by using *Recap Transaction*

Video: A video showing you how to record and deposit a receipt is on the DVD

Self-test exercise 4.2

Have the file dem41.myo open.

Enter the following daily cash sales of books and materials for the craft business. Enter each of these as single deposits direct to the bank, with the 'Payor" as "Daily Banking". All amounts shown are GST-inclusive, and the tax code should be GST. **Note:** Before clicking on the *Record* button, check your entries with the answers to self-test questions supplied at the end of the chapter. You should also use the *Edit – Recap Transaction* facility to verify the entries to the general ledger accounts.

4/7: Total deposit of cash $874.50 for sales of craft material $423.50 and sale of books $451.00

5/7: Total deposit of cash $400.95 for sale of books $361.90 and a charge for cartage $39.05 (credit the account "Cartage Charged on Sales" account number 4-7000 with this cartage charged)

Using an "Undeposited Funds" account

If a business receives a number of payments in a single day and deposits all these receipts together in a single deposit to the bank, it will be necessary to group these receipts first and then make a **single** deposit for the total amount to the bank. In *MYOB AccountRight* this is achieved by using a clearance account called "Undeposited Funds", which is set up as a bank account and linked as such. Each receipt is recorded against this account and then all these receipts are deposited to the actual bank account by using the *Prepare Bank Deposit* option. This option will transfer all these separate receipts to the bank account as a single amount by crediting the "Undeposited Funds" account and debiting the bank account with the total amount. This is very useful when reconciling a bank account with a bank statement (see later in this chapter).

In the *Receive Money* window you need to select the option *Group with Undeposited Funds*. The use of an "Undeposited Funds" account can be set as the default through the *Setup* pull-down menu and *Preferences* menu item.

For this chapter, all demonstration exercise files will already have "Undeposited Funds" account in the *Accounts List* and linked as required.

How to set up "Undeposited Funds" *as the default*

Step	Instruction
1	Select the *Setup* pull-down menu.
2	Select the *Preferences* menu item.
3	Click on the tab for *Banking*.
4	Click to place a tick in the box for 'When I Receive Money, I Prefer to Group It with the Other Undeposited Funds [System-wide]'.
5	Click on the *OK* button to close the *Preferences* window.

Example 4.2—Setting "Undeposited Funds" *as a default*

1. Make sure that you have the file dem41.myo open.
2. Select the *Setup* pull-down menu.
3. Select the *Preferences* menu item.
4. Click on the tab for *Banking*.
5. Click to place a tick in the box for 'When I Receive Money, I Prefer to Group It with the Other Undeposited Funds [System-wide]'. The *Preferences* window should look like Figure 4.6 on the next page.
6. Click on the *OK* button to close the *Preferences* window.

My preference is for a real mouse.

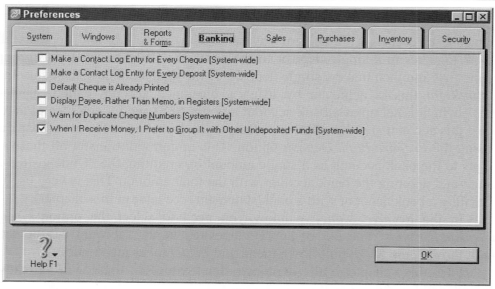

Figure 4.6: Preference setting "Undeposited Funds" as the default

Video: A video showing you how change preferences is on the DVD

How to record money received using the Undeposited Funds account

Step	Instruction
1	Select the *Banking* command centre.
2	Select the *Receive Money* option.
3	If not already selected, the option button for '*Group with Undeposited Funds:*' should be selected ↵.
4	Look at the 'Tax Inclusive' box and change if necessary.
5	Leave the ID #. This is automatically incremented by one for each new deposit.
6	Type in the date ↵. If the month and year are already correct, only type in the day of the month.
7	If a card exists for this payor (see later), type in the first few letters of the payor's name and ↵. If several receipts are being deposited, an entry for "Daily Deposit" can be made ↵.
8	Enter the total amount of the deposit and ↵.
9	Select a payment method. Type this in or use the selection *List* button ▦ at the end of the 'Payment Method' field and select from the list ↵. You may also enter details of cheques or credit cards by clicking on the *Details* button.
10	Enter a memo for this transaction and ↵. This might appear on transaction listings, so it should describe the transaction fully.

(continued on the next page)

Step	Instruction
11	Enter the account (name or number depending on your preference) for the account to be credited for the first receipt being deposited and use the TAB key.
12	Enter the amount of the first receipt.
13	TAB to the 'Job' column and enter a job number if you are using jobs.
14	TAB and enter a memo (optional) to further explain the line entry.
15	TAB to the Tax column and enter the three-character code for the GST tax involved ↵.
16	Continue entering all receipts making up the day's deposit.
17	Click the *Record* button.

Example 4.3—Recording receipts and crediting Undeposited Funds

1. Make sure that you have the file dem41.myo open.

2. On 8 July 2011, two amounts of money are received: A cheque No 101864 for a cash sale of books amounting to $2,260.30 (including the GST) *and* cash of $5,000 additional capital contributed by the owner (tax code "N-T"). The receipts will be banked together as one deposit of $7,260.30.

3. Use *Receive Money* and record the cheque No 101864 for $2,260.30 received for cash sales. Follow the instructions on pages 4-5 to 4-8 on recording money received. Click on the *Details* button and enter the cheque details: "BSB 456-789", bank account number "65432198" and account name "BJ Richards". Add a note "Driver's Licence #6875MU expires 12/3/10". The *Applied Payment Details* window should look like Figure 4.7:

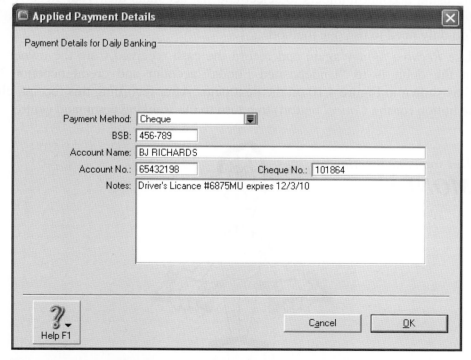

Figure 4.7: *Applied Payment Details* **window showing cheque details**

4. Make sure that the *Group with Undeposited Funds* option is selected at the top of the window and credit the account 4-1200 'Sales – Books'. Your *Receive Money* window using account names should look like Figure 4.8:

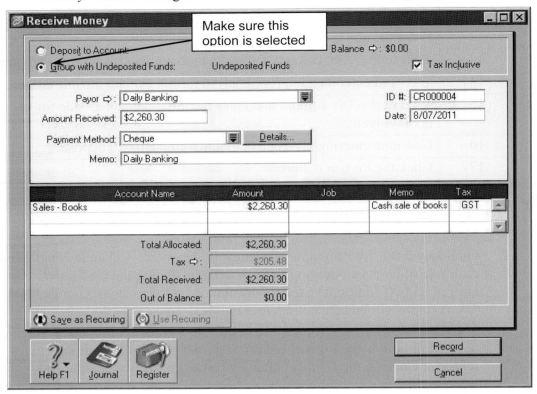

Figure 4.8: Cheque received for cash sales debited to "Undeposited Funds"

If you are using account numbers to select and list accounts then your *Receive Money* window for the cheque received will look like Figure 4.9 on the next page **Note:** You only need to use one method.

Use *Receive Money* again and record the cash received from the owner. Make sure that the debit is to "Undeposited Funds" account and credit account 3-1100 'Capital' as shown in Figure 4.10 on the next page. After recording this receipt, click on the *Close* button (or the *Cancel* button) to return to the *Banking* command centre.

Did someone mention
MONEY?

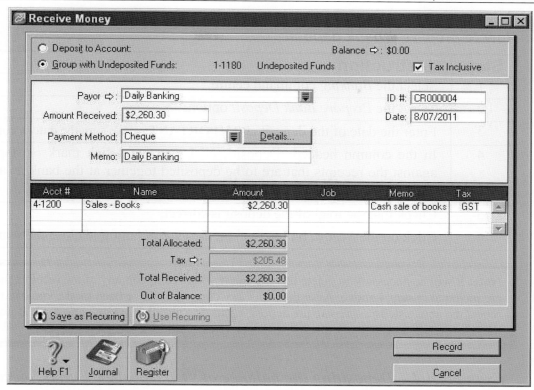

Figure 4.9: *Receive Money* window using account numbers

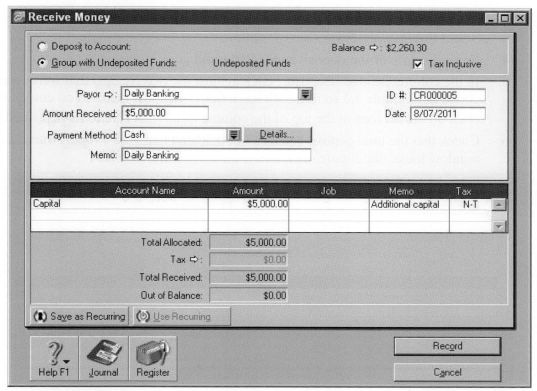

Figure 4.10: Cash from owner debited to "Undeposited Funds" account

How to prepare a bank deposit

Step	Instruction
1	Select the *Banking* command centre.
2	Select the *Prepare Bank Deposit* option.
3	Enter the date of the deposit ↵ (**IMPORTANT:** make sure the date is correct.)
4	In the column headed 'Deposit', click (so that a tick mark ✓ appears) against the receipts that are to be deposited together at the bank as at that date. If all items listed are to be deposited, click on the 🔲 icon.
5	Check that the total of the deposit is correct.
6	Click on the *Record* button then on the *Cancel* button to close the window.

Note: It will be necessary to <u>delete</u> this deposit if you need to edit any of the receipts that are included in step 4 above. After the necessary corrections have been made, you can then repeat the above steps to prepare the deposit again. See also the box on page 4-18. Refer to the 'How to …' in Chapter 1 on how to delete a transaction.

Example 4.4—Depositing the balance of "Undeposited Funds" account

1. Make sure that you have the file dem41.myo open.
2. Select the *Banking* command centre.
3. Select the *Prepare Bank Deposit* option.
4. Enter the date of the deposit as 8/7/2011 and ↵.
5. In the column headed 'Deposit', click against the two receipts that were recorded above in Example 4.3 so that each has a tick ✓ against them. (You could also click on the 🔲 icon at the top of the column as all items are to be deposited.)
6. Check that the total deposit equals $7,260.30 and that your *Prepare Bank Deposit* window looks like Figure 4.11:

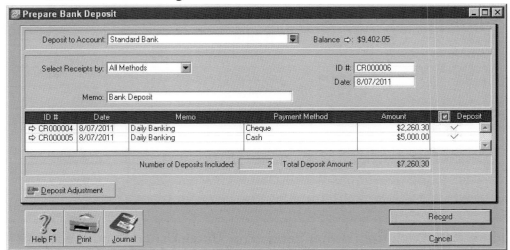

Figure 4.11: Undeposited funds now deposited at the bank

7.   Before recording the deposit, select the *Edit* pull-down menu and *Recap Transaction* menu item and examine the entries that will be posted in the general ledger. The recap transaction should look like Figure 4.12:

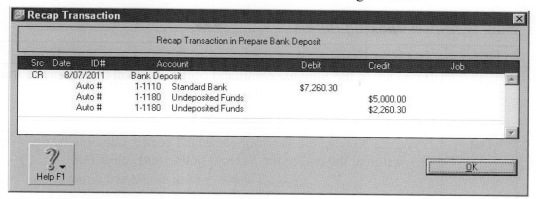

Figure 4.12: The *Recap Transaction* window for banking undeposited funds

8.   Close the *Recap Transaction* window.

9.   Click on the *Record* button.

10. Click the *Cancel* button to exit the *Prepare Bank Deposit* window.

Video: A video on using undeposited funds is on the DVD

Self-test exercise 4.3

Have the file dem41.myo open.

Enter the following receipts using *Receive Money* and group with "Undeposited Funds". All amounts include the GST. For <u>each</u> day's receipts, deposit the amount that is in the "Undeposited Funds" account at the bank (Standard Bank).

11 July: Cheque received from Black's Auction House $8,937.50 for sale of books. Credit "Sales – Books" account. The cheque details are: BSB 456-789, account name BLACKS AUCTIONS, account No 63018420 and cheque No 333128.

Cash sales totalling $2,964.50 for sale of craft material $1,892.00 and sale of books $1,072.50.

Prepare a single deposit of $11,902.00 to Standard Bank for these receipts.

18 July: Received $2,654.85 for the sale of materials (cheque number 100359 from Edgar Poe drawn on Varsity Bank BSB 551-111, account No 43212345) and $2,340.50 cash for the sale of books.

Prepare a single deposit of $4,995.35.

22 July: Obsolete stationery sold to staff member for $198.00 (cheque number 214127, BSB 441-556 drawn on Dave Robinson's account number 84201234). Credit the Stationery (account number 6-0450).

Cash sales totalling $3,201.80 for sale of craft material $1,595.55 and sale of books $1,606.25.

Prepare a single deposit of $3,399.80.

31 July: Received $1,744.60 for the sale of materials (cheque number 100380 from Edgar Poe drawn on Varsity Bank BSB 551-111, account number 43212345) and $1,078.00 cash for the sale of books.

Prepare a single deposit of $2,822.60.

Printing reports from the *Banking* command centre

Several reports will need to be printed when going through the rest of this chapter.

How to print a banking report

Step	Instruction
1	If you are in the *Banking* command centre, click on the *Reports* button (see bottom of the command centre window). Click ⟶ Reports ▼
OR	If you are NOT in the *Banking* command centre, click on the drop-down *List* button at the end of the *Reports* button and select *Banking*. Reports ▼ ◀—Click drop-down arrow Accounts ◀— Banking reports selected GST/Sales Tax Sales Time Billing Purchases Payroll Inventory Card File Custom
2	Click on the report you want to select.
3	Click on the *Customise* button at the foot of the window. Click ⟶ 🛈 Customise
4	Make selections from the resulting *Report Customisation* window. Under the *Report Fields* tab, select or deselect report fields to be printed. Under the *Finishing* tab select or de-select other items that may appear on the report.
5	Preview the report on the screen by selecting the *Display* button.
6	Click on the *Print* button at the bottom left of the screen to obtain a printout.

Example 4.5—Print the bank deposits for July

1. Start *MYOB AccountRight* and open the file dem41.myo.
2. Select the *Banking* command centre.
3. Click on the *Reports* button at the bottom of the command centre window.
4. Click on the "Bank Deposit Slip" report as shown in Figure 4.13 on the next page.
5. Click on the *Customise* button and enter the 'Dated From:' date as "1/7/2011" and TAB to enter the 'To' date as "31/7/2011". Leave the *Report Fields* and *Finishing* as they are. The *Advanced Filters* window is shown in Figure 4.14 on the next page.

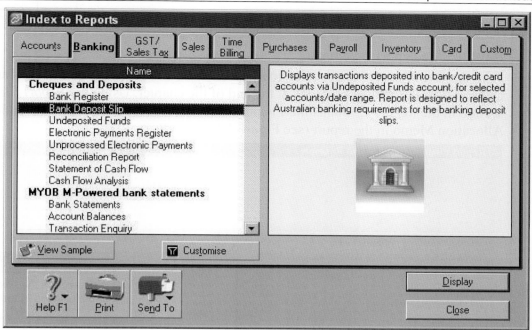

Figure 4.13: "Bank Deposit Slip" report selected from *Index to Reports* window

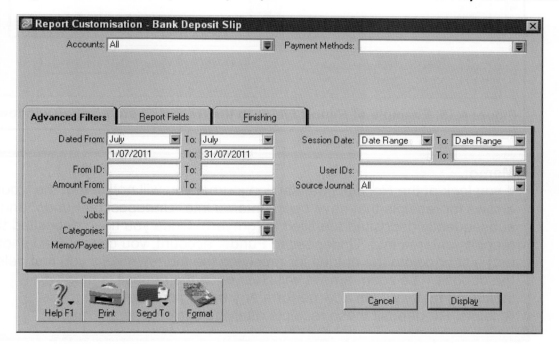

Figure 4.14: Advanced Filters in the Report Customisation window

6. Click on the *Display* button to view the report on the screen. Change the 'View' to "Print Preview". You can maximise the report window and use the scroll bars to see the whole report.

7. If you want a hard copy, click on the *Print* button at the foot of the window to print the report. Otherwise, click on the *Close* button.

Video: A video about printing reports is on the DVD

Self-test exercise 4.4

Have the file dem41.myo open.

Print the *Cash Receipts* transaction journal for all of the July 2011 transactions and check it with the answer provided at the end of the chapter. Using the *Report Fields* section in the *Report Customisation* window, de-select the 'Job' field and include the Allocation Memo in the report (see Figure 4.15).

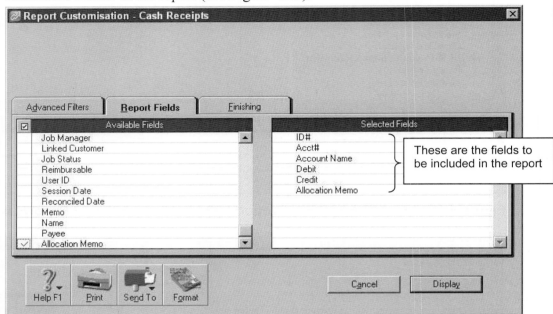

Figure 4.15: Example of *Report Fields* in the *Report Customisation* window

Memo:

If you look at the *Receipts* transaction journal you will notice that the 'zoom' arrows for receipts that have been entered into "Undeposited Funds" and subsequently deposited are filled in (greyed). Once you have deposited the receipts entered into "Undeposited Funds" account, you cannot (and should not) edit or delete the entries for receiving the money *unless* you first delete the deposit. The zoom arrows will clear once the deposit is deleted indicating that you can now perform any editing or deletion to these receipts. Re-deposit these receipts after the corrections are made.

I am "greyed out" but the cat still likes me!

Cash payments

All payments (disbursements) are made by 'writing a cheque' using the *Spend Money* option. This option is used even in a situation where there is no physical cheque involved – such as recording a bank charge from a bank statement or paying cash for an expense.

How to record a payment using Spend Money

Step	Instruction
1	Select the *Banking* command centre.
2	Select the *Spend Money* option.
3	Change the bank account <u>if necessary</u> by clicking on the *List* button ▣ at the end of the 'Pay from Account' field for the bank and selecting from the list.
4	Check that the 'Tax Inclusive' checkbox is correct for the particular transaction. A tick in this checkbox means that any dollar amounts entered in the 'Amount' column will be considered as GST-inclusive (includes the GST). Click this checkbox on if amounts are tax-inclusive. Clear it if the amounts are *plus* the GST.
5	You need to enter the first cheque number of each cheque book. After that the cheque numbers automatically increment by one for each new cheque. If no cheque is issued, change this (for example – "B/S" for bank statement) ↵.
6	Type in the date ↵. If the month and year are already correct, only type in the day of the month.
7	Enter the amount of the cheque ↵.
8	At the 'Card' field, enter the first few letters of the payee and TAB twice. **Only do this if a card exists for the payee**, or you want to add a card to the card file. Otherwise, skip this field by using TAB three times.
9	If you have not used a card, type in the payee name and TAB.
10	Type in a memo or leave the payee's name in the 'Memo' field ↵.
11	Enter the account name or the account number for the account to be debited or credited. <u>You</u> may enter the first few letters (or numbers) and click the *List* button ▣ and select the correct account from the list. Using the Enter key will list all accounts for selection. TAB to the 'Amount' column.
12	Enter the amount. If the 'Tax Inclusive' checkbox is on (ticked), enter the amount <u>including</u> any tax, otherwise enter the amount excluding the tax and the tax (if any) will be automatically calculated and added to the total transaction. The amounts, excluding tax, will be debited to the nominated account for each line. Enter the amount as negative to credit the accounts instead. TAB to the 'Job' column and enter any job number, if required.
13	TAB to the 'Memo' column and enter any additional allocation information for this line (this is optional and may appear on reports).
14	TAB to the 'Tax' column and edit, if necessary, the tax code for the GST involved and ↵ .
	(continued on the next page)

Step	Instruction
15	Enter any additional lines for the cheque. Enter credit entries as a minus figure – for example, group tax deducted from the gross amount of wages.
16	Click on the *Record* button to record the cheque.

Entering and recording a cheque in *Spend Money* will automatically credit the bank account nominated as a *Bank* account with the amount of the cheque. You must therefore nominate the accounts to be debited (or credited if entered as negative) making up the cheque total. If the amounts in the details section do not match the cheque amount you will not be able to post (record) the transaction.

Example 4.6—Recording a payment using Spend Money

The following instructions are for the payment of $2,882.00, including the GST, to Castle Hill Art Galleries for craft materials purchased on 1 July 2011. This business does not keep perpetual inventory accounts and purchases of craft materials and craft books are debited to purchases accounts in the *Cost of Sales* section in the general ledger. If you are using account numbers rather than account names, these accounts have a prefix of "5" (for example, purchases of craft materials will be debited to account "5-1110 Purchases – Materials").

1. The file dem41.myo should be used in this example.
2. Select the *Banking* command centre.
3. Select the *Spend Money* option.
4. The amount for this purchase includes the GST. Check that the checkbox for 'Tax Inclusive' at the top of the *Spend Money* window is on (there is a tick in the box).
5. The cheque number should be "145663". The cheque number will automatically increment by 1 for the next cheque.
6. Set the date to "1/7/2011" ↵.
7. Enter the GST-inclusive amount as 2882 (this is $2,620.00 plus $262.00 GST) ↵.
8. At the 'Card' field, type in "c" ↵. This should select the payee as Castle Hill Art Galleries as per a card that has already been set up.
    Note: If a card does not exist *and* you do not want to set one up, leave the 'Card' field blank and TAB through to the 'Payee' field and enter in the details.
9. TAB through to the 'Memo' field and in this exercise leave this as "Castle Hill Art Galleries"↵.
10. Enter the account. The preference set up in this file is to list and select accounts by name. In the column headed 'Account Name' type in the account name "Purchases – Materials" (you may type in the first few letters "pu" and use the *List* button 🔲 to select the correct account from the list). If you have changed the preference to use account numbers instead of account names, enter "5-1120" as the account number. TAB through to the 'Amount' column.

    Note: If you hit Enter instead of TAB you will be on the second line – use the "up" arrow key or point and click the mouse to go back to the first line.

11. $2,882.00 should be highlighted in the 'Amount' column. TAB through to the column headed 'Memo' (this chapter does not use Jobs – see Chapter 9 about using Jobs).

12. Type in an allocation memo (an additional explanation of this line in the account allocation section) as "Payment for craft material purchased" and ↵ (the tax code should be "GST").

13. Make sure your screen looks like Figure 4.16 and edit any fields that have errors. **Note:** At the foot of the *Spend Money* window the total amount of the GST is shown in grey indicating that it is already included in the 'Total Allocated'.

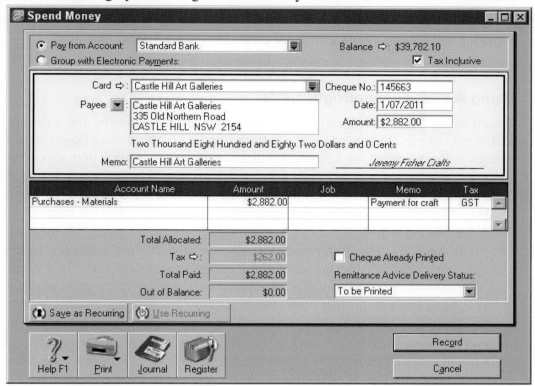

Figure 4.16: Payment for purchases using the *Spend Money* option

14. Before recording the cheque, you can examine how the amounts will be recorded in the general ledger. Select the *Edit* pull-down menu at the top of the screen and then select the *Recap Transaction* menu item. The resulting window will look like Figure 4.17 on the next page.

15. Click on the *OK* button to close the *Recap Transaction* window.

16. Click the *Record* button.

17. Click the *Cancel* button to close *Spend Money*.

Video: A video on making payments using **Spend Money** *is on the DVD*

Figure 4.17: *Recap Transaction* **for payment using** *Spend Money*

Using *MYOB AccountRight* cards

A card called "Daily Banking" has already been used for deposits, and a card for Castle Hill Art Galleries was used in the last example. *MYOB AccountRight* uses a set of records called "cards" for keeping relatively permanent information about customers, suppliers, employees and personal contacts. A card should be set up whenever there will be regular transactions with people and organisations. Care should be taken not to overdo the use of cards as they take up space in the data file – and the bigger the file gets the slower the performance!

In the *Sales*, *Purchases* and *Payroll* command centres, cards are essential. For example, you cannot issue an invoice for a customer unless there is a card for that customer. Similarly you need cards for suppliers and employees to issue purchase orders or pay wages. The use of cards in the *Banking* command centre, however, is optional.

Cards can be created or viewed using the *Card File* command centre. The creation of cards will be covered in the following chapters for accounts receivable, accounts payable and payroll (Chapters 5, 6 and 8). You can refer to the 'How to …' boxes in these chapters if you wish to create any cards. However, in this chapter the necessary cards are already included on the files provided and you will not be required to create any cards.

A diversion!

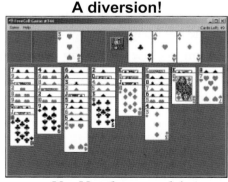

No. Not those cards!

Self-test exercise 4.5

Have the file dem41.myo open.

Enter in the following payments using *Spend Money*. The first cheque number should be "145664", and the 'Tax Inclusive' checkbox should be ticked. The GST-inclusive amount for each cheque is in the 'Cheque Amount' column below. This is also the amount to be entered in the 'Amount' column.

Enter the 'details' in the allocation 'Memo' column.

Jul	Chq No	Cheque Amount	GST Amount	Tax Code	Payee/Details	Account
4	664	$984.50	$89.50	GST	I.G.O. Pty Ltd – for general insurance premiums	Insurance – Account 6-0200
4	665	$2,079.55	$189.05	GST	Hornsby Artico Pty Ltd – for books purchased	Purchases – Books – Account 5-2120

Using a petty cash "bank" account

A separate "bank" type account (Detail – Bank) can be used to record small payments of cash. Instead of paying these small amounts with individual cheques, an amount called a "float" is drawn and kept by one person usually in a "petty cash tin". Small payments for expenses like taxi fares, staff amenities, postage etc. are made from this float. When the float is nearly all spent, a cheque called a "re-imbursement cheque" is drawn for all the expenses paid out of the petty cash tin and this brings the float back to the original amount. In a hand-written bookkeeping system, a separate book called the "Petty Cash Book" is usually kept to record all expenses and re-imbursements.

With a computerised system, a "bank" type account called 'Petty Cash' or 'Petty Cash Float' can be used to <u>record</u> the payments made from petty cash and there is no need for a separate petty cash book. Payments are recorded using the *Spend Money* option from the *Banking* command centre and is exactly the same as shown in the instructions on pages 4-19 and 4-20 earlier in this chapter. Note however, that this is NOT an account at a bank, and payments are not really by way of a cheque (even though a cheque form is used to record the petty cash payments).

Example 4.7—Making petty cash payments

1. Make sure that you have the file dem41.myo open. This file already has a "Petty Cash" account (account number 1-1150) with $300 as the "float".
2. Select the *Banking* command centre.
3. Select the *Spend Money* option.
4. In the 'Pay from Account:' field at the top, select the "Petty Cash" account.
5. Check that the checkbox for 'Tax Inclusive' is on (there is a tick in the box).
6. The cheque No should be "1". (This is a reference number rather than a cheque #.)
7. Set the date to "1/7/2011".
8. Enter the amount as "66.88" ↵.
9. At the 'Card' field, type in "pe" ↵. This should select a card called "Petty Cash".
10. TAB through to the 'Memo' field and in this exercise leave this as "Petty Cash"↵.

11. In the 'Account Name' column type "Tr" and select "Travel". If you are using account numbers, enter "6-0510". TAB through to the 'Amount' column.

12. Type in "$39.60" in the 'Amount' column. TAB through to the 'Memo' column.

13. Type in an allocation memo as "Taxi fares for sales manager" and ↵ (the tax code should be "GST").

14. On the next line, enter in a petty cash payment of "$27.28" (including GST) for "Urgent taxi truck delivery". Use the account called "Parcel Delivery" (account number
   "6-0030") and ↵ (the tax code should be "GST").

15. Make sure your screen looks like Figure 4.18 and edit any fields that have errors:

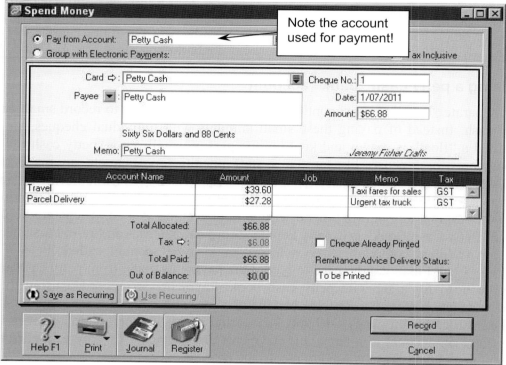

Figure 4.18: A petty cash payment using *Spend Money*

Video: A video showing you how to keep petty cash is on the DVD

Self-test exercise 4.6

Have the file dem41.myo open.

On 4 July 2011, use the "Petty Cash" bank account to record some petty cash expenses. Petty cash cheque Number 2 is for $138.32 and the expenses paid were:

$46.20 (including GST) for taxi fares to the airport for the accountant. Debit the account "Travel" (account number 6-0510).

$59.52 (including GST) for diesel fuel for sales representative's vehicle. Debit the account "Motor Vehicle Running Costs" (account number 6-0250).

$32.60 (GST-free) for staff tea, coffee and sugar purchased. Debit the account "Staff Amenities Expense" (account number 6-0110) and the tax code is "FRE".

Petty cash re-imbursement

A cash cheque is drawn to put back into the petty cash account (physically into the petty cash tin) the total of the petty cash paid out. This should return the "Petty Cash" account to the original float.

In the example and exercise above, the total petty cash expenses paid out amount to $205.20 and the balance of the "Petty Cash" account in the general ledger is $94.80 (original float of $300.00 less the total expenses paid of $205.20). You should verify the balance by selecting *Accounts List* in the *Accounts* command centre. A cheque is cashed at the bank for $205.20 to return the balance back to $300.00.

Example 4.8—Petty cash re-imbursement cheque

1. Make sure that you have the file dem41.myo open.
2. Select the *Banking* command centre.
3. Select the *Spend Money* option.
4. The bank account for this cheque is "Standard Bank".
5. As this entry is an internal transfer of cash, no GST is involved and it does not matter whether you have the 'Tax Inclusive' checkbox selected or not.
6. The cheque number should be "145666".
7. Enter the date as "5/7/2011" ↵.
8. Enter the amount as "205.20" ↵.
9. No card is required so TAB to the 'Payee' field and type in "Cash".
10. TAB to the 'Memo' field and type in "Petty cash re-imbursement"↵.
11. In the column headed 'Account Name' type in the account name "Petty Cash" (you may type in the first few letters "pe" and this should select this account). If you have changed the preference to use account numbers instead of account names, enter "1-1150" as the account number.
12. TAB twice and the amount of $205.20 should be in the 'Amount' column. The TAX code should be "N-T". There is no need for a line memo. If your *Spend Money* window looks like Figure 4.19 on the next page, click on the *Record* button.

Memo:
The big danger with using the "Petty Cash" account as a "bank" type account is to forget to change the 'Pay from Account' field at the top of the *Spend Money* window. The same problem will also arise if the business has (and uses) more than one bank account to record receipts and payments.

Therefore, it is *always* a good idea when recording payments to check your first entry for the accuracy of the following: the bank account, the first cheque number and the starting date.

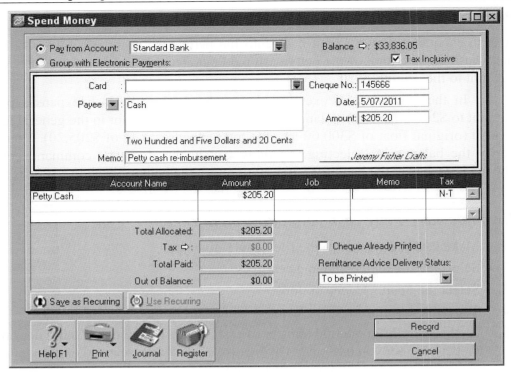

Figure 4.19: A petty cash re-imbursement cheque

Recurring cheques

There are payments that must be made at regular intervals. Some examples are rent, leases, superannuation, payroll deductions, GST and Pay-As-You-Go (PAYG). A cheque can be set up as a "Recurring Entry" that can be recalled, adjusted (if necessary) and recorded as a new payment at regular intervals or as needed. Using a recurring entry is similar to using a template in Microsoft products – the basic entry is already set up and only requires minimum editing such as the date and occasionally the amounts.

How to create a recurring payment

Step	Instruction
1	Prepare a payment using the *Spend Money* option in the *Banking* command centre (see "*How to record a payment using Spend Money*" on page 4-19) but <u>do not record it</u> straight away – until step 6.
2	Click on the *Save as Recurring* button.
3	Type in a unique name for the recurring entry.
4	Click the drop-down arrows to change the frequency and set up the *Schedule*, *Alerts* and *Transaction* options.
5	Click on the *Save* button to save the template of the recurring entry – note that this does not *record* the entry as a transaction in the journal.
6	Click on the *Record* button to save the payment.

Example 4.9—Creating a recurring payment

Have the file dem41.myo open. The payment transactions that follow later in Self-Test Exercises 4.7 and 4.8 include cheques for the weekly salary of an employee called 'Sally Hubble'. As this transaction takes place every week, the cheque for 7 July should be saved as a recurring payment <u>before</u> being recorded. You will also know that while the payment is made out for the net pay, $544.50, it is the Gross pay that is recorded as the expense. Deductions from the gross pay, such as PAYG withholding, superannuation etc, must be credited to current liability accounts for payment in the next month. There is no GST involved with salary transactions. To record the pay cheque on 7 July:

1. Select the *Spend Money* option from the *Banking* command centre.

2. The cheque number should be "145667". Enter the date as "7/7/2011" ↵.

3. Enter the amount as "544.50" ↵.

4. In the 'Card' field type "hu" and select "Hubble, Sally" ↵.

5. TAB through to the 'Memo' field and edit to "Weekly salary – Sally Hubble" ↵.

6. The account to be debited with the gross salary is "Wages & Salaries" – account number 6-0130. Type in the account name (or number if you are using account numbers) and TAB to the 'Amount' field.

7. Enter the gross salary as "835" and TAB to the allocation line 'Memo' column.

8. Type in "Gross pay for a week" as the allocation line memo and ↵ (the 'Tax' field should have "N-T" as the code).

9. Type in the account "PAYG Withholding" number "2-1420" and TAB.

10. As "PAYG Withholding" is to be credited, enter the amount as a negative – type the minus sign followed by the amount " – 250.50".

11. TAB to the allocation line 'Memo' column and enter "PAYG tax withheld" and ↵ (the 'Tax' field should have "N-T" as the code).

12. Type in the account "Payroll Deductions" number 2-1410 and TAB.

13. Enter the amount as "– 40.00" (amount should appear as the default balance).

14. TAB to the allocation line memo column and enter "Medical and union fees deducted" and ↵ (the Tax field should have "N-T" as the code).

15. The *Spend Money* window should be as per Figure 4.20 on the next page – <u>DO NOT</u> record this yet.

16. Click on the *Save as Recurring* button.

17. Leave the name of the recurring entry "Weekly salary – Sally Hubble". Use the drop-down arrow at the end of the 'Frequency' field and select "weekly".

18. The 'Starting on' field is used by *MYOB Accounting* to issue 'To Do List' reminders. As we are not using this feature enter any future date.
    Note: You cannot enter a <u>starting</u> date prior to the <u>current</u> financial year.

19. The *Edit Recurring Schedule* window should look like Figure 4.21 on the next page.

20. Click on the *Save* button to save the recurring transaction template.

21. In the *Spend Money* window click on the *Record* button to now record cheque number 145667 on 7 July 2011.

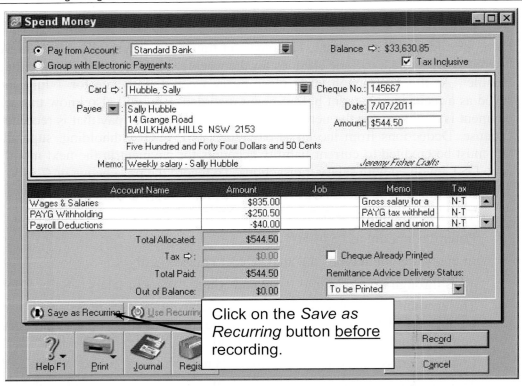

Figure 4.20: Wages cheque for Sally Hubble – to be saved as a recurring entry

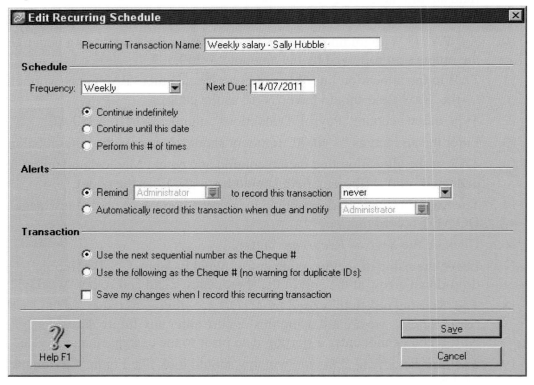

Figure 4.21: The *Edit Recurring Schedule* window

 Video: A video on creating and using recurring entries is on the DVD

Self-test exercise 4.7

Have the file dem41.myo open. This exercise follows on from previous exercises and the examples above. The total amount for each cheque is in the *Cheque Amount* column, and it includes the GST (tax-inclusive) where applicable. Enter in the following payments using *Spend Money*. Pay amounts from the **Standard Bank** (first cheque number 145668) and for petty cash expenses, pay the amounts from the **Petty Cash** bank account (first cheque number 3):

Make sure that you use the correct bank account and cheque number!

Jul	Chq No	Cheque Amount	GST Amount	Tax Code	Payee/Details	Account
7	668	$524.00	$0.00	N-T	Australian Taxation Office – PAYG withholding for June	PAYG Withholding (account number 2-1420)
8	669	$400.00	$0.00	N-T	Cash – Cash taken by the proprietor	Drawings (account number 3-1300)
8	Petty Cash 3	$136.95	$12.45	GST	Petty cash – repairs to door	Maintenance & Repairs (account number 6-0220)
11	670	$251.35	$22.85	GST	Mobil Castle Hill – Petrol and oil for June	Motor Vehicle Running Costs (6-0250)
12	671	$250.00	$0.00	N-T	PMA Society – superannuation deductions for June	Payroll Deductions (2-1410)
12	672	$100.00	$0.00	N-T	St. George Savings – employee voluntary savings deducted	Payroll Deductions (2-1410)
13	Petty Cash 4	$61.16	$5.56	GST	Petty cash $31.46 for cleaning materials	Shop Expenses (6-0400)
				GST	$29.70 for taxi fares	Travel (6-0510)

Print the *Cash Disbursements* **Transaction Journal** for the period 7/7/2011 to 13/7/2011 and check the printout with the answer provided at the end of the chapter. Show the allocation line details in the report, and do not print the 'Job' column (refer to pages 4-16 and 4-18 for instructions on printing *Banking* command centre reports).

How to use a recurring payment

Step	Instruction
1	Select the *Spend Money* option from the *Banking* command centre.
2	Click on the *Use Recurring* ⟨ Use Recurring ⟩ button.
3	In the *Select a Recurring Transaction* window (Figure 4.22 on the next page), select the recurring entry required by clicking on it.
4	Click on the *Select* button to return to the *Spend Money* window.
5	Edit the cheque details if necessary – for example, change the date.
6	Click on the *Record* button.

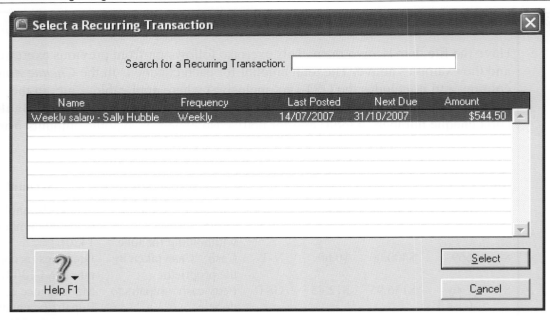

Figure 4.22: Selecting a recurring transaction

Self-test exercise 4.8

Have the file dem41.myo. This exercise follows on from Exercise 4.7. Select *Spend Money* and the cheque number for the Standard Bank should already be 145673.

Click on *Use Recurring* button and select "Weekly Salary – Hubble" (see Figure 4.22). Change the date to 14/7/2011 and record. There is no GST on salaries and wages.

Jul	Chq No	Cheque Amount	GST Amount	Tax Code	Payee	Details
14	673	$544.50	$0.00	N-T	Sally Hubble	Wages – Gross $835.00 less Group tax $250.50 and deductions $40 (**Note:** These details should already be shown if you have used the recurring entry!)

Once a recurring transaction is created, it can be used (as demonstrated above), deleted (if it is no longer required) or modified. The modification can be either to the transaction details or to its schedule details. Modifications are only necessary if the changes are of a permanent nature. The recurring transaction can also be copied as a shortcut solution to creating another similar recurring transaction.

How to use, modify, delete or copy recurring transactions

Step	Instruction
1	Click on the *Lists* pull-down menu.
2	Select the *Recurring Transactions* menu item. A list of <u>ALL</u> available recurring transactions created from any command centre will be displayed.

(continued on the next page)

Step	Instruction
3	To use a recurring transaction, select (highlight) a transaction and click on the [ⓘ Use Recurring] button.
4	To delete a recurring transaction that is no longer required, select the transaction and click on the [🗑 Delete] button.
5	To copy a recurring transaction, select the transaction you wish to make a copy of and click on the [📋 Create Copy] button. You will need to edit the copy as necessary. **Note:** This is useful in situations where a recurring transaction with similar details as an existing transaction is required.
6	To modify the transaction details (account names, amounts etc), select the transaction and click on the [Edit] button.
7	To Modify (change) the transaction name, the frequency, the starting date etc, select the transaction and click on the [Edit Schedule] button.

Self-test exercise 4.9

Have the file dem41.myo open. This exercise follows on from Exercise 4.8. The amount for each cheque is in the 'Cheque Amount' column, and includes the GST where applicable. Pay amounts from the "Standard Bank" account (first cheque number should be 145674) except for those shown for petty cash expenses. For petty cash expenses, pay the amount from the "Petty Cash" account ("Petty Cash" first cheque number should be 5).

Enter in the following payments. New cards are <u>not</u> required. If a card does not exist, type in the payee name in the 'Payee' field. Recurring salary transaction should be used when paying Sally Hubble. Account names and codes are given in the column headed 'Account':

Jul	Chq No	Cheque Amount	GST Amount	Tax Code	Payee/Details	Account
16	674	$100.00	$0.00	FRE	Salvation Army – Donation to special appeal	Donations – account number 6-0060
16	675	$465.30	$42.30	GST	Skillett and Sons – repairs to office partitions	Maintenance & Repairs – account number 6-0220
16	676	$1,650.00	$150.00	GST	E. G. O'Brien Pty Ltd – *Yellow Pages* advertisement	Advertising – account number 6-0010
18	677	$3,619.00	$329.00	GST	Wholesale Craft Pty Ltd – purchase of books	Purchases – Books – account number 5-2120
19	Petty Cash 5	$92.40	$8.40	GST	Petty cash – sundry stationery items	Stationery – account number 6-0450
19	678	$290.51	$0.00	N-T	Cash – Petty cash re-imbursement	Petty Cash – account number 1-1150

(continued on the next page)

Self-test exercise 4.9 *(continued)*

Jul	Chq No	Cheque Amount	GST Amount	Tax Code	Payee/Details	Account
20	679	$544.50	$0.00	N-T	Sally Hubble – as per recurring entry	As per the recurring entry. Click *Use Recurring* button
21	680	$1,955.80	$177.80	GST	Hornsby Artico Pty Ltd – purchase of craft materials	Purchases – Materials account number 5-1120
23	681	$550.00	$50.00	GST	Paul and Dainty – fees for special investigation	Accounting Fees – account number 6-0005
23	Petty Cash 6	$107.06	$6.26	GST	Petty cash - $68.86 for petrol and oil	Motor Vehicle Running Costs – account number 6-0250
			$0.00	FRE	$38.20 for staff tea and coffee	Staff Amenities Expense – account number 6-0110
25	682	$3,608.00	$328.00	GST	Castle Hill Art Galleries – purchase of craft materials	Purchases – Materials account number 5-1120
25	683	$66.00	$6.00	GST	Australia Post – parcel delivery of books	Parcel Delivery – account number 6-0030
28	684	$544.50	$0.00	N-T	Sally Hubble – as per recurring entry	As per the recurring entry. Click on the *Use Recurring* button.
30	Petty Cash 7	$141.35	$12.85	GST	Petty Cash – sundry shop expenses	Shop Expenses – account number 6-0400
30	685	$2,024.00	$184.00	CAP	Sarcom Electronics – purchase of a laser printer for office	Equipment – at cost – account number 1-2210
31	686	$39.05	$3.55	GST	Hills Transport – urgent parcel delivery	Parcel Delivery – account number 6-0030
31	687	$264.88	$24.08	GST	Powerplus – electricity account for the quarter	Electricity – account number 6-0310

Print the Cash Disbursements Transaction Journal for the period 14/07/2011 to 31/07/2011. Customise the report to show the allocation memo, and not to print the 'Job' column (refer to page 4-16 for instructions on printing "Banking" reports).

Check your printout with the answer provided at the end of this chapter. Modify any errors if necessary.

> **Note:**
> Check that the bank balance of the Standard Bank account is $15,294.96
> <u>after</u> recording all these entries.

Bank reconciliation

A bank statement received from the bank should be checked against the general ledger account for that bank. This is an essential task that should be carried out regularly. Errors can be detected and bank charges or interest (paid or earned) recorded into the ledger account. The checking process should be carried out methodically and carefully, and the computer reconciliation follows closely the reconciliation that would be done in a manual system.

A file of transactions can be downloaded from the bank and this provides you with an automatic reconciliation of items between your records and the bank's records.

How to reconcile the bank account with the bank statement

Step	Instruction
1	Select the *Banking* command centre.
2	Select the *Reconcile Accounts* option.
3	Type in or use the *List* button 🔳 and select the "General Ledger" account for the bank account.
4	TAB to the 'New Statement Balance:' field and type in the **closing** balance as per the bank statement and ↵. **IMPORTANT:** Enter the balance as <u>negative</u> if the closing balance is <u>overdrawn</u> (i.e. debit balance as per bank statement).
5	Enter the 'Bank Statement Date:'.
6	**If** you have downloaded a statement electronically from the bank, click on the *Actions* button, select *Get Statement* and find the downloaded file. Actions: Undo Reconciliation, Bank Entry, **Get Statement**, Spend Money, Pay Bills, Receive Money, Receive Payments, Transfer Money, Record Journal Entry, Settle Returns and Credits, Settle Returns and Debits, Find Transactions, View Bank Register, Print Last Reconciliation Report Click on the *Actions* button Select for reconciling ← with a downloaded statement *(continued on the next page)*

Step	Instruction
7	Click the button for your transaction order preference (transactions can be listed (sorted) in either date or ID# order). Click [Date] **OR** Click [ID#]
8	Click in the left-hand column to mark a tick ✓ against all items that appear on the bank statement. At the same time mark the items on the bank statement that reconcile. This will also apply to any items not matched when using an electronically downloaded statement.
9	To enter items that are on the bank statement that need to be entered into the bank account in the general ledger, click on the *Action* button and select *Bank Entry*. Actions Undo Reconciliation Click on the *Actions* button Get Statement → Select to enter items from bank statement Spend Money Pay Bills Receive Money Receive Payments Transfer Money Record Journal Entry Settle Returns and Credits Settle Returns and Debits Find Transactions View Bank Register Print Last Reconciliation Report
10	In the top part of the window called *Record Service Charges and Interest Earned* enter details for bank charges (amount, date, account number to debit, tax code (FRE for bank charges)) and memo.
11	Enter any credits for interest received from the bank in the bottom part of the *Record Service Charges and Interest Earned* window.
12	Click on the *Record* button to record bank charges etc.
13	If the 'Out of Balance' field is zero, click on the *Reconcile* button.
14	Click on the second *Reconcile* button to clear all items that have been matched (ticked) and print the final reconciliation statement.
15	If you find an error in the accounts after completing a reconciliation, you can undo the last reconciliation by clicking on the *Action* button and selecting *Undo Reconciliation*. See the 'How to …' instructions on page 4-39 for more information.
16	Use the *Print* button to print the reconciliation statement.

Memo:
A direct deposit from an accounts receivable (a customer) will need to be entered into *MYOB AccountRight* using the *Sales* command centre, *Receive Payments* option – see Chapter 5. A payment to an accounts payable (a supplier) direct from your bank account will need to be entered using the *Purchases* command centre, *Pay Bills* option – see Chapter 6.

Note:
Make sure that standard bank account balance in your general ledger is
$15,294.96 <u>before</u> starting the following example.

Example 4.10—Bank reconciliation using "paper" bank statement

The statement from the Standard Bank to be used in this example is shown on the next page. The file is dem41.myo. This business has not obtained the statement electronically and does not have a file for reconciliation. You will need a pencil to "tick" off items in this bank statement that reconcile (agree) with items in the bank account in the general ledger.

1. Select the *Banking* command centre.

2. Select *Reconcile Accounts* option.

3. Enter the general ledger account number for the Standard Bank. Use the *List* button ⬇ next to the 'Account:' field to select the account "Standard Bank" from the account list (if you are using account numbers this account will be 1-1110).

4. TAB to the 'New Statement Balance:' field and enter the bank statement balance at 31 July 2011 – this is the closing balance on the bank statement "$15,337.34" and ↵.

5. The date on the bank statement is 31/07/2011. Enter this date in the 'Bank Statement Date' field ↵ (Ignore any date warning). (The 'Out of Balance' figure should show –$10,422.74 – **Note:** If you do not have this figure, you may find that the *MYOB* program has placed a tick against some items in the left-hand column and you will need to click on these to remove the tick mark.)

6. Transactions can be displayed in either 'date' or 'reference number' order. To show transactions sorted in date order, click on the *Date* button at the foot of the *Reconcile Accounts* window or to show transactions sorted in reference number order, click on the *ID#* button. The latter will group all deposits together and all cheques together and this is especially useful for reconciling cheques – as cheques are not necessarily cleared in date order.

7. Click in the left-hand column to produce a tick ✓ for all items that are on the bank statement that agree with the ledger bank account – i.e. the items that reconcile. The *Reconcile Accounts* window (expanded) is shown in Figure 4.23 on page 4-37.

8. The figure of $28.25 shown in the 'Out of Balance:' field in Figure 4.23 represents bank charges on the bank statement not yet recorded in the ledger account for Standard Bank (i.e. not yet entered in *MYOB AccountRight*).

9. Click on the *Action* button at the bottom of the *Reconcile Accounts* window and select *Bank Entry* from the list of actions to record these bank charges. This is shown on Figure 4.24 on page 4-37.

10. Enter $28.25 in the 'Amount:' field and TAB to the date field (<u>do not press</u> ↵).

11. Enter the date as "4/7/11" and TAB.

12. Type in "Bank Charges" (account number 6-0025) for the 'Expense Account' or click on the *List* button ⬇ and select the account "Bank Charges".

13. TAB through to the 'Memo' field and type in the memo as "Bank Charges from the bank statement".

14. Click on the *List* button ⬛ for 'Tax Code' and select the code FRE if it is not already selected.

15. Check that the *Bank and Deposit Adjustments* window looks like Figure 4.25 on page 4-38 and edit any incorrect fields.

16. Click on the *Record* button.

Bank statement for example 4.10

Standard Bank		Statement for July 2011			31/07/2011	
Jeremy Fisher Crafts						
		Debit	**Credit**	**Balance**	
1/7/11	Brought forward			4,914.60	CR
	Deposit		3,212.00	8,126.60	CR
4/7/11	Bank Fees	28.25			
	Deposit		874.50	8,972.85	CR
5/7/11	Chq 145666	205.20		8,767.65	CR
7/7/11	Chq 145663	2,882.00			
	Chq 145664	984.50			
	Chq 145667	544.50			
	Deposit		400.95	4,757.60	CR
8/7/11	Chq 145669	400.00			
	Deposit		7,260.30	11,617.90	CR
11/7/11	Chq 145665	2,079.55			
	Chq 145668	524.00			
	Deposit		11,902.00	20,916.35	CR
14/7/11	Chq 145673	544.50		20,371.85	CR
15/7/11	Chq 145670	251.35			
	Chq 145671	250.00			
	Chq 145672	100.00		19,770.50	CR
18/7/11	Deposit		4,995.35	24,765.85	CR
19/7/11	Chq 145678	290.51		24,475.34	CR
21/7/11	Chq 145679	544.50		23,930.84	CR
22/7/11	Deposit		3,399.80	27,330.64	CR
25/7/11	Chq 145680	1,955.80		25,374.84	CR
26/7/11	Chq 145681	550.00			
	Chq 145676	1,650.00		23,174.84	CR
27/7/11	Chq 145683	66.00		23,108.84	CR
28/7/11	Chq 145684	544.50			
	Chq 145677	3,619.00		18,945.34	CR
29/7/11	Chq 145682	3,608.00		15,337.34	CR

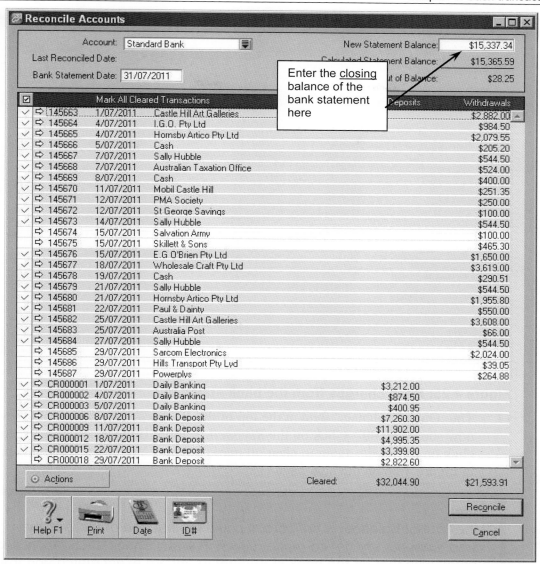

Figure 4.23: Reconciling the ledger account with the bank statement

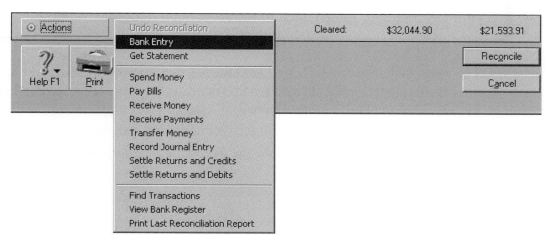

Figure 4.24: Selecting *Bank Entry* from the *Actions* menu

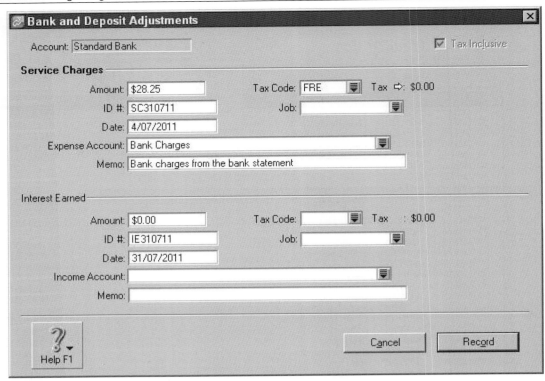

Figure 4.25: Bank charges from the bank statement

17. The 'Out of Balance:' field at the top of the *Reconcile Accounts* window should now show "$0.00". Click on the *Reconcile* button. If the accounts are reconciled, click on *Reconcile* again to clear all marked items. Your screen should appear as in Figure 4.26 on the next page.

Note:
If the 'Out of Balance' is not zero, it could be that one or more of the ticked amounts are not correct or ticked in error. Check each reconciled amount with that on the bank statement to ensure exact match and the amounts are not transposed, e.g. 970 instead of 790 etc. Click on the zoom arrow of a transaction with a wrong amount, fix the error and click on the *OK* button to return back to the *Reconcile Accounts* window.

18. The items that are not yet cleared are cheques that have not yet been presented at your bank (Unpresented cheques), and a deposit that was not banked on Friday 29 July 2011 (an Outstanding Deposit).

19. Click on the *Print* button and print the reconciliation statement.

20. Click on the *Cancel* button to close the *Reconcile Accounts* window.

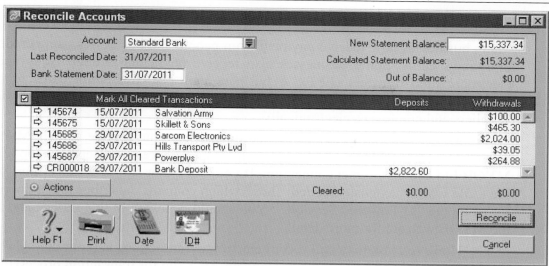

Figure 4.26: Final reconciliation statement

 Video: A video on completing a bank reconciliation is on the DVD

Reverse (undo) a previous bank reconciliation
If you have completed a bank reconciliation and you find that an error has been made, you can reverse the last completed reconciliation.

 How to reverse a completed bank reconciliation

Step	Instruction
1	In the *Reconcile Accounts* window (see Figure 4.26 above), click on the *Action* button and select *Undo Reconciliation*.
2	Read the warning message and click on the *Back Up* button in the *Undo Last Reconciliation* window if you want to complete a backup (refer to the 'How to …' instructions in Chapter 3 on backing up a data file for more detailed instructions on backups).
3	Click on the *Undo Reconciliation* button.
4	Click the *OK* button when you receive the message that the undo operation has been successful.

Electronic transactions and reconciliation

Many businesses now receive payment from people and businesses using credit, debit or savings cards. Some businesses also receive payments through BPay and other electronic fund transfers (EFT). A business may also use credit cards to pay for purchases (for example, petrol station expenses) and will also make payments to suppliers and employees electronically.

MYOB software provides an additional electronic service called "M-Powered Services Centre". This is not covered in this book as it requires separate application to MYOB Ltd and an internet connection. If your computer shows systems files, you will see a file with an extension called ".box" which contains data, logs and authorisations for using the "M-Powered Services". You should be aware of this service and look up the MYOB website for more details.

However, you may still record electronic transactions without the "M-Powered Services Centre" and provide a bank with an ABA file for transaction processing.

Receipts and payments are recorded in exactly the same way as shown earlier in this chapter. The main differences are in recording the deposit of receipts for which credit cards have been accepted, preparing an ABA file for payments and using a downloaded bank statement file from the bank to assist with electronic bank reconciliation.

Recording payments received by credit card

The cash received transaction is recorded in the normal way using the *Receive Money* option in the *Banking* command centre. Some credit card receipts (for example, American Express and Diners Club) will appear on the bank statement after the deduction of merchant fees. When a deposit is created, these merchant fees can be deducted to show the net amount in the general ledger bank account. Credit card receipts are therefore grouped with all other undeposited funds but must be deposited individually to assist with the bank reconciliation.

 ### *Example 4.11—Recording a credit card payment received*

1. A new file called file dem42.myo is used. Open this file and sign on as usual as the Administrator without a password. This business is a wholesale florist.  **NEW FILE**

2. Use the *Company Information* item in the *Setup* menu and insert your name in the company address field where shown.

3. On 18 July 2011, the customer D Brokoff using her MasterCard pays for a cash sale of flowers for $980.86 (including GST). Details of this card are: Card Number 1234 5645 7893 5562; Expiry Date 12/13; Name on Card D Brokoff. The Authorisation code is 876.

4. Use *Receive Money* and record the cash sale. Follow the instructions on pages 4-10 to 4-11 for recording money received that is grouped with Undeposited Funds. Use a card called "Cash Sales" and select "MasterCard" as the 'Payment Method'. Click on the *Details* button and enter in the MasterCard details. Your *Applied Payment Details* window should look like Figure 4.27 on the next page (note that the checkbox for 'Update Customer Card with Payment Details' is NOT selected, otherwise all sales using the card called "Cash Sales" would contain these MasterCard details!).

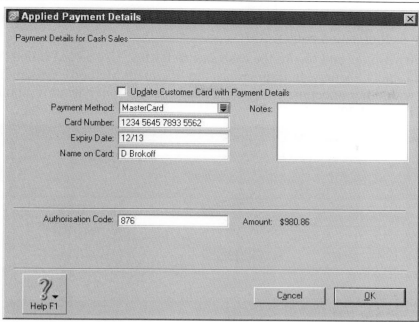

Figure 4.27: *Applied Payment Details* **window showing MasterCard details**

5. Make sure that the *Group with Undeposited Funds* option is selected at the top of the window and credit the account "Flower Sales" (account number 4-1000). Your *Receive Money* window using account names should look like Figure 4.28:

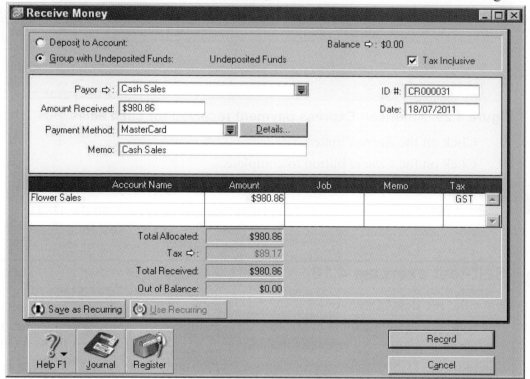

Figure 4.28: MasterCard payment received for cash sales

6. Click on the *Record* button.

7. On the same day (18 July 2011), the customer P May using an American Express card pays $625.60 (including GST) for a cash sale of flowers. Details of this card

are: Card Number 6541 3214 7896 4562; Expiry Date 08/13; Name on Card P May. The Authorisation code is 071.

8.   Use *Receive Money* and record the cash sale to P May. Use a card called "Cash Sales" and select "American Express" as the 'Payment Method'. Group this payment with other undeposited funds. Your *Receive Money* window should look like Figure 4.29:

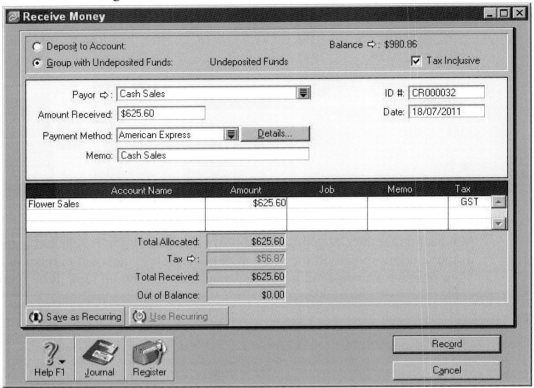

Figure 4.29: American Express payment received for cash sales

9.   Click on the *Record* button.

10.   Click on the *Cancel* button to complete.

Video: A video on recording credit card payments received is on the DVD

Self-test exercise 4.10

Have the file dem42.myo open.

Enter the following receipts on 22 July 2011 using *Receive Money* and *Group with Undeposited Funds*. All amounts include the GST. Do NOT deposit these receipts.

Cash sale to D Cheong for sale of plants $798.00 (including GST). Cheong pays using MasterCard Number 3456 7890 1234 9876 having an expiry date of 12/13 and authorisation code 192.

Cash sale for sale of novelty items to P May $329.00 (including GST). P May pays using an American Express card Number 6541 3214 7896 4562 with Expiry Date 08/13 and authorisation code 071.

Depositing credit card payments received

The proceeds from some credit cards such as MasterCard and Visa will appear on the bank statement on the following day. The merchant fees on these receipts are usually charged on the bank statement in one amount at the end of the month. For other credit cards like American Express and Diners Club, the merchant fees are deducted before the net proceeds are deposited in the bank account. These credit card proceeds often take up to one week to be shown on the bank statement. As the credit card receipts will appear separate from other deposits, they should be recorded as separate deposits. You can also record the net proceeds only (provided you know the net proceeds from the bank statement).

Example 4.12—Depositing credit card payments received

1. Make sure that you have the file dem42.myo open.
2. Select the *Banking* command centre.
3. Select the *Prepare Bank Deposit* option.
4. Enter the date of the deposit as "18/7/11" and ↵.
5. The MasterCard payment received is to be deposited. Tick (click) in the column headed 'Deposit', against the MasterCard amount of "$980.86" ✓ .
6. Check that the total deposit equals $980.86 and that your *Prepare Bank Deposit* window looks like Figure 4.30:

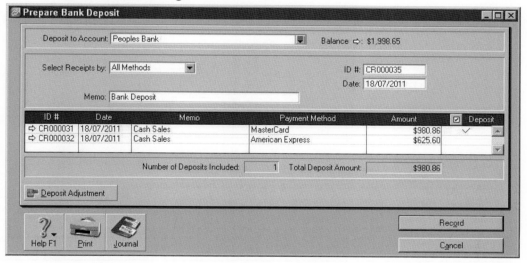

Figure 4.30: MasterCard payment received now deposited at the bank

Note:
If there are a number of receipts you can select to display them by their payment method. For example, to display only those receipts where a MasterCard was used, select this as the payment method in the *Prepare Bank Deposit* window.

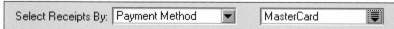

7. Click on the *Record* button.

8. Select the *Prepare Bank Deposit* option again. The American Express payment received, less merchant fees of $10.60, is to be deposited on 18 July 2011. In the column headed 'Deposit', click against the American Express amount of $625.60 so a tick ✓ appears against it. Do not record the transaction yet.

9. Click on the *Deposit Adjustment* button in the *Prepare Bank Deposit* window.

📠 <u>D</u>eposit Adjustment

10. In the *Bank and Deposit Adjustments* window, type in the amount of "10.60".

11. TAB through to the 'Expense Account' field and enter "Merchant fees" (account number 6-1024).

12. TAB to the 'Memo' field and type in "Merchant fees on American Express receipt".

13. If your *Bank and Deposit Adjustments* window looks like Figure 4.31, click on the *Record* button.

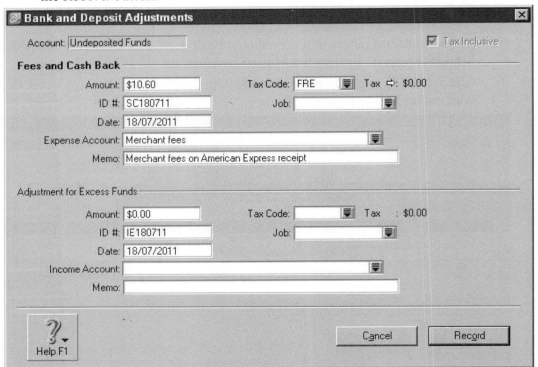

Figure 4.31: Merchant fees recorded as deduction from American Express receipt

14. The *Prepare Bank Deposit* window will now show a net deposit of $615.00 as shown in Figure 4.32 on the next page.

15. Click on the *Record* button to record the deposit.

16. Click the *Cancel* button to exit the *Prepare Bank Deposit* window.

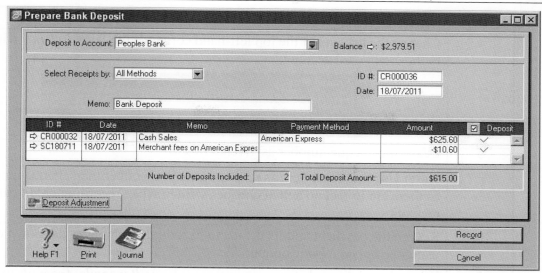

Figure 4.32: Bank deposit after deducting merchant fees from credit card receipt

Video: A video on depositing credit card payments received is on the DVD

Self-test exercise 4.11

Have the file dem42.myo open.

On 22 July 2011, record a deposit for each of the credit card receipts received on that day. For the American Express receipt, record a deduction of $5.60 for merchant fees.

Using a credit card for payments

Credit cards are now a popular method of paying for small items in addition to the use of petty cash. There are two main ways of accounting for costs incurred using a credit card: record each item as incurred using the credit card receipts, or record the costs direct from the credit card statement received. Where each receipt is recorded, the detailed cheque account set up for credit card transactions can be reconciled with the credit card statement in exactly the same way as shown earlier for a bank reconciliation.

The following instructions, example and exercises show how to enter credit card receipts using a detailed cheque account. You will then be required to reconcile this account with the credit card statement.

How to record credit card transactions from receipts

Step	Instruction
1	A credit card type account will be required under the *Liabilities in the Accounts List* (see Chapter 3 for editing the *Accounts List*).
2	Select the *Banking* command centre.
3	Select the *Spend Money* option.

(continued on the next page)

Step	Instruction
4	Change the account at the top left-hand corner of the *Spend Money* window to the credit card account. ![Spend Money window showing Pay from Account: Visa] **Spend Money** ⦿ Pay from Account: Visa ○ Group with Electronic Payments:
5	Leave the cheque number as given. **Note:** Use these numbers as reference numbers rather than cheque numbers as there are in fact no actual cheques written when recording credit card receipts.
6	Record the payment and its details in exactly the same way as shown earlier using the *Spend Money* option.
7	When the credit card statement is received, use *Reconcile Accounts* to reconcile the statement with the detailed credit card account.
8	Use *Spend Money* with the normal bank account to record the payment of the amount owing on the credit card statement, debiting the detailed credit card account.

Example 4.13—Recording a Visa credit card receipt

Using the file dem42.myo, a Visa card is used on 12 July 2011 to pay $62.75 to Mobil Castle Hill for motorcar parts.

1. Select the *Banking* command centre.
2. Select *Spend Money* option.
3. Change the "bank" account at the top left-hand corner of the *Spend Money* window to the account "Visa", account number 2-1140. This account is a 'Credit Card' liability account type.
4. This transaction is to be recorded at the GST-inclusive amount, so make sure that 'Tax Inclusive' checkbox at the top of the window is ticked.
5. Leave the cheque number as given (it should be "1") and enter the date as 12 July 2011 ↵.
6. Enter the amount as $62.75 ↵.
7. Use the card for "Mobil Castle Hill" (type in or use the *List* button).
8. TAB to the 'Memo' field and enter "Motor car parts purchased using Visa card" ↵.
9. Type in "Mo" to enter the account "Motor car expenses" (or if you are using account numbers enter "6-1050") and TAB to the 'Amount' column.
10. The amount of "$62.75" should be in the 'Amount' column. TAB to the allocation line 'Memo' column and enter "Spare car parts purchased" and ↵. The Tax code should be "GST". If your cheque looks like Figure 4.33 on the next page, click on the *Record* button.

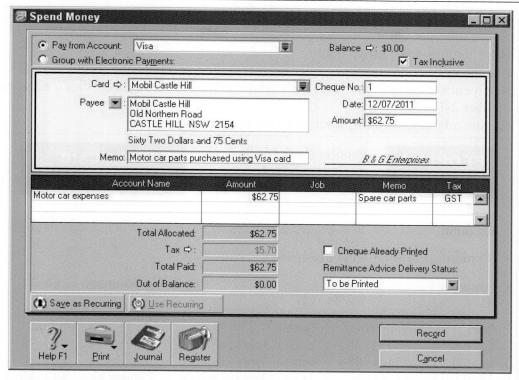

Figure 4.33: Recording a Visa card receipt (a receipt for a payment made)

Video: A video on making credit card payments is on the DVD

Self-test exercise 4.12

Have the file dem42.myo open.

Record the following two Visa card payments. The amounts shown for both payments include the GST and the tax code is "GST":

Date	Amount	Payee	Details	Account
18/7/11	$74.80	Sonic Taxi Trucks	Special delivery	Freight Paid 6-1700
28/7/11	$82.00	Interflora	Flowers sent to staff member in hospital	Staff Amenities (6-5110)

Reconciling the Visa card statement

Where the individual credit card receipts are recorded as above, you will need to reconcile the statement received with the details in the detail credit card account. This reconciliation is carried out in exactly the same way as reconciling a statement from the bank.

Self-test exercise 4.13

Have the file dem42.myo open.
Use the instructions learned earlier for reconciling accounts and reconcile the statement shown in Figure 4.34 with details in the account called "Visa", account number 2-1140.
(Ignore any date warning when entering the statement date)

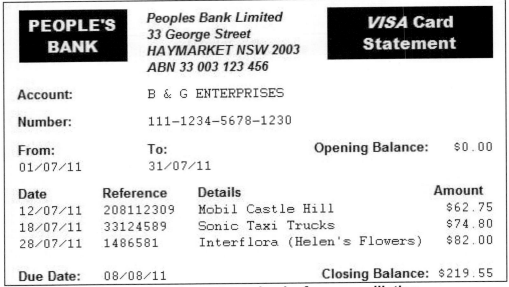

Figure 4.34: Visa card statement received – for reconciliation

Recording payments from the credit card statement

Where the individual credit card receipts are not recorded, the amount owing on the credit card statement will be paid using *Spend Money* using the normal detail cheque account. The details will be posted to the various expense accounts directly from this payment. In this case, a separate "Detail Card" account will not be required.

Bank reconciliation using downloaded statement file

In the bank reconciliation demonstrated earlier in this chapter, each transaction on the bank statement was checked manually against the bank entries in the general ledger account. A statement can be downloaded from a bank and *MYOB AccountRight* will automatically check off all of the items that agree. You then complete the reconciliation process manually for items that have not been agreed.

Most banks will provide a statement file that is compatible with *MYOB AccountRight*. For example, the Commonwealth Bank's NetBank allows you to export your statement in a number of formats as shown in the example in Figure 4.35 on the next page.

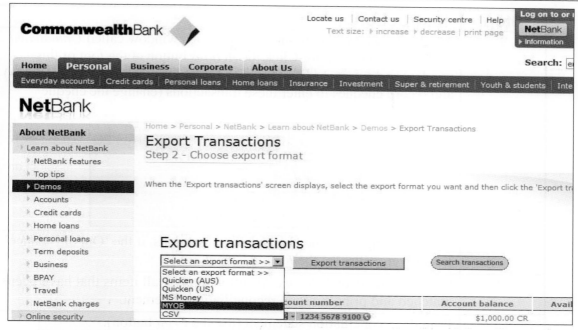

Figure 4.35: Download a bank statement from the Commonwealth Bank

How to reconcile the bank account with a downloaded bank statement

Step	Instruction
1	Select the *Banking* command centre.
2	Select the *Reconcile Accounts* option.
3	Type in or use the *List* button ▤ and select the general ledger account for the bank account.
4	TAB to the 'New Statement Balance:' field and type in the closing balance as per the bank statement and ↵.
5	Enter the 'Bank Statement Date:'.
6	Make sure no ticks ✓ appear in the left-hand column against any item (for example, because you had already started a reconciliation). Click on the ☑ button once or twice to clear all ticks. This button toggles between selecting all items and clearing all ticks (i.e. selecting none).
7	If you have downloaded a statement electronically from the bank, click on the *Actions* button, select *Get Statement* and find the downloaded file. Click the *Actions* button ⊙ Actions Undo Reconciliation Bank Entry Get Statement Click for reconciling with downloaded statement
8	You will receive a message stating the number of transactions that have been read successfully from the bank statement file. Click on *OK*.
	(continued on the next page)

4-49

Step	Instruction
9	*MYOB AccountRight* produces a report in a window called *Unmatched Statement Transactions*. Click the *Actions* button at the foot of this window and select *Add Transaction* button (or one of the other options) and record cheques to enter these transactions (change the cheque number to "B/S"). Click → ⊙ Actions Add Transaction Match Transaction ? Help F1 Spend Money Pay Bills Receive Money Select an action
10	After entering all of the unmatched transactions, if the 'Out of Balance' field is zero, click on the *Reconcile* button.
11	Click on the second *Reconcile* button to clear all items that have been matched and print the final reconciliation statement.
12	Print the reconciliation statement (use the *Print* button). Click Print

Example 4.14—Bank reconciliation using downloaded file

The statement from the People's Bank to be used in this example is shown on the next page. You will also have to use a file called "BS for dem42.qif" that is the "downloaded" bank statement file for this example. You should have obtained this file from this book's CD using the menu provided. The example accounting file is dem42.myo.

1. Open the file dem42.myo.

2. Select the *Banking* command centre.

3. Select *Reconcile Accounts* option.

4. Enter the general ledger account name for the People's Bank. Type "Pe" and/or use the *List* button 🔽 next to the 'Account:' field to select the account "People's Bank" from the account list.

5. TAB to the 'New Statement Balance:' field and enter the bank statement balance at 31 July 2011– this is the closing balance on the bank statement shown here as $4,289.55 and ↵.

6. The date on the bank statement is 31/07/11. Enter this date in the 'Bank Statement Date' field ↵ – Ignore any date warning. (The 'Out of Balance' figure should show – $1,802.95).

7. To make sure that no items are already matched (ticked), click on the button at the top of the tick column ☑ that toggles between all and no items being selected (this is essential if you have already tried to reconcile and have some items "ticked" as the electronic matching will not match these items a second time).

Bank statement for example 4.14

People's Bank		Statement for July 2011		31/07/2011	
B & G Enterprises 8 Jimmy Henriks Street, Mapleton					
Account # 321-468 22479689					
		Debit	**Credit**	**Balance**	
1/7/11	Brought forward			2,486.60	CR
	Deposit		4,589.40	7,076.00	CR
4/7/11	Prev Month Acct Fee	25.00			
	Prev Month Trans Fee	18.00			
	Cash 123457	2,356.80		4,676.20	CR
6/7/11	MasterCard		587.60	5,263.80	CR
8/7/11	Collisimo Wsale 123456	2,589.30			
	Deposit		6,857.95		
	Cash 123458	568.60		8,963.85	CR
11/7/11	Caltex Carlingford	133.36			
	ABWDL Cstle Twr 2347	250.00			
	Deposit		3,859.00		
	Cash 123460	2,564.00		9,875.49	CR
12/7/11	MasterCard		698.50		
	American Express (Fees $8.30)		481.30	11,055.29	CR
15/7/11	Garden Springs 123459	3,879.00			
	Deposit		5,875.00	13,051.29	CR
18/7/11	Cash 123462	2,564.00		10,487.29	CR
19/7/11	MasterCard		980.86	11,468.15	CR
22/7/11	Clear & Bright 123461	3,456.00		8,012.15	CR
25/7/11	American Express (Fees $10.60)		615.00		
	MasterCard		798.00		
	Huston and Huston 123463	2,895.00			
	Cash 123464	2,564.00		3,966.15	CR
29/7/11	American Express (Fees $5.60)		323.40	4,289.55	CR

8. Click on the *Actions* button and select *Get Statement*.

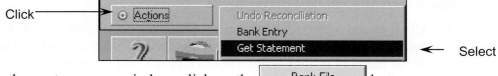

9. In the next message window, click on the Bank File button.

10. Select and open the "BS for dem42.qif" file from the disk (and/or directory) in which you have stored it.

11. You will receive a message as shown in Figure 4.36 on the next page that states the number of transactions that have been read successfully from the bank statement file. Click on the *OK* button.

12. When *MYOB AccountRight* has completed the matching process it will produce an "Unmatched Statement Transactions" report. The items on this report have usually been processed by the bank, but have not yet been recorded in your accounts. Figure 4.37 on the next page shows four unmatched transactions – bank charges ($25.00 and $18.00), a petrol station account that has been debited direct ($133.36) and a cash withdrawal from an automatic teller ($250.00):

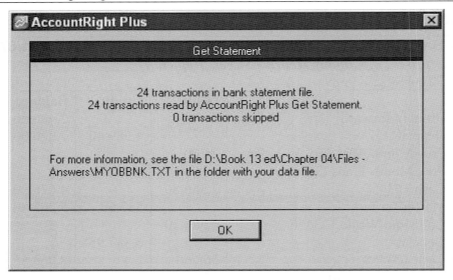

Figure 4.36: Message about number of transactions read

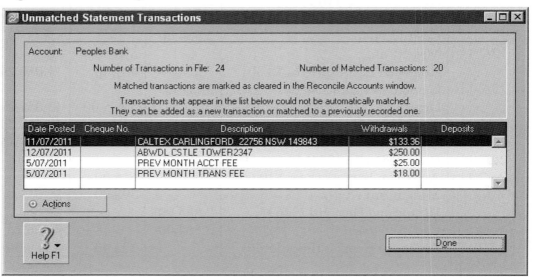

Figure 4.37: Unmatched transactions

13. Click on the *Actions* button, select *Add Transaction* and record "Cheques" to record these transactions (or select the *Spend Money* action). Do not enter these at the moment as they will be entered in self-test exercise 4.14.

14. Click on the [Done] button. Click *OK* when you receive the message about unmatched transactions. Your *Reconcile Accounts* window should show an 'Out of Balance' figure of $426.36 (the total of the four unmatched transactions).

Reconciled at last!

Self-test exercise 4.14

Have the file dem42.myo open. Use the *Actions* button and select *Add Transactions* in the *Reconcile Accounts* window and record each the four unmatched items from the above Example. Use "B/S" for the cheque number and nominate the account to debit as shown below. Check entries with the solutions at the end of the chapter.

The accounts to debit for the four items shown in Figure 4.37 above are:

11/7/11 Caltex Carlingford $133.36 (tax code "GST") – debit "Motor Car Expenses" account number 6-1050.

12/7/11 ABWDL Castle Towers $250.00 (tax code "N-T") – debit "Drawings" account 3-1200 (ignore the warning that you should use an expense account). This is an ATM withdrawal by the owner.

05/7/11 Bank charges $25.00 (tax code "FRE") – debit "Bank Fees" account 6-1022.

05/7/11 Bank charges $18.00 (tax code "FRE") – debit "Bank Fees" account 6-1022.

Complete the reconciliation of the People's Bank account with the bank statement at 31 July 2011.

How to list account transactions

Step	Instruction
1	Click on the arrow at the end of the *Find Transactions* option at the foot of a command centre window and select *Account*. Find Transactions ▼ ←——Click ←—— Select Account Card Invoice Bill Job Payroll Category
2	Type in the account name or number or select from a list.
3	Change the 'Dated From' and 'To' dates if necessary.
4	Use the *Print* button if a printout of the bank account is required.

Self-test exercise 4.15

Have the file dem42.myo open.

Use the instructions listed above. Display and print the "People's Bank" account (#1-1110) for the month of July 2011.

Business Activity Statement (BAS) and GST report

At the end of a tax period, a business is required to prepare a Business Activity Statement (BAS) and remit any taxes owing to the Australian Taxation Office (ATO). The tax period is quarterly unless annual turnover is greater than $20 million, in which case your tax period is monthly. You may elect to have a monthly tax period if your turnover is less than $20 million.

The BAS contains sections for all taxes collected or due. This includes the GST, Pay-As-You-Go Withholding from employees, income tax instalment, wine equalisation tax, luxury car tax, fringe benefits tax and other withholding taxes. **See Chapter 2 for instructions on completing a Business Activity Statement.**

Using the *MYOB AccountRight* tax codes allows the user to produce a report that will show the various income and expense tax categories for entry on to the BAS, especially the optional GST calculation sheet. Please refer to Chapter 2 for the 'How to print a GST Report for Cash or Accrual Basis' before attempting the next example to print a "Cash Basis" GST report.

Example 4.15—Print a summary cash GST report for July 2011

1. Open the file dem42.myo.
2. Click on the arrow at the end of the *Reports* option at the foot of a command centre window and select *GST/Sales Tax*.
3. Click on the report called "GST [Summary – Cash]".
4. Click on the *Customise* button.
5. If it is not already selected, select "All" for 'Tax Codes'.
6. Select "Both Collected and Paid" in the 'Collected/Paid:' field.
7. Enter the period dated from 1/7/11 to 31/7/11. The *Report Customisation* window should look like Figure 4.38:
8. Click on the *Display* button to produce the report on screen.
9. Click on the *Print* button. The report should be as shown in Figure 4.39:
10. Click the *Close* button to exit the display and click the *Close* button to return to a command centre.
11. Exit from the file dem42.myo and open the previous file **dem41.myo**.

B & G Enterprises
Demonstration File dem42.myo
GST [Summary – Cash]
1/07/2011 To 31/07/2011

Code	Description	Rate	Sale Value	Purchase Value	Tax Collected	Tax Paid
FRE	GST Free	0.00%		$169.80		
GST	Goods & Services Tax	10.00%	$25,690.51	$13,638.51	$2,335.51	$1,239.85
N-T	Not Reportable	0.00%		$10,298.80		
			Total:		**$2,335.51**	**$1,239.85**

Figure 4.39: GST [Summary – Cash] report for B & G Enterprises

Video: A video on printing reports is on the DVD

Self-test exercise 4.16

Open the file dem41.myo used earlier in this chapter.

Print a "GST [Summary – Cash]" report for the period 1 July 2011 to 31 July 2011. This should be for all codes and include both GST collected and paid.

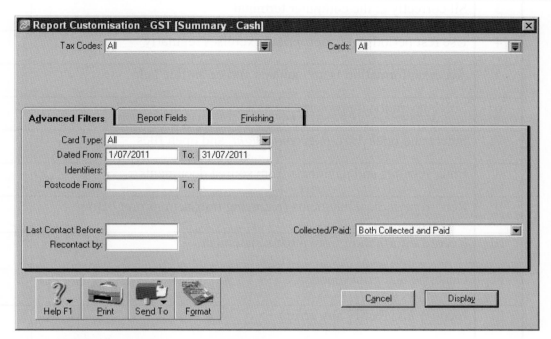

Figure 4.38: Report Customisation for GST report

Competency checklist

	I can now do the following:	✔
1	Switch the computer and screen on	
2	Adjust chair and equipment to suit ergonomic requirements	
3	Sit correctly at the computer terminal	
4	Use rest periods and appropriate exercises regularly	
5	Access information from manuals and/or on-line help	
6	Solve operational problems	
7	Select and open *MYOB AccountRight*, and open files	
8	Enter receipts and payments from source documents	
9	Record periodical payments (recurring transactions and PBAs)	
10	Record information from a bank statement	
11	Generate and print reports	
12	Identify and rectify any errors	
13	Carry out a bank reconciliation and print the bank reconciliation statement	
14	Apply techniques to minimise paper wastage such as using screen inquiries and recycling paper from printouts	

Chapter 4: Assessment exercises

Note: Throughout the following practical exercises you should continually observe relevant Occupational Health and Safety practices and apply recycling techniques to minimise paper wastage. In addition, you should use the on-line help facilities (the F1 key and/or Windows *Help* menu) and the notes to solve any problems you encounter.

4.1 The exercise month is July 2011. Start *MYOB AccountRight*.
Open an existing file called ass41.myo.
Use the **Setup** drop-down menu, **Company Information** item and enter your name in the business address field.

(a) Enter the following deposits for July 2011. The file is set up to debit "Undeposited Funds" account as the default. You need to group multiple receipts on a single day in to the "Undeposited Funds" accounts first and then deposit each day's receipts as a single deposit in to the "General Ledger" bank account.

You may ignore line memos in this exercise.

All amounts are GST-inclusive except for interest received which is GST free.

2011 July	Transaction	Payment Method	Amount $	Tax Code
3	Cash sales of electrical goods	Cash	2,117.06	GST
4	Cash sales of plumbing items	Cash	2,816.55	GST
6	Interest received from Gasworks Ltd. (BSB 555-555, account # 45612345)	Cheque #412098	1,200.00	FRE
	Consultancy fees received for plans from Treloar Pty Ltd (BSB 432-987, account # 32012564)	Cheque #109876	2,200.00	GST
9	Cash sales of electrical goods	Cash	1,635.15	GST
11	Consultancy fees from ULUG Shire Council (BSB 654-765, account # 0764876)	Cheque # 125328	4,235.00	GST
13	Cash sales of electrical goods	Cash	2,068.00	GST
	Cash sales of plumbing items to D. Hinds (BSB 145-879, account # 81097534)	Cheque #112365	2,374.46	GST
18	Commission received from Electric Bulb Co (BSB 467-432, account # 2387298)	Cheque #210987	2,750.00	GST
25	Cash sales of plumbing items	Cash	1,342.66	GST
30	Cash sales of electrical goods	Cash	3,909.62	GST
	Cash sales of plumbing items to D. Hinds (BSB 145-879, account # 81097534)	Cheque #112375	1,714.13	GST
31	Consultancy fees received for plans from Treloar Pty Ltd (BSB 432-987, account # 32012564)	Cheque #109888	2,200.00	GST

(b) Enter the following cheques for July 2011. All amounts are tax-inclusive, except those with a tax code of "N-T" or "FRE". Weekly wages has been set up as a recurring entry but you may need to edit the amounts as given below. Use the "Petty Cash" account (account number 1-1130) to record petty cash expenses on 16 July.

2011 July	CHQ No.	Transaction	Cheque Amount $	Tax Code
3	118561	Paid Opus for telephone account	933.52	GST
4	118562	Paid rent to U.J. Pty Ltd	3,300.00	GST
5	118563	Cash cheque for wages (Gross $2,795.00, PAYG $645.00)	2,150.00	N-T
9	118564	Purchased a computer from OME Pty Ltd	4,070.00	CAP
	118565	Sales commission to Peter Rabbit	1,320.00	GST
12	118566	MRNA P/L – General Insurance	2,734.60	GST
	118567	Cash cheque for wages (Gross $2,628.00, PAYG $580.00)	2,048.00	N-T
13	118568	Purchased fax machine from Tasco Comp	2,084.50	CAP

16	Petty Cash 1	Petty cash expenses:
		    Postage 42.35
		    Staff amenities expense 47.08
		    Travel 73.54
		    Printing & Stationery 97.46
			260.43	GST
				FRE
				GST
				GST

19	118569	Cash cheque for wages (Gross $2,890.00, PAYG $634.00)	2,256.00	N-T
	118570	Cash purchases of trade goods from Arco Ltd	3,584.52	GST
20	118571	Cash – petty cash re-imbursement (debit Petty cash Account 1-1130)	260.43	N-T
25	118572	Cash drawings by proprietor	1,000.00	N-T
26	118573	Cash cheque for wages (Gross $2,795.00, PAYG $645.00)	2,150.00	N-T
30	118574	Paid Integer Power for electricity	1,014.92	GST
31	118575	Paid Mobil for July petrol etc	1,263.52	GST

(c) Complete the bank reconciliation using the bank statement shown on the next page and/or the downloaded bank statement in file "BS for ass41.qif" that is provided on the CD. The bank statement includes two bank charges – use the *Actions* button and *Add Transactions* to record each of these. Use "B/S" as the ID#.

Ignore any date warning when entering the statement date.

(d) Print the following:
> Transaction journals for July 2011 (all transactions)
> Bank Reconciliation report at 31 July 2011
> GST [Detail – Cash] report for July 2011

Bank statement for assessment exercise 4.1

Bank of Hong Kong	Statement for July 2011			31/07/2011	
		Debit	**Credit**	**Balance**	
1/7/11	Brought forward			5,951.35	CR
3/7/11	Deposit		2,117.06	8,068.41	CR
4/7/11	Deposit		2,816.55	10,884.96	CR
5/7/11	118563	2,150.00		8,734.96	CR
6/7/11	118561	933.52			
	Deposit		3,400.00	11,201.44	CR
9/7/11	Deposit		1,635.15		
	June account fee	17.25			
	June service fees	15.70		12,803.64	CR
11/7/11	118562	3,300.00			
	Deposit		4,235.00	13,738.64	CR
12/7/11	118567	2,048.00		11,690.64	CR
13/7/11	118564	4,070.00			
	118565	1,320.00			
	Deposit		4,442.46	10,743.10	CR
18/7/11	Deposit		2,750.00	13,493.10	CR
19/7/11	118569	2,256.00		11,237.10	CR
20/7/11	118571	260.43		10,976.67	CR
25/7/11	118568	2,084.50			
	118570	3,584.52			
	118572	1,000.00			
	Deposit		1,342.66	5,650.31	CR
26/7/11	118573	2,150.00		3,500.31	CR
30/7/11	118566	2,734.60			
	Deposit		5,623.75	6,389.46	CR

4.2 The exercise month is July 2011.
Start *MYOB AccountRight.*
Open an existing file called ass42.myo.
Use the **Setup** drop-down menu, **Company Information** item and enter your name in the business address field.
Print the Accounts List [Summary].

(a) Code and enter the following deposits for July 2011. The file is set up to debit "Undeposited Funds" account as the default. Make sure that you deposit each day's receipts as a single deposit in the general ledger "Common Bank" account.

2011 July	Transaction	Payment method	GST-inclusive $	Deposit amount $
2	Cash sales of hardware – Tax code "GST"	Cash	2,085.16	2,085.16
6	Cash sales of software – Tax code "GST"	Cash	3,041.50	3,041.50

2011 July	Transaction	Payment method	GST-inclusive $	Deposit amount $
9	Commission received – Tax code "GST"	Cash	880.00	
	Training fees received from Acme Trading (BSB 204-812, Account # 18042631) – Tax code "GST"	Cheque #321046	2,750.00	3,630.00
12	Cash sales of software – Tax code "GST"	Cash	1,568.05	1,568.05
16	Consultancy fees from Limberges (BSB 108-231, Acct # 62041238)– Tax "GST"	Cheque #109873	5,808.00	5,808.00
18	Cash sales of hardware to J. H. Menon (BSB 321-612, Acct# 4263182)–Tax GST	Cheque #218765	644.60	
	Cash sales of software – Tax code "GST"	Cash	1,925.00	2,569.60
23	Training fees received from Acme Trading (BSB 204-812, Account # 18042631) – Tax code "GST"	Cheque #321098	2,750.00	2,750.00
26	Cash sales of software – Tax code "GST"	Cash	1,039.50	1,039.50
27	Cash sales of hardware –Tax code "GST"	Cash	4,730.00	
	Cash sales of hardware to J. H. Menon (BSB 321-612, Acct # 4263182–Tax GST	Cheque #218798	1,633.50	6,363.50
31	Training fees received from Acme Trading (BSB 204-812, Account # 18042631) – Tax code "GST"	Cheque #321106	2,750.00	2,750.00

(b) Enter the following cheques for July 2011. All amounts with a tax code of "GST" include the GST. Weekly wages has been set up as a recurring entry and the amount shown is the net amount. Use the Petty Cash account (account number 1-1130) to record petty cash expenses on 15 July.

2011 July	Cheque No.	Transaction		Cheque Amount $	Tax Code
2	248345	Paid Energy Oz for electricity		535.54	GST
4	248346	Paid rent to L.J. Hooker		3,080.00	GST
	248347	Cash cheque for wages		1,778.70	N-T
6	248348	Accountancy fees paid to Elgin Company		1,980.00	GST
9	248349	Sales commission to Jeremy Fisher		880.00	GST
11	248350	I.G.O. for Fidelity Insurance		550.00	GST
	248351	Cash cheque for wages		1,778.70	N-T
12	248352	Paid Koko Pty Ltd for advertising		5,038.00	GST
13	248353	Cash purchases of software for re-sale		3,184.50	GST
	248354	Cash drawings by proprietor		1,000.00	N-T
15	Petty Cash 1	Petty cash expenses:		210.82	
		Postage	47.08		GST
		Staff amenities expense	28.00		FRE
		Travel	93.94		GST
		Printing & Stationery	41.80		GST

2011 July	Cheque No.	Transaction	Cheque Amount $	Tax Code
18	248355	Cash cheque for wages	1,778.70	N-T
25	248356	Cash - petty cash re-imbursement (debit Petty Cash account 1-1130)	210.82	N-T
	248357	Cash cheque for wages	1,778.70	N-T
30	248358	Paid Telsatra telephone account	1,375.55	GST
31	248359	Paid Mobil Castle Hill for July petrol Debit: "Motor vehicle running costs"	1,263.52	GST

(c) Complete the bank reconciliation using the bank statement shown below and/or the downloaded bank statement in file "BS for ass42.qif" that is provided on the CD. The bank statement includes bank charges – use the *Actions* button and *Add Transactions* to enter each of these. Use "B/S" as the ID#. (Ignore any date warning)

(d) Print the following:
Transaction journals for July 2011 (all transactions)
Bank Reconciliation report at 31 July 2011
GST [Summary – Cash] report for July 2011

Bank statement for assessment exercise 4.2

Common Bank	Statement for July 2011			31/07/11	
		Debit	**Credit**	**Balance**	
1/7/11	Brought forward			8,135.65	CR
2/7/11	Deposit		2,085.16	10,220.81	CR
4/7/11	248347	1,778.70		8,442.11	CR
6/7/11	248345	535.54			
	Deposit		3,041.50	10,948.07	CR
9/7/11	Bank Charges	22.45			
	Deposit		3,630.00	14,555.62	CR
11/7/11	248346	3,080.00			
	248351	1,778.70		9,696.92	CR
12/7/11	Deposit		1,568.05	11,264.97	CR
14/7/11	248348	1,980.00			
	248349	880.00		8,404.97	CR
16/7/11	Deposit		5,808.00	14,212.97	CR
18/7/11	Deposit		2,569.60		
	248355	1,778.70		15,003.87	CR
23/7/11	Deposit		2,750.00	17,753.87	CR
25/7/11	248357	1,778.70			
	248356	210.82		15,764.35	CR
26/7/11	Deposit		1,039.50	16,803.85	CR
27/7/11	Deposit		6,363.50	23,167.35	CR
30/7/11	248352	5,038.00			
	248353	3,184.50		14,944.85	CR
31/7/11	248354	1,000.00		13,944.85	CR

4.3   Start *MYOB AccountRight* and open an existing file called ass43.myo.
Use the ***Setup*** drop-down menu, ***Company Information*** item and enter your name in
the business address field.
Print the Accounts List [Summary].
In this exercise, line memos for receipts and payments do not need to be entered.
The bank reconciliation report at 30 June 2011 shows:

Balance as per bank statement at 30 June 2011	$11,242.25	Credit
Less: Unpresented cheque number 248344	1,689.65	
Balance as per bank account 1-1-1110	$9,552.60	Debit

(a)   Enter the following GST-inclusive deposits for July 2011. The file is set up to
debit "Undeposited Funds" account as the default. Make sure that you deposit
each day's receipts as a single deposit in the "General Ledger" bank account.

2011 July	Transaction	Payment Method	Amount $	Tax Code
3	Cash sales of stationery	Cash	2,186.36	GST
4	Cash sales of books	Cash	3,166.90	GST
6	Commission received from Doogood Books (BSB 654-143, Account #3451987)	Cheque #198564	1,100.00	GST
	Contracting fees received from Ace Sales Pty Ltd (BSB 311-111, account #712897)	Cheque #216998	3,300.00	GST
11	Cash sales of stationery	Cash	1,703.85	GST
13	Project management fees received from Ace Sales Pty Ltd (BSB 311-111, account #712897)	Cheque #217003	5,610.00	GST
16	Cash sales of books	Cash	2,087.25	GST
	Cash sales of stationery to MNM Pty Ltd (BSB 221-098, Account #4478765)	Cheque #335876	3,946.36	GST
20	Contracting fees received from Ace Sales Pty Ltd (BSB 311-111, account #712897)	Cheque #217018	3,300.00	GST
25	Cash sales of stationery	Cash	1,195.70	GST
30	Cash sales of books	Cash	5,940.00	GST
	Cash sales of stationery to Helen Richards (MasterCard # 3456 1234 7895 1126, Expiry Date 12/13, Auth. Code 1087428)	Master Card	2,805.00	GST
31	Contracting fees received from Ace Sales Pty Ltd (BSB 311-111, account #712897)	Cheque #217027	3,300.00	GST

(b)   Enter the following cheques for July 2011. All amounts include the GST where
applicable (they are tax-inclusive). Weekly wages has been set up as a recurring
entry and the cheque amount shown is the net amount. Use the "Petty Cash"
account (account number 1-1130) to record petty cash expenses on 15 July.

2011 July	CHQ No.	Transaction	Cheque Amount $	GST Code
3	248345	Paid Pacific Power for electricity	684.86	GST
4	248346	Paid rent to G.R. Beverage	3,300.00	GST
6	248347	Cash cheque for wages (Gross wages $2,780.00, PAYG Withholding $794.35)	1,985.65	N-T
	248348	Accountancy fees paid to J. Smith	4,310.00	GST
	248349	Sales commissions to Spock, Ramon	1,320.00	GST
10	248350	I.G.M. for Insurance on stock	2,035.00	GST
13	248351	Cash cheque for wages (Gross wages $2,780.00, PAYG Withholding $794.35)	1,985.65	N-T
	248352	Paid Moyo for advertising	6,663.80	GST

16	Petty Cash 1	Petty cash expenses:
		    Postage 35.75
		    Staff amenities expense 40.59
		    Travel 108.13
		    Printing & Stationery 73.37
			257.84	GST
				FRE
				GST
				GST

20	248353	Cash cheque for wages (Gross wages $2,780.00, PAYG Withholding $794.35)	1,985.65	N-T
	248354	Cash – petty cash re-imbursement (debit "Petty Cash" account 1-1130)	257.84	N-T
25	248355	Purchase of books from Obay	6,028.66	GST
	248356	Cash drawings by proprietor	4,000.00	N-T
27	248357	Cash cheque for wages (Gross wages $2,780.00, PAYG Withholding $794.35)	1,985.65	N-T
30	248358	Paid Telsatra telephone account	1,078.55	GST
	248359	Paid Shell Castle Hill for July petrol	821.37	GST

(c) Complete the bank reconciliation using the bank statement shown on the next page and/or the downloaded bank statement in file "BS for ass43.qif" that is provided on the CD. The bank statement includes bank charges and a direct payment by authority – use the *Actions* button and *Add Transactions* to enter each of these. Use "B/S" as the ID#. (Ignore any date warning.)

(d)   Print the following:
          Transaction journals for July 2011 (all transactions)
          Bank Reconciliation report at 31 July 2011
          GST [Detail – Cash] report for July 2011

Bank statement for assessment exercise 4.3

Friendly Bank of Australia		Statement for July 2011		31/07/2011	
		Debit	**Credit**	**Balance**	
1/7/11	Brought forward			11,242.25	CR
3/7/11	Deposit		2,186.36	13,428.61	CR
4/7/11	Deposit		3,166.90	16,595.51	CR
6/7/11	248347	1,985.65			
	248345	684.86			
	Deposit		4,400.00	18,325.00	CR
10/7/11	Prev Mth Acc Fee	35.65		18,289.35	CR
11/7/11	248346	3,300.00			
	Deposit		1,703.85	16,693.20	CR
13/7/11	Deposit		5,610.00	22,303.20	CR
	248351	1,985.65			
	248348	4,310.00			
	248349	1,320.00			
16/7/11	Deposit		6,033.61	20,721.16	CR
20/7/11	248353	1,985.65			
	Deposit		3,300.00	22,035.51	CR
	248354	257.84		21,777.67	CR
24/7/11	248352	6,663.80		15,113.87	CR
25/7/11	Deposit		1,195.70	16,309.57	CR
26/7/11	248356	4,000.00		12,309.57	CR
27/7/11	248344	1,689.65			
	248357	1,985.65			
	248355	6,028.66		2,605.61	CR
30/7/11	Deposit		5,940.00	8,545.61	CR
31/7/11	MasterCard		2,805.00		
	Telcomet PA	1,450.00			
	MasterCard fees	18.20		9,882.41	CR

Notes:

- The entry on the bank statement on 31 July for Telcomet is a monthly payment by authority (PA) from the bank account to pay for an operating lease of telephone equipment. Debit the account "Telephones" 6-2100 with this GST-inclusive payment.

- MasterCard fees include the GST.

4.4 The month for this exercise is July 2011.
Start *MYOB AccountRight* and open an existing file called ass44.myo.
Use the **Setup** drop-down menu, **Company Information** item and enter your name in the business address field.
Line memos are not required in this exercise.

A bank reconciliation for the manual system at 30 June 2011 shows:

Balance as per bank statement	$13,183.10	Cr
Add: Outstanding deposit 30 June	2,376.00	
	15,559.10	
Less: Unpresented cheques:		
Cheque Number 118560	1,000.00	
Balance as per bank account in ledger (1-1110)	$14,559.10	Dr

(a) Enter the following deposits for July 2011. Amounts are GST-inclusive where the GST applies. The file is set up to debit "Undeposited Funds" account as the default. Make sure that you deposit each day's receipts in the "General Ledger" bank account.

2011 July	Transaction	Payment Method	Amount $	GST Code
3	Cash sales of hardware	Cash	2,704.35	GST
4	Cash sales of software to J May (AMEX Card # 5412 3321 4412 2224, Expiry Date 12/13, Authorisation Code 546321. Merchant fees $21.40)	American Express	3,900.16	GST
6	Interest received from ABC Ltd (BSB 218-345, Account # 312765)	Cheque #209561	848.75	FRE
	Consultancy fees received from Fate Pty Ltd (BSB 670-765, Account #87197650)	Cheque #404167	2,332.00	GST
11	Cash sales of hardware to Tryiton Pty Ltd (MasterCard # 4568 1234 7895 1112, Expiry Date 12/10, Auth. Code 7412480)	Master-Card	2,087.69	GST
12	Consultancy fees received from Fate Pty Ltd (BSB 670-765, Account #87197650)	Cheque #404180	4,235.00	GST
15	Cash sales of hardware to J May (AMEX Card # 5412 3321 4412 2224, Expiry Date 12/13, Authorisation Code 546321. Merchant fees $18.30)	American Express	2,068.00	GST
	Cash sales of software to J Peters (BSB 441-221, Account #31967854)	Cheque #512780	2,563.00	GST
19	Commission received from Comsar Pty Ltd (BSB 341-569, Account #22367331)	Cheque #217443	2,062.50	GST
22	Cash sales of software to J Peters (BSB 441-221, Account #31967854)	Cheque #512795	1,342.66	GST
27	Cash sales of hardware	Cash	3,909.62	GST
	Consultancy fees received from Fate Pty Ltd (BSB 670-765, Account #87197650)	Cheque #404203	1,714.13	GST
31	Monthly rent for attached flat received from G Cheung (Visa Card #2345 3487 1250 8888, Expiry date 06/14, Authorisation # 082)	Visa Card	1,200.00	ITS

(b) Enter the following cheques for July 2011:
Note: The computer purchased on 7 July and the fax machine purchased on 14 July were for office use and not for re-sale. Cheque amounts are GST-inclusive where the GST applies. Weekly wages has been set up as a recurring entry but you may need to edit the amounts to those given below. Use the "Petty Cash" account (account number 1-1130) to record petty cash expenses on 18 July and 26 July.

2011 July	CHQ No.	Transaction	Cheque Amount $	GST Code
3	108561	Paid Telsatra for telephone account	535.48	GST
6	108562	Paid monthly rent to G Beveridge	3,080.00	GST
	108563	Cash cheque for wages (Gross pay $2,902.00 and PAYG $752.00)	2,150.00	N-T
9	108564	Purchased a computer from Comsar P/L	4,070.00	CAP
	108565	Sales commission to Mr Brown	1,320.00	GST
11	108566	MAMI Insurance – Insurance	3,826.46	GST
13	108567	Cash cheque for wages (Gross pay $2,765.00 and PAYG $717.00)	2,048.00	N-T
	108568	Purchased fax machine from Tasco Comp	2,084.50	CAP
18	Petty Cash 1	Petty cash expenses: Postage 20.46; Staff amenities expense 69.85; Travel 92.40; Printing & Stationery 83.16	265.87	GST FRE GST GST
20	108569	Cash cheque for wages (Gross pay $3,045.00 and PAYG $789.00)	2,256.00	N-T
23	108570	Cash purchases of hardware from Elecro Macs	3,584.46	GST
25	108571	Cash drawings by proprietor	3,000.00	N-T
26	Petty Cash 2	Petty cash expenses: Postage 34.32; Travel 105.60; Printing & Stationery 70.40	210.32	GST GST GST
26	108572	Cash – petty cash re-imbursement (debit Petty Cash account 1-1130)	476.19	N-T
27	108573	Cash cheque for wages (Gross pay $2,902.00 and PAYG $752.00)	2,150.00	N-T
30	108574	Paid Integer Power for electricity	792.88	GST
31	108575	Paid Shell OK for July petrol etc.	1,040.38	GST

(c) Complete the bank reconciliation using the bank statement on the next page and/or the downloaded bank statement in file "BS for ass44.qif" that is provided on the CD. The bank statement includes some additional items – a dishonoured cheque that had been used to pay for cash sales of hardware, a dishonour fee (debit this to "Bank Charges"), interest received (GST free) and bank charges. **Note:** Merchant fees include the GST. The dishonoured cheque is debited to the

"Commission Received" account and the dishonour fee is debited to "Bank Charges".

Use the *Actions* button and *Add Transactions* to enter each of these. Use "B/S" as the ID#. (Ignore any date warning.)

Bank statement for assessment exercise 4.4

ZNA Bank	Statement for July 2011				31/07/11
		Debit	**Credit**	**Balance**	
1/7/11	Brought forward			13,183.10	CR
3/7/11	Deposit		2,376.00	15,559.10	CR
4/7/11	Deposit		2,704.35	18,263.45	CR
6/7/11	108563	2,150.00			
	108560	1,000.00			
	Deposit		3,180.75	18,294.20	CR
7/7/11	108561	535.48		17,758.72	CR
8/7/11	Prev Mth Account Fee	16.85			
	Prev Mth Service Fees	35.40			
	108562	3,080.00		14,626.47	CR
11/7/11	108564	4,070.00			
	108565	1,320.00			
	AMEX (Less fees $21.40)		3,878.76	13,115.23	CR
12/7/11	MasterCard		2,087.69		
	Deposit		4,235.00	19,437.92	CR
13/7/11	108567	2,048.00		17,389.92	CR
15/7/11	Deposit		2,563.00	19,952.92	CR
19/7/11	Deposit		2,062.50	22,015.42	CR
20/7/11	108569	2,256.00			
	AMEX (Less fees $18.30)		2,049.70	21,809.12	CR
21/7/11	Chq Dishonoured: RTD Comsar Pty Ltd	2,062.50			
	Dishonour fee	15.00		19,731.62	CR
22/7/11	CBF Securities – Interest on 9% Mortgage		1,312.50		
	Deposit		1,342.66	22,386.78	CR
25/7/11	108568	2,084.50			
	108571	3,000.00		17,302.28	CR
26/7/11	108572	476.19		16,826.09	CR
27/7/11	108573	2,150.00			
	Deposit		5,623.75	20,299.84	CR
30/7/11	108570	3,584.46			
	Merchant Fees (MasterCard)	17.60		16,697.78	CR

(d) Print the following:

Transaction journals for July 2011 (all transactions)
Bank Reconciliation report at 31 July 2011
GST [Detail – Cash] report for July 2011

4.5 Abbott Costello runs a small health food business. Sales and purchases are recorded on a cash basis. The business uses *MYOB AccountRight* and accounts for GST on a cash basis.

A bank reconciliation report at 30 June 2011 shows:

Balance as per bank statement at 30 June 2011	$2,600.85 Cr
Add: Outstanding deposit	2,485.00
	5,085.85
Less: Unpresented cheque number 130333	1,500.00
Balance as per bank account 1-1100	$3,585.85

Open the file "ass45.myo" and enter your name in the company address field. Print the *Accounts List [Summary]*.

Record the following cash receipts and payments for July 2011. You may ignore line memos in this exercise. Reconcile the bank account with the printed bank statement provided and/or the downloaded bank statement file "BS for ass45.qif" that has been provided on the CD. (Ignore any date warning when entering the statement date.)

Note: All cash sales and cash purchases of trade goods for this business in July 2011 are GST-free (food that is GST-free) and the tax code for these is "FRE". The exercise shows when GST is included in items.

Cash receipts:

The file is set up to debit "Undeposited Funds" account as the default. Make sure that you deposit each day's receipts as a single deposit in the "General Ledger" bank account.

July
4   Cash sales $480.00.
    Received cheque number 318773 for $1,344.50 being cash sales to Calorie Control Pty Ltd. Cheque details are: BSB 338-222, Account #6013452.
5   Sold stock for cash $590.00.
    Sold to Sam Harris old furniture at book value $638 (including $58 GST – tax code GST). Sam Harris paid using an American Express card (Card Number 1234 5678 9123 4567, Expiry date 11/13, Authorisation #2219870). Merchant fees on this receipt $7.40 including GST.
8   Cash sales $1,895.00.
    Received cheque number 218775 for $982.60 being cash sales to Double Life. Cheque details are: BSB 476-227, Account #49810921.
11 Additional capital introduced by Costello $4,000.00 cash (no GST involved).
15 Cash sales $2,880.50.
18 Received cheque number 318797 for $603.50 from Calorie Control Pty Ltd for cash sales. Cheque details are: BSB 338-222, Account #6013452.
20 Cash sales $1,999.50.
21 Payment received for cash sales to Waugh and Waugh $500.00 Cheque #412333 details are: BSB 411-666, drawn by Peace Collection Agency, account #21988724.
22 Cash sales $890.00.

Cheque number 412887 for cash sales to Crean and Evans of $2,650.00. Cheque details are: BSB 712-222, Account #911765.

25 Cash sales $4,100.60.

30 Payment received from Calorie Control Pty Ltd $1,780.90 for cash sales. Cheque #318805 details are: BSB 338-222, Account #6013452.

31 Payment received for cash sales to Waugh and Waugh $500.00. Cheque #412348 details are: BSB 411-666, drawn by Peace Collection Agency, account #21988724.

Cash payments: (First cheque number should be 130334)

Weekly wages has been set up as a recurring entry but you may need to edit the amounts to those given below. Line memos are not required.

Date	Chq. No.	Amount $	Details
July			
3	334	389.00	D Tortillo – Cash purchases of trade goods
5	335	1,120.90	Wages (Gross pay $1,460.50 and PAYG $339.60)
	336	1,789.60	Paid Associated Foods Ltd for cash purchases of trade goods
	337	957.00	James Dobell for advertising leaflets – includes GST of $87.00
8	338	509.08	Inertia Electricity – electricity for the quarter – amount includes GST of $46.28
11	339	590.60	D Tortillo – Cash purchases of trade goods
	340	2,844.50	Paid Livelong Herbal Co for cash purchases of trade goods
12	341	1,120.90	Wages (Gross pay $1,460.50 and PAYG $339.60)
	342	6,490.00	Techno Advance – purchase of a computer system – amount includes GST of $590.00 and tax code is CAP
13	343	2,156.00	Richard Dreyfus – annual Insurance premiums – GST included in the amount is $196.00
14	344	505.78	Mears Stationery – purchase of office stationery – amount includes GST of $45.98
18	345	2,908.50	Paid Associated Foods Ltd for cash purchases of trade goods
19	346	1,210.40	Wages (Gross pay $1,573.50 and PAYG $363.10)
21	347	772.30	D Tortillo – Cash purchases of trade goods
22	348	1,842.00	Paid Livelong Herbal Co for cash purchases of trade goods
26	349	1,210.40	Wages (Gross pay $1,573.50 and PAYG $363.10)
27	350	204.22	Mears Stationery – purchase of office stationery – amount includes GST of $18.57
30	351	1,417.90	Harbottle Jaques – purchase of fax machine – amount includes GST of $128.90 and the tax code is CAP
31	352	5,000.00	Loan repayment to C Twitty (no GST involved)
	353	926.20	Paid Shellmob Service Station including $84.20 GST for motor vehicle repairs and petrol. 10% of this account is for the private use by the owner (tax code is "NON")

Bank statement for the month of July 2011:

July		Debit	Credit	Balance	
	Federated Bank To: Abbott Costello		Statement for month of July 2011		
1	Balance brought forward			2,600.85	Cr
3	Deposit		2,485.00	5,085.85	Cr
4	Cheque 333	1,500.00			
	Deposit		1,824.50	5,410.35	Cr
5	Cheque 335	1,120.90			
	Deposit		590.00	4,879.45	Cr
7	Bank account keeping fee	28.90			
	Bank services fee	18.40		4,832.15	Cr
8	Cheque 334	389.00			
	Cheque 336	1,789.60			
	Deposit		2,877.60	5,531.15	Cr
11	Cheque 338	509.08			
	Deposit		4,000.00		
	AMEX (less merchant fees $7.40)		630.60	9,652.67	Cr
12	Cheque 337	957.00			
	Cheque 341	1,120.90		7,574.77	Cr
15	Deposit		2,880.50	10,455.27	Cr
18	Cheque 340	2,844.50			
	Cheque 342	6,490.00			
	Cheque 343	2,156.00			
	Cheque 339	590.60			
	Deposit		603.50	−1,022.33	Dr
19	Cheque 344	505.78			
	Cheque 346	1,210.40		−2,738.51	Dr
20	Deposit		1,999.50	−739.01	Dr
21	Deposit		500.00	−239.01	Dr
22	Cheque 345	2,908.50			
	Deposit		3,540.00	392.49	Cr
25	ABC Finance – Interest		250.00		
	Deposit		4,100.60	4,743.09	Cr
26	Cheque 349	1,210.40			
	Overdrawn account charge	100.00		3,432.69	Cr
30	Dishonoured Cheque #412333 – Peace Collection Agency	500.00			
	Dishonoured cheque fee	18.00			
	Deposit		1,780.90	4,695.59	Cr
31	Cheque 348	1,842.00			
	Interest on overdrawn amount	4.10		2,849.49	Cr

Note: The dishonoured cheque is debited to the "Sales" account and the dishonour fee is debited to "Bank Charges". Use the *Actions* button and *Add Transactions* to enter each of these and the other bank statement items. Use "B/S" as the ID#.

Print the following:

(a) Cash receipts journal transaction listing
(b) Cash disbursements (payments) listing
(c) Final bank account reconciliation statement
(d) GST [Detail – Cash] report for July 2011
(e) Trial Balance as at 31 July 2011

Chapter 4: Answers to self-test exercises

4.1 Check Chapter 1 or the videos if you cannot open a file and edit company information.

4.2

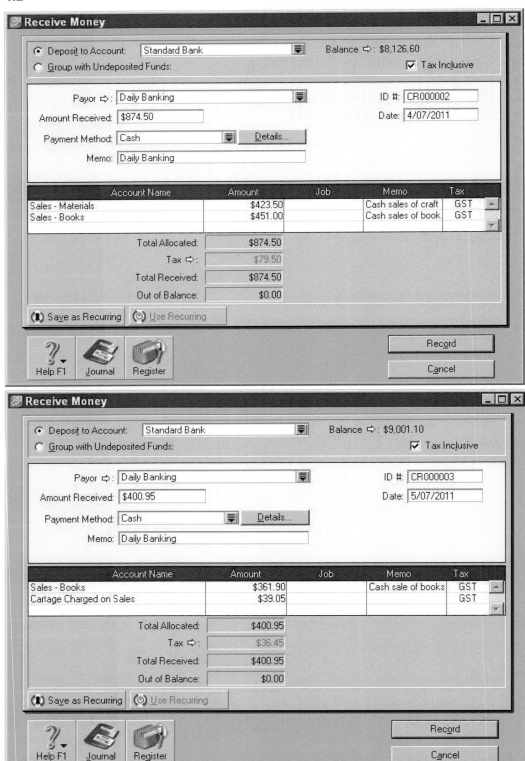

4.3

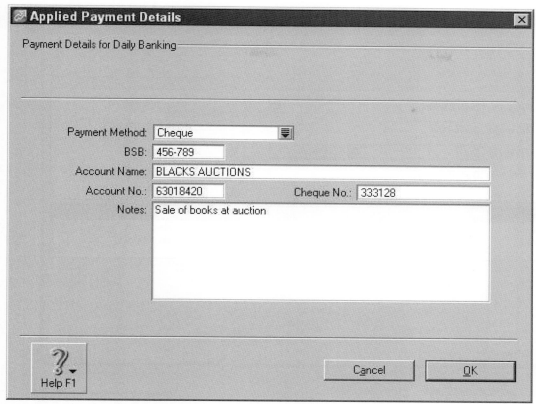

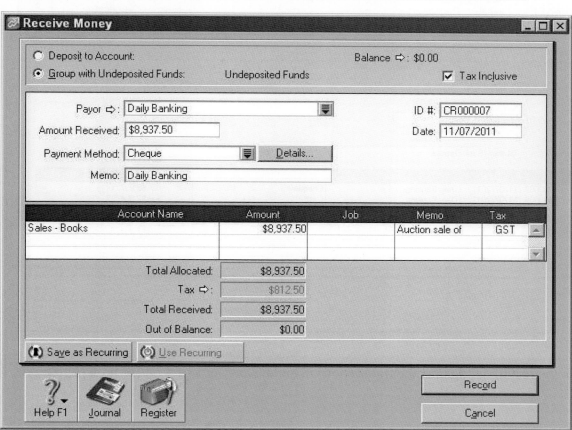

4.3 *(continued)*

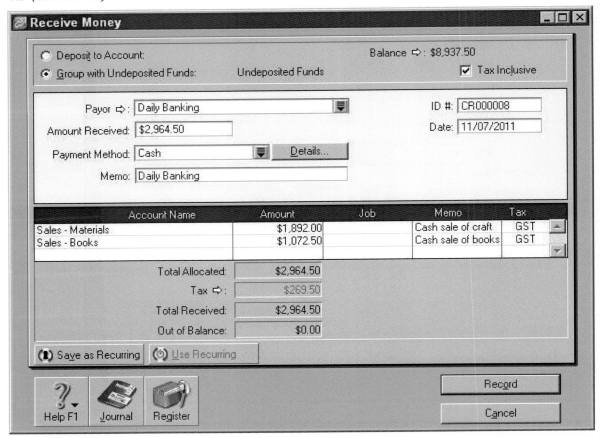

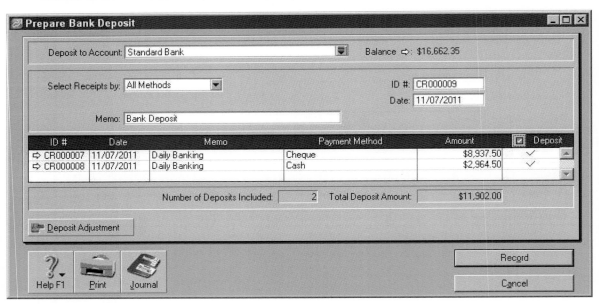

Check the rest of 4.3 against the transactions using the answer to 4.4 on the next page.

4.4

Jeremy Fisher Crafts
Cash Receipts Journal

1/07/2011 To 31/07/2011

Page 1

	ID#	Acct# Account Name	Debit	Credit	Allocation Memo
CR	**3/07/2011**	**Daily Banking**			
	CR000001	1-1110 Standard Bank	$3,212.00		
	CR000001	4-1200 Sales – Books		$2,920.00	Cash sales of books for the day
	CR000001	2-1210 GST Collected		$292.00	
CR	**4/07/2011**	**Daily Banking**			
	CR000002	1-1110 Standard Bank	$874.50		
	CR000002	4-1100 Sales – Materials		$385.00	Craft materials sold
	CR000002	4-1200 Sales – Books		$410.00	Craft books sold
	CR000002	2-1210 GST Collected		$79.50	
CR	**5/07/2011**	**Daily Banking**			
	CR000003	1-1110 Standard Bank	$400.95		
	CR000003	4-1200 Sales – Books		$329.00	Craft books sold
	CR000003	4-7000 Cartage Charged on Sales		$35.50	Cartage charged
	CR000003	2-1210 GST Collected		$36.45	
CR	**9/07/2011**	**Daily Banking**			
	CR000004	1-1180 Undeposited Funds	$2,260.30		
	CR000004	4-1200 Sales – Books		$2,054.82	Craft books sold
	CR000004	2-1210 GST Collected		$205.48	
CR	**9/07/2011**	**Additional capital from owner**			
	CR000005	1-1180 Undeposited Funds	$5,000.00		
	CR000005	3-1100 Capital		$5,000.00	Additional capital
CR	**9/07/2011**	**Bank Deposit**			
	CR000006	1-1110 Standard Bank	$7,260.30		
	CR000006	1-1180 Undeposited Funds		$5,000.00	
	CR000006	1-1180 Undeposited Funds		$2,260.30	
CR	**11/07/2011**	**Sale of books at auction**			
	CR000007	1-1120 Undeposited Funds	$8,937.50		
	CR000007	4-1200 Sales – Books		$8,125.00	Books sold at auction
	CR000007	2-1210 GST Collected		$812.50	
CR	**11/07/2011**	**Cash sales**			
	CR000008	1-1180 Undeposited Funds	$2,964.50		
	CR000008	4-1100 Sales – Materials		$1,720.00	Craft materials cash sales
	CR000008	4-1200 Sales – Books		$975.00	Craft books cash sales
	CR000008	2-1210 GST Collected		$269.50	
CR	**11/07/2011**	**Bank Deposit**			
	CR000009	1-1110 Standard Bank	$11,902.00		
	CR000009	1-1180 Undeposited Funds		$2,964.50	
	CR000009	1-1180 Undeposited Funds		$8,937.50	
CR	**18/07/2011**	**Cash sale of materials**			
	CR000010	1-1180 Undeposited Funds	$2,654.85		
	CR000010	4-1100 Sales – Materials		$2,413.50	Craft material sold
	CR000010	2-1210 GST Collected		$241.35	
CR	**18/07/2011**	**Cash sale of books**			
	CR000011	1-1180 Undeposited Funds	$2,340.50		
	CR000011	4-1200 Sales – Books		$2,127.73	Craft books sold for cash
	CR000011	2-1210 GST Collected		$212.77	
CR	**18/07/2011**	**Bank Deposit**			
	CR000012	1-1110 Standard Bank	$4,995.35		
	CR000012	1-1180 Undeposited Funds		$2,340.50	
	CR000012	1-1180 Undeposited Funds		$2,654.85	

4.4 *(continued)*

Jeremy Fisher Crafts
Cash Receipts Journal

1/07/2011 To 31/07/2011

Page 2

	ID#	Acct# Account Name	Debit	Credit	Allocation Memo
CR	**22/07/2011 Sale of obsolete stationery**				
	CR000013 1-1180 Undeposited Funds		$198.00		
	CR000013 6-0450 Stationery			$180.00	Obsolete stationery sold to staff
	CR000013 2-1210 GST Collected			$18.00	
CR	**22/07/2011 Cash sales**				
	CR000014 1-1180 Undeposited Funds		$3,201.80		
	CR000014 4-1100 Sales – Materials			$1,450.50	Craft materials cash sales
	CR000014 4-1200 Sales – Books			$1,460.23	Craft books cash sales
	CR000014 2-1210 GST Collected			$291.07	
CR	**22/07/2011 Bank Deposit**				
	CR000015 1-1110 Standard Bank		$3,399.80		
	CR000015 1-1180 Undeposited Funds			$3,201.80	
	CR000015 1-1180 Undeposited Funds			$198.00	
CR	**31/07/2011 Sale of materials to Edgar Poe**				
	CR000016 1-1180 Undeposited Funds		$1,744.60		
	CR000016 4-1100 Sales – Materials			$1,586.00	Craft material sold
	CR000016 2-1210 GST Collected			$158.60	
CR	**31/07/2011 Cash sale of books**				
	CR000017 1-1180 Undeposited Funds		$1,078.00		
	CR000017 4-1200 Sales – Books			$980.00	Craft books cash sales
	CR000017 2-1210 GST Collected			$98.00	
CR	**31/07/2011 Bank Deposit**				
	CR000018 1-1110 Standard Bank		$2,822.60		
	CR000018 1-1180 Undeposited Funds			$1,078.00	
	CR000018 1-1180 Undeposited Funds			$1,744.60	
		Grand Total:	$65,247.55	$65,247.55	

4.5

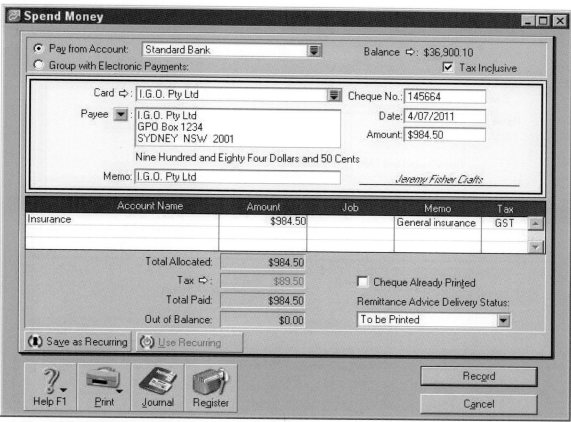

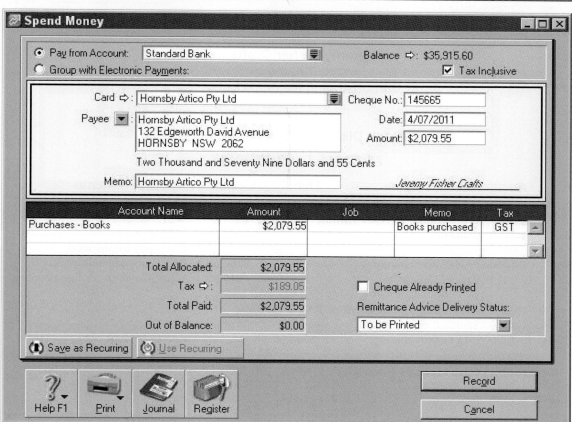

4.6

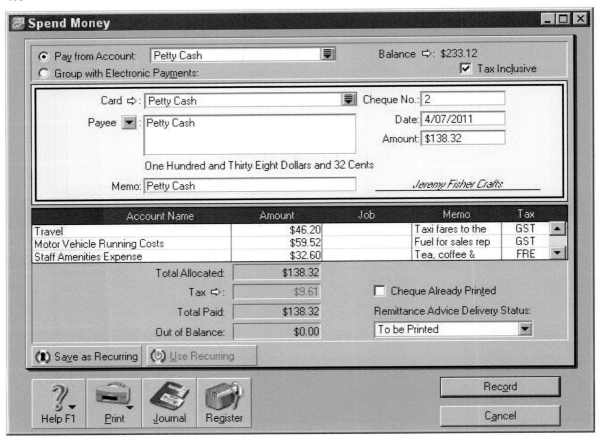

4.7

Jeremy Fisher Crafts
<< your name >>
Demonstration file dem41.myo

Cash Disbursements Journal

7/07/2011 To 13/07/2011

ID#	Acct#	Account Name	Debit	Credit	Allocation Memo
CD	**7/07/2011**	**Weekly salary - Sally Hubble**			
145667	1-1110	Standard Bank		$544.50	
145667	6-0130	Wages & Salaries	$835.00		Gross pay for the week
145667	2-1420	PAYG Withholding		$250.50	PAYG tax withheld
145667	2-1410	Payroll Deductions		$40.00	Medical and union dues deducted
CD	**7/07/2011**	**Australian Taxation Office PAYG for June**			
145668	1-1110	Standard Bank		$524.00	
145668	2-1420	PAYG Withholding	$524.00		PAYG for June
CD	**8/07/2011**	**Cash taken by proprietor**			
145669	1-1110	Standard Bank		$400.00	
145669	3-1300	Drawings	$400.00		Cash for owner

(continued on the next page)

4.7 *(continued)*

CD	**8/07/2011**	**Petty Cash**			
3	1-1150	Petty Cash		$136.95	
3	6-0220	Maintenance & Repairs	$124.50		Repairs to door
3	2-1230	GST Paid	$12.45		
CD	**1/07/2011**	**Mobil Castle Hill**			
145670	1-1110	Standard Bank		$251.35	
145670	6-0250	Motor Vehicle Running	$228.50		Petrol & oil for June
145670	2-1230	GST Paid	$22.85		
CD	**12/07/2011**	**PMA Society**			
145671	1-1110	Standard Bank		$250.00	
145671	2-1410	Payroll Deductions	$250.00		Superannuation for June
CD	**12/07/2011**	**St George Savings**			
145672	1-1110	Standard Bank		$100.00	
145672	2-1410	Payroll Deductions	$100.00		Voluntary savings
CD	**13/07/2011**	**Petty Cash**			
4	1-1150	Petty Cash		$61.16	
4	6-0400	Shop Expenses	$28.60		Cleaning materials
4	6-0510	Travel	$27.00		Taxi fares
4	2-1230	GST Paid	$5.56		
		Grand Total:	$2,558.46	$2,558.46	

4.8

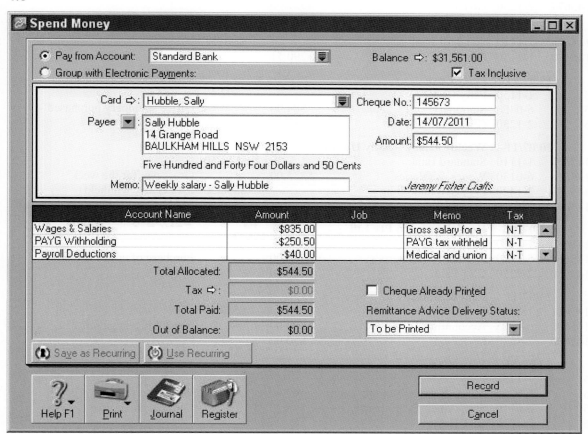

4.9

Jeremy Fisher Crafts
Cash Disbursements Journal

14/07/2011 To 31/07/2011

ID#	Acct#	Account Name	Debit	Credit	Allocation Memo
CD	**14/07/11**	**Weekly salary – Sally Hubble**			
145673	1-1110	Standard Bank		$544.50	
145673	6-0130	Wages & salaries	$835.00		Gross pay for the week
145673	2-1420	PAYG Withholding		$250.50	PAYG Tax withheld
145673	2-1410	Payroll Deductions		$40.00	Medical and Union fees deducted
CD	**16/07/11**	**Salvation Army**			
145674	1-1110	Standard Bank		$100.00	
145674	6-0060	Donations	$100.00		Donation to special appeal
CD	**16/07/11**	**Skillett & Sons**			
145675	1-1110	Standard Bank		$465.30	
145675	6-0220	Maintenance & Repairs	$423.00		Office partitions repaired
145675	2-1230	GST Paid	$42.30		
CD	**16/07/11**	**E.G. O'Brien Pty Ltd**			
145676	1-1110	Standard Bank		$1,650.00	
145676	6-0010	Advertising	$1,500.00		Yellow Pages advertisement
145676	2-1230	GST Paid	$150.00		
CD	**18/07/11**	**Wholesale Craft Pty Ltd**			
145677	1-1110	Standard Bank		$3,619.00	
145677	5-2120	Purchases – Books	$3,290.00		Books purchased
145677	2-1230	GST Paid	$329.00		
CD	**19/07/11**	**Petty cash re-imbursement**			
145678	1-1110	Standard Bank		$290.51	
145678	1-1150	Petty Cash	$290.51		
CD	**19/07/11**	**Petty Cash**			
5	1-1150	Petty Cash		$92.40	
5	6-0450	Stationery	$84.00		Office stationery purchased
5	2-1230	GST Paid	$8.40		
CD	**20/07/11**	**Weekly salary – Sally Hubble**			
145679	1-1110	Standard Bank		$544.50	
145676	6-0130	Wages & salaries	$835.00		Gross pay for the week
145679	2-1420	PAYG Withholding		$250.50	PAYG Tax withheld
145679	2-1410	Payroll Deductions		$40.00	Medical and Union fees deducted
CD	**21/07/11**	**Hornsby Antico Pty Ltd**			
145680	1-1110	Standard Bank		$1,955.80	
145680	5-1120	Purchases – Materials	$1,778.00		Purchase of craft materials
145680	2-1230	GST Paid	$177.80		
CD	**23/07/11**	**Paul & Dainty**			
145681	1-1110	Standard Bank		$550.00	
145680	6-0005	Accounting	$500.00		Special investigation
145680	2-1230	GST Paid	$50.00		
CD	**23/07/11**	**Petty Cash**			
6	1-1150	Petty Cash		$107.06	
6	6-0250	Motor Vehicle Running Costs	$62.60		Petrol and oil
6	6-0110	Staff Amenities Expense	$38.20		Staff tea and coffee
6	2-1230	GST Paid	$6.26		

(continued on the next page)

4.9 *(continued)*

ID#	Acct#	Account Name	Debit	Credit	Allocation Memo
CD	**25/07/11**	**Castle Hill Art Galleries**			
145682	1-1110	Standard Bank		$3,608.00	
145682	5-1120	Purchases – Materials	$3,280.00		Purchase of craft materials
145682	2-1230	GST Paid	$328.00		
CD	**25/07/11**	**Australia Post**			
145683	1-1110	Standard Bank		$66.00	
145683	6-0030	Parcel Delivery	$60.00		Parcel delivery of books
145683	2-1230	GST Paid	$6.00		
CD	**28/07/11**	**Weekly salary – Sally Hubble**			
145684	1-1110	Standard Bank		$544.50	
145684	6-0130	Wages & salaries	$835.00		Gross pay for the week
145684	2-1420	PAYG Withholding		$250.50	PAYG Tax withheld
145684	2-1410	Payroll Deductions		$40.00	Medical and Union fees deducted
CD	**30/07/11**	**Sarcom Electronics**			
145685	1-1110	Standard Bank		$2,024.00	
145685	1-2210	Equipment – at cost	$1,840.00		Laser printer for the office
145685	2-1230	GST Paid	$184.00		
CD	**30/07/11**	**Petty Cash**			
7	1-1150	Petty Cash		$141.35	
7	6-0400	Shop Expenses	$128.50		Sundry shop expenses
7	2-1230	GST Paid	$12.85		
CD	**31/07/11**	**Hills Transport Pty Ltd**			
145686	1-1110	Standard Bank		$39.05	
145686	6-0030	Parcel Delivery	$35.50		Urgent parcel delivery
145663	2-1230	GST Paid	$3.55		
CD	**31/07/11**	**Powerplus Corporation**			
145687	1-1110	Standard Bank		$264.88	
145687	6-0310	Electricity	$240.80		Electricity for the quarter
145687	2-1230	GST Paid	$24.08		
		Grand Total:	$17,478.35	$17,478.35	

4.10

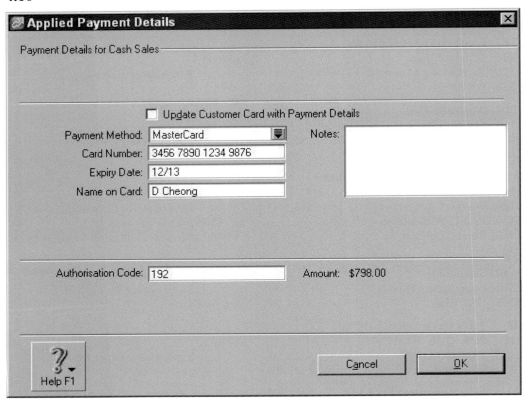

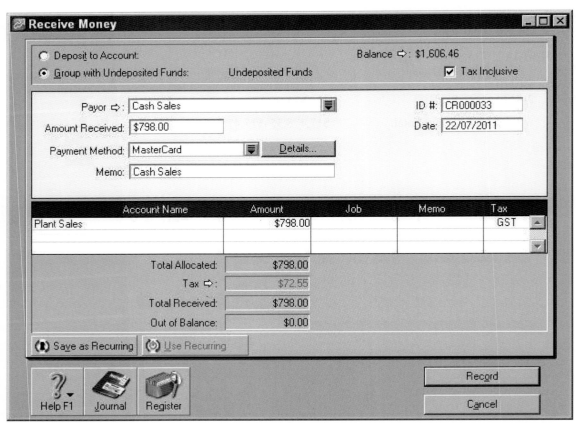

4.10 *(continued)*

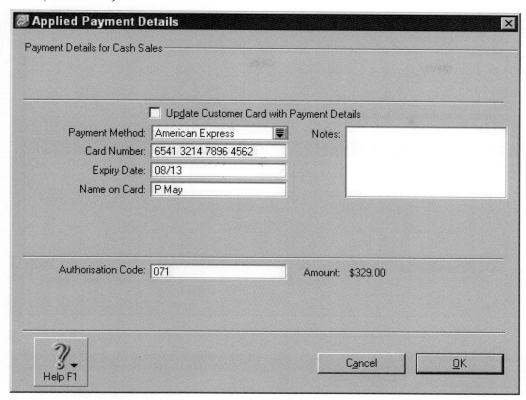

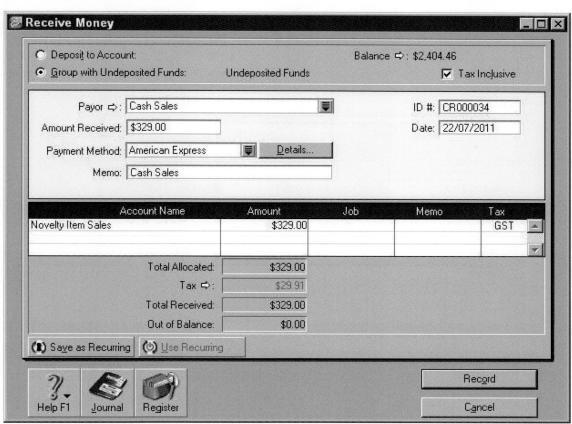

4.11

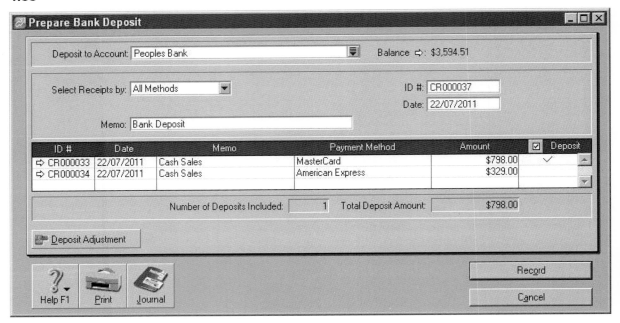

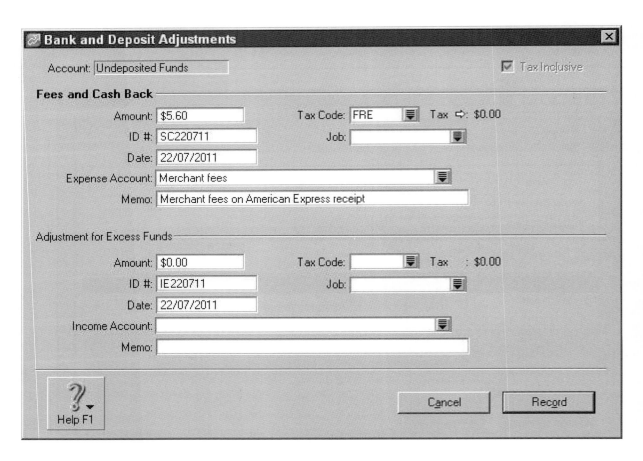

4.11 *(continued)*

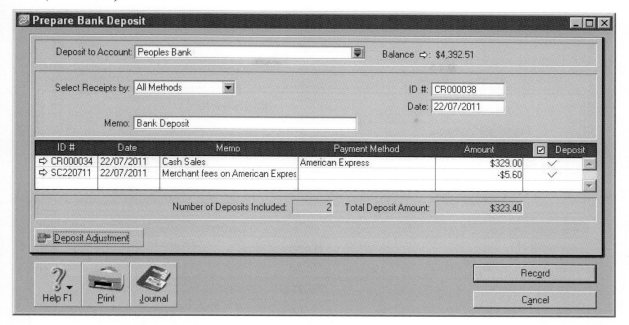

4.12

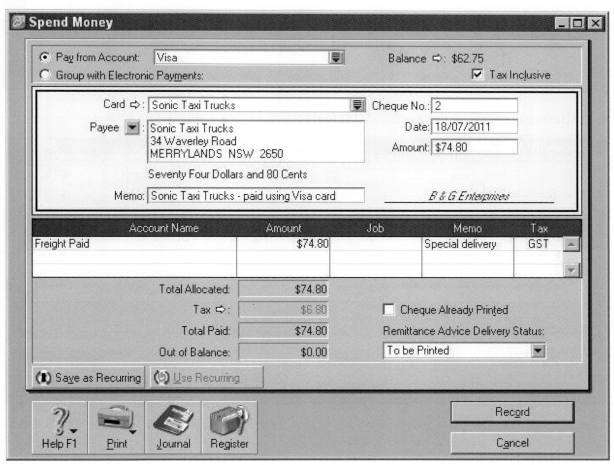

4.12 (continued)

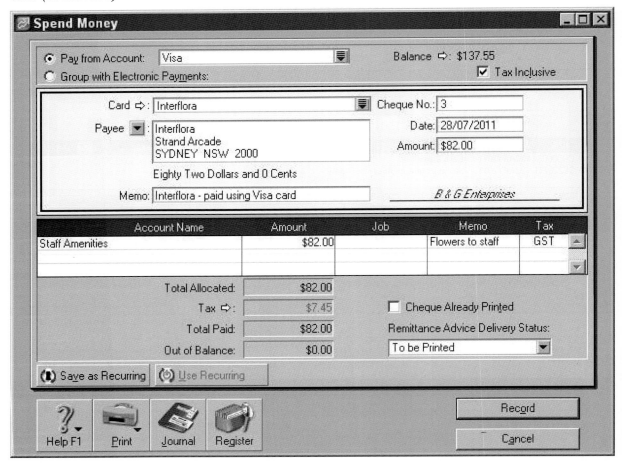

4.13 (Before clicking on the *Reconcile* button!)

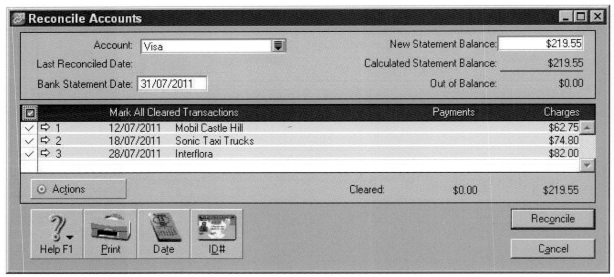

4.14

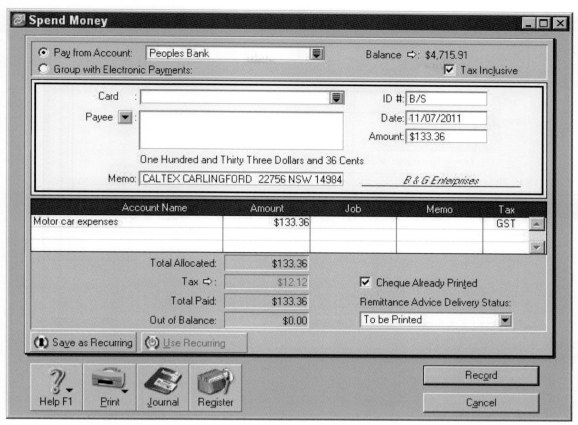

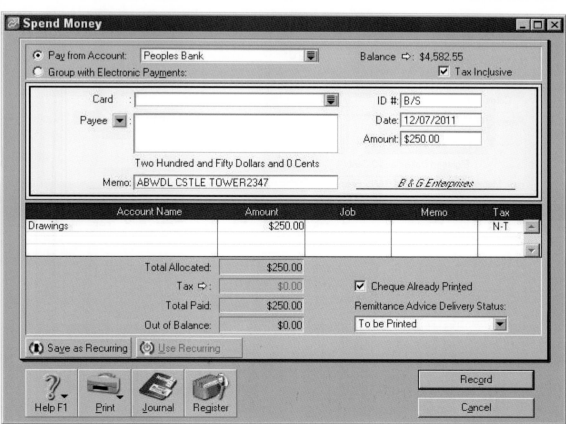

4.14 (continued)

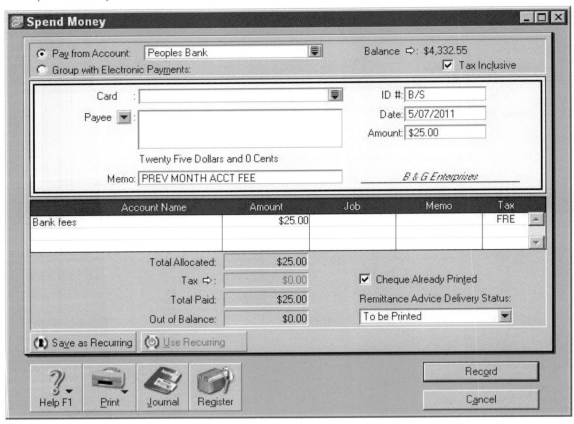

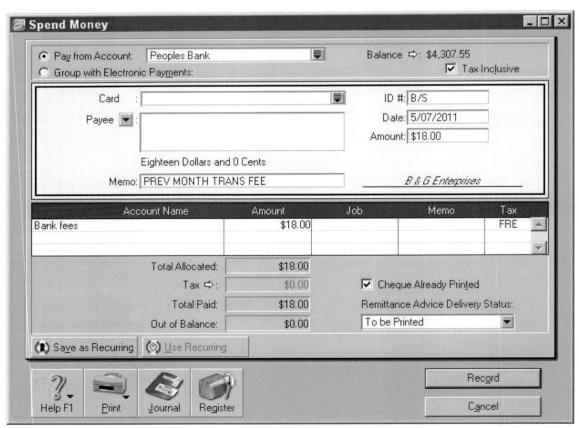

4.14 (continued)

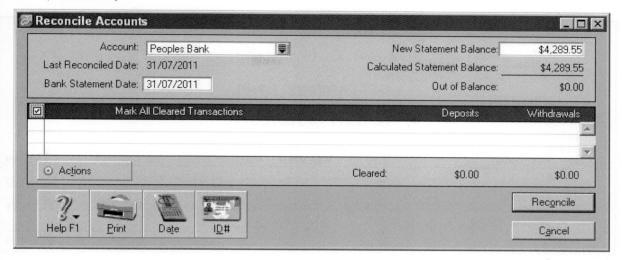

4.15

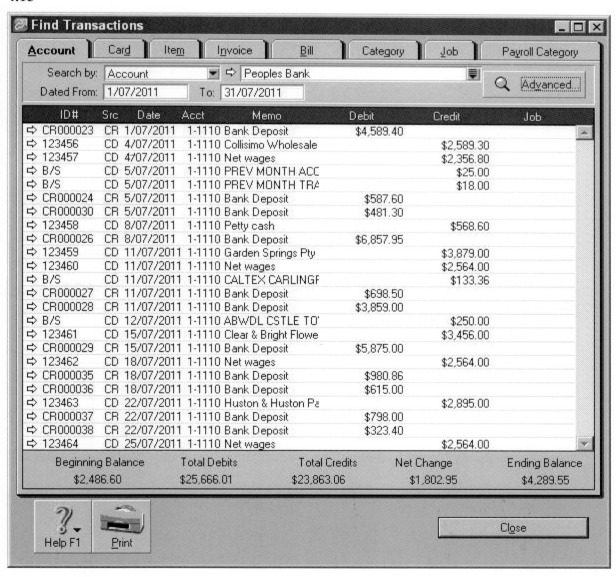

4.16

<table>
<tr><td colspan="7" align="center">**Jeremy Fisher Crafts**
<< your name >>
Demonstration file dem41.MYO</td></tr>
<tr><td colspan="7" align="center">**GST [Summary - Cash]**</td></tr>
<tr><td colspan="7" align="center">**1/07/2011 To 31/07/2011**</td></tr>
<tr><td colspan="4">19/07/2010
10:53:30 AM</td><td colspan="3" align="right">**Page 1**</td></tr>
<tr><td>**Code**</td><td>**Description**</td><td>**Rate**</td><td>**Sale Value**</td><td>**Purchase Value**</td><td>**Tax Collected**</td><td>**Tax Paid**</td></tr>
<tr><td>CAP</td><td>Capital Acquisitions</td><td>10.00%</td><td></td><td>$2,024.00</td><td></td><td>$184.00</td></tr>
<tr><td>FRE</td><td>GST Free</td><td>0.00%</td><td></td><td>$199.05</td><td></td><td></td></tr>
<tr><td>GST</td><td>Goods & Services Tax</td><td>10.00%</td><td>$29,867.50</td><td>$19,088.75</td><td>$2,715.22</td><td>$1,735.34</td></tr>
<tr><td>N-T</td><td>Not Reportable</td><td>0.00%</td><td>$5,000.00</td><td>$3,947.71</td><td></td><td></td></tr>
<tr><td></td><td></td><td></td><td></td><td align="right">Total:</td><td>$2,715.22</td><td>$1,919.34</td></tr>
</table>

Accounts receivable 5

Creating and maintaining customer records, recording invoices on credit and payments received from customers. Printing invoices, statements and reports.

After completing this chapter you will be able to:

1 Set up the Sales & Receivables.

2 Create and maintain customer information on cards.

3 Enter starting historical data for accounts receivable.

4 Integrate the accounts receivable records with the general ledger.

5 Record sales quotes, orders and invoices.

6 Change quotes to orders and orders to invoices.

7 Record special transactions such as bad debts and credit notes.

8 Record receipts from customers using an open item system and automatically deducting any cash discount for early settlement.

9 Use "Undeposited Funds" account to allow for daily deposits.

10 Print/email documents and reports from the accounts receivable.

11 Print "GST" reports.

12 Combine duplicate Customer Records (cards).

13 Record customer dishonoured cheques.

Introduction

The *Sales* command centre is used primarily for invoicing credit sales, recording credit notes against those sales, and recording payments received from customers. Records are also kept for individual accounts receivable (customers). It is also used to issue and keep records of quotes given to customers and orders received from them.

The *Sales* command centre (or its full name: '**Sales and Receivable**') cannot be used without certain minimum accounts in a general ledger. The general ledger setup has to be completed before this command centre can be used. At least two accounts must appear in the general ledger accounts list – "Accounts Receivable" and "Bank". For the first part of this lesson, the general ledger setup has been completed for you.

> **TIP:**
> The notes, examples and exercises that follow assume that you have read and gone through the basic instructions in Chapters 1 and 2, and that you can:
> - Start the *MYOB AccountRight Plus* application;
> - Change the business name and/or address;
> - Select command centres and options within those command centres; and
> - Recognise the conventions used in this book (for example, the sign ↵ is an instruction to tap the *Enter* key).
>
> **You may need to refer back to Chapter 1 to do these tasks. A quick way of finding the place for instructions is to use the 'How to ...' index at the front of the book.**
> **Throughout this chapter, you need to sign on as the "Administrator" for all the exercises and assessments.**

An open item system

Many computer packages allow for two methods of accounting for payments received from customers, and the issue of credit notes against credit transactions. These are known as "balance forward" and "open item". A *balance forward* system applies money and/or credit notes against the opening balance (or first invoice). An *open item* system applies money received from a customer or credit notes against the relevant invoice(s) involved.

In *MYOB AccountRight Plus* you can select either method. For example, if you choose you can set a preference so that all payments are applied against the earliest invoice first. In this book an *Open Item* system is used. Money received from a customer, or credits given to the customer, must be *applied* (matched) against the invoices concerned. Until a receipt or credit is applied, the invoice is shown as *OPEN*. Once a receipt or credit is applied to the total amount owing on an invoice, the invoice is shown as *CLOSED*. Closed invoices have a balance owing of zero. To reduce the size of the file, closed items should be regularly purged (removed from the file) – after making a permanent backup of course!

Recording a sale on credit

When you record a sale on credit using the *Sales* command centre, the program will charge the customer with the total sales value and automatically debit the same amount to the linked "accounts receivable" account. It will also record any GST and freight to the relevant accounts (e.g. "GST Collected" and "Freight Collected"). In this chapter the *Service* layout will be used and you will have to nominate the account(s) that need to be credited (or debited for credit notes). This account is usually an income account such as "Sales for Goods Sold" or *"Consulting Fees"* for an example of a service given to a customer. In Chapter 7 the *Item* layout will be used instead of the *Service* layout and you will not have to enter the account to be credited as that will be set up for each item.

Account name or account number?

A general ledger account in *MYOB AccountRight* has an account number (code) and an account name. Whenever you are required to enter a general ledger account, you may choose to select the account to be used either by its name or by its number, depending on the way your data file is set up (see later). If the data file you are using is set up to use account *names* you can type in the account name in full, just type in the first few letters of the name until you see the correct account displayed or you can use the *List* button ▤ to list the accounts and make your selection from the displayed list. Alternatively, if the file is set up for account *numbers* you may type in the account number or select it by using the *List* button.

    To set up the data file to list accounts **either** by name or by number, you need to access the *Preferences* option from the *Setup* drop down menu and click on the *Windows* tab. Figure 5.1 shows preferences used in this chapter – accounts will be selected and listed by account name as indicated by the fourth checkbox. If you prefer to use account numbers, de-select this selection. In all the exercises and whenever a general ledger account is required, you will be given its number *and* name. Throughout this book, you may use whichever option you prefer.

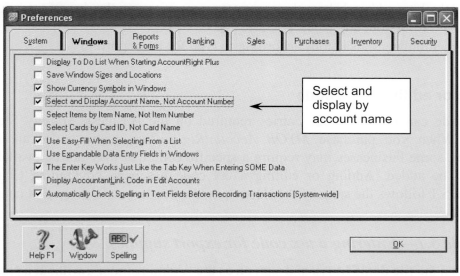

Figure 5.1: Preference for selecting and displaying accounts by name

Check spelling before recording transactions

Before recording sales, purchases or adding new inventory items, you can check the spelling. *MYOB AccountRight Plus* spell checker mainly checks spelling in the 'Description' fields for sales and purchases and the 'Name' field for the inventory items.

You have the option of whether or not to use this feature. To set up *MYOB AccountRight Plus* to spell check your entries before recording them, you need to access the *Preferences* option from the *Setup* drop down menu and click on the *Windows* tab. Figure 5.1 shows preferences used in <u>this chapter</u> – transactions will be automatically checked for spelling before recording as indicated by the last checkbox. If you prefer not to use this feature, de-select this selection. If you de-select this option you can still check the spelling manually at any time before recording a transaction by clicking on the *Spell* button at the bottom of any form.

When you record a transaction the spell checker will display the misspelled words. You have the option to accept the suggestion by clicking *Change* or *Change All*, ignoring the suggestion by selecting *Ignore* or *Ignore All*, or alternatively you may add the word to the dictionary used by selecting "Add".

You can also control the way the spell checker will perform its functions. In the *Windows* tab of the preferences, click on the *Spelling* button. The *Spell Check Preferences* window will appear where you can fine tune the spell checker performance. You can, for example, select that the spell checker ignores words that start with capitals or email addresses and so on.

MYOB AccountRight Plus tax codes

A tax code is used in a transaction to:

- Calculate, add and show the correct amount of tax on the document evidencing the transaction; and
- Accumulate transactions according to type for tax reporting.

Adding or editing a tax code

A tax code can be set up for entries required on the Business Activity Statement (BAS). When you purchase *MYOB AccountRight Plus*, many codes are set up. However, some businesses may require a specific code that may not be available and needs to be added. Adding or editing a tax code has been covered in Chapter 2. Example 5.1 follows the steps of the 'How to add/edit a tax code' from that chapter.

Example 5.1—Entering a tax code for export supplies

1. Open the file **dem51.myo** and sign on as the "Administrator", without a password.
2. Select the *Lists* pull-down menu and select the *Tax Codes* menu item.
3. Click on the *New* button.

4. Enter a three character tax code as "EXP" ↵.

5. Type in the description as "Export Sales" ↵.

6. The type of tax is "Goods & Services Tax" ↵.

7. The tax rate is 0% (export sales are *GST-free*) ↵.

8. Select account "GST Collected" (number 2-1310) as the linked account for GST collected by the business from customers (type the name or number in or use the *List* button 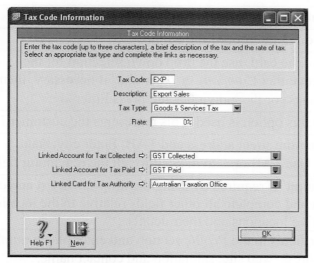 and select from the accounts list).

9. Select "GST Paid" (account number 2-1330) as the linked account for GST paid by the business to suppliers of goods and services.

10. Select the "Australian Taxation Office" as the linked tax authority to be paid.

11. The window should look like Figure 5.2. Edit any incorrect part and click the *OK* button to finish, then click on *Close* button to exit to the command centre.

Figure 5.2: New tax code for export sales

Video: A video on adding tax codes is on the DVD

Self-test exercise 5.1

The file is dem51.myo.

Enter a new tax code as: "ITS"

Description:	Rate	Tax Type:	Linked Acc. for Tax Collected:	Linked Acc. for Tax Paid
Input Taxed Sales	0%	Goods & Services Tax	GST Collected 2-1310	GST Paid 2-1330

As well as the codes entered in the previous example and exercise, there should already be the following codes: "GST", "FRE" and "CAP".

Businesses registered for the GST, should enter a tax code for all income and for all expenses and acquisitions. This is necessary for the Business Activity Statement.

Creating customer records (card file)

MYOB AccountRight Plus uses a "card file" system to record the relatively permanent data (records) about customers, suppliers and employees. Each customer making up *Accounts Receivable* must have a card. This card will contain the address, phone etc as well as credit and sales terms. Unless a customer has a card, you will not be able to issue an invoice. You can create customer cards (or edit existing ones) using the *Card File* command centre. A card can also be created at the time when issuing an invoice.

How to create a card for a customer

Step	Instruction
1	Select the *Card File* command centre.
2	Select the *Cards List* option.
3	Select the *Customer* tab at the top of the window.
4	Click on the *New* button at the foot of the window.
5	In the *Profile* section of the card, use the drop down selection for the 'Designation' and select either *Company* or *Individual* if necessary, then type in the name of the business or the individual and press Enter ↵.
6	Type in the Card ID if this option is used. This represents the customer ID.
7	Using 'Address 1', enter the street address and TAB. Enter city, state, postcode and country. Use TAB or ↵ to move through the remaining fields.
8	Select any other 'Location' if required by using the drop-down list and enter in address information and complete all other fields relative to the location. You can record up to five locations and their details.
9	TAB through the other fields in the *Profile* section and enter phone numbers, fax numbers, email address, web site, salutation and contact name.
10	Click on the *Card Details* Tab and enter any of the optional information. Select 'Identifier' and a 'Custom List' if these have been set up (they are used to select cards for reports based on certain criteria).
11	Click on the *Selling Details* tab at the top of the window.
12	On the left-hand side of the *Selling Details* section defaults for an order or invoice may be entered (these are optional).
13	Enter the customer's ABN and, if applicable, the branch ABN.
14	Set the default GST code for goods and services sold to this customer and for freight charged to the customer. Use the *List* button 🔽 and select the code or type it in. These codes would be used if the customer's tax code is to be used.
15	Click on the *Actions* button ⊙ Actions (at the bottom left side) to select 'Edit Credit Limit & Hold' item from the list and enter the credit information.
16	In the bottom of the *Selling Details* enter in the terms of trade (see next page).
17	Click on the *OK* button to complete.

TRADING TERMS

Trading terms for *Account Customers* (those who buy goods and services on credit) are set in the *Selling Details* window of the *Customers' Cards*.

Credit Limits

You need to set a credit limit for each customer. Customers can buy goods on credit to the extent of their "credit limit". Once they exceed that limit *MYOB AccountRight Plus* gives a warning before processing any invoice. You can then make a decision whether to extend the credit limit to cater for the sale or request a payment from the customer for the difference between the available credit and the total sale.

There are numerous ways that you can request customers to settle their accounts:

Settlement Terms	Select **this** in the field 'Payment is Due:'
Pay in advance before dispatching the goods.	Prepaid
Pay for the goods when delivered. **C**ash **O**n **D**elivery.	C.O.D.
Pay in so many days after the date of the Invoice (days after sale).	In a given # of Days
Pay in so many days after *the end of the month* of sale.	# of Days after EOM.
Pay for <u>all outstanding</u> invoices on a day of the month – each month. For example, on the 15th of each month pay for all invoices.	On a Day of the month
Pay, on a specific day *this* month, for all *last* month's sales (invoices).	Day of Month after EOM
Letter of Credit (*see boxed text on page 5-13*).	C.O.D.

Cash Discounts: A customer can receive a discount for paying early, i.e. *before* the due date as set above. Enter the discount rate (%) in the field '% Discount for Early Payment' and enter in the field 'Discount Days' or 'Discount Date', the number of days (or date), after sale, a payment can be made to qualify for this discount.

Volume Discount: For "Item" layout invoices you can nominate a discount rate for customers who buy large volumes of merchandise (e.g. wholesalers). This discount appears on the invoice and automatically discounts the prices set for inventory items. This feature will have no effect on "Service" layout invoices.

Example 5.2—Creating a card for a customer (account receivable)

1. Make sure that you have the file dem51.myo open.
2. Change the 'Company Information' by entering your name in the address field.
3. Select the *Card File* command centre.
4. Select the *Cards List* option.
5. Click on the *Customer* tab at the top of the *Card List* window.
6. Click on the *New* button at the bottom of the window.
7. If it is not already selected, the 'Designation' is "Company". Type in the name of the company "David James Ltd" ↵.
8. Type in "DAVID" as the Card ID ↵.
9. The 'Location' field should have "Address 1: Bill To" selected. TAB and enter in the address as "134 Goodwood Avenue, RYDE, NSW, 2112, AUSTRALIA".
10. TAB and enter the phone #1 as "(02) 9702 1223" ↵.
11. Enter Phone #2 as "0419 268 324".
12. TAB through to the fax number and enter "(02) 9702 4433" ↵.
13. Type in "echee@dj.com.au" as the email address and ↵.
14. Enter "www.dj.com.au" as the website address ↵.
15. At the 'Salutation' field enter "Eileen" ↵.
16. Enter the 'Contact' as "Eileen Chee".
17. The *Profile* section of the supplier's card should look like Figure 5.3:

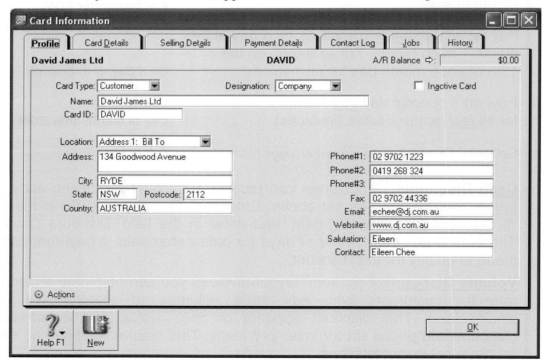

Figure 5.3: Profile section for a new customer card

18. Click on the drop-down arrow and change the 'Location' field to "Address 2: Ship To" and enter "46 Garfield Street, RICHMOND, VIC, 3121, AUSTRALIA".

19. TAB and enter phone #1 as "(03) 9214 4455". The *Profile* window will now look like Figure 5.4:

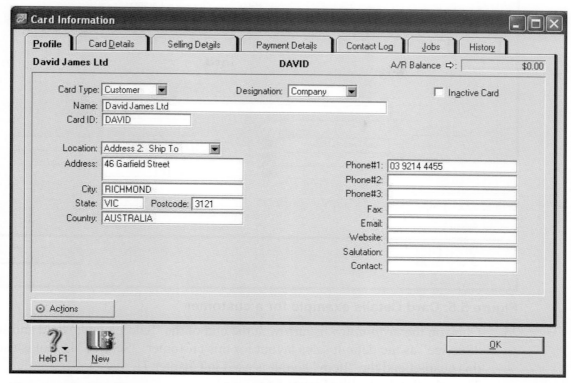

Figure 5.4: Profile window showing the "Ship To" address

20. Click on the *Card Details* tab at the top of the *Card Information* window.

21. Click on the *Identifiers* button and tick the selection box "R" (this business uses "R" to identify this customer as a retailer). Identifiers can be used to filter data in reports. Click on the *OK* button.

22. Use the *List* button ▼ at the end of the 'Custom List #1' field and select "Sales Territory NSW" as the list. Custom Lists can be used as selection criteria when filtering reports (see later when printing reports).
    Note: Three *Custom Lists* for customers have already been added for this file. You can add (or edit) a list to the *Custom Lists* using the *Custom Lists – Customers* option from the *Lists* drop-down menu. (More on setting up these lists in Chapter 6.)

23. Click on the 'Notes' field and type in "New customer in July 2011. Locations throughout Australia and Singapore". You may type in any notes pertinent to the customer. The *Card Details* window should look like Figure 5.5 on the next page.

24. Select the *Selling Details* tab at the top of the *Card Information* window.

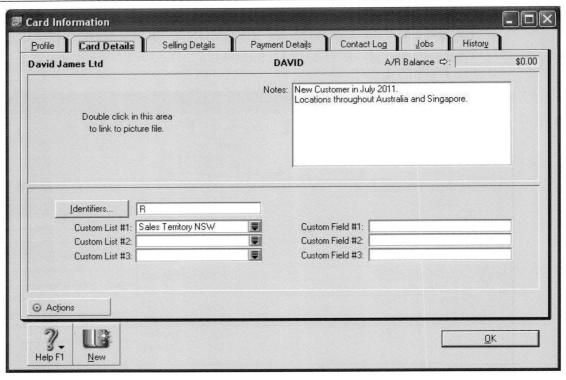

Figure 5.5: Card Details example for a customer

25.   Click on the *drop-down* list arrow at the end of the 'Sale Layout:' field and select "Service" as the default sales layout for this customer. "Service" layout is used in this chapter and the "Item" layout is used in Chapter 7.
      The selection looks like Figure 5.6:

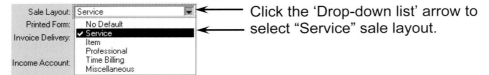

Figure 5.6: "Service" type layout selected

26.   Use the *List* button ▼ at the 'Printed Form' field and select "AccountRight Plus's Plain Paper Invoice" (used when no pre-printed invoice is available).

27.   Select "To be Printed" in the 'Invoice Delivery' field.

28.   Use the *List* button ▼ for 'Salesperson:' and select "Chopin, Frederic".

29.   Use the *List* button ▼ for 'Shipping Method:' and select "Hills Transport".

30.   Click on the *Actions* button ⊙ Actions (at the bottom left side) to select 'Edit Credit Limit & Hold' item from the list and enter the credit limit "$100,000" ↵

31.   At the 'A.B.N' field, enter "22 111 345 678" ↵.

32.   Leave the 'Tax Code' field as "GST" and the 'Freight Tax Code' as "GST". The 'Use Customer's Tax Code:' checkbox should not be ticked for this customer.

33.   Use the drop-down list in the 'Payment is Due' field and select "In a Given # of Days". This customer is to make payment within 30 days after invoice date.

34.   In the 'Balance Due Days' field, enter "30" (no discount).

35. Your *Selling Details* window should look like Figure 5.7. Click on any field to edit any errors.

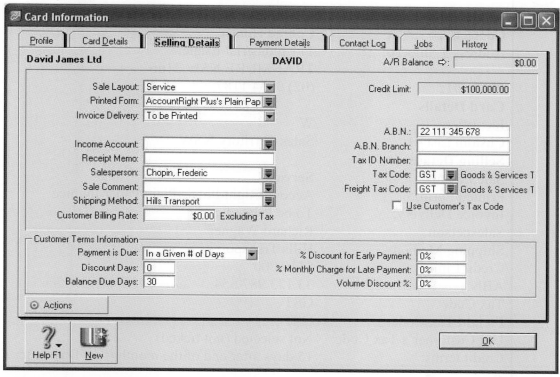

Figure 5.7: Selling Details set up for a customer

36. As this is a new customer, and Jobs are not used in this chapter, the other Options in Card Information (Payment Details, Jobs, History, and Contact Log) are not used. Click on the *OK* button to complete the card set up. (Jobs are covered in chapter 9.)

Video: A video on creating a customer card is on the DVD

Self-test exercise 5.2

Have the file dem51.myo open and create the following *new* customer cards:
Customer 1:
Profile

Designation	Company
Name:	Pharmaceutical Distribution Pty Ltd
Card ID:	PHARM
Address 1 Bill To:	42 Bossworth Street
	BAULKHAM HILLS NSW 2153
Phone #1:	(02) 9623 8416
Fax #:	(02) 9623 1133
Email:	ConH@fishpond.com.au
Website:	www.phd.com.au

(continued on the next page)

Self-test exercise 5.2 *(continued)*

Salutation:	Mr Hunter
Contact:	Conrad Hunter
Address 2 Ship To:	111 Industrial Estate
	TRANMURE NSW 2166
Phone #1:	(02) 9854 1187
Card Details	
Identifier:	W
Custom List #1:	Sales Territory NSW
Selling Details	
Sale Layout:	Service
Printed Form:	AccountRight Plus's Plain Paper Invoice
Invoice Delivery:	To be Printed
Salesperson:	Richard Wagner
Shipping Method:	Hills Transport
Credit Limit:	$110,000
ABN:	33 123 987 654
Tax Code:	GST
Freight Tax Code:	GST
Use Customer's Tax Code:	Not selected (not ticked)
Credit terms:	15 days after end of the month (# of Days after EOM)

Customer 2:
Profile

Designation	Individual
Last Name:	Devlin
First Name:	Maureen
CARD ID:	DEVLI
Address 1 Bill To:	4 Green Street
	GLADSTONE SA 5473
Phone #1:	(086) 432 1184
Fax #:	(086) 444 5575
Email:	mdevlin@optusnet.com.au
Salutation:	Maureen
Contact:	Maureen Devlin
Card Details	
Identifier:	R
Custom List #1:	Sales Territory SA
Selling Details	
Sale Layout:	Service
Printed Form:	AccountRight Plus's Plain Paper Invoice
Invoice Delivery:	To be Printed
Salesperson:	Albert Dvorak
Shipping Method:	Hills Transport
Credit Limit:	$15,000

(continued on the next page)

Self-test exercise 5.2 *(continued)*

ABN:	55 192 873 756
Tax Code:	GST
Freight Tax Code:	GST
Use Customer's Tax Code:	Not selected (not ticked)
Credit terms:	15 days after end of the month (# of Days after EOM)

Customer 3:

Profile

Company name:	Anzamate Ltd
CARD ID:	ANZAM
Address 1 Bill To:	29 Maupitu Street
	DEVONDALE New Zealand
Phone #1:	8623 2345
Fax #:	8623 3311
Email:	anzamate@kiwitel.com.nz
Website:	www.anzamate.com.nz
Salutation:	Peter
Contact:	Peter Wong
Ship to:	Same address

Card Details

Identifier:	E
Custom List #1:	Export Sales

Selling Details

Sale Layout:	Service
Printed Form:	AccountRight Plus's Plain Paper Invoice
Invoice Delivery:	To be Printed
Salesperson:	Stephanie Bach
Shipping Method:	International
Credit Limit:	$150,000
ABN:	No ABN – New Zealand Company!
Tax Code:	EXP
Freight Tax Code:	FRE
Use Customer's Tax Code:	YES (box is ticked)
Credit terms:	Letter of Credit
	(select *C.O.D.* in 'Payment is Due' see memo below)

Letter of Credit (L/C) is the most commonly used payment term in **International** Trade. This method protects both parties. The buyer pays for the goods in advance to his banker, who issues a L/C and advises the seller's bank. The seller is guaranteed payment, by his bank, when he fulfils all the terms of the L/C and ships the goods.

In *MYOB AccountRight Plus* select *C.O.D.* for our *customers* and *Prepaid* for our *suppliers* for the payment term *Letter of Credit*.

Maintaining a customer card

An existing customer card can be edited to update its data. If a customer's account needs to be temporarily or permanently cancelled then his/her card can be made inactive or deleted. A customer's card <u>cannot be deleted</u> if there are any outstanding transactions recorded for that customer. In this situation the card can be made inactive. No transactions can be recorded to an 'inactive' card.

It is also possible to <u>combine</u> duplicate cards (see later in this chapter).

How to maintain a customer's card

Step	Instruction
1	Select the *Cards List* option from the *Card File* command centre.
2	Select the *Customer* tab at the top of the window.
3	Click on the detail arrow ⇨ next to the customer's card to be modified or deleted to open it.
4	To edit a card: Select a view (window) by clicking on its tab at the top. To correct any errors, click on the field concerned and overtype or edit to make the necessary changes in that view. To make a card inactive: In the *Profile* view, click on the 'Inactive' field to turn it on, ☑ Inactive Card and click *OK* to accept the warning/message. You have indicated that this record is inactive. It will no longer display in Select From List options. To make this record active again, just deselect the checkbox. **Note:** No transactions can be recorded for inactive customers. To delete a card: Click on the *Edit* menu and select "Delete Card".
5	Click the *OK* button.

Self-test exercise 5.3

Have the file dem51.myo open.

Edit the <u>existing</u> card for the customer: Abnego Pty Ltd. Click on the *Selling Details* tab and <u>change</u> the 'Tax Code' to "EXP", the 'Freight Tax Code' to "FRE", the 'Payment is Due' to "C.O.D." and tick the 'Use Customer's Tax code' box.

Important: When the card option 'Use Customer Tax Code' is selected (ticked), that will override the default tax code for the accounts used to record the sale of goods and services. In the above exercise it is necessary to <u>change</u> the GST codes to "EXP" and "FRE" as the customer is an *overseas* customer and as such does not pay the goods and services tax. However, for <u>local customers</u> this field <u>must not</u> be ticked.

Setting up sales linked accounts to the general ledger

There are six *default* general ledger accounts used by *MYOB AccountRight Plus* to automatically prepare the necessary journal entries when recording invoices for sales to, or payments received from, accounts receivable (customers). Two out of these six accounts are compulsory minimum linked accounts that need to be nominated (i.e. the "Accounts Receivable" control account and a bank account). The other four are optional.

How to set up the sales linked accounts

Step	Instruction
1	Select the *Setup* pull-down menu at the top of the screen.
2	Click the *Linked Accounts* option and select the *Sales Accounts*.
3	Enter an asset account to record amounts owing by Accounts Receivable ↵.
4	Enter a bank account to record payments by Accounts Receivable ↵.
5	If customers are charged for freight, tick on the optional link for recording freight charges and enter an income account ↵.
6	If customers are required to pay deposits, tick on the optional link for recording deposits paid by customers and enter a liability account ↵.
7	If customers are given discounts for early payment, tick on the optional link for recording any discounts allowed and enter an expense account ↵.
8	If customers are charged for late payments, tick on the optional link for recording any additional charges paid by customers for late payments and enter an income account ↵.
9	Click *OK*.

In the demonstration file dem51.myo, the *Sales Linked Accounts* are already set up. You can view the setup by selecting "Setup/Linked Accounts/Sales Accounts" option.

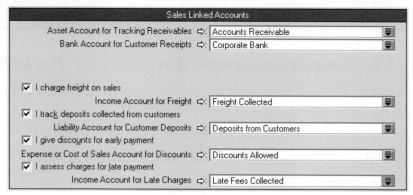

Note: The accounts can be displayed by their numbers instead. If that option is selected (see page 5-3) the account numbers will be (from top to bottom):
1-1210, 1-1110, 4-5000, 2-1600, 6-2100 and 8-3000.

Video: A video about setting link accounts is on the DVD

Opening customer balances (amounts owing by accounts receivable)

When *MYOB AccountRight Plus* is used for the **first** time (the conversion date), if customers have outstanding balances, the invoices that make up the Accounts Receivable balance (pre-conversion invoices), must be recorded (entered). At the end of all subsequent years, however, customer balances are automatically carried forward and need not be entered.

How to enter the opening customer invoices owing

Step	Instruction
1	Open an *MYOB AccountRight Plus* file.
2	Select the *Setup* pull-down menu at the top of the screen.
3	Select the *Balances – Customer Balances* option.
4	Select a customer by clicking on the detail arrow ⇨ next to the customer's name.
5	Select the *Add Sale* button.
6	If the customer name is correct and highlighted, tap the enter key or TAB to the invoice number field.
7	Type in the sales invoice number ↵.
8	Enter the date of the invoice ↵.
9	Enter the customer's purchase order number (PO #).
10	The standard memo suggested is "Pre-conversion sale". Change this if you want another detail to appear on a statement (e.g. "Invoice") ↵.
11	Enter the amount of the invoice.
12	Enter or edit the tax code if necessary.
13	Click on the *Record* button. Read the message regarding cash basis income and simplified tax system and click *OK* to continue.
14	Repeat steps 4 to 13 until all balances are entered. You will receive a congratulations message to that fact. Click the *Close* button.

Example 5.3—Entering a pre-conversion invoice for Abacus Pty Ltd

1. Open the *MYOB AccountRight Plus* file dem51.myo (if not already open).
2. Select the *Setup* pull down menu.
3. Select the *Balances* option and *Customer Balances*.
4. Click on the detail arrow ⇨ next to the name Abacus Pty Ltd.
5. Select the *Add Sale* button.
6. The name Abacus Pty Ltd should be highlighted. Tab to the 'Invoice #' field.
7. Enter the invoice number as "5637" ↵.
8. Enter the invoice date as "18/5/2011" ↵.

9.   Enter "N300" as the 'Customer PO #' ↵.

10. Change the memo to "Invoice" ↵.

11. Enter the amount as "$24,621.20" ↵.

12. The tax code is "GST".

13. Your screen should look like Figure 5.8:

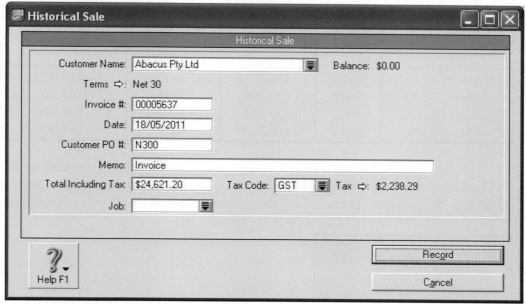

Figure 5.8: Historical sale for Abacus Pty Ltd

14. Leave the 'Job' field blank (Jobs will be covered in Chapter 9).

15. Select the *Record* button, then *OK* for the message regarding cash basis income.

16. Your Customer balances window should now look like Figure 5.9.
     (**Note**: 'Out of Balance Amount' indicates more sales need to be entered.)

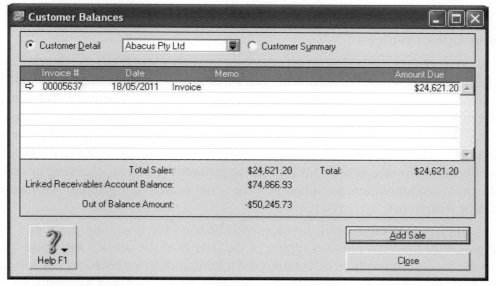

Figure 5.9: Receivable balances after entering Abacus historical invoice

Video: A video on pre-conversion sales (invoices) is on the DVD

Self-test exercise 5.4

Have the file dem51.myo open.
Enter the following pre-conversion invoices:

Customer	Inv. No.	Date	Customer PO#	Amount	Tax Code
Abacus Pty Ltd	5650	24/6/2011	N315	$3,248.63	GST
Colzmier Pty Ltd	5642	11/6/2011	C8560	$21,148.50	GST
Em-Kart Pty Ltd	5643	16/6/2011	848-1450	$25,290.60	GST
Kiss Me Quick	3849	24/7/2009	442	$558.00	GST

After entering the above pre-conversion invoices, they (together with Invoice 5637 entered in the previous example) should total the amount that is shown in the Accounts Receivable account in the general ledger and you should receive a "Congratulations" message as shown in Figure 5.10:

Figure 5.10: Congratulations – if you balance

If you do not balance, check your answer. Select *Transaction Journals* option – and select the *Sales* tab. Change the date range to: From: 24/7/2009 To: 31/7/2011to include all the above transactions. Click on a detail arrow ⇨ next to any incorrect invoice and edit the historical entry.

Credit sales invoices

There are five types of sales invoice layouts available in *MYOB AccountRight Plus* – an *Item* invoice which is used with the *Inventory* command centre, a *Professional* invoice for continuous recording of work carried out for clients, a *Service* invoice (used in this chapter), a *Time Billing* invoice for charging times and a *Miscellaneous* invoice. This does not preclude a professional engineer from using an *Item* invoice to charge set rates per hour or a retailer selling items using a *Service* invoice. The *Miscellaneous* invoice is used for internal adjustments, such as, charging or crediting a customer's account where an actual invoice is not issued (not printed) – for example, a bad debt written off.

In this chapter, *Service* invoices will be used for invoicing items and services. Using *Service* invoices requires typing in the details of the service and goods provided on to the invoice, as well as calculating the total amounts for each item or service sold. You will also need to nominate the account to be credited (usually an income account).

Item invoice layout will be used in Chapter 7 'Inventory and Integration'.

The *Enter Sales* option in the *Sales* command centre allows for three different entries:

1. **A Quote:** Entering in a quotation given to a customer. A saved quote is not recorded in the double-entry accounting system, but may be retrieved at a later date and converted to an order (or an invoice) when the customer accepts the quotation and places an order (see later in this chapter);

2. **An Order:** Entering an order received from a customer. An order is also not recorded in the double-entry accounting system, but is taken into account when using Item inventory (see Chapter 7 for using inventory items). The order may be converted to an invoice when the goods are picked up or delivered; or

3. **An Invoice:** An invoice is recorded without first having recorded a quote or an order. An invoice is recorded in the double-entry accounting system and the customer is charged with the invoice total amount.

The entry of an invoice directly (without first having recorded a quote or an order) will be demonstrated first in the following pages and later in the chapter the use of Quotes, Orders and the Sales Register will be shown.

How to enter a service type invoice directly

Step	Instruction
1	Select the *Sales* command centre.
2	Select the *Enter Sales* option.
3	A tick should appear in the 'Tax Inclusive' checkbox if the amounts to be entered include tax. Clear the tick box if the amounts entered are tax exclusive (prices *plus* tax). If this option is **not** ticked then the tax amount (if any) is calculated and <u>added</u> to the total. **Important:** The Invoice <u>total</u> should be the same regardless of whether this box is ticked or not (i.e. amount *plus* tax *or* amount including tax). ☑ Tax Inclusive ☐ Tax Inclusive Prices *Include* GST Prices *Plus* any GST
4	"INVOICE" should be the default set up at the top of the *Sales – New Service* window. INVOICE ← Entering an invoice Customer :
5	Click on the 'Customer' field and enter the customer name. Type in the first few letters or use the *List* button ▤ and select from the list. Tab through the 'Ship to' field (do not press *Enter* <u>unless</u> you are changing the details).
	(continued on the next page)

5-19

Step	Instruction
6	The invoice type appears in the window title bar (e.g. *Sales – New Service*). To change a sale type, if necessary, click on the *Layout* button at the bottom of the *Sales* window, and make your selection. Click [Layout] **Remember:** You can set a default layout for a customer on the customer card (Figure 5.7).
7	TAB through to the invoice number field, change if necessary and TAB.
8	Enter the invoice date ↵ (or press the space bar to activate the *Calendar*).
9	Type in the customer's purchase order number if it is available. You can enter other details if a number is not available – for example, "Email 14/7" ↵.
10	Type in the details of the goods sold or service provided and TAB.
11	Enter the account name or number for the income account to be credited or you may use ↵ to list all accounts and select from the list. If you are using account number you can type in '4' and ↵ to show income accounts, otherwise ↵ and scroll down to the *Income* accounts. Make your selection by clicking on the desired account and click the *Use Account* button and TAB.
12	Enter the amount of the line item *or* you may press the space bar to activate *MYOB Calculator* to calculate the amount for this line. You can type your calculations or click on the calculator to enter your calculations. You may use *numbers* and the " + * – / " signs when typing your calculations and press the "=" sign or ↵ to enter result in this field, and TAB.
13	Enter a job number, if income is to be recorded for a particular job, and TAB.
14	Enter *or* change the tax code if necessary. Use the *List* button ▼ to select.
15	Enter any other line items as above.
16	Enter any freight or delivery charges in the 'Freight' field. If necessary, change the GST code next to this field.
17	In the 'Paid Today' field enter any amount paid today (e.g. a deposit). For 'Cash Sales' enter the **total** invoice amount here. If an amount is entered it might be necessary to also complete the 'Payment Method' details.
18	The 'Salesperson', 'Comment', 'Ship via' and 'Promised Date' fields are optional. Click on the *List* button ▼ next to the field and select from the list. Use the *New* button to <u>add</u> any new entry required.
19	To view the terms of this invoice *or* to change them, if necessary, click on the detail arrow ⇨ next to 'Terms' field on top of the form. **Note:** If you change the terms in this field, these changes will apply to <u>this invoice only</u>. Permanent changes to the terms must be completed on the customer's card.
20	Change the journal memo, if necessary.
21	Click on the *Record* button.

Example 5.4—Entering a 'tax-inclusive' service invoice

Enter the following invoice for a sale to Colzmier Pty Ltd. The invoice is to show tax-inclusive amounts, including freight. The sales person was Gustav Mahler and Hills Transport delivered the goods.

1. Have the file dem51.myo open.

2. Select the *Sales* command centre.

3. Select the *Enter Sales* option.

4. Check that "INVOICE" is selected.

5. Check that the invoice amounts are to be entered as tax-inclusive.

6. The customer is Colzmier Pty Ltd. Remember that you may type in the first few letters (say "co"), hit ↵ and select from a list, or use the *List* button ⬇.

7. Make sure that the invoice type is *Sales – New Service* in the title bar at the top.

8. TAB through to the 'Invoice Number' field so that the 'Ship to' address remains (i.e. do not press Enter in the 'Ship To' field). Enter "5651" as the invoice number↵.

9. Enter the date as 7/7/2011. Remember that if the date field displays a date in July 2011, you only have to type "7" ↵.

10. The customer's purchase order number (#) is "C8621". Type this in and ↵.

11. Enter the description as "75 cartons of Roseanne Face Cream @ $475.20 per carton" and TAB to the next field.

12. The account to be credited is "Sales – Cosmetics" which has an account # of "4-1100". Enter this (or use the *List* button ☰ and select from the accounts list) and TAB to the amount field.

13. In the amount column enter $35,640.00 (this is the GST-inclusive amount for this line of the invoice). You can either type "75 * 475.20" and ↵ or "35640".

    (**Note**: When entering amounts it is <u>not necessary</u> to type the dollar sign or the commas).

14. TAB through the 'Job' column to the 'Tax' column.
    (**Note**: Jobs will be covered in Chapter 9 'Categories and Jobs').

15. The 'Tax' column should show a GST code of "GST"; press ↵, otherwise change the code to "GST" and ↵ to the next line.

16. Enter the description on the next line as "15 cartons of Moshi Face Pack @ $126.50 per carton" and TAB to the next field.

17. The account to be credited is "Sales – Cosmetics" which has an account # of "4-1100". Enter this and TAB to the amount field.

18. The amount to enter is $1,897.50 (this is the GST-inclusive amount for this line of the invoice). Type "15 * 126.50" and ↵.

19. TAB through to the 'Tax' column and if necessary change the code to "GST" ↵.

20. Click on the field for entering freight and enter "$165.00" ↵ (the tax code for this freight should show "GST").

21. The 'Salesperson' field should show "Gustav Mahler" as the salesperson and the company that carried the goods was "Hills Transport".

22. The 'Comment' field should show "We appreciate your business". These are the defaults set up on the card for Colzmier Pty Ltd.

23. Leave the rest of the invoice as is. The invoice should look like Figure 5.11. To correct any errors, click on the field concerned and overtype or edit.

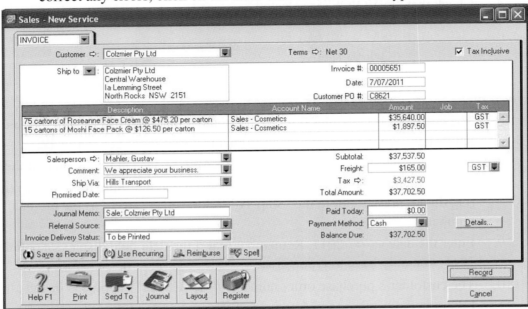

Figure 5.11: Completed tax-inclusive service layout invoice for Colzmier Pty Ltd

24. The spell checker will try to change 'Roseanne' and 'Moshi', click on Ignore for both.

25. Click on the *Record* button to complete this invoice.

The term 'Tax Inclusive' ☑ Tax Inclusive means that the amounts and prices entered in the invoice already include tax. The tax amount will be shown in grey to indicate that the tax amount is *included* in the total.

The term 'Tax Exclusive' ☐ Tax Inclusive does not mean tax free. It simply means the prices and amounts entered are *plus* tax. The tax amount will be calculated and *added* to the total.

The amount of tax will depend on the 'Tax code' used (i.e. *either* at 10% *or* 0%).

Note: The total of an invoice will be the same whether you enter amounts *plus* tax or enter the amounts *including* tax (e.g. $100 + $10 is the same as $110).

Video: A video on entering Invoices directly is on the DVD

Self-test exercise 5.5

Have the file dem51.myo open.

Enter the following tax-inclusive service type invoice on 14 July 2011:

Invoice number 5652 to David James Ltd on 14/7/2011. Customer PO # is D44311. Description: "150 cartons of Rafiki Hand Cream @ $211.20 per carton". This sale is to be credited to the account "Sales - Cosmetics" (account # 4-1100). The price is GST inclusive. Use the *MYOB Calculator* in the amount field to calculate the 'Amount'. The tax code is "GST". Freight on this invoice is $88.00 (GST-inclusive). The salesperson was Frederick Chopin and Hills Transport delivered the goods. Ignore changing the spelling for 'Rafiki'.

Example 5.5—Entering a tax-exclusive service invoice

Enter the following invoice for a sale to Pharmaceutical Distribution Pty Ltd. The invoice is to show amounts excluding the GST, with the GST added at the foot of the invoice. The sales person was Richard Wagner and Hills Transport delivered the goods.

1. Have the file dem51.myo open.
2. Select the *Enter Sales* option from the *Sales* command centre.
3. Make sure that the invoice type is *Sales – New Service.*
4. Check that "INVOICE" is selected.

5. Check that the invoice amounts are shown as tax exclusive.

   No tick if tax exclusive ➔ ☐ Tax Inclusive

6. The customer is Pharmaceutical Distribution Pty Ltd. Remember that you may type in the first few letters (say "ph"), use the ENTER key and select from a list, or use the *List* button ▤.
7. TAB to the Invoice number field so that the 'Ship to' address remains. The invoice number should be "5653" ↵.
8. Enter the date as "18/7/2011". Remember that if the date field is a date in July 2011, you only have to type "18" ↵ (or press the space bar to activate *MYOB Calendar*).
9. The customer's purchase order number (#) is "9876" ↵.
10. Enter the description as "80 cartons of Roseanne Face Cream @ $432.00 per carton" and TAB to the next field.
11. The account to be credited is "Sales – Cosmetics" which has an account # of "4-1100". Enter this and TAB to the amount field.
12. The amount to enter is $34,560.00 (this amount does not include the GST). Type "80 * 432" and ↵ or "34560".

13. The 'Tax' column should show a GST code of "GST".

14. Click on the field for entering freight and enter "$165.00" (the tax code is "GST").

15. "Richard Wagner" is the salesperson and the goods were shipped by "Hills Transport".

16. Click on the *List* button 🔳 for the 'Comment' field and select "We appreciate your business".

17. Leave the rest of the invoice as is. The invoice should look like Figure 5.12. To correct any errors, click on the field concerned and overtype or edit.

18. Click on the *Record* button to complete this invoice.

    NOTICE: Tax $3,472.50 which is 10% of the sale amount and the freight has been added to the invoice total.

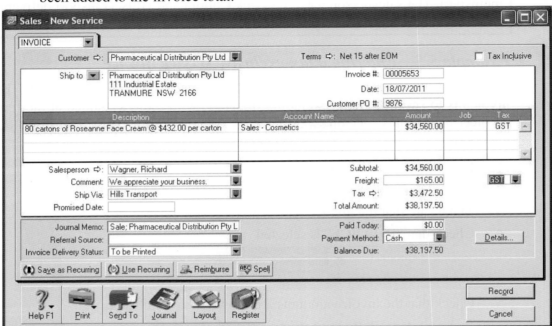

Figure 5.12: Invoice with GST exclusive amounts

Video: A video on entering Invoices directly is on the DVD

Self-test exercise 5.6

Have the file dem51.myo open.

Enter the following GST-exclusive service type invoice in July 2011:

Invoice number 5654 to Bioteam Wholesale Pty Ltd on 18/7/2011. Customer PO # is 873. Description: "50 cartons of Nature's Friend Cream @ $180.00 each plus GST". This sale is to be credited to "Sales – Cosmetics" (account 4-1100). The tax code is "GST". Freight on this invoice is $92.00 *plus* GST. Ship Via: "Road Freight". The salesperson was Gustav Mahler. Enter comment "We appreciate your Business".

Example 5.6—Entering an invoice for GST-free goods or services

Enter the following invoice for a sale to Em-Kart Pty Ltd. The invoice is to show amounts including the GST where the goods or services are taxable.

1. Have the file dem51.myo open.
2. Select the *Enter Sales* option from the *Sales* command centre.
3. Make sure that the invoice type is *Sales – New Service*.
4. Check that "INVOICE" is selected.

5. Check that the invoice amounts are to be entered as tax-inclusive.

   Make sure the checkbox 'Tax Inclusive' ☑ Tax Inclusive is ticked.
6. The customer is Em-Kart Pty Ltd. You may type in the first few letters (say "em"), use the *ENTER* key and select from a list, or use the *List* button ⬇
7. <u>TAB</u> to the 'Invoice number' field so that the 'Ship to' address remains. The invoice number should be "5655" ↵.
8. Enter the date as "21/7/2011" (or press the space bar and select the date).
9. The customer's purchase order number (#) is "848-1465" ↵.
10. Enter the description as "100 cartons of Skinpro SP 30+ Sunscreen @ $300 per carton" and TAB to the next field.
11. The account to be credited is "Sales – Sunscreens" which has an account # of "4-1200". Enter this and TAB to the amount field.
12. The amount to enter is $30,000.00. Type "100 * 300 = ".
13. The tax code is "FRE", if necessary, TAB to the 'Tax' column and change it. ↵.
14. On the second line of the invoice, enter the description as "20 cartons of Skinpro Tanning Lotion @ $220.00 including GST per carton" and TAB.
15. The account to be credited is "Sales – Sunscreens" which has an account # of "4-1200". Enter this and TAB to the amount field.
16. The amount to enter is $4,400.00 including GST. Type "20 * 220 = ".
17. Change the tax code in the 'Tax' column to "GST" (while sunscreens are GST-free, sun tanning lotions are taxable) ↵.
18. Click on the field for entering freight and enter "$103.40" including GST (the tax code for this freight should show "GST").
19. The 'Salesperson' is "Jacques Offenbach" and the goods are shipped by "Hills Transport".
20. Click on the *List* button ⬇ for the 'Comment' field and select "Thank you!".
21. Leave the rest of the invoice as is. The invoice should look like Figure 5.13 on the next page. To correct any errors, click on the field concerned and overtype or edit. Ignore any spell check regarding the product names.

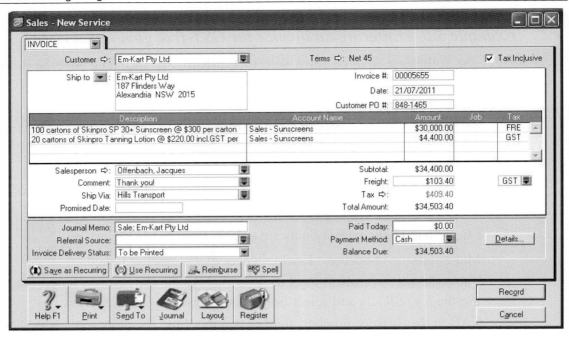

Figure 5.13: Mixed taxable and GST-free invoice

Self-test exercise 5.7

Have the file dem51.myo open.

Enter the following *service* type invoices in July 2011.

Make sure the 'Tax Inclusive' box is <u>ticked</u> for all three invoices: ☑ Tax Inclusive

Note: for all these invoices click on 'IGNORE ALL' in the spell checker.

Invoice number 5656 to Colzmier Pty Ltd on 25/7/2011. Customer PO # is C8689. Description: "95 cartons of 'Skinpro SP 30+ Sunscreen' @ $300.00 per carton". Account name to be credited is "Sales – Sunscreens" account 4-1200. Amount $28,500.00 GST-free (95 * 300). The tax code is "FRE".

Freight on this invoice is $66.00 (GST-inclusive), payable to the carrier "Hills Transport". The salesperson was "Gustav Mahler". Comment: "Thank you!".

Invoice number 5657 to Abnego Pty Ltd on 28/7/2011. Customer PO # is NZ332. Description: "130 cartons of 'SOL SP15+ Sunscreen (Export)' @ $192.00 per carton". Credit "Sales – Sunscreens" account 4-1200. Amount 130 * 192 equals $24,960.00. As this is an **export sale**, change, *if necessary*, the tax code to "EXP".

Freight on this invoice is $198.00 (GST-free, and tax code of "FRE"), payable to the carrier International. The salesperson was "Stephanie Bach". Comment: "Thank you!".

Invoice number 5658 to Francis Gilberti on 29/7/2011 for "Residential rent for August 2011". Credit "Rent Received" account 8-5000. Enter the amount as "1400" and change the tax code to "ITS". Change the memo to "Rent; Gilberti".

Mr Gilberti acts as night caretaker and rents a flat attached to the warehouse.

Make sure to use the account "Rent Received" <u>NOT</u> "Rent" (which is an expense).

Using Quotes, Orders, Invoices and the Sales Register

It may be useful to record quotations given to customers. When a customer accepts the quotation and places an order, the quotation recorded in *MYOB AccountRight Plus* can be converted to an order. A quotation does not usually create an obligation by the customer to buy – it is simply an offer by the seller to sell goods or services at given terms and conditions. An order, on the other hand, is an acceptance of a quote (verbal or written) and a commitment or an offer to buy goods or services at given terms and conditions.

The difference between quotes and orders, as far as recording the transaction in *MYOB AccountRight Plus*, is not so important when services are being supplied, as there is no inventory commitment. However, for review purposes and good management it will be useful to keep records of all outstanding quotes (not yet converted to orders) and what orders have not yet been fulfilled, delivered and invoiced within the promised time. The conversion of <u>quotes to orders</u> and <u>orders to invoices</u> can be achieved using the *Sales Register* option in the *Sales* command centre. Quotes may be converted <u>directly</u> to invoices if the quotes are accepted and goods are shipped (delivered or picked up). *Preferences* can be set up to delete quotes once converted. The *Sales Register* can also be used to review invoices, credit notes and recurring templates.

Quotes and orders are only saved when recorded <u>without</u> charging the customer and without debiting or crediting any general ledger accounts (**except** where a deposit is paid).

Quotes and orders can be kept on file until modified, deleted or converted.

How to enter a quote using the service layout

Step	Instruction
1	Select the *Sales* command centre.
2	Select the *Enter Sales* option.
3	A tick may appear in the 'Tax Inclusive' checkbox. Turn this on or off depending on whether the amounts entered are to include or exclude the GST. ☑ Tax Inclusive — Amounts to include the GST ☐ Tax Inclusive — Amounts *plus* the GST
4	Change the default "INVOICE" set up at the top of the *Sales – New Service* window to "QUOTE". QUOTE / ✔ QUOTE / ORDER / INVOICE Entering a quotation
5	Click on the 'Customer' field and enter the customer name.
6	The invoice type appears in the window title bar (e.g. *Sales – New Service*). To change a sale type, if necessary, click on the *Layout* button at the bottom of the window and select *Service* layout. Click [Layout] *(continued on the next page)*

7	Tab through to the invoice number field, change if necessary, and TAB.
8	Enter the quotation date ↵.
9	Type in the customer's reference number if it is available. You can enter other details if a number is not available - for example, "Email 14/6" and ↵.
10	Type in the description of the service to be provided and TAB. **Remember:** TAB *across* a 'line of entry' and ENTER to go to the next line.
11	Enter the account number or name for the income account to be credited and TAB. If the account number or name is *not* known, you may use ↵ or the *List* button 🔽 to list all accounts and select from the list. If using account numbers type in "4" (should be the default) and ↵ to show the income accounts. If using account names press ↵ or 🔽 and scroll down the list to the "Income" accounts. Make your selection from the list of accounts by double clicking the account, or use a single click on it and ↵ or click on the *Use Account* button.
12	Enter the amount of the line item and TAB (you do not have to enter a dollar sign or comma in money amounts). You can press the space bar to activate *MYOB Calculator* or use the keyboard to type a formula to calculate the amount if necessary. You can type using *numbers* and any of the following signs in your calculation: "+, –, * and / ". To enter the result type "=" or ↵.
13	Enter a job number if income is to be recorded for a particular job and TAB. (Refer to Chapter 9 for Jobs.)
14	Change the tax code, if necessary, and ↵.
15	Repeat steps 10 to 14 above to enter any other line items.
16	Enter any freight to be charged on the invoice in the 'Freight' field. Change the tax code for the freight, if necessary.
17	The 'Salesperson', 'Comment', 'Ship via', 'Promised Date' and 'Referral Source' fields are optional. Click on the *List* button 🔽 and select from the list or type any new entry and click on the *Easy-Add* button to add it.
18	To view or edit the terms of settlement for this quote click on ⇨ next to the 'Terms' field on top of the form. (**Note**: any changes to the terms entered here will only apply to this quote and will not affect any future sales.)
19	Change the 'Journal Memo:' to add the word "quote", if necessary.
20	Select the *Save Quote* button.

Example 5.7—Entering a quote given to a customer

Enter the following quotation for a sale to Maureen Devlin. Our invoices show amounts including the GST (Tax Inclusive) where the goods or services are taxable.

1. Have the file dem51.myo open.

2. Select the *Sales* command centre.

3. Select the *Enter Sales* option.

4. Click on the drop-down arrow next to *INVOICE* and select "QUOTE".

5. Check that the figures entered in to the amount column are to be printed as tax inclusive where GST is applicable.

6. The customer is "Maureen Devlin". You may type in the first few letters i.e. "de", use the ENTER key or use the *List* button ▤ and select from a list.
   Remember: if the customer is an *individual* the name is sorted in <u>surname</u> order (i.e. filed under Devlin not Maureen).

7. Make sure that the invoice type at the top is *Sales – New Service*. If necessary, click on the *Layout* button, at the bottom of the form, select *Service* and click *OK*.

8. The 'Invoice' number should be "5659". (If necessary, TAB to the 'Invoice number' and change it.) ↵.
   (**Note:** You can change the number if you wish to keep a different sequence for quotations or orders.)

9. Enter the date as "4/7/2011". If the date in the date field is a date in July 2011, you only have to type '4' and ↵. Alternatively, you can activate *MYOB Calender* by pressing the space bar and select the date.

10. As this is only a quotation, skip the 'Customer PO #' field press ↵ or TAB.

11. In the description field enter:
    "40 cartons of Skinpro Tanning Lotion @ $209.00 each incl. GST"
    and TAB to the next field.

12. The account to be credited is "Sales – Sunscreens" (account # 4-1200).
    Enter this account name or number and TAB to the amount field.

13. The amount to enter is $8,360.00 (you may type "8360" or "40 * 209 =").

14. TAB to the 'Tax' column and change it, if necessary, to "GST" ↵.

15. Click on the 'Freight' field and enter $100. The tax code for this freight should show "GST". This freight charge is only an <u>estimated</u> amount at this stage (the <u>exact</u> amount will be obtained from the shipping company once the quote is accepted).

16. The 'Salesperson' is "Albert Dvorak" and the goods will probably be shipped by "Hills Transport". No comment is necessary at this stage.

17. Click on the *List* button ▤ for the 'Referral Source:' field and select "Internet".

18. Change the 'Memo:' to read "Quote; Devlin, Maureen".
    The Quote should look like Figure 5.14 on the next page – check your answer.

19. To correct any errors, click on the field concerned and overtype or edit.

20. Click on the *Save Quote* button to save it on file.

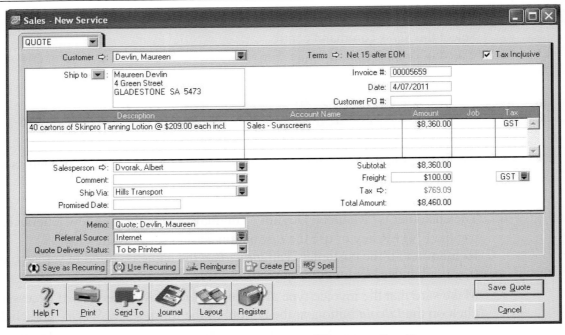

Figure 5.14: Quotation given to a customer: Maureen Devlin

Video: A video on entering Quotes, Orders and Invoices is on the DVD

Self-test exercise 5.8

Have the file dem51.myo open.

Enter a quote (#5660 dated 7 July 08) to "Anzamate". The quote is for "200 cartons SOL SP 15+ Sunscreen @ $180 per carton". Credit account "Sales – Sunscreens" (4-1200). Amount (200 * 180 = 36,000). The tax code is "EXP".
Freight is expected to be about $200.00, tax code "FRE". Ship via: "International".
Salesperson: "Stephanie Bach" and the Referral source: "Dealer/Consultant".

If the tax code is "FRE" or "EXP", it does not matter whether the checkbox 'Tax Inclusive' is ticked or not. If it *is* ticked the amount will include a tax amount of $0.00. and if it is not ticked the amount will be *plus* $0.00 tax!

Quotes and Orders Preferences

Quotes and Orders once saved can be modified, deleted or converted. A Quote can either be converted to an Order or to an Invoice. An Order can be converted to an Invoice.

The conversion of quotes and orders can be <u>controlled</u> through the sales preferences (*Setup/Preferences/Sales*). In the following exercise, the authors have set up the sales preferences in regard to quotes and orders as follows:

☑ Retain Original Invoice Number on Backorders [System-wide]
☑ Retain Original Invoice Number when Quotes Change to Orders or Invoices [System-wide]
☑ Delete Quotes upon Changing to and Recording as an Order or Invoice [System-wide]

This means that the invoice number is set to be the same number when quotes and orders are converted. Quotes are set to be deleted once converted to an order or to an invoice. Orders, on the other hand, will always be deleted when converted to invoices regardless of the preferences!

Changing a quote to an order

When a customer accepts a quote and places an order, the quote recorded in the *MYOB AccountRight Plus* file can be converted to an order.

How to change a quote to an order

Step	Instruction
1	Select the *Sales* command centre.
2	Select the *Sales Register* option.
3	Click on the *Quotes* tab at the top of the *Sales Register* window.
4	Make sure that the 'From' and 'To' dates are for the period you want.
5	You can set the 'Search by:' field to "All Customers" or a specific customer.
6	Select (highlight) the quote to be converted to an order.
7	Click on the *Change to Order* button (bottom left).
8	Edit any field (for example, "Invoice #", date and 'Customer PO #' or any other changes to the original quote that is agreed upon by the buyer and the seller). **Note:** you can set the *Preferences* (Setup/Preferences/Sales) to retain the same Invoice numbers as used in Quotes when converting.
9	Click on the *Record* button to save the order.

Example 5.8—Changing a quote given to Maureen Devlin to an order

1. Have the file dem51.myo open.
2. Select the *Sales* command centre.
3. Select the *Sales Register* option.
4. Select the *Quotes* tab at the top of the *Sales Register* window.
5. Set the date from "1/7/2011" to "31/7/2011" and 'Search by:' to "All Customers".
6. The quote to Maureen Devlin entered earlier will be highlighted (selected) as shown in Figure 5.15 on the next page.
7. Click on the *Change to Order* button.
8. The Invoice # should be "5659" ↵.
9. Change the date of the order to "25/7/2011" ↵.
10. Click on the 'Customer PO #:' field and enter the customer order # "453" ↵.
11. Click on the 'Journal Memo:' field and edit it to: "Order; Devlin, Maureen".

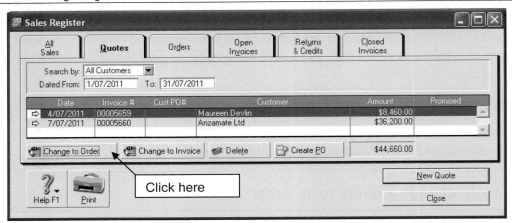

Figure 5.15: The *Sales Register* showing Quote to Maureen Devlin highlighted

12.　The Order will look like Figure 5.16:

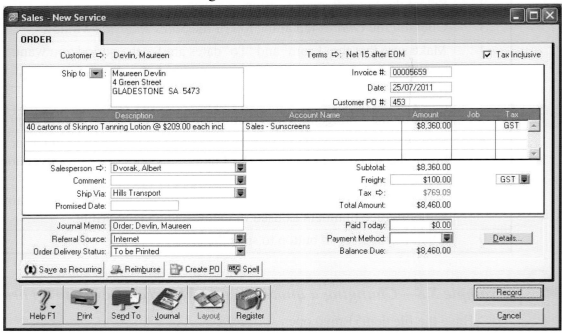

Figure 5.16: Quote now changed to an Order

13.　Click on the *Record* button to save the order on file.

14.　Click on *Ignore All* in the spell checker. (**Note:** You can also select *Add* if you wish.)

15.　Click on the *Cancel* button to close the *Sales – New Service* window and you will be returned to the *Sales Register* window.

16.　Select the *Orders* tab and check the order you have just recorded:

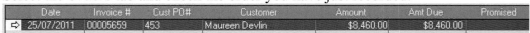

17.　Click on the *Close* button to finish with the *Sales Register*.

 Video: A video on changing Quotes and Orders is on the DVD

Chapter 5: Accounts receivable

Self-test exercise 5.9

Have the file dem51.myo open.

The quote given to Anzamate Ltd on 7 July is accepted and Anzamate Ltd places Order # "A1098" based on the quote. Change the *quote* to an *order* on 26/7/11 with the same invoice number "5660". Update the 'Journal Memo' to "Order; Anzmate Ltd". Change the 'Freight' to "$204.50", which was acceptable to Anzamate Ltd, and *Record* the order.

Changing an order to an invoice

When goods or services that have been ordered are delivered and invoiced, the order recorded in *MYOB AccountRight Plus* can be changed to an invoice.

How to change an order to an invoice

Step	Instruction
1	Select the *Sales* command centre.
2	Select the *Sales Register* option.
3	Click on the *Orders* tab at the top of the *Sales Register* window.
4	You can set the 'Search by:' field to "All Customers" or a specific customer.
5	Make sure that the 'From' and 'To' dates are for the period you want.
6	Select (highlight) the order to be converted to an invoice.
7	Click on the *Change to Invoice* button.
8	Edit any field (for example, 'Invoice #', date and 'Customer PO #').
9	Click on the *Record* button to save the invoice.

Example 5.9—Changing an order from Maureen Devlin to an invoice

1. Have the file dem51.myo open.
2. Select the *Sales* command centre.
3. Select the *Sales Register* option.
4. Select the *Orders* tab at the top of the *Sales Register* window.
5. Make sure the date criteria is 'Dated From' "1/7/2011" 'To' "31/7/2011" and the 'Search By:' field is set to "All Customers".
6. The order from Maureen Devlin entered earlier will be highlighted (selected) as shown in Figure 5.17 on the next page.
7. Click on the *Change to Invoice* button.
8. The Invoice # should be "5659". Change it if necessary.
9. Change the date to "30/7/2011" and the freight amount to "$118.80" including "GST", which was accepted by Maureen Devlin.

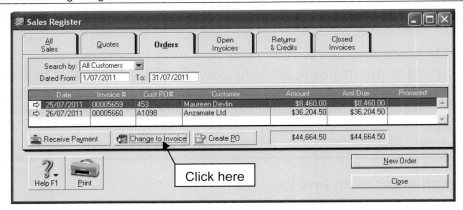

Figure 5.17: The *Sales Register* window showing Orders on file

10. Click on the 'Journal Memo:' field and edit to "Sale; Devlin, Maureen". The Invoice should look like Figure 5.18.

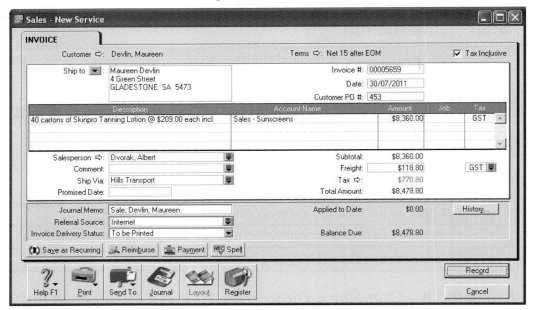

Figure 5.18: Order now changed to an Invoice

11. Click on the *Record* button to save the invoice.

12. Click on *Ignore All* in the spell checker and Ignore date message, click *OK*.

13. Click on the *Cancel* button to close the *Sales – New Service* window and you will be returned to the *Sales Register* window.

14. Click on the *Close* button to finish with the *Sales Register*.

Self-test exercise 5.10

Have the file dem51.myo open.
Goods ordered by Anzamate Ltd are now despatched and invoiced. Change the order recorded for Anzamate to an invoice – dated 30/7/2011 (same invoice# 5660). Ignore any warning regarding spelling or pre-date – click *Ignore All* or *OK*.

> **Note:**
> You have probably realised that you can enter an order without having first entered a quote – that is, for example, customers who are buying goods and/or services from a set price list will not have to obtain a quote first before they place an order. The entry is the same as for an invoice except for selecting ORDER before entering. The order can be changed to an invoice as was done in the previous example and self-test exercise.

Cash received from customers (accounts receivable)

This is **MOST IMPORTANT**.

To record money received from a debtor (a customer) you use the *Receive Payments* option in the *Sales* command centre. **DO NOT** use the *Receive Money* option in the *Banking* command centre. Using the *Receive Payments* option will record the receipt and update the customer's record as well as updating the account receivable control account.

Listen Mate:
*The bloke says this is **important!***
Make a note – or forever hold your peace!

How to record a receipt from a customer (accounts receivable)

Step	Instruction
1	Select the *Sales* command centre.
2	Select the *Receive Payments* Option.
3	Enter the customer's name. Either type in the first few letters or tap the Enter key and select from a *List* ▼ ↵.
4	Enter the amount received ↵.
5	Use the *List* button 🔳 and select a payment method (or type the first few letters of the method) ↵.
6	Click on the *Details* button and enter in the details relating to the method of payment. Click the *OK* button to record the payment details ↵.
7	Change the memo if necessary and/or ↵.
8	Leave the ID# (a cash receipt reference number) as shown ↵.
9	Enter the date ↵.
10	Select an option button for either depositing into a bank account or, if more than one receipt on the day, debiting them to "Undeposited Funds" first.
11	Tab to the last column and apply the amount against the correct invoice(s) (in this chapter, an "open item" system of accounts receivable is used).
12	Make sure the 'Finance Charges' field is zero unless a charge for late payment is being made.
13	Click on the *Record* button.

Example 5.10—Entering a payment received from a customer

1. Open the file dem51.myo (if not already open).

2. From the *Sales* command centre select the *Receive Payments* option.

3. For the *Deposit to Account* option select "Corporate Bank" (account #1-1110).

4. Select Abacus Pty Ltd as the 'Customer' (type "aba" or use the *List* button ⬇ and select from the list) and press ↵ twice.

5. Click in the 'Amount Received' field and enter $24,621.20 ↵.

6. Abacus Pty Ltd has paid by cheque. In the 'Payment Method' field type "ch" or use the *List* button ⬇ to select "Cheque" as the payment method.

7. Click on the *Details* button and enter in the details: BSB 337-765, account name "ABACUS PTY LTD", Account No. 67105567 and cheque No. 145987. The payment method details will look like Figure 5.19:

BSB:	337-765
Account Name:	ABACUS PTY LTD
Account No.:	67105567	Cheque No.:	145987

Figure 5.19: Cheque details for payment from Abacus Pty Ltd

8. Click on the *OK* button to complete cheque details ↵↵↵ .

9. Leave the memo as is ↵.

10. Leave the 'ID#' (a cash receipt reference number) as shown on the screen ↵.

11. Enter the date as "4/7/2011" ↵.

12. Click in the 'Amount Applied' column so that $24,621.20 appears applied against invoice number 5637 dated 18 May 2011 and ↵.
    (Make sure after pressing Enter the 'Out of Balance' and 'Finance Charge' show $0.00.)

13. Click on the *Record* button if your screen looks like Figure 5.20 on the next page.

Video: A video on entering customer payments is on the DVD

Self-test exercise 5.11

Have the file dem51.myo open.

Enter the following payments received from customers in July. Deposit these direct to the Corporate Bank account 1-1110.

Date	Customer	Payment Method	Amount	Apply To Invoice #
7/7/2011	Colzmier Pty Ltd (BSB 299-218, Account No 4312666)	Cheque 288341	$21,148.50	5642
8/7/2011	Abacus Pty Ltd (BSB 337-765, Account No. 67105567)	Cheque 146018	$3,248.63	5650
14/7/2011	Em-Kart Pty Ltd (BSB 466-608, Account No. 47713345)	Cheque 312889	$25,290.60	5643

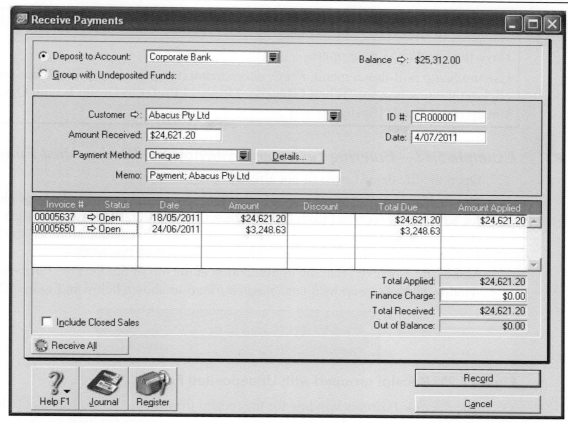

Figure 5.20: Customer payment applied to invoice

Using the Undeposited Funds facility

In real life a business may have a number of receipts <u>in a single day</u>, including cheques, cash and credit cards. These receipts are usually grouped and put into the bank in a single deposit. This is achieved in *MYOB AccountRight Plus* by debiting receipts to a temporary account that is called "Undeposited Funds". Once all of the day's receipts are entered, the *Prepare Bank Deposit* option is used to credit the "Undeposited Funds" account and debit a single amount representing the actual deposit to the bank account on that day. This single entry in the general ledger bank account can then be reconciled to the deposit that will appear on the statement received from the bank.

The 'How to …' instructions on page 5-35 still apply, with the debit going to "Undeposited Funds" account instead of directly into the bank account.

It is a good idea to make the "Undeposited Funds" account the default – that is, to set up the preferences so that all money received will be put into "Undeposited Funds" unless this default is changed. Full instructions can be found in the 'How to set up Undeposited Funds as the default' in Chapter 4.

Self-test exercise 5.12

Have the file dem51.myo open.

Use the *Setup* pull-down menu, *Preferences* menu item, *Banking* preferences and click on the tick box for 'When I Receive Money, I Prefer to Group It with Other Undeposited Funds [System-wide]'.

Example 5.11—Entering customer payments into "Undeposited Funds"

1. Open the file dem51.myo (if not already open).

2. Use the *Receive Payments* option in the *Sales* command centre and record cheque for $31,768.00 received from David James Ltd on 28/7/2011 paying invoice 5652 (Cheque details: BSB 457-238, Account No. 2143355, Cheque Number 409111). Follow the instructions on the previous pages to record this receipt.

    Make sure, however, that the option button at the top of the *Receive Payments* window shows *Group with Undeposited Funds* as shown below in Figure 5.21:

Figure 5.21: Receipt grouped with Undeposited Funds

3. The *Receive Payment* window for the receipt from David James Ltd should look like Figure 5.22:

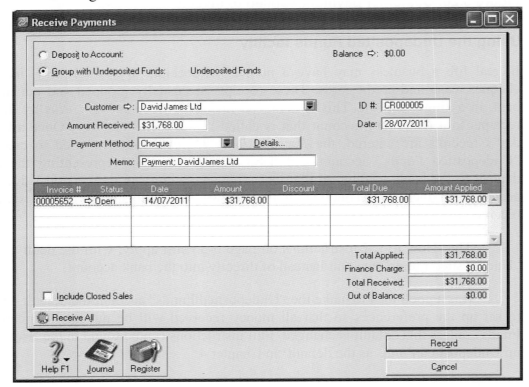

Figure 5.22: Payment from David James grouped with Undeposited Funds

4. Click in the 'Amount Applied' column to apply the amount to Invoice 5652 and ⏎.

5. Make sure 'Out of Balance' and 'Freight Charge' both show $0.00.

6. Click on the *Record* button but do not click *Cancel* in order to record the next receipt.

7. Record a second customer payment received from Colzmier Pty Ltd on the same day i.e. 28/7/2011 by a cheque for $37,702.50 (Cheque details: BSB 299-218, Account No. 4312666 – Cheque # 288395). Apply this amount to Invoice # 5651.

8. Make sure that the option button at the top of the *Receive Payments* window is still set to *Group with Undeposited Funds* (account 1-1180).

9. Click on the *Record* button if the *Receive Payment* window for the cheque received from Colzmier Pty Ltd looks like Figure 5.23 below:

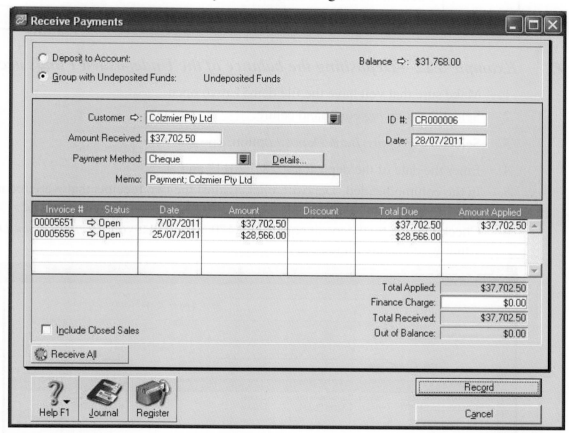

Figure 5.23: Payment from Colzmier grouped with Undeposited Funds

10. Click *Cancel.*

Preparing a bank deposit

The two cheques received and recorded in Example 5.11 above totalling $69,470.50 were debited to account 1-1180 "Undeposited Funds" (you can check this by going to the *Accounts* command centre, *Accounts List* option and looking at the balance of this account in the *Assets* section). This amount needs to be deposited at the bank. A deposit is recorded by using the *Prepare Bank Deposit* option in the *Banking* command centre.

How to prepare a bank deposit

Step	Instruction
1	Select the *Banking* command centre.
2	Select the *Prepare Bank Deposit* option.
3	Enter the date of the deposit ↵.
4	In the column headed 'Deposit', click against the receipts that are to be deposited at the bank.
5	Check that the 'Total Deposit Amount' at the bottom, is correct.
6	Click on the *Record* button.
7	Click on the *Cancel* button to close the window.

Example 5.12—Depositing the balance of the Undeposited Funds account

1. Make sure that you have the file dem51.myo open.

2. Select the *Banking* command centre.

3. Select the *Prepare Bank Deposit* option. | Prepare Bank Deposit |

4. Enter the date of the deposit as "28/7/2011" and ↵.

5. In the column headed 'Deposit', click against the two receipts that were recorded previously in Example 5.11.

6. Check that the total deposit equals $69,470.50 and that your *Prepare Bank Deposit* window looks like Figure 5.24:

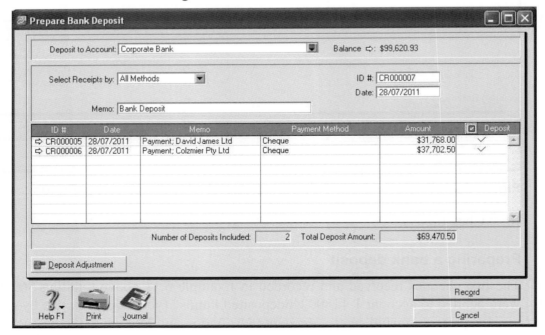

Figure 5.24: Undeposited Funds now deposited at bank

7. Before recording the deposit, select the *Edit* pull-down menu and *Recap Transaction* menu item and examine the entries that will be posted in the general ledger. The transaction should look like Figure 5.25:

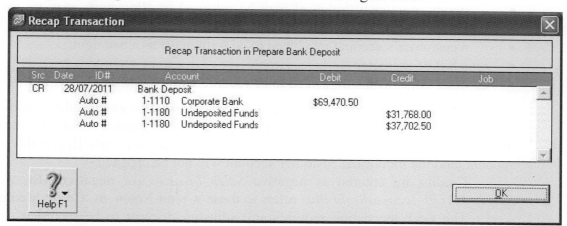

Figure 5.25: Recap Transaction showing how Undeposited Funds are transferred to Corporate Bank as a single deposit

8. Click *OK* to close the *Recap Transaction* window.

9. Click on the *Record* button and then click on the *Cancel* button to exit.

Video: A video on preparing a bank deposit is on the DVD

Self-test exercise 5.13

Have the file dem51.myo open.
Enter the following cheques received from customers on 30/7/2011.
Record these through the "Undeposited Funds" account (account number 1-1180) :

Customer	Cheque Number	Amount	Apply To Invoice #
Bioteam Wholesale Ltd (BSB 608-113, Account No. 48761233)	109667	$10,001.20	5654
Francis Gilberti (BSB 476-881, Account No. 22728791)	200228	$1,400.00	5658

Prepare a single deposit ($11,401.20) to bank these two cheques as at 30/7/2011.

Memo:
Cash discounts for early settlement can be set on the customer's card. If a payment is received within the specified period, *MYOB AccountRight* will automatically calculate not only the amount of discount allowed, but also the refund of the *proportion* of any GST charged on the <u>original</u> sale. A Credit Note (Credit Memo) is also automatically generated and applied to the relevant sale.

Credits to customer accounts

There are many reasons why a credit may be required on a customer's account:

- goods previously invoiced may be returned or allowances may be given for damaged, overcharge or incorrect goods;
- a customer's account may need to be written off as a bad debt;
- a bill of exchange (bills receivable) may have to be recorded; *or*
- other adjustments may need to be recorded.

All credits involving a receivables account *must* be entered through the *Sales* command centre. A common error is to use the general journal – but this means that the entry will only be recorded to the general ledger Accounts Receivable control account, and the individual customer account will not be credited.

Credits are entered as negative *Sales Invoices* (or negative *Miscellaneous Sales*). *MYOB AccountRight Plus* refers to these 'Credit Notes' as 'Credit Memos'.

The GST legislation requires any adjustment event to be recorded using an 'Adjustment Note', except where the GST effect of discount is clearly shown on a Tax Invoice.

It is important to enter annotation in the memo that describes the purpose for the credit, as it is this memo that will be printed on a customer's statement.

Once a 'Credit Note' has been recorded it must *either*:

(a) be **applied** against the relevant (original) invoice(s) *or*

(b) **refunded** to the customer.

To do this you use the *Sales Register* option in the *Sales* command centre.

 How to write out a credit note (negative invoice)

Step	Instruction
1	Select the *Sales* command centre.
2	Select the *Enter Sales* option.
3	Set the 'Tax Inclusive' check box depending on whether GST is included in the amount or the amount is GST-exclusive. ☑ Tax Inclusive ☐ Tax Inclusive Amount Includes GST Excludes GST (Amount plus GST)
4	"INVOICE" should be the default set up at the top of the *Sales – New Service* window. INVOICE ← Entering a *negative* invoice Customer :
5	Click on the 'Customer' field and enter the customer name. Type in the first few letters or use the *List* button ▼ and select a customer from the list.
6	The invoice type appears in the window title bar. To change a sale type, click on the *Layout* button at the bottom of the Sales window. Select a *Service* layout if a copy of the credit needs to be printed for the customer; alternatively, if a print is not required then select a *Miscellaneous* layout.
	(continued on the next page)

Step	Instruction
7	Enter a credit note number ↵.
8	Enter a date ↵.
9	Type in a description of the credit, making reference to the original invoice involved and TAB to the account number field.
10	Type in the account name or number to be debited and TAB.
11	Enter the amount as a <u>minus</u> (you may type a formula to calculate the amount but start with a minus sign and complete the calculation with an "=" sign or ↵ to enter the negative amount).
12	TAB and change the tax code *if necessary*.
13	Type in a sensible memo – for example, "Credit for overcharge" – and change any other optional field as necessary.
14	Click on the *Record* button.

Memo:
Enter a negative *quantity* instead of a negative amount when using *Item* invoices to record item returns. This will update the inventory item count and calculate the negative amount for the credit note. Refer to Chapter 7.

Example 5.13—Creating a negative invoice credit note

1. Make sure that you have the file dem51.myo open.
2. Select the *Enter Sales* option from the *Sales* command centre.
3. Enter the customer as "Colzmier Pty Ltd" – you only need to type in "co".
4. As a copy of this credit note needs to be printed make sure the layout is set to "Service". *Sales – New Service* should be displayed in the title bar above.
5. TAB to the 'Invoice #' field and enter "CN100" ↵.
6. Type in "28/7/2011" as the date ↵.
7. Type in "DN836-24" in the 'Customer PO#' field ↵. (This is their Debit Note #.)
8. Enter a description as "Return of 5 cartons Skinpro SP 30+ @ $300 per carton".
9. TAB to 'Account Name' column and enter the account to be debited "Sales-Sunscreens" account number 4-1200. TAB to the next column.
10. Type in the amount, start with a **minus** sign, as " –1500" or type " – 5 * 300 = ".
11. If necessary, TAB to the 'Tax' column and enter a tax code of "FRE" ↵.
12. The salesperson is Gustav Mahler. No 'Comment' or 'Ship Via' entries.
13. Click on the 'Journal Memo:' field and enter: "Returns from Colzmier Pty Ltd" ↵.
14. Your credit note should look like Figure 5.26.
15. Make sure the 'Total Amount' is negative either as "–$1,500.00" or ($1,500.00).
16. Click on the *Record* button (ignore any spelling errors for the product names).

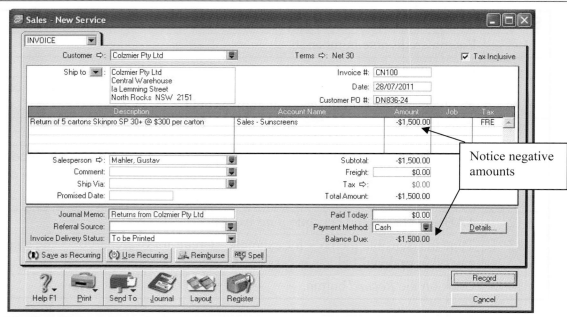

Figure 5.26: Credit note to Colzmier Pty Ltd for returns

Video: A video on preparing a credit note (negative invoice) is on the DVD

Self-test exercise 5.14

Have the file dem51.myo open.

A quarterly volume rebate for the quarter ended 31 July 2011 is to be credited to Em-Kart Pty Ltd. The date is 31/7/2011, the 'Invoice #' is "CN101" (no customer P.O.) and the total rebate amount is $4,715.70. This rebate relates to two products:

- $3,685.00 incl. tax is for a rebate relating to cosmetic sales – debit account "Sales – Cosmetics" account number 4-1100, (tax code "GST").

- The balance of the rebate, $1,030.70, is relating to sunscreen sales – debit account "Sales – Sunscreen" account number 4-1200 (tax code "FRE").

Remember to enter the amounts as negative and the total is negative –$4,715.70. The salesperson is Jacques Offenbach. As a copy of this credit note is required to be printed and sent to the customer, use a *Service* layout.

When an *Open Item* system is used (the most usual case), a credit or adjustment to an account must either be:

(a)   applied against the open invoice involved so as to reduce its balance, *or*

(b)   refunded to the customer if the invoice involved has already been paid.

How to settle a credit

Step	Instruction
1	Select *Sales Register* option from the *Sales* command centre.
2	Click on the *Returns & Credits* tab at the top of the *Sales Register* window.
3	Highlight the credit to be settled to select it.
4	If the amount is to be refunded, click on the *Pay Refund* icon at the foot of the window and complete the resulting cheque – make sure to change cheque number and date as necessary.
OR	
5	If the credit is to be applied against an invoice (matched), click on the *Apply to Sale* button and enter the amount in the 'Applied' column against the correct invoice. Change the date if necessary (to be the same date as the credit note).

Example 5.14—Credit note applied against invoice

1. Open the *MYOB AccountRight Plus* file dem51.myo.
2. Select the *Sales* command centre.
3. Select the *Sales Register* and click on the *Returns & Credits* tab.
4. The credit for Colzmier Pty Ltd should be highlighted in the window of the *Sales Register* as shown in Figure 5.27:

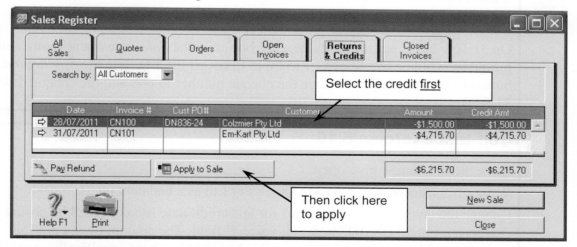

Figure 5.27: Colzmier credit selected

5. Click on the *Apply to Sale* button.
6. Enter the date as "28/7/2011" – same date as the credit note.
7. Click in the 'Amount Applied' column for invoice number 5656 so that the credit of $1,500 is applied against that invoice and press ↵.
8. If the *Settle Returns and Credits* window looks like Figure 5.28 on the next page, click on the *Record* button and then the *Close* button to close the *Sales Register*.

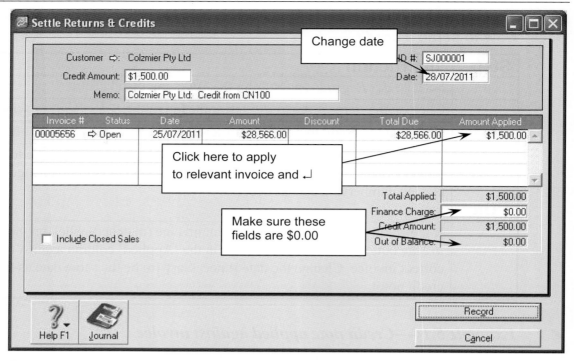

Figure 5.28: Credit applied against an open invoice

 Video: A video on applying or refunding a credit note is on the DVD

Self-test exercise 5.15

Have the file dem51.myo open.

On 31 July 2011, use the *Sales Register* option in the *Sales* command centre and refund the volume rebate of $4,715.70 to Em-Kart Pty Ltd. Use the *Pay Refund* button to issue a cheque. Change the cheque number to 668 and the cheque date to 31/7/2011.

Self-test exercise 5.16

Have the file dem51.myo open.

Write off the account of Kiss Me Quick Pty Ltd as a bad debt on 31/7/2011.

Change the layout to *Miscellaneous* for this credit note (no copy will be posted to the customer). Enter "CN102" in the 'Invoice #' field. The amount owing is $558 including GST (tax code "GST"). As this bad debt has been specifically considered when setting the allowance for doubtful debts, the account to debit is the "Allowance for Doubtful Debts" account (account number 1-1220) – a warning will be given that sales are usually credited to an income account. Click *OK*.

Use the *Sales Register* option, *Returns & Credits* tab, in the *Sales* command centre and apply this credit against Invoice# 3849, enter date as "31/7/2011".

Make this customer's card inactive. Open the card for editing and tick on the check box for 'Inactive Card' ☑ Inactive Card in the *Profile* window of the card and click *OK*.

Printing or emailing invoices

With *MYOB AccountRight* several options exist for printing (or emailing) sales forms. A *Review Sales Before Delivery* window allows various combinations of selections.

 How to print or email an invoice

Step	Instruction
1	Select the *Sales* command centre.
2	Select the *Print/Email Invoices* option. A *Review Sales Before Delivery* window appears with two tabs – *To Be Printed* and *To Be Emailed*.
3	<u>To print an invoice:</u> Select the *To Be Printed* tab to display all invoices that have been set to be printed.
4	Click on the *Advance Filters* button.
5	In the *Advanced Filters* window make the necessary selections such as: • Select a particular customer *or* "All Customers" • Select a 'Sale Type' such as "Service", "Item", "Professional" etc. • Select a Sales Status such as 'Open', 'Closed', 'All Sales', 'Quotes' etc. • Tick or clear the tick for 'Unprinted or Unsent Sales Only' to hide or display invoices that have already been printed or emailed. • You can specify specific sales by a date range and/or by invoice numbers. • Note: If not sure un-tick all boxes and select "All Sales" Select a form layout – Click on the *List* button 📄 next to the 'Selected Form for Sale:' field and select the print form required for an invoice to be printed (or emailed) from the resulting list. Click *OK* to close the *Advance Filters* window.
6	Enter the number of copies to be printed of each selected invoice, packing slips and labels (TAB or ↵ after each entry).
7	Tick any invoice listed that you do want to print. To print ALL, use the *tick-all* ☑ button above the tick column to select (or de-select) *all* invoices.
8	Click the *Print* button to print or the *Cancel* button to cancel the printing.
9	**OR** <u>To email an invoice:</u> Select the *To Be Emailed* tab to display all invoices that have been set to be emailed.
10	Click on the *Advance Filters* button and repeat step 5 above for the invoices to be emailed.
11	Tick any invoice listed that you do want to email. Use the *tick-all* ☑ button above the tick column to select or de-select *all* invoices.
	(continued on the next page)

Step	Instruction
12	Click on the invoices to be emailed one at a time and check for <u>each</u> invoice:
	• The email address (change if necessary)
	• Add a subject and a message (or change the default ones).
	Repeat for all other invoices to be emailed.
13	Click the *Send Email* button to email all the ticked invoices else click *Cancel*.

Example 5.15—Printing a customer invoice

1. Open the *MYOB AccountRight Plus* file dem51.myo.

2. Select the *Sales* command centre.

3. Select the *Print/Email Invoices* option. A *Review Sales Before Delivery* window will be displayed. Select the *To Be Printed* tab.

4. Click on the *Advanced Filters* button to open the *Advance Filters* window.

5. Select customer: "Em-Kart Pty Ltd".

6. Select the 'Sales Type' as "Service" and the 'Sale Status' as "Open".

7. As this invoice was not printed before, leave the box for 'Unprinted' ticked. **Note**: you will need to clear this box if you wish to re-print this invoice for whatever reason.

8. Click on the *List* button ⬇ for "Selected Form for Sale" and select "AccountRight Plus's Plain Paper Invoice" as the *invoice form* to use, as shown in Figure 5.29:

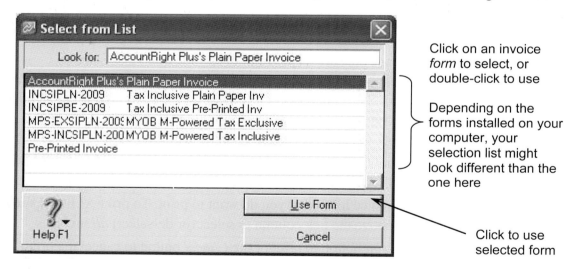

Figure 5.29: Selecting the invoice form to use

9. If your *Advanced Filters* window looks like Figure 5.30 on the next page, click on the *OK* button to return to the *Review Sales Before Delivery* window.

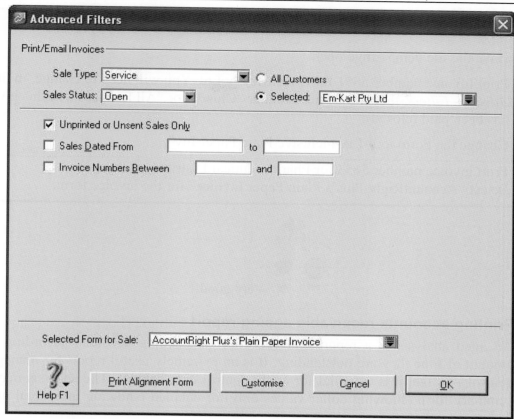

Figure 5.30: The *Advanced Filters* window

10. Tick the invoice to be printed # 5655 for Em-Kart Pty Ltd.

11. If your screen looks like Figure 5.31, click on the *Print* button.

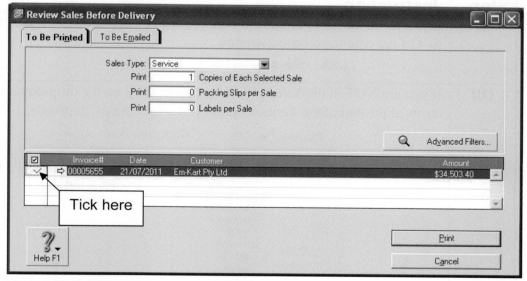

Figure 5.31: Invoice number 5655 selected to be printed

Video: A video on printing customer invoice is on the DVD

Self-test exercise 5.17

Have the file dem51.myo open.

Print Invoice number 5651 for Colzmier Pty Ltd. You will need to change, in the *Advance Filters*, the Sale Status to either "Closed" or "All Invoices", as this invoice has been paid (closed).

Change the Form to: "Tax-inclusive Plain Paper Inv".

Print invoice number 5653 for Pharmaceutical Distribution Pty Ltd.
Select "AccountRight Plus's Plain Paper Invoice" for the invoice form.

Very good!!

Printing accounts receivable ageing report

An aged analysis is a report that classifies outstanding accounts according to the amount of time they are outstanding. It is an extremely useful report for management control – in fact it is essential for credit control over debtors. The analysis may be in summary form (showing dollar values only) or detailed (showing individual invoices and credit notes).

How to print accounts receivable ageing report

Step	Instruction
1	If you are in the *Sales* command centre, click on the *Reports* option at the foot of the command centre window. Click → Reports ▼
OR	If you are NOT in the *Sales* command centre, click on the drop-down list arrow at the end of the *Reports* option and select "Sales" reports. Reports ▼ ← Click drop-down arrow Accounts Banking GST/Sales Tax Sales ← Sales reports selected Time Billing Purchases Payroll Inventory Card File Custom
2	Select the report from the resulting list of "Sales" reports. Select either "Ageing Summary" or "Ageing Detail".
3	Click on the *Customise* button.
	(continued on the next page)

Step	Instruction
4	Select the customers to be included in the report. By default "All" customers are selected. If necessary, click on the 'Customers:' *List* button ⊟ and select the customers to be included. Similarly you can make selections from the three custom lists.
5	In the *Advanced Filters* window enter the report date, customer card identifiers and the ageing method. Click on the relevant fields or their down arrows to change the selections as necessary. For example: To print an "Ageing Summary" report for "all" customers as at "31/7/2011" and using the "number of days from invoice date" as the ageing method, your screen should look like Figure 5.32.
6	In the *Report Fields* window select the fields to be included in the report by checking the fields on the left pane. The selected fields will be listed on the right pane.
7	In the *Finishing* window select the inclusion of any of the following: • $0.00 balances; • Company Name and Address; • Report Date.
8	Click on the *Display* button to see the report on screen (you may need to maximise the window and use the scroll bars to examine the report).
9	Click on the *Print* button to send the report to the printer.

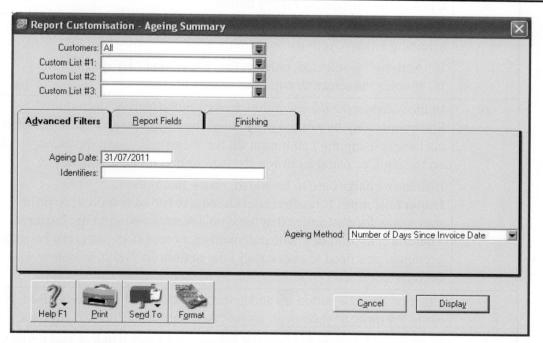

Figure 5.32: Report Customisation for Ageing Summary using invoice terms

Self-test exercise 5.18

Have the file dem51.myo open.

Print a receivables ageing summary report for all customers at 31 July 2011. Use the "Number of Days Since Invoice Date" as the ageing method.

Do not include customers with $0.00 balances.

Printing accounts receivable statements

A normal business practice is to issue statements to accounts receivable at least once a month. Statements may be printed for all customers, a selected customer or a group of customers with the same identifier.

There are two types of statements: 'Invoice' or 'Activity'. The *Invoice* type lists all open invoices and their outstanding balances. The *Activity* type lists all transactions for the customer in the given date range.

How to print/email a statement for an account receivable

Step	Instruction
1	Select the *Sales* command centre.
2	Select the *Print/Email Statements* option.
3	Statements can be printed, emailed (or printed *and* emailed) In the *Review Statements Before Delivery* window select either the "*To Be Printed*" or the "*To Be Emailed*" tab.
4	Click on the *Advanced Filters* button.
5	Select the 'Statement Type' by pointing to the drop-down arrow and selecting either "Activity" or "Invoice". If "Activity" is selected, enter in the 'From' and 'To' dates. If "Invoice" is selected, enter the statement date.
6	In the *Advanced Filters* window make your selections as required. Statements may be printed or emailed for a single customer or selected customers using the *List* button ▤ for 'Selected', using the *identifier* field on the card, or using a *custom list* (see setting up cards earlier). If finance charges are to be added, check that option. **Important note:** It is often considered a waste of resources to print statements for customers that have no amounts owing to the business. Therefore, to print or email statements for customers with <u>zero balance accounts</u>, you need to check (tick) the option: *Include Customers with Zero Balances*.
7	Click on the *List* button ▤ and select the statement form to be used. If not using Pre-printed statement, select "AccountRight Plus's Plain Paper" form.
8	Click the *OK* button to close the *Advanced Filters* window and return to the *Review Statements Before Delivery* window.
	(continued on the next page)

Step	Instruction
9	Make sure that the customers whose statements that you need printed or emailed are ticked and for all the others the ticks are turned off (cleared).
10	Enter number of statements to be printed per customer if you are printing or check and edit as necessary email addresses, subjects and messages if emailing.
11	Click on the *Print* or the *Send Email* button to print or email selected statements.

Example 5.16—Printing a single statement

1. The *MYOB AccountRight Plus* file is dem51.myo.
2. Select the *Sales* command centre.
3. Select the *Print/Email Statements* option.
4. Click on the *Advanced Filters*   Q Advanced Filters... button.
5. Click on the drop-down box for the 'Statement Type' field and select "Activity" as the statement type.
6. The statement is for the month of July 2011. Enter the 'From:' date as "1/7/2011" and the 'to:' date as "31/7/2011".
7. Click on the option button for *Selected* and use the *List* button ▼ to select the customer: "Colzmier Pty Ltd".
8. Click on the *List* button ▣ for 'Selected Form For Statement' and select "AccountRight Plus's Plain Paper Statement" as shown in Figure 5.33 and click *Use Form*.

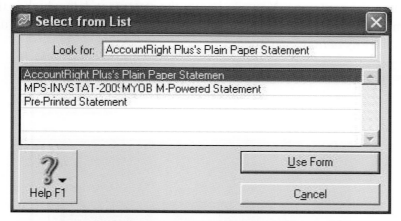

Figure 5.33: Statement form type selected

9. Click the *OK* button if your selections are as per Figure 5.34:

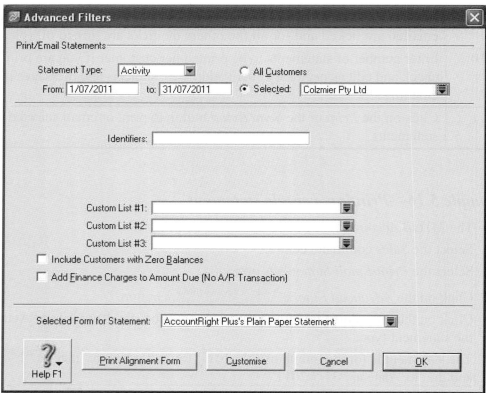

Figure 5.34: Completed forms selection window for an Activity type statement

10. Enter the number of copies per customer to print or leave the default as "1".

11. Check (tick) next to "Colzmier Pty Ltd" to select it for printing.

12. If your screen looks like Figure 5.35, click on the *Print* button and check your print with that on the next page. You can ignore the statement date which is the date the statement is printed. Make sure, however, that the 'date from' and 'date to' are correct for this *activity* statement.

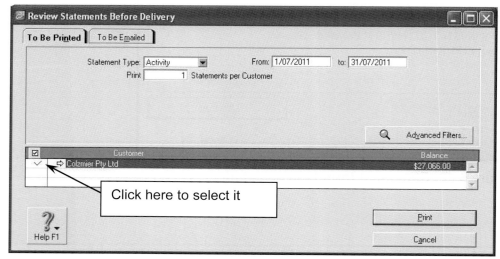

Figure 5.35: Selection for printing a single statement for Colzmier Pty Ltd

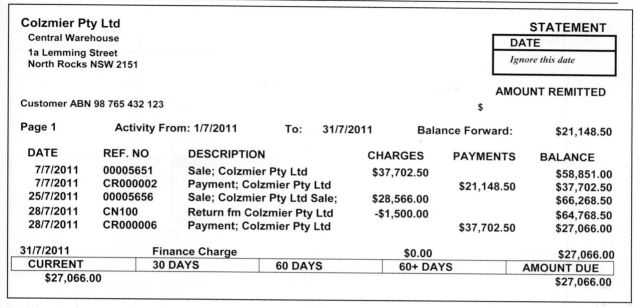

| **Colzmier Pty Ltd** | | | | | **STATEMENT** |
| Central Warehouse | | | | | |

Colzmier Pty Ltd
Central Warehouse
1a Lemming Street
North Rocks NSW 2151

STATEMENT
DATE
Ignore this date

Customer ABN 98 765 432 123

AMOUNT REMITTED
$

| Page 1 | | Activity From: 1/7/2011 | To: 31/7/2011 | | Balance Forward: | $21,148.50 |

DATE	REF. NO	DESCRIPTION	CHARGES	PAYMENTS	BALANCE
7/7/2011	00005651	Sale; Colzmier Pty Ltd	$37,702.50		$58,851.00
7/7/2011	CR000002	Payment; Colzmier Pty Ltd		$21,148.50	$37,702.50
25/7/2011	00005656	Sale; Colzmier Pty Ltd Sale;	$28,566.00		$66,268.50
28/7/2011	CN100	Return fm Colzmier Pty Ltd	-$1,500.00		$64,768.50
28/7/2011	CR000006	Payment; Colzmier Pty Ltd		$37,702.50	$27,066.00
31/7/2011		Finance Charge	$0.00		$27,066.00

CURRENT	30 DAYS	60 DAYS	60+ DAYS	AMOUNT DUE
$27,066.00				$27,066.00

Video: A video on printing customer statement is on the DVD

Self-test exercise 5.19

Have the file dem51.myo open.

Print a statement. Select "Activity" as the statement type with dates from "1/7/2011" to "31/7/2011". Select "All Customers". Use the *List* button ⊟ for 'Custom List #1:' and select "Sales Territory NSW" to print *all* NSW customers.

Custom List #1:	Sales Territory NSW	⊟
Custom List #2:		⊟
Custom List #3:		⊟

Print an "AccountRight Plus's plain paper" statement for Pharmaceutical Distribution Pty Ltd from the resulting list (i.e. only <u>one</u> NSW customer!).

Customer transaction detail

At the foot of each command centre in *MYOB AccountRight Plus* there is a *Find Transactions* option. You can use the *Find Transactions* option to access *Find Transactions window*. This window has tabs on the top so that inquiries can be made on any type (account, card etc). Select the type and enter the date range to display relevant transactions.

Are we nearly finished?
It's playtime!

How to display customer transactions

Step	Instruction
1	Click on the arrow at the end of the *Find Transactions* option that is at the foot of a command centre window and select 'Card' as the type.
2	Type in the customer name, or use the *List* button ☑ and select from the list.
3	Change the 'from' and 'to' dates if necessary.
4	You can select the *Advanced* button on the top, if necessary, to make a more specific selection – such as 'sorted by'.
5	To obtain a printout, select the *Print* button at the foot of the window.

Self-test exercise 5.20

Have the file dem51.myo open.

Display the details for Colzmier Pty Ltd from 1/7/2011 to 31/7/2011. Compare your display with the answer at the end of the chapter. Click on *Print* to obtain a hard copy or *Close*.

Printing GST reports

The *MYOB AccountRight Plus* package produces a GST report that assists with the preparation of the Business Activity Statement (BAS).

If you are not using the BAS link you will need to print one of the GST reports available and fill in the BAS from that. You select the report depending on whether you are using a *cash* or an *accrual* basis for reporting your GST.

Refer to Chapter 2 if you want to see how to use GST reports for filling in a Business Activity Statement (BAS).

Example 5.17—Printing the GST Report

1. Use the file dem51.myo.
2. Click on the arrow at the end of the *Reports* option and select *GST/Sales Tax* tab.
3. Select the "GST [Summary – Accrual]" report as shown in Figure 5.36.

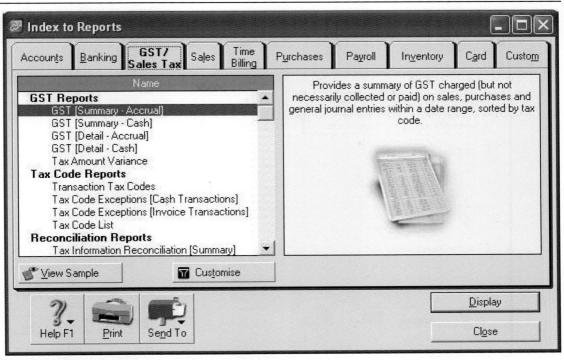

Figure 5.36: GST report selected from list

4. Click on the *Customise* button. Enter the dates from "1/7/2011" to "31/7/2011" and "Both Collected and Paid" in the 'Collected/Paid' field as per Figure 5.37.

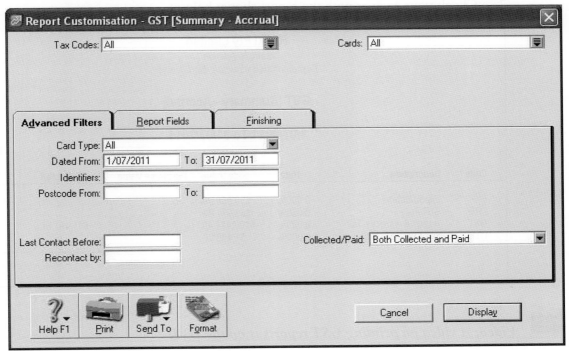

Figure 5.37: Report customisation *Advanced Filters* window for a GST report

5. In the *Finishing* window select to display sales and purchase values as 'Tax Inclusive'. Your screen should look like Figure 5.38 on the next page.

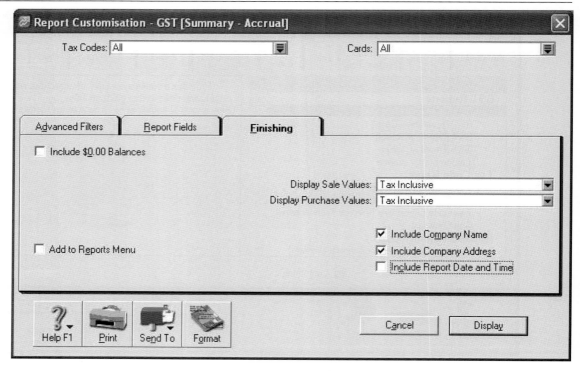

Figure 5.38: Report Customisation *Finishing* window for a GST report

6. Click the *Display* button to accept the settings and show the report on screen.
7. Check your answer with the report shown below:

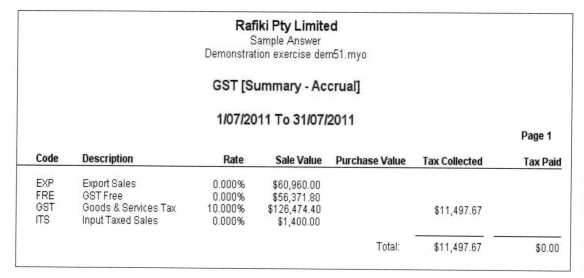

 Video: A video on printing GST reports is on the DVD

Back up before combining customer cards

You should be able to combine and delete a duplicate *general ledger account,* a duplicate *customer card* or a duplicate *supplier card.* On the following pages we will cover *Combining Customer Cards.*

The program <u>combines</u> the two cards into one card or the two accounts into one account by merging their transactions and balances.

Once combined and merged the duplicate card or account is deleted and you cannot undo or reverse this action. It is, therefore, **very important** that you **back up** the data file **before** combining cards or accounts (see Chapter 1 for backup instructions).

Combining customer cards

A situation may occur where a customer has two cards recording the transactions of a single business. The duplicate card could have been created intentionally or in error. For example, a customer may have two cards because there are two branches and each branch has its own card. Another example is where an existing customer buys the business of another existing customer. In these situations it *may* be necessary to combine the two cards into one. Before combining two customer cards a decision has to be made <u>first</u> as to which card will have <u>all</u> the transactions <u>merged</u> onto it (this card will be called the '**Primary**' card), and which card will be deleted (the '**Secondary**' card) after all its transactions are transferred to the 'Primary' card.

The cards to be combined or merged <u>need not</u> be with the same customer name or details. To combine cards they only need to be of the *same type* and both *active.* For example both are 'Customer' cards and neither of the cards is an 'Inactive' card.

How to combine customer cards

Step	Instruction
1	Select the *Card File* command centre.
2	Select the *Cards List* option.
3	Click on the ⊙ Actions button (below the card list) and select the *Combine Cards* option from the list of options.
4	In the 'Primary' field click the *List* button 🔽 to select the customer card where all the transactions will be combined, and click on the *Use Card.* This card will not be deleted and will have all the transactions from both cards.
5	In the 'Secondary' field click the *List* button 🔽 to select the second card of the customer whose transactions will be transferred to the primary card. The secondary card will be deleted after the transfer.
6	Click on the Combine Cards button.
7	Read the warning message and click the *OK* button to confirm your wish to combine the cards.

Note:
If more than two cards are to be combined for a single business, it will be necessary to carry out the above process *once* for *each* of the 'secondary' cards. For example if a business has three customer cards, it will be necessary to carry out the above process *twice* to eliminate the extra *two* duplicate cards and transfer all their transactions onto the 'Primary' card.

Example 5.18— Combining two customer cards

Combine the cards of 'Colzmier' and 'Em-Kart'. Colzmier is to be the *primary* card.

1. Make sure that you have the file dem51.myo open.
2. Select the *Cards List* option from the *Card File* command centre..
3. Click on the ⊙ Actions button at the bottom of the cards list then select the *Combine Cards* option.
4. In the 'Primary' field click the *List* button ▼ to select the customer card "Colzmier Pty Ltd" where the transactions of the two cards will be combined.
5. In the 'Secondary' field click the *List* button ▼ to select the second card "Em-Kart Pty Ltd" which is the customer whose transactions will be transferred to the primary card. This secondary card *Em-Kart Pty Ltd* will be deleted after the transfer of all its transactions to the primary card.
6. If your screen looks like figure 5.39, click on the *Combine Cards* button.

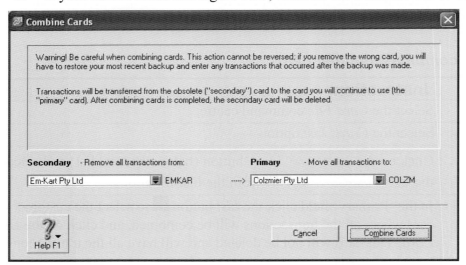

Figure 5.39: Combining two customer cards

Note:
Steps 3 and 4 above may be reversed. You can start by selecting (highlight) the primary customer card and then click on the ⊙ Actions button and select the *Combine Cards* option. The *Combine Cards* dialogue box as in Figure 5.39 above will open with the primary card already entered.

7. Read the warning message.

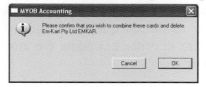

Figure 5.40: A warning message before deleting customer card

and click the *OK* button to confirm your wish to combine the cards and delete the secondary card. Check the customer *Cards List* to confirm that Em-Kart is deleted.

Video: A video on combining customer cards is on the DVD

Self-test exercise 5.21

Have the file dem51.myo open.

Use *Find Transactions/Card* (from 1/7/2011to 31/7/2011) and select Colzmier to check that invoice # 5655, previously invoiced to Em-Kart, is now listed with Colzmier.

Exit (close) **dem51.myo** and open **dem52.myo** to complete the next exercise.

Dishonoured and re-presented cheques

No matter how careful a business is in accepting cheques from customers, there are occasions when cheques are returned unpaid. These are commonly known as *dishonoured cheques*. On other occasions a cheque, which was rejected on the first attempt to clear it, is subsequently paid after the bank has re-presented it a second time.

A *re-presented cheque* is a cheque that was not honoured (not paid) within the period banks usually allow for deposited cheques. The bank then deposits the cheque a second time and if the conditions that caused the cheque not to be paid in the first instance are now cleared, the cheque will be honoured (paid). A debit and a credit entry will appear on the bank statement. No *accounting* action is necessary, simply contra both entries on the bank statement (tick them both). Sometimes the bank charges a fee for this service. It may be necessary, then, to charge the customer for it.

The term "dishonoured cheques" refers to customers' cheques that are returned unpaid by their banks. The bank may dishonour (not pay for) a cheque for any one of the following reasons:

*   Lack of sufficient funds in the customer's bank account to cover the cheque.
*   Signature is missing or incorrect.
*   Cheque is defective in any manner (torn, missing pieces, not legible etc.).
*   The cheque is incorrectly filled out.
*   Amount in figures and words do not match or not correctly filled in.
*   Payee's name is missing or not the same as the depositor.
*   Post dated or date is too old.
*   Account is closed.
*   The customer has put a 'stop payment' order on the cheque at his/her bank.

A customer's dishonoured cheque must be recorded as a *negative* receipt. As the receipt of the cheque was originally recorded in the *Sales* command centre using the *Receive Payments* option, then the dishonour of the cheque (the negative entry) must *also* be recorded in the *Sales* command centre in order to update the customer's record. This is achieved by:

1. Reversing the original receipt;
2. Charging the customer for any *discount given* for early payment;
3. Charging the customer for any *bank charges* incurred; and if applicable,
4. Charging the customer for *late payment fees* (if applicable).

Remember: For all of the above entries you will need to change the *memos* to describe the nature of the entries and, if necessary, also change the transaction dates.

You cannot record *negative* receipts using the *Receive Payments* option in the *Sales* command centre. The only way to enter a negative 'Receive Payments' is to reverse the original receipt.

This action (reversing the original receipt) will:

1. update the customer's balance,
2. update the invoice total, and
3. update the balances of the general ledger accounts that relate to this transaction, i.e. the "Bank" account and "Accounts Receivable" account.

It does not, however, reverse any discount given, but it does give a warning message to that effect.

You need to charge the customer for any discount previously given for early settlement.

How to record a customer's dishonoured cheque

Step	Instructions
1	Select the *Setup* pull-down menu.
2	Select the *Preferences* menu item and click on the *Security* tab on the top.
3	If not already ticked, tick on the first checkbox. Click ☑ Transactions CAN'T be Changed; They Must be Reversed [System-wide]
4	Click *OK* to exit *Preferences*.
5	Select *Transaction Journal* from any command centre then click on the *Receipts* tab.
6	Change the date range, if necessary, to include the date of the original receipt for the dishonoured cheque and click on its detail arrow ⇨ to open it.
	(continued on the next page)

Step	Instructions
7	When the *Receive Payments* window is displayed check that it is the correct transaction to reverse (i.e. the original receipt for the dishonoured cheque).
8	Click on the *Edit* pull-down menu and select *Reverse Payment* option.
9	*MYOB AccountRight Plus* will prepare a reversal entry, which will need to be edited before recording it.
10	Change the date on the reversal (enter the date of dishonour).
11	Change the memo. For example: "Dishonoured Cheque".
12	Click the *Record* button. **Note:** To change the preferences back – repeat the first three steps above, but un-tick the checkbox in step 3. ☐ Transactions CAN'T be Changed; They Must be Reversed [System-wide]
13	If you receive a message that a discount was given for the original payment, you will need to prepare an invoice and charge the customer for the amount of the discount. Use the original discount account and the tax code. **Note:** Use a *Service* layout invoice for this charge as a *Tax* invoice. However, if the customer does not need a tax invoice, a *Miscellaneous* invoice can be used instead.
14	If there are any bank charges or any other charges you wish to make for this dishonoured cheque, you can include them on the same invoice created in step 13 or issue a separate invoice.

Example 5.19—Recording a dishonoured cheque from a customer

1. Open the *MYOB AccountRight Plus* file **dem52.myo**. and sign on as the "Administrator" without a password.

2. Select the *Setup* pull-down menu. ⬅ **NEW FILE**

3. Select the *Preferences* menu item.

4. Click on the *Security* tab, and if not already selected, tick on the first checkbox
   ☑ Transactions CAN'T be Changed; They Must be Reversed [System-wide]
   then click *OK* to exit *Preferences*.

5. Select *Transaction Journal* from any command centre, and then

6. Click on the *Receipts* tab on the top.

7. Change the date range: 'Dated From' "1/7/2011" To "31/7/2011".

8. Click on the detail arrow next to the receipt on "20/7/2011" from "Sahara Garden Supplies" for "$277.00" to open it – see Figure 5.41 on the next page.

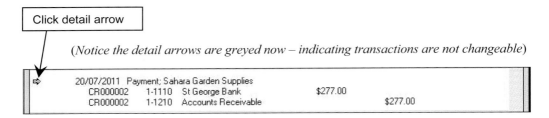

Figure 5.41: Transaction of the dishonoured cheque

9.   In the *Receive Payments* window, check that the correct transaction to be reversed is open.

10.   Click on the *Edit* pull-down menu and select the *Reverse Payment* option.

11.   Enter "Dishonoured Cheque; Sahara Garden Supplies" in the 'Memo' field ↵.

12.   Change the 'ID #' to "BS" ↵.

13.   Change the 'Date' to "23/7/2011" ↵.

14.   If your screen looks like Figure 5.42 click on the *Record* button:

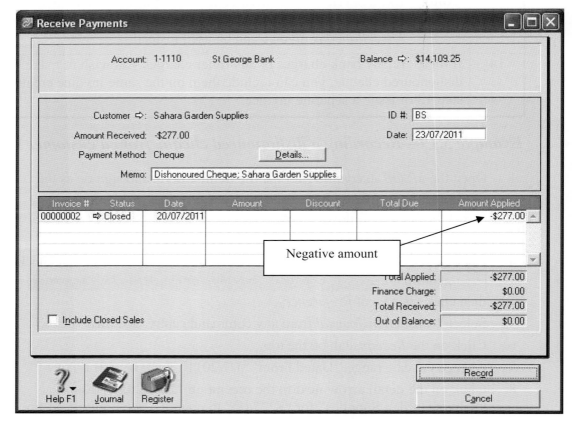

Figure 5.42: Dishonoured Cheque – *negative* 'Receive Payment' entry

15.   Restore the preferences. If necessary, access the *Security* tab of *Preferences* (as above) and un-tick the first checkbox and click *OK*.

Un-tick ➝ ☐ Transactions CAN'T be Changed; They Must be Reversed [System-wide]

16. Re-select the *Receipts* tab of the *Transaction Journal*. The original and reversal entries should be as in Figure 5.43:

⇨	20/07/2011	Payment; Sahara Garden Supplies		
	CR000002	1-1110	St George Bank	$277.00	
	CR000002	1-1210	Accounts Receivable		$277.00
⇨	23/07/2011	Dishonoured Cheque; Sahara Garden Supplies		
	BS	1-1110	St George Bank		$277.00
	BS	1-1210	Accounts Receivable	$277.00	

Figure 5.43: Original receipt and its reversal in the cash receipts journal

Close **Dem52.myo** and open **Dem53.myo** to complete the following exercises.

Default setup for Sales

An alternative method to set up the accounts receivable module is to use the setup wizard the *Easy Setup Assistant* which can be accessed at any time from the *Setup* menu.

How to use the Easy Setup Assistant *for accounts receivable*

Step	Instruction
1	Select the *Setup* pull-down menu and click on *Easy Setup Assistant* menu item.
2	Click on the *Sales* button. Click
3	Read the message in the window and click on the *Next* button.
4	The first setup item is to select the default sales layout of invoices. Click on the option button to make this selection and click the *Next* button.
5	In the *Selling Details* window enter the default income account and the default credit limit that is applicable for most customers and click the *Next* button.
6	In the *Tax Codes* window enter the tax codes often used with customers for sales as well as for freight charged. Click the *Next* button.
7	In the *Payment Information* window make the following selections. Click on the *List* button 🔽 next to the 'Payment Method' field and make a selection. Click on the 'Payment is Due' field and drag down to select from the list. Click and edit the fields for 'Discount Days', 'Balance Due Days', '% Discount for Early Payment', '% Monthly Charge for Late Payment'. Click on the *Next* button.
	(continued on the next page)

Step	Instruction
8	In the *Linked Accounts* window. Accept or change the two main linked accounts for "Customer Receipts" and "Undeposited funds". Click on the *Next* button.
9	In the *Customer Cards* window you can add "New Customers", edit or delete existing ones. This was done earlier in this chapter but can be done using this option. Click on the *Next* button.
10	Enter outstanding customer balances in the *Historical Sales* window. This was demonstrated earlier in this chapter but can also be done using this option. Click on the *Next* button.
11	Click on the *Close* button in the last (Conclusion) window.

Example 5.20—Using Easy Setup Assistant for accounts receivable

1. Open the *MYOB AccountRight Plus* file **dem53.myo** and sign on as "Administrator" without a password.

2. Select the *Setup* pull-down menu.

3. Select the *Easy Setup Assistant* menu item.

4. Click on the *Sales* button. Read the "Welcome" message and click *Next*.

5. In the *Layout* window click on the option button to select *Service* layout invoices as the default and click on the *Next* button.

6. In the *Selling Details* window use the *List* button ▼ at the 'Income Account' field and scroll down to the income accounts and select "Catering Fees" (or account No 4-3000) as the usual income account. Type in a credit limit of "$20,000". Your selling details should look like Figure 5.44 on the next page. Click the *Next* button.

7. Leave the tax codes as "GST" for both sales and freight and click *Next*.

8. In the payment information setup, use the *List* button ▼ and select "Cheque" as the usual payment method. Use the dropdown arrows and select the default credit terms as "In a given # of days" with balance due in 30 days. In the 'Discount Days' field enter "7" and in the '% Discount for Early Payment' field enter "1%". The payment information window should look like Figure 5.45 on the next page. Click *Next*.

9. Use the *List* button ▼ and select "St George Bank" as the account for tracking customer receipts. Leave the account for "Undeposited Funds" and click *Next*.

10. For this exercise, leave the customer list and click *Next*, as well as for the historical sales – click *Next*.

11. Accept the well-deserved congratulations and click on the *Close* button.

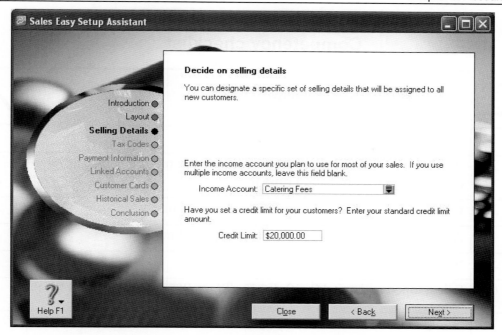

Figure 5.44: Selling details in *Easy Setup Assistant*

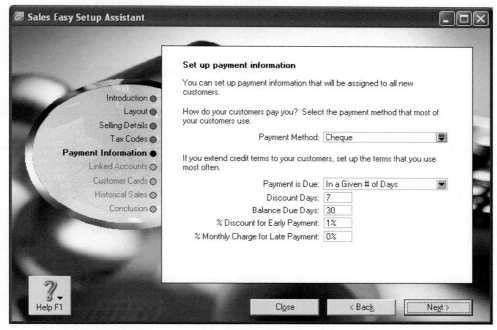

Figure 5.45: Default customer terms using *Easy Setup Assistant*

Competency checklist

	I can now do the following:	✓
1	Switch the computer and screen on	
2	Adjust chair and equipment to suit ergonomic requirements and sit correctly at the computer terminal	
3	Use rest periods and appropriate exercises regularly	
4	Access information from manuals and/or on-line help	
5	Solve operational problems	
6	Select, open and exit *MYOB AccountRight Plus* or Premier and files	
7	Set up GST codes for sales and print BAS reports	
8	Enter and maintain customer information (customer cards)	
9	Enter debtors' (accounts receivable) opening balances	
10	Set up accounts receivable for automatic posting to the general ledger (set up the linked accounts for 'Sales')	
11	Record sales *Quotes, Orders* and *Invoices* and check for accuracy	
12	Convert quotes to orders and orders to invoices	
13	Enter receipts from customers and apply to open invoices	
14	Create credit notes and apply to relevant invoices *or* refund	
15	Perform special operations such as change tax rates, write off bad debts, charging freight and charging interest	
16	Print/Email invoices, credit notes and statements	
17	Print various sales and accounts receivable reports	
18	Access information about an account	
19	Combine customer cards by merging their transactions and deleting the duplicate cards	
20	Record customers' dishonoured and re-presented cheques	
21	Apply techniques to minimise paper wastage such as using screen inquiries and recycling paper from printouts	

Chapter 5: Assessment exercises

Note: Throughout the following practical exercises you should observe relevant occupational health and safety practices and apply recycling techniques to minimise paper wastage. In addition, you should use the help facilities to solve problems you may encounter.

Spell checker: For all the following assessments you may choose to use the spell checker or to stop it. Select *Setup/Preferences* then *Windows* tab and select or de-select the last option.

5.1 Gates & Murdock have a business of selling electronic equipment. They started using *MYOB AccountRight Plus* from 1 July 2011. Their accountant started the necessary *MYOB AccountRight Plus* file, set up the general ledger accounts list and entered the opening balances as at the conversion date.

You are required to create the cards for the customers and enter the amounts owing by them (the *Customer Balances*), which should agree with the control account (accounts receivable) balance in the general ledger. You will also be required to enter July's accounts receivable transactions (sales, credit notes and receipts) and print the reports listed at the end of this assessment.

The exercise month is July 2011.
Start *MYOB AccountRight Plus* (or Premier) and open an existing file called **ass51.myo**.
Use the **Setup** drop-down menu, **Company Information** item and change the business address to "Your full name – Assessment 5.1".

The *Goods & Services* tax is set at 10%.
The Tax Code = GST (unless otherwise stated).
Note: ALL GOODS AND SERVICES in this exercise are taxable.

Create the following customer cards:

1. Super Electronics Pty Limited – Customer number (card ID): "SE-001"
   Billing address (address 1): PO Box 911, Flemington VIC 3031.
   Telephone: (03) 9922 1712 and fax: (03) 9922 1722.
   Email address is superelec@ar.com.au. Salutation Mr Morse and the contact person is Mr Samuel Morse.
   Delivery address (address 2): 100 Henley St., Flemington VIC 3031.
   Telephone: (03) 9922 1111 and fax: (03) 9922 1122.
   Identifier: R.   Sale Layout: Service. Printed Form: AccountRight Plus's plain paper. Income Account: 4-1000 Sales. Credit Limit $75,000. ABN: 22 199 877 711. Tax code and Freight Tax code: GST. Do not use customer tax code.
   Credit terms: 30 days after end of month (select: # of days after EOM).
   No discounts are given.

2. One Stop Digital Pty Limited – Customer No "OSD010".
   Billing and delivery addresses: 20 Bright St., Melbourne VIC 3000.
   Telephone: (03) 9634 4191 and fax: (03) 9634 4444. Email address:
   digi@sos.com.au. Salutation: John and the contact person is John Wong.
   Identifier D. Sale Layout: Service. Printed Form: AccountRight's plain
   paper. Income Account: 4-1000 Sales. Credit Limit $50,000.
   ABN: 27 099 750 811. Tax code and Freight Tax code: GST. Do not use
   customer tax code. Credit terms: 30 days after end of month. No discount.

3. Phones Galore – Customer No "PG003". **Billing address**: P.O. Box 21,
   Brisbane QLD 4001. Telephone and fax: (04) 9144 7060. Email address:
   pg@aone.com. Salutation Bill McIntosh and the contact person: Sofia
   McIntosh. **Delivery address**: 11 Church Street, Brisbane QLD 4000.
   Identifier: D. Sale Layout: Service. Printed Form: AccountRight's plain
   paper. Income Account: 4-1000 Sales. Credit limit: $100,000 (due 30 days
   after EOM). Tax Code: GST. Freight Tax code: GST. ABN: 81 399 625
   447.

**Enter the outstanding (historical or opening) balances owing by the above
customers as at 1/7/2011. Tax code for these entries: GST.**

Customer	Invoice #	Dated	Amount
Super Electronics Pty Limited	2026	30/4/2011	$77.00
	2345	10/5/2011	4,290.00
	2388	30/6/2011	1,787.50
One Stop Digital	2387	30/6/2011	7,986.00
Phones Galore	2386	29/6/2011	3,053.60

Select *Service* as invoice layout for this assessment.
Enter the following sales in July 2011:

ALL sales are TAX INCLUSIVE ☑ Tax Inclusive
Remember: You can type a formula in the 'Amount' field to calculate the amount.

Invoice # 2398 dated 3 July 2011 to Phones Galore. Their P.O.# is 133. The
sale is for 10 Canon Compact-X Mobile Phones at $330 each incl. GST and 10
Heavy Duty Batteries for the Compact-X at $154 each incl. GST. Freight $55
incl. GST. Deliver by "Australia Post". Total invoice should be $4895.00 incl.
GST.

Invoice # 2399 dated 13 July 2011 to One Stop Digital. Their P.O.# is 501C.
The sale is for 1 Desktop Computer cost $6,457.00 and training fees of
$924.00 (GST inclusive both items). The carrier is "Best Way" and freight of
$66 (incl. GST). Total invoice should be $7447.00 incl. GST.

Invoice # 2400 dated 28 July 2011 to Phones Galore. Their P.O.# is 186. The
sale is for 20 Leather Cases to fit the Compact-X at $330 each incl. GST. The
order is posted (Aust. Post) – the delivery charge is $11.00 incl. GST. Total
invoice should be $6611.00 incl. GST.

Invoice # 2401 dated 28 July 2011 to Super Electronics. Their P.O.# is 905. The sale is for 3 Millennium Pentium IV 4Ghz Computers at $3,300 each incl. GST and 2 copies of Microsoft *Office 2010 Pro Upgrades* at $440 each incl. GST. Goods were picked up by customer (no freight charges). Total invoice should be $10,780.00 incl. GST.

Enter the following receipts from customers:
(**Note**: No details are necessary for the following payment methods.)

Customer	Date	Method	Amount	Apply to INV #
Phones Galore	5/7/2011	Cheque	$3,053.60	2386
One Stop Digital	12/7/2011	Visa	$7,986.00	2387
Phones Galore	20/7/2011	Cash	$4,895.00	2398
Super Electronics	31/7/2011	Cheque	$6,077.50	2345 & 2388
One Stop Digital	31/7/2011	MasterCard	$7,337.00	2399

Issue the following Credit Notes on 31 July 2011 for goods returned.
Use *Tax Inclusive* **invoices.** Select '4-100 Sales' for the account.
Remember: *Enter all amounts in negative.*
Don't forget to **apply** each credit note to its specified invoice **as at 31/7/2011**.

Customer	Invoice #	Amount	Tax Code	Apply to INV #
Super Electronics	CN8	$77.00	GST	2026
One Stop Digital	CN9	$110.00	GST	2399

Required prints (for Assessment 5.1):
Print all invoices
   (select '*All Sales*' as status
   and "AccountRight Plus's Plain Paper Invoice" as form);
Print the Sales and Receivables Journal for the month of July 2011;
Print the Cash Receipts Journal for the month of July 2011;
Print a statement for Super Electronics (use AccountRight Plain Paper form):
   Statement Type: *Activities* from 30/4/2011 to 31/7/2011;
Print GST [Details Accrual] report for July 2011 – All Taxes and "Both Collected and Paid" with tax inclusive amounts for sales and purchases.

5.2 The exercise month is July 2011.

Start *MYOB AccountRight Plus* and open an existing file called ass52.myo.

Use the ***Setup*** menu, ***Company Information*** item and change the business address to "Your full name – Assessment 5.2".

Create the following customer cards:

(**Note:** Do not specify default *Income Accounts* for these customers)

Lomond Computers (Card ID: Cust_03)
Address for both billing and delivery: 345 Victoria Road, Castle Hill NSW 2154. Telephone # is (02) 9634 1419 and fax # is (02) 9680 2255. Salutation is Michael and the contact person is M. Tang. No email. Credit terms are 30 days from date of sale with a limit of $40,000 and 2% discount for early payment within 7 days. Sales layout: Service. Printed Form: "Tax Inclusive Plain Paper Invoice". Tax Code (& Freight) = GST. ABN 40 901 198 611.

Serendipity Electronics (Card ID: Cust_02)
Address for both billing and delivery: 327 George Street, Sydney NSW 2000. Telephone and fax # is (02) 9238 4455. Salutation is Warren and the contact person is Warren Dennis. Email address: wd@ccb.org.au. Sales layout: Service. Printed Form: "Tax Inclusive Plain Paper Invoice". Credit terms are 30 days from date of sale (In a given # of days) and 1% discount for early payment within 7 days.
Credit limit: $85,000. Tax Code (& Freight) = GST. ABN 30 991 198 654.

Silver Star Computers Pty Ltd (Card ID: Cust_01).
Address for both billing and delivery: 5149 Oxford Street, Darlinghurst NSW 2010. Telephone # is (02) 9203 6545 and fax # is (02) 9203 1111. Salutation is Petro and the contact person is Peter Davey. No email address and no ABN. Enter the following in the 'Notes' field: "Customer is no longer in Oxford Street and all the phones are disconnected. Outstanding balance is to be written off. Credit terms are changed to Prepaid with a credit limit of $0, for the time being". Sales layout: Service. Printed Form: "Tax Inclusive Plain Paper Invoice". Credit terms: Prepaid. Credit limit: $0. Tax Code (& Freight) = GST.

Create a customer card as 'Cash Sales' – (Card ID: CS) – Set the credit limit to $0 and credit term to C.O.D. – no other details are necessary. This card will be used for customers with no accounts and who pay for the goods at the time of sale.
Note: For cash sales enter the total amount of the invoice in the field 'Paid Today'.

Enter the following historical balances at 1 July 2011 (Tax code = GST):

Silver Star Computers	INV # 3909	13/4/2009	$125.00
Serendipity	INV # 5122	29/5/2011	$1,486.50
	INV # 5134	28/6/2011	$2,480.80
Lomond Computers	INV # 5135	29/6/2011	$1,427.70

The *Goods & Services* tax is set at 10%. The Tax Code is GST (unless otherwise stated). Note: ALL GOODS AND SERVICES in this exercise are taxable.

Enter the following invoices for credit sales in July 2011.

Use *Service* type Invoices for this assessment.

All amounts are TAX INCLUSIVE: ☑ Tax Inclusive

Note: For *all* the following invoices, select the appropriate income account for each item sold. For example for computer systems use the income account '4-1100 Sales – Computers' and for software use '4-1200 Sales – Software'.

Invoice #5136 dated 6 July 2011 to Serendipity Electronics. Their P.O. #1228. The sale was for a Computer System $4,235 incl. GST together with bundled Software $638.00 incl. GST. These goods were picked up (no freight charges).

Invoice # 5137 dated 20 July 2011 to Lomond Computers. Their P.O. # 11256. The sale was for a Computer System $4,200 incl. GST. The carrier was *International*. Freight: $35.00 incl. GST.

Invoice #5138 dated 29 July 2011 to Serendipity Electronics. Their P.O.#1231. The sale was for 2 Computer Systems $4,235 each incl. GST plus bundled Software totalling $1,276 incl. GST. These goods were picked up.

Invoice #5139 dated 31 July 2011 is a *Cash Sale*. No P.O. number. Use account '4-1300 Sales – Other' for all the following items. The sale was for a HP Printer CP2000 and Cables $187 incl. GST. A box of black toner for CP2000 $55 incl. GST as well as a box of colour toner $71.50 incl. GST. Goods were picked up and the total of the invoice was paid in cash. Enter the total in the field 'Paid Today'.

Write-off the outstanding balance by Silver Star Computers.

Issue a *Credit Note* for the outstanding unpaid balance of this customer. Debit "Bad Debts" account – ignore warning.

Use a *Miscellaneous* layout for this credit note:

Reminder: Enter all amounts for credit notes as negative!

Customer	C/Note #	Date	Amount	Tax	Apply to
Silver Star	CN1	1/7/2011	$125.00	GST	Inv.#3909

For security and to disable any future sales to this customer, after applying this credit note to invoice 3909, access the customer's card and make it inactive. ☑ Inactive Card

Enter the following Credit Note to record the correction for an overcharge:
(Use: *Service* layout for this credit note. Enter amount as negative.)
All amounts are TAX INCLUSIVE. Debit: '4-1100 Sales – Computers'

Date Issued	Customer	Apply to INV. #	Amount	Tax Code	Credit Note No.
10/7/2011	Serendipity	5136	$97.46	GST	CN2

Reminder: Apply the above credit note to the specified invoice!

Enter the following receipts from customers

All receipts are paid by cheques – no cheque details required for this exercise.
Make sure the 'Finance Charge' is $0.00 for each of the following receipts.

IMPORTANT: Enter the receipt dates correctly for the discount to be calculated automatically.

(*)Use "Undeposited Funds" account to group the two receipts on 9/7/11 **and** prepare a single deposit to the "Bank" account. Bank all *other* receipts directly to the "Bank" account.

Customer	Date	Amount	Apply to INV #	Discount
*Serendipity Elec.	09/7/2011	$2,480.80	5134	0.00
*Lomond Computers	09/7/2011	$1,427.70	5135	0.00
Serendipity Elec.	15/7/2011	$1,486.50	5122	0.00
Serendipity Elec.	21/7/2011	$4,775.54	5136	0.00
Lomond Computers	22/7/2011	$4,150.30	5137	$84.70

Note: Click on *Print Later* when asked regarding printing the credit memo.

Issue the following Credit Note to refund an overcharge:

29/7/2011 <u>Refunded</u> to Lomond Computers $66 ($60 plus Tax). C/Note #: CN3.
Cheque No 1112 (Memo: Re Overcharge on Invoice # 5135). TAX code: GST.
Use *Service* layout and debit account '4-1100 Sales – Computers'.

Required prints (for Assessment 5.2):

Print the following invoices: (use form: "<u>Tax Inclusive</u> plain paper invoice")
No 5138 (status = "Open") and No 5137 (status = "Closed");
Print the following *Transaction Journals* for the month of July 2011:
'Sales and Receivable' Journal
'Cash Receipts' Journal
'Cash Disbursements' Journal;
Print Statements for Serendipity and Lomond.
Select *Activity* type statements from 1/5/2011 to 31/7/2011.
Tick on the box 'Include Customers with Zero Balances' and select the statement form as: "AccountRight Plus's Plain Paper Statement";
Select *Ageing Detail* to print Aged Receivable (Detail) report as at 31 July 2011;
Print GST [Detail Accrual] report for July – All Taxes and "Both Collected and Paid" with tax inclusive amounts for sales and purchases. (No 0.00 balances.)

5.3 **Create and maintain customer records:**

The exercise month is July 2011.

Start *MYOB AccountRight Plus* and open an existing file called **ass53.myo**.

Use the ***Setup*** menu, ***Company Information*** item and change the business address to "Your full name – Assessment 5.3 (ass53.myo)".

Set up the following customer cards.

Note: for all the following customer cards:

No email addresses for any of these cards (unless otherwise stated).

Except for export sales *do not* use customer tax code when invoicing.

Set the 'Sale Layout' for all the following customers as *Service* and the 'Printed Form:' as "Tax Inclusive Plain Paper".

David Pumps Pty Ltd (Customer #: DAVI01)
Billing address: P.O. Box No 16, Newcastle NSW 2301. Telephone and Fax: (02) 472 4481, salutation is Trevor and contact person is Trevor Dean.
Delivery address: 23 Peripheral Street, Newcastle, NSW 2300.
Identifier is "T". The credit limit is $40,000.00. Net 30 days after invoice date. (Select: "In a given # of days"). Tax Code: GST. Freight Tax Code: GST. ABN: 65 552 900 873.

Dortmund Robotics Pty Ltd (Customer #: DORT01)
Billing and delivery address: 23 Park Road, Adelaide SA 5000.
Telephone (08) 9221 3321, Fax # same number, salutation is Ms Hall and contact is Betty Hall. Identifier is "T". The credit limit is $15,000.00.
Tax Code: GST. Freight Tax Code: GST. Credit term is net 30 days after end of month. ABN 15 515 662 320.

Jamieson Gears and Pumps (Customer #: JAMI01)
Billing and delivery address: 50 Queen Street, Brisbane Markets QLD 4106.
Telephone (07) 9634 8774, Fax # (07) 9634 2222, Email: jgp@star.com.au, salutation is Mr Fox and contact is Francois Reynard. Identifier: "T".
The credit limit is $48,000.00. Credit term is net 7 days after invoice date.
Tax Code: GST. Freight Tax Code: GST. ABN 21 212 332 223.

Note: For the next customer create a *new* tax code: "**EXP**" (Export Sales), Rate: 0%. Link to (2-1310) GST Collected and (2-1330) GST Paid.

UNDP (Customer #: UNDP01)
Billing and shipping address: 214 Independence Ave, Dar Es Salaam, Tanzania. Telephone (0011) 94 6641. Fax # (0011) 94 6982. Salutation is Mr Parker and contact is Winston Mujemula. Identifier is "O". No credit terms – all payments are by "Letters of Credit" (select "Prepaid" or "C.O.D."). No ABN.
TAX Code: EXP. Freight Tax Code: FRE. Use customer's tax code.

The *Goods & Services* tax is set at 10%. **ALL GOODS AND SERVICES in this exercise are taxable. The Tax Code is GST except for exported goods; it is EXP.**

IMPORTANT: Check that the Sales linked accounts for Freight Collected (8-0100) and Discount Allowed (6-2010) are set up properly before recording the invoices:

Enter the following service invoices:
IMPORTANT: ALL prices <u>in this exercise</u> are plus tax i.e. <u>NOT</u> TAX INCLUSIVE.

> Invoice # 8703 dated 10 July 2011 to Dortmund Robotics Pty Ltd. The P.O. # D45/N and the invoice is for "Reconditioning a WX Pump" (account: 4-2300 Repairs Income). The amount is $2,000.00 plus GST.
> Salesperson: Betty Hall. Promised date 17/7/2011.

> Invoice #8704 dated 15 July 2011 to David Pumps. The customer ordered these in a letter dated 24/6/2011. The invoice is for the "Supply of a WZ Pump" (account: 4-1110 Sales Pumps). The price is $3,800.00 (plus GST).
> Freight is $300 (plus GST). Carrier: Federal Express. Salesperson: J. Hayes.

> Invoice #8705 dated 20 July 2011 to Jamieson Gears and Pumps. The P.O.# 487. This was for "Feasibility study on manufacture of activators" (account: 4-2100 Consultancy fees) – total cost is $6,500.00 plus GST.
> Salesperson: Helen Richards.

> Invoice #8706 dated 25 July 2011 to UNDP, Tanzania. This is a government contract reference UN2020. The invoice is for the "Supply of 20 RX Activators @ $1,000.00 each" (account: 4-1100 Sales Activators). Tax code: EXP, and $700 freight – Tax code: FRE. Ship via QANTAS. Salesperson: Helen Richards.

> Invoice #8707 dated 28 July 2011 to Dortmund Robotics. Their order #W28. This invoice is for the "Supply of 3 TX Activators @ $1,000.00 each" (4-1100 Sales Activators) and "2 TX Pumps @ $1,300 each" (account: 4-1110 Sales Pumps). Both items are plus GST. Freight is $125 plus GST. The carrier: Kwikasair (delivery 31/7/2011). Salesperson: Hall.

Enter the following credit notes:
Use Tax Exclusive Service Invoices.

> Credit note #112 dated 20 July 2011 issued to Dortmund Robotics – for an overcharge on invoice # 8703 for $50 plus $5 GST. (Refer to the original invoice for account number to use.)

> Credit note #113 dated 29 July 2011 issued to David Pumps – for an overcharge on invoice # 8704 being an error on the amount charged for the freight. Amount charged $300 and it should be $30. Prepare a credit note for the difference $270 (use "8-0100 Freight Collected") plus $27 GST (total credit $297.00).

Apply *ALL* Credits against their relevant invoices. Make sure to use the credit notes dates when applying these credits to the invoices.

Change the card details for the following (existing) customer:

For "Dortmund Robotics Pty Ltd":

Copy the current address to 'Address 2 Ship to:' and

for the 'Address 1 Bill to', enter: P.O. Box 9123, ADELAIDE SA 5001;

Add an email address: dort@aol.com; and

Increase the credit limit *by* an additional $20,000.

Record the following payments (cheques) received from customers:

22 July 2011 – Jamieson Gears and Pumps paid $7,150.00 by cheque number 634 to be applied against invoice #8705.

25 July 2011 – Dortmund Robotics Pty Ltd paid $2,145.00 by cheque number 000667 to be applied against invoice #8703.

28 July 2011 – David Pumps Pty Ltd paid $4,213.00 – by cheque number 50228 to be applied against invoice #8704.

Record the following direct payment credited to the bank account in regard to a *Letter of Credit* from UNDP of Dar Es Salaam, Tanzania:

31 July 2011 – amount received $20,700.00 in settlement of invoice #8706. (Use *Receive Payment* option in *Sales* command centre to record this receipt. Method = 'Other' and for details enter "Proceeds re Letter of Credit".)

Record the following customer dishonoured cheque:

26 July 2011 – Jamieson Gears and Pumps cheque No 634 for $7,150.00 was returned by the bank unpaid (dishonoured).

Print the following forms and reports:

1. Invoice # 8704 (Status: Closed. Form: use Tax Inclusive plain paper).

2. Invoice # 8705 (Status: Open.   Form: use Tax Inclusive plain paper).

3. A Statement [Activities: 1/7/2011 to 31/7/2011] for Dortmund Robotics Pty Ltd – Use AccountRight Plus's Plain Paper form for this statement.

4. An Aged Receivable (Detail) report at 31 July 2011.
   (Select '*Ageing Detail*' to print this report and use *Customise* to enter report date and to select *All Customers.*)

5. A transaction journal (Sales & Receivable) for the month of July 2011.

6. A transaction journal (Cash Receipts) for the month of July 2011.

7. Print GST [Details Accrual] report for July – Select "*All Tax codes*" and "*Both Collected and Paid*" with tax inclusive amounts for sales and purchases.

5.4 **Accounts Receivable, Cash Transactions and General Ledger integrated.**
To satisfactorily complete this exercise, chapters 1 to 5 should have been covered.

Helen Richards has a franchise business distributing and servicing new commercial
and industrial heavy duty vacuum cleaners. The franchise has expanded rapidly and
the accounting systems are to be converted to *MYOB AccountRight Plus* on 1 July
2011.

The balance sheet at 30 June 2011 was:

Assets
  Current Assets

National bank		1,560.80	
Petty cash		500.00	
Accounts receivable	14,980.70		
Provision for doubtful debts	-950.00	14,030.70	
Inventories		21,540.00	
Total Current Assets			37,631.50

  Non-Current Assets

Motor vehicle – at cost	36,500.00		
Accumulated depreciation	-4,562.00	31,938.00	
Furniture and equipment – at cost	19,780.00		
Accumulated depreciation	-1,484.00	18,296.00	
Total Non-Current Assets			50,234.00
Total Assets			87,865.50

Liabilities
  Current Liabilities

Accounts payable	12,980.80	
Credit Card (Visa)	2,000.00	
GST Collected	1,000.00	
GST Paid	-500.00	
Total Current Liabilities		15,480.80

  Non-Current Liabilities

Long Term Loan	15,000.00	
Total Non-Current Liabilities		15,000.00
Total Liabilities		30,480.80

Net Assets	57,384.70

Capital – H. Richards	57,384.70

Required:

The exercise month is July 2011.

1.   Copy a data file called **ass54.myo** to your disk or folder.
   Start *MYOB AccountRight Plus* and open this data file.
   This is a new file with a minimum number of accounts.
   Use the ***Setup*** menu, ***Company Information*** item and change the business
   address to "Your full name – Assessment 5.4 (ass54.myo)".

2.   Read through the whole exercise and design an *Accounts List* (Chart of
   Accounts) that will <u>at least</u> cover the accounts required. The *Cost of Sales*
   section should show the typical "Cost of Goods Sold" section of a P&L
   Statement (i.e. Opening inventory *plus* Purchases *less* Closing inventory).
   Enter this *Accounts List*.
   Enter the general ledger account opening balances (as at 1 July 2011) using the
   Balances option from the *Setup* menu.

3.   Set up the linked accounts for the *Sales* command centre. Link Freight to
   '*Freight Collected*' and discount for early payments to '*Discount Allowed*'.
   (From the *Setup* pull-down menu use either the *Linked Sales Accounts* option
   or the *Easy Setup Assistant* option.)

4.   Create Customer Records (Cards) and enter in the historical invoices making
   up the accounts receivable balance at 30 June 2011.

5.   Record the transactions for July 2011.

6.   Print the required forms and reports mentioned at the end of this exercise.

Details of the accounts receivable balance of $14,980.70 at 30 June 2011:

> **Note**: For *ALL* customers in this exercise:
>
> Do not use Card IDs;
>
> For '*net 30 days*' select: '*In a given# of days*' Balance Due 30 days. No
> discount.
>
> The tax code for Sales and Freight, on all customer cards, is GST.

Hot Shot Appliances of 321 Parramatta Road, Camperdown, NSW 2050.
Telephone (02) 9550 6551, Fax (02) 9550 4333. Email hot@msn.com.
Credit limit is $30,000 and term is net 30 days. ABN: 43 763 103 449.

Invoices owing by Hot Shot Appliances are:

			Tax Code
Invoice # 215	3/6/2011	$4,550.50	GST
Invoice # 225	28/6/2011	$3,730.20	GST

Taylor Square Whitegoods of 277 Oxford Street, Darlinghurst, NSW 2010.
Telephone (02) 9360 5412, Fax # (02) 9360 1212. No Email.
Credit limit is $40,000.00 and term is net 30 days. ABN: 88 789 001 002.

Invoices owing by Taylor Square Whitegoods are:			**Tax Code**
Invoice # 219	14/6/2011	$3,540.00	GST
Invoice # 224	26/6/2011	$3,010.00	GST

Harry Trelawn of 33 Standard Street, Rooty Hill, NSW 2766. Phone (02) 9832 5541 (no other details available).

Invoice owing by customer:			**Tax Code**
Invoice # 120	4/1/2009	$150.00	GST

Create a customer card as '*Cash Sales*' – Use "Service" as the default layout. Credit terms C.O.D. with $0 credit limit – Tax codes are "GST" – no other details are necessary. This will be used for cash sales and customers with no credit accounts.
Note: For 'cash sales' enter the total amount of the invoice in the field 'Paid Today'.

During July 2011 the following transactions took place:

Note: In this exercise: <u>ALL Goods & Services are subject to 10% GST.</u>
Tax CODE for all sales and all Credit Notes (adjustments) is "GST".

<u>Note</u>**: Amounts for all sale invoices and credit notes are:**
TAX EXCLUSIVE (i.e. price plus tax).

Clear the 'Tax Inclusive' tick box.

☐ Tax Inclusive

July 2011	Details
3	Sold Model Turbo B vacuum cleaners to Taylor Square Whitegoods. Invoice #226. Order # 885 $2,850 plus GST.
5	Cash sales – Inv #227. Vacuum cleaners $1,590 (plus GST). (Use the card *Cash Sales* to record this invoice. Enter in *Paid today* $1749.00.) Paid $528.77 cheque # 123554 for Telephone account $480.70 plus GST.
9	Paid $1,375.00 cheque # 123555 for months rent $1,250 plus GST. Received from Hot Shot Appliances $4,550.50 – Inv. # 215.
10	3 vacuum cleaners returned as damaged by Taylor Square Whitegoods. Credit Note #21 for $-750 plus GST. Apply to Invoice # 226.
11	Cheque # 123556 $1,760.00 for purchase of vacuum cleaners for cash for $1,600 (plus GST). (Use *Spend Money* in *Banking* command centre. Debit *Purchases*.)

July 2011	Details
12	Create a card for a new credit customer Mad Discounts (218 Sunnyholt Road, Blacktown NSW 2148, Phone (02) 9831 7055. Credit Limit $15,000 – ABN 00 011 530 019) – Terms 7 days after sale. Tax code GST.
	Sold Model Turbo B vacuum cleaners to Mad Discounts for $3,800 (plus GST) – Invoice # 228 – Their order # 010710.
	Sold to Hot Shot Appliances Compact vacuum cleaners for $3890.70 (plus GST) on Invoice # 229. (No order number.)
15	Paid $537.90 cheque # 123557 for repairs to computer $489 (plus GST).
	Paid $2,028 Cheque # 123558 for fortnightly salaries (gross $2,600 less PAYG Withholding $572). Tax code N-T. (Enter the PAYG as negative.)
17	Received from Taylor Square Whitegoods $6,550, paying June account.
19	Sold vacuum cleaners for $2,416 cash (plus GST). Invoice # 230. (Use Cash Sales and enter $2657.60 as paid to-day.)
20	Received from Mad Discounts a cheque for $4180 paying Inv # 228.
	Sold Barrel cleaners to Taylor Square Whitegoods for $4,320.60 (plus GST) on Invoice #231.
23	Purchased new colour printer for cash for $1,290 (plus GST) – cheque # 123559 for $1,419. Debit "Furniture and Equipment" account – Tax code: CAP.
26	Received from Hot Shot Appliances $3,730.20, paying Inv # 225.
	Paid Macquarie Stationery cash for stationery – $621.90 (plus GST) on cheque # 123560 for $684.09.
	Invoice # 232 sent to Taylor Square Whitegoods for $100 (plus GST) being an undercharge on Invoice # 231.
29	Paid Bill Shylock accounting fees of $1,000 (Plus GST) – cheque # 123561 for $1,100.
	Paid fortnightly salaries (gross $2,600 less tax $572). Cheque # 123562 for $2,028.
30	Harry Trelawn cannot be traced and his account is to be written off as bad. Create a credit note (# CN22) for the balance owing $136.36 plus GST. (Make sure to enter this amount as negative.) Debit *Bad Debts* and apply the credit to his outstanding invoice. Make his card *Inactive* and add an appropriate remark in the card's 'Note' field.
31	Invoice # 233 – sale of discontinued models to Mad Discounts for $2,988 plus freight of $120 – both items plus GST.

Required prints (for Assessment 5.4):

1.   Print the following from the *Sales* command centre:

(a)   Tax Invoice #233 to Mad Discounts
(use form: "Tax Inclusive Plain Paper Invoice")

(b)   A statement (Activity: 1/7/11 to 31/7/11) for Taylor Square Whitegoods.
(use form: 'AccountRight Plus's Plain Paper')

2.   Print the following reports:

(a)   Aged Receivables (detailed) at 31 July 2011
(Use the report name: *Ageing Detail* and enter "31/7/2011" as the report date in the report customisation window)

(b)   The following transaction listings –
all for the period: 1 July 2011 to 31 July 2011:
Cash Receipts Journal
Cash Disbursement Journal
Sales and Receivable Journal

(c)   Print two account inquiries (select *Find Transactions* then *Account*)
for the following general ledger accounts:
Enter date range as: 1/7/2011 to 31/7/2011 (for both accounts)
Bad Debts and
Sales

(d)   Print a Standard Balance Sheet as at 31/7/2011. Include $0 balances.

(e)   Print GST [Details – Accrual] report for July – All Taxes and "*Both Collected and Paid*" with tax inclusive amounts for sales and purchases.

5.5   *Integrates general ledger, accounts receivable and cashbook.*

Assessment requirements:

This assessment exercise requires you to:

- Enter opening balances for the general ledger to convert hand-written accounts to *MYOB AccountRight Plus*.
- Create Accounts Receivable
- Set up the Sales and Receivables linked accounts and enter the historical invoice details agreeing with the general ledger accounts receivable control account
- Record accounts receivable transactions for the month of July 2011
- Print various forms and reports.

The business (*Adam's Garden*) is a *fresh food supplier and distributor*.
An *Accounts List* has been adopted from those supplied with *MYOB AccountRight Plus* and been modified by an accountant to comply with their normal reporting style.

Important: You may need to add accounts as you progress through the exercise. The exercise month is July 2011.

Start *MYOB AccountRight Plus* and open an existing file called **ass55.myo.**

Use the ***Setup*** menu, ***Company Information*** option and change the business address to "Your full name – Assessment 5.5 (ass55.myo)".

- Select *Balances* from the *Setup* menu to enter the following account opening balances as at 1 July 2011:

	Debit	Credit
St George Bank	5,481.35	
Petty Cash	500.00	
Accounts Receivable	17,126.10	
Provision for Doubtful Debts		1,780.00
Inventory	18,431.85	
Prepayments	3,800.00	
Cool Rooms & Refrigerators	124,380.00	
Accum. Depreciation – Cool Rooms & Refrigerators		31,480.60
Furniture and Fittings	23,450.60	
Accum. Depreciation – Furniture and Fittings		9,540.90
Office Equipment	24,290.00	
Accum. Depreciation – Office Equipment		18,990.00
Motor Car	18,500.00	
Delivery Truck	31,600.00	
Acc Dep. Motor Vehicles		40,100.00
Improvements	31,900.00	
Improvements Amortisation		7,975.00
Accounts Payable		7,026.10
GST Collected		80.75
GST Paid	1,000.00	
PAYG Withholding Payable		3,954.75
Payroll Deductions Payable		1,180.50
Capital		100,000.00
Retained Earnings		78,351.30
	300,459.90	300,459.90

- Set up Accounts Receivable (customer) records using the *Card File* Command centre as follows: (assume second address is the same as the first). No email addresses.

  For '*net/30*' select: "In a given # of days" Balance Due Days = 30. No discount.

Name	Address	Phone	Fax	Contact	$ Limit	Terms
Excelsior Restaurant	345 Mary Street Silverwater 2141 ABN:77 797 401 402	9714 0865	9714 0777	Nick Savini	80,000	net/30
Sunny Restaurant	82 Queen Street Granville 2141 ABN:14 497 466 484	9682 4412	9637 5543	Ted Jones	50,000	net/30
7H Restaurant	78 Shenton Av Seven Hills 2147 ABN:90 900 111 111	9624 3332	9624 6648	Bill Deutrom	40,000	net/30
Granville Delight	136 Terminus St Granville 2141 ABN:30 308 644 848	9637 2558	9637 1110	Zack Romero	30,000	net/30
Ace Food Bar	144 Showground Road Castle Hill NSW 2154 ABN:11 212 337 609	9680 2217	9680 2255	Sheralyn	25,000	net/30
GIBB Restaurant	1 Church Street Castle Hill 2154 ABN:11 311 819 991	9634 9914	9634 5550	Russell Balding	80,000	net/30
The Nutt Bar	45 Brunker Road Homebush 2140 ABN 21 844 696 115	9763 4444	9763 4419	Peter Taylor	50,000	net/30
Boowana Canteen	50 Pittwater Road Hunters Hill 2110 No ABN	9637 1288		Ziggy	500	net/30

- Enter the following invoices (opening balances as at the conversion date) making up the balance in the general ledger for accounts receivable of $17,126.10:

  Note: Tax code is **FRE** for all sales in this exercise (fresh food).

Account Receivable	Invoice	Date	Amount – $
Boowana Canteen	7066	25/1/2009	100.00
Excelsior Restaurant	8410	5/6/2011	2,448.50
	8500	24/6/2011	1,899.00
Sunny Restaurant	8470	15/6/2011	3,228.60
7H Restaurant	8501	24/6/2011	800.00
Granville Delight	8407	2/6/2011	448.90
	8510	29/6/2011	1,045.60
GIBB Restaurant	8472	15/6/2011	2,175.00
The Nutt Bar	8408	3/6/2011	105.40
	8450	13/6/2011	150.50
	8480	21/6/2011	100.00
	8522	29/6/2011	124.60
Ace Food Bar	8445	12/6/2011	4,500.00
	Total	Receivable	17,126.10

- Enter the linked account numbers for Sales.
  (Select the *Setup* Menu, *Linked Accounts* option then *Sales Accounts* option.)

- Enter the following credit invoices. They are for the sale of fresh food (fit for human consumption) and as such are GST Free. First Invoice number should be #8523.

Note: All Amounts given <u>exclude</u> the GST. Tax CODE: **FRE** for all items.

Date	Account Receivable	Invoice	Amount	Sales detail
3/7/2011	Sunny Restaurant	8523	1,568.80	Fresh Meat
4/7/2011	Granville Delight	8524	480.50	Fresh Fruit
6/7/2011	The Nutt Bar	8525	65.80	Fresh Vegetables
7/7/2011	GIBB Restaurant	8526	1,077.00	Fresh Meat
7/7/2011	Ace Food Bar	8527	280.00	Fresh Meat
10/7/2011	The Nutt Bar	8528	142.80	Fresh Fruit
11/7/2011	Excelsior Restaurant	8529	1,888.75	Fresh Vegetables
14/7/2011	Sunny Restaurant	8530	985.60	Fresh Meat
17/7/2011	The Nutt Bar	8531	95.70	Fresh Fruit
18/7/2011	The Nutt Bar	8532	105.20	Fresh Vegetables
19/7/2011	GIBB Restaurant	8533	2,440.80	Fresh Meat
21/7/2011	Ace Food Bar	8534	829.00	Fresh Fruit
24/7/2011	7H Restaurant	8535	800.00	Fresh Vegetables
24/7/2011	Sunny Restaurant	8536	1,225.00	Fresh Meat
25/7/2011	Cash sales (Enter $440 in 'Paid Today' field)	8537	440.00	Fresh Meat
26/7/2011	Excelsior Restaurant	8538	1,030.60	Fresh Vegetables
26/7/2011	Cash sales (Enter $132 in 'Paid Today' field)	8539	132.00	Fresh Fruit
31/7/2011	Elgin Refreshments <u>New Account:</u> 3 Brisbane Rd, Castle Hill 2154 Phone: 9963 1419. ABN: 79 888 888 181	8540	1,429.00	Fresh Vegetables Contact: Willy Credit Limit $50,000 Terms: net/30 days
31/7/2011	The Nutt Bar	8541	180.50	Fresh Fruit

- At the end of the month, write off as bad the balance owing by Boowana $100. Use a negative sale invoice and apply it to Invoice # 7066. Make this customer card inactive.

- Enter the following cash receipts.
  IMPORTANT! When receiving payments from customers:
  use *Receive Payments* from the *Sales* command centre; and for *all* other receipts use *Receive Money* from the *Banking* command centre.
  <u>For multiple receipts on the same day use '***Group with Undeposited Funds***' and prepare a single deposit for that day</u>. Deposit all other single day receipts directly to the bank account. All the following receipts are paid by cheques (no details).

Date	Amount – $	Details
4/7/2011	448.90	Granville Delight – paying Inv # 8407
	350.00	Rent Income (Tax code GST)
10/7/2011	2,448.50	Excelsior Restaurant – paying Inv # 8410
12/7/2011	4,500.00	Ace Food Bar – paying Inv # 8445
14/7/2011	3,228.60	Sunny Restaurant – paying Inv # 8470
17/7/2011	2,175.00	GIBB Restaurant – paying Inv # 8472
18/7/2011	255.90	The Nutt Bar – paying Inv # 8408 $105.40 and Inv # 8450 $150.50
24/7/2011	1,899.00	Excelsior Restaurant – paying Inv # 8500
	500.00	Interest Income (Tax code FRE)
	800.00	7H Restaurant – paying Inv # 8501
	100.00	The Nutt Bar – paying Inv # 8480
28/7/2011	10,000.00	Additional Capital
31/7/2011	124.60	The Nutt Bar – paying Inv # 8522

- Print the following:
  (a)   Invoice # 8540 (select: "AccountRight Plus's Plain Paper Invoice");
  (b)   Statement for Excelsior Restaurant
      (Select Activity 1/6/11 to 31/7/11 – Form: AccountRight plain paper);
  (c)   Aged Receivable (detailed) at 31 July 2011
      (Select report name: *Ageing Detail*. Customise the report to <u>include</u> customers with $0.00 balances and enter date: 31/7/2011);
  (d)   Transaction listing for each of the following journals:
          Cash Receipts Journal for 1/7/2011 to 31/7/2011
          Sales & Receivable Journal for 1/1/2005 to 31/7/2011;
  (e)   Trial balance as at 31 July 2011. Do <u>*NOT*</u> include $0 balances.

Chapter 5: Answers to self-test exercises

5.1

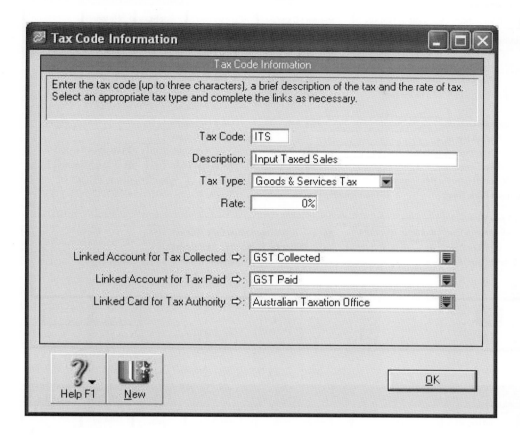

5.2

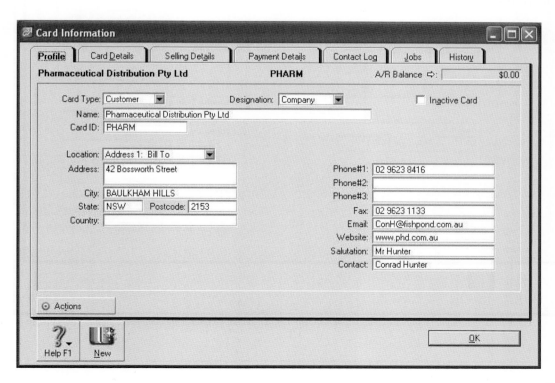

5.2 *(continued)*

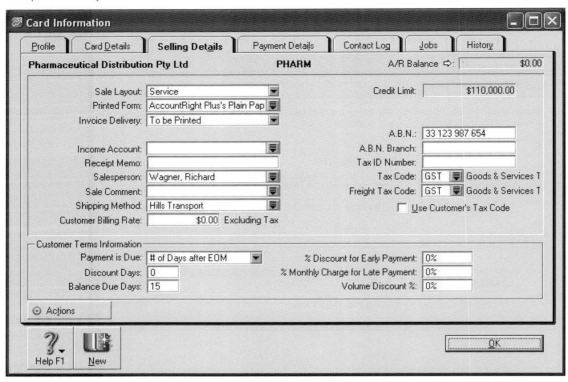

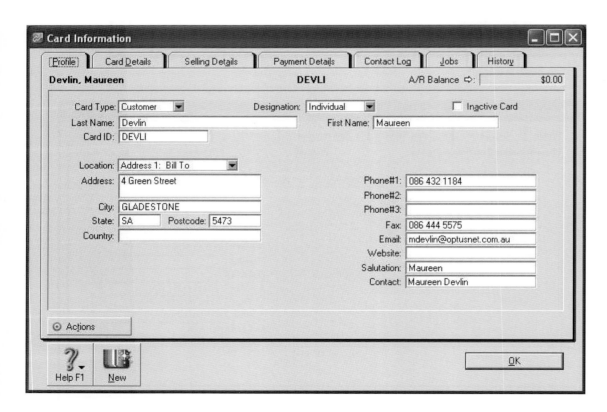

5.2 *(continued)*

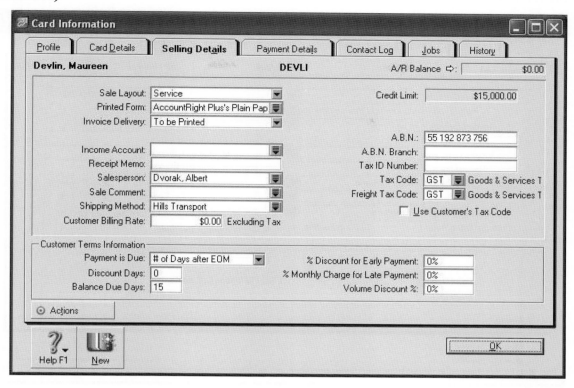

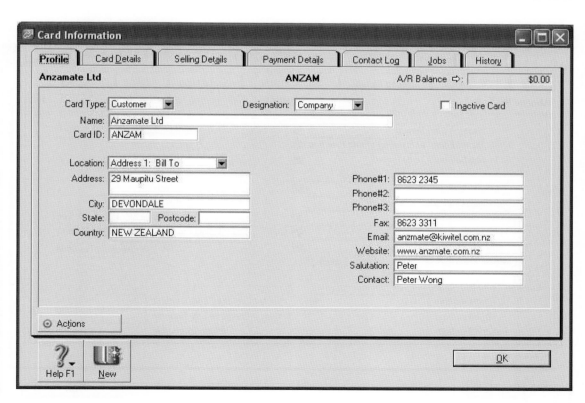

5.2 *(continued)*

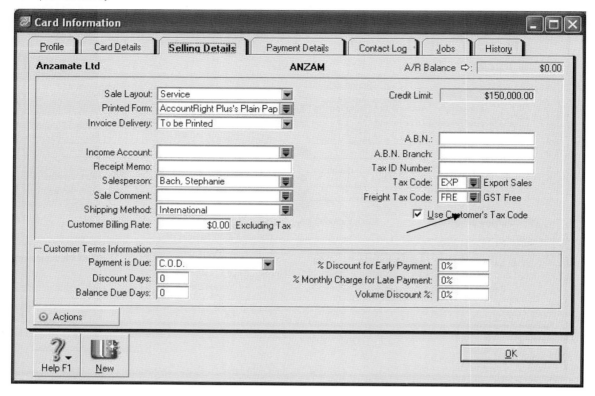

5.3

5.4

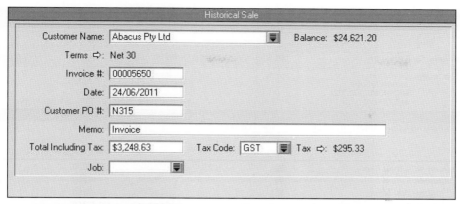

Historical Sale

Customer Name: Abacus Pty Ltd   Balance: $24,621.20
Terms ➪: Net 30
Invoice #: 00005650
Date: 24/06/2011
Customer PO #: N315
Memo: Invoice
Total Including Tax: $3,248.63   Tax Code: GST   Tax ➪: $295.33
Job:

Historical Sale

Customer Name: Colzmier Pty Ltd   Balance: $0.00
Terms ➪: Net 30
Invoice #: 00005642
Date: 11/06/2011
Customer PO #: C8560
Memo: Invoice
Total Including Tax: $21,148.50   Tax Code: GST   Tax ➪: $1,922.59
Job:

Historical Sale

Customer Name: Em-Kart Pty Ltd   Balance: $0.00
Terms ➪: Net 45
Invoice #: 00005643
Date: 16/06/2011
Customer PO #: 848-1450
Memo: Invoice
Total Including Tax: $25,290.60   Tax Code: GST   Tax ➪: $2,299.15
Job:

Historical Sale

Customer Name: Kiss Me Quick Pty Ltd   Balance: $0.00
Terms ➪: Net after EOM
Invoice #: 00003849
Date: 24/07/2009
Customer PO #: 442
Memo: Invoice
Total Including Tax: $558.00   Tax Code: GST   Tax ➪: $50.73
Job:

5.5

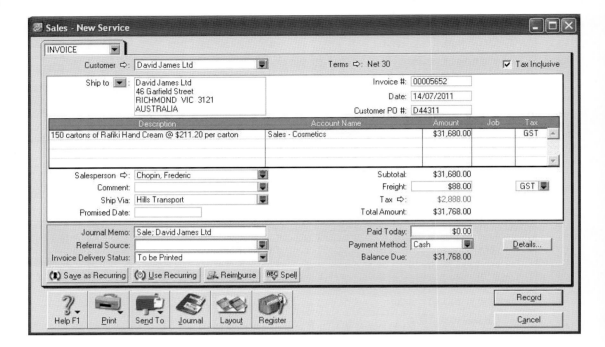

5.6

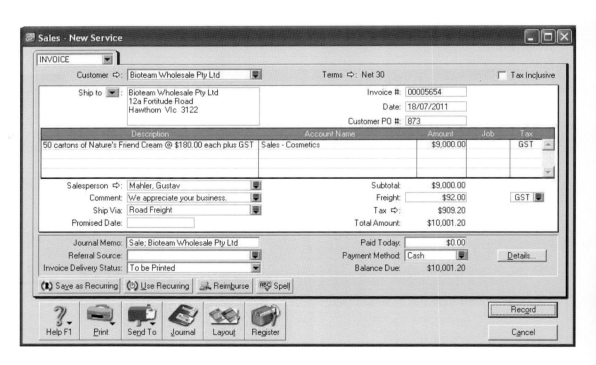

5.7

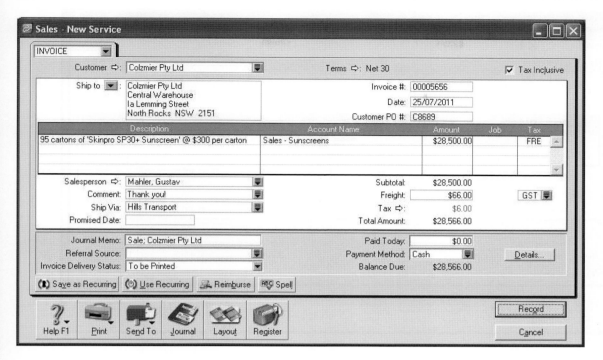

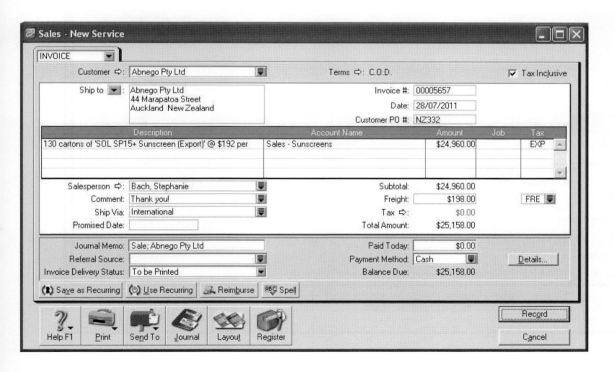

5.7 *(continued)*

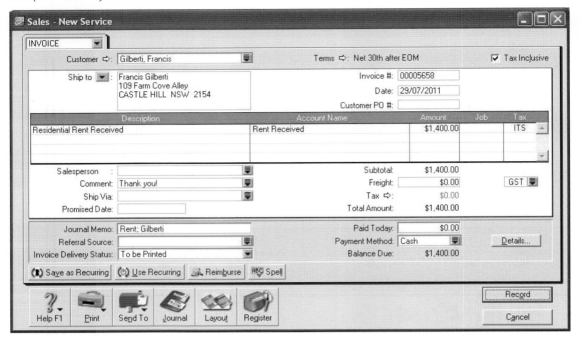

5.8

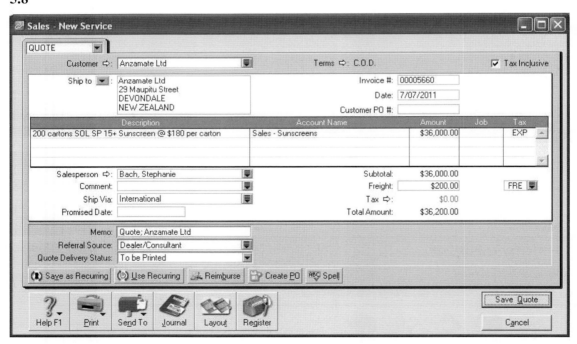

5.9

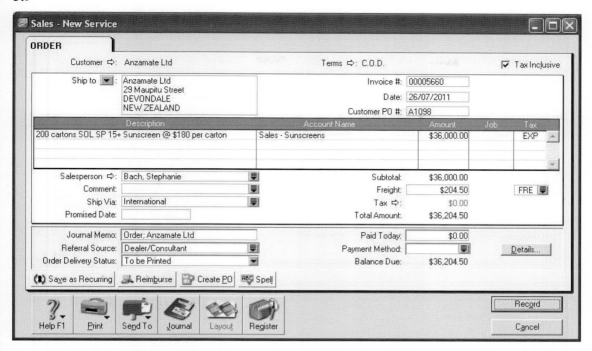

5.10

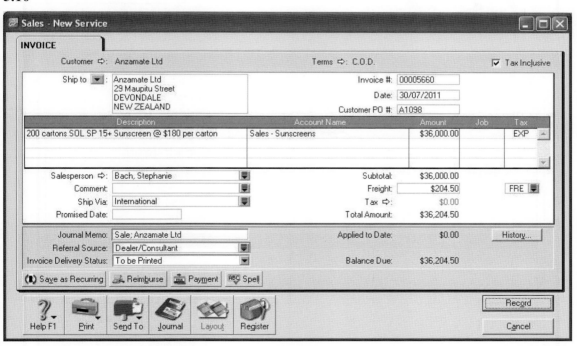

5.11

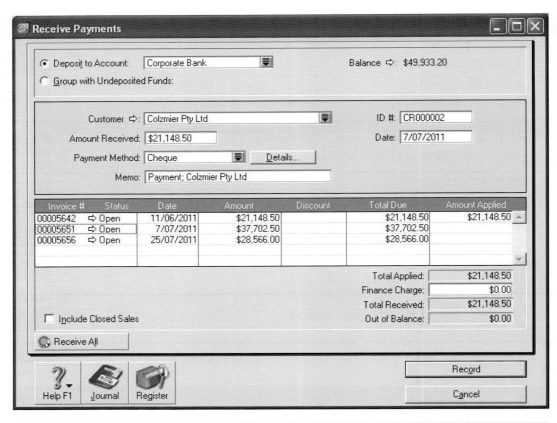

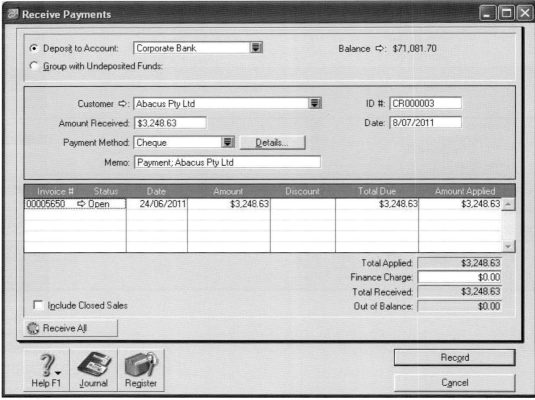

5.11 *(continued)*

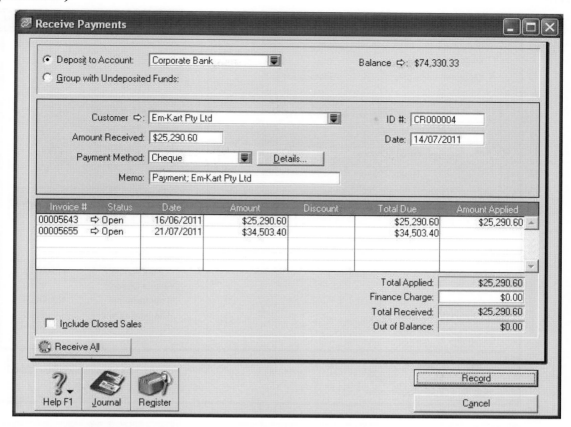

5.12

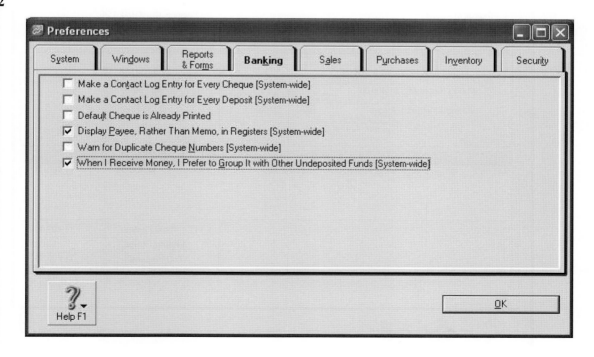

5.13

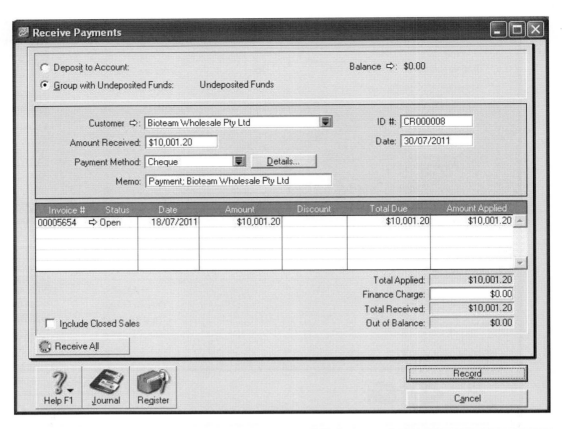

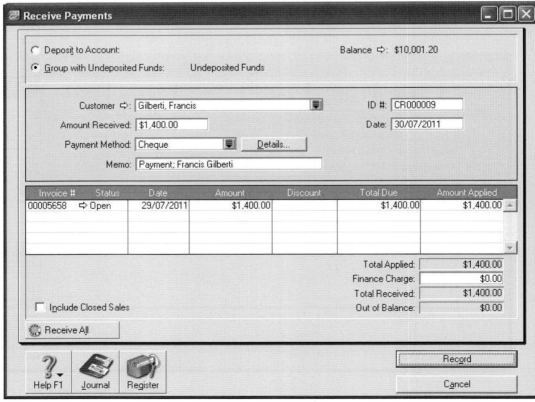

5.13 *(continued)*

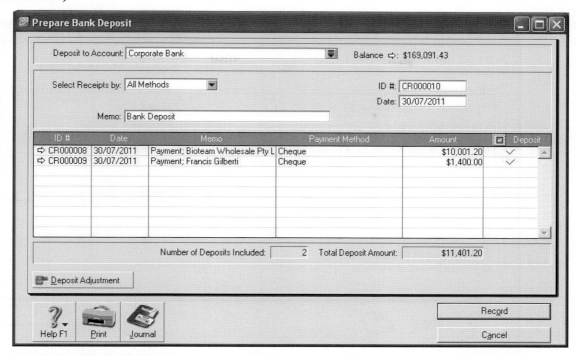

5.14

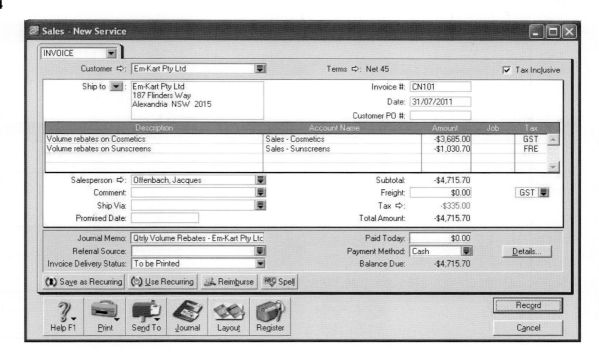

5.15

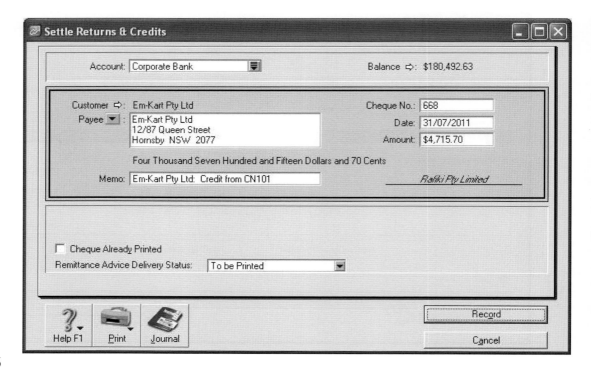

5.16

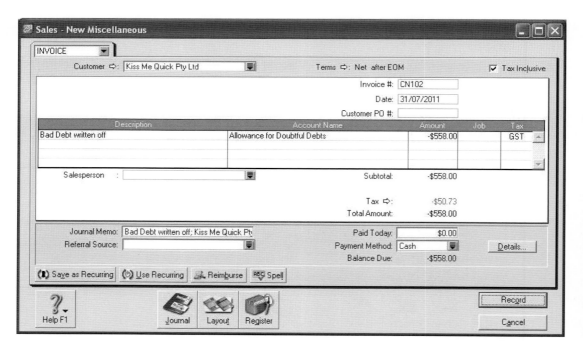

5.16 *(continued)*

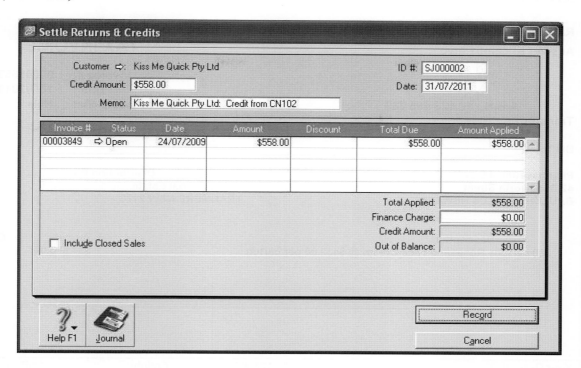

5.17

Rafiki Pty Ltd

Answer to dem51.myo

TAX INVOICE

Invoice #:	00005651
Date:	7/7/2011
Ship Via:	Hills Transport
Page:	1

A.B.N.: 12 123 456 789
A.C.N.:

Bill To:

Colzmier Pty Ltd
Central Warehouse
1a Lemming Street
North Rocks NSW 2151

Ship To:

Colzmier Pty Ltd
Central Warehouse
1a Lemming Street
North Rocks NSW 2151

Description	Amount	Code
75 cartons Roseanne Face Cream @ $475.20 per carton	$35,640.00	GST
15 cartons Moshi Face Pack @ $126.50 per carton	$1,897.50	GST

Your Order #: C8621			Customer ABN: 98 765 432 123		Freight:	$165.00	GST
Shipping Date:			Terms: Net 30		GST:	$3,427.50	
COMMENT	CODE	RATE	TAX	SALE AMOUNT	Total Inc GST:	$37,702.50	
We appreciate your business	GST	10%	$3,427.50	$34,275.00	Amount Applied:	$37,702.50	
					Balance Due:	$0.00	

5.17 *(continued)*

Rafiki Pty Ltd

Answer to dem51.myo

TAX INVOICE

Invoice #:	00005653
Date:	18/7/2011
Ship Via:	Hills

A.B.N.: 12 123 456 789

Transport

A.C.N.:   Page: 1

Bill To: Ship To:

Bill To:	Ship To:
Pharmaceutical Distribution P/L	Pharmaceutical Distribution P/L
42 Bossworth Street	111 Industrial Estate
BAULKHAM HILLS NSW 2153	TRANMERE NSW 2166

Description	Amount	Code
80 cartons Roseanne Face Cream @ $432.00 per carton	$34,560.00	GST

Your Order #: 9876	Customer ABN: 33 123 987 654			Freight:	$165.00	GST
Shipping Date:	Terms: Net 30			GST:	$3,472.50	
COMMENT	CODE	RATE	TAX	SALE AMOUNT	Total Inc GST:	$38,197.50
We appreciate your business	GST	10%	$3,472.50	$34,725.00	Amount Applied:	$0.00
					Balance Due:	$38,197.50

5.18

Rafiki Pty Limited
Sample Answer
Demonstration exercise dem51.myo

Aged Receivables [Summary]

31/07/2011

Page 1

Name	Total Due	0 - 30	31 - 60	61 - 90	90+
Abnego Pty Ltd	$25,158.00	$25,158.00	$0.00	$0.00	$0.00
Anzamate Ltd	$36,204.50	$36,204.50	$0.00	$0.00	$0.00
Colzmier Pty Ltd	$27,066.00	$27,066.00	$0.00	$0.00	$0.00
Maureen Devlin	$8,478.80	$8,478.80	$0.00	$0.00	$0.00
Em-Kart Pty Ltd	$34,503.40	$34,503.40	$0.00	$0.00	$0.00
Pharmaceutical Distribution	$38,197.50	$38,197.50	$0.00	$0.00	$0.00
Total:	$169,608.20	$169,608.20	$0.00	$0.00	$0.00
Ageing Percent:		100.0%	0.0%	0.0%	0.0%

5.19

Click here to select "Sales Territory NSW"

Rafiki Pty Ltd
Answer to dem51.myo

Ignore this date. It refers to the date the report was printed – not necessarily the statement date!

STATEMENT

A.B.N.:	12 123 456 789
A.C.N.:	123 456 789

DATE
31/7/2011

Pharmaceutical Distribution Pty Ltd
42 Bossworth Street
BAULKHAM HILLS NSW 2153

Check these dates!

AMOUNT REMITTED

$

Customer ABN: 33 123 987 654

Page 1   Activity From: 01/7/2011   To: 31/7/2011   Balance Forward: $0.00

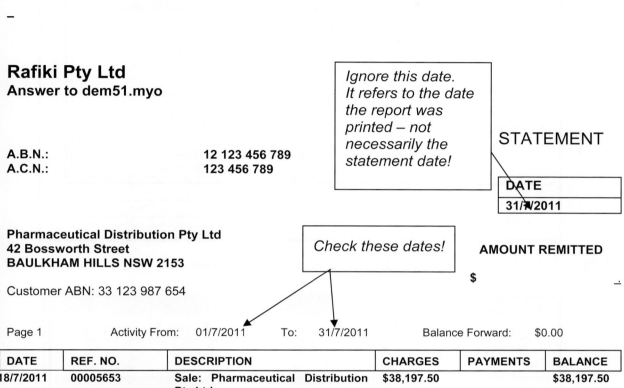

DATE	REF. NO.	DESCRIPTION	CHARGES	PAYMENTS	BALANCE
18/7/2011	00005653	Sale: Pharmaceutical Distribution Pty Ltd	$38,197.50		$38,197.50

31/7/2011		Finance Charges	$0.00		$38,197.50

CURRENT	30 DAYS	60 DAYS	60+ DAYS	AMOUNT DUE
$38,197.50				$38,197.50

5.20 *Colzmier*'s transactions <u>before</u> the merger with *Em-Kart*

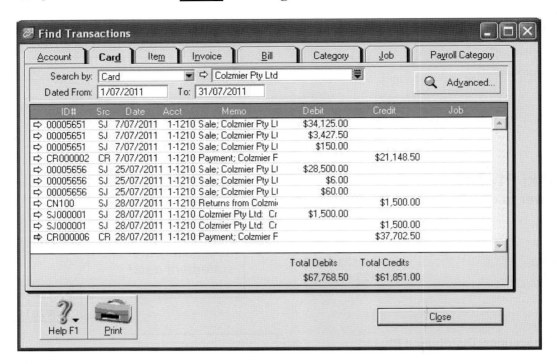

5.21 *Colzmier*'s transactions <u>after</u> the merger with *Em-Kart*

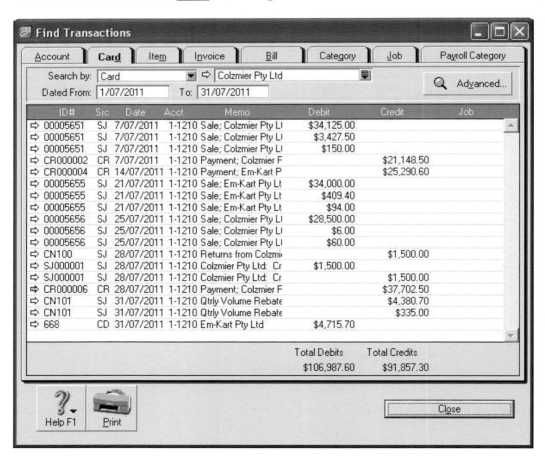

Accounts payable   6

Creating and maintaining supplier records, recording bills on credit and debit notes, payments to suppliers. Printing reports.

After completing this chapter you will be able to:

1   Set up the Purchases and Payables.

2   Create and maintain supplier information on cards.

3   Enter starting historical data for accounts payable.

4   Integrate (link) the accounts payable records with the general ledger.

5   Record purchase quotes, orders or invoices (bills) and payments to suppliers using an 'open item' method.

6   Record special transactions such as suppliers' credit notes.

7   Print/email documents and reports from the accounts payable.

8   Print GST reports.

9   Combine duplicate Supplier Records (cards).

10   Contra amounts owing against amounts owed.

Introduction

The *Purchases* command centre is used for preparing purchase orders or supplier invoices, recording credit notes against purchases (internal debit notes), and recording payments to accounts payable. Records are also kept for individual accounts payable (suppliers of goods and services on credit).

The *Purchases* command centre (or its full name 'Purchases and Payable') cannot be used without certain minimum accounts in a general ledger. The general ledger setup has to be completed before this command centre can be used. At least two accounts must appear in the general ledger *Accounts List* – "Accounts Payable" and "Bank". For this chapter, the general ledger set up has been completed for you.

> The notes, examples and exercises that follow assume that you have read and gone through the basic instructions in Chapter 1, and that you can:
>
> - Start the *MYOB AccountRight Plus* application;
> - Change the business name and/or address;
> - Select Command Centres and options within those command centres; and
> - Recognise the conventions used in this book (for example, the sign ↵ is an instruction to tap the *Enter* key).
>
> You may need to refer back to Chapter 1 to do these tasks. A quick way of finding the place for instructions is to use the 'How to ...' index at the front of the book – listed by chapters and by functions.
>
> In this chapter the authors have elected to use accounts selected and listed by **account numbers** rather than by account names. Throughout this book, you may use whichever option you prefer.

An open item system

Many computer packages allow for two methods of accounting for payments, and the recording of credit notes against credit transactions. These are known as "balance forward" and "open item". A balance forward system applies money and/or credit notes against the opening balance (or first supplier's invoice). An open item system applies money and/or credit notes against the <u>relevant</u> invoice(s) involved.

The *MYOB AccountRight Plus* accounts payable can be set up as a "balance forward" system by selecting *Setup – Preferences – Purchases* and turning this option on. However, in this chapter, examples and exercises use an open item system. Payments to a supplier, or credits received from the supplier, <u>must</u> be *applied* (matched) against the invoices (bills) concerned. Until a payment or credit is applied to the <u>full</u> balance of the invoice, the invoice is shown as *OPEN*. Once a payment or credit is applied to an invoice and no outstanding balance is owing, the invoice is shown as *CLOSED*. Closed invoices have balances of zero.

Check spelling before recording transactions

Before recording a transaction you can check the spelling. *MYOB AccountRight Plus* spell checker mainly checks spelling in the text fields.

You have the option of whether or not to use this feature automatically. In <u>this chapter</u>, the authors have selected to use the spell checker <u>manually</u>. To set up this option, you need to access the *Preferences* option from the *Setup* drop down menu, click on the *Windows* tab and clear the tick box of the last option:

| Clear this box | 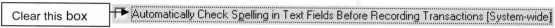 Automatically Check Spelling in Text Fields Before Recording Transactions [System-wide] |

The transactions therefore will not be automatically checked for spelling before recording. You can check the spelling manually at any time before recording any transaction by clicking on the *Spell* button at the bottom of any form.

However, if you prefer to use this option automatically, tick the box of the last option "Automatically Check Spelling in Text Fields Before Recording Transactions".

When the spell checker is activated (manually or automatically) it will display the misspelled words. You have the option to accept the suggestion by clicking *Change* or *Change All*, ignoring the suggestion by selecting *Ignore* or *Ignore All*, or alternatively you may add the word to the dictionary used by selecting *Add*.

You can control the way the spell checker will perform its functions. In the *Windows* tab of the preferences, click on the *Spelling* button at the bottom.

The *Spell Check Preferences* window will appear where you can fine tune the spell checker's performance. You can, for example, select that the spell checker ignores words that start with capitals or email addresses and so on.

MYOB AccountRight Plus tax codes

A tax code is used in a transaction to:

- calculate, add and show the correct amount of tax on the document evidencing the transaction; and
- accumulate transactions according to type for tax reporting.

Adding or editing a tax code

A tax code can be set up for entries required on the Business Activity Statement (BAS). When you purchase *MYOB AccountRight Plus*, many codes are set up. However, some businesses may require a specific code that may not be available and needs to be added. Adding or editing a tax code has been covered in Chapter 2. Example 6.1 follows the steps of the 'How to add/edit a tax code' from that chapter.

 Example 6.1—Entering a tax code for capital purchases

1. Open the file **dem61.myo** and sign on as the "Administrator", without a password.
2. Select the *Lists* pull-down menu.
3. Select the *Tax Codes* menu item and click on the *New* button.
4. Enter a three character tax code as "CAP" ↵.
5. Type in the description as "Capital Acquisitions" ↵.
6. The type of tax is "Goods & Services Tax" ↵.

7. The tax rate is "10%" ↵.

8. Select account number "2-1310" 'GST Collected' as the linked account for GST collected by the business from customers.

9. Select account number "2-1330" 'GST Paid' as the linked account for GST paid by the business to suppliers of goods and services.

10. Select the "Australian Taxation Office" as the linked tax authority that is to be paid.

11. The window should look like Figure 6.1. Edit any incorrect part and click the *OK* button to finish, then click on *Close* button to return to the command centre.

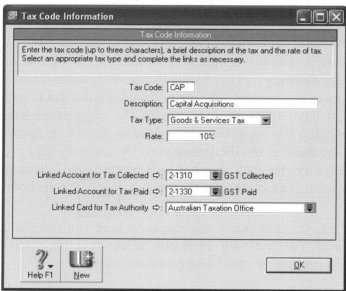

Figure 6.1: New tax code for capital acquisitions (purchases)

Video: A video showing you how to add or edit tax codes is on the DVD

Self-test exercise 6.1

The file is dem61.myo.

Enter a new Tax Code as: "NON".

Description:	Rate	Tax Type:	Linked Acc. for Tax Collected:	Linked Acc. for Tax Paid
Non-Deductible/ Private Use	0%	Goods & Services Tax	GST Collected 2-1310	GST Paid 2-1330
This tax code will be used for entry in G15 on a GST calculation worksheet for the Business Activity Statement (BAS). It relates to purchases of items for private use or other non-deductible items for income tax purposes.				

As well as the codes entered in the previous example and exercise, there should already be the following codes: "GST" and "FRE".

Recording a purchase on credit

When you record a purchase on credit using the *Purchases* command centre, the program will automatically credit the total purchase value to the linked accounts payable account. It will also record any GST and freight to the relevant accounts. If you are not using an *Item* purchase (see Chapter 7 for *item purchases*), you will have to nominate the account that needs to be debited. This account is usually a trading expense account such as "Purchases", but it can also be an asset, a service or an office supplies account, if they are purchased on credit. When recording a purchase you can specify the cost or charges against specific jobs. Jobs and categories will be covered in Chapter 9.

Setting up custom lists and field names for suppliers' cards

A card must be created for each supplier before any purchases are able to be processed for that supplier. There are certain custom fields and lists that will be used with these cards and they need to be set up (named and added) first.

Supplier cards come with a number of standard fields. However, a business may have a particular need to include certain information on the suppliers' cards that may not be available. In this situation *MYOB AccountRight Plus* offers up to three extra fields and three extra lists that can be customised and used for this purpose.

In the *Card Details* window of any card (see later) there are three *custom lists* and three *custom fields*. These can be customised and used to enter data on the cards.

The custom lists and custom fields are set up from the *Lists* pull-down menu, but used from the *Card Details* window of all suppliers' cards.

Setting up *Custom Fields*
The setting up mainly involves giving each field a label name that describes its use. Once you name the custom fields you can enter relevant information in these fields in the same manner as you would for any other field on the card.

Setting up *Custom Lists*
The setting up of the three custom lists is achieved in two steps – 1) giving a label name to each list used, and 2) adding items to the lists. Once you create a list you can make a selection from any supplier's card by simply clicking on the down-arrow next to the relevant list and selecting an item by clicking on it. You can add new items to each list or edit or delete existing items from any list. These are done from the *Lists* pull-down menu.

How to label or name custom lists and fields for suppliers' cards

Step	Instruction
1	Select the *Lists* pull-down menu at the top of the window.
2	Select the *Custom List and Field Names* menu item then select *Suppliers*.
3	Enter a list label name for each custom list in the first three boxes.
4	Enter a field label name for the three custom fields in the last three boxes.
5	Click *OK* to exit the *Custom List and Field Names* window.

Example 6.2—Naming the custom lists and the custom fields

1. Make sure that you have the file dem61.myo open.
2. Select the *Lists* pull-down menu.
3. Select the *Custom List and Field Names* menu item then select *Supplier*.
4. Enter three labels for the three lists and three labels for the three fields as per Figure 6.2 and click the *OK* button.

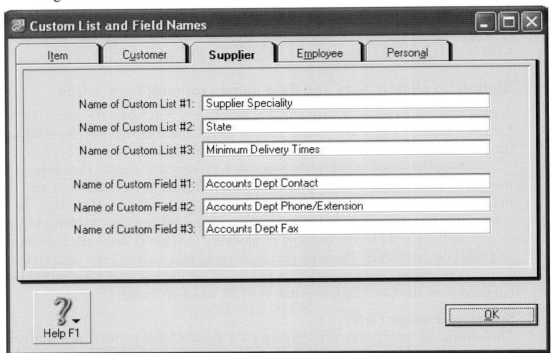

Figure 6.2: Supplier section of the *Custom List and Field Names*

How to add items to custom lists for suppliers' cards

Step	Instruction
1	Select the *Lists* pull-down menu at the top of the window.
2	Select the *Custom List* menu item then select *Suppliers*.
3	Click on the 'Custom List:' selection box and from the resulting drop-down box select the list you wish to add items to.
4	Click on the *New* button and type the item's name to be added.
5	To add more items click on *New* to record the entry and add the next item.
6	To record the last item click the *OK* button and then the *Close* button to exit.

Example 6.3—Naming the custom lists and the custom fields

1. Make sure that you have the file dem61.myo open.
2. Select the *Lists* pull-down menu.
3. Select the *Custom List* menu item then select *Suppliers*.
4. Click on 'Custom List:' box and select "Supplier Speciality".

5. Click on the *New* button and type "Cosmetic Suppliers".

6. Click on *New* button and type "Sunscreen Consultants" to add the next item.
7. Click on *New* button and type "Sunscreen Suppliers" to add the last item.
8. Click on *OK* to record the last item and on *Close* to exit.

Video: A video showing you how to set up custom lists and fields is on the DVD

Self-test exercise 6.2

Have the file dem61.myo open.

Add the following items to the *State* custom list:

"ACT", "NSW", "NT", "SA", "TAS", "QLD", "VIC" and "WA".

Creating supplier records in a card file

MYOB AccountRight Plus uses a "card file" system to record the relatively permanent data about customers, suppliers and employees. Each supplier making up the "Accounts Payable" (as well as cash suppliers) <u>must</u> have a card. This card will contain the address, phone etc as well as credit and purchasing terms. A card can be established at any time when using the *Purchases* command centre, but if a number of cards are to be created or maintained (altered), the separate *Card File* command centre should be used.

How to create a card for a supplier

Step	Instruction
1	Select the *Card File* command centre.
2	Select the *Cards List* option.
3	Select the *Supplier* tab at the top of the window. A list of suppliers for which cards have been prepared is displayed (if any).
4	Click on the *New* button at the foot of the window.
5	In the *Profile* section of the card, type in the name of the business or individual and ⏎. (Use the drop down selection for the 'Designation' and select either '*Company*' or '*Individual*' if necessary.)
6	Type in the 'Card ID' if this option is used. This represents the supplier ID.
7	Using 'Address 1', enter the street address and TAB. Enter city, state, postcode and country.
8	TAB or ⏎ to move through the other fields in the *Profile* section and enter phone and fax numbers, email address, web site, salutation and contact name.
9	Select any other 'Location' if required by using the drop-down list and enter in address information. Repeat steps 7 & 8 above for the other addresses (if any).
10	Click on the *Card Details* Tab and enter any of the optional information. Select *Identifier* and a *Custom List* if these have been set up (they are also used to select (or sort) cards for reports based on certain criteria).
11	Click on the *Buying Details* tab at the top of the window.
12	On the left-hand side of this section bill defaults may be entered. For example, a default layout, printed form, shipping method etc. These defaults can be changed on the actual bill (if necessary).
13	On the right-hand side of this section enter the credit limit, the supplier's ABN and, if applicable, the branch ABN.
14	Set the default GST code for goods and services purchased from this supplier and for freight charged by the supplier. Type a code or use the *List* button 🔽 and select it. These codes will be used if the supplier's tax code is to be used.
15	In the bottom of this section enter in the terms of trade. (See next page.)
16	Click on the *New* button to add more cards.
17	Click on the *OK* button to complete the last card and on the *Close* button to exit the *Cards List* window.

SUPPLIER TRADING TERMS

When creating a Supplier's card, we need to record the supplier's terms and conditions. As you add suppliers' cards, refer to this page for explanations of terms used by *MYOB AccountRight Plus*.

Credit Limits

We need to set a credit limit for each supplier. Goods can be purchased on credit from the supplier to the extent of this 'Credit limit'. Once this limit is exceeded, *MYOB AccountRight Plus* gives a warning before processing any bill. The supplier can then be contacted to either extend the credit limit to cater for the purchase, or, alternatively, make a payment for the difference between the available credit and the total.

There are numerous ways that a supplier's bill can be settled depending on the agreed terms of settlement:

Settlement Terms	Select **this** in the field **'Payment is Due:'**
Pay in advance before goods are dispatched.	**Prepaid**
Pay for the goods when delivered. **C**ash **O**n **D**elivery	**C.O.D.**
Pay in so many days after the date of the Bill (days after purchase date).	**In a given # of Days**
Pay in so many days after *the end of the month* of purchase.	**# of Days after E.O.M.**
Pay for all outstanding bills on a day of the month – each month. For example, on the 15th of each month pay for all bills (purchases).	**On a Day of the month**
Pay, on a specific day next month, for this month's purchases (bills).	**Day of Month after EOM**
Letter of Credit.	**Prepaid**

Discounts

A supplier may offer a discount for paying bills early i.e. *before* the due date as set above. Enter the discount rate (%) in the field '% Discount for Early Payment' and enter in the field 'Discount Days' or 'Discount Date', the number of days (or Date), after purchase, a payment can be made to qualify for this discount.

If a volume (or quantity) discount is offered by the supplier for bulk buying, you can enter the discount rate (%) in the 'Volume Discount %' field. This discount appears on the bill and automatically discounts the prices set for inventory items. This feature can only be used with *Item* layout bills.

Example 6.4—Creating a card for a supplier (account payable)

1. Make sure that you have the file dem61.myo open.
2. Change the *Company Information* by entering your name in the address field.
3. Select the *Card File* command centre.
4. Select the *Cards List* option.
5. Click on the *Supplier* tab at the top of the *Cards List* window.
6. Click on the *New* icon button at the bottom of the *Cards List* window.
7. If it is not already selected, the designation is "Company". Type in the name of the company "Skincare Labs Pty Ltd" ↵.
8. Type in "SKINC" as the card ID ↵.
9. The 'Location' field should have "Address 1" selected. Use the TAB or ENTER key and enter in the address as "4/32 O'Briens Road, BUSSELTON, WA, 6280".
10. TAB and enter the phone #1 as "(08) 9244 6678" ↵.
11. TAB through to the fax number and enter "(08) 9243 2222" ↵.
12. Type in "scheong@sl.com.au" as the email address and ↵.
13. Enter "www.sl.com.au" as the web address ↵.
14. At the salutation field enter "Samantha" ↵.
15. Enter the contact name as "Samantha Cheong".
16. The *Profile* section of the supplier's card should look like Figure 6.3:

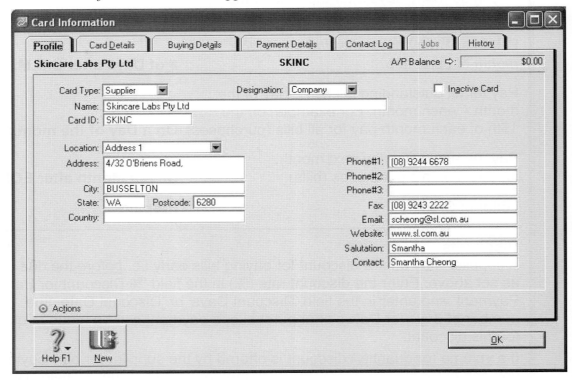

Figure 6.3: Profile section for a new supplier card

17. Click on the *Card Details* tab at the top of the *Card Information* window.

18. Click on the *Identifiers* button and tick the selection box "M" (this business uses "M" to identify this customer as a manufacturer) and click the *OK* button. Identifiers can be used to customise reports.

19. Use the *List* button ⏷ at the end of the 'Supplier Speciality' field and select "Cosmetic Suppliers" from the list, and select "WA" for the 'State'. Custom Lists can be used as selection criteria when customising or filtering reports.

20. Click on the 'Notes' field (top right) and type in "New Supplier in July. Specialises in creams made from natural ingredients". You may type in any notes pertinent to the supplier.

21. Click on the field 'Accounts Dept Contact' created earlier in the previous example, and type "Kerry Wilde".

22. Click on the new field 'Accounts Dept Phone/Ex' and type "(08) 9243 6682".

23. Click on the new field 'Accounts Dept Fax' and type "(08) 9243 6680". The *Card Details* window should look like Figure 6.4:

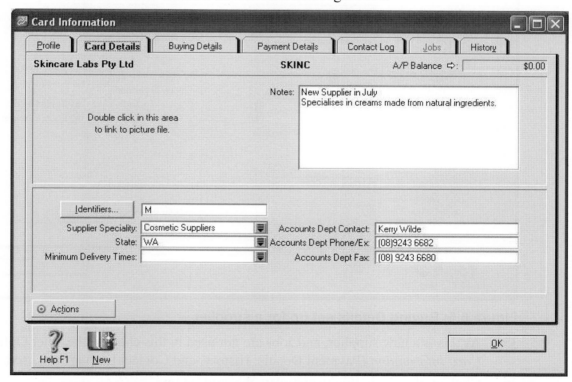

Figure 6.4: Card Details example for a supplier

24. Select the *Buying Details* tab at the top of the *Card Information* window.

25. Click on the drop-down list arrow at the end of the 'Purchase Layout:' field and select "Service" as the layout (this layout is used in this chapter and the "Item" layout is used in Chapter 7).

26. Use the *List* button ⏷ at the end of the 'Printed Form' field and select "AccountRight Plus's Plain Paper P.O.", and "To be Printed" for the 'Purchase Order Delivery'.

27. Click on the 'Credit Limit' field and enter "$60,000" ↵.

28. At the 'A.B.N' field, enter "84 342 645 879" ↵.

29. Leave the 'Tax Code' field as "GST" and the 'Freight Tax Code' as "GST". The 'Use Supplier's Tax Code' check box <u>should not</u> be ticked for <u>this</u> supplier.

30. Use the drop-down list in the 'Payment is Due' field and select "# of Days after EOM". This supplier requires payment within 30 days after the end of the month.

    IMPORTANT: Make sure to refer to the explanations of the trading terms on page 6-9.

31. In the 'Discount Days' field. Type in "7".

32. In the 'Balance Due Days' field, type in "30".

33. In '%Discount for Early Payment' field, type in "1" for 1%.

34. Your *Buying Details* window should look like Figure 6.5:

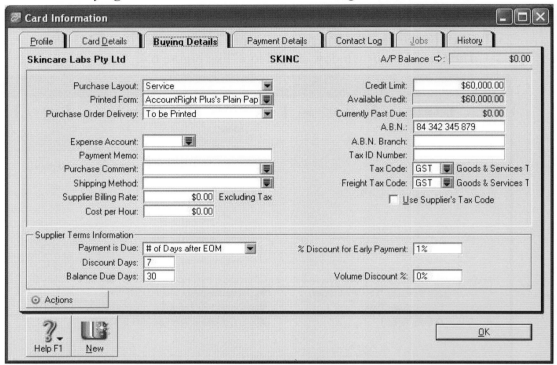

Figure 6.5: Buying Details set up for a supplier

35. As this is a new supplier, and Jobs are not used in this chapter, the other Options in *Card Information* (Payment Details, History, and Contact Log) are not used.

36. Click on the *OK* button to complete the card set up.

37. Click on the *Close* button to close the *Cards List* window.

> **Memo:**
> When cash discount terms are entered in a supplier's card, *MYOB AccountRight Plus* will calculate the amount of discount **and** will also calculate a refund of the proportion of any GST paid on the discounted amount. However, no discount will be automatically recorded unless the bill (less the discount) is paid in full <u>within the discount days</u>. A discount amount can <u>also</u> be <u>manually</u> entered or modified by the user, if necessary. The program will create a credit note (a debit memo) and apply it to the relevant bill.

Video: A video showing you how to create supplier cards is on the DVD

Self-test exercise 6.3

Have the file dem61.myo open and create the following Supplier cards:

First Card (Individual):

Profile

Last Name:	Hoy
First Name:	David
Card ID:	HOYDA
Address 1:	148 The Esplanade
	JACOBS WELL QLD 4208
Phone #1:	(07) 9287 2137
Phone #2:	0415 567 879
Fax #:	(07) 9287 9111
Email:	PhilB@fishpond.au
Salutation:	Philip
Contact Name:	Philip Ball

Card Details

Identifier:	C
Supplier Speciality:	Sunscreen Consultants
State:	QLD

Buying Details

Purchase Layout:	Service
Printed Form:	AccountRight Plus's Plain Paper P.O.
Credit Limit:	Not supplied
ABN:	44 123 456 789
Tax Code and Freight Tax Code:	GST
Use Supplier's Tax Code:	Do not select (not ticked)
Credit terms:	15 days after end of month (# of Days after EOM)

Second Card (Company):

Profile

Company name:	Davis Manufacturing Ltd
CARD ID:	DAVIS
Address 1:	124 Grange Street
	HORNSBY NSW 2077
Phone #1:	(02) 9623 2345
Fax #:	(02) 9623 3311
Email:	torpitz@davis.com.au
WW web:	www.davis.com.au
Salutation:	Bill
Contact Name:	William Torpitz

(continued on the next page)

Second Card (Company – *continued*):
Card Details

Identifier:	M
Supplier Speciality:	Cosmetic Suppliers
State	NSW
Accounts Dept Contact:	M/s Peta Costello

Buying Details

Purchase Layout:	Service
Printed Form:	AccountRight Plus's Plain Paper P.O.
Credit Limit:	$50,000
ABN:	12 176 543 123
Tax Code:	GST
Freight Tax Code:	GST
Use Supplier's Tax Code:	Do not select (not ticked)
Credit terms:	30 days after the end of the month/ 2% Discount for early payment (Discount Days = 7)

Setting up Purchases linked accounts to the general ledger

There are six *default* general ledger accounts *MYOB AccountRight Plus* uses to automatically prepare the necessary journal entries when recording bills for purchases, or payments to accounts payable (suppliers). Two out of these six linked accounts are compulsory minimum accounts that need to be nominated. The other four are optional.

 How to set up the purchases linked accounts

Step	Instruction
1	Select the *Setup* pull-down menu at the top of the screen.
2	Click on the *Linked Accounts* option and select the *Purchases Accounts*.
3	Enter a liability account to record amounts owing to Accounts Payable ↵.
4	Enter a bank account to record payments to Accounts Payable ↵.
5	Leave the *Optional* link 'I can receive items without a Supplier bill' un-ticked, as this link only applies to *Item* purchases (see Chapter 7).
6	If the supplier charges for freight, tick on the *Optional* link for recording freight charges and enter an expense account ↵.
7	If the supplier requires deposits to be paid, tick on the *Optional* link for recording deposits paid to suppliers and enter an asset account ↵.
8	If the supplier gives discounts for early payment, tick on the *Optional* link for recording any discounts received and enter an income account ↵.
9	If the supplier charges for late payments, tick on the *Optional* link for recording any additional charges paid to suppliers for late payments and enter an expense account ↵.
10	Click the *OK* button.

Video: A video showing how to set up the purchases link accounts is on the DVD

In the file dem61.myo, the purchases linked accounts are already set up:

Purchases Linked Accounts			
Liability Account for Tracking Payables ⇨:	2-1200		Accounts Payable
Bank Account for Paying Bills ⇨:	1-1110		Corporate Bank
☐ I can receive items without a Supplier bill			
☑ I pay freight on purchases			
Expense or Cost of Sales Account for Freight ⇨:	6-2300		Freight Charges
☑ I track deposits paid to suppliers			
Asset Account for Supplier Deposits ⇨:	1-2200		Deposits Paid
☑ I take discounts for early payment			
Expense (or Contra) Account for Discounts ⇨:	8-2000		Discounts Received
☑ I pay charges for late payment			
Expense Account for Late Charges ⇨:	6-2500		Late Fees Paid

Opening supplier balances (amounts owing to accounts payable)

If there are amounts owing to suppliers at conversion date (the date when the *MYOB AccountRight Plus* is *first* used), the invoices (bills) that make up the "Accounts Payable" balance must be entered. This is a "once-only" exercise, but needless to say, must be done carefully. When the total of the amounts entered for individual accounts payable agrees with the general ledger balance for accounts payable, a congratulatory message is received! The MYOB program refers to these balances as *Historical* or *Pre-conversion*.

How to enter the historical purchase invoices

Step	Instruction
1	Select the *Setup* pull-down menu at the top of the screen.
2	Select the *Balances – Supplier Balances* option.
3	Select a supplier by clicking on its name.
4	Click on the *Add Purchase* button.
5	If the supplier name is correct and highlighted, tap the enter key or TAB to the 'PO #:' field and type in the purchase order (bill) number ↵.
6	Enter the date of the purchase ↵.
7	Type in the supplier's invoice number (optional) ↵.
8	The standard memo suggested is "Pre-conversion purchase". Change this if you want another detail to appear in the account (for example, you may want "Invoice" to appear) ↵.
9	Enter the amount of the purchase (or outstanding balance) owing.
10	Check or change the tax code if necessary. If the purchase included GST the tax amount should show.
11	Click on the *Record* button. Read the warning and click *OK* to continue: Please Note: If you are reporting income on a cash basis, the payment of this purchase will not be included in Simplified Tax System reports.

Example 6.5—Entering a pre-conversion invoice for Cretian Cosmetics

1. Open the *MYOB AccountRight Plus* file dem61.myo.
2. Select *Setup* pull-down menu.
3. Select the *Balances* option and *Supplier Balances*.
4. Click on the details arrow ➪ next to the name 'Cretian Cosmetics Pty Ltd'.
5. Select the *Add Purchase* button.
6. The name Cretian Cosmetics Pty Ltd should be highlighted. Tap the enter key or TAB to the 'PO #:' field.
7. Enter the purchase number as "3125" ↵.
8. Enter the purchase date as "11/6/2011" ↵.
9. Enter the "Supplier Inv #" as "08212" ↵.
10. Leave the memo as "Pre-conversion purchase" ↵.
11. Enter the amount as "$21,262.25" ↵.
12. The tax code should be "GST" and the tax amount shown should be $1,932.93.
13. Your screen should look like Figure 6.6:

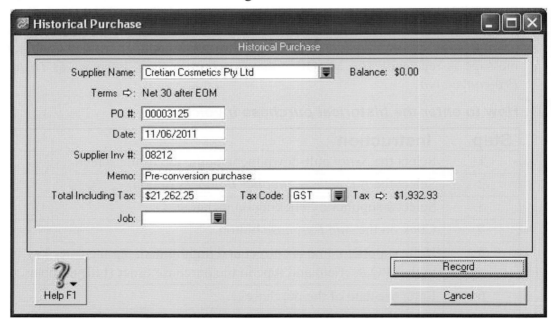

Figure 6.6: Pre-conversion invoice for Cretian Cosmetics Pty Ltd

14. Edit any incorrect field and click on the *Record* button. (Ignore the warning.)
15. Your *Supplier Balances* window should now look like Figure 6.7 on the next page. The 'Out of Balance Amount' indicates more balances need to be entered.

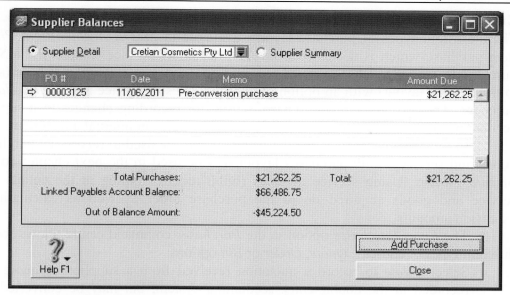

Figure 6.7: Payable balances after entering an invoice

Video: A video showing you how to enter suppliers opening balances is on the DVD

Self-test exercise 6.4

Have the file dem61.myo open. The exercise month is July 2011.
Enter the following pre-conversion purchases (all with tax code GST).
See solution at back of the chapter for this self-test exercise 6.4.
Ignore the warning in regard to the STS for Cash Basis Income for the following:

	Purch. #	Date	Supplier #	Amount
Cretian Cosmetics Pty Ltd	3147	30/6/2011	08250	$3,286.20
Davis Manufacturing Ltd	3122	7/6/2011	W286	13,260.30
Natural Bliss Pty Ltd	3144	29/6/2011	1234	4,052.90
Organic Beauty Supplies	3120	6/6/2011	993	10,000.00
Skincare Labs Pty Ltd	3140	24/6/2011	T819	14,625.10

A 'Congratulations' message, as shown in Figure 6.8, will indicate that all the entries of the outstanding (pre-conversion) purchases were entered correctly (i.e. equal the balance of the linked general ledger "Accounts Payable") and that you're ready to use the *Purchases* Command Centre!:

Figure 6.8: Congratulations – if you balance

If you do not balance, check your answer. Click on a detail arrow ⇨ next to any incorrect purchase in the *purchases* transaction journals for June 2011 and edit the entry.

Credit purchases

There are four types of purchase layouts available in *MYOB AccountRight Plus*: an *Item* purchase which is used when the *Item list* is set up (see Chapter 7), a *Service* purchase to record purchases of services <u>and</u> goods, a *Professional* purchase (similar to the *Service* layout) with an option of entering dates of service and a *Miscellaneous* purchase. The *Miscellaneous* purchase is used for recording changes to a supplier's account where no printouts are necessary – for example, an internal adjustment.

In this chapter, *Service* purchases layout will be used to record the purchase of goods and services. *Item* purchases layout will be used in the next chapter covering *Inventory items*. Using service invoices (bills) requires typing in the details of the service and goods acquired on to the purchase order as well as calculating the extension amounts.

The *Enter Purchases* option in the *Purchases* command centre allows for three different types of entries – *Quote*, *Order* or *Bill* options:

1.   Select **Quote** to record a quotation received from a supplier. A quote is not recorded in the double-entry accounting system, but may be converted to an *Order* (or a *Bill*) when the quotation is accepted and an order is placed with the supplier;

2.   Select **Order** to record an order placed with a supplier where a quotation has not been received. An *Order* is not recorded in the double-entry bookkeeping system, but is taken into account when using Item inventory (see Chapter 7 for using inventory items). The *Order* may be converted to a *Bill* when the goods and a supplier invoice are received;

3.   Select **Bill** (supplier's invoice) to record a purchase without first having recorded a quote or an order.

Note: There is a fourth option called **Received Items** which is used to record items received on existing *Item* orders before a bill is received. It is only available when *Item* layout is selected. This is covered in Chapter 7 – *Inventory and Integration*.

The entry of a purchase invoice (bill) directly will be demonstrated <u>*first*</u> and then the use of *Quotes*, *Orders* and the *Sales Register* will be shown.

How to enter a service purchase

Step	Instruction
1	Select the *Purchases* command centre.
2	Select the *Enter Purchases* option.
3	Click on the 'Supplier:' field and enter the supplier name. Type in the first few letters or use the *List* button ▼ and select a supplier from the list.
4	The purchase layout appears in the window title bar. Purchases - New Service To change the layout, click on the *Layout* button at the bottom of the window and select the option for a *Service* type layout. Layout
	(continued on the next page)

Step	Instruction
5	Tick the 'Tax Inclusive' box *on* if the prices and amounts to be entered already include the GST, otherwise clear it (un-tick the box). ☑ Tax Inclusive ☐ Tax Inclusive Amounts include GST GST (*if any*) will be added to the amounts
6	"BILL" should be the default set up at the top of the *Purchases - New Service* window. BILL ⬅ Entering a Bill Supplier :
7	TAB through to the purchase number field, change if necessary and TAB.
8	Enter the transaction date ↵ (or press the space bar to activate the *Calendar*).
9	Type in the supplier's invoice number if an actual purchase is being recorded. You can enter other details if a number is not available – for example, "Email 14/6" or "Fax – 14/6" etc. ↵.
10	Type in the description of the goods or services purchased and TAB.
11	Enter the account number (or the account name) for the asset or expense account to be debited and TAB. If the account number or name is not known, you may use ↵ to list all accounts and select from the list.
12	Enter the amount of the line item and TAB. You can use the keyboard and type your calculations or click on the calculator. You may press the space bar to activate *MYOB Calculator* to calculate the total amount payable. You may use *numbers* and the " + * – / " signs when typing your formula and press the "=" sign or ↵ to enter result.
13	Enter a job number if the amount is to be recorded against a particular job and TAB. **Note**: Jobs and Categories are covered in Chapter 9.
14	Accept or change the tax code ↵.
15	Enter any other line items as above.
16	Enter any freight charged on the invoice in the 'Freight' field. Change the default GST code for freight, if necessary.
17	If any deposit is paid today click in the 'Paid Today' field and enter amount.
18	The 'Comment', 'Ship via' and 'Promised Date' fields are optional. Click on the *List* button ▼ next to the field and select from the list. Use the *New* button to add any new entry required.
19	To view the settlement terms of this purchase or to change them, if necessary, click on the detail arrow ⇨ next to 'Terms' field on top of the form. **Note:** If you change the terms in this field, these changes will <u>only</u> apply to this bill. For a permanent change to the terms, enter the changes on the supplier's card.
20	Change the *Journal Memo* if necessary.
21	Select the *Record* button.

Example 6.6—Entering a purchase from Davis Manufacturing Pty Ltd

Enter the following purchase from Davis Manufacturing Pty Ltd on 4 July 2011. The purchase is for 150 cartons of Rafiki Hand Cream @ $126.50 per carton. "Best Way" delivered the goods and freight charged was $357.45. All prices include the GST.

1. Have the file dem61.myo open.

2. Select the *Purchases* command centre.

3. Select the *Enter Purchases* option.

4. The supplier is Davis Manufacturing Pty Ltd. Remember that you may type in the first few letters (say "Da"), hit enter and select from a list, or use the *List* button ⬇.

5. Make sure the purchase layout is *Purchases New Service.*

    If the layout is not *Service*, change it to *Service*.

    Click on the *Layout* button.

     ⬅ Click

    select the option *Service*  and click *OK*.

6. Check that the default "BILL" is selected in this exercise.

BILL ▼
Supplier : ▤

7. Check that the tax-inclusive box is ticked.   ☑ Tax Inclusive

8. TAB to the 'Purchase #' field so that the 'Ship to:' address remains. Enter "3148" as the purchase number ↵.

9. Enter the date as "4/7/2011". Remember that if the date in this field is a date in July 2011, you only have to type "4" ↵ (alternatively, press the spacebar or right click and select a date from the calendar).

10. The supplier's invoice number (#) is "W301" ↵.

11. Enter the description as "150 cartons of Rafiki Hand Cream @ $126.50 per carton" and TAB to the next field.

12. The account to be debited is account # 5-2100 "Purchases – Cosmetics". Enter this and TAB twice to amount field.

13. The amount to enter is $18,975.00 (this is the GST-inclusive amount for this line of the bill). You can either type "150 * 126.50 =" *or* "18975" and ↵.

14. The 'Tax' column should show a tax code of "GST".

15. Click on the 'Freight' field and enter "$357.45" which already includes the GST. The Tax code for freight should already show "GST".

16. Click on the 'Ship Via:' field and enter "Best Way". You may type in the first few letters or click on the *List* button ▤ and select from the list ↵.

17. Leave the rest of the purchase as is. The form should look like Figure 6.9:

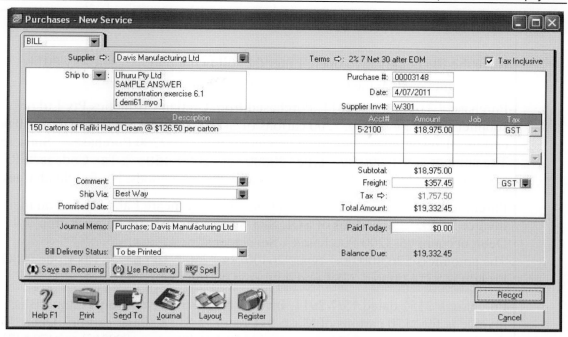

Figure 6.9: Completed tax-inclusive service purchase

18.	To correct any errors, click on the field concerned and over-type or edit.

19.	Before recording, use the *Edit* menu – *Recap Transaction* menu item and look at the effect on the ledger accounts. This is shown in Figure 6.10:

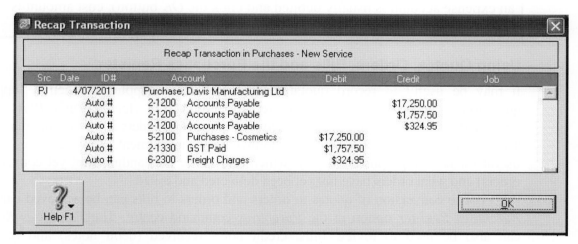

Figure 6.10: Recap transaction using a bill for service type purchase

20.	Click on the *OK* button to close the *Recap Transaction* window.

21.	Click on the *Record* button to record the purchase.

Video: A video showing you how to enter a purchase from a supplier is on the DVD

Self-test exercise 6.5

Have the file dem61.myo open. Enter the following purchases in July 2011 (all amounts include the GST where applicable): ☑ Tax Inclusive

Purchase # 3149 on 8/7/2011. Purchased from Cretian Cosmetics Pty Ltd on supplier Invoice # 08260, "200 cartons of Skinpro SP30+ Sunscreen @ $150 per carton". This purchase should be debited to Acc# "5-2200 Purchases – Sunscreens". The amount is $30,000.00 – type "30000" or "200 * 150 =". Tax Code is "FRE" for GST-free supply. Best Way Transport delivers these goods. No freight charges.

Purchase # 3150 on 12/7/2011. Purchased from Skincare Labs Pty Ltd on their invoice T840, "250 cartons of SOL SP5 Sunscreen @ $105.60 per carton". Debit account "5-2200 Purchases – Sunscreens". The amount is $26,400.00 – type "26400" or "250 * 105.6 = ". Tax Code is "GST". Freight is $314.60 incl. GST and delivered by International.

Purchase # 3151 dated 15/7/2011. Invoice # 1248 received from Natural Bliss. This invoice is for "170 cartons of Maso-to Cream @ $173.80 per carton". Debit "5-2100 Purchases – Cosmetics". The amount is $29,546.00 – type "29546" or "170 * 173.8 =". Tax Code = "GST". Hills Transport delivered these goods. Free delivery.

Purchased from Blue Leaf Computers on 28/7/2011 (Purchase # 3152, Supplier Invoice 462). Record the purchase of a "Dell – File server Model BLC-FS1000". Account # 1-3210 "Computer Equipment" is to be debited (ignore the warning that an expense account is usually debited and click the *OK* button), cost amount is $7,480.00 and the tax code is "CAP" for GST on capital acquisitions.

Using Quotes, Orders, Bills and the Purchases Register

It may be useful to record quotations received from suppliers. When a supplier's quotation is accepted, the quotation recorded in *MYOB AccountRight Plus* can be converted to an order. The difference between quotes and orders is not so important when services are being acquired, as there is no inventory commitment. However, it will still be useful for review purposes to know which quotes are outstanding (not yet converted to orders) and what orders have not yet been delivered and billed.

The conversion of quotes to orders and orders to bills can be achieved using the *Purchases Register* option in the *Purchases* command centre. The *Purchases Register* can also be used to review bills, credit notes received (debit notes) and recurring templates.

How to enter a supplier's quote using the service layout

Step	Instruction
1	Select the *Purchases* command centre.
2	Select the *Enter Purchases* option.

(continued on the next page)

Step	Instruction
3	Click on the 'Supplier:' field and enter the supplier's name. Type in the first few letters or use the *List* button ▼ and select a supplier from the list.
4	The *Purchase* layout appears in the window title bar. To change a purchase type, click on the *Layout* button at the bottom of the window and select *Service* as the layout.
5	A tick may appear in the 'Tax Inclusive' check box. Turn this *on* or *off* (tick or no tick) depending on whether the amounts entered are to be shown including or excluding the GST.
	☑ Tax Inclusive ☐ Tax Inclusive
	Includes GST Excludes GST
6	Change the default "BILL" set up at the top of the *Purchases – New Service* window to "QUOTE".
	Entering a supplier's quotation
7	TAB through to the purchase number field, change if necessary and TAB.
8	Enter the quotation date ↵.
9	Type in the supplier's quotation reference or number if it is available. You can enter other details if a number is not available – for example, "Letter 14/6", "Email 14/6" or "Fax – 14/6/2011" etc. and ↵.
10	Type in the description of the goods or services to be supplied or provided and TAB.
11	Enter the account number or name for the expense or asset account to be debited and TAB. If the account number or name is not known, you may use ↵ to list all accounts and select from the list. You select an account from the list by double clicking on it, or use a single click on the account and a click on the *Use Account* button.
12	Enter the amount of the line item and TAB (you do not have to enter a dollar sign or comma in money amounts). You can make use of *MYOB Calculator* in this field by typing in the calculation using digits (0 – 9) and any of these signs (+ – * /); enter result by typing "=" or ↵ (or Press the spacebar and use the mouse and click on the calculator buttons to calculate the amount).
13	Enter a job number if a cost is to be recorded for a particular job and TAB.
14	Enter or change the tax code.
15	Enter any other line items as above.

(continued on the next page)

Step	Instruction
16	Enter any freight quoted by the supplier in the 'Freight' field, if known. To change the default GST code, click on the *List* button next to the 'freight' field and select the code.
17	The 'Comment', 'Ship via' and 'Promised Date' fields are optional. Click on the *List* button next to the field and select from the list. Use the *New* or *Easy-Add* buttons to add any new entry required.
18	Change the journal 'Memo:' if necessary.
19	If the terms for this quote are different from the usual terms given by this supplier, click on the detail arrow ⇨ next to 'Terms' field on top of the form and modify as necessary. This change will only apply to this purchase.
20	Select the *Save Quote* button.

Example 6.7—Entering a quote received from a supplier

Enter the following quotation from Cretian Cosmetics Pty Ltd. Their invoices show amounts including the GST where the goods or services are taxable.

1. Have the file dem61.myo open.
2. Select the *Purchases* command centre.
3. Select the *Enter Purchases* option.
4. The supplier is Cretian Cosmetics Pty Ltd. You can either type the name in full or you may type in the first few letters (say "cr") and the program will "auto complete" the full name. Alternatively, use either the ENTER key or the *List* button to select the supplier's name from the displayed list.
5. Make sure that the purchase type is *Purchases – New Service.*
6. Click on the drop down arrow next to "BILL" and select "QUOTE".

7. Check that the figures entered in to the amount column are to be entered and displayed as tax-inclusive amounts where GST is applicable. ☑ Tax Inclusive
8. TAB through to the 'Purchase #:' field so that the ship to address remains. The purchase number should be 3153 ↵ (note that you could change the number if you want to keep a different sequence for quotations or orders).
9. Enter the date as "5/7/2011". Remember that if the date in this field is already a date in July 2011, you only have to type "5" ↵.
10. There is no supplier invoice number as this is only a quotation ↵.
11. Enter the description as "150 cartons of Rozeanne Face Cream @ $286.00 per carton including GST" and TAB to the next field.
12. The account to be debited is number 5-2100 "Purchases – Cosmetics". TAB to the amount field.

13. The amount to enter is $42,900.00. Type "42900" or "150 * 286 =".

14. The 'Tax' column should show "GST" ⏎.

15. Click on the field for entering freight and enter "$200", an estimated amount (the tax code for this freight should show "GST").

16. Change the 'Memo:' to read "Quote; Cretian Cosmetics Pty Ltd".
The Quote should look like Figure 6.11.

17. To correct any errors, click on the field concerned and overtype or edit.

18. Click on the *Save Quote* button to save it on file.

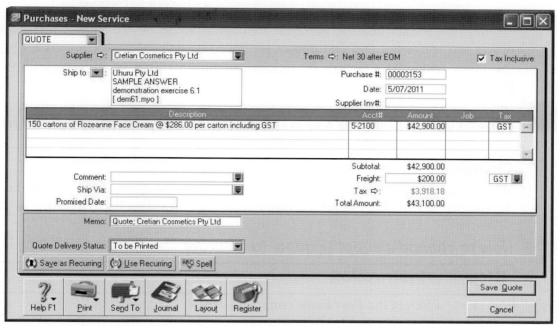

Figure 6.11: Quotation received from a supplier

Video: A video showing you how to enter a quote from a supplier is on the DVD

Self-test exercise 6.6

Have the file dem61.myo open.

Enter a quote (#3154 dated 6 July 2011) received from Bronco Skincare Pty Ltd. The quote is for "200 cartons of SOL SP-5 Sunscreen @ $104.50 incl. GST per carton". The account to be debited is number 5-2200 "Purchases – Sunscreens". The amount is (200 * 104.50 equals $20,900.00). The tax Code is "GST". Freight on this shipment is quoted at $220.00 including GST.

Quotes and orders preferences

Quotes and *Orders* once saved can be modified, deleted or converted. A *Quote* can be converted to either an *Order* or a *Bill*. An *Order* can be converted to a *Bill*.

The conversion of quotes and orders can be <u>controlled</u> through the purchases preferences (*Setup/Preferences/Purchases*). In the following exercise, the authors have set up the purchases preferences in regard to quotes and orders as follows:

> ☑ Retain Original PO <u>N</u>umber on Backorders [System-wide]
> ☑ Retain Original PO Number when <u>Q</u>uotes Change to Orders or Bills [System-wide]
> ☑ Delete <u>Q</u>uotes upon Changing to and Recording as an Order or Bill [System-wide]

This means that the purchase number is set to be the same when quotes and orders are converted and that quotes are set to be deleted once converted. <u>Orders</u>, on the other hand, <u>will always be deleted</u> when converted to bills regardless of the preferences.

Video: A video showing you how to set up the purchases preferences is on the DVD

Changing a quote to an order

When a quote is accepted and an order is placed, the quote recorded in the *MYOB AccountRight Plus* file can be converted to an order (or directly to a bill).

How to change a supplier quote to an order

Step	Instruction
1	Select the *Purchases* command centre.
2	Select the *Purchases Register* option.
3	Click on the *Quotes* tab at the top of the *Purchases Register* window.
4	Change the 'Dated from' and 'To' dates, if necessary.
5	Select (highlight) the quote to be converted to either an order or a bill.
6	Click on the *Change to Order* or *Change to Bill* button. **Note:** The quote can also be modified (edited) or deleted, if necessary.
7	Edit any field (for example, 'Purchase #', 'Date' and 'Supplier Inv #').
8	Click on the *Record* button to save the order.

Example 6.8—Changing a quote received to an order

1. Have the file dem61.myo open.
2. Select the *Purchases* command centre.
3. Select the *Purchases Register* option.
4. Select the *Quotes* tab at the top of the *Purchases Register* window.
5. Make sure the date criteria is 'Dated From' "1/7/2011 'To' 31/7/2011.
6. The quote from Cretian Cosmetics entered earlier will be highlighted (selected) as shown in Figure 6.12 on the next page.

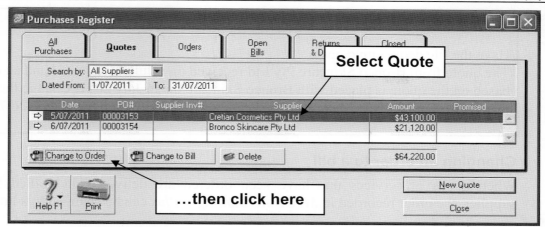

Figure 6.12: Purchases Register with quote from Cretian Cosmetics highlighted

7. Click on the *Change to Order* button.

8. As this business maintains the same purchase number for the quote, order and the actual bill, make sure the 'Purchase #' is 3153.

9. TAB through and <u>change</u> the date to "25/7/2011" and ↵.

10. Click on the 'Journal Memo:' field and edit to "Order; Cretian Cosmetics Pty Ltd". The order will look like Figure 6.13:

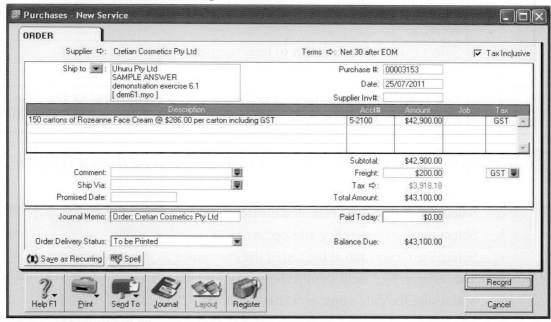

Figure 6.13: Supplier's quote now changed to an order

11. Click on the *Record* button to save the order on file.

12. Click on the *Cancel* button to close the *Purchases – New Service* window and you will be returned to the *Purchases Register* window and click on the *Close* button to finish and exit the *Purchases Register*.

 Video: A video showing you how to change quotes to orders is on the DVD

Self-test exercise 6.7

Have the file dem61.myo open.

The quote from Bronco Skincare Pty Ltd received on 6 July is accepted and an order based on the quote is placed with Bronco Skincare on 26 July 2011. Change the quote to an order on that date. Make sure the 'Purchase #' is 3154 and the date is 26/7/2011.

Changing an order to a bill

When goods or services that have been ordered are delivered and billed by the supplier, the order recorded in *MYOB AccountRight Plus* can be changed to a bill.

How to change an order to a bill received from a supplier

Step	Instruction
1	Select the *Purchases* command centre.
2	Select the *Purchases Register* option.
3	Click on the Orders tab at the top of the *Purchases Register* window.
4	Make sure that the 'Dated From' and 'To' dates are for the period you want and the 'Search By' field "All Suppliers" *or* a particular supplier's name is entered.
5	Select (highlight) the order to be converted to a bill.
6	Click on the *Change to Bill* button.
7	Edit any field (for example, 'Purchase #', 'date' and 'Supplier Inv #').
8	Click on the *Record* button.

Example 6.9—Changing an order to a bill received from a supplier

1. Have the file dem61.myo open.
2. Select the *Purchases* command centre.
3. Select the *Purchases Register* option.
4. Select the *Orders* tab at the top of the *Purchases Register* window.
5. The 'Search by:' field should show "All Suppliers".
6. Make sure the date range is 'Dated From' 1/7/2011 'To' 31/7/2011.
7. The order on Cretian Cosmetics entered earlier will be highlighted (selected) as shown in Figure 6.14 on the next page.
8. Click on the *Change to Bill* button.
9. TAB to the date field of the *Bill* and change it to "31/7/2011" ↵.
10. Enter the supplier's invoice number as "3180" ↵.
11. Click in the 'Freight:' field and change the amount to "209.00" (including GST).
12. Click on the 'Journal Memo:' field and edit to "Purchase: Cretian Cosmetics".

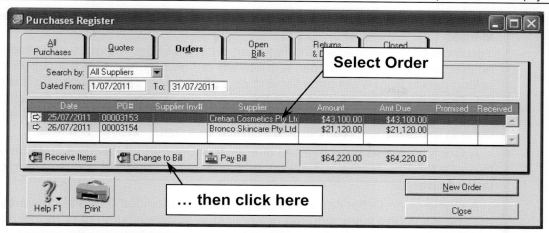

Figure 6.14: The purchases register window showing orders on file

13. The Bill should look like Figure 6.15:

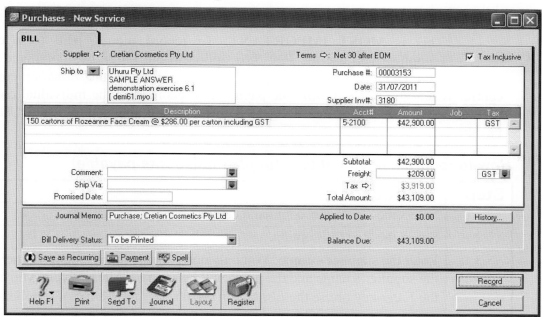

Figure 6.15: Order now changed to a bill received from supplier

14. Click on the *Record* button to save the bill (ignore any warnings about the date).

15. Click on the *Cancel* button to close the *Purchases – New Service* window.

Video: A video showing you how to change orders to bills is on the DVD

Self-test exercise 6.8

Have the file dem61.myo open.
Goods ordered from Bronco Skincare are now received together with their bill.
Change the *Order* placed with Bronco Skincare to a *Bill* on 31/7/2011.
Leave the Purchase # as 3154, Supplier's Inv# 5519. Ignore any date warning.

> **Memo:**
> You have probably realised that you can enter an Order without having first entered a Quote. For example, a quote will not be required where a supplier is selling goods from a set price list and an order can be placed based on the price list. The entry is the same as for a Bill (supplier's invoice) except for selecting "ORDER" before entering any details. The order can be changed to a Bill as was done in the previous example and self-test exercise.
>
> A Quote can also be converted directly to a Bill without having it first converted to an Order. For example, if the quote was accepted and the goods were picked up or delivered.
>
> A Quote or an Order can be saved (recorded), modified (edited), converted, or deleted if it is no longer required or applicable. A cancellation of or modification to a firm order is usually done with mutual agreement between the parties (the customer and the supplier).

Payments to suppliers (accounts payable)

This is **MOST IMPORTANT**. To record money paid to a creditor (supplier) you use the *Pay Bills* option in the *Purchases* command centre. You **DO NOT** use the *Spend Money* option in the *Banking* command centre. When you use *Pay Bills* the payment is recorded to the individual creditor's account as well as the general ledger control accounts (e.g. "Bank" and "Accounts Payable").

How to record a payment to a supplier (accounts payable)

Step	Instruction
1	Select the *Purchases* command centre.
2	Select the *Pay Bills* option.
3	Enter the supplier's name. You only need to type in the first few letters of the supplier's name and the name will be entered. Alternatively, you can tap the *Enter* key or use the *List* button 🔽 to select from a list of suppliers ↵.
4	TAB to the 'Memo' field and change if necessary ↵.
5	TAB to the 'Cheque No:' field and change if necessary ↵.
6	Enter the date ↵. **Note:** The discount for early payment is offered based on this date (the date of payment). Make sure it is entered correctly.
7	Enter the amount being paid ↵.
8	TAB to the last column and apply the amount against the correct purchase and ↵. **Remember:** You can apply to more than one purchase as long as the total amounts applied agree with the cheque amount entered in step 7.
9	Check the amount in the 'Discount' column. **Note:** You can edit or modify the discount amount if necessary.

(continued on the next page)

Step	Instruction
10	Make sure the 'Finance Charges' field is zero unless a charge for late payment is being made.
11	Click on the *Record* button.
12	If a discount amount was entered in the 'Discount' column you will get a message informing you that a 'Debit Memo' (supplier Credit Note) will be issued and automatically applied. If this is incorrect click on *Cancel* button otherwise click on either *Print Now* or *Print Later* to record the credit note. Print Now *or* Print Later
13	To enter more payments repeat steps 3 to 12 above or click on *Close* to exit.

Example 6.10—Recording a payment made to a supplier

1. Open the *MYOB AccountRight Plus* file dem61.myo.
2. Select the *Pay Bills* option from the *Purchases* command centre.
3. Type "Cr" for Cretian Cosmetics Pty Ltd and ↵.
4. The 'Cheque No:' should be "120346" (change it if necessary).
5. TAB through to the 'Date:' field and enter the date as "11/7/2011" ↵.
6. Enter the amount being paid $21,262.25 (you may enter it as "21262.25") ↵.
7. TAB to (or click in) the 'Amount Applied' column so that $21,262.25 appears applied against 'Purchase #' 3125 dated 11/06/2011.
8. Press the *Enter* key and then check that the 'Out of Balance' and 'Finance Charge' fields both show '$0.00'.
9. Click on the *Record* button if your screen looks like Figure 6.16:

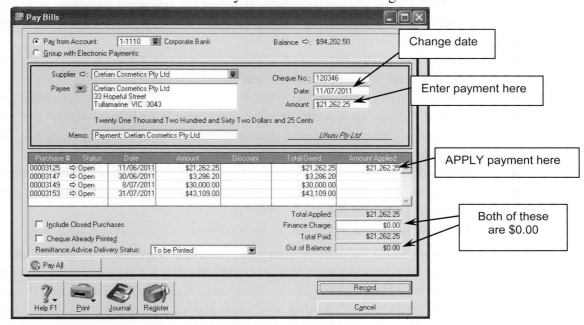

Figure 6.16: Payment to Cretian Cosmetics Pty Ltd for PO #3125

Video: A video showing you how to record payments to suppliers is on the DVD

Self-test exercise 6.9

Have the file dem61.myo open.

Enter the following amounts paid to suppliers:

Important: *Make sure the dates are entered correctly for the following payments*:

Date	Supplier (Account Payable)	Cheque Number	Amount	Apply To Purchase:
13/7/2011	Davis Manufacturing Pty Ltd	120347	$13,260.30	3122
19/7/2011	Skincare Labs Pty Ltd	120348	$14,625.10	3140
25/7/2011	Cretian Cosmetics Pty Ltd	120349	$3,286.20	3147
27/7/2011	Natural Bliss Pty Ltd	120350	$4,052.90	3144
28/7/2011	Davis Manufacturing P/d **	120351	$18,945.80	3148

** A 2% discount of $386.65 has been deducted when paying Davis Manufacturing.

Click on *Print Later* to record the *Debit Memo* (Debit Note).

Check the transaction journals in the *Purchases* tab to make sure that this discount is recorded **and** applied (see solution at back of the chapter for this self-test exercise 6.9).

Debits to suppliers' accounts

The amount owing to a supplier can be reduced by making a payment as seen in the previous exercise or by recording a *debit note* (a *debit memo*). A debit adjustment may be necessary to record any of the following:

- Goods previously purchased may be returned or allowances may be received for damaged goods or goods incorrectly delivered;
- The quantity or price on the supplier's invoice was incorrect (overcharged);
- Cash discounts or volume rebates may have been agreed to. In the previous exercise a cash discount was done automatically at the time of paying the bill, however, there are occasions where this needs to be done manually;
- A credit may be required from the supplier to write off a disputed amount;
- A bill of exchange (bills payable) may have to be recorded (to debit the supplier's account and credit "bills payable"); or
- Other adjustments may need to be recorded.

A *Credit Note* is usually received from the supplier for any of the above circumstances. The important point to remember is that ***all*** debits involving a payables account must be entered through the *Purchases* Command Centre, not through the *Accounts* command centre, as this will only record a debit entry to the "Accounts Payable" control account **and not** to the individual supplier's account.

When a *Credit Note* is received from a supplier, it is necessary to record its details as an internal adjustment i.e. record a *Debit Note*. As we have already received the printed copy of the *Credit Note* from the supplier and therefore no prints are necessary, use the negative *Miscellaneous* purchase layout to record these adjustments. In cases where a print is required, then use a negative *Service* purchase layout instead. The accounting outcome will be the same regardless of which *layout* is used. The main difference between the two layouts is that the *Service* layout <u>can be printed</u> while the *Miscellaneous* layout cannot.

For auditing purposes and good record keeping, it is important to enter a *journal memo* that fully describes the nature (or reason) for the debit (i.e. the credit received).

Once a debit (negative purchase) has been recorded it <u>must either</u> be:
1.   <u>applied</u> against the relevant bill(s), *or*
2.   recorded as a <u>refund</u> amount received and deposited.

To do this you use the *Purchases Register* option in the *Purchases* command centre.

 ### How to record a credit note received (or an internal debit note)

Step	Instruction
1	Select the *Purchases* command centre.
2	Select the *Enter Purchases* option.
3	Make sure the 'Tax Inclusive' tick box is correct. Turn this on (tick) if the amounts on the credit note include GST and clear it if they don't: ☑ Tax Inclusive ☐ Tax Inclusive Amounts *Include GST* Amounts *Exclude GST*
4	"BILL" should be the default set at the top of the *Purchases* window. ┌ BILL ◄── ┐ Entering a Supplier : negative bill
5	Click on the 'Supplier:' field and enter the supplier's name (or at least the first few letters of the name), or click on the *List* button 🔽 and select the supplier.
6	Click on the *Layout* button at the foot of the window and change the type to *Miscellaneous* (or *Service* if a print is required) then click the *OK* button. **Important note:** Use *Item* layout when recording item returns (see Chapter 7).
7	Click on the 'Purchase #' field and enter an internal debit note number ⏎.
8	Enter a date ⏎.
9	Enter a credit note number from a supplier (if any) ⏎.
10	Type in a description of the credit, making reference to the supplier invoice involved and TAB to the account number (or account name) field.
11	Type in the account number or name to be credited and TAB. *(continued on the next page)*

Step	Instruction
12	Enter a negative amount (as a <u>minus</u> amount or a <u>minus</u> calculation). To activate the calculator and use the mouse you can press the spacebar or "=", alternatively just type the calculation using digits (0 – 9) and any of the following signs (– + * /). Enter the result by typing ↵ or "=". <u>Make sure the result is negative.</u>
13	TAB and enter a job number, if jobs are being used.
14	TAB and edit the tax code, if necessary ↵.
15	Click on the 'Journal Memo' field and type in a sensible memo – for example, "Credit for overcharge" ↵.
16	Click on the *Record* button.

Note:
If you are using *Item* layout (Chapter 7) to record the return of items, select *Item* layout bill or invoice and enter <u>the quantity returned</u> as negative (not the amount). That is necessary to update the item count and cost.

Example 6.11—Creating an adjustment (debit) note

1. Open the *MYOB AccountRight Plus* file dem61.myo.
2. Select the *Purchases* command centre.
3. Select the *Enter Purchases* option.
4. Check that the tax-inclusive box is ticked.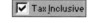
5. Enter the supplier as "Natural Bliss Pty Ltd" - or type in the first few letters "Na".
6. Click on the *Layout* button and change the purchase layout to "Miscellaneous" and click on the *OK* button.

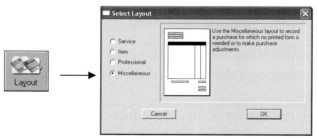

7. Select the 'Purchase #' field.
8. Enter the 'Purchase #' as "D3151" ↵.
   (**Note:** This business uses the same Purchase # as the original purchase plus the letter "D")
9. Enter the date as "18/7/2011" ↵.
10. Enter 'Supplier inv #' as "CN100" ↵ or TAB to the 'Description' column.
11. Enter a description as "Return 10 cartons of Maso-to Cream @ $173.80 each incl. GST" and TAB.
12. The account number to be credited is "5-2100" for "Purchases – Cosmetics".
13. Type in the amount as "–1738"   or "–10 * 173.8=" (**notice the minus sign**) TAB.

14. If the tax code is not "GST", TAB to the 'Tax' column and enter in "GST" ↵.

15. Click on the 'Journal Memo:' field and change it to read "Damaged Goods returned to Supplier " ↵.

16. Your debit note should look like Figure 6.17– make sure that the dollar amounts are shown as negatives and click the *Record* button.

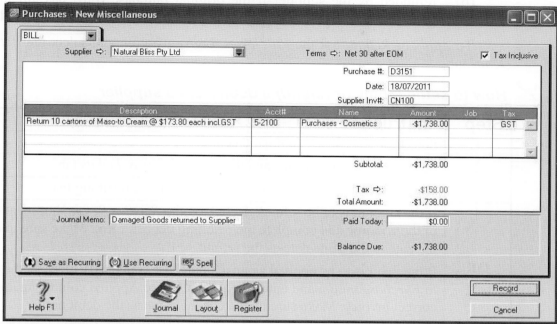

Figure 6.17: Debit note for discount received

Video: A video showing how to record debits to suppliers' accounts is on the DVD

Self-test exercise 6.10

Have the file dem61.myo open.

Enter a credit note received from Cretian Cosmetics Pty Ltd on 22/7/2011. Click on the *Enter Purchases* button and change the layout to *Miscellaneous*.

The 'Purchase #' is "D3149", date is 22/7/2011 and 'Supplier Inv #' is "CN7".

This credit is for "Return of 10 cartons Skinpro SP30+ Sunscreen @ $150 per carton" and the account to credit is "5-2200 Purchases – Sunscreen".

Enter the amount as "–1500" (*minus* 1500) *or* "–10 * 150 =" and TAB.

The tax code is "FRE", as these goods were purchased GST-free. Change the memo to: "Returns; Cretian Cosmetics Pty Ltd". Make sure the total is negative.

As previously stated a debit or adjustment to a supplier's account must *either* be applied against a purchase *or* refunded. When an *Open Item* system is used the debit must be:

(a)   applied against the purchase involved so as to remove it as an open item,
or

(b)   refunded by the supplier if the original purchase (bill) has already been paid. A cheque received from the supplier needs to be entered as a deposit.

To *Apply* or *Refund* use the *Purchases Register* option and select the *Returns & Debits* tab.

How to settle (apply or refund) a debit from a supplier

Step	Instruction
1	Select the *Purchases* command centre.
2	Select *Purchases Register* and then the *Returns & Debits* tab.
3	Highlight (select) the debit to be settled from the resulting list.
4	If the amount is to be refunded, click on the *Receive Refund* button at the foot of the window and complete the resulting deposit form. Make sure to change the date to the same date as the refund.
OR 5	If the debit is to be applied against a purchase (matched), click on the *Apply to Purchase* button and enter the amount in the Applied column against the correct invoice. Make sure the date is the same as the debit note.

Example 6.12—Applying a credit received against a purchase invoice bill)

1.   Open the *MYOB AccountRight Plus* file dem61.myo.

2.   Select the *Purchases* command centre.

3.   Select the *Purchases Register* – then the *Returns & Debits* tab.

4.   The debit to "Natural Bliss Pty Ltd" should be highlighted. Select this debit as shown in Figure 6.18:

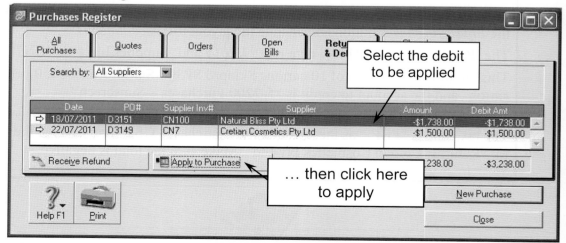

Figure 6.18: Debit for Nature Bliss selected from the list

5. Click on the *Apply to Purchase* button.

6. Enter the date as "18/07/2011" (same date as the debit note or memo) ↵.

7. The amount is to be applied against Purchase #3151.

8. Click in the 'Amount Applied' column for the Purchase #3151 or TAB to this field so that the amount appears there as the amount applied ↵.

9. Your *Settle Returns & Debits* window should look like Figure 6.19:

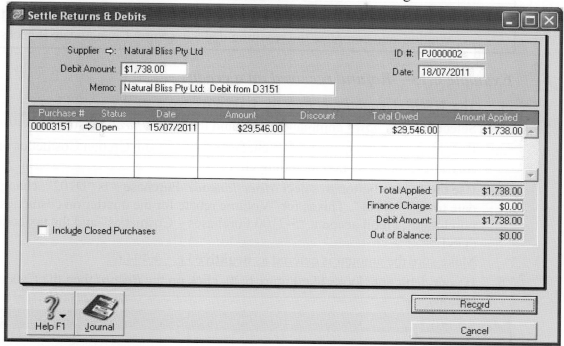

Figure 6.19: Debit applied against purchase #3151

10. Click the *Record* button.

Video: A video showing you how to apply a debit to a purchase is on the DVD

Self-test exercise 6.11

Have the file dem61.myo open.

On 22/7/2011, apply the debit of $1,500.00 made out to Cretian Cosmetics Pty Ltd to Purchase #3149.

Entering a deposit for credit refund received

Sometimes the credit received from a supplier will be accompanied by a refund cheque. This will happen when a purchase invoice (bill) has already been paid and the credit might not be offset against an upcoming purchase. It may also happen when a rebate (e.g. volume rebate) is received from the supplier. Instead of applying the credit to an existing purchase as shown above, the money received (the refund) is deposited.

How to enter a deposit for credit refund received

Step	Instruction
1	Select the *Purchases* command centre.
2	Select the *Purchases Register – Returns & Debits* tab.
3	Highlight (select) the debit to be settled from the resulting list.
4	Click on the *Receive Refund* ⟨ Receive Refund ⟩ button at the foot of the window and complete the resulting deposit. (**Note**: Change date if necessary.)

 Example 6.13—Refund received on a credit

1. The *MYOB AccountRight Plus* file is dem61.myo.
2. Select the *Purchases* command centre and the *Enter Purchases* option.
3. Record an adjustment note and a cheque received from Cretian Cosmetics on 29 July 2011, for $4,494.60 including GST.
4. Use the *Layout* button to select *Miscellaneous*. Purchase # is "D102", change the date to "29/7/2011". This is for "Volume rebate for the quarter on cosmetics purchased", credit account "5-2100 Purchases – Cosmetics" and the tax code is "GST".
   Make sure the amount is entered as **negative** i.e. –4,494.60.
5. If your debit note looks like Figure 6.20, click on the *Record* then the *Cancel* buttons.

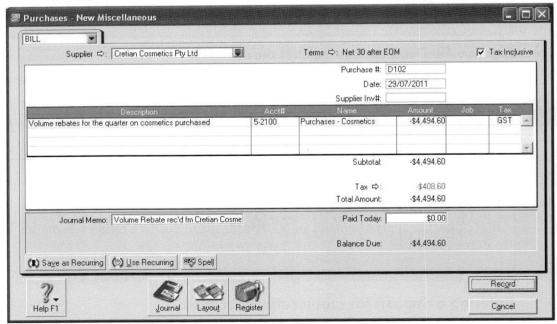

Figure 6.20: Volume rebate received from Cretian Cosmetics

6. Select *Purchases Register* then *Returns & Debits* tab.
7. Select the debit to Cretian Cosmetics as shown in Figure 6.21 on the next page.
8. Click on the *Receive Refund* button.

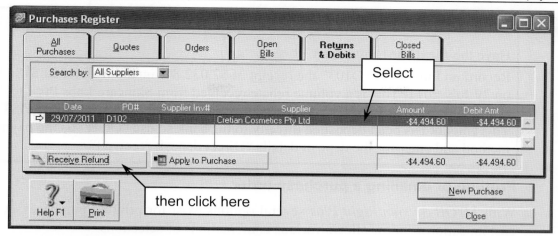

Figure 6.21: Debit for Cretian Cosmetics selected

9. In the *Settle Returns & Debits* window change the date to "29/7/2011" ↵.

10. The correct amount of $4,494.60 should be highlighted ↵.

11. Enter the payment method as a "Cheque".

12. Click on the *Details* button and enter the cheque's details: 'BSB:' as "333-444", the 'Account Name:' as "Cretian Cosmetics", the 'Account No.:' as "65438765" and the 'Cheque No.:' as "345678". Click the *OK* button to continue.

13. Change the 'Memo:' to "Volume rebate rec'd from Cretian Cosmetics" ↵.

14. Click the *Record* button if your screen looks like Figure 6.22:

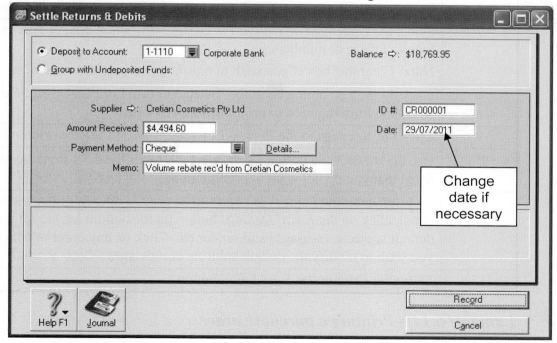

Figure 6.22: Refund from Cretian recorded through Settle Returns & Debits

15. Back at the *Purchase Register* window click on *Close* to exit.

Video: A video showing you how to record refunds from suppliers is on the DVD

Self-test exercise 6.12

Have the file dem61.myo open.

Record on Purchase# "D103" the <u>receipt</u> of $2,032.80 (including GST of $184.80) on 29 July 2011. This is a volume rebate received from Skincare Labs Pty Ltd. The account to credit is 5-2100 "Purchases – Cosmetics" and the Tax Code is "GST". This amount has been deposited directly to the bank so use "Other" as the payment method and enter for the deposit details "Direct deposit received".

Printing or emailing a purchase order

With *MYOB AccountRight Plus* several options exist for printing purchases. A report customisation window allows various combinations of selections.

 How to print or email a purchase order

Step	Instruction
1	Select the *Purchases* command centre.
2	Select the *Print/Email Purchase Orders* option.
3	In the *Review Purchases Before Delivery* window select either "To Be Printed" or "To Be Emailed" tab.
4	Select the 'Purchase Type' (e.g. "Service", "Item" or "Professional").
5	Click on the *Advanced Filters* button.
6	Select a purchase status by pointing and dragging (e.g. "Open", "Closed").
7	Select the *Unprinted or Unsent Purchases only* option box, or type in required dates or numbers. **Note:** Clear this box if you wish to reprint a purchase a second time.
8	Click on the *List* button ⏷ at the 'Selected Form For Purchase:' field and select the form required to print the purchase order.
9	Click *OK* to return to the *Review Purchases before Delivery* window.
10	Use the *All* or *None* button ☑ to select all. Clear the ticks from any order listed that you do not want to print or email.
11	To print, enter the number of copies to be printed of each order, and to email, click on the *Email Defaults* button (at the bottom left) to set up the default subjects, messages and sender etc. Click on any order in which you wish to modify the default subjects or messages.
12	Select the *Print* or the *Send Email* button.

 Example 6.14—Printing a purchase order

1. Open the *MYOB AccountRight Plus* file dem61.myo.
2. Select the *Purchases* command centre.
3. Select the *Print/Email Purchase Orders* option and then the *To Be Printed* tab.
4. Click on the *Advanced Filters* button.
5. Select the Purchase Type as "Service" and the status as "Open".

6. Clear (un-tick) the box for 'Unprinted or Unsent Purchases'.

7. Click on the *List* button 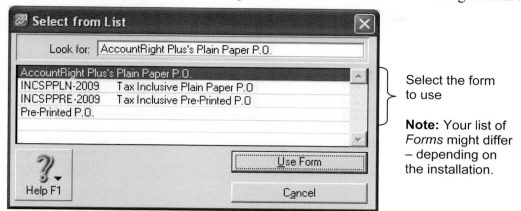 at the 'Selected Form For Purchase:' field and select "AccountRight Plus's Plain Paper P.O." as the form to use. See Figure 6.23:

Figure 6.23: Selecting a form to use for printing a purchase order

8. Click on the *Use Form* button.

9. The *Advanced Filters* window should look like Figure 6.24:

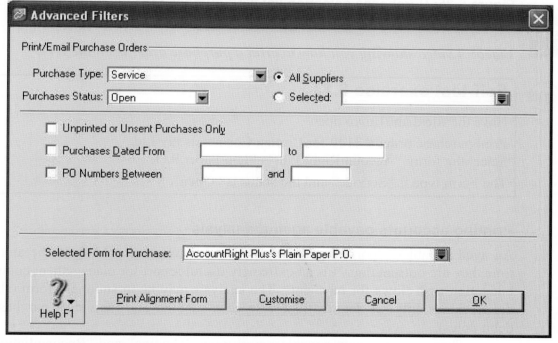

Figure 6.24: The Print Purchase *Advanced Filters* window

10. Select the *OK* button to return to the *Review Purchases Before Delivery* window to make your selection of the purchases to be printed.

11. The purchase to print is number 3151 for Natural Bliss Pty Ltd. – click next to "3151" to select it.

12.   If your screen looks like Figure 6.25, click on the *Print* button.

☑	Purchase#	Date	Supplier	Amount
⇨	00003149	8/07/2011	Cretian Cosmetics Pty Ltd	$28,500.00
⇨	00003150	12/07/2011	Skincare Labs Pty Ltd	$26,714.60
✓ ⇨	00003151	15/07/2011	Natural Bliss Pty Ltd	$27,808.00
⇨	00003152	28/07/2011	Blue Leaf Computers Pty Ltd	$7,480.00
⇨	00003153	31/07/2011	Cretian Cosmetics Pty Ltd	$43,109.00
⇨	00003154	31/07/2011	Bronco Skincare Pty Ltd	$21,120.00

Figure 6.25: Purchases selection list with number 3151 selected for printing.

Video: A video showing you how to print a purchase order is on the DVD

Self-test exercise 6.13

Have the file dem61.myo open.

Print purchase order # 3149 for Cretian Cosmetics Pty Ltd.
Select the form: "AccountRight Plus's Plain Paper P.O."

The Form type is "Service" and the status is "Open".

Printing accounts payable ageing analysis

An aged payables report classifies outstanding accounts according to the amount of time they are outstanding. It is an extremely useful report for management control and budgeting cash flows for payments. The analysis may be in summary form (showing dollar values only) or detailed (showing each supplier and individual purchases and debit notes).

There are two main payable report types, "Ageing" and "Reconciliation" and each can be in a summary or detailed form. The main difference is that the "Ageing" reports display the <u>current</u> supplier balances regardless of the specified 'Ageing date', while the "Payable Reconciliation" reports show the position of the purchases as at the ageing date entered. The total of the 'Payable Reconciliation' report should agree with the balance of general ledger 'accounts payable' account, as at the 'Ageing' date, while the 'Aged Payables' total is the <u>current</u> balance of accounts payable regardless of the 'Ageing Date' specified for the report in the customisation window. For the exercises in this chapter we will be using the "Ageing" reports – both in the detailed and summary forms.

How to print/email an accounts payable ageing analysis

Step	Instruction
1	If you are in the *Purchases* command centre, click on the *Reports* button (this button is located at the bottom of the command centre).
OR	If you are NOT in the *Purchases* command centre, click on the drop-down arrow at the end of the *Reports* button and select "Purchases".
2	Under the *Payables* heading select "Ageing Detail" or "Ageing Summary" report by clicking once on it.
3	Click on the *Customise* button to open the *Customisation* window.
4	Make sure the report Customisation window is correctly filled in. By default "All" suppliers are selected. If necessary, click on the *List* button next to the 'Suppliers' field and change the selection.
5	Click on the *Advanced Filters* tab and enter the ageing date in the 'Ageing Date' field. If necessary, change the 'Ageing Method' field (click on the down arrow and click on the selection). For example, to print an "Ageing Summary" report for ___all___ suppliers at 31 July 2011 with ageing method "Number of Days since P.O. Date", your screen should look like Figure 6.26 on the next page.
6	Click on the *Report Fields* tab. From the left pane check the fields to be included on the report by placing a tick next to them. The fields that will be on the report will be listed on the right pane.
7	Click on the *Finishing* tab and make any other selection as necessary. **Note:** No ageing report will be printed for suppliers with no amounts outstanding to them, unless the option 'Include $0.00 Balances' is checked (ticked).
8	Click on the *Display* button then change the 'View' to "Print Preview" to see the report on screen.
9	Click on the *Print* button at the foot of the window to send the report to the printer. **Note:** Use the *Send To* button to email/fax a copy of this report. You can also export the report to 'Excel' or create a text, a PDF or an HTML file.

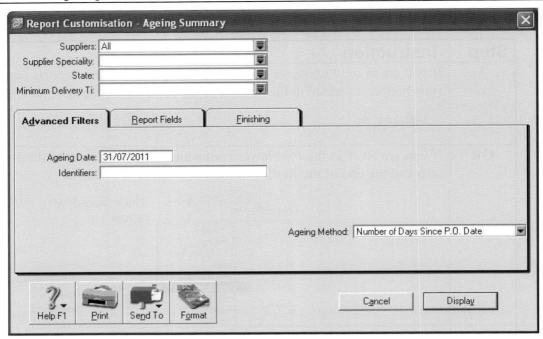

Figure 6.26: Selections made for *Ageing Summary* report

Video: A video showing you how to print aged payable reports is on the DVD

Self-test exercise 6.14

Have the file dem61.myo open.

Print an "Aged Payables [Summary]" report for all suppliers as of: 31 July 2011. (In the *Purchases* reports window select *Ageing Summary* under the *Payables* heading.)

Customise – use "Days Overdue Using Purchase Terms" as the ageing method, and do **not** include $0.00 balances in your report.

Click on *Display* button and change the view in the *Report Display* window to *Print Preview* – check the report on screen before printing.

This is an extremely useful report!

Supplier transaction detail

Each command centre in *MYOB AccountRight Plus* has a *Find Transactions* button to access an inquiry screen. Clicking on the arrow at the end of the *Find Transactions* button results in a drop-down list of inquiry types from which to make a selection. Alternatively you can click on the *Find Transaction* button and select the required tab.

How to display and print supplier transactions

Step	Instruction
1	Click on the arrow at the end of the *Find Transactions* button and drag down to select "Card" as the type.
2	Type in the supplier name, or use the *List* button 🔽 and select from the list.
3	Change the 'from' and 'to' dates if necessary.
4	View all the transactions. To view any particular transaction click on the detail arrow next to it to open it. After viewing any transaction click on the *OK* button to return to this view. To obtain a printout, click on the *Print* button at the foot of the window.
5	Modify the above to make a new inquiry or click on *Close* to exit.

 Video: A video showing you how to print supplier transactions is on the DVD

 Self-test exercise 6.15

Have the file dem61.myo open.

Display the transaction details for Cretian Cosmetics Pty Ltd from 1/06/2011 to 31/07/2011.
Check your screen with the answer at the back of the chapter – no prints required.

Back up before combining supplier cards

You should be able to combine and delete a duplicate *general ledger account*, a duplicate *customer card* or a duplicate *supplier card*. On the following pages we will cover *Combining Supplier Cards*.

The program <u>combines</u> the two cards into one card or the two accounts into one account by merging their transactions and balances.

Once combined and merged the duplicate card or account is deleted and you will not be able to undo or reverse this action. It is therefore ***very important*** that you <u>back up</u> the data file <u>before</u> combining cards or accounts.

Combining supplier cards

A situation may occur where there are two cards recording a single supplier's transactions. The duplicate card may have been created intentionally or in error. For example, a supplier may have two cards because there are two branches and each branch has its own card. Another example, two of our suppliers combine their businesses, i.e. one supplier acquires the business of the other. In these situations it *may* be necessary to combine the two cards into one. Before combining two supplier cards a decision has to be made <u>first</u> as to which card will have <u>all</u> the transactions <u>merged</u> onto it (this card will be called the '**Primary**' card), and which card will be deleted (the '**Secondary**' card) after all its transactions are transferred to the 'Primary' card.

The cards to be combined or merged <u>need not</u> be with the same supplier name or details. To combine two cards they only need to be of the *same type* and both *active*. For example both are 'Supplier' cards and neither of the cards is an 'Inactive' card.

 ### *How to combine supplier cards*

Step	Instruction
1	Select the *Card File* command centre.
2	Select the *Cards List* option.
3	Select (highlight) the *primary* supplier card *first* from the card list.
4	Click on the [⊙ Actions] button below the card list and select the *Combine Cards* option. The primary supplier should already be selected in the 'Primary' field. This supplier card will **not** be deleted and will have all the transactions from both cards.
5	In the 'Secondary' field click the *List* button [▼] to select the second card of the supplier whose transactions will be transferred to the primary card. The secondary card **will be deleted** after the transfer.
6	Click on the [Combine Cards] button.
7	Read the warning message and click the *OK* button to confirm your wish to combine the cards and delete the secondary card.

 Memo:
If more than two cards are to be combined for a single business, it will be necessary to carry out the above process *once* for *each* of the 'secondary' cards. For example if a business has three supplier cards it will be necessary to carry out the above process *twice* in order to eliminate the extra *two* duplicate cards and transfer all their transactions onto the 'Primary' card.

Example 6.15— Combining two supplier cards

You have been advised that 'Cretian Cosmetics Pty Ltd' has acquired the business of 'Organic Beauty Supplies'. It is therefore will be necessary to combine the two relevant cards. Cretian Pty Ltd is to be the ***primary*** card.

1. Make sure that you have the file dem61.myo open.
2. Select the *Cards List* option from the *Card File* command centre.
3. Select (highlight) the supplier card "Cretian Cosmetics Pty Ltd" where the transactions of the two cards will be combined.
4. Click on the ⊙ Actions button at the bottom of the cards list and select *Combine Cards* option.
5. In the 'Secondary' field click the *List* button 📥 to select the second card "Organic Beauty Supplies", which is the supplier whose transactions will be transferred to the primary card. This secondary card *Organic Beauty Supplies* will be deleted after the transfer of all its transactions to the primary card.
6. If your screen looks like figure 6.27, click on the *Combine Cards* button.

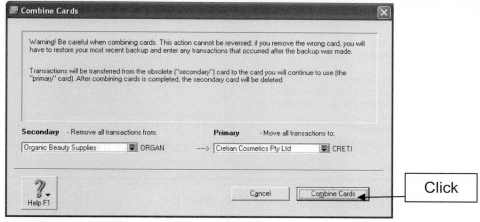

Figure 6.27: Combining two supplier cards

7. Read the warning message and click the *OK* button to confirm your wish to combine the cards and delete the secondary card:

Video: A video on combining cards is on the DVD

Self-test exercise 6.16

Have the file dem61.myo open.

Use *Find Transactions/Card* (from 1/6/2011 to 31/7/2011) and select "Cretian Cosmetics" to check that Purchase # 3120 dated 6/6/2011, previously recorded to "Organic Beauty Supplies", is now listed with Cretian Cosmetics' transactions.

Printing GST reports

The *MYOB AccountRight Plus* package produces a GST report that assists with the preparation of the Business Activity Statement (BAS).

Refer to Chapter 2 if you want to see how to <u>print</u> and <u>use</u> GST reports to fill a Business Activity Statement (BAS).

Example 6.16—Printing the GST report

1.   Make sure the file dem61.myo is open.

2.   Click on the arrow at the end of the *Reports* option.

3.   Select *GST/Sales Tax.*

4.   Select the "GST [Summary – Accrual]" report as shown in Figure 6.28:

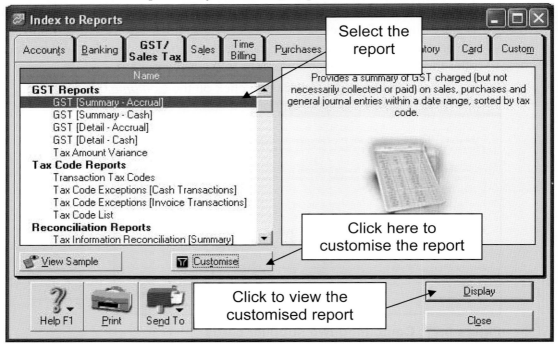

Figure 6.28: GST report selected from list

5.   Click on the *Customise* button.

6.   In the *Report Customisation – GST [Summary – Accrual]* window enter the dates from "1/07/2011" to "31/07/2011" .

7.   Make sure "Both Collected and Paid" in the 'Collected/Paid' field is selected. Your screen should look like Figure 6.29 on the next page.

8.   Select the *Finishing* tab and make sure to select to display sales and purchase values as "Tax Inclusive".
     Your screen should look like Figure 6.30 on the next page.

9.   Click the *Display* button to accept the settings and show the report on screen. Check your answer with the report shown on page 6-50.

10. If a hard copy is required, click on the *Print* button.

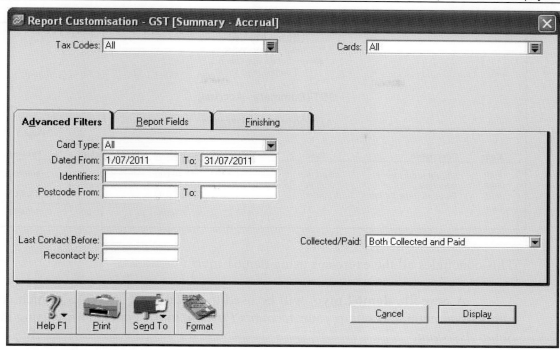

Figure 6.29: Report customisation *Advanced Filters* window for a GST report

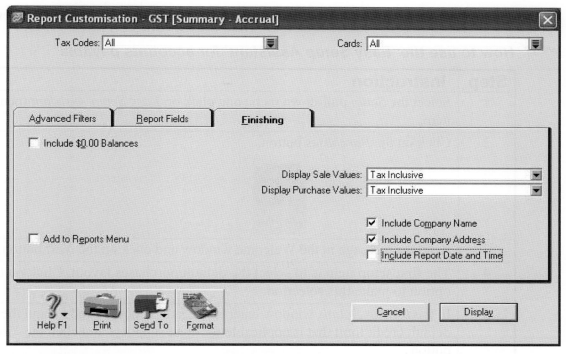

Figure 6.30: Report customisation *Finishing* window for a GST report

Uhuru Pty Ltd
SAMPLE ANSWER
demonstration exercise 6.1
[dem61.myo]

GST [Summary - Accrual]

1/07/2011 To 31/07/2011

Page 1

Code	Description	Rate	Sale Value	Purchase Value	Tax Collected	Tax Paid
CAP	Capital Acquisitions	10.000%		$7,480.00		$680.00
FRE	GST Free	0.000%		$28,500.00		
GST	Goods & Services Tax	10.000%		$131,170.00		$11,924.55
				Total:	$0.00	$12,604.55

This concludes all the exercises using dem61.myo.

A new file **dem62.myo** will be used to do the next exercises, which cover an alternative method to set up your *Accounts Payable* in the company file using the *Easy Setup Assistant*.

Default setup for purchases

The setup "Assistant" can be accessed at any time from the *Setup* pull-down menu.

 How to use the 'Easy Setup Assistant' for accounts payable

Step	Instruction
1	Select the *Setup* pull-down menu and click on *Easy Setup Assistant* menu item.
2	Click on the *Purchases* button.
3	Read the message in the Welcome window and click on the *Next* button.
4	The first setup item is to select the default purchases layout. Click on the option to make this selection.
5	In the *Buying Details* window enter the default expense account and the default credit limit that is applicable for most suppliers and click the *Next* button.
6	In the *Tax Codes* window enter the tax codes often used by suppliers for purchases as well as for freight charged.
	(continued on the next page)

Step	Instruction
7	In the *Payment Information* window make the following selections: • Click on the *List* button next to the 'Payment Method' field and make a selection. • Click on the 'Payment is Due' field and drag down to select from the resulting list. • Click and edit the fields for 'Discount Days', 'Balance Due Days', '% Discount for Early Payment', '% Monthly Charge for Late Payment'. • Click on the *Next* button.
8	In the Linked accounts window accept or change the linked account for paying bills (usually a bank account). Click on the *Next* button. **Note:** You need to use *Setup/Linked Accounts/Purchases Accounts* to set any other linked accounts for purchases (such as the account for "Discount Allowed").
9	In the *Supplier Cards* window you can add new suppliers, edit, combine or delete existing ones. Click on the *Next* button.
10	Click on *Add Purchase* to enter outstanding customer balances in the *Historical Purchases* window. When all balances are entered, click on the *Next* button.
11	Click on the *Close* button in the last (Conclusion) window.

Example 6.17—Using Easy Setup Assistant for accounts payable

1. Open the *MYOB AccountRight Plus* file dem62.myo. Sign on as "Administrator" (no password).

2. Select the *Setup* pull-down menu.
3. Select the *Easy Setup Assistant* menu item.
4. Click on the *Purchases* button, read the message and click on the *Next* button.
5. Click on the option to select *Service* layout for purchases as the default and click on the *Next* button.
6. Leave the expense account blank and enter "$10,000" as the credit limit. Click *Next*.
7. Leave the tax codes as GST for both purchases and freight and click *Next*.
8. In the *Payment Information* window, use the *List* button and select "Cheque" as the *usual* payment method. Use the drop-down arrows and select the default credit terms as "In a given # of days" with "0" for 'Discount Days' and "30" 'Balance Due Days'. Your screen window should look like Figure 6.31 on the next page.
9. Click on the *Next* button.
10. Enter the bank linked account as shown in Figure 6.32 on the next page.
11. Click on the *Next* button.

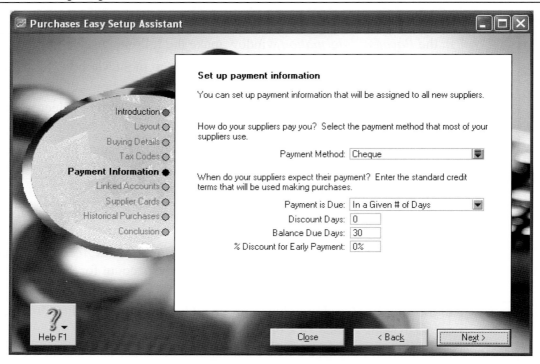

Figure 6.31: Default supplier terms using *Easy Setup Assistant*

Figure 6.32: The linked account for paying supplier bills

12. You can add supplier cards here. However, there are no supplier cards to enter at this stage. Click on the *Next* button.

13. If there are any opening (historical) supplier balances, they can be added here. As there are no historical purchases to be entered, click on the *Next* button.

14. Click on the *Close* button to finish and exit.

Exit dem62.myo and open **dem63.myo** to do the next exercise on contra accounts payable against accounts receivable.

NEW FILE

Recording contra receipts and payments

It is very likely that a business can have dealings with a supplier who is, at the same time, also a customer of the business. The business can purchase certain types of goods from a supplier and sell to them (the supplier) other lines of goods or services. As a result of these transactions, both businesses will owe money to each other.

The normal process in settling the two accounts is that each business will pay the other for the amount owing by them. To minimise these transactions, there is a process that is sometimes used in these situations, whereby only one business pays the other for the difference between the two accounts and contras (writes off) the balance owing in one account against the balance owing by the other. The other business will do the same to the two account balances in their books, but will receive the difference.

For example, if the business owes a supplier $10,000 and the supplier owes the business $8,000, then the amount to contra is $8,000 (the lesser amount). The business then has to pay only the balance owing to the supplier i.e. $2,000.

To be able to do that in *MYOB AccountRight Plus*, it is necessary to create a clearing account as a "Bank" type similar to the 'Undeposited Funds' account. That account can be named any reasonable name such as "Contra".

It is also necessary, if not already created, to create **two** cards for the other business, one as a supplier and the other as a customer.

Record a payment to the supplier *and* a receipt from the customer for the same amount, but use the "Contra" bank account to record these two transactions. These actions will result in reducing both the supplier's and the customer's balances by the same amount. After recording both transactions the clearance bank account "Contra" should have a zero balance.

To set up and use this facility, you need to do the following:

1. Create a new current asset account as a 'bank' type, and name it: "Contra"

2. Determine the amount to be applied in the contra transaction. The amount to be used is the lesser amount owing by the customer or owed by the business to the supplier. Remember, the supplier and the customer in this situation is the same person.

3. Make two transactions – a receipt and a payment for the same amount as determined in step 2 above:

    (a) record and apply a payment to the supplier, and

    (b) record and apply a receipt from the customer.

4. Pay or receive the amount of any balance still owing or owed.

To create an account as a 'bank' type refer to Chapter 3 'General Ledger' and the 'How to enter a detail cheque account in the Accounting List'.

Note: An account called "Contra" has already been created as a bank type account to be used in the Example 6.18.

To record the payment to the supplier (step 3a above), follow the steps of the earlier 'How to …', namely 'How to record a payment to an accounts payable' but select the "Contra" account in the 'Pay from Account' field at the top instead of a bank account. All other steps are the same.

To record the payment received from the customer (step 3b above), follow the steps in the 'How to …', namely 'How to record a payment from an accounts receivable' from Chapter 5 'Accounts Receivable', but select the "Contra" account in the 'Deposit to Account' field instead of a bank account. All other steps are the same.

Example 6.18—Contra accounts receivable and accounts payable

In this example contra an amount owing by the business to a supplier named "Ray Repairs & Maintenance" of $200 against an amount owing by the same business as a customer:

1. Open the file dem63.myo and sign on as the "Administrator" without a password.
2. Select the *Purchases* command centre.
3. Select the *Pay Bills* option to open the *Pay Bills* window.
4. Select "1-1120 Contra" as the bank account in the 'Pay From Account' field at the top.
5. TAB to the 'Supplier' field and select "Ray Repairs & Maintenance".
6. TAB to the 'Memo' field and type "Contra accounts receivable".
7. TAB to the 'Cheque No:' field and enter "Contra" and ↵.
8. Enter the date as "31/7/2011" and ↵.
9. In the 'Amount' field enter "200" and ↵.
10. Click in the 'Amount Applied' column against Purchase # 14 to enter the amount to be applied (i.e. $200.00) and ↵.
11. If your screen looks like Figure 6.33 on the next page, click on the *Record* button and then click on the *Cancel* button.
12. Select the *Sales* command centre.
13. Select the *Receive Payments* option to open the *Receive Payments* window.
14. Change the bank account at the top to "1-1120 Contra".
15. TAB to the 'Customer' field and select "Ray Repairs & Maintenance" and ↵.
16. TAB to the 'Amount Received' field and enter "200" and ↵.

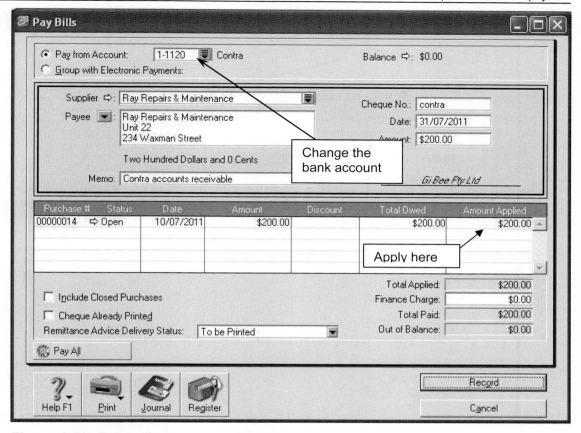

Figure 6.33: Recording a contra payment to a supplier

17.   In 'Payment Method' field select "Other" and ⏎.

18.   Click on the *Details* button and type "Contra amounts owing" in the 'Notes' box and click *OK*.

19.   TAB to the 'Memo' field and type "Contra accounts payable" and ⏎.

20.   In the 'ID #' enter "Contra" and ⏎.

21.   Enter the date as "31/7/2011" and ⏎.

22.   Click in the 'Amount Applied' column against Invoice #876 to enter the amount to be applied (i.e. $200.00) and ⏎.

23.   If your screen looks like Figure 6.34 on the next page, click on the *Record* button and then click on the *Cancel* button.

The contra bank account balance should be zero now (debited and credited with $200). The amount owing to "Ray Repairs & Maintenance" is now Nil and the balance owing by them is now $150 ($350 less $200), which they will have to pay in due course.

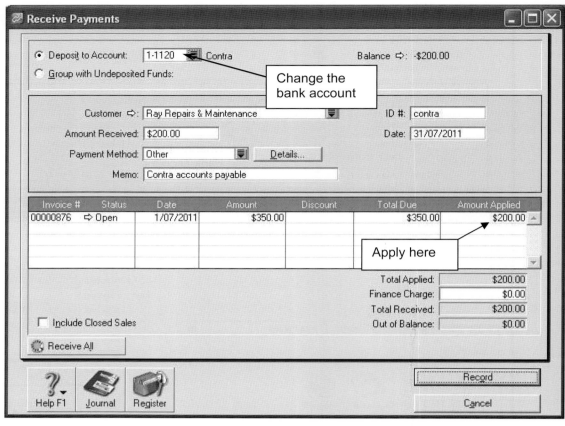

Figure 6.34: Recording a contra receipt from a customer

Competency checklist

	I can now do the following:	✓
1	Turn the computer and screen on	
2	Adjust chair, desk and equipment to suit ergonomic requirements and sit correctly at the computer terminal	
3	Use rest periods and appropriate exercises regularly	
4	Select and start *MYOB AccountRight Plus* or *MYOB Premier* and open existing data files or create new ones	
5	Access information from manuals and/or on-line help	
6	Apply techniques to minimise paper wastage such as using screen inquiries and recycling paper from incorrect printouts.	
7	Maintain supplier information (records)	
8	Enter credit purchases data and check for accuracy	
9	Enter payments to creditors and check for accuracy	
10	Solve operational problems	
11	Use the *Reports* pull-down menu and print/email various reports	
12	Set up accounts payable for automatic posting to the general ledger	
13	Perform special operations such as enter credits received (Returns & Debits), add or modify GST codes, record freight and interest charged	
14	Access information about a supplier's account	
15	Combine supplier cards and merge their transactions onto one card to eliminate duplicate records (cards)	
16	Print/email purchase orders: quotations, orders and bills	
17	Contra an amount payable to a supplier against an amount receivable from the same business	

Chapter 6: Assessment exercises

Note: Throughout the following practical exercises you should continually observe relevant occupational health and safety practices and apply recycling techniques to minimise paper wastage. In addition, you should use the on-line help facilities to solve any problems you encounter.

Select '*Service*' as the purchase layout for the following assessments (6.1 to 6.5).

6.1 Markos Fashion Shoes are in the business of selling fashion shoes and accessories. Their accountant started the necessary *MYOB AccountRight Plus* file, set up the accounts list and entered the general ledger opening balances as at the conversion date.

      You are required to create the cards for the suppliers and enter the amounts owing to them (the historical balances), which should agree with the control account (accounts payable) balance in the general ledger. You will also be required to enter July's accounts payable transactions and print the reports listed at the end of this assessment.

The exercise month is July 2011.
Start *MYOB AccountRight Plus* and open an existing file called **ass61.myo.**
Use the **Setup** menu, **Company Information** item and change the business address to "Your full name – Assessment 6.1 (ass61.myo)".

The *Goods & Services* tax is set at 10%. The tax code is "GST".
Note: ALL GOODS AND SERVICES in this exercise are taxable.

Create the following suppliers' cards:

    For *ALL* the following supplier cards:

> Select **"Service"** as the default '**Purchase Layout**'.
> Printed Form select **"AccountRight Plus's Plain Paper P.O."**
> Select **"5-1120 Purchases"** as the default expense account.
> For '**Tax Code**' & '**Freight Tax Code**' select **"GST"**.
> Do not select **"Use Supplier's Tax Code"** for any of these cards.

1. Cool Fashions Pty Limited (Card ID CF-1) of 197 Station St., Flemington VIC 3031. Telephone: (03) 9922 1712 and fax: (03) 9922 1722. No email. Salutation Michael and the contact person is Mr Michael Schoemann. ABN: 00 111 222 333. TERMS: Payments are due 30 days after the End of month (EOM). Credit limit: $125,000. No discount is allowed.

2. One Stop Shoes Pty Limited (Card ID OSS-2) of 1 High St., Castle Hill NSW 2154.
   Telephone: (02) 9634 4191 and fax: (02) 9634 4444. Email address: onestop@onetel.com.au. Salutation John and the contact person is John Pablo.
   TERMS: Payments are due 30 days from date of purchase. ABN 41 445 566 733.
   Credit limit: $140,000. No discount is allowed.

3. Shoes Galore (Card ID: SG-3) of 1 Good Street, Brisbane QLD 4000.
   Telephone: (04) 9144 7060 and the fax is the same number as the telephone.
   Salutation Bill and the contact person is William McIntosh. Email address: Loch@noness.com.au.
   TERMS: Payments are due 21 days from date of purchase. Credit limit: $100,000.
   ABN: 33 498 756 111. No discount is allowed. Tax code: GST.

Enter the outstanding (historical) balances owing to the above suppliers as at 1/7/2011:

Supplier	Purchase #	Tax Code	Dated	Amount
Cool Fashions	1190	GST	30/09/2009	$10.00
	2080	GST	10/12/2010	1,500.00
	2204	GST	30/01/2011	855.50
One Stop Shoes	2598	GST	30/06/2011	1,396.50
Shoes Galore	2596	GST	29/06/2011	25,466.00

Enter the following purchases (Bills) in July 2011:

Prices are GST inclusive. ☑ Tax Inclusive

Use *'Service'* layout and account: *'5-1120 – Purchases'* for all purchases.

Purchase # 2600 dated 3 July 2011 from Shoes Galore. Their Invoice number is 133. The purchase was for 10 pairs Pump Peacock shoes @ $125 each incl. GST and 20 Bottles Heavy Duty Shoe Polish @ $2 each incl. GST.
Freight is $55 incl. GST. Delivered by Southern Cross.

Purchase # 2601 dated 12 July 2011 from One Stop Shoes. Their Invoice number is 501C. Purchased 100 pairs Men's Hi Spirits socks @ $19.25 each incl. GST. These goods were picked up.

Purchase # 2602 dated 28 July 2011 from Shoes Galore. Their invoice number is 186. The purchase was for 20 Leather 'Compact-X' Purses at $25 each incl. GST. The order was sent by Australia Post – there was no delivery charge.

Purchase #2603 dated 28 July 2011 from Cool Fashions. Their invoice number is 01-905. The purchase was for 30 *Millennium* Leather Bags at $100 each incl. GST and 10 *Office 2K* Leather Briefcases at $40 each incl. GST. Freight charges $61.60 incl. GST. Delivered by "Virgin Blue".

Enter the following payments to suppliers (use *Pay Bills*):

Paid	Cheque #	Date Paid	Amount	Apply to PO #
Shoes Galore	5032	15/7/2011	$25,466.00	2596
Shoes Galore	5041	20/7/2011	$1,345.00	2600
One Stop Shoes	5094	25/7/2011	$1,396.50	2598
Cool Fashions	5135	31/7/2011	$2,355.50	2080 & 2204

Received the following Credit Note. Tax code: GST. Credit "Purchases" account:

Being a credit for an overcharge, remember to enter amount as a negative and to apply the credit note to the original purchase # 1190.

Supplier	Debit Note#	Dated	Amount	Apply to PO #
Cool Fashions	DN99-1190	30/7/2011	$10.00	1190

Required:

Print all July's Purchases

Select *Service* type –"All Purchase" status and *AccountRight Plain Paper* form;

Print the Purchases and Payables Journal for the month of July 2011;

Print the Cash Disbursements Journal for the month of July 2011;

Print Cool Fashions' account details from 30/9/**2009** to 31/7/2011

Select *Find Transactions* then *Card* – select supplier and enter date range;

Print Aged Payables (Detail) report at 31 July 2011

Select *Reports* then *Purchases* – select *Ageing Detail* report. Use *Customise* to enter report date and *All Suppliers*. For the 'Ageing Method' select "Days Overdue Using Purchase Terms";

Print GST (Summary Accrual) report for July 2011.

6.2 The exercise month is July 2011.

Start *MYOB AccountRight Plus* and open an existing file called ass62.myo.

Use the ***Setup*** menu, ***Company Information*** item and change the business address to "Your full name – Assessment 6.2 (ass62.myo)".

Mark Seinfield trading as: ***Pink Computers***, selling computers and accessories.

Create the following suppliers cards

Select "*Service*" as the default '*Purchase Layout*' for all suppliers.

Tax code for all the following suppliers (Purchases & Freight) is "*GST*".

Do not select '*Use Supplier's Tax Code*' for any of these cards.

Darling Computers Pty Ltd (Card ID SUP010) of 8/179 Darling Street Darlinghurst 2010. Telephone # is (02) 9207 1545 and fax # is (02) 9993 1631. Salutation is Pietro and the contact person is Peter Davey. ABN 91 111 011 637. Email: darling@donttell.com.au. Credit terms are 30 days from date of purchase (In a Given # of Days) with a limit of $125,000. No discount is allowed.

Micro Electronics (Card ID SUP011) of 915 Pitt Street Sydney NSW 2010. Telephone # is (02) 9298 4005 and fax # is (02) 9283 2432. Salutation is Warren and the contact person is Warren Dennis. Email: me@bng.com.au. ABN 83 472 122 745. Credit terms are 30 days from date of purchase with a credit limit of $135,000, 1% discount for early payment and discount days is 7.

Larry's Computers (Card ID SUP012) of 888 Victoria Road Drummoyne NSW 2047. Telephone # is (02) 9181 1419 and fax # is (02) 9880 2255. Salutation is Michelle and the contact person is Michelle Tang. Email: lcomp@wot.com.au. ABN 45 455 900 522. Credit terms are 30 days from date of purchase with a limit of $140,000. "1%" discount for early payment and discount days is "7".

Enter the following historical balances at 1 July 2011:   **TAX CODE**

Darling Computers	PO # 3095	21/5/2011	$35.00	GST
Darling Computers	PO # 3110	6/6/2011	$6,750.50	GST
Micro Electronics	PO # 3125	17/6/2011	$9,252.00	GST
Larry's Computers	PO # 3130	29/6/2011	$3,367.50	GST
Total Accounts Payable:			**$19,405.00**	

The *Goods & Services* tax is set at 10%. The tax code is GST.
Note: ALL GOODS AND SERVICES in this exercise are taxable.

Enter the following purchases in July 2011 (including an order and a quote):
Prices are GST Inclusive. ☑ Tax Inclusive   Use *'Service'* layout.

Purchase # 3136 dated 4 July 2011 from Micro Electronics. Their invoice # is 34. The purchase was for a desktop Computer System (5-1110) $4,235 including $385 GST together with bundled Software (5-1120) $638 incl. GST $58. These goods were picked up. No freight charged.

Purchase # 3137 dated 17 July 2011 from Larry's Computers. Their invoice # is 125. The purchase was for a desktop Computer System $4,235.00 incl. GST $385.00. The carrier was *International*. No freight charged.

Purchase # 3138 dated 28 July 2011 from Micro Electronics. Their invoice # is 89. The purchase was for 3 desktop Computer Systems @ $4,235.00 each incl. $385 GST each. These goods were picked up. No freight charged.

Record an Order # 3139 dated 28 July 2011 given to Darling Computers. Their invoice # is 888. The purchase is 3 Toshiba P4 Laptops @ $2,750 each incl. $250 GST each. The carrier is *Virgin Blue* (no delivery charges).

Received a Quote # 3140 dated 31 July 2011 from Larry's Computers for the purchase of 10 desktop Computer Systems @ $3,850 incl. $350 GST each.

Change Darling Computers Order # 3139 to a Bill as at 31/7/2011. Retain same purchase # and ignore any date warning.

Enter the following payments to suppliers made in July 2011:

Paid To	Cheque #	Date Paid	Amount	Discount	Apply to PO #
Micro Elec.	101	9/7/2011	$9,252.00	0.00	3125
Larry's Computers	102	10/7/2011	$3,367.50	0.00	3130
Darling Comp.	103	20/7/2011	$6,750.50	0.00	3110
Micro Elec.	104	21/7/2011	$4,873.00	0.00	3136
Larry's Computers	105	22/7/2011	$4,192.65	$42.35	3137

(To record the discount for Larry and apply the debit – select *Print Later*)

Received the following credit note for an overcharge on the original purchase:
> **Remember** to enter amount as a negative.

Supplier	Debit Note #	Date	Amount	TAX	Apply to PO #
Darling	DN1	11/7/2011	$35.00	GST	3095

Credit: *Purchases Hardware – Computer.*

Received the following credit note for 5% volume discount ($577.50 plus Tax)

Supplier	Debit Note #	Date	Amount	TAX	Apply to PO #
Micro Elect.	DN2	31/7/2011	$635.25	GST	3138

Credit: *Purchases Hardware – Computer*:

Received the following credit note together with a refund cheque:

29/7/2011 received a refund of $66 ($60 plus Tax) (overcharge) on computer hardware purchased from Larry's Computers. TAX code: GST. Create a negative purchase then record the receipt of the refund.

Required:
> Print Purchase order No 3137
>> Form Layout: "*Service*". Status: "*Closed*" and Form: "AccountRight plain paper P.O."
>
> Print the Purchases and Payables Journal for the month of July 2011;
>
> Print the Cash Disbursements Journal for the month of July 2011;
>
> Print the Cash Receipts Journal for the month of July 2011;
>
> Print Darling's Account Details from 1/5/2011 to 31/7/2011
>> Select *Find Transactions* then *Card* tab. Enter supplier, date range and print.
>
> Print Aged Payables (Detail) report at 31 July 2011:
>> Select *Reports* then *Purchases* – select *Ageing Detail* report. Use *Customise* to enter report date (*31/7/2011*) and select *All Suppliers*
>
> Print GST [Detail Accrual] for July 2011 – All Tax Codes "*Both Collected and Paid*" with tax inclusive amounts.

6.3 The exercise month is July 2011.

Start *MYOB AccountRight Plus* and open an existing file called **ass63.myo**.

Use the *Setup* menu, *Company Information* item and change the business address to "Your full name – Assessment 6.3".

Set up the following supplier cards for *Loch Ness Engineering*:

There are no second or email addresses on the following cards:

Walga Pneumatics Ltd (Card ID TC01) of 207 Pacific Parade, St Leonards, Victoria 3223. Telephone (052) 9221 3321, Fax # (03) 9221 5571. Salutation is Ms Ball and contact is Melissa Ball. Identifier is "T". The credit limit is $85,000.00. Credit term is net 30 days after end of month. ABN 85 854 290 290. TAX code: GST.

Sattler Electronics (Card ID TC02) of 23 Peripheral Street, Newcastle, NSW 2300. Telephone (049) 972 4481, Fax # (02) 972 1199. Salutation is Trevor and contact person is T Deanne. Identifier is "T". ABN 88 541 244 290. The credit limit is 60,000.00. Net 30 days after date of purchase. TAX code: GST.

C.M.S. Stationery Supplies Pty Ltd (Card ID OC01), Unit 44, Tryhurst Avenue, Castle Hill, NSW 2154. Telephone (02) 9634 8774, Fax # (02) 9634 2222. Salutation is Mr Fox and contact is Francois Reynaldo. Identifier is "O". ABN 09 141 444 090. The credit limit is $38,000.00. Net 30 days after date of purchase. TAX code: GST.

Graf Spey Engineering Pty Ltd (Card ID TC03) of 32 Dry Street, Mount Walker, WA 6369. Telephone (09) 924 5538. Salutation is Mr Pritchard and contact is Peter Pritchard. Identifier is "T". ABN 79 451 774 097. No credit terms have been agreed to. TAX code: GST.

Yella Terra Machining Pty Ltd (Card ID TC04) of 33 Treloar Avenue, Seven Hills, NSW 2147. Telephone (02) 8394 6641. Fax # (02) 8394 2982. Salutation is Mr Speed and contact is Bozo Speed. Identifier is "T". ABN 79 461 762 111. Credit limit: $25,000. Net 30 days after invoice date. TAX code: GST.

Change the card details for the following *existing* suppliers:

Daintree Alternatives. Change the contact name to Max Prokofiev. Add ABN: 30 404 504 904 (Tax codes for purchases and freight: GST) and increase the credit limit to $75,000.

Deponse Engineering Pty Ltd. The address shown at present should be the second address. The postal address for the invoice is PO. Box 28, Wagga Wagga, 2650. Add the ABN 76 461 762 061 (TAX codes for purchases and freight: GST) and increase credit limit to $50,000.

Spence Pneumatics. Add ABN: 39 388 611 966 (Tax code: GST).

Enter the following historical balances at 1 July 2011 – (Tax code for all = "GST"):

Daintree Alternatives	PO # 3000	1/6/2011	2,037.00
Deponse Engineering	PO # 3021	14/6/2011	$9,268.00
Spence Pneumatics	PO # 3010	6/6/2011	$12,680.00
Total Accounts payable:			**$23,985.00**

Enter the following purchases in July 2011: Prices are <u>GST inclusive</u>. ☑ Tax Inclusive

Purchase # 3031 dated 3 July 2011 from Sattler Electronics. Their invoice # is 3321. Details are "Design and supply actuating arm as per specifications". The amount is $5,489.00 (incl. $499 GST). Debit *Purchases – Engineering*. (5-1110)
Goods delivered by *Road Freight*.

Purchase # 3032 dated 10 July 2011 from Graf Spey Engineering Pty Ltd. Their invoice # is G210. Details are "Machining of parts to order". The amount is $5,005.00 (incl. $455 GST) and Hills Transport will deliver the parts. Debit *Purchases – Engineering* (5-1110). Enter $5,005.00 in *"Paid Today:"* field to record a cheque accompanying the P.O.
(After recording this purchase click *OK* to accept the advice about cheque No.)

Purchase # 3033 dated 17 July 2011 from C.M.S. Stationery Supplies Pty Ltd. Their invoice # is 4426. Details are "Stationery supplies as per order". The amount is $748.00 (incl. $68 GST) and the goods were picked up.
Debit *Printing and Stationery* (6-2560).

Purchase # 3034 dated 20 July 2011 from Yella Terra Machining Pty Ltd. Their invoice # is I443. Details are "High tolerance precision machining of tubes as per specifications". The amount is $5,854.09 (incl. $532.19 GST) and these were delivered by *Hills Transport*. Debit *Purchases – Engineering* (5-1110).

Purchase # 3035 dated 26 July 2011 from Walga Pneumatics . Their invoice # is 21030. Details are "Supply of 20 only T44 arms". The amount is $5,489.00 (incl. $499 GST) and is delivered by Road Freight.
Debit *Purchases – Equipment* (5-1120).

Record the following payments to suppliers:

8 July 2011 – paid Deponse Engineering Pty Ltd $9,268.00 for purchase #3021 dated 14 June 2011. Enter the cheque number as 301624.

9 July 2011 – paid Sattler Electronics $5,379.22 for purchase #3031 dated 3 July 2011. Cheque #301625.

15 July 2011 – paid Spence Pneumatics Pty Ltd $12,680.00 for Purchase #3010 date 6 June 2011. Cheque #301626.

22 July 2011 – paid Daintree Alternatives $2,037.00 for Purchase #3000 of 1 June 2011. Cheque #301627.

26 July 2011 – paid Yella Terra Machining Pty Ltd $5,854.09 for Purchase #3034 of 20 July 2011. Cheque #301628.

31 July 2011 – paid C.M.S. Stationery Supplies $594.00 of their account. Cheque #301629.

Record the following debit notes (credit notes received from suppliers):

Debit Note #112 dated 20 July 2011 and a <u>refund cheque</u> received from Graf Spey Engineering for an overcharge on invoice # G210 (our order #3032 dated 10 July 2011). The credit is for $462.00 ($420.00 plus $42 GST). Tax Code: GST.

Debit Note #113 dated 29 July 2011 received from C.M.S. Stationery Supplies Pty Ltd for return of stationery incorrectly supplied. The credit is for $154.00 incl. $14 GST and <u>should be **applied** against Purchase # 3033</u>.

Debit Note #114 dated 29 July 2011 from Sattler Electronics being discount received for early payment. Amount of discount is $109.78 incl. $9.98 GST. Credit *Discount Received (8-1000)*. <u>Apply to Purchase # 3031</u>.

Note: As this supplier does not always offer discounts, any discount received is recorded by issuing a debit note and then applying it against the original bill.

Print the following:

Purchase #3034 (Status: "Closed" and form: "AccountRight Plus's plain paper P.O.");

A detailed report for Graf Spey Engineering account for July 2011 (use the *Find Transactions/ Card* select supplier, enter date range – and print);

An Aged Payables (Detail) report at 31 July 2011 and include zero balances; (use the *Ageing Detail* report and use the report customise button to enter date);

A transaction journal (all journals) for the month of July 2011;

GST [Detail Accrual] for July 2011 – All Tax Codes "Both Collected and Paid".

6.4 Accounts payable, cash transactions and general ledger integrated.

To satisfactorily complete this exercise, Chapters 1 to 6 should have been covered.

Required: The exercise month is July 2011.

1.   Start *MYOB AccountRight Plus* and open an existing file called **ass64.myo.** This is a new file with <u>a minimum number of accounts</u>.

2.   Use the **Setup** menu, **Company Information** item and change the business <u>address</u> to: "Your full name – Assessment 6.4 (ass64.myo)".

3.   Read through the whole exercise and design an *Account List* that will <u>at least</u> cover the accounts required.
     Enter this *Accounts List* – add **new** accounts and headers or **edit** existing ones. The *Cost of Sales* section should show the typical "Cost of Goods Sold" set up (i.e. Opening inventory *plus* Purchases accounts and *less* Closing Inventory).

4.   Enter the opening general ledger account balances as at 1 July 2011. Using the *Setup* pull-down menu select *Balances* then *Account Opening Balances*.

5.   Set up the linked accounts for the *Purchases Accounts*.
   Note: Do <u>not</u> set a link for 'I can receive Items without a Supplier Bill'.

6.   Create suppliers records (Cards) and enter in the historical invoices making up the accounts payable balance at 30 June 2011.

7.   Record the transactions for July 2011.

8.   Print the reports listed at the end of this assessment.

Andrey Yelysyeyev has a battery franchise (*Batteries 4U*). The franchise has expanded rapidly and the accounting systems are to be converted to *MYOB AccountRight Plus* on 1 July 2011. The balance sheet at 30 June 2011 was:

Assets
     Current Assets

ANZ bank		2,180.60	
Petty cash		300.00	
Accounts receivable	18,248.75		
Provision for doubtful debts	−1,000.00	17,248.75	
Inventories		18,648.20	
Total Current Assets			38,377.55
Non-Current Assets			
Motor vehicle – at cost	42,800.00		
Accumulated depreciation	−5,800.00	37,000.00	
Furniture and equipment – at cost	22,684.80		
Accumulated depreciation	−8,120.40	14,564.40	
Fork Lift – at cost	31,280.00		
Accumulated depreciation	−12,120.00	19,160.00	
Total Non-Current Assets			70,724.40
Total Assets			109,101.95

Liabilities
     Current Liabilities

Accounts payable	14,268.60	
GST Collected	3,900.00	
GST Paid	−800.00	
Total Current Liabilities		17,368.60
Non-Current Liabilities		
Loan from A.D. Finance	16,000.00	
Total Non-Current Liabilities		16,000.00
Total Liabilities		33,368.60
Net Assets		75,733.35

Capital – A. Yelysyeyev	50,000.00	
Retained Earnings	25,733.35	
Total Equity		75,733.35

Details of the accounts payable balance of $14,268.60 at 30 June 2011:

Try-Us Imports Pty Ltd of 68 Stevens Road, Camperdown, NSW 2050. Telephone (02) 9550 1245, Fax (02) 9550 1222. Credit limit is $80,000 and payment is due net 30 days. ABN 11 122 522 901. Purchases owing at 30 June 2011:

Purchase # 6814	04/6/2011	$4,828.50	Tax code GST
Purchase # 6830	26/6/2011	3,326.40	Tax code GST

Denman Manufacturing Pty Ltd of 24 Adamson Street, Leichhardt, NSW 2040. Telephone (02) 9568 4463, Fax # (02) 9568 1426. Credit limit is $90,000.00 and term is net 30 days. ABN 71 177 711 604. Purchases owing were:

Purchase # 6820	11/6/2011	$4,268.40	Tax code GST
Purchase # 6835	28/6/2011	1,624.80	Tax code GST

Torpur Products Pty Ltd of 1 Richmond Road, Blacktown, NSW 2148. Credit limit $5000, net 30 days. ABN 21 100 947 432. Purchase outstanding at 30 June 2011:

Purchase # 5104	18/10/09	$220.50	Tax code GST

Note: In this exercise ALL Goods & Services are subject to 10% GST. Tax code for all purchases and adjustments is "GST".

During July 2011 the following transactions took place (excluding sales and accounts receivable): Prices are tax inclusive:

July 2011		Amount incl. GST
1	Paid a month's rent $4,180 (incl. GST) to Davis Estate Management. Chq #302103.	$4,180.00
4	Purchase 200 'A9' batteries @ $33 (incl. GST) each, from Denman Manufacturing Pty Ltd. Purchase # 6836. Invoice #11240.	6,600.00
5	Purchased from Try-Us Imports and paid cash for 100 'Zorro' batteries @ $11 each (incl. GST). Purchase #6837 – cheque #302104. (For cash purchases enter $1,100 in 'Paid Today' field. Balance due should = 0.)	1,100.00
10	Paid electricity account to Integral Electricity. Chq #302105.	902.00

(continued on the next page)

July 2011		Amount incl. GST
12	Paid Try-Us Imports against Purchase #6814. Chq #302106.	4,828.50
	Paid salaries (Gross 2,480.00 less PAYG tax of $512.00) Cheque #302107. Credit Tax liability to Acc. #2-1520.	1,968.00
15	Purchased 100 'Delta' Heavy Duty batteries @ $30.80 each (incl. GST) from Robsons Pty Ltd (new supplier) Address: 418 Terminus Street, Adelaide SA 5000. Phone (08) 9214 126 Fax (08) 9214 3333. Purchase #6838. Their invoice #442. Credit term is Net 30 days after invoice date. Credit limit is $15,000. ABN 98 800 700 666.	3,080.00
17	Owner contributed further capital.	20,000.00
19	Paid Denman Manufacturing Pty Ltd – Purchase #6820. Cheque # 302108.	4,268.40
22	Paid Dobel Stationery for stationery. Cheque # 302109.	528.00
23	Paid Robsons Manufacturing amount owing – Chq # 302110.	3,080.00
26	Paid salaries (Gross 2,818.00 less PAYG tax $546) – Cheque # 302111.	2,272.00
29	Paid Try-Us for purchase # 6830 – Cheque # 302112.	3,326.40
30	Purchased 200 'A9' batteries @ $33 each incl. GST from Denman Manufacturing – purchase # 6839. Invoice #11250.	6,600.00
31	Paid Denman for purchase # 6835.	1,624.80
	Purchased 100 'Try-Us' batteries @ $30.80 each incl. GST, from Try-Us Imports purchase # 6840. Invoice #684.	3,080.00
	Received a credit note CN1 from Denman for return of 3 batteries @ $33 each incl. GST. Apply to purchase #6836.	99.00
	Torpur Products have now agreed on a disputed amount since 2009. Prepare a credit note (CN #TP629), credit purchases (Tax code: GST) and apply to purchase #5104.	220.50

Print the following:

Purchase #6838 – Robsons Pty Ltd

Status: *Closed*, Form: "AccountRight Plus's Plain Paper P.O."

Details of Denman Manufacturing transactions during July 2011

(Select *Find Transactions* then *Card,* select supplier, enter dates and print)

Aged Payable (detailed) at 31 July 2011

Select report name: "Ageing Detail"

Transaction listing (all journals) – for July 2011.

Accounts List (Summary) include account numbers.

6.5 **Integrates general ledger, accounts payable and cashbook. Uses batch mode entry.**

Assessment requirements:

This assessment exercise requires you to:

- Enter opening balances for the general ledger to convert hand written accounts to *MYOB AccountRight Plus*.

- Create Accounts Payable.

- Set up the Purchases linked accounts and enter the historical invoice details agreeing with the general ledger accounts payable control account.

- Record accounts payable transactions for the month of July 2011.

- Print various forms and reports.

The business *Northern Printery* is a small printery that leases premises in Old Northern Road, Castle Hill. An *Accounts List* has been adopted from those supplied with *MYOB AccountRight Plus* and has been modified by an accountant to comply with their normal reporting style.

Important: You may need to add accounts as you progress through the exercise. Print an accounts list summary and use it for reference.

The exercise month is July 2011.
Start *MYOB AccountRight Plus* and open an existing file called **ass65.myo.**
Use the ***Setup*** menu, ***Company Information*** item and change the business address to "Your full name – Assessment 6.5 (ass65.myo)".

- The Current fiscal (financial) year is 2012 and the year ends on 30 June.

- Enter the linked accounts for Purchases.
  Select *Setup* menu, *Linked Accounts* and *Purchases Accounts* options.

  (2-1100 for payable and 1-1110 for bank are already set)
  Use:
          5-1190 for freight,
          1-1410 for deposits,
          8-3000 for discounts *and*
          6-2460 for late fees payable.

*Ignore any error messages regarding type of accounts **usually** linked.*

(continued on the next page)

- Use *Balances* from the *Setup* menu to enter the following opening general ledger account balances at 1 July 2011:

	Debit	Credit
St George Bank	101,398.45	
Petty Cash	500.00	
Accounts Receivable	21,209.00	
Provision for Doubtful Debts		1,780.00
Inventory	18,431.85	
Prepayments	3,800.00	
Leasehold Improvements	31,900.00	
Accumulated Depreciation – Leasehold Improvements		7,975.00
Printing Equipment	124,380.00	
Accumulated Depreciation – Printing Equipment		31,480.60
Furniture and Fittings	23,450.60	
Accumulated Depreciation – Furniture and Fittings		9,540.90
Office Equipment	24,290.00	
Accumulated Depreciation – Office Equipment		18,990.00
Accounts Payable		17,026.10
Accrued Expenses		1,980.75
GST Collected		4,395.00
GST Paid	1,395.00	
Payroll Deductions Payable		280.50
PAYG Withholding Payable		954.00
Esanda Finance Ltd (repayable $7,000 per annum) i.e. $7,000 Current and $21,000 Non-current		28,000.00
Capital		150,000.00
Retained Earnings		78,352.05
	350,754.90	350,754.90

- Set up Accounts Payable (suppliers' records) using the *Card* command centre as follows: (assume no second address and no email. Tax code = GST for all).

Name	Address	Phone	Fax	Contact	$ Limit	Terms
Tessorini Papers Pty Ltd ABN:12345888999	345 Mary Street Silverwater NSW 2141	9714 0865	9714 0777	Nick Savini	90,000	net/30
Printing Supplies Pty Ltd ABN:12345888777	82 Queen Street Granville NSW 2141	9682 4412	9637 5543	Ted Jones	82,000	net/30

(continued on the next page)

Suppliers' cards *(continued)*

Name	Address	Phone	Fax	Contact	$ Limit	Terms
Deutrom Cleaning ABN:12342220757	78 Shenton Ave Seven Hills NSW 2147	9624 3332	9624 6648	Bill Deutrom	61,000	net/30
B.T. Printer Repairs Pty Ltd ABN:90011172277	13 Terminus St Granville NSW 2141	9637 2558	9637 1110	Zack Romero	63,000	net/30
Acer Action Church Graphics ABN:12345022277	14 Showground Road Castle Hill NSW 2154	9680 2217	9680 2255	Sheralyn	85,000	net/30
Ace Binding & Packaging Pty Ltd ABN:12345811227	1 Church Street Castle Hill NSW 2154	9634 9914	9634 5550	Russell Balding	88,000	net/30
Hills Transport Pty Ltd ABN:12345000733	4 Brunker Road Homebush NSW 2140	9763 4444	9763 4419	Peter Taylor	75,000	net/30

Note: Terms: "net/30" means "Balance due days" = "30" and "Discount days" = "0"

- Enter the following invoices (pre-conversion) making up the balance in the general ledger for accounts payable of $17,026.10. Tax code = "GST":

Account Payable	Purchase #	Supplier Invoice #	Date	Amount – $
Tessorini Papers Pty Ltd	8410	445	5/6/2011	2,448.50
	8500	483	24/6/2011	1,899.00
Printing Supplies Pty Ltd	8470	IN2283	15/6/2011	3,228.60
Deutrom Cleaning	8501	1112	24/6/2011	800.00
B.T. Printer Repairs Pty Ltd	8407	R0122	2/6/2011	448.90
	8510	R0140	29/6/2011	1,045.60
Ace Binding & Packaging Pty	8472	I1076	15/6/2011	2,175.00
Hills Transport Pty Ltd	8408	100776	3/6/2011	105.40
	8450	111221	13/6/2011	150.50
	8480	118012	21/6/2011	100.00
	8522	122115	29/6/2011	124.60
Acer Action Graphics	8445	A338	12/6/2011	4,500.00
			Total	17,026.10

• Enter the following invoices for goods and services purchased on credit:
Note: All Amounts are excluding GST. ☐ Tax Inclusive ← **Note**: NOT inclusive.
You need to Code each item with the Tax Code: GST (unless otherwise stated)
First (*Bill*) Purchase number should be #8523.

GST to be added to all amounts & prices - (unless otherwise stated)

Date	Ref.	Account Payable	Amount excl.GST	Detail ☐ Tax Inclusive	Purch. #
3/7/11	IN2295	Printing Supplies Pty Ltd	1,568.80	Purchases – Ink	8523
4/7/11	R0151	B.T. Printer Repairs P/Ltd	480.50	Repairs to equipment	8524
6/7/11	123000	Hills Transport Pty Ltd	65.80	Cartage (use 6-4050)	8525
7/7/11	I1080	Ace Binding & Pac. P/L	1,077.00	Subcontracting (use 5-1220)	8526
7/7/11	A342	Acer Action Graphics	280.00	Subcontracting	8527
10/7/11	122555	Hills Transport Pty Ltd	142.80	Cartage	8528
11/7/11	AD147	PKWU Magazine (148 Sussex St, Sydney NSW 2000. Phone 9201 7772 ABN 09 404 540 682)	450.00	Advertising	8529
11/7/11	501	Tessorini Papers Pty Ltd	1,888.75	Purchases – Paper	8530
14/7/11	IN2308	Printing Supplies Pty Ltd	985.60	Purchases – Ink	8531
17/7/11	123034	Hills Transport Pty Ltd	95.70	Cartage	8532
18/7/11	123126	Hills Transport Pty Ltd	105.20	Cartage	8533
19/7/11	I1085	Ace Binding & Packaging P/L	2,440.80	Subcontracting	8534
21/7/11	A348	Acer Action Graphics	829.00	Subcontracting	8535
24/7/11	1149	Deutrom Cleaning	800.00	Cleaning – Office and Workshop	8536
24/7/11	IN2401	Printing Supplies Pty Ltd	1,225.00	Purchases – Stamps $385 and Toner $840.00	8537
26/7/11	511	Tessorini Papers Pty Ltd	1,030.60	Purchases – Paper	8538
26/7/11	8012	Shelley Wilson Travel (1 Bay St., Coogee 2034 ABN 96 651 543111)	840.00	3 day seminar (Staff training 6-5115)	8539

(continued on the next page)

Date	Ref.	Account Payable	Amount excl.GST	Detail ☐ Tax Inclusive	Purch. #
27/7/11	AC228	Frost & Partners (245 Old Northern Road, Castle Hill 2154 – 9680 3345 ABN 00 556 771 876)	600.00	Accounting Fees	8540
31/7/11	D287	Elgin Business Information Systems (3 Brisbane Rd, Castle Hill 2154 – 9634 1419 ABN 18 763 321 123)	4,290.00	Computer Accounting System – Equipment, software and installation (debit Office Equipment) Tax Code "CAP" Ignore error message!	8541
31/7/11	125004	Hills Transport Pty Ltd	180.50	Cartage	8542

- Enter the following cash payments.
  Remember to use *Pay Bills* when paying a supplier, and *Spend Money* for the other payments.
  The first cheque number should be 148101:

Important Note: Tax code for Wages, PAYG Tax and Deductions = "N-T"

CHQ #	Date	Amount – $	Details ☐ Tax Inclusive ← Note
148101	4/7/11	$448.90	B.T. Printer Repairs – paying Inv # R0122 Purchase #8407
148102	6/7/11	1,869.40	Wages: Printers Salaries (5-1210) $1,080.00, Clerical wages (6-5130) $1,400, less Tax (2-1520) -$545.60, less deductions (2-1510) –$65.00 (Tax Code = N-T for all these) *Save this payment as recurring before recording it!*
148103	7/7/11	3,954.00	ATO – June's BAS return. Tax Code N-T for all. PAYG deductions (2-1520) $954.00, GST Collected (2-1310) $4395.00, less GST Paid (2-1330) –$1395.00
148104	7/7/11	278.96	Petty Cash Re-imbursement – Postage $88.90, travel $48.00, staff amenities $48.70, cartage $68.00 (all plus GST)
148105	10/7/11	2,448.50	Tessorini Papers – paying Inv # 445 – Purchase# 8410
148106	10/7/11	535.15	Telstra – telephone ($486.50 plus GST)
148107	12/7/11	4,500.00	Acer Action Graphics – paying Inv # A338
148108	13/7/11	1,869.40	Wages: Printers $1,080.00, Clerical $1,400.00, less Tax –$545.60, deductions –$65.00 (Tax Code = N-T for all these)
148109	14/7/11	3,228.60	Printing Supplies – paying Inv # IN2283 – Purchase #8470
148110	17/7/11	2,175.00	Ace Binding & Packaging – paying Inv # I1076 – Purchase # 8472

(continued on the next page)

CHQ #	Date	Amount – $	Details ☐ Tax Inclusive ← Note
148111	18/7/11	255.90	Hills Transport – paying Inv # 100776 $105.40 and Inv # 111221 $150.50 (P.O. 8408 & 8450)
148112	18/7/11	202.90	AMP – Payroll deduction (2-1510) (Tax code = N-T)
148113	18/7/11	77.60	PKWU – Payroll deduction (2-1510) (Tax code = N-T) (*Don't use the PKWU Magazine card for this entry*)
148114	19/7/11	396.77	Petty Cash Re-imbursement – Postage $105.80, travel $66.30, staff amenities $78.60, cartage $110.00 (all plus GST)
148115	20/7/11	1,869.40	Wages: Printers $1,080.00, Clerical $1,400.00, less Tax –$545.60, deductions –$65.00. (Tax = N-T for these)
148116	21/7/11	137.50	Subscription to Trade paper ($125 plus GST)–(6-1400)
148117	24/7/11	1,899.00	Tessorini Papers – paying Inv # 483 – Purchase # 8500
148118	24/7/11	800.00	Deutrom Cleaning – paying Inv # 1112 – Purchase # 8501
148119	25/7/11	100.00	Hills Transport – paying Inv # 118012 – Purchase # 8480
148120	25/7/11	440.00	Cash purchase – ink ($400 plus GST)
148121	25/7/11	238.15	Petty Cash Re-imbursement – Postage $55.70, travel $44.80, staff amenities $56.00, cartage $60.00 (all plus GST)
148122	26/7/11	132.00	Cash purchase – postage stamps ($120 plus GST)
148123	27/7/11	1,869.40	Wages: Printers $1,080.00, Clerical $1,400.00, less Tax –$545.60, deductions –$65.00. (Tax = N-T for these)
148124	31/7/11	124.60	Hills Transport – paying Inv # 122115
148125	31/7/11	1,980.00	Ray White Real Estate – Rent (6-4400) $1800 plus GST

Required the following reports:

> Print purchase # 8541 (use "AccountRight Plus's Plain Paper P.O." form);
>
> Print details of Tessorini Papers transactions – 1/07/2011 to 31/07/2011
> (Select *Find Transactions* then *Card,* select supplier, enter dates and print)
>
> Print "Aged Payables (detail)" at 31 July 2011;
> (Select *Reports* then *Purchases* – select *Ageing Detail* report. Use *Customise* to enter report date (31/07/2011) and select *All Suppliers*)
>
> Print the "Purchases and Payables" Journal for the month of July 2011;
>
> Print the "Cash Disbursements" Journal for the month of July 2011;
>
> Print a "Trial Balance" report for July 2011 (Do *NOT* include zero balances)
>
> Print "GST [Detail Accrual]" for July 2011 –
> Select all Tax Codes "Both Collected and Paid" with tax inclusive amounts.

Chapter 6: Answers to self-test questions

6.1

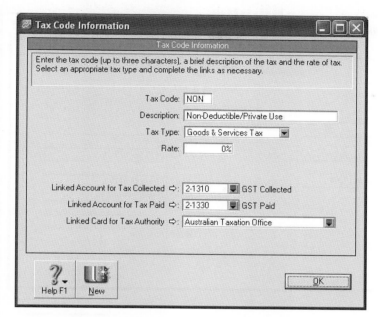

6.2 Only the first custom list is shown here – the others are similar.

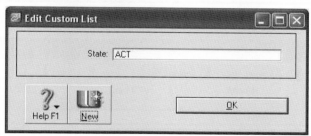

The complete 'Custom list'

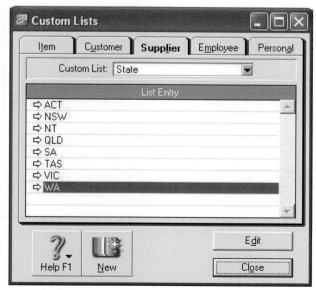

6.3

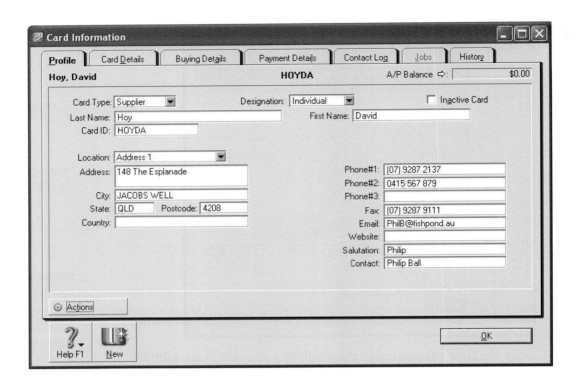

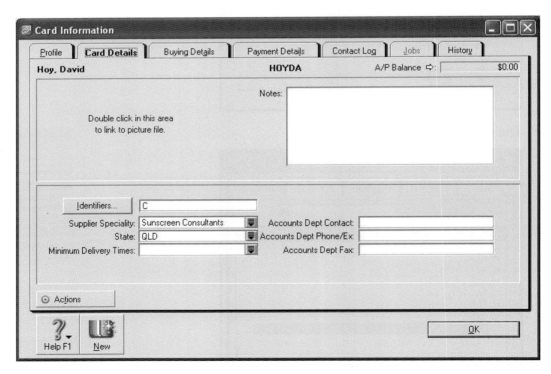

6.3 *(continued)*

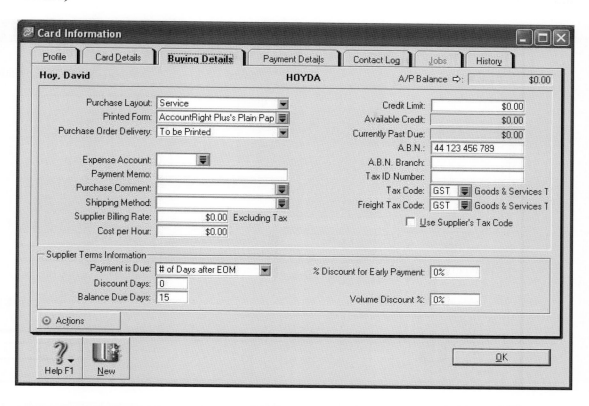

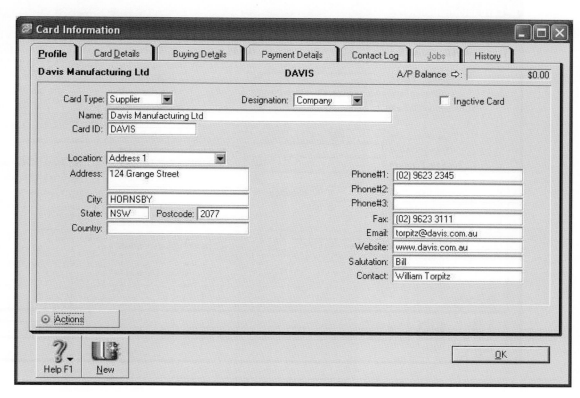

6.3 *(continued)*

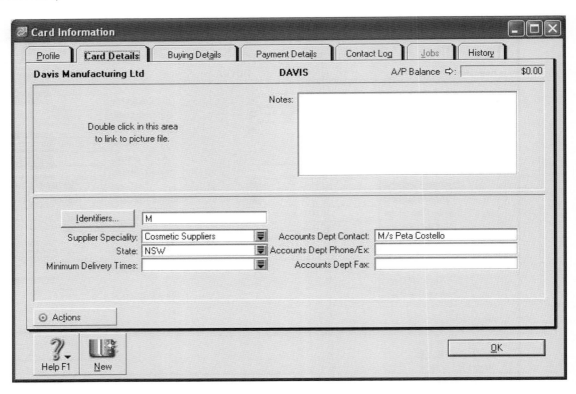

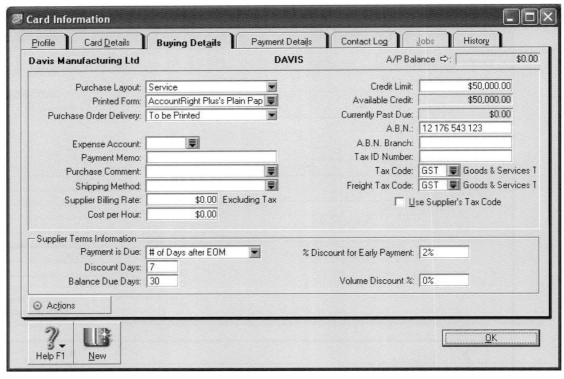

6.4

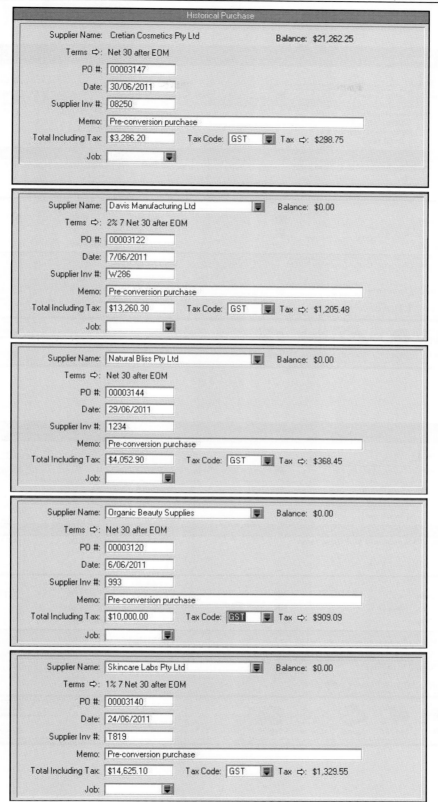

6.5

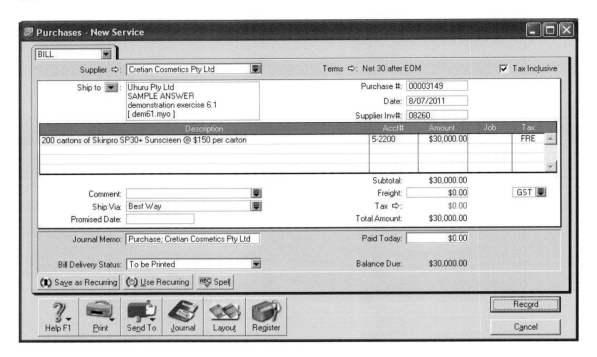

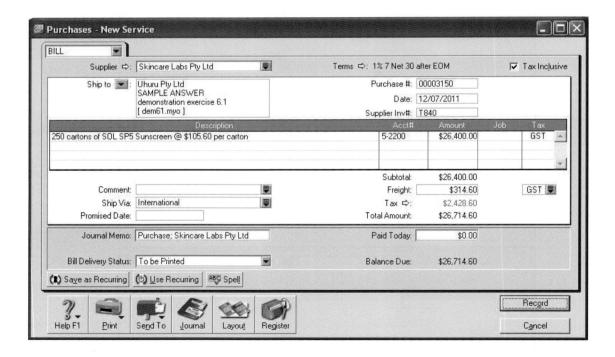

6.5 *(continued)*

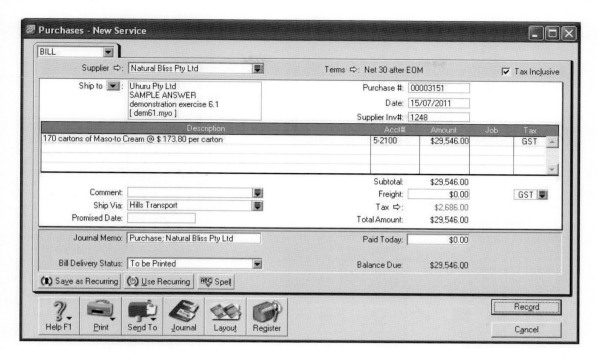

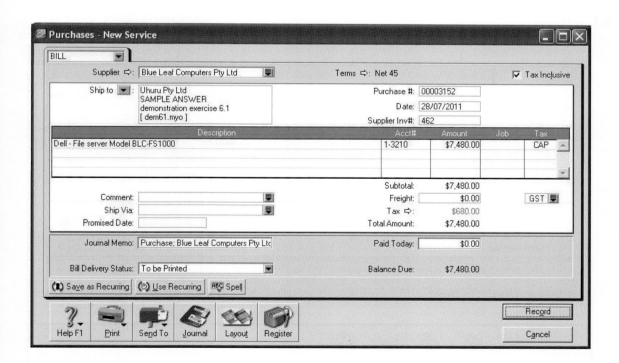

6.6

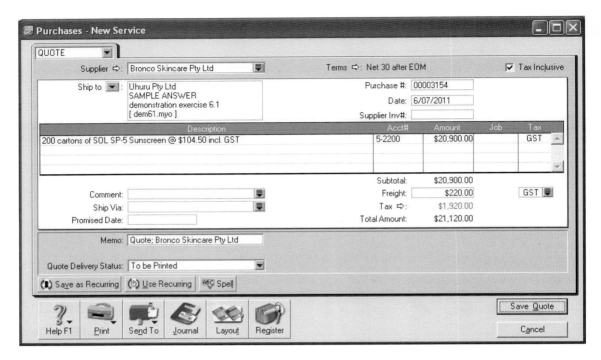

6.7

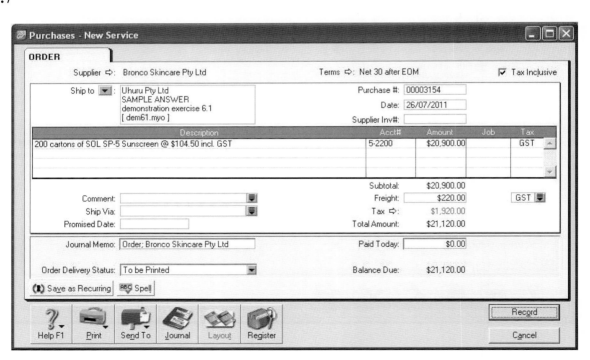

6.8

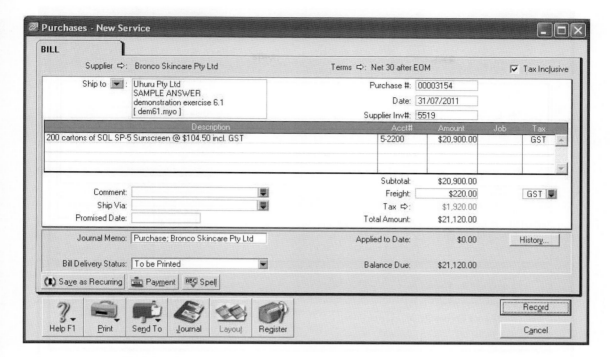

6.9

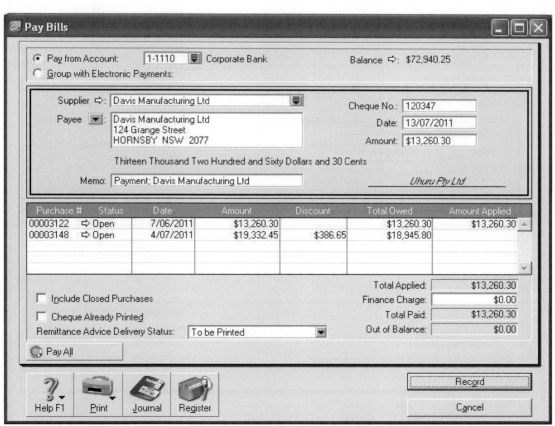

6.9 *(continued)*

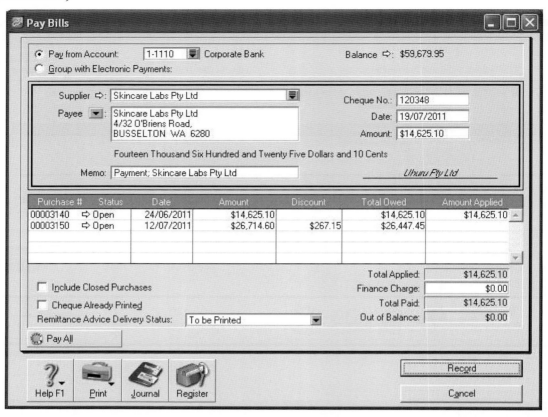

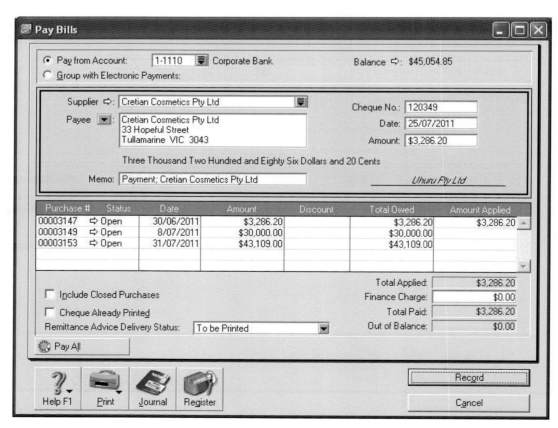

6.9 *(continued)*

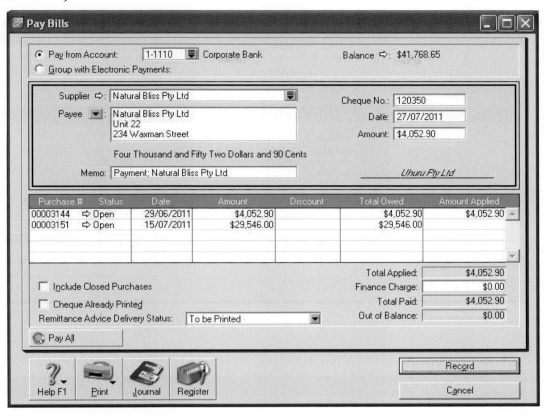

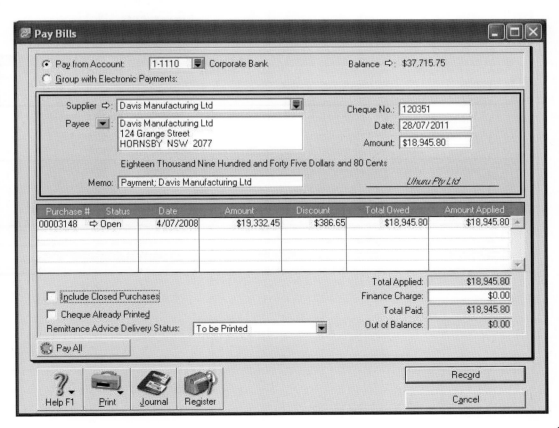

6.9 *(continued)*

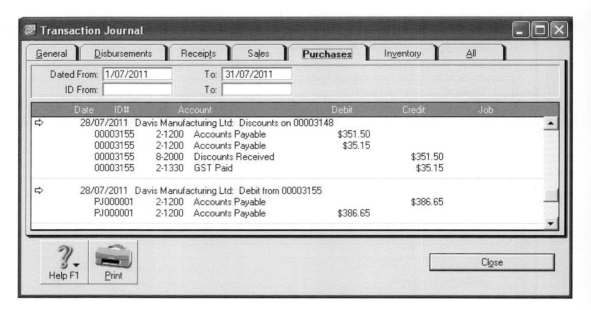

6.10

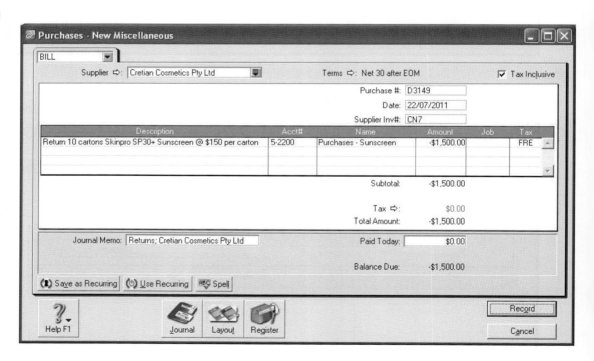

6.11

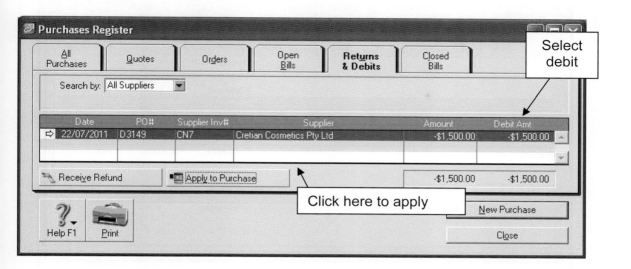

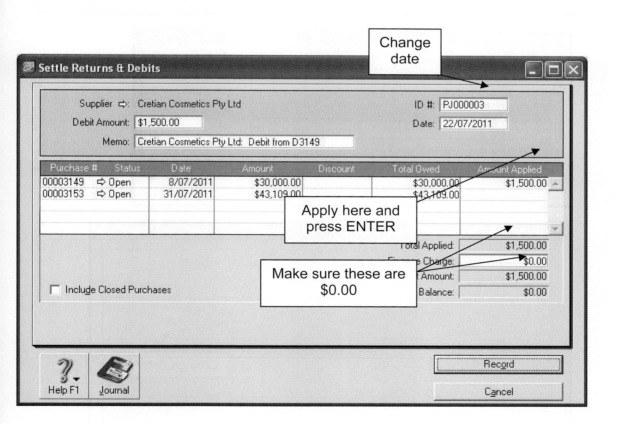

6.12

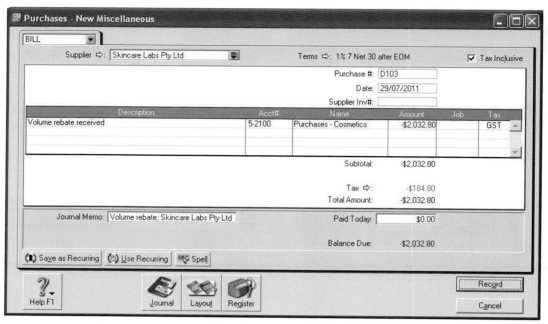

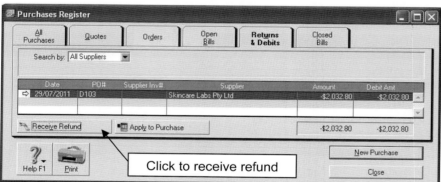

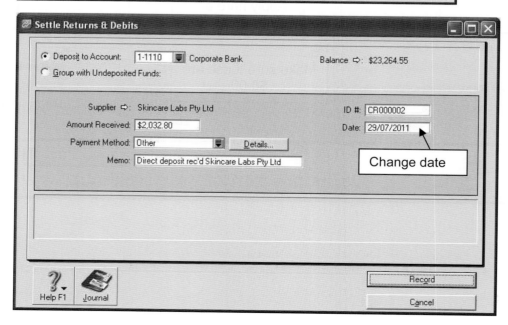

6.13

Uhuru Pty Ltd
Demonstration File dem61.myo
Recipient Created Tax Invoice

	Purchase #: 00003149
	Date: 8/07/2011
A.B.N.: 98 999 999 999	Ship Via: Best Way
A.C.N.:	Page: 1

Ship To:

Cretian Cosmetics Pty Ltd
33 Hopeful Street
Tullamarine VIC 3043

Uhuru Pty Ltd
Demonstration exercise 6.1
[dem61.myo]

Description	**Amount**	**Code**
200 cartons of Skinpro SP30+ Sunscreen @ $150 per carton	$30,000.00	FRE

Your Invoice #: 08260	Supplier ABN: 23 123 678 908		Freight:	$0.00	GST
Shipping Date:	Terms: Net 30 after EOM		GST:	$0.00	
COMMENT	CODE	RATE	TAX SALE AMOUNT		
	FRE	0%	$0.00	$30,000.00	Total Amount: $30,000.00
	GST	10%	$0.00	$0.00	Amount Applied: $1,500.00
					Balance Due: $28,500.00

6.14

Uhuru Pty Ltd
SAMPLE ANSWER
demonstration exercise 6.1
[dem61.myo]

Aged Payables [Summary]

31/07/2011

Page 1

Name	Total Due	Current	1 - 30	31 - 60	60+
Blue Leaf Computers Pty Lt	$7,480.00	$7,480.00	$0.00	$0.00	$0.00
Bronco Skincare Pty Ltd	$21,120.00	$21,120.00	$0.00	$0.00	$0.00
Cretian Cosmetics Pty Ltd	$71,609.00	$71,609.00	$0.00	$0.00	$0.00
Natural Bliss Pty Ltd	$27,808.00	$27,808.00	$0.00	$0.00	$0.00
Organic Beauty Supplies	$10,000.00	$0.00	$10,000.00	$0.00	$0.00
Skincare Labs Pty Ltd	$26,714.60	$26,714.60	$0.00	$0.00	$0.00
Total:	$164,731.60	$154,731.60	$10,000.00	$0.00	$0.00
Ageing Percent:		93.9%	6.1%	0.0%	0.0%

6.15 *Cretian Cosmetics'* transactions <u>before</u> the merger with *Organic*

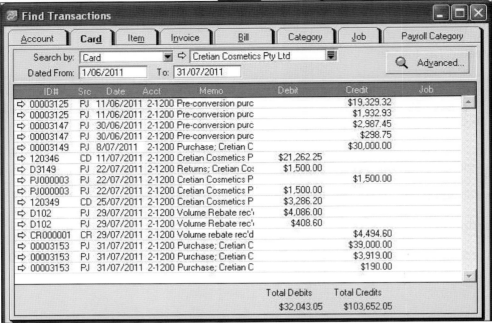

6.16

Cretian Cosmetics' transactions <u>after</u> the merger with *Organic*

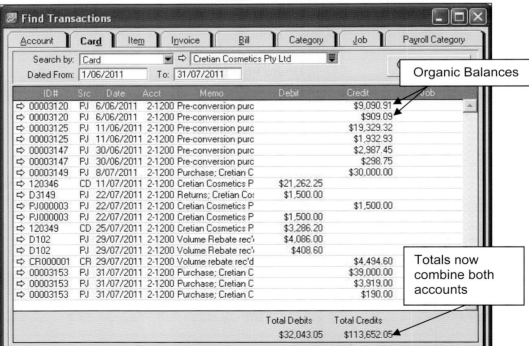

Inventory and integration

7

Setting up inventory items and integrating transactions through accounts receivable, accounts payable and the general ledger.

After completing this chapter you will be able to:

1 Set up inventory items for goods to purchase, store and/or sell.

2 Set up items to be included on invoices that are not stocked.

3 Enter in the opening balances – count and cost – of inventory.

4 Enter in cost values agreeing with the balance of inventory accounts in the general ledger.

5 Record transactions involving inventory and the items list.

6 Record item returns with adjustment to inventory count and balance.

7 Maintain and update item records.

8 Make adjustments to item count to comply with the actual periodical physical stocktake.

9 Integrate inventory, accounts receivable, accounts payable and general ledger modules.

10 Print/email item invoices, bills and reports including GST reports.

Introduction

The *Inventory* command centre is used to set up items of inventory (goods purchased, stored and sold in the normal course of business). It is the final link between Sales, Purchases and Inventory and must be set up correctly to ensure that the correct accounts are debited and credited in the general ledger.

The *Inventory* command centre is used to keep a perpetual inventory of each inventory item, and to set up invoice items that are to be charged at set amounts but are not carried in inventory.

The notes, examples and exercises that follow assume that you have read and gone through the basic instructions in Chapters 1 and 2, and that you can:

- Start the *MYOB AccountRight Plus* application;
- Change the business name and/or address;
- Select command centres and options within those command centres; and
- Recognise the conventions used in this book (for example, the sign ↵ is an instruction to tap the *ENTER* key).

You may need to refer back to Chapter 1 to do these tasks. A quick way of finding the place for instructions is to use the 'How to ...' index at the front of the book.

In this chapter the authors have elected to use accounts, selected and listed, by account <u>numbers</u> rather than by account names. Throughout this book, you may use whichever option you prefer. **If you so wish, you may need to refer back to previous chapters (e.g. Chapters 1 and 5) for instructions on how to change this preference.**

Item list

The *Inventory* command centre is used whenever a similar *item* is regularly bought or sold. Using an Item invoice or Item bill, items can be set up with a standard description, cost or price. This means that only the quantity and item number or ID need to be entered at the keyboard and the description, extension, tax and total will be automatically generated. If the item is inventoried using the perpetual inventory system, a purchase or sale will automatically update the inventory item count record and the postings to the relevant general ledger accounts.

An item is not necessarily an inventory item that is purchased, inventoried and sold. It may be consulting hours charged by an engineering consultancy, a financial adviser charging by the hour or it may be labour charged by a motor vehicle repairer. It may also be a charge such as insurance added to a customer's account. The type of item gives rise to different accounting entries.

Setting up items

Setting up item information depends on the type of item. In *MYOB AccountRight Plus*, the *Item Information* window has several tabs (or views) that only become active depending on starting selections on the *Item Profile* tab. Clicking on the three options for buying, selling and stocking activates the other optional tabs for purchasing and sales information.

When setting up a new item, the three option boxes in the *Item Profile* may be selected in various combinations. The following are the main combinations for setting up items, each with an example of the 'boxes' which need to be selected.

How to start an entry for a new item

Step	Instruction
1	Select the *Inventory* command centre.
2	Select the *Items List* option.
3	Click on the *New* icon button.
4	Enter an 'Item Number' ↵.
5	Type in the 'Name' of the item ↵.

Example 7.1—Starting an inventory item

1. Start *MYOB AccountRight Plus* and open an existing file called dem71.myo. Sign on as the "Administrator" – without a password.
2. Select the *Inventory* command centre.
3. Select the *Items List* option.
4. Click on the *New* button.
5. Enter "P360" in the 'Item Number:' field and ↵.
6. Type in "Underwater Pump Type 360" as the 'Name:' of the item ↵.
7. The *Item Profile* window should look like Figure 7.1 on the next page.
8. Click on the *OK* button.
9. Click on the *Close* button to exit.

These tabs become active when the relevant tick boxes are selected

Item Information

| Profile | Item Details | Buying Details | Selling Details | History | Auto-Build |

Item Number: P360

Name: Underwater Pump Type 360

☐ Inactive Item

☐ I Buy This Item
☐ I Sell This Item
☐ I Inventory This Item

Click on these boxes to select the type of item to be recorded

Copy From   ABC Spell

Use this button to copy the setup from a previous item

Help F1   New

OK

Figure 7.1: Starting an item profile

How to edit/add an item purchased, inventoried and sold

Step	Instruction
1	Select the *Inventory* command centre.
2	Select the *Items List* option.
3	To <u>edit</u> an existing item click on the detail arrow ⇨ next to it, *or* To <u>add a new</u> item click on the *New* button.
4	Enter/edit the 'Item Number' ↵.
5	Type in or edit the 'Name' of the item ↵.
6	Click on the option checkboxes for 'I Buy This Item', 'I Sell This Item' and 'I Inventory This Item' to turn them on as necessary.
7	Enter the expense account for entering cost of goods sold (account # 5-xxxx). Alternatively, click on the *List* button 🔽 or press ↵ and scroll down to the "Cost of Sales" section and make your selection.
8	Enter the income account for tracking sales (account # 4-xxxx). Alternatively, click on the *List* button 🔽 or press ↵ and scroll down to the "Income" section and make your selection.
9	Enter the asset account for item inventory (account # 1-xxxx). *(continued on the next page)*

Step	Instruction
10	Click on the *Item Details* Tab at the top and enter any <u>optional</u> details such as a description, use any of the customised lists or fields and insert an item's picture (if available). **Note:** If the description is to be used (instead of the item's name) on the invoices and the purchases, tick the checkbox: 'Use Item Description on Sales and Purchases'.
11	Click on the *Buying Details* Tab at the top of the *Item Information* window.
12	TAB and enter a 'Standard Cost' price (optional). This is the cost price, <u>including tax</u>, that will be used on purchases (orders or bills), if selected in the *Setup/Preferences/Inventory* to be used. ☑ Use Standard Cost as the Default Price on Purchase Orders and Bills [System-Wide]
13	TAB and type in the buying unit of measure (each, unit, kilo, dozen etc.) ↵.
14	Enter the number of items making up the buying unit of measure (for example, enter "10" if the buying unit of measure is a 'carton', with each carton holding 10 items. However, in most cases the buying unit of measure is 1) ↵.
15	Set the 'Tax Code When Bought:' – type it in or use the *List* button 🔽 and select from the tax code list. This is only a "default" tax code.
16	Enter any <u>optional</u> re-stocking information: TAB and enter a minimum level of stock when an alert will be given. Use the *List* button and select a <u>default</u> supplier. TAB and enter any supplier reference (item) number. TAB and enter the <u>default</u> order quantity.
17	Click on the *Selling Details* Tab at the top of the *Item Information* window.
18	TAB and enter in the 'Base Selling Price' ↵.
19	Enter the selling unit of measure ↵.
20	Type in the number of items per selling unit (refer to step 14 above) ↵.
21	TAB and set the 'Tax Code When Sold:' – use the *List* button 🔽 and select from the tax code list.
22	Toggle the 'Inclusive/Exclusive' option box on or off depending on your choice of having the sales price (entered in step 18 above) include tax or plus tax (if any). If the base selling price includes the GST, make sure that the 'Inclusive/Exclusive' option box is ticked to show that GST is included: Inclusive/Exclusive: ☑ Prices are Tax Inclusive However, if the selling price <u>does not</u> include tax, clear this checkbox. The tax, if any, will then be <u>added</u> to this price by *MYOB AccountRight Plus*.
23	GST should always be calculated on *actual* selling price, so leave this last option at that. Click on the *OK* button to complete the edit of an existing item or the addition of a new item.

Example 7.2—Editing or adding an item that is purchased, inventoried and sold

Retailers and wholesalers have items that are purchased, inventoried and sold. On purchase, the cost is debited to inventory and credited to the supplier. The quantity is also added to the inventory count of the item. When an item is sold, the sale amount is credited to an income account (e.g. sales) and debited to an accounts receivable (or bank). The <u>cost</u> of the item sold (not the sale amount) is debited to a 'cost of goods sold' account and credited to the inventory account (reducing its balance). The quantity of the item sold is also removed (deducted) from the inventory count of that item.

1. Have the file called dem71.myo open. Sign on as "administrator" (no password).
2. Select the *Inventory* command centre.
3. Select the *Items List* option.
4. Click on the detail arrow ⇨ next to item "P360" started in exercise 7.1 above.
5. Click on the three option boxes: 'I Buy This Item', 'I Sell This Item', and 'I Inventory This Item' so that a tick appears in each one.
6. Click on the *List* button 🔽 to find the expense account for entering cost of goods sold and select 5-0120 "COGS – Pumps".
7. Click on the *List* button 🔽 to find the income account for entering sales and select 4-0120 "Sales – Pumps". Alternatively, press ↵ and scroll to the income accounts section in the *Accounts List*, and make your selection.
8. The inventory account number to enter is 1-0300 "Inventory". Enter this if it is not already there and ↵.
9. The *Item Profile* should look like Figure 7.2:

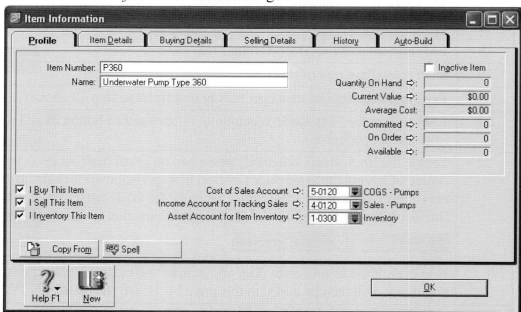

Figure 7.2: The item profile for P360 Underwater Pump

10. Click on the *Buying Details* Tab at the top of the *Item Information* window.

11. TAB and enter "$990.00" as the standard cost (including the GST) ↵.

12. Enter the buying unit of measure as "each" ↵.

13. Enter the number of items per buying unit as "1" ↵.

14. Enter the tax code when bought as "GST" ↵.

15. TAB and enter "3" as the minimum level for restocking alert ↵.
(this is also known as "Re-order point ROP".)

16. Select "Walga Pneumatics Ltd" as the primary supplier for reorders ↵.

17. TAB and enter the Walga Pneumatics supplier number as "360" ↵.

18. TAB and enter "5" as the default reorder quantity (i.e. "Re-order quantity ROQ").

19. The *Buying Details* should look like Figure 7.3:

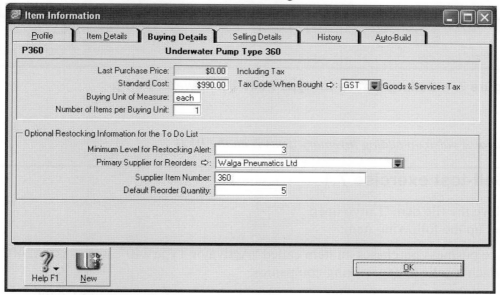

Figure 7.3: Buying details for type P360 Underwater Pump

20. Click on the *Selling Details* Tab at the top of the *Item Information* window.

21. TAB and enter in the 'Base Selling Price' as "2046" (this will result in $2,046.00)↵.

22. Enter the selling unit of measure as "each" ↵.

23. Type in "1" as the number of items per selling unit ↵.

24. Set the 'Tax Code When Sold:' to "GST" – type it in or use the *List* button ▼ and select from the tax code list.

25. The base selling price entered above includes the GST. Make sure that the 'Inclusive/Exclusive' option box is ticked to show that GST is included:

> Inclusive/Exclusive: ☑ Prices are Tax Inclusive

26. GST is always calculated on actual selling price, so leave this last option at that.

27. The *Selling Details* should look like Figure 7.4 on the next page.

28. Click on the *OK* button to complete the edit or addition.

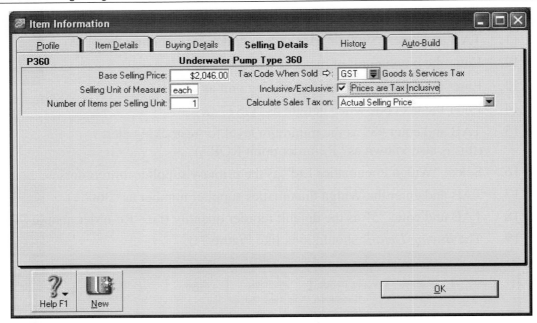

Figure 7.4: Selling details for type P360 Underwater Pump

Video: A video on adding inventory items is on the DVD

Self-test exercise 7.1

Have the file dem71.myo open.
Set up the following item:

The business purchases an item called "Activator Type 240", item # is "A240" which it sells to engineering companies.

When these are purchased they are placed into inventory account "1-0300 Inventory" and when they are sold the cost of sales account is "5-0110 COGS – Activators", and the income sales account is "4-0110 Sales – Activators".

The buying unit of measure is "each", and there is 1 item purchased per buying and selling unit. Standard cost price (including tax) is $935.00. The Tax Code on purchase or sale is "GST". The minimum inventory level for a restocking alert (Re-Order Point) is 2 units. These Activators are usually purchased from Tartha Pty Ltd who gives item number 240 to this unit. The default reorder quantity is 5 units.

The selling price is $1,452.00 each item (including the GST).

The next three "Item" information setups are alternatives to the more usual idea of inventory. In fact, the *Item List* can be used for any charge that is regular, apart from using the *Time Billing* command centre.

The first of these setups is for items that are purchased but <u>not put into inventory</u> (immediate expense), and are used up in the business rather than sold. Therefore only the *Buying Details* and an expense account need to be set up.

How to set up an item for purchase and immediate expense

Step	Instruction
1	Select the *Inventory* command centre.
2	Select the *Items List* option.
3	Click on the *New* button.
4	Enter an 'Item Number' and ↵.
5	Type in the 'Name' of the item and ↵.
6	Click on the option for 'I Buy This Item' (do not turn the other options on).
7	Click on the *List* button ▼ to find the expense account and select it from the list. An alternative is to type "6" and ↵, and this will take you to the expense accounts in the *Accounts List*.
8	Click on the *Buying Details* TAB at the top of the *Item Information* window.
9	TAB and enter the 'Standard Cost' if available and/or used.
10	TAB and enter the buying unit of measure (carton, dozen, litre, kilo etc.) ↵.
11	Enter the number of items per buying unit.
12	TAB and set the 'Tax Code When Bought:' – use the *List* button ▼ and select from the tax code list.
13	Click on the *OK* button.

Example 7.3—Setting up a regular expense as an item

This refers to an item of expense that is regularly purchased but not kept in inventory – for example, a small engineering business may regularly purchase the same lubricant for specialised machinery as and when required. The lubricant can be set up as an item with an expense account "Lubricants" to be debited.

1. Have the file dem71.myo open. Sign on as "administrator", without a password.
2. Select the *Inventory* command centre.
3. Select the *Items List* option.
4. Click on the *New* button.
5. Type in the 'Item Number' as "L1102" ↵.
6. Enter the 'Name' as "Graphite G330" ↵.
7. Click on the option box for 'I Buy This Item'. Do not select the other two options.
8. The account number to enter is 6-0030 – "Lubricants". Press ↵ and select the account from the list ↵.
9. The *Item Profile* for the Graphite G330 should look like Figure 7.5 on the next page.

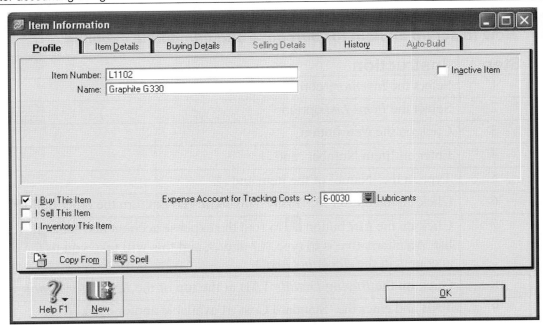

Figure 7.5: Item profile for item purchased and expensed

10. Click on the *Buying Details* Tab at the top of the *Item Information* window.

11. There is no 'Standard Cost', TAB through to the 'Buying Unit of Measure' field and type in "litre".

12. The 'Tax Code when Bought' is "GST" – type this in or use the *List* button and select from the tax code list.

13. This lubricant is usually purchased from "Engineering World". The 'Supplier Item Number' is "G330" and 'Default Reorder Quantity' is "10" litres.

14. If your screen looks like Figure 7.6, click on the *OK* button.

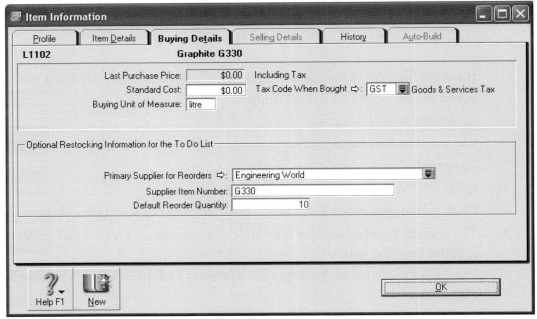

Figure 7.6: Buying details for lubricant purchased and expensed

Self-test exercise 7.2

Have the file dem71.myo open.

The business purchases special pallets for delivering pumps and activators. These are purchased as and when required. Set up an item "P100" called "Pallets". The expense account number to debit is 5-0200 "Pallets". The buying unit of measure is "each" and GST is payable. Neither the standard cost nor the restocking information are necessary.

It may be useful to keep an inventory record of expensive items that are purchased but not used immediately. This will provide better control over the item, as a perpetual inventory record will show how many or how much of the item should be on hand.

How to set up an item purchased, kept in inventory and used

Step	Instruction
1	Select the *Items List* option from the *Inventory* command centre.
2	Click on the *New* button.
3	Enter an 'Item Number' and ↵.
4	Type in the 'Name' of the item ↵.
5	Click on the options for 'I Buy This Item' and 'I Inventory This Item' (do **not** click on the option for 'I Sell This Item').
6	Enter the account number for inventory (an asset account).
7	Click on the *Buying Details* TAB at the top of the *Item Information* window.
8	TAB and enter the 'Standard Cost' for this item (if available or used).
9	TAB and enter the buying unit of measure (carton, dozen, litre, kilo etc.) ↵.
10	Enter the number of items per buying unit.
11	TAB and set the 'Tax Code When Bought:' if necessary – use the *List* button ▼ and select from the tax code list.
12	Enter any optional restocking information.
13	Click on the *OK* button.

Example 7.4—Entering an inventory item to be inventoried and used

An item that is used up in manufacturing a product and is also included in inventory can be set up. This example is for the purchase of a high-priced "Activator". On purchase, the cost will be debited to inventory and the quantity recorded as an increase in inventory. When used the item count is reduced and the cost will be transferred from inventory to an expense account. Note that these types of items are *bought*, *inventoried* and *used* but not sold as such.

1. Have the file called dem71.myo open (sign on as "administrator" and no password).
2. Select the *Inventory* command centre.
3. Select the *Items List* option.
4. Click on the *New* button.
5. Type in the 'Item Number' as "A300" ↵.
6. Enter the 'Name' as "Activator Type 300" ↵.
7. Click on the option box for 'I Buy This Item'.
8. Click on the option box for 'I Inventory This Item'.
9. The inventory account number to enter is "1-0300". Enter this ↵.
10. Your *Item Profile* should look like Figure 7.7:

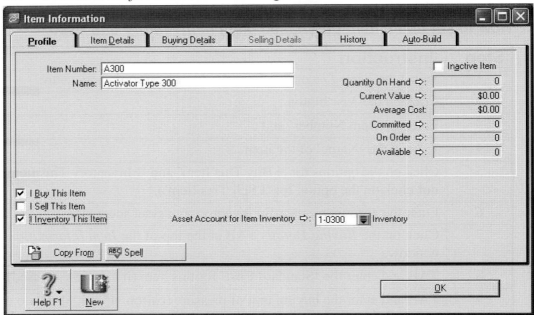

Figure 7.7: Item profile for an item purchased and entered into inventory

11. Click on the *Buying Details* Tab at the top of the *Item Information* window.
12. There is no 'Standard Cost', TAB through to the 'Buying Unit of Measure' field and type in "each" ↵.
13. The number of items per buying unit is "1". Enter this.
14. If necessary, TAB and set the 'Tax Code When Bought:' to "GST" – use the *List* button ▼ and select from the tax code list.
15. TAB and enter "4" as the minimum level for restocking alert ↵.
16. Select "Sattler Electronics" as the primary supplier for reorders.
17. TAB and enter the Sattler Electronics supplier number as "A300" ↵.
18. Enter "6" as the default reorder quantity.
19. The *Buying Details* should look like Figure 7.8 on the next page. Click on the *OK* button to complete the entry.

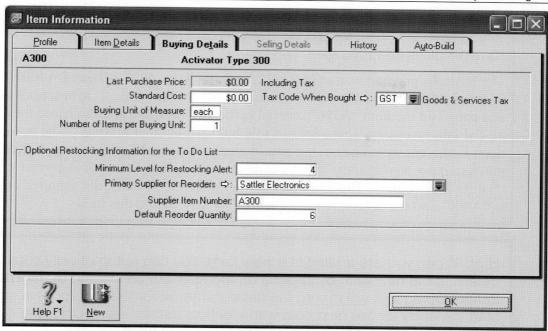

Figure 7.8: Buying details for item purchased and inventoried

If there are a number of similar products from the same supplier, entering time can be saved by using the *Copy From* button. This will copy details from an inventory item that has already been set up. All that is then required is to edit any minor changes.

How to use the Copy From *button*

Step	Instruction
1	Select the *Inventory* command centre.
2	Select the *Items List* option.
3	Click on the *New* button.
4	Enter the 'Item Number' and ↵.
5	Enter the 'Name' of the item.
6	Click on the *Copy From* button (accept warning) and select an existing item from the list that has a similar setup Copy From and click *OK* after reading any warning message.
7	Select an item to copy (double click on it or click once and click on the *Use Item* button).

Self-test exercise 7.3

Have the file dem71.myo open.

The business purchases an expensive "Activator Type 400" – (Item # A400). Create this new item. Try the *Copy From* button as per the 'How to …' instructions above, and copy/edit the item "A300" entered earlier. When these are purchased they are placed into inventory. These are not sold but used in other products. The account to debit is "Inventory". The buying unit of measure is "each", and there is "1" item purchased per buying unit. The tax code is "GST". This Activator is purchased from "Sattler Electronics". The minimum reorder point is "3" units, the supplier's number is "A400" and the default reorder quantity is "10". Set up this item.

Hint! When you are adding in a new item, you can automatically copy its details to the next item by clicking on the *New* button instead of the *OK* button. Doing that <u>will record</u> the details entered for the current item <u>and</u> start the entry for the next item with identical details – except for the item's number and name. Make sure to edit the selling price.

The final "Item" that can be entered into inventory is an item that is to be charged only. This is better done through the *Time Billing* command centre, but where employees' times are not recorded there, it is possible to use an item invoice. However, in situations where items sold/purchased include charges for labour (such as parts and labour invoices) it would be more practical to include the labour as an item together with the other trading items.

How to set up an item to be used as a charge-out rate

Step	Instruction
1	Select the *Items List* option from the *Inventory* command centre.
2	Click on the *New* button.
3	Enter an 'Item Number' and ↵.
4	Type in the 'Name' of the item.
5	Click on the option 'I Sell This Item' (do **not** select the other options).
6	Enter the account number that will record the income.
7	Click on the *Selling Details* tab at the top of the *Item Information* window.
8	Type in the charge rate (either excluding or including GST).
9	Enter the selling unit of measure as a charge rate – usually per hour.
10	Select the appropriate 'Tax Code When Sold' – usually "GST" – type the code in or – use the *List* button ▼ and select from the tax code list.
11	Toggle the 'Inclusive/Exclusive' option box on or off depending on your choice of having the charge rate include GST or not.

Example 7.5—Setting up an item to be used as a charge-out rate

This example shows the set up for an engineering firm charging consultancy fees to a client:

1. If not already open, open dem71.myo (sign on as "administrator" and no password).
2. Select the *Inventory* command centre.
3. Select the *Items List* button and click on the *New* button.
4. Type in the 'Item Number' as "Cons" ↵.
5. Enter the 'Name' as "Consultancy Fees".
6. Click on the option box for 'I Sell This Item' (do not select the other options).
7. The income account for recording the sale is "4-0200" (Consultancy).
8. The *Item Profile* should look like Figure 7.9:

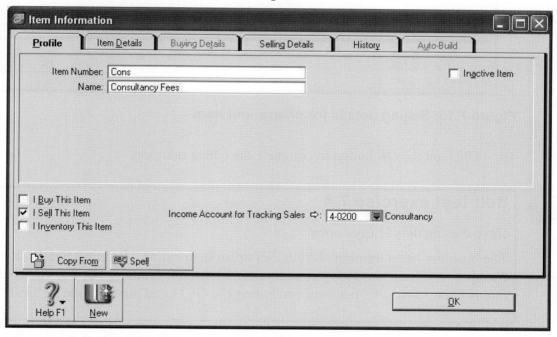

Figure 7.9: Item profile for an item charged out

9. Click on the *Selling Details* tab at the top of the *Item Information* window.
10. The charge rate is $198.00 (including the GST). TAB and enter "198" in the 'Base Selling Price' field ↵.
11. Type in "hour" as the selling unit of measure ↵.
12. The 'Tax Code When Sold' should be "GST" – if necessary, type this in or use the *List* button ▤ and select from the tax code list.
13. The base selling price entered above (the charge rate) includes the GST. Make sure that the 'Inclusive/Exclusive' option box is ticked to show that GST is included.

    Inclusive/Exclusive: ☑ Prices are Tax Inclusive
14. GST is always calculated on actual selling price, so leave this last option at that.

15. The *Selling Details* should look like Figure 7.10:

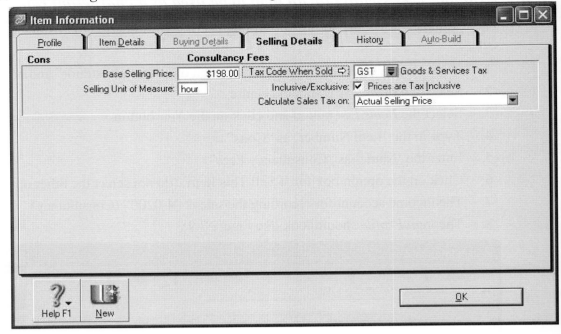

Figure 7.10: Selling details for charge-out item

16. Click on the *OK* button to complete the edit or addition.

Self-test exercise 7.4

Have the file dem71.myo open.

The business has a training section. Set up an item called "Training Fees" ('Item Number' is "Train" and income account is # "4-0300 Training Fees"). The charge rate is to be "$165.00" per hour (including the GST) and the tax code is "GST".

Maintaining the item list

Entries have already been made to add items to the item list. The same procedures can be used to change any of the details for each item. A new purchase price can be entered on a purchase order and will be reflected in the cost price of the item. Changes in the selling price of items can be made using the *Set Item Prices* option in the *Inventory* command centre. The process of setting new prices can be automated for general price changes, or can be entered separately for each item. Care should be taken when using the automated mark-ups option.

How to change the selling price for an individual item

Step	Instruction
1	Select the *Inventory* command centre.
2	Select the *Set Item Prices* option.
3	Click on the selling price that is to be changed in the column headed 'Current Price' and enter the new price. (You can use the *Shortcuts* button for making changes to all or a number of items at a time.)
4	Click on the *OK* then on the *Close* buttons.

Example 7.6—Changing the selling price of an item

1. Have the file called dem71.myo open (sign on as "administrator" – no password).
2. Select the *Inventory* command centre.
3. Click on the *Set Item Prices* option.
4. Click on the current price of $2,046.00 for the "P360 Underwater Pump" and enter "$1,969.00" as the new (lower) selling price ↵.
5. Your screen should look like Figure 7.11. Click on the *OK* button.

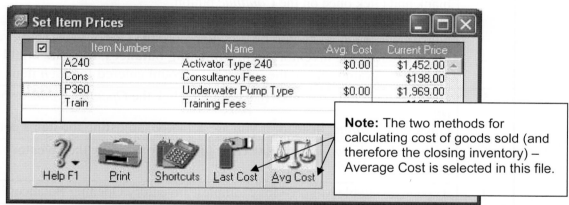

Figure 7.11: *Set Item Prices* **window with new price for item P360**

Video: A video on changing items' selling prices is on the DVD

Self-test exercise 7.5

Have the file dem71.myo open.

Change the charge rate for consultancy from $198.00 to $209.00 per hour.

Note: You can also change the selling price or charge rate for an item by editing the information in the *Item List* – i.e. select *Item List* and then the item, and change the selling price. However, this method is not practical if you are changing the selling prices of a number of items.

Entering an initial inventory count (inventory items opening balances)

When the inventory command centre first used in *MYOB AccountRight Plus* and the item list is created, you will need to enter <u>an initial inventory count</u> for all the inventoried items. A physical stocktake needs to be conducted to determine the actual count of every item in stock. The cost of each item needs to be entered on the list. The balance of the *Inventory* asset account should equal the aggregate of the cost of all the items in stock (i.e. "items count" x "cost of each item" = "inventory account" balance).

How to enter opening inventory balances or inventory adjustments

Step	Instruction
1	Select the *Count Inventory* option from the *Inventory* command centre.
2	Enter the inventory count for each item in the 'Counted' column, using the *ENTER* key after each one. If you are recording the opening inventory count, the same amount entered in the 'Counted' column will appear in the 'Difference' column.
3	Click on the *Adjust Inventory* button.
4	For items opening balances leave the 'Default Adjustment Account' field blank and click <u>once</u> on the *Continue* button. **Note:** If you are recording an inventory adjustment an "inventory adjustment" account should be used to record the loss or gain. However, when entering the inventory items' **opening balances**, leave this field blank and the program will use the inventory account entered for *each* item.
5	If entering opening balances <u>make sure to click</u> the *Opening Balances* button. *OR:* Click on *Continue*, instead, if you are actually "adjusting the items count".
6	In the *Adjust Inventory* window enter the date for starting the inventory system.
7	Type in a suitable Memo – for example, "Inventory Opening Balances".
8	Enter the unit costs in the 'Unit Cost' column. Use the down arrow key to move down the column. **Note:** These costs *always* <u>exclude</u> any GST.
9	Check the entry very carefully – edit any errors. Check that the date, quantities and amounts are correctly entered <u>and</u> to the correct item numbers. If you are entering opening balances, the total amounts in the 'Amount' column should add up to the inventory account (or accounts) balance(s).
10	Click on the *Record* button.

Example 7.7—Entering opening balances

1. Have the file dem71.myo open.
2. Select the *Inventory* command centre.
3. Select the *Count Inventory* option.

4. Enter in the following numbers of items on hand in the 'Counted' column, using the *ENTER* key after each one. The same amount will appear in the 'Difference' column as these are new (opening balance) inventory items.

Item #	Name	Counted
A240	Activator Type 240	3
A300	Activator Type 300	5
A400	Activator Type 400	5
P360	Underwater Pump Type 360	5

5. The *Count Inventory* window should look like Figure 7.12:

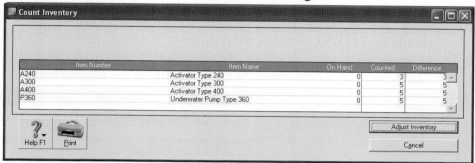

Figure 7.12: The completed *Count Inventory* window

6. Make sure that you have entered the correct figures before continuing (click on any incorrect figure and correct it, if necessary).

7. Click on the *Adjust Inventory* button. [Adjust Inventory]

8. The cursor should be in the field waiting for a default inventory adjustment account. As we are entering items' opening balances and <u>not</u> doing an adjustment, leave this field blank and click once on the *Continue* button.

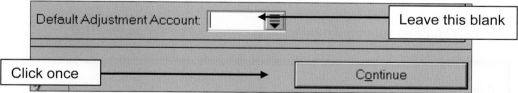

Figure 7.13: Default Adjustments Account

Note: When this field is left blank and you click on *Opening Balances* button (next step), *MYOB AccountRight Plus* will debit and credit the inventory account entered for <u>each</u> item.

> If you are entering your opening inventory balances, click the button called Opening Balances. Otherwise click Continue.

9. Make sure to click on the *Opening Balances* [Opening Balances] button (and <u>not</u> *Continue* again).

10. At the next screen *Adjust Inventory* enter in the date as "1/7/2011" ↵.

11. Change the 'Memo' field to "Opening Inventory Count".

12. Click in the 'Unit Cost' column and enter in the cost per item from the following table. You can use the down arrow key to go down the column.
    IMPORTANT: These prices must be entered <u>excluding any GST paid or payable</u>.

Item #	Name	Unit Cost $
A240	Activator Type 240	$850
A300	Activator Type 300	$400
A400	Activator Type 400	$600
P360	Underwater Pump Type 360	$900

13. If you add up the figures in the *Amount* column as shown in Figure 7.14, the total should be $12,050, which is the balance of the asset account "1-0300 Inventory". (Alternatively, you can select "Recap Transactions" from the *Edit* menu.) Check and correct any errors before clicking on the *Record* button.

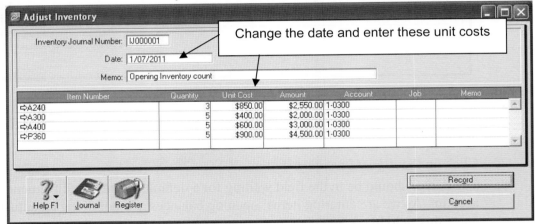

Figure 7.14: Inventory adjustments window with unit costs

Video: A video on entering inventory item count and cost is on the DVD

If you entered the 'Amount' instead of the 'Unit Cost' in the *Adjust Inventory* window, *MYOB AccountRight Plus* will calculate and enter the 'Unit Cost'.

WARNING: If the total in the 'Amount' column of the *Adjust Inventory* window is <u>greater</u> than the balance of the nominated 'Inventory' account(s), then the difference will be considered by *MYOB AccountRight Plus* as an 'out of balance' amount and will be added to the "Historical Balance" account in the general ledger. If that occurs, an adjustment to these balances will be necessary.

Close dem71.myo and open **dem72.myo** which will be used for the demonstration exercises in the remainder of this chapter.

Perpetual inventory system

To use the *Inventory* command centre you will need to know how a perpetual inventory system works and the use of a "Cost of Goods Sold" account in the general ledger. If you are already familiar with that, you can skip this section.

A perpetual inventory system is one in which there is a continual recording of purchases (increasing inventory) and sales or usage (decreasing inventory) in the accounting records. The balance in the inventory records *should* reflect the actual inventory on hand. The decreasing cost of computers and point-of-sale systems has led to smaller businesses being able to adopt this method. The main advantages of a perpetual inventory system are:

- Instant calculation of the cost of goods sold upon the sale of goods and, therefore, the Gross Profit (or Gross Loss).
- Instant allocation of material costs where job costing is used.
- Internal control over the inventory (records should agree with physical inventory). Major variations could indicate poor recording and/or possible theft.

The alternative to perpetual inventory is called periodic inventory. The account for inventory is usually only adjusted <u>at the end</u> of an accounting period to reflect the value of a stock count. Cost of Goods Sold is not an account in the ledger but is *calculated*, that is determined by adjusting the Purchases for opening and closing inventories. Figure 7.15 shows the difference in the inventory systems for a retailer or a wholesaler:

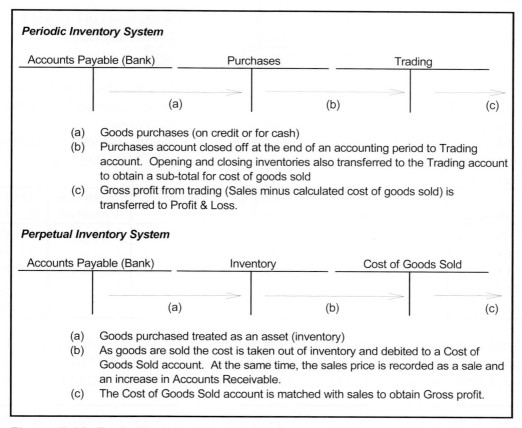

Figure 7.15: Periodic v perpetual inventory systems – retailer

Self-test exercise 7.6

Open the file **dem72.myo** provided.
Sign on as "Administrator", no password.

NEW FILE

Create a <u>non-inventory</u> item "Consulting Fees" (Item Number: "Consulting") with a charge rate of $140.00 per **hour** (<u>excluding</u> the GST) `Inclusive/Exclusive: ☐ Prices are Tax Inclusive` and a tax code of "GST". Obviously we neither buy nor stock this item, we only sell it. Use "4-5000 Consulting Fees" as the income account for this item.

Create <u>inventory</u> items and enter the following Opening Inventory and Unit Costs at 1/7/2011. All items are <u>bought, put into inventory</u> and <u>sold</u>. The accounts to use for all the following items are:

  For Cost of Sale Account: use   "5-1000 Cost of Goods Sold"
  For Income Account: use   "4-1000 Sales" and
  For Inventory Account: use   "1-1400 Inventory"

     The buying and selling unit of measure is "each" for <u>all</u> items. The Tax code in all cases is "GST" and **no** restocking information needs to be entered and **no** 'Standard Cost' will be used for the following items.

Hint: You can make use of the *Copy From* button discussed earlier to speed up entry of items. You can also use the *New* button instead of the *OK* button to add more items. **Remember** to edit the selling price for each item.

All selling prices listed here are *plus* GST – that is, they exclude GST (if any). The 'Inclusive/Exclusive' checkbox **should not** be ticked for any item:

`Inclusive/Exclusive: ☐ Prices are Tax Inclusive`

Figures 7.16, 7.17 and 7.18 starting on the next page show the three windows for the first item (G100 "Noise Generator"). For the other items and entering the opening balances, check your answers with those at the end of the chapter.
Make sure that the final dollar values shown in the *Inventory Adjustments* window add up to the 'opening balance' of the *Inventory* account (i.e. $7,600.00), before recording*.

Item #	Name	Selling price (each) (Excluding GST)	Open Bal Counted	Unit Cost (Excl. GST)
G100	Noise Generator	$780.00	2	$463.00
LOG1	Logger Station	$3,150.00	2	$2,100.00
LOG2	Logger Analyser	$840.00	1	$560.80
PC1	PC1501 Computer	$878.00	2	$584.60
R25	A25X2 Receiver	$450.00	3	$248.00

Print an *Item List Summary* for all items. Refer to page 7-52 for instructions on how to print this report. Use *Customise* to select "Include Zero Quantities" from the *Finishing* tab. Check your prints with the solution answers (for 7.6) at the end of this chapter.

*Hint: You may use *Recap Transaction* option from the *Edit* pull down menu to check the total.

Item Prices and the GST – If an item *is* taxable:
Always <u>INCLUDE</u> the GST when entering a 'Standard Cost' for an item;
Always <u>EXCLUDE</u> the GST when entering unit costs for the opening balances or
any inventory adjustments. The selling prices for items can be entered <u>including or
excluding</u> the GST. However, you need to indicate this by checking or clearing the
relevant box.

Inclusive/Exclusive: ☐ Prices are Tax <u>I</u>nclusive

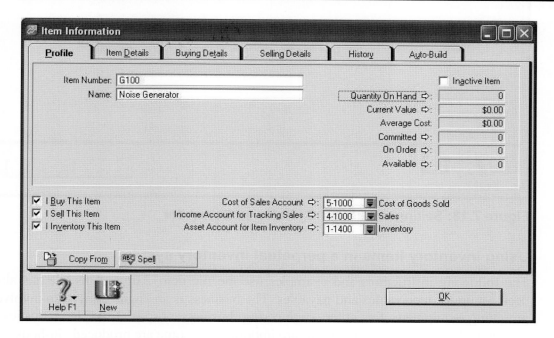

Figure 7.16: Item profile for G100 Noise Generator

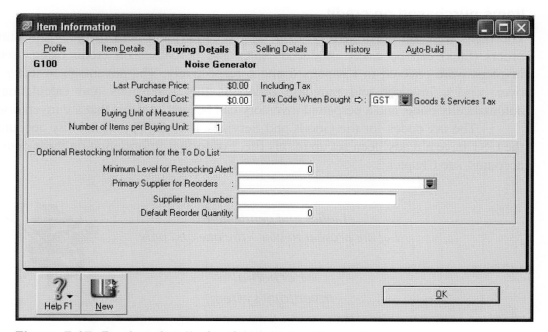

Figure 7.17: Buying details for G100 Noise Generator

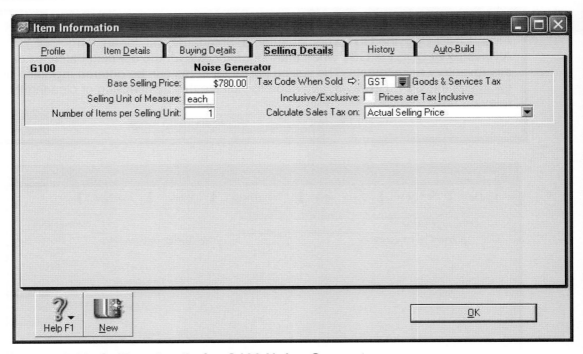

Figure 7.18: Selling details for G100 Noise Generator

Using inventory items in a perpetual inventory system

The following instructions and examples use the file dem72.myo. This file has already been set up for receivables and payables. The business is an engineering firm involved in providing equipment for other engineering businesses specialised in acoustics and mechanical engineering. Some items are imported and some are produced "in-house".

Items purchased on credit

The items were set up in self-test exercise 7.6 earlier, and item invoices and purchase orders (bills) can be easily produced. Sales and purchases on credit using "service" invoices were covered in Chapters 5 and 6 respectively. The advantage in using items over service invoices and purchase orders is that extensions and calculations are automatically done, and a perpetual inventory can be kept of items that are inventoried.

The tax codes for the Goods and Services Tax (GST) and liability accounts for the GST have already been set up in this file. For further information on these codes and accounts, see Chapter 2.

Ladies and gentlemen...
Let me present to you – the one and only

Perpetual
inventory system!

How to record an item purchased on credit or returned to supplier

Step	Instruction
1	Select the *Purchases* command centre.
2	Select the *Enter Purchases* option.
3	Click on the 'Supplier:' field and enter the supplier name. Type in the first few letters or use the *List* button ▣ and select a supplier from the list.
4	The purchase layout type appears in the window title bar. Make sure it is 'Purchases – New Item'. To change the type of purchase, if necessary click on the *Layout* button at the bottom of the window and select the "Item" type layout option button. **Note:** If the supplier's card is set to use "Item" purchases, the layout will automatically change to this layout.
5	Make sure the 'Tax Inclusive' checkbox is correct. Turn this off if the supplier invoice is to show the item at tax exclusive price. ☑ Tax Inclusive **OR** ☐ Tax Inclusive Includes GST Excludes GST
6	"BILL" should be the default set up at the top of the *Purchases – New Item* window. BILL ← Entering a bill Supplier :
7	TAB through to the purchase number field, change if necessary and TAB.
8	Enter the transaction date ↵.
9	Type in the supplier's invoice number if an actual purchase is being recorded. You can enter other details if a number is not available – for example, "Email 14/6" or "Fax – 14/6/2011" etc. ↵.
10	In the 'Bill' column enter the quantity billed and TAB. **Note:** To record goods returned enter a negative quantity here (for example: –2).
11	Enter any backorder quantity (if not in stock) and TAB. **Note:** You cannot select or use the 'Received' column, it is calculated automatically.
12	Enter the Item # of the item being purchased (or returned). Type this in or use the *ENTER* key and select from the list. Use TAB to go to the price field.
13	Enter the unit price of the purchase and TAB. If the price includes GST, the 'Tax Inclusive' option at the top of the window should be ticked first.
14	Enter any discount or any job number (if used) and TAB to the 'Tax' column.
15	Enter the tax code or click on ▣ and pick from the list and ↵.
	(continued on the next page)

Step	Instruction
16	Enter other lines for the purchase.
17	Enter other fields (such as 'Comment' and 'Ship Via') if required – use the *List* button and select from the list.
	Note: If the comment or shipping method is not in the list, type it in and click on *Easy Add* from within the relevant list to add it in.
18	Enter any freight. Change the tax code on freight if necessary by typing it in or by using the *List* button and selecting the code.
19	TAB to the 'Paid Today' field and enter any amount paid at the time of purchase (e.g. deposit paid).
	Note: For 'Cash purchases' enter the <u>total</u> bill amount here.
20	Click the *Record* button.

Example 7.8—Purchasing an item on credit

Record a purchase of 5 PC1501 computers at $584.60 (plus GST) each from Carsom Electronics on 3/7/2011 as follows:

1. Have the file dem72.myo open.

2. Select the *Enter Purchases* option from the *Purchases* command centre.

3. The supplier is Carsom Electronics Pty Ltd. Remember that you may type in the first few letters (say "ca"), hit *ENTER* and select from a list, or use the *List* button .

4. Check that the default BILL is selected in this example.

5. Make sure that the purchase type is 'Purchases – New Item':

   If it is not, click on the *Layout* button, select the 'Item' option and click *OK*.

Click ⟶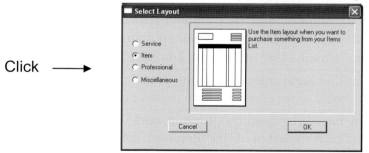

6. Check that the tax-inclusive box is ticked.

7. Enter the purchase number as "899".

8. TAB to the date field and enter "3/7/11". If the date field displays a date in July 2011, you only need to type "3"↵. You can also activate the *MYOB AccountRight Plus* calendar by pressing the spacebar in this field – use the 'left' and 'right' arrows on the top of the calendar to change the month, then click on the day.

9. The supplier's invoice number (#) is "W228" ↵.

10. Enter "5" as the quantity billed and TAB to the next field. The same quantity is automatically displayed in the 'Received' column.

11. TAB again to leave the 'Backorder' field blank (a backorder would be recorded if the supplier could not supply some items at the present time).

12. Enter the 'Item Number' as "PC1" or use the *List* button and select from the list. Enter this and TAB through to the 'Price' field.

13. Enter "$643.06" ↵. (This is the GST-inclusive price i.e. $584.60 plus tax $58.46).

14. The 'Tax' code should be "GST" (the default code set up earlier for this item).

15. Click on the 'Ship Via:' field and enter "Pick up". ↵.

16. Leave the rest of the purchase as is. The form should look like Figure 7.19:

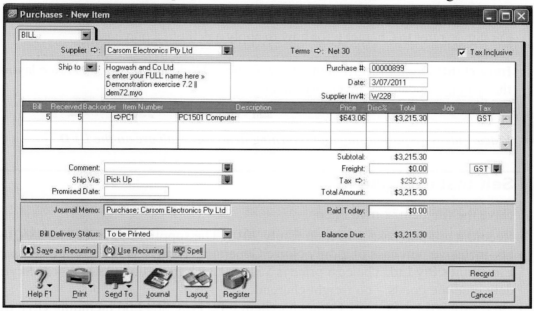

Figure 7.19: A bill for purchase of an item

17. To correct any errors, click on the field concerned and over-type or edit.

18. Before recording, use the *Edit* menu – *Recap Transaction* menu item and look at the effect on the ledger accounts—this is shown in Figure 7.20 below. Click on the *OK* button.

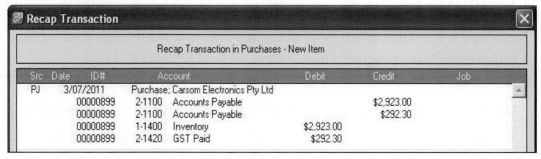

Figure 7.20: The Recap Transaction

19. Click on the *Record* button to record the purchase.

Return of items purchased on credit (credit notes received)

The return of inventory items purchased on credit is recorded in the same manner as items purchased using an *Item* layout bill. You will need, however, to enter a <u>negative</u> quantity in the 'Bill' column, for each item returned. It is advisable to enter a memo briefly explaining the reason for the return. The 'Purchase #' field can be used to record the internal debit note number and the 'Supplier's Inv #' field can be used to record the 'credit note' number received from the supplier.

Once you record a negative item purchase (bill), you need to *either*

1. <u>Apply</u> the debit to the relevant purchase *or*

2. Record a <u>refund</u> when received from the supplier.

Select the *Purchase Register* then *Returns & Debits* to perform *either* action.

(You may refer to Chapter 6 for how to apply a debit to a purchase.)

Important: Do <u>not</u> record item returns using a *Miscellaneous* or a *Service* layout bill as that <u>will not</u> update the inventory count.

Video: Videos on purchasing and returning items on credit are on the DVD

Self-test exercise 7.7

Have the file dem72.myo open.

Record a bill purchase # 900, on 6 July 2011. The supplier's invoice # is 386, for the tax-inclusive purchase of 2 only Noise Generators (Item # G100) from Dempson Electronics Pty Ltd. The cost price is $517.00 each including GST. Wards Skyroad delivered the goods – no freight charged.

On 6 July 2011 1 PC1501 Computer (Item # PC1) @ $643.06 including GST was returned to Carsom Electronics Pty Ltd. Use a negative *Item* layout Bill to record this debit. The 'Purchase #' should be changed to "D899" and for the 'Supplier Inv #' enter the number of the credit note received from the supplier: "CN1". Remember to enter in the 'Bill' column "–1" (**minus** 1). Enter a memo: "Faulty computer returned to suppliers".

This computer was originally purchased on 3 July 2011. Use *Returns & Debits* from the *Purchases Register* in the *Purchases* command centre to apply this debit to purchase # 899. Change the date, when applying, to 6/7/2011 (same as the debit note).

Important: Make sure the 'Finance Charge' field is $0.00.

Using Quotes, Orders (Receive Items), Bills and the Purchases Register

It may be useful to record quotations received from suppliers. When a supplier's quotation is accepted, the quotation recorded in *MYOB AccountRight Plus* can be converted to an order. For good customer relations it is useful to know which quotes are outstanding (not yet converted to orders) and what orders have not yet been delivered and billed. In this way, customers can be kept informed of the likely arrival of outstanding goods (backorders).

The conversion of quotes to orders and orders to invoices can be achieved using the *Purchases Register* option in the *Purchases* command centre. The *Purchases Register* can also be used to review bills and debit notes (supplier credit notes).

How to enter a supplier's quote using the item layout

Step	Instruction
1	Select the *Purchases* command centre.
2	Select the *Enter Purchases* option.
3	Click on the 'Supplier:' field and enter the supplier's name. Type in the first few letters or use the *List* button ▼ and select a supplier from the list.
4	The purchase type appears in the window title bar. To change a purchase type, click on the *Layout* button at the bottom and select "Item" as the layout. Layout
5	A tick may appear in the 'Tax Inclusive' checkbox. Turn this off or on depending on whether the amounts are to be shown excluding or including the GST. ☑ Tax Inclusive ☐ Tax Inclusive Price includes GST Price excludes GST
6	Change the default "BILL" set up at the top of the *Purchases – New Item* window to "QUOTE". QUOTE ▼ ✔ QUOTE ORDER RECEIVE ITEMS BILL Entering a supplier's quotation
7	TAB through to the 'Purchase #' field, change if necessary and TAB.
8	Enter the quotation date ↵.
9	In the 'Supplier Inv#' field enter the supplier quote number if it is available. You can enter other details if a number is not available – for example, "Email 14/6" or "Fax – 14/6/2011" etc. and ↵.
10	Enter the quantity quoted and TAB.

(continued on the next page)

Step	Instruction
11	Enter the 'Item Number' of the item being quoted. Type this in or use the *ENTER* key and select from the list. Use TAB to go to the price field.
12	Enter the unit price of the purchase and TAB.
	Hint: *Before* entering the price, make sure the 'Tax Inclusive' checkbox is either ticked or cleared as the case may be.
13	The 'Disc%' column will display any volume discount rate entered on the supplier's card. You can edit this and manually enter any promised volume discount (if applicable) and TAB.
14	Enter a job number if jobs are used and TAB.
15	Enter the tax code ↵.
16	Enter other lines for the purchase quote.
17	Complete any other fields (such as 'Comment' and 'Ship Via') if required – use the *List* button 🔽 and select from the list.
18	Enter any freight. Change the tax code on freight if necessary by typing it in or by using the *List* button 🔽 and selecting the code.
19	Click on the *Save Quote* button.

Example 7.9—Entering a quote received from a supplier

Enter the following quotation from Dempson Electronics Pty Ltd. Their invoices show amounts including the GST where the goods or services are taxable.

1. Have the file dem72.myo open.

2. Select the *Purchases* command centre.

3. Select the *Enter Purchases* option.

4. The supplier is Dempson Electronics Pty Ltd. Remember that you may type in the first few letters (say "de"), use the *ENTER* key (or use the *List* button 🔽) and select from a list.

5. Make sure that the purchase type is *Purchases – New Item*.
   Click on the *Layout* button and change layout to "Item", if necessary.

6. Check that the figures entered in to the amount column are to be displayed as tax-inclusive where GST is applicable. ☑ Tax Inclusive

7. Click on the drop down arrow next to BILL and select "QUOTE".

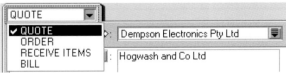

8. TAB to the 'Purchase #' field and enter "901".

9. TAB to the 'Date' field and enter the date as "7/7/2011".
   Note: If the date in this field already shows a date in July 2011, you can type "7" ↵. Alternatively, to use the calendar, right click or press the spacebar.

10. There is no supplier invoice number as this is only a quotation ↵.

11. Enter "3" in the 'Quantity' column and TAB to the 'Item Number' column.

12. Enter the 'Item Number' as "R25" or use the *List* button ☰ and select from the list. Enter this and TAB through to the 'Price' column.

13. Enter the price as "$272.80" (this is the GST-inclusive price) ↵.

14. The 'Tax' column should show a tax code of "GST"

15. Click on the field for entering freight and enter "88.00" (this includes the GST), an estimated amount (the tax code for this freight should show "GST").

16. Modify the memo but leave the rest of the quote as is.
    The form should look like Figure 7.21:

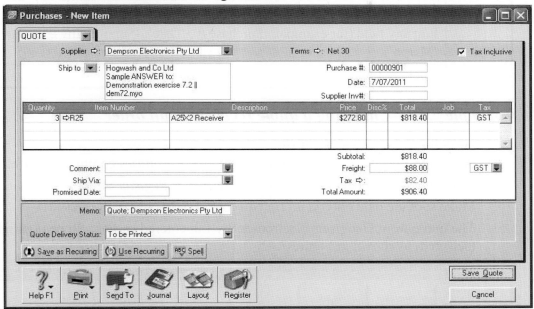

Figure 7.21: Quote for items received from Dempson Electronics Pty Ltd

17. To correct any errors, click on the field concerned and over type or edit.

18. Click on the *Save Quote* button [Save Quote] to save it on the data file.

Video: A video on entering a quote received from a supplier is on the DVD

Self-test exercise 7.8

Have the file dem72.myo open.

Enter a quote (#902 dated 8 July 2011) received from Elgin Business Info Systems. The quote is for 3 LOG2 Logger Analyser @ $616.88 each including the GST. The tax code is "GST", and freight on this shipment is quoted at $110.00 including GST.

Changing a quote to an order

When a quote is accepted and an order is placed, the quote recorded in the *MYOB AccountRight Plus* file can be converted to an order.

How to change a supplier item quote to an order

Step	Instruction
1	Select the *Purchases* command centre.
2	Select the *Purchases Register* option.
3	Click on the *Quotes* tab at the top of the *Purchases Register* window.
4	Change the 'Search By:', 'Dated From:' and 'To:' fields, if necessary.
5	Select (highlight) the quote to be converted to either an order, a bill or deleted.
6	Click on the *Change to Order* button.
7	Edit any field (for example, 'Purchase #', 'Date', 'Supplier Inv #' and 'Memo').
8	Click on the *Record* button to save the order.

Example 7.10—*Changing a quote received to an order*

1. Have the file dem72.myo open.
2. Select the *Purchases Register* option from the *Purchases* command centre.
3. Select the *Quotes* tab at the top of the *Purchases Register* window.
4. Make sure the date criteria is 'Dated From' 1/7/2011 'To' 31/7/2011.
5. The quote from Dempson Electronics Pty Ltd entered earlier will be highlighted (selected) as shown in Figure 7.22.

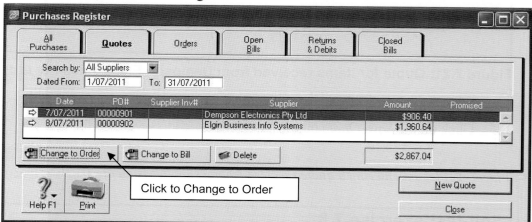

Figure 7.22: The purchases register showing quotes

6. Click on the *Change to Order* [Change to Order] button.
7. Make sure the 'Purchase #' is 901 (same as the quote number).

8. TAB through and change the date to "14/7/2011" and ↵.

9. The supplier offered a 5% volume discount, as well as free delivery, if the quantity quoted is changed from 3 to 10. This offer was accepted. Change the quantity in the 'Order' column to "10" and TAB to the 'Disc%' column.

10. Enter "5" in the 'Disc%' column.

11. Click in the 'Freight' field and enter "0.00" and ↵.

12. Modify the memo – change "Quote" to "Order".
The *Order* should look like Figure 7.23:

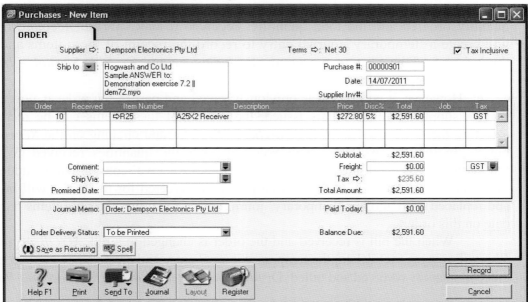

Figure 7.23: Quote from Dempson Electronics now converted to an order

13. Click on the *Record* button to save the order on file.

14. Click on the *Cancel* button to close the *Purchases – New Item* window and you will be returned to the *Purchases Register* window.

15. Click on the *Orders* tab in the *Purchases Register* to check that the quote 901 is changed to an order with the same Purchase #.

Video: A video on changing a quote received to an order is on the DVD

Self-test exercise 7.9

Have the file dem72.myo open.

The quote from Elgin Business Information Systems received on 8 July is accepted and an order based on the quote is placed with them on 15 July 2011. Change the quote to an order – same purchase #. Change the date to 15/7/2011. (Ignore any date warning.)

Recording the receipt of items before the supplier's bill arrives

For items received from a supplier without a bill, use the *Receive Item* view to record the quantities received. If a purchase price is not known, use an approximate price.

Quantities ordered are entered in the 'Ordered' column and items received are recorded in the 'Receive' column, using the *Receive Item* view of *Enter Purchases* option:

Ordered	To Date	Receive	Item Number	Description

The second column 'To Date' cannot be used or modified. It is automatically updated to accumulate the quantities entered to date in the 'Receive' column.

When this transaction is recorded it will be saved as an *Order* showing the quantity ordered and the total quantities received <u>to date</u>. *MYOB AccountRight Plus* will create a 'temporary' journal entry to record the receipt of these items and update the balance of the inventory account: Dr *Inventory* and Cr A/P *Accrual – Inventory* (no GST is recorded).

However, if an order was previously saved and part of the order is now received from a supplier, but no bill is issued, the receipt of these items can be recorded by selecting the *Order* first from the *Purchases Register* and clicking on the *Receive Items* button. In the *Receive Item* view you can enter the quantities received. When this transaction is recorded, the quantity entered in the 'Receive' column will be added to the 'To Date' total. Any temporary journal previously created for this order will be deleted and replaced with another 'temporary' journal entry recording the <u>total</u> items received <u>to date</u> on this order.

When the bill is received and the order is changed to a bill, *MYOB AccountRight Plus* will <u>reverse</u> (not delete) the temporary journal entry and create a new journal entry for the <u>total</u> quantity received and billed: Dr *Inventory* Dr *GST Paid* and Cr *Accounts Payable*.

How to record receipt of items ordered but not billed

Step	Instruction
1	Select the *Purchases* command centre.
2	**If an *Order* was previously saved:** • Select the *Purchases Register* option and click on the *Orders* tab. • Change the 'Search By:', 'Dated From:' and 'To:' fields, if necessary. • Select (highlight) the order for which items are received. • Click on the *Receive Items* button ⬛ Receive Ite<u>m</u>s (go to step 4).
3	**If NO order was previously saved:** • Select *Enter Purchases*, change the view to "Receive Items" and RECEIVE ITEMS ▼ QUOTE ORDER ✓RECEIVE ITEMS BILL • Enter the quantity ordered in the 'Ordered' column and TAB.
4	Enter quantity received in the 'Received' column. **Note:** The 'Total Amount' of the order changes to reflect <u>only</u> what is <u>actually</u> received, <u>not what is ordered.</u>
5	Edit any other field (for example, date and memo).
6	Click on the *Record* button to save the *Order* (or save the changes).

Example 7.11— Recording receipt of items ordered but not billed

1. Have the file dem72.myo open.
2. Select the *Purchases Register* option from the *Purchases* command centre.
3. Select the *Orders* tab at the top of the *Purchases Register* window.
4. Make sure the date criteria is 'Dated From' 1/7/2011 'To' 31/7/2011.
5. The order on Dempson Electronics Pty Ltd entered earlier will be highlighted.
6. Click on the *Receive Items*  button.
7. Change the date to 16/7/2011.
8. Enter "3" in the 'Receive' column. The total amount will change to reflect only what is actually received i.e. $777.48 incl. GST – (or $706.80 excl GST).
9. Use the *Edit* menu – *Recap Transaction* menu item to view the journal entry that will be recorded as shown in Figure 7.24. Click on the *OK* button.

Src	Date	ID#	Account	Debit	Credit	Job
PJ	16/07/2011		Order; Dempson Electronics Pty Ltd			
		00000901	2-1120 A/P Accrual - Inventory		$706.80	
		00000901	1-1400 Inventory	$706.80		

Figure 7.24: Recap transaction for the 'temporary' journal entry

10. If your screen looks like Figure 7.25, click on *Record* to save the changes to the order.

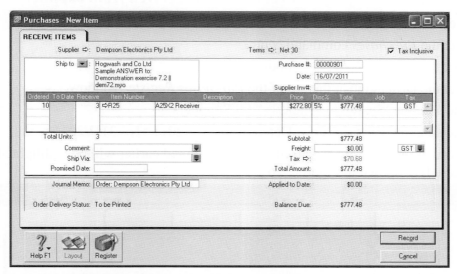

Figure 7.25: 'Receive item' view recording the receipt of three items

Self-test exercise 7.10

Have the file dem72.myo open.
On 16 July 2011 Elgin Business Information Systems delivered: 1 LOG2 Logger Analyser. This is part of the order previously saved, no bill received as yet. Record this partial receipt (make sure the date is 16/7/2011). **Note:** The total amount of the order will change to reflect only the items received so far (to-date).

Changing an order to a bill

When goods or services that have been ordered are delivered and billed by the supplier, the order recorded in *MYOB AccountRight Plus* can be changed to a bill.

How to change an order to a bill received from a supplier

Step	Instruction
1	Select the *Purchases* command centre.
2	Select the *Purchases Register* option.
3	Click on the *Orders* tab at the top of the *Purchases Register* window.
4	Make sure that the search by showing 'All Suppliers' or the specific supplier you are searching and the 'From' and 'To' dates are for the period you want.
5	Select (highlight) the order to be converted to a Bill.
6	Click on the *Change to Bill* [Change to Bill] button.
7	Edit any field (for example, 'Purchase #', 'Date', 'Supplier Inv #' and 'Memo').
8	Click on the *Record* button to save the order.

 Example 7.12—Changing an order to a bill received from supplier

1. Have the file dem72.myo open.
2. Select the *Purchases* command centre.
3. Select the *Purchases Register* option.
4. Select the *Orders* tab at the top of the *Purchases Register* window.
5. Make sure the 'Search by:' field is "All Suppliers".
6. Make sure the date criteria is 'Dated From' 1/7/2011 'To' 31/7/2011.
7. The order on Dempson Electronics Pty Ltd entered earlier will be highlighted (selected) as shown in Figure 7.26:

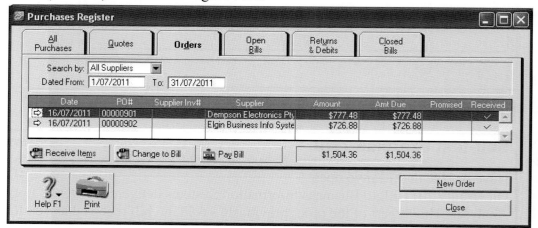

Figure 7.26: The *Purchases Register* window showing orders on file

8. Click on the *Change to Bill* 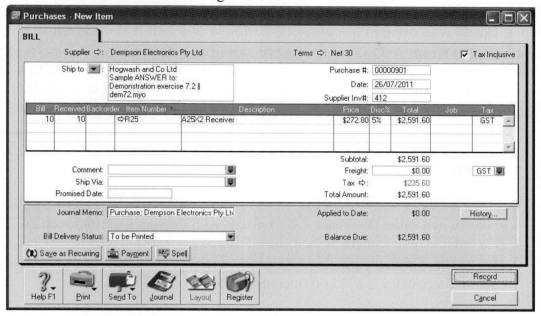 button.
9. Change the date to "26/7/2011", enter 'Supplier's invoice #' as "412" and modify the memo – change "Order" to "Purchase".
10. The Bill should look like Figure 7.27:

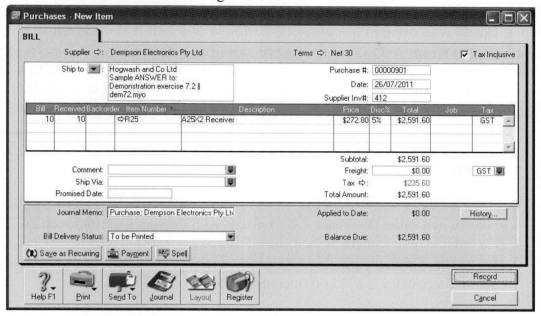

Figure 7.27: Order now changed to a bill received from supplier

11. Click on the *Record* button to save the bill (ignore any warnings about the date).
12. Click on the *Cancel* button to close the *Purchases – New Item* window and you will be returned to the *Purchases Register* window.
13. Click on the *Close* button to finish with the *Purchases Register*.

Video: A video on changing an order to a bill is on the DVD

Self-test exercise 7.11

Have the file dem72.myo open.

The balance of the goods ordered from Elgin Business Information Systems (Purchase # 902) is now received together with their invoice # 4129 on 31 July 2011.

Change the order placed with Elgin Business Information to a Bill.
Modify the memo, change the date to 31/7/2011 and enter the invoice number.
Ignore any warning about the date.

I often modify my 'memoirs' and change my 'dates'!

Note: <u>You can enter an 'Order' without having first entered a 'Quote':</u>
For example, a quote will not be required where a supplier is selling goods or services from a set price list. An order can then be placed based on that price list. To enter an 'Order' refer to the 'How to ...' on page 7-25, except in step 6 select "ORDER" instead of "BILL". The order can be changed to a Bill as was done in the previous example and self-test exercise.

ALSO Note: <u>A 'Quote' can be converted to a 'Bill' without having first been converted to an 'Order':</u> For example, a quote can be converted to a bill if it was accepted and the goods were received (delivered or picked up).

Self-test exercise 7.12

Have the file dem72.myo open.

Record a new order (Purchase # 903) placed with Carsom Electronics on 26/7/2011. This order is for a Logger Station (Item # LOG1) at a cost of $2,310.00 (incl. GST).

The promised delivery date is 28/8/2011 by "Best Way" and freight to be paid to Carsom Electronics is $132.00 (including the GST).

Items sold on credit

A major advantage of a perpetual inventory system is the automatic continuous updating of the inventory records. When a sale is made, the quantity sold is removed from inventory. Other advantages of the *MYOB AccountRight Plus* inventory module are the ease of producing item invoices and the automatic updating of the total cost of goods sold and of the general ledger accounts.

How to record an item sold on credit or returned from customer

Step	Instruction
1	Select the *Sales* command centre.
2	Select the *Enter Sales* option.
3	Click on the 'Customer:' field and enter the customer name. Type in the first few letters or use the *List* button ▼ and select a customer from the list.
4	The invoice layout appears in the window title bar. To change the type of sale, if necessary, click on the *Layout* button at the bottom of the *Sales* window and click on the *option* button next to *Item* ⊙ Item to select it. **Note:** If the customer's card is set to use 'Item' invoices, the layout will automatically change to this layout. *(continued on the next page)*

Step	Instruction
5	A tick may appear in the 'Tax Inclusive' checkbox. Turn this on or off depending on whether the amounts are to be shown including or excluding Tax: ☑ Tax Inclusive ☐ Tax Inclusive Prices *Include* GST Prices *Plus* any GST
6	"INVOICE" should be the default view set up at the top of the *Sales – New Item* window. INVOICE ◄—— Entering an Invoice Customer :
7	TAB through to the invoice number field, change if necessary and TAB.
8	Enter the transaction date ↵.
9	Type in the customer's purchase order number. You can enter other details if a number is not available – e.g. "Email 14/06/2011" or "Fax 14/06/2011" and ↵.
10	Enter the quantity of the item sold in the 'Ship' column and TAB. **Note:** To record goods returned enter a **negative** quantity here (e.g. –2).
11	Enter any backorder quantity or leave blank and TAB. **Note:** Any quantity entered in this column will automatically create an order from the same customer and for the same item entered in the next step.
12	Enter the Item # of the item being sold (or returned). Type this number in or press *ENTER* and select from the list of available items and TAB.
13	Edit the sales price, the discount rate and/or the tax code if necessary. **Note:** If recording **return** of items, match these details with the original invoice.
14	Enter or modify other optional fields ('Salesperson', 'Comment', 'Ship Via', 'Promised Date' and 'Referral Source') if required.
15	Enter freight (if any) and change the tax code on freight if necessary.
16	Enter any amount received in the 'Paid Today' field. For example a part payment (a deposit) or for the full invoice amount. If any amount is entered here you will need to complete the 'Payment Method' and 'Details' fields as necessary. **Note:** For "Cash Sales" enter the **full** invoice amount here (i.e. the "Total Amount").
17	Change the Journal Memo if necessary.
18	Click on the *Record* button.

Example 7.13—Selling an item on credit

To create and record an invoice to Darvil Engineering Pty Ltd on 5 July 2011 for 2 only Logger Station and 5 hours consulting you:

1. Start *MYOB AccountRight Plus* and open the file called dem72.myo, if it is not already open. Sign in as "Administrator", no password.
2. Select the *Sales* command centre.
3. Select the *Enter Sales* option.
4. Enter the customer as Darvil Engineering Pty Ltd., the invoice number as "8411" and make sure that the invoice layout is *Sales – New Item*.
5. Check that "INVOICE" view is selected.
6. Check that the invoice amounts are to be entered as tax-inclusive.
7. TAB to the 'Invoice #' field (or click in the field) and enter "8411" ↵
8. Enter "5/7/2011" as the date ↵.
9. Enter "881" as the 'Customer's PO #' ↵.
10. The quantity to ship is "2". Enter this and TAB to the 'Item Number' column.
11. The 'Item Number' is "LOG1". Enter this and ↵.
    The tax-inclusive sales price and the tax code of "GST" should now be shown taken from the details in the item list. The 'Total' is automatically calculated and entered.
12. The second line item is 5 hours consulting. Enter "5" as the quantity, TAB to the 'Item Number' column and enter "Consulting" ↵.
13. Click on the *List* button for the 'Ship Via:' field and select "Pick up". Click on the *List* button for the 'Referral Source:' field and select "Yellow Pages".
14. Make sure the invoice looks like Figure 7.28. Edit and modify any errors:

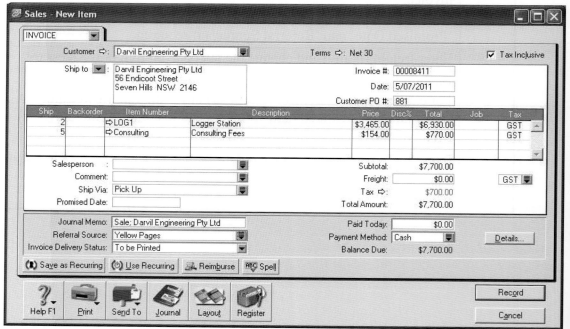

Figure 7.28: Completed item invoice to Darvil Engineering Pty Ltd

15. Before recording, use the *Edit* menu – *Recap Transaction* menu item and look at the effect on the ledger accounts. This is shown in Figure 7.29 on the next page, and click on the *OK* button.

16. Click on the *Record* button to record the sale.

Src	Date	ID#		Account	Debit	Credit
SJ	5/07/2011			Sale; Darvil Engineering Pty Ltd		
		Auto #	1-1210	Accounts Receivable	$7,000.00	
		Auto #	1-1210	Accounts Receivable	$700.00	
		Auto #	4-1000	Sales		$6,300.00
		Auto #	4-5000	Consulting Fees		$700.00
		Auto #	2-1410	GST Collected		$700.00
		Auto #	5-1000	Cost of Goods Sold	$4,200.00	
		Auto #	1-1400	Inventory		$4,200.00

Figure 7.29: The *Recap Transaction* window

Video: A video on selling items on credit is on the DVD

Return of items sold on credit (credit notes issued to customers)

The return of inventory items sold on credit is recorded in the same manner as items sold using an *Item* layout invoice. You will need, however, to enter a <u>negative</u> quantity in the 'Ship' column, for each item returned. It is advisable to enter a memo briefly explaining the reason for the return. The 'Invoice #' field can be used to record the credit note number and the 'Customer PO #' field can be used to record any 'debit note' number received from the customer (if any).

Once you record a negative item invoice (the Credit Note), you need to ***either***:

1. <u>Apply</u> the credit to the relevant invoice ***or***

2. Record a <u>refund</u> if the credit is paid (refunded) to the customer.

To perform ***either*** action, select the *Sales Register* then *Returns & Credits*.

(You may refer to Chapter 5 for how to apply a credit to a customer.)

<u>**IMPORTANT**</u>: The return of inventory <u>items</u> from a customer must be recorded using an *Item* layout invoice. Do <u>**not**</u> record item returns using a *Miscellaneous* or a *Service* layout invoice as that will only update the customer balance and the account receivable account in the general ledger, but <u>**will not**</u> update the inventory count, <u>**will not reduce**</u> the cost of goods sold balance and <u>**will not increase**</u> the inventory account balance.

Video: A video on returning an item sold on credit is on the DVD

Self-test exercise 7.13

Have the file dem72.myo open.

Record the sale of 2 only Noise Generators ('Item Number' G100) on 7 July 2011 to Dravo Computer Supplies Pty Ltd. The 'Tax Inclusive' option should be ticked as the sales price is GST-inclusive ☑ Tax Inclusive. The invoice number is 8412 and the customer's purchase order number is 1122. The selling price should appear as $858.00 each (tax inclusive) and the tax code as "GST". Wards Skyroad delivered the goods, and the sale is in response to a request on the company's web site.

On 6 July 2011 1 Logger Station (Item # LOG1) @ 3465.00 including GST was returned from Darvil Engineering Pty Ltd (faulty). Use a negative *Item* invoice to record a credit note. The 'Invoice #' is "CN8411". Remember to enter in the 'Ship' column "–1" (**minus** 1). Change the memo to: "Faulty Logger Station".

This item was originally sold on 5 July 2011. Use *Return & Credits* from the *Sales Register* to apply this credit to Invoice # 8411 (change the date – same as C/N).

Using Quotes, Orders, Invoices and the Sales Register

It may be useful to record quotations given to customers. When a customer accepts the quotation and places an order, the quotation recorded in *MYOB AccountRight Plus* can be converted to an order. Recording orders in item inventory shows the number of the item that has been committed to customers and therefore not available for sale to others.

The conversion of quotes to orders and orders to invoices can be achieved using the *Sales Register* option in the *Sales* command centre. The Sales Register can *also* be used to create, review, edit or delete quotes, orders, invoices and credit notes.

Once a quote is converted, it is either deleted or kept on file depending on your selection in the preferences (*Setup/Preferences/Sales*). Orders, on the other hand, are always deleted once converted to invoices. You can also select, in the preferences, whether to retain the same invoice numbers for invoices and orders as that of the quotes.

These are the preferences selected for this exercise:

☑ Retain Original Invoice Number when Quotes Change to Orders or Invoices [System-wide]

☐ Delete Quotes upon Changing to and Recording as an Order or Invoice [System-wide]

How to enter a quote using the item layout

Step	Instruction
1	Select the *Sales* command centre.
2	Select the *Enter Sales* option.
3	Click on the 'Customer:' field and enter the customer name. Type in the first few letters or use the *List* button 🔽 and select a customer from the list.
	(continued on the next page)

Step	Instruction
4	The invoice layout appears in the window title bar. To change a sale layout, click on the *Layout* button at the bottom of the window and select *Item* layout.
5	A tick may appear in the 'Tax Inclusive' checkbox. Turn this off or on depending on whether the amounts are to be shown excluding or including the GST. ☑ Tax Inclusive Includes GST ☐ Tax Inclusive Excludes GST
6	Change the default view at the top of the *Sales – New Item* window from INVOICE to QUOTE. Entering a quotation QUOTE ✔ QUOTE ORDER INVOICE
7	TAB through to the invoice number field, change if necessary and TAB.
8	Enter the quotation date ↵.
9	Type in the customer's reference number if it is available. You can enter other details if a number is not available – for example, "Letter – 14/6", "Email – 14/6/2011" or "Fax – 14/6/2011" etc. and ↵.
10	Enter the quantity that is to be shipped and TAB.
11	Enter the item number or press *ENTER* and select from the list.
12	TAB to the price field and edit the price if necessary and TAB.
13	Enter a job number if income is to be recorded for a particular job and TAB.
14	Change the tax code if necessary.
15	Enter any other line items (repeat steps 10 to 14 above).
16	Enter any freight to be charged on the invoice in the 'Freight' field. To change the default GST code, click on the *List* button 🔽 next to the 'Freight' field and select the code.
17	The 'Salesperson', 'Comment', 'Ship Via' and 'Promised Date' fields are optional. Click on the *List* button next to the field and select from the list. Use the *New* button to add any new entry required not on the list.
18	Change the 'Journal Memo:' if necessary.
19	Select the *Save Quote* button.

Example 7.14—Entering a quote given to a customer

Enter the following quotation given to Trahurn Accoustics Pty Ltd. Our invoices show amounts including the GST where the goods or services are taxable:

1. Have the file dem72.myo open.

2. Select the *Enter Sales* option from the *Sales* command centre.

3. The customer is Trahurn Accoustics Pty Ltd. You may type in the first few letters of the name, use the *Enter* key or the *List* button ☒ and select from the list.

4. Make sure that the invoice layout is *Sales – New Item.* Change it if necessary.

5. Click on the drop down arrow next to INVOICE and select QUOTE.

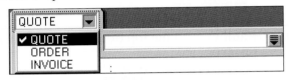

6. Check that the figures entered in to the 'amount' field are to be entered and displayed as tax-inclusive where GST is applicable. ☑ Tax Inclusive

7. TAB to (or click in) the 'Invoice #' field and enter "8413" ↵.
   (**Note:** You may change the number if you want to keep a different sequence for quotations or orders by modifying the preferences.)

8. Enter the date as "5/7/2011". If the date in this field displays a date in July 2011, you only have to type "5" ↵. To select a date using the calendar press the spacebar (or right click) and make your selection by clicking on the date.

9. There is no customer's purchase order number as this is only a quotation ↵.

10. Enter the 'Ship' quantity as "3" and TAB to the 'Item Number' column.

11. The quote is for Item Number "R25". Type this in or press ENTER to select from the list.

12. The sales price should already show $495.00 with a total of $1,485.00, and the 'Tax' column should show "GST". Modify if necessary ↵.

13. Click on the 'Freight' field and enter "35.20" tax inclusive, an <u>estimated</u> amount. The tax code for this freight is "GST".

14. Change the word "Sale" in the 'Memo' to "Quote".

15. The Quote should look like Figure 7.30 on the next page:

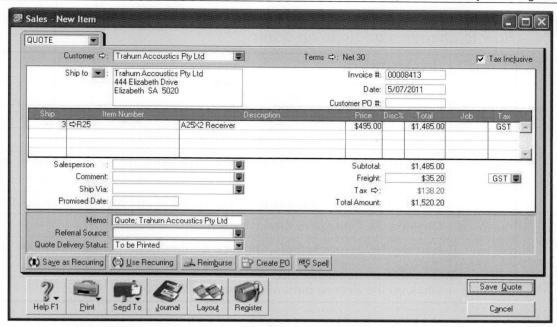

Figure 7.30: Quotation given to a customer

16. To correct any errors, click on the field concerned and over type or edit.

17. You can click on the *Spell* button to check the spelling before saving. Ignore any errors for brand or item names.

18. Click on the *Save Quote* button [Save Quote] to save it on file.

Video: A video on entering a quote given to a customer is on the DVD

Self-test exercise 7.14

Have the file dem72.myo open.

Enter a quote (#8414 dated 8 July 2011) to Marrickville City Council.

The quote is for one "PC1501 Computer" item # "PC1" @ $965.80 including the GST. Modify the memo.

No freight or other details are to be entered on the quote.

Changing a quote to an order

When a customer accepts a quote and places an order, the quote recorded in the *MYOB AccountRight Plus* file can be converted to an order.

How to change a quote to an order

Step	Instruction
1	Select the *Sales* command centre.
2	Select the *Sales Register* option.
3	Click on the *Quotes* tab at the top of the *Sales Register* window.
4	Make sure that the 'Dated From' and 'To' dates are for the period you want and the 'Search By:' displays "All Customers" or a specific customer.
5	Select (highlight) the quote to be converted to an order (or to an invoice).
6	Click on the *Change to Order* button.
7	Edit any field (for example, 'Invoice #', the 'Date', 'Customer PO #', and 'Memo').
8	Click on the *Record* button to save the order.

Example 7.15—Changing a quote to an order

1. Have the file dem72.myo open.
2. Select the *Sales* command centre.
3. Select the *Sales Register* option.
4. Select the *Quotes* tab at the top of the *Sales Register* window.
5. Make sure the date criteria is 'Dated From' 1/07/2011 'To' 31/07/2011.
6. The quote to Trahurn Accoustics Pty Ltd entered earlier will be highlighted (selected) as shown in Figure 7.31 on the next page.

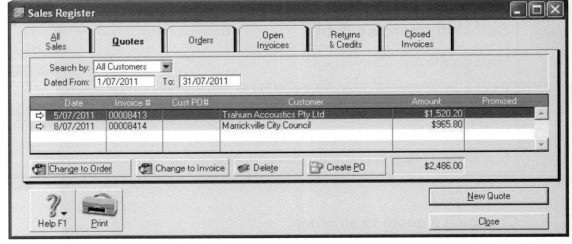

Figure 7.31: *Sales Register* window showing quote Trahurn Accoustics highlighted

7. Click on the *Change to Order* button. Change to Order
8. Change the date to "14/7/2011" and ↵.
9. Click on the 'Customer PO #:' field and enter "T331".
10. Edit the 'Journal Memo' – replace "Quote" with "Order".

11. The order should look like Figure 7.32:

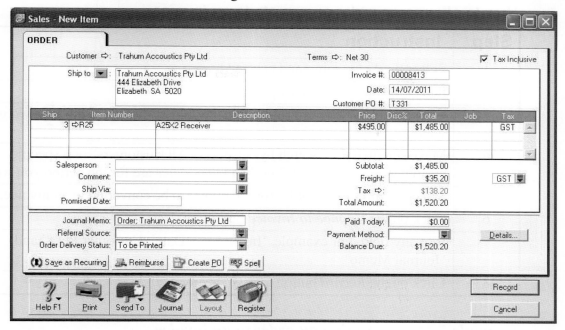

Figure 7.32: Quote now changed to an order

12. Click on the *Record* button to save the order on file.

13. Click on the *Cancel* button to close the *Sales – New Item* window and you will be returned to the *Sales Register* window.

14. Click on the *Close* button to finish with the *Sales Register*.

Video: A video on changing a quote given to a customer to an order is on the DVD

Self-test exercise 7.15

Have the file dem72.myo open.

The quote given to Marrickville City Council on 8 July is accepted and they placed an order # RD1120 on 18 July 2011 based on the quote.
Change the quote to an order on 18 July 2011 (modify the journal memo).

Changing an order (or a quote) to an invoice

When goods or services that have been ordered are delivered and invoiced, the order recorded in *MYOB AccountRight Plus* can be changed to an invoice.

A quote can also be converted to an invoice without been converted to an order first if the quote was accepted and the goods were received by the customer.

How to change an order or a quote to an invoice

Step	Instruction
1	Select the *Sales* command centre.
2	Select the *Sales Register* option.
3	Click on the *Orders* tab (or the *Quotes* tab) at the top of the *Sales Register* window.
4	Make sure that the 'Search by' displays "All Customers" or a specific customer and the 'Dated From' and 'To' dates are for the period you want.
5	Select (highlight) the order (or the quote) to be converted to an invoice.
6	Click on the *Change to Invoice* button.
7	Edit any field. For example, 'Invoice #', 'Date', Customer PO #' and 'Journal Memo'.
8	Click on the *Record* button to save the invoice.

Example 7.16—Changing an order to an invoice

1. Have the file dem72.myo open.
2. Select the *Sales* command centre.
3. Select the *Sales Register* option.
4. Select the *Orders* tab at the top of the *Sales Register* window.
5. Make sure the search is for "All Customers" and dated from "1/07/2011" to "31/07/2011".
6. The order from Trahurn Accoustics Pty Ltd entered earlier will be highlighted (selected) as shown in Figure 7.33 on the next page.

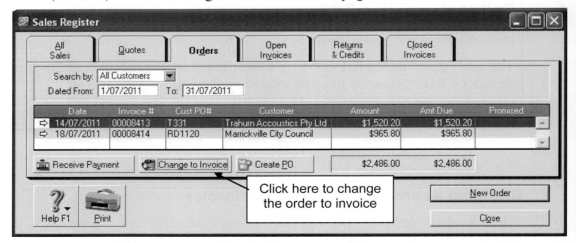

Figure 7.33: The *Sales Register* window showing orders on file

7. Click on the *Change to Invoice* button.

8. Change the date to "28/07/2011" and update the memo – change "Order" to "Sale". The invoice should look like Figure 7.34:

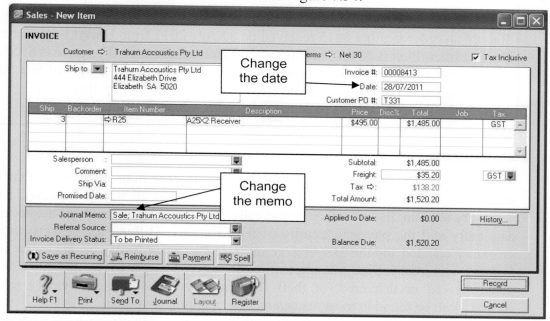

Figure 7.34: Order now changed to an invoice

9. Click on the *Record* button to save the invoice (ignore any error message regarding the date – click *OK*).

10. Click on the *Cancel* button to close the *Sales – New Item* window and you will be returned to the *Sales Register* window.

11. Click on the *Close* button to finish with the *Sales Register*.

Video: A video on changing an order received to an invoice is on the DVD

Self-test exercise 7.16

Have the file dem72.myo open.

Goods ordered by Marrickville City Council are now invoiced and despatched on 31 July 2011.

Change the order recorded for Marrickville City Council to an invoice. Use the same Purchase # as the quote, change the date to 31/07/2011 and modify the journal memo.

(Ignore any date warning – click *OK*.)

You can of course enter an order from a customer without having first provided a quote, especially if the customer is ordering from a price list. The entry is the same as for an invoice except that the ORDER view is selected instead of INVOICE before entering. The order can be changed to an invoice as was done in the previous example and self-test exercise.

Self-test exercise 7.17

Have the file dem72.myo open.

Record an order number 8415 received on 31 July 2011 from Darvil Engineering Pty Ltd (their PO# is "4482") for one G100 Noise Generator. The price is $858.00 (including the GST) and Darvil Engineering has agreed to pay freight of $93.50 (including the GST). Promised date 8/8/2011 to be delivered by Best Way. Modify the journal memo – replace "Sale" with "Order".

Stocktaking

A perpetual inventory system is useful for knowing the number of items that are (or should be) on hand, and for item invoicing. Things can go wrong, however, and it is necessary to count the inventory periodically. This serves as a check on the accuracy of data entry and the physical security of the inventory. Differences between the actual inventory counted and the *MYOB AccountRight Plus* records may be due to one or more factors – incorrect entries, missing entries, damage, spoilage, wrong quantities or wrong item received or delivered, or theft. The methods of counting inventory to ensure accuracy can be found in most management accounting textbooks.

In *MYOB AccountRight Plus*, an *Inventory Count Sheet* can be printed from the *Reports* pull-down menu. This allows for two separate counts to be entered, preferably by two independent counters. A general ledger account must be set up so that adjustments to the *Item List* can be made to bring them into line with the count.

How to enter the stocktake figures

Step	Instruction
1	Select the *Inventory* command centre.
2	Select the *Count Inventory* option.
3	Enter the stocktake amounts (quantity of items) in the column headed 'Counted'.
4	If there are differences, click on the *Adjust Inventory* button.
5	Enter a 'Default Adjustment Account' number. This will usually be an expense or cost of sales account.
6	Click on the *Continue* button.
7	Enter the date of the stocktake and this adjustment.
8	Change the memo if required.
9	Click on the *Record* button.

Select the option *Count Inventory* from the *Inventory* command centre; you will notice there are three quantity columns (see Figure 7.35 on the next page):

'**On Hand**', '**Counted**' and '**Difference**'.

The amounts in the column 'On Hand' are what ***should be*** in stock according to *MYOB AccountRight Plus* records. In the 'Counted' column <u>you enter</u> the ***actual*** stocktake count. In the 'Difference' column *MYOB AccountRight Plus* will calculate and display the discrepancies, if any, otherwise it will display '0'. A negative *difference* will indicate a shortage and a positive *difference* will indicate a gain. The reasons for the differences can be attributed to any of the following causes: errors in recording, errors in counting, wrong items delivered or received, or loss of items due to theft, damage, spoilage or being misplaced.

Example 7.17—Entering an inventory count

1. Start *MYOB AccountRight Plus* and open the file called dem72.myo.
2. Select the *Inventory* command centre.
3. Select the *Count Inventory* option and enter the stocktake amounts listed here in the column headed '**Counted**':

Item Number	On Hand	Counted	Difference
G100	2	"**2**"	no difference
LOG1	1	"**1**"	no difference
LOG2	4	"**4**"	no difference
PC1	5	"**5**"	no difference
R25	10	"**8**"	-2

(-2 should appear as shortage for item No. R25)

The *Count Inventory* window should look like Figure 7.35:

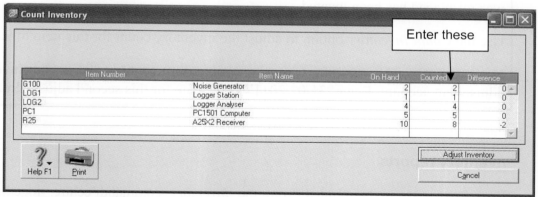

Figure 7.35: The *Count Inventory* window

4. Click on the *Adjust Inventory* button. [Adjust Inventory]
5. Enter "9-1000 Inventory Count Adjustment" as the 'Default Adjustment Account' and click on the *Continue* button.

    Default Adjustment Account: 9-1000 ▼ Inventory count adjustment

6. The date of the stocktake should be entered as "31/07/2011" and the 'Memo' should be changed to "Inventory count adjustment".

7. If your screen looks like Figure 7.36, click the *Record* button.

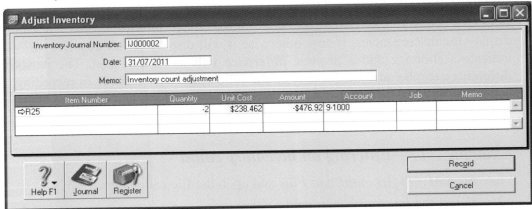

Figure 7.36: Inventory adjustment transaction

 Video: A video on entering inventory items count is on the DVD

 ## Self-test exercise 7.18

Have the file dem72.myo open.

Following on from Example 7.17 above, an additional R25 'A25X2 Receiver' that was misplaced has been located.

Use the *Count Inventory* option to adjust the inventory count for this item to 9.

Use account number "9-1000 Inventory count adjustment" as the default inventory adjustment account. Enter "31/07/2011" as the date for this second adjustment.

Inventory reports

Several reports can be printed from the *Inventory* command centre, together with transaction listings from all command centres. An 'Inventory Count List' can be printed upon which stock counts can be manually entered for later input to the computer. A most important report is the *Item List*, which can be printed in summary or in detail.

How to print an item list

Step	Instruction
1	If you are in the *Inventory* command centre, click on the *Reports* button (this button is located below the command centre). Reports◄▼ ──── Click
OR	If you are NOT in the *Inventory* command centre, click on the drop-down list arrow at the end of the *Reports* button and select "Inventory" (the example shows "Inventory" selected while in the *Accounts* command centre). Reports ▼◄── Click on drop-down arrow Accounts Banking GST/Sales Tax Sales Time Billing Purchases Payroll Inventory reports selected ──► Inventory Card File Custom
2	Click on the *Items List* "Summary" **or** *Items List* "Detail" report to select it **Note:** You can use these 'How to …' instructions to print any inventory report by selecting an alternative report in this step.
3	Click on the *Customise* icon button. ▼ Customise
4	There are three customisation windows (views). Click on the tab of each Advanced Filters | Report Fields | Finishing and select the print options required.
5	Click on the *Display* button to view the report on screen. You may have to maximise the screen and use the scroll bars to see the report.
6	Click on the *Print* button to obtain a printout Print and then click on *Close* to exit the *Index to Reports* window.

Example 7.18—Printing a summary item list

1. Have the file called dem72.myo open.
2. Select the *Inventory* command centre.
3. Click on the arrow on the *Reports* button and drag down to select the *Inventory* command centre.
4. Click on the *Items List* "Summary" report.
5. Click on the *Customise* icon button at the foot of the window.
6. Change or make sure the options are for all suppliers and all items, sorted by item number, and include zero quantities.
7. Click on the *Display* button to see the report on screen.
8. If your screen looks like Figure 7.37, click on the *Print* button and then on the *Close* button to exit.

Items List [Summary]						Page 1
Item #	Item Name	Supplier	Units On Hand	Total Value	Average Cost	Current Price
Consulting	Consulting Fees		0	$0.00	$0.00	$140.00
G100	Noise Generator		2	$933.00	$466.50	$780.00
LOG1	Logger Station		1	$2,100.00	$2,100.00	$3,150.00
LOG2	Logger Analyser		4	$2,243.20	$560.80	$840.00
PC1	PC1501 Computer		5	$2,923.00	$584.60	$878.00
R25	A25X2 Receiver		9	$2,146.16	$238.4622	$450.00
			Grand Total:	$10,345.36		

Figure 7.37: *Items List [Summary]* **report**

Self-test exercise 7.19

Have the file dem72.myo open.

Print the "Analyse Inventory Summary" report. Use the *Customise* button and select 'Sort by' "Item Number" and in the *Finishing* Tab to 'Include Zero Quantities'.

> **Hint:** Follow the steps listed in the previous 'How to …' but in step 2 select the "Analyse Inventory Summary" report.

> **Notice:** This report takes into consideration the outstanding orders. Orders to customers are listed in the 'Committed' column and orders from suppliers are in the 'On Order' column. The 'Available' column shows the actual quantities available for sale.

Finished!!

Competency checklist

	I can now do the following:	✔
1	Adjust office furniture including chair and computer equipment to suit ergonomic requirements	
2	Sit with the correct posture in front of the computer	
3	Take proper breaks and exercise regularly	
4	Use *MYOB* Help (Manuals/On line Help/Site Help)	
5	Turn the computer system on	
6	Solve operational problems	
7	Start *MYOB AccountRight Plus* and open data files	
8	Access the accounts, banking, sales, purchases and inventory command centres	
9	Set up inventory items to be purchased, sold and stored (inventoried)	
10	Enter opening balances of inventory items (count and cost prices)	
11	Enter sales and purchases quotes, orders and invoices/bills	
12	Record partial receipts of items on order	
13	Integrate inventory with accounts receivable, account payable, cash book and the general ledger modules	
14	Record purchases returns (credit notes received or internal debit notes) and apply the debit from the supplier to a previous purchase or record the refund received	
15	Record sales returns (credit notes) and apply the credit to a previous invoice or record the refund paid to the customer	
16	Maintain inventory list records (add, edit, delete inventory items)	
17	Process item transactions and associated accounts receivable and payable, including changes in inventory cost price and selling price during a period	
18	Process entries to correct errors in the inventory	
19	Reconcile the inventory list with the general ledger inventory account after periodical stocktakes	
20	Produce relevant reports (print or email) from all command centres as well as GST and BAS reports	

Chapter 7: Assessment exercises

Note: Throughout the following practical exercises you should continually observe relevant Occupational Health and Safety practices and apply recycling techniques to minimise paper wastage. In addition, you should use the on-line help facilities (the F1 key and/or windows Help menu) and the notes to solve any problems you encounter.

Unless otherwise stated, select '*Item*' as the layout for the invoices (sales) and bills (purchases) in the following assessments.

7.1 Inventory maintenance, purchases and sales

Dogmatic Pty Ltd is an importer and wholesaler of pet food ingredients from Africa. It has been using *MYOB AccountRight Plus* for some time, but they would like to set up and use the *Inventory* command centre and a perpetual inventory system from 1 July 2011.

Start *MYOB AccountRight Plus*. The month for this exercise is July 2011.

Open the existing file ass71.myo (sign on as "Administrator" – no password).

Change the company information to show your name in the address field.

(a)   Set up the following inventory items. All items are purchased, held in inventory and sold. **The selling prices given do <u>not</u> include the GST**.

Inclusive/Exclusive: ☐ Prices are Tax Inclusive

Item #	D100	D200	D300
Name	Buffalo Biltong	Salted Reedbuck	Posho
Buying unit	Sack	Sack	Sack
# per buying unit	1	1	1
Buying tax code	GST	GST	GST
Selling price	$240.00	$180.00	$75.00
Selling unit	Sack	Sack	Sack
# per selling unit	1	1	1
Selling tax code	GST	GST	GST
Inclusive/Exclusive	Exclusive	Exclusive	Exclusive

Item #	D400	D500	D600
Name	Ground Tilapia	Dried Tuna	Couscous
Buying unit	Drum	Sack	Sack
# per buying unit	1	1	1
Buying tax code	GST	GST	GST
Selling price	$580.00	$110.00	$90.00
Selling unit	Drum	Sack	Sack
# per selling unit	1	1	1
Selling tax code	GST	GST	GST
Inclusive/Exclusive	Exclusive	Exclusive	Exclusive

(b)   Enter the following opening balances at 1 July 2011:

Item #	Name	Qty on Hand	Cost per buying unit (Excluding GST)
D100	Buffalo Biltong	80 Sacks	$162.00
D200	Salted Reedbuck	20 Sacks	$100.80
D300	Posho	40 Sacks	$40.00
D400	Ground Tilapia	5 Drums	$210.00
D500	Dried Tuna	0 Sacks	No stock
D600	Couscous	20 Sacks	$51.80

Important: Open the *Recap Transaction* option from the *Edit* drop down menu to check and make sure the total 'Amount' in the *Adjusted Inventory* window adds up to $18,662.00, which is the Inventory account balance, before recording.

(c)   Record the following *Item* layout purchases for July 2011. **All purchase prices exclude the GST** (i.e. Price *plus* GST) and the tax code should be "GST" by default. Ignore customs duty in this question.
       All prices are in Australian dollars.
       FIS: "free into store" means Price includes freight and/or insurance.

       IMPORTANT: Make sure the layout for all purchases is "ITEM".
                           First Purchase # is "**1001**"

       The 'Tax Inclusive' box on the purchase order should <u>not</u> be ticked:

       ☐ Tax Inclusive

       4 July 2011   Received the following goods from the National Trading
                      Corporation, Tanzania. on their invoice 48721 FIS:
                      300 sacks "Posho" @ $40 per sack
                        50   Drums "Ground Tilapia" @ $220.80 per drum

       9 July 2011   Purchased from Gopal Enterprises, Kenya on their invoice
                      EXP560, the following goods FIS:
                      140   sacks "Dried Tuna" @ $57.80 per sack

       15 July 2011   Purchased from Mwangi Mills, Kenya on their invoice AUS33,
                      the following goods FIS:
                      200   sacks "Couscous" @ $50.00 per sack
                      120   sacks "Posho" @ $46 per sack

       25 July 2011   Purchased from Direct Imports, Melbourne,
                      Their invoice number is 4438
                      30   drums "Ground Tilapia" @ $220.80 per drum.

30 July 2011   Purchased from Mambo Trading, Kenya, the following goods
FIS on their invoice AB556:
110 sacks "Salted Reedbuck" @ $104.60 per sack
 40 sacks "Buffalo Biltong" @ $162.00 per sack

(d)   Record the return on 28 July 2011 of 5 drums "Ground Tilapia" to Direct
Imports. Use an *Item* layout bill and enter returned item as negative quantities.
Change the 'Purchase #' to "DN1004" and the 'Supplier Inv #' to "CN1".
Enter –5 (**minus** 5) in the 'Bill' column. These were purchased on 25 July on
their invoice number 4438. They are being returned because tests show the
contents to contain excess preservative 220.
Apply this debit to Purchase # 1004.

(e)   Record the following item sales for July 2011. All sales are taxable and have a
tax code of "GST" (including the GST on freight). First Invoice # is "**3501**".

IMPORTANT: Make sure the layout is *ITEM* for all these Invoices.
Sales invoices must show tax-inclusive prices – the 'Tax Inclusive' box must
be ticked: ☑ Tax Inclusive

3 July 2011   Sold to Carter's Pet Kennels against their order number 558:
20 sacks "Posho" and
40 sacks "Buffalo Biltong".
Add freight to this invoice of $52.80 (including the GST) and
the carrier was Hills Transport.

8 July 2011   Sold to Kondoa Pet Supplies. Their order number was P1100.
100 sacks "Posho",
 20 drums "Ground Tilapia" and
 20 sacks "Buffalo Biltong".
Hills Transport delivered the goods. Enter freight charge of
$93.06 (including the GST).

18 July 2011   Invoiced Bushies Pet Foods for their phone order:
100 sacks of "Couscous" and
 10 sacks of "Salted Reedbuck".
Hills Transport delivered the goods. Add freight $81.62 (incl.
GST).

24 July 2011   Sold to Kondoa Pet Supplies against their order number P1156.
180 sacks of "Posho" and
 80 sacks of "Dried Tuna"
Hills Transport delivered the goods. Freight is $101.42
(incl.GST).

31 July 2011   Invoiced Bushies Pet Foods for their phone order, for
75 sacks of "Salted Reedbuck" and
40 drums of "Ground Tilapia".
Hills Transport delivered the goods. Freight $92.62 (incl. GST).

(f)   Record on the 21 July 2011 a credit note (a negative item invoice) issued to Bushies Pet Foods for "2 sacks of Salted Reedbuck" returned by them to be checked for quality (suspected impurities). The 'Invoice #' should be changed to "CN1", the 'Tax Inclusive' box should be ticked and the number of items returned to be entered as a negative i.e. –2 (**minus 2**). This credit note is to be applied to the invoice# 3503 issued to them on 18 July 2011.

(g)   Print the following:

   (i)   An items list (detail)
   (ii)   A "GST [Summary – Accrual]" report for July 2011
   (iii)   Transaction journal for July 2011 (select "All" journals as the source)
   (iv)   Invoice# 3501 (Type: "Item" and "AccountRight Plain Paper" form)
   (v)   Purchase# 1004 (Type: "Item" and "AccountRight Plain Paper" form)

7.2   Inventory maintenance, purchases and sales, restocking and stocktaking

Just in Time OK Ltd wholesales top quality Australian-made classical guitars. It has been in business and using *MYOB AccountRight Plus* for some time. They have decided to start using the *Inventory* command centre to control their stock. They are converting their accounting system to a perpetual inventory as from 1 July 2011.

Start *MYOB AccountRight Plus*. The month for this exercise is July 2011.
Copy and open the existing file ass72.myo.
Change the business address: Enter your full name and "Assessment 7.2".

Set up the sales and purchases linked accounts (especially for Freight).

(a)   **Set up the following inventory items.** All items are purchased, held in inventory and sold. **The selling prices given do not include the GST.**

Inclusive/Exclusive: ☐ Prices are Tax Inclusive

Item #	WEST100	WEST030	WEST200
Name	Westralis Classical	Westralis Student	Westralis Original
Buying unit	Each	Each	Each
# per buying unit	1	1	1
Buying tax code	GST	GST	GST
Selling price	$700.00	$130.00	$1,500.00
Selling unit	Each	Each	Each
# per selling unit	1	1	1
Selling tax code	GST	GST	GST
Inclusive/Exclusive	Exclusive	Exclusive	Exclusive
Minimum level	2	2	0
Principal supplier	Westralis Guitars Ltd	Westralis Guitars Ltd	Westralis Guitars Ltd
Supplier item #	28C	28S	28O
Reorder quantity	6	5	2

continued (more items) on the next page

Item #	LEV010	WIND500	WIND400
Name	Levin Classical	Windsor Ace	Windsor 3/4
Buying unit	each	Each	Each
# per buying unit	1	1	1
Buying tax code	GST	GST	GST
Selling price	$1,300.00	$920.00	$260.00
Selling unit	each	Each	Each
# per selling unit	1	1	1
Selling tax code	GST	GST	GST
Inclusive/Exclusive	Exclusive	Exclusive	Exclusive
Minimum level	2	2	2
Principal supplier	G.B. Instruments P/L	Katoomba Guitars	Katoomba Guitars
Supplier item #		WIND500	WIND400
Reorder quantity	2	3	3

(b)   Enter the following opening balances at 1 July 2011:

Item #	Name	Qty on Hand	Cost per buying unit (Excluding GST)
LEV010	Levin Classical	4	$920.00
WEST030	Westralis Student	3	$ 85.00
WEST100	Westralis Classical	8	$480.00
WEST200	Westralis Original	0	No stock
WIND400	Windsor 3/4	0	No stock
WIND500	Windsor Ace	5	$520.00

Important notice: Inventory account balance at 1/07/2011 is $10,375.00.

(c)   Record the following item purchases for July 2011. All purchase prices are GST inclusive and the tax code is "GST". The 'Tax Inclusive' box should therefore be ticked in this exercise: ☑ Tax Inclusive

Note: First Purchase # is "**501**". (Use *Item* layout.)

8 July 2011   Purchased from Westralis Guitars on their invoice number 11280:
6   only WEST100 Classical guitars @ $528.00 each
5   only WEST030 Student guitars @ $93.50 each

10 July 2011   Purchased from G.B. Instruments on their invoice number 5870:
2   only LEV010 Levin Classical guitars @ $1,012.00 each

25 July 2011   Purchased from Katoomba Guitars on their invoice number M662:
3   only WIND500 Windsor Ace guitars @ $572.00 each
1   only WIND400 Windsor 3/4 guitar @ $198.00

30 July 2011   Purchased from Westralis Guitars on their invoice number 11289:
6   only #WEST100 Classical guitars @ $528.00 each
5   only #WEST030 Student guitars @ $93.50 each

(d)   Record the following 'Quote' received:

30 July 2011   A 'Quote' was received from G.B. Instruments for the purchase of
2 LEV010 Classical guitars @ $1,144.00 each including GST.
Enter 'Purchase #' as "505" and save the quote.

(e)   Record a credit note received from Westralis Guitars on 12 July for the return of a damaged WEST030 guitar. Enter "DN1" as the 'Purchase #', and "CN182" as the 'Supplier Inv #'. This guitar was purchased from Westralis Guitars on 8 July for $93.50 (including GST).
Use a negative 'Item' Bill (enter –1 in the 'Bill' column). Make sure to apply the debit to the invoice of 8 July. (Purchase # 501.)

(f)   Change the 'Quote' received from G.B. Instruments Pty Ltd to an 'Order'. Use the same purchase # as the quote and change the date to 31 July 2011. Wards Skyroad will deliver the order by 31 August 2011.

(g)   Record the following credit sales: (Use the *Item* layout invoice). Sales in Australia have a tax code of "GST". The export sale to Murray's Music on 22 July will be coded "EXP" for the items and "FRE for the international freight.

Sales prices on the invoices for this business are to show the tax-inclusive prices where applicable, so the 'Tax Inclusive' box should be ticked:

☑ Tax Inclusive

First invoice number should be "**3801**".

4 July 2011   Sold to Hills Symphonic Pty Ltd against their order #487:
6 only WEST100 Westralis Classical guitars
2 only LEV010 Levin Classical guitars
Freight $57.20 (incl. GST). The carrier was Best Way.

12 July 2011   Sold to Guitars Classique Pty Ltd on their order #1986:
6 only WEST030 Westralis Student guitars
These were shipped by Best Way but no freight is charged to the customer.

22 July 2011   Export sale to Murray's Music Pty Ltd on their order #NZ333:
2 only LEV010 Levin Classical guitars. Tax code "EXP".
4 only WIND500 Windsor Ace Guitars. Tax code "EXP".
Freight $148.00 (GST-free) is added to the invoice.
The carrier was Kwikasair.

29 July 2011   Sold to Musica Professionals on their fax order dated 28/7/2011:
6 Only WEST100 Westralis Classical guitars
1 only WIND400 Windsor 3/4 guitars
Add Freight $59.40 (incl. GST), the carrier being Federal Express.

31 July 2011   Sold to Hills Symphonic Pty Ltd on their order #492:
4   only WEST100 Westralis Classical guitars
2   only WEST030 Westralis Student guitars
2   only WIND500 Windsor Ace guitars
A delivery charge of $61.60 (which includes GST) is to be added to the invoice, and the carrier was Best Way.

(h)   At 31 July 2011 management decided, since the cost to purchase LEV010 has increased it will be necessary to increase the selling price for this item to $1,500.00 each plus GST (i.e. price is excluding the GST). Modify the selling price for this item accordingly.

(i)   Management carried out a physical stock take on 31 July 2011. All items counted agreed with *MYOB AccountRight Plus* records <u>except</u> for item # WEST100.
According to *MYOB AccountRight Plus* there should be 4 guitars but only 3 were found. Adjust the inventory count for this item to 3 (use *Count Inventory*) and use account 9-1000 as the default adjustment account to record this loss.

(j)   Print the following reports and forms:
(i)   An *Items List* (detail) report (include items with zero quantities)

(ii)   An "Analyse Inventory Summary" (include items with zero quantities)

(iii) A "GST [Summary – Accrual]" report for the month of July 2011

(iv)   The "Sales & Receivables Journal" for July 2011

(v)   The "Purchases & Payables Journal" for July 2011

For the next three prints select "Item" as the sale or purchase 'Type' and "AccountRight Plus's Plain Paper" as the 'Selected Form' for sales and purchases:

(vi)   Print the Invoice to Murray's dated 22/7/2011

(vii) Print the bill (purchase) from Westralis dated 8/7/2011
(Change the 'Purchase Status' to "All Purchases")

(viii) Print the Order to purchase from G.B. Instruments dated 31/7/2011
(Change the 'Purchase Status' to "Orders")

7.3   Comprehensive exercise

This exercise integrates all the modules covered between Chapter 1 through to this chapter. It does not cover payroll and asset manager (Chapters 8 and 9).

Business background

Rafiki Pty Ltd was incorporated a few years ago. It is a small wholesaler of fruit juices. It purchases these products in bulk from a small number of suppliers (including import), and sells to major supermarket companies and catering suppliers. Rafiki Pty Ltd also owns its own premises, which consists of the company's warehouse and office. The company's only other assets are motor vehicles, fixtures and fittings, office furniture and office equipment (including computers).

It has used a hand-written bookkeeping system to date, but due to rapid expansion plans and the accounting requirements of the GST, management has decided to computerise the accounting process. They also feel that the use of a perpetual inventory system will avoid problems related to stock control that have occurred. The management and owners are also keen to have more regular profit reporting, and a greater control over accounts receivable and payable through regular aged analysis reports.

A decision has been made for the accounts to be converted to *MYOB AccountRight Plus* on 1 July 2011.

Required:

(a) Start *MYOB AccountRight Plus* and open the file called **ass73.myo**.

(b) ***Enter Company Information***
Type in your full name in the address field and "assessment 7.3" on the second line of the address. The company's ABN Number is 33 001 895 564.

(c) ***Report Design***
Design how you want the Balance Sheet and the Profit and Loss Statement to appear. As a minimum, these must comply with company legislation and Australian Accounting Standards. In addition, include in your design, headings, columns, sub-totals and totals that you want to appear. The Profit and Loss must show full details of income, cost of goods sold and expenses under appropriate headings. This design forms the basis for setting up your *Accounts List* (see (d) next).

(d) ***Edit the* Accounts List**
Edit the *Accounts List* that is already in the file. The *Accounts List* at present contains most of the accounts you will require, but is not correct and needs alteration to put it in good form. You must edit the *Accounts List* to ensure that after recording transactions correctly, financial reports will be printed exactly as per your design.

This requires you to enter some headings into the *Accounts List* and to nominate whether you want a total for the accounts coming under that heading. You will need to rearrange some accounts, and change some reporting levels. Refer to the 'How to ...' instructions for entering and editing different types of accounts.

(e) ***Opening General Ledger Account Balances***
    The general ledger trial balance at 30 June 2011 is given. Enter these balances into the accounts as at 1/7/2011, using the *Setup* pull-down menu, *Balances* menu item and *Account Opening Balances*. You may need to add accounts as necessary. (See the 'How to ...' instruction list).

Remember: Asset accounts with *credit* balances and liability accounts with *debit* balances are to be entered as negative (i.e. minus amounts).

General Ledger Trial Balance
As At 30 June 2011

Account Name	Debit	Credit
St George Bank	4,029.50	
Term Deposit	2,000.00	
Accounts Receivable	24,866.93	
Provision for Doubtful Debts		1,500.00
Inventory	31,606.00	
Freehold Land	1,204,000.85	
Building	238,263.15	
Accumulated Depreciation – Building		7,428.00
Motor Cars	42,558.00	
Accumulated Depreciation – Motor Vehicles		12,887.00
Furniture and Fixtures	28,756.80	
Accumulated Depreciation – Furniture and Fixture		4,996.00
Office Equipment	54,500.00	
Accumulated Depreciation – Office Equipment		10,900.00
Accounts Payable		18,486.75
GST Collected		17,596.40
GST Paid	15,530.65	
PAYG Withholding Payable		7,621.48
Payroll Deductions Payable		3,503.98
Provision for Income Tax		18,777.40
Issued Capital – $1 "A" Shares		1,400,000.00
Retained Earnings		142,414.87
	1,646,111.88	1,646,111.88

VERY IMPORTANT MESSAGE!
Make sure that the account "Historical Balancing" equals zero when you have finished entering the above balances.

Check that the above accounts are included in the *Accounts List*, as well as the income and expenditure accounts listed below. Do the necessary additions or modifications and remember to add the necessary header accounts and adjust the accounts' levels to enhance the appearance and to correctly group accounts under their respective headings.

Group the expense accounts under these headings: "**Marketing Expenses**", "**General & Administrative Exp.**", "**Employment Expenses**" and "**Financial Expenses**"

IMPORTANT:

For this exercise make sure that ***all*** header accounts display a subtotal for their group:

Account Name:	Account Classification
Sales – Retail	Income
Sales – Catering	Income
COGS – Retail & Catering	Cost of Sales
Freight & Insurance Inwards	Cost of Sales
Advertising	Expense
Sales Commission	Expense
Accounting & Audit	Expense
Bank Charges	Expense
Depreciation – Buildings	Expense
Depreciation – Motor Vehicles	Expense
Depreciation – Furniture & Fixtures	Expense
Depreciation – Office Equipment	Expense
Electricity	Expense
General Expenses	Expense
Insurance	Expense
Motor Vehicle Running	Expense
Postage	Expense
Printing & Stationery	Expense
Repairs & Maintenance	Expense
Salaries and Wages	Expense
Staff Amenities	Expense
Telephones & Faxes	Expense
Travel	Expense

(f) ***Add a tax code for Export Sales***

Export sales are GST free. Add a tax code for export sales.

				Linked accounts for GST	
Tax Code	Description	Tax Rate	Tax Type	Collected	Paid
EXP	Export Sales	0%	Goods & Services	GST Collected	GST Paid

Hint: Select "Tax Codes" from the *Lists* pull-down menu then click on *New*.

(g) ***Create an Accounts Receivable (Customer) Card***

Some customer cards have already been set up for you. Create a new customer card for the following customer:

Company Name:	Abnego Pty Limited
Card ID:	C1007
Address:	345 Smith Lane
	THORNLEIGH NSW 2120
Ship to:	44 Marapatoa Street
	Auckland New Zealand
Phone #1:	(02) 9980 1234
Fax #:	(02) 9980 1288
Identifier:	W
Salutation:	Fiona
Contact Name:	Fiona Garth
Credit Limit:	$125,000
Sale Layout:	Item
Credit Terms:	30 days after End of Month (# of days after EOM)
Tax Code:	EXP
Freight Tax Code:	FRE
Use Customer's Tax Code:	Yes (tick its box ON)

(h) ***Create Accounts Payable (Supplier) Card***

Several supplier cards have already been set up for you. Create a new supplier card for the following supplier:

Company Name:	Bronco Orchards Pty Ltd
Card ID:	S08
Address:	4/32 O'Briens Road
	BUSSELTON WA 6280
Phone #1:	(08) 9752 2345
Fax #:	(08) 9752 3333
Identifier:	T
Salutation:	Samantha
Contact Name:	Ms Samantha Cheong
Credit Limit:	$50,000
Purchase Layout:	Item
Credit Terms:	30 days after the EOM (# of Days after EOM)
ABN:	44 123 456 789
Tax Code:	GST
Freight Tax Code:	GST
Use Supplier's Tax Code:	No (clear the box tick OFF)

(i) *Add Inventory Items*

These items are all **purchased**, kept in **inventory** and **sold**.

An item with an 'Item#' that starts with an "**R**" is a retail item. Retail items are purchased and sold by the carton (Buying and Selling Unit of Measure is "**CTN**"). An 'Item#' that starts with a "**C**" is a catering item which is purchased and sold by the "**CASE**". The number of items per buying *and* selling unit (for *all* items) is "1". The linked accounts are:

"Cost of Sale" account:	"5-2000 COGS – Retail & Catering"
"Inventory" account:	"1-1300 Inventory".
"Income" account for the **retail** items:	"4-1100 Sales – Retail" *and*
"Income" account for the **catering** items:	"4-1200 Sales – Catering".

The following selling prices do *not* include **GST**:

Inclusive/Exclusive: ☐ Prices are Tax Inclusive

Item #:	Name:	Tax Code Buying	Tax Code Selling	ROP*	Order Qty*	Selling Price (Excluding the GST)
C0001	Narchi Conc 10 litre	FRE	FRE	10	50	$367.50
C0002	Mzuri Orange 20 litre	GST	GST	10	50	$200.00
C0003	Sana Mango 20 litre	GST	GST	10	80	$560.00
R0001	Narchi Conc. 500 ml	FRE	FRE	10	50	$134.40
R0002	Mzuri Orange 250 ml	GST	GST	10	80	$56.00
R0003	Sana Mango 250 ml	GST	GST	5	100	$70.00

(*****) Enter quantities for 'ROP' (Reorder point) in '*Minimum Level for Restocking Alert*' field and 'Order Qty' in '*Default Reorder Quantity*' field.

(j) *Enter in the following inventory 'Opening Balances' and costs at 1 July 2011:*

Item #:	Name:	QTY (CTN/CASE)	Unit Cost (Excluding GST)
C0001	Narchi Conc 10 litre	38	$210.00
C0002	Mzuri Orange 20 litre	38	$115.00
C0003	Sana Mango 20 litre	29	$320.00
R0001	Narchi Conc. 500 ml	72	$84.00
R0002	Mzuri Orange 250 ml	44	$32.00
R0003	Sana Mango 250 ml	63	$40.00

(k) *Enter customer historical balances*

Enter in the following outstanding customer invoices:
(Leave the 'Customer PO#' field blank)

Customer	Date	Inv. No.	Amount	Tax Code
Kiss Me Quick	1/5/2010	3861	$558.00	GST
Abnego Pty Ltd	18/5/2011	5637	$4,621.20	EXP
	24/6/2011	5650	$3,248.63	EXP
Colzmier Pty Ltd	11/6/2011	5642	$11,148.50	GST
Em-Kart Pty Ltd	16/6/2011	5643	$5,290.60	GST
			$24,866.93	

(l) ***Enter supplier historical balances***
Enter in the following outstanding supplier invoices (bills) – (Tax code is GST):

Supplier	Date	PO. No.	Amount
Cretian Juices Pty Ltd	11/6/2011	3125	$5,262.25
	30/6/2011	3147	$3,286.20
Davis Manufacturing Pty Ltd	7/6/2011	3122	$3,260.30
Natural Bliss Pty Ltd	29/6/2011	3144	$2,052.90
Bronco Orchards Pty Ltd	24/6/2011	3140	$4,625.10
			$18,486.75

(m) ***Enter the following credit transactions for July 2011***

Purchases on credit for July 2011 (use *Item* layout)
First Purchase number is "3148". All purchases are to show the GST-inclusive prices, where applicable. Tick the ☑ Tax Inclusive box before entering amounts:

4/7   Davis Manufacturing Pty Ltd – Purchase # 3148. Supplier Invoice # is 18003. All prices include the GST. Received:
350   cartons Item # R0002 "Mzuri Orange 250 ml" @ $35.20 per CTN and
180   cases Item #C0002 "Mzuri Orange 20 litre" @ $126.50 per case.
Delivered (Shipped) by "Best Way".

8/7   Cretian Juices Pty Ltd – Purchase # 3149. Supplier Invoice # is 4424. Received:
200   cartons Item # R0001 "Narchi Conc. 500 ml" @ $84.00 per CTN (GST-free). Delivered by "Best Way".

12/7   Bronco Orchards P/L – Purchase # 3150. Supplier Invoice # is 1234. Received:
150   cartons Item # R0003 "Sana Mango 250 ml" @ $44.00 per CTN (incl. GST). Delivered by "International".

15/7   Natural Bliss Pty Ltd – Purchase # 3151. Supplier Invoice # is 847. Received:
150   cases Item # C0003 "Sana Mango 20 litre" @ $352 per case (incl. GST). Delivered by "International".

25/7   Cretian Juices Pty Ltd – Purchase # 3152. Supplier Invoice # is 4430. Received:
150   cases Item # C0001 "Narchi Conc 10 litre" @ $210 per case (GST-free), and 100   cartons R0001 "Narchi Conc. 500 ml" @ $84.00 per CTN (GST-free). Delivered by "Best Way".

Purchase Returns for July 2011 –
26/7 Use *Item* layout bill to record a return to Cretian Juices Pty Ltd, 'Purchase #:' "D3152" and 'Supplier Inv#:' "CN71", of:
1 case Item # C0001 "Narchi Conc 10 litre" @ $210 per case (GST-free)
Enter –1 (minus 1) in the 'Bill' column.
Apply this debit (on 26/7/2011) to Purchase # 3152 dated 25/7/2011.

Sales Invoices for July 2011 (use *Item* layout)

First invoice number is "5651". All invoices are to show the GST-inclusive prices, where applicable. Tick the ☑ Tax Inclusive box before entering amounts:

6/7   Colzmier Pty Ltd – Invoice # is 5651. Customer PO # is C8621. Shipped:
- 40   cartons of Item # R0002 "Mzuri Orange 250 ml" and
- 45   cartons of Item # R0001 "Narchi Conc. 500 ml".

Salesperson was Gustav Mahler. Hills Transport delivered the goods.

11/7   Em-Kart Pty Ltd – Invoice # is 5652. Customer PO # is 848-1465. Shipped:
- 50   cartons of Item # R0003 "Sana Mango 250 ml".

Salesperson was Jacques Offenbach and goods are delivered by International.

13/7   Abnego Pty Ltd – Invoice # is 5653. Customer PO # is NZ331. Shipped:
- 130   cartons of Item # R0001 "Narchi Conc. 500 ml" (Tax code "EXP"), and
- 80   cases of Item # C0002 "Mzuri Orange 20 litre". (Tax code "EXP")

Freight charged $298.75 (Tax code is "FRE"). Salesperson is Stephanie Bach. Goods are delivered to New Zealand by International.

18/7   Colzmier Pty Ltd – Invoice # is 5654. Customer PO # is C8689. Shipped:
- 95   cartons of Item # R0002 "Mzuri Orange 250 ml". Salesperson was Gustav Mahler and goods are delivered by Hills Transport.

19/7   David James Ltd – Invoice # is 5655. Customer PO # is D44311. Shipped:
- 150   cases of Item # C0003 "Sana Mango 20 litre".

Salesperson was Jacques Offenbach and International delivered the goods.

22/7   P.H. Distribution Pty Ltd – Invoice # is 5656. Customer PO # is 9876. Shipped:
- 100   cases of Item # C0001 "Narchi Conc. 10 litre" and
- 100   cases of Item # C0002 "Mzuri Orange 20 litre".

Salesperson was Jacques Offenbach and goods are delivered by Hills Transport.

28/7   Abnego Pty Ltd – Invoice # is 5657. Customer PO # is NZ332. Shipped:
- 130   cartons of Item # R0001 "Narchi Conc. 500 ml" (Tax code: "EXP") and
- 140   cartons of Item # R0002 "Mzuri Orange 250 ml" (Tax code: "EXP")

Freight charged $186.50 (GST-free) and the salesperson is Stephanie Bach. International delivered these goods.

(n)   *Record the Purchase of a Going Concern*

1/7   Enter a journal entry to record a purchase of a going concern from Pepi Cosmetics Pty Ltd for $329,996.00. As a going concern the purchase is GST-free. Assets acquired at agreed values are:

		Tax Code
Motor cars	$78,248.00	FRE
Delivery Trucks	$192,480.00	FRE
Furniture and Fixtures	$19,268.00	FRE
Goodwill	$40,000.00	FRE
Create a current liability account for "Pepi Cosmetics Pty Ltd".		N-T

(o) **Record cheques received from Accounts Receivable in July 2011**
Apply to oldest open invoices:

Note: All deposits are made to St George Bank account.

4/7	Received from Abnego Pty Ltd	$7,869.83
8/7	Received from Colzmier Pty Ltd	11,148.50
15/7	Received from Colzmier Pty Ltd	8,512.00
20/7	Received from Em-Kart Pty Ltd	5,290.60
21/7	Received from Abnego Pty Ltd	33,770.75
27/7	Received from David James Pty Ltd	92,400.00
28/7	Received from Colzmier Pty Ltd	5,852.00

(p) **Record other money received in July 2011**

Note: All deposits are made to St George Bank account.

14/7   Interest Received (from St George Bank) $38.90. Tax code "FRE".

18/7   Received from "Advance Stock Brokers" $100,000 by direct deposit for the issue of 100,000 "B" Shares fully paid. Tax "N-T".

29/7   Received $180,000 "5% Mortgage Loan" from St George Bank. This loan is repayable in July 2013. Tax code "N-T".

(q) **Record cheques drawn in July 2011**
Note: First cheque number is "**21**".

1/7   Cash Cheque # 21 drawn to create $600 imprest petty cash float. Tax code "N-T".

7/7   Cheque # 22 – Lease payment to ACDC Finance for $5,379.00 <u>incl. GST</u>. Debit "Lease Payment".

14/7   Cheque # 23 – Paid Loden Motors Pty Ltd $55,000 (<u>which includes GST</u>) for second hand delivery truck. Tax code "CAP".

15/7   Cash Cheque # 24 – Petty Cash re-imbursement for $419.65
Postage .... $81.95 (including the GST)
Travel .... $173.80 (including the GST)
Staff Amenities .... $163.90 (including the GST)

20/7   Cheque # 25 – Paid Australian Taxation Office $9,687.23 ($17,596.40 GST Collected *less* $15,530.65 GST Paid *plus* PAYG Withholding Payable $7,621.48).

21/7   Cheque # 26 – Paid MA Union $180.00. Tax code: "N-T".
Debit "Payroll Deductions Payable".

21/7   Cheque # 27 – Paid CM Superannuation Fund $2,348.20. Tax code: "N-T". Debit "Payroll Deductions Payable".

21/7   Cheque # 28 – Paid IOG Workcover $975.78   Tax code: "N-T"
Debit "Payroll Deductions Payable".

22/7   Cheque # 29 – Paid Hogans Stationery for printing $2,418.68 including the GST.

25/7   Cheque # 30 – Paid for a new laser printer $4,730.00 (incl. GST) purchased from Lightblaster. Debit "Office Equipment".

28/7   Cheque # 31 – Paid Pepi Cosmetics Pty Ltd $329,996.00 for the purchase of the going concern.

(r) **Record money paid to Account Payable in July 2011** (Next cheque # **32**)

31/7   Cheque # 32   Paid Cretian Juices Pty Ltd $8,548.45

Cheque # 33   Paid Davis Manufacturing Pty Ltd $3,260.30

Cheque # 34   Paid Bronco Orchards Pty Ltd $11,225.10

(s) **Record Depreciation for the month of July 2011**

This entry requires a debit to the depreciation expense accounts and a credit to the relevant accumulated depreciation accounts:

Buildings $309.50
Furniture and Fixtures $179.50
Office Equipment...$210.00
Motor Vehicles $676.50

(t) **Complete a Bank Reconciliation as at 31 July 2011**

Complete a bank reconciliation using the Bank Statement from St George Bank dated 31 July 2011 (on the next page). Print the bank reconciliation report at 31/7/2011.

Note: A loan fee on 29/7 is to be debited to "Bank charges" account. Tax code: "**FRE**". The Interest received on 14/7 should have _already_ been recorded on that date from the transaction listed earlier.

(u) **Print (and hand in) the following reports**
     (i)   "Standard Balance Sheet" (as at 31/7/2011)
     (ii)   "Profit & Loss (Accrual)" for July 2011
     (iii) "Bank Reconciliation" report at 31/7/2011 as printed in (t) above.
     (iv)   "Aged Receivables [Detail]" – for July 2011
        (Select _Sales_ report called "Ageing Detail" and enter date as "31/7/2011")
     (v)   Aged Payables [Detail] – for July 2011
        (Select _Purchases_ report called "Ageing Detail" and enter date as "31/7/2011")
     (vi)   "GST [Summary – Accrual]" for 1/7/2011 to 31/7/2011
     (vii) "Item List Summary" (Select "All" Items)
     (viii) Transaction journals for the period 1/5/2010 to 31/7/2011
        (Print all transaction journals as separate reports or alternatively you can use the '_All_' tab to print all journals in a single report.)

St George Bank

Statement for July 2011
31/7/2011

Date	Description	Deposits	Withdrawals	Balance
1/7/2011	Balance B/FWD			$4,029.50 Cr.
	Cheque # 21		$600.00	$3,429.50 Cr.
6/7/2011	Deposit	$7,869.83		$11,299.33 Cr.
9/7/2011	Deposit	$11,148.50		$22,447.83 Cr.
11/7/2011	Cheque # 22		$5,379.00	$17,068.83 Cr.
14/7/2011	Interest on Term Deposit	$38.90		$17,107.73 Cr.
15/7/2011	Cheque # 24		$419.65	$16,688.08 Cr.
17/7/2011	Deposit	$8,512.00		$25,200.08 Cr.
18/7/2011	Deposit	$100,000.00		$125,200.08 Cr.
21/7/2011	Deposit	$5,290.60		$130,490.68 Cr.
	Cheque # 23		$55,000.00	$75,490.68 Cr.
22/7/2011	Deposit	$33,770.75		$109,261.43 Cr.
25/7/2011	Cheque # 27		$2,348.20	$106,913.23 Cr.
	Cheque # 25		$9,687.23	$97,226.00 Cr.
	Cheque # 28		$975.78	$96,250.22 Cr.
28/7/2011	Deposit	$92,400.00		$188,650.22 Cr.
29/7/2011	Deposit	$5,852.00		$194,502.22 Cr.
	Cheque # 30		$4,730.00	$189,772.22 Cr.
	Cheque # 31		$329,996.00	($140,223.78) Dr
	5% Mortgage Loan	$180,000.00		$39,776.22 Cr.
	Cheque # 26		$180.00	$39,596.22 Cr.
	Loan fees		$3,499.10	$36,097.12 Cr.

Note: The loan fee on 29/7/2011 is to be debited to 'Bank charges' account Tax code: **"FRE".**

7.4   Inventory and integration

This business is an engineering consultancy concentrating on problems of pressure in air supply lines. It also supplies and installs a limited range of pressure accelerators. It keeps a small stock of some accelerators and buys in the more expensive ones for specific jobs.

(a) Open the file called **ass74.myo**. The month for this exercise is **July 2011**.

(b) *Select Setup – Company Information* and change the business address to include "Your full name – Assessment 7.4".

(c) **Important:** This exercise will require you to add a number of accounts to those that are already in the *Accounts List*. You are advised to print the existing *Accounts List* first, and then go through the whole exercise to establish which new accounts are required and then add them in to the list *before* starting the exercise (*Recommended*). Alternatively, you can of course add these accounts as you go. You are also required to add cards as necessary.

(d) Print a "Profit and Loss" (include accounts with zero balances) so that you can see how income and expense is to be recorded.

(e) All goods and services in this exercise are taxable supplies with a tax code of "GST".

(f) Enter the following transactions for the month of July 2011:

Reverse accrued expenses at 1 July using the General Journal entry
Note that the salaries and wages for consulting and installation are considered "direct" expenses and are debited to accounts in the *Cost of Sales* section in the *Accounts List*. For this journal entry use "N-T" as the tax code:

Salaries Consulting (5-1100)	$ 350
Salaries Installation (5-2100)	1,700
Salaries & Wages – Administration (6-1120)	1,230
Motor Vehicle Running Expenses (6-1065)	530

Purchases and services on credit.
Use the *Layout* button to select *Item* type purchases for purchase of inventory items, and *Service* type purchases for acquisition of assets and expenses. First purchase # "14008".

Note: All prices are <u>tax-exclusive</u> (price *plus* tax).   ☐ Tax Inclusive

1/7   Sarcom Pumps – 5 AP430 Accelerators @ $840 each plus GST on Invoice # "1145".

4/7   Reynolds & Reynolds – printing and stationery purchased for $410 plus GST.

7/7   Gordon Robotics P/L – Robot Mole $5,200 plus GST (this is not for resale but is equipment used to place accelerators in pipes. Do NOT put this item into inventory – it is a non-current asset. Ignore the warning about using an asset account). Create an asset account "Plant & Equipment" (Tax code: "CAP") and debit it.

13/7   Koshnitsky Pneumatics P/L (New Supplier: 18 Angel Place, Happy Valley, SA 5020. Credit limit = "50,000", Terms 30 days, ABN "18 463 848 216") Invoice # "984": 4 Type 860 Accelerators (Item # AP860) @ $1,100 each plus GST.

18/7   Target Electronics Ltd – 8 AP200 Accelerator @ $550 each plus GST. Change the selling price of this inventory item from $850 to $935 <u>excluding</u> tax. (Inventory command centre – *Set Item Prices*)

21/7   Yeltsin Advertising – Invoice No 332 for production and supply of advertising brochures $2,190 plus GST (debit advertising expense).

28/7   Sarcom Pumps – 4 AP430 Accelerators @ $840 each plus GST on Invoice # "1150".

Sales Invoices for July (use 'Item' invoice layout)

Sales invoices are to show tax-inclusive sales prices:

4/7   Dorf Plumbing Supplies P/L – Invoice Number is "786"
Supply and Installation of: 4 AP430 Accelerators and 24 hours installation.

7/7   Tye Piping Company – 10 hours consulting

11/7   Hagar Pumping P/L – 6 hours consulting

15/7   P.G.A. Plastics P/L – Supply and installation of:
2 AP860 Accelerators and 40 hours installation

18/7   Hagar Pumping P/L – Supply and installation of:
4 AP860 accelerators and 56 hours Installation

20/7   Elcom P/L (New customer: 323 Castlereagh St, Sydney. Credit Limit: "10000", Terms 30 days, ABN 30 848 163 557) – 32 hours consulting and design

25/7   AJS Compressed Air (New customer: 34 Ridgeway Street, Newcastle 2300) – supply and installation of: 8 AP200 accelerators and 42 hours installation. The customer paid in full by cheque# "00012". Enter the total in the 'Paid Today' field.

Money received in July

(Use *Receive Payments* option in the *Sales* command centre to record customer payments and *Receive Money* option in the *Banking* command centre for other receipts.)

1/7   P.G.A. Plastics P/L – $11,700 for Invoice No 784

4/7   Refund of a deposit on tender $1,000 received from State Rail (credit the account called "Deposits on Tenders" and tax code "N-T")

7/7   National Bank Loan $15,000. Re-payable $5,000 on 31 March 2012 and remainder on 31 March 2013 (tax code "N-T")

15/7   Dorf Plumbing Supplies – $4,200

18/7   Tye Piping Company – $5,000 on account

25/7   Dorf Plumbing Supplies – $7,867.20

29/7   Additional capital $5,000

(Money received – continued on the next page)

29/7   Sold used printer for $550 ($500 plus $50 GST). Original cost was $3,600 and accumulated depreciation to date is $2,800 (i.e. loss on disposal is $300).

> **Hint:**   Use *Receive Money* from the *Banking* command centre.
> Un-tick 'Tax Inclusive' box before entering these amounts:
>
> **Note:** to debit an account in *Receive Money* enter the amount as **negative**.
>
> Debit the loss on disposal account (i.e. minus –$300) tax code "GST" debit "Accum. Dep. Office Equipment " (i.e. minus. –$2800) tax "GST" and credit "Office Equipment" $3600. Tax code "GST".

Money paid in July. Tax codes are "N-T" unless GST is stated as being involved.

4/7   Cash cheque for fortnight's salaries and wages $3,495 as follows:

Gross:			
	Consulting (5-1100)	$550	
	Installation (5-2100)	2,400	
	Administration (6-1120)	1,760	$4,710
Less:			
	PAYG Withholding Payable (2-1310)		–1,130
	PMA Superannuation (2-1330)		–85

> **Note:**   Debit the gross salaries and wages for consulting and installation to the cost of sales section and the gross wages for administration to expenses. Enter the PAYG Withholdings Payable and superannuation as negative (**minus** amounts) so that they are credited to the liability accounts.

7/7   Paid PAYG Withholdings Payable $2,280 to ATO

8/7   Paid Sarcom Pumps $2,500

11/7   Petty Cash re-imbursement $250 including any GST as follows:

Postage		$88	(Incl. GST)
Stationery		110	(Incl. GST)
Staff Amenities Expense		30	(GST-free)
Travel		22	(Incl. GST)

14/7   Paid Desmond Compressors amount owing
Paid Mobil Castle Hill $583 (incl. GST) for petrol (Motor Vehicle Running)

18/7   Cash cheque for fortnight's salaries and wages $2,747 as follows:

Gross:			
	Consulting	$250	
	Installation	1,750	
	Administration	1,680	3,680
Less:			
	PAYG Withholdings Payable		–848
	PMA Superannuation		–85

28/7   Purchased a Flat-bed Plotter for office from Printers Galore Pty Ltd $6,820 including the GST. (Debit Office Equipment. Tax code is "CAP").

28/7   Paid Target Electronics $3,600
Paid Gordon Robotics $800

29/7   Paid Energetic County Council $330 (including GST) for electricity

29/7   Loan (staff advance) made to Joan Teo, a staff member $1,000
(Tax code: "N-T")

End of Month adjustments (no GST involved – Tax code: "N-T")

Accrued Salaries and Wages	Consulting	$800
	Installation	$1,680
	Administration	$1,400

Accrued Expenses:

| Motor Vehicle expenses | $410 |
| Telephone expenses | $270 |

Depreciation:

Plant and equipment	$43
Office equipment	$155
Motor Vehicle	$400

Create a provision for doubtful debts of $1,000. Make sure that you re-design the Balance Sheet to account for this provision (add a header and adjust the levels).

Record July's insurance expense $300.

This business uses *Standing Journals* to account for prepaid expenses. It will be necessary to write off $300 from 'Prepaid Insurance' (i.e. debit *Insurance 6-1060* expense and credit *Prepaid Insurance 1-1400* – Tax code for this adjustment transaction is "N-T").

Hint: This transaction has already been saved as recurring. You can select this recurring transaction from the *Use Recurring* list, change the transaction date to 31/7/2011, and record it.

(g)   **Print the following reports:**

"Standard Balance Sheet" as at 31 July 2011

"Profit & Loss [Accrual]" for July 2011

"Aged Receivables (Detail)" as at 31 July 2011
         (Select *Sales* report called "Ageing Detail")

"Aged Payables (Detail)" as at 31 July 2011
         (Select *Purchases* report called '*Ageing Detail*')

Transaction details for the general ledger account 'Prepaid Insurance' for the period 1/7/2011 to 31/7/2011. (Click on *Find Transactions* then *Account* tab – select account, enter date range and print)

"GST [Summary – Accrual]" report for July 2011

"Item List Summary"

Transaction journals for July 2011:
         (Print all transaction journals as separate reports or alternatively you can use the '*All*' tab to print all journals in a single report.)

Chapter 7: Answers to self-test exercises

7.1

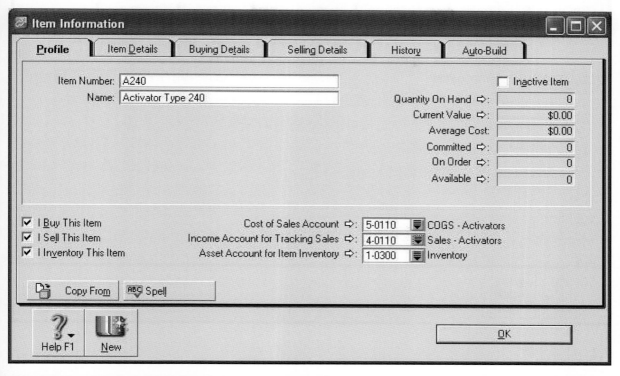

7.1 *(continued)*

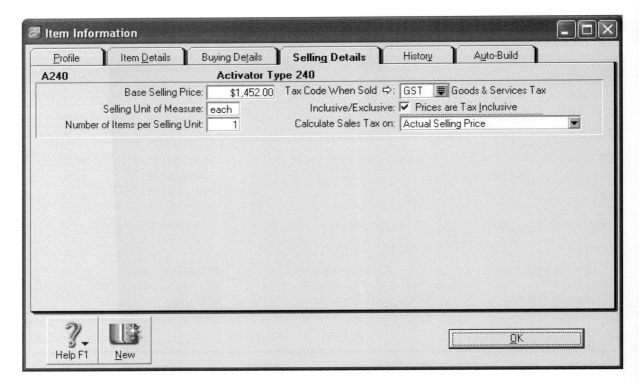

7.2

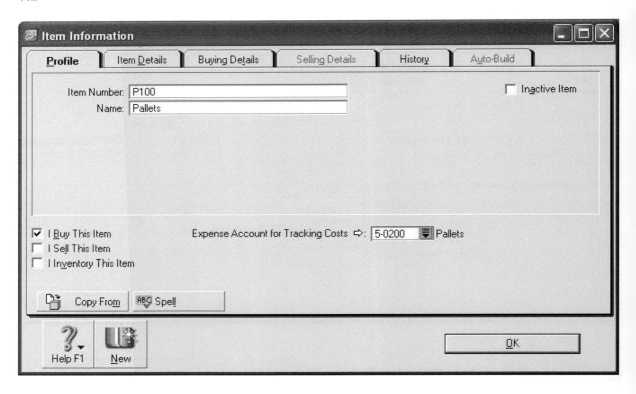

7.2 *(continued)*

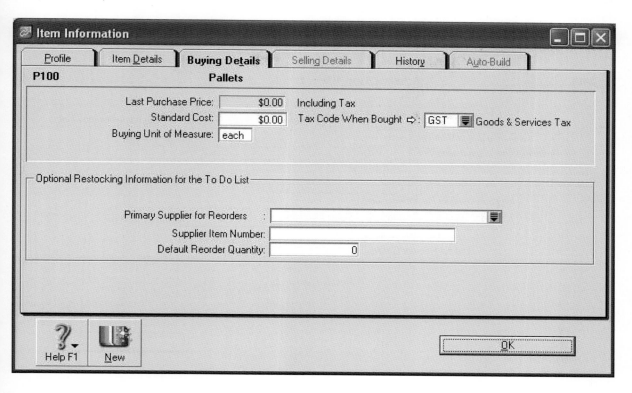

7.3

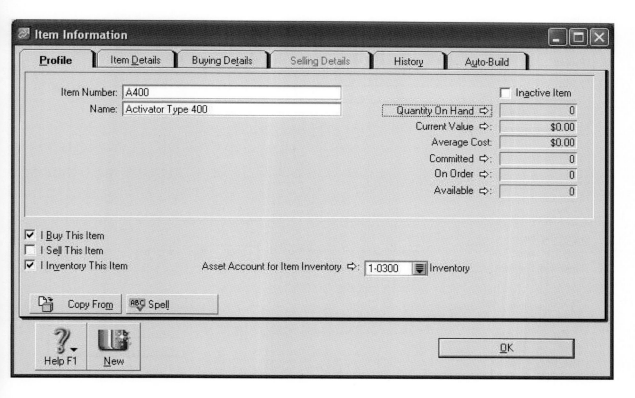

7.3 *(continued)*

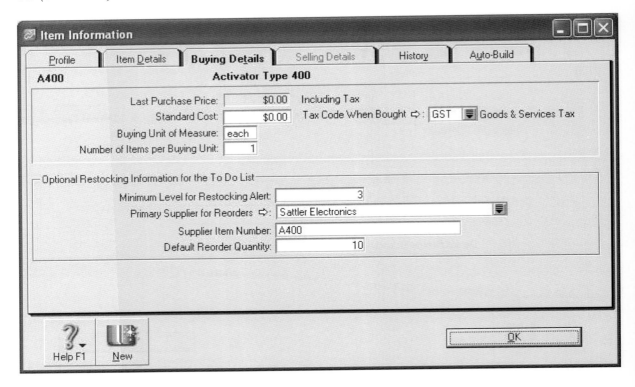

7.4

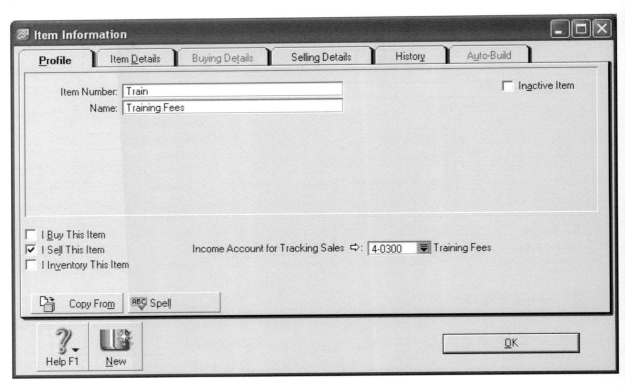

7.4 *(continued)*

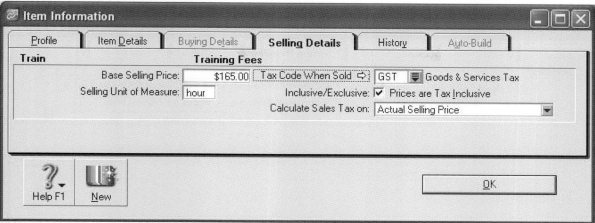

7.5

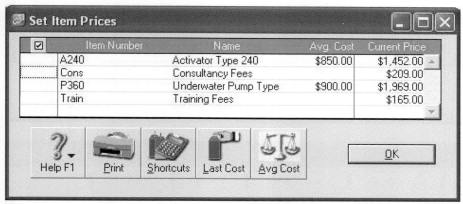

7.6

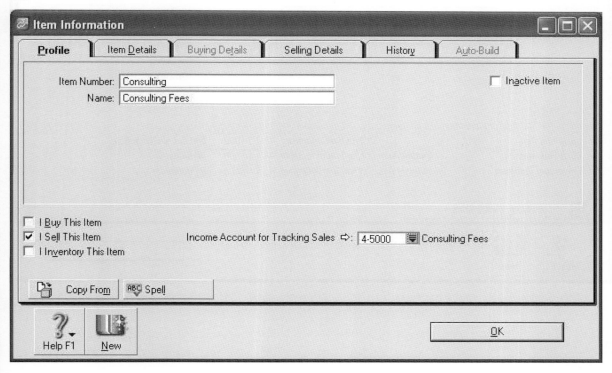

7.6 *(continued)*

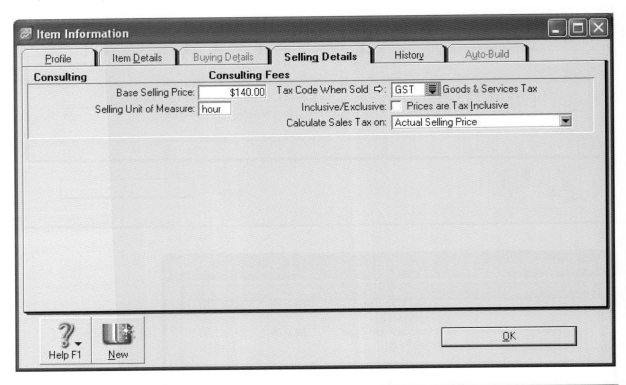

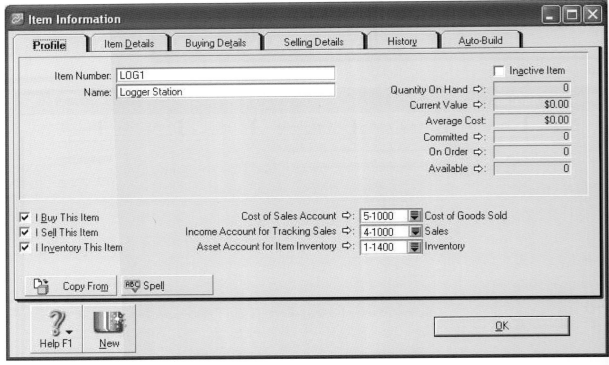

7.6 *(continued)*

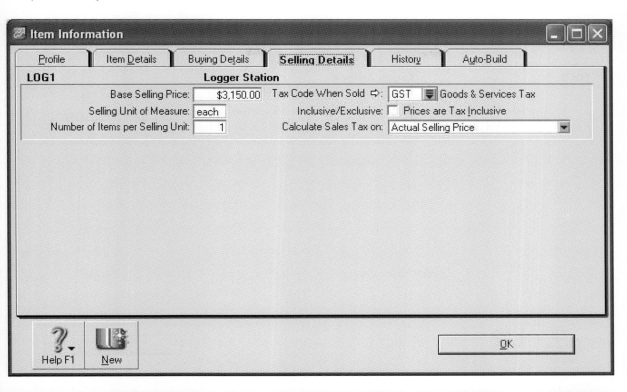

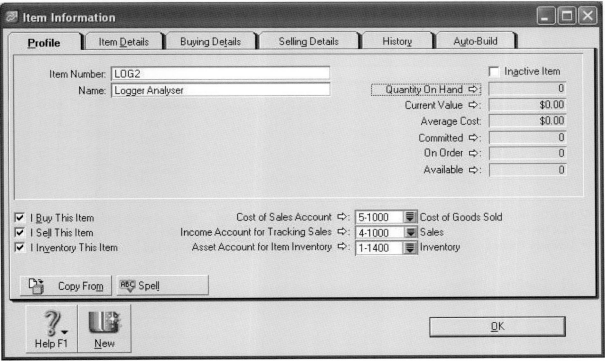

7.6 *(continued)*

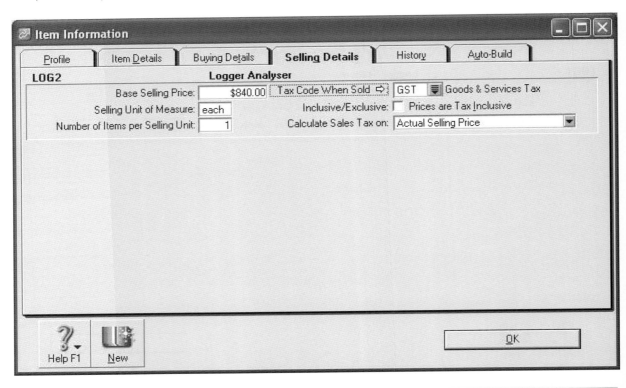

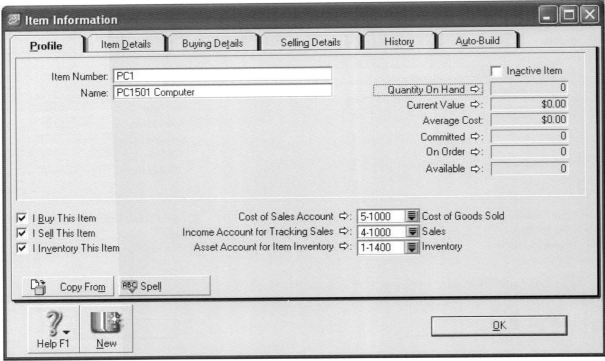

7.6 *(continued)*

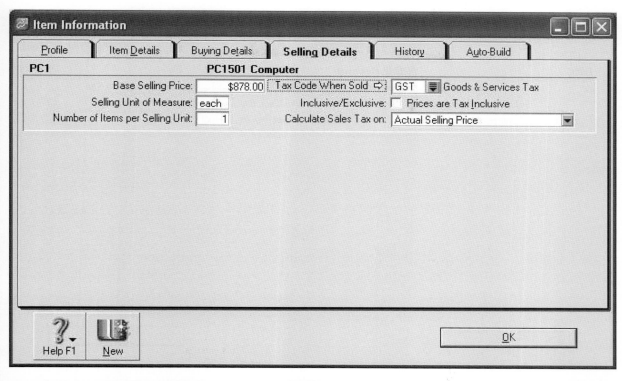

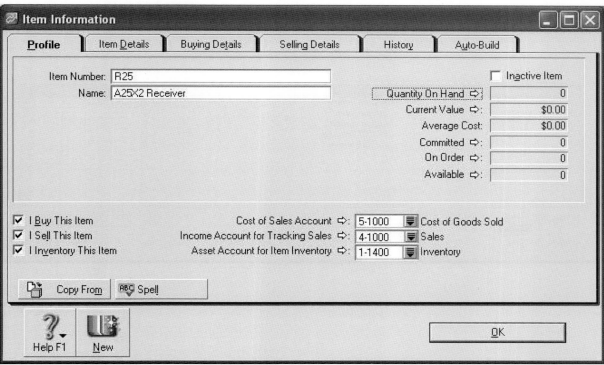

7.6 *(continued)*

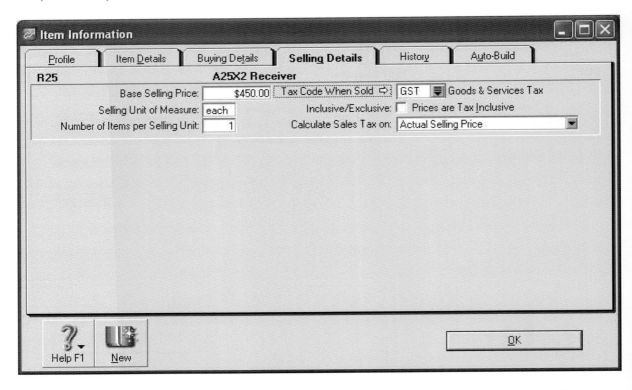

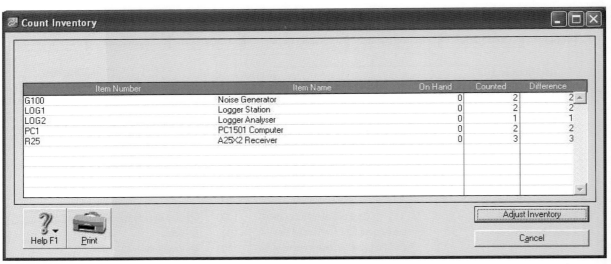

7.6 *(continued)*

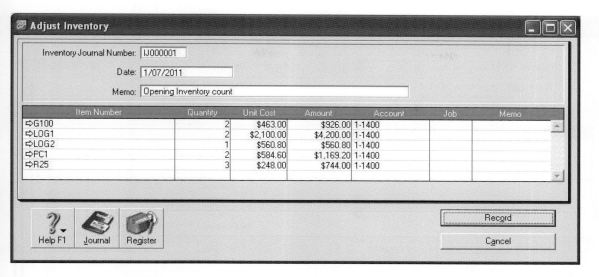

Items List [Summary]

Item #	Item Name	Supplier	Units On Hand	Total Value	Average Cost	Current Price
Consulting	Consulting Fees		0	$0.00	$0.00	$140.00
G100	Noise Generator		2	$926.00	$463.00	$780.00
LOG1	Logger Station		2	$4,200.00	$2,100.00	$3,150.00
LOG2	Logger Analyser		1	$560.80	$560.80	$840.00
PC1	PC1501 Computer		2	$1,169.20	$584.60	$878.00
R25	A25X2 Receiver		3	$744.00	$248.00	$450.00
			Grand Total:	$7,600.00		

7.7

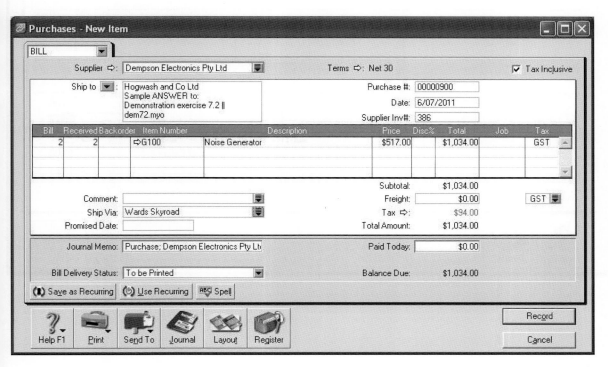

7.7 *(continued)*

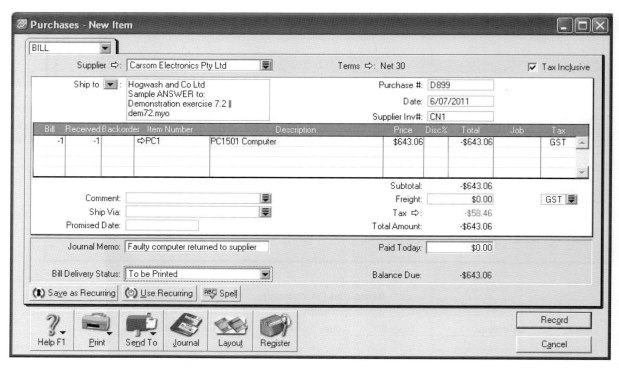

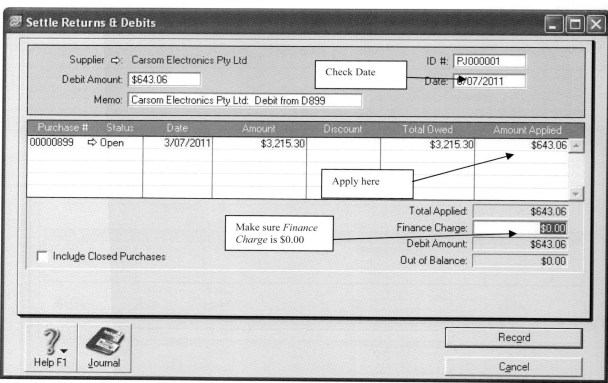

7.8

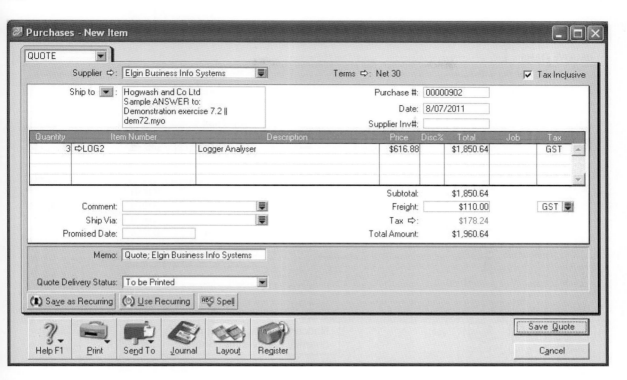

7.9

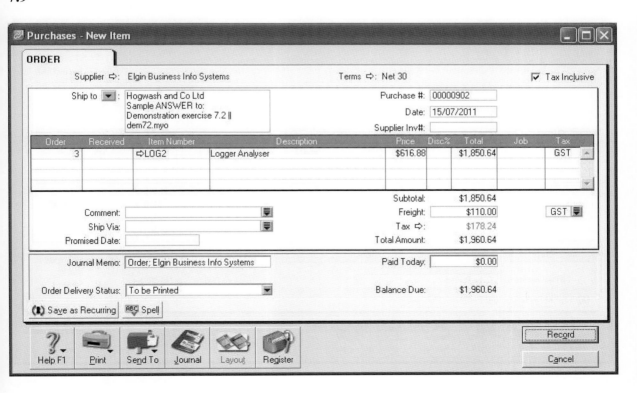

7.10

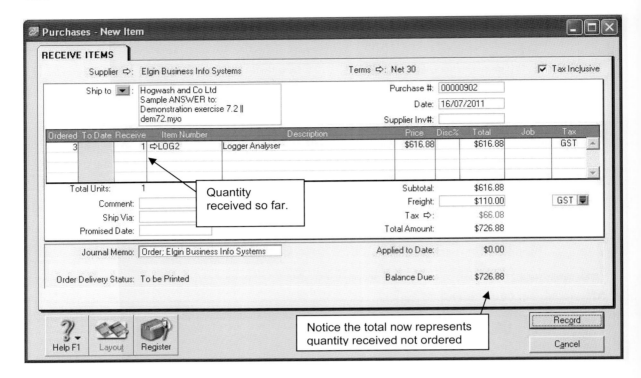

7.11

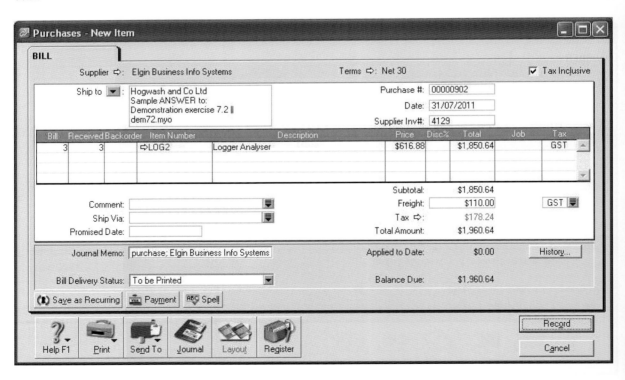

7.12

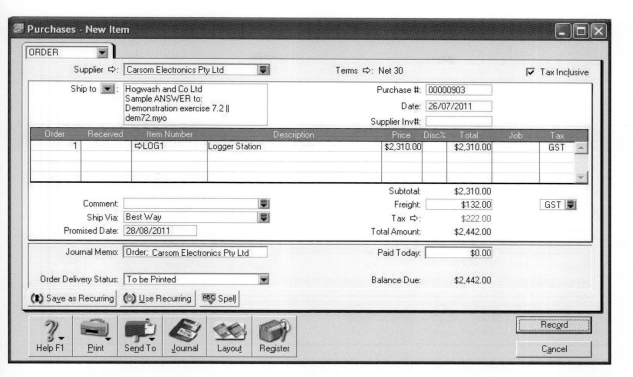

7.13

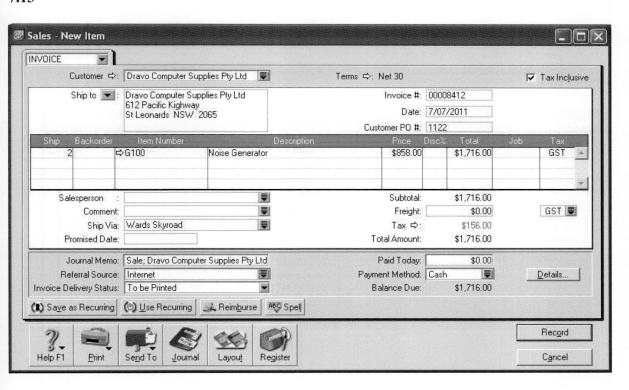

7.13 *(continued)*

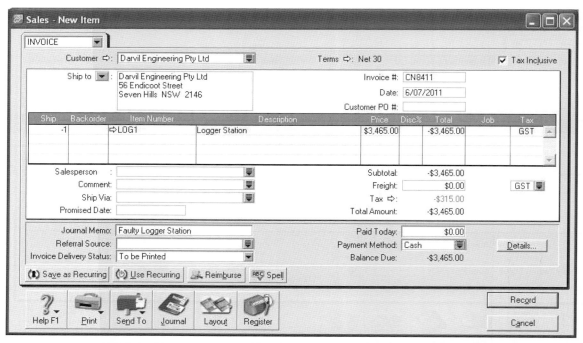

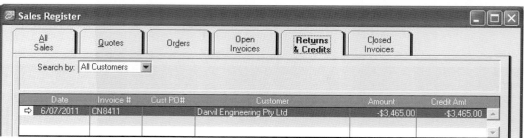

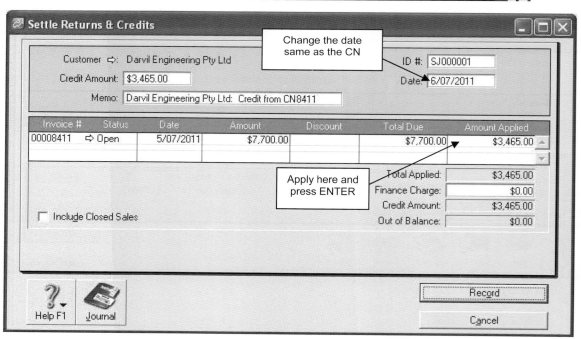

7.14

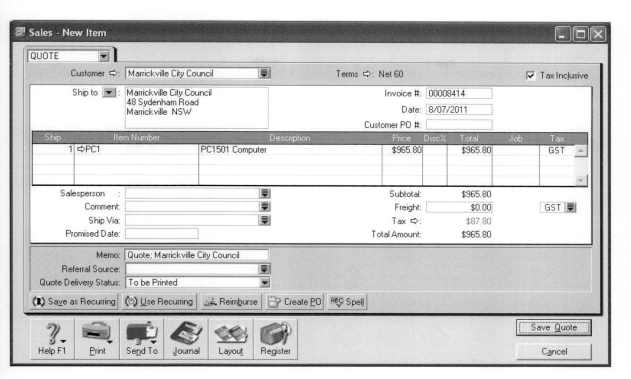

7.15

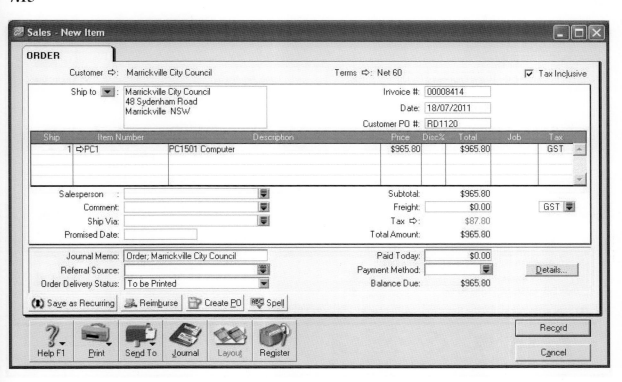

7.16

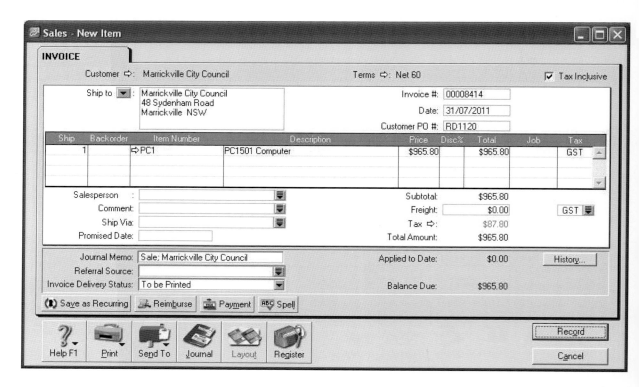

7.17

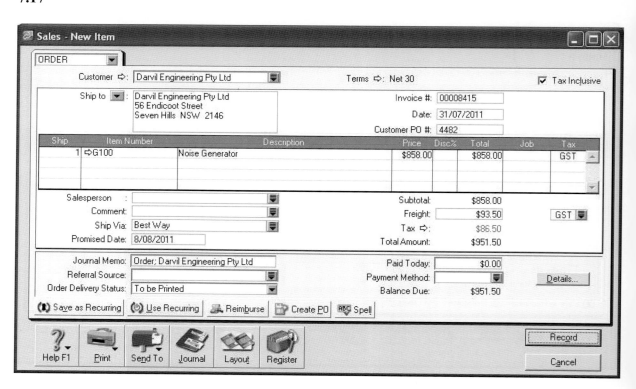

7.18

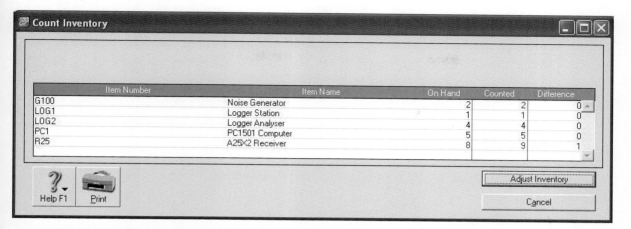

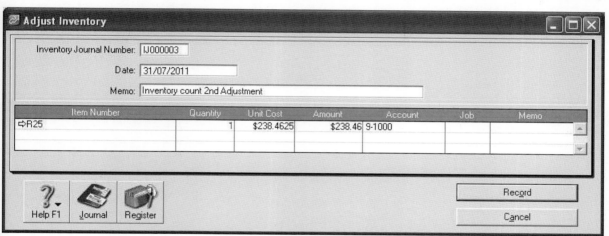

7.19

Analyse Inventory [Summary]

Page 1

Item #	Item Name	On Hand	Committed	On Order	Available
Consulting	Consulting Fees	0	0	0	0
G100	Noise Generator	2	1	0	1
LOG1	Logger Station	1	0	1	2
LOG2	Logger Analyser	4	0	0	4
PC1	PC1501 Computer	5	0	0	5
R25	A25X2 Receiver	9	0	0	9

Payroll

8

Setting up employee and payroll information.
Paying employees and payroll liabilities.
Printing payment summaries and other reports.

After completing this chapter you will be able to:

1   Set up a payroll in *MYOB AccountRight Plus*.

2   Enter general payroll and employee information.

3   Set up wage categories, deduction types, allowances and employer expenses.

4   Record recurring payroll details for each employee.

5   Prepare a weekly payroll with adjustments for overtime, annual leave and sick leave.

6   Pay monthly or quarterly payroll liabilities.

7   Produce payslips, payroll summaries, payment summaries (*group tax certificates*) and analysis reports.

8   Produce various customised payroll reports detailed or summarised.

Introduction

The payroll module in *MYOB AccountRight Plus* is specifically set up for Australia's industrial policy and income tax system. It is fully functional and can do <u>most</u> of the necessary jobs that more expensive "off-the-shelf" payroll systems perform.

The notes, examples and exercises that follow assume a basic knowledge of payroll accounting, that you have read through the instructions in Chapter 1, and that you can:

- Start the *MYOB AccountRight Plus* application;
- Change the business name and/or address;
- Select command centres and options within those command centres; and
- Recognise the conventions used in this book (for example, the sign ↵ is an instruction to tap the *ENTER* key).

In this chapter the authors have elected to use accounts selected and listed by account names rather than by account numbers. Throughout this book, you may choose and use whichever option you prefer.

For <u>ALL</u> the exercises in this chapter, open the data files (demonstrations and assessments) by signing on as the "Administrator" without a password.

Self-test exercise 8.1

Start *MYOB AccountRight Plus*.

Open the file dem81.myo and sign on as the "Administrator" without a password.

Change the company information by entering your name in the address field.

If you are not sure how to start *MYOB AccountRight Plus* and open an existing file or change the company information, refer to the 'How to …' instructions for Chapter 1 (look up the index of the 'How to …' instructions at the front of this book).

TAX TABLE:
MYOB AccountRight Plus is constantly updating the tax tables as new rates or changes take place.
The revision date for the *Tax Tables* used in the exercises in this chapter is 1/7/2014.
If your answers have tax figures that are different from those figures given in this chapter, this <u>may</u> indicate that the tax tables installed on the computer system you are using are different from the one used by the authors at the time of writing this text. Of course, if your tax figures are different then your *Net Pay* figures will also be different.

Gross pay, deductions and net pay

The amount to be paid to an employee for a period of time (the payroll period) is the gross pay earned less deductions. Examples of these deductions are the Income tax PAYG (*Pay As You Go*) salary deductions and other deductions required by the employee such as union dues, voluntary superannuation and medical benefit fund contributions.

It is important to understand that the salary or wages cost to a business is the *Gross* salary or wages earned by the employee, plus other expenses required to be paid for or on behalf of the employee or as a consequence of their employment such as *SGC* superannuation, *WorkCover* insurance, fringe benefits, tax on fringe benefits, training and any state payroll tax.

The gross wages paid to an employee will include the wages earned for the period as well as any other payments due to the employee including **allowances** such as overtime, sick or holiday pay, uniforms, housing, motor vehicle running expenses and **incentive pays** such as bonuses and commissions. *Wages* is the term used by *MYOB AccountRight Plus* to refer to any of these payments to employees. These wages may be calculated on an *hourly* or *salary* basis.

Employees are entitled to receive certain benefits as stated in their awards or employment agreements. Certain benefits such as holiday pay and sick pay are calculated per annum and therefore each pay period they accumulate a proportion of the total entitlement. The **entitlements** to these specific benefits are earned as their employment progresses, that is, the longer they are employed the more benefits they will accumulate. When a benefit is received, such accumulated balance is reduced by the amount of benefit taken (accrued less paid). *MYOB AccountRight Plus* can be set to calculate and keep track of these accrued benefits in one of the entitlements categories. When these entitlements are subsequently paid to the employee one of the corresponding wages categories is used. To keep track of the balances of each entitlement the relevant category is usually linked to the corresponding wages category. For example "Holiday Leave Accrual" (entitlements category) is linked to the "Holiday Pay" (wages category), so when a holiday is taken the entitlement is reduced accordingly.

Deductions from the gross wages are handled by two payroll categories: **Deductions** and **Taxes**. The tax deductions are calculated and withheld in a liability account and in due course remitted to the Australian Taxation Office (ATO). Other deductions from the gross pay are <u>generally</u> made as requested by the employee on behalf of external parties (for example: union dues and medical fund). Again these amounts withheld must be kept in a liability account and subsequently paid over to those external parties.

Superannuation category is a category that lists all superannuation entries. It combines <u>both</u> superannuation **expenses** <u>and</u> superannuation **deductions**. The superannuation <u>expenses</u> are those paid for by the **employer** on behalf of the employee and superannuation <u>deductions</u> are those that are deducted from the **employee's** pay.

The net pay (Gross Wages less Deductions) is then paid to the employee. Paying employees can take many different forms such as: cash, cheque, direct debt and electronic fund transfers.

The accounting entries for a payroll period for an employee will follow the scheme in Figure 8.1 below.

Gross wages		600.00	Debit Wage Expense account
Less: Deductions:			
PAYG Tax	132.00		Credit liability account for PAYG tax
Union fees	18.50		Credit liability account for the union
Medicare	24.50		Credit liability account for medical benefit
Staff loan	50.00		Credit the staff loan account (an asset)
Total deductions		−225.00	
Net Pay		$375.00	Credit bank – amount paid to employee.

Figure 8.1: Example of general accounting entries for a wage payment

An employer may also be required (or elect) to pay other ***expenses*** related to a person's employment. *WorkCover* insurance is an example of such expense. Unlike deductions these amounts are not deducted from the employee's gross pay but rather they are additional expenses paid by the employer. These amounts are not paid to the employee but paid on behalf of or for the benefit of the employee to third parties. These amounts are calculated and debited to the appropriate expense accounts and credited to a liability account and subsequently paid out. When this is payable, the payroll system is set up to carry out the accounting entry similar to the one shown in Figure 8.2:

WorkCover Insurance expense	48.00		Debit an Expense account
Payroll Withholdings		48.00	Credit a Current Liability account

Figure 8.2: Example of the accounting entry for the expense category

The above ***wages***, ***superannuation***, ***entitlements***, ***deductions***, ***expenses*** and ***taxes*** represent the six payroll categories used by *MYOB AccountRight Plus*.

PAYG and the 'Activity Statement'

The employer is required by law to deduct tax before paying the employee. This deduction is calculated using tax tables provided from time to time by MYOB and based on specific ATO formulas. The amount of income tax deduction is not only based on the amount of wages paid but also on each employee's circumstances. An employee might or might not have quoted a Tax File Number (TFN), desire to claim the general tax exemption if this is his or her main employer and whether there are other amounts to be taken into consideration such as entitlement to tax rebates or the employee wishes to pay extra amounts of tax. These tax deductions must be kept in a liability account and paid to the taxation department (ATO), usually every three months. If the amount of Pay As You Go tax (PAYG) withheld by the business per annum is substantially high, this period could be altered to monthly or weekly. A special form (an activity statement) is used to report the amount of wages paid and the PAYG deductions made. This *activity statement* can be one of two main types: a *Business Activity Statement* (BAS) if the business or *entity* is registered for GST, otherwise the business uses an *Instalment Activity Statement*. These forms are used to report to the taxation department PAYG deductions from wages, PAYG withholding (amounts withheld from others and payable to ATO), the business's own PAYG tax instalments and any Fringe Benefit Tax payable. If the business is registered for GST they will use the same form (BAS) to report their GST obligations.

At the end of the financial year the employer is required to prepare and issue a **Payment Summary** for each employee. This summary must show (among other things) the total gross payments made during the year as well as the total amount of income tax deducted (withheld and paid to ATO). In some circumstances (beyond the scope of this book) the employer will be required to report amounts of any *reportable* fringe benefit made to the employee. The employee uses this *Payment Summary* to complete his or her own annual income tax return. These *Payment Summaries* replace the old *Group Certificates* for all payments made after 1 July 2000.

The payroll system for *MYOB AccountRight Plus*

The *MYOB AccountRight Plus* payroll system follows the general operations common to most computerised payroll systems. The five main steps are:

1. Setting up the payroll system and categories.
2. Setting up individual employee records and standard pays.
3. Paying the employees each pay period.
4. Paying the payroll liabilities.
5. Carrying out end of year functions.

Setting up the payroll system and payroll categories

It is extremely important to set up the payroll system correctly. This can be fairly time consuming, but once the payroll is set up correctly very little work is involved from then on. The steps in setting up the payroll system are:

1. Loading the tax tables so that the correct amount of income tax is deducted from the employees' pay;
2. Setting (or modifying) the payroll link (default) accounts to the general ledger;
3. Recording the general *Payroll Information* (e.g. the payroll year, the default weekly hours, the rounding of net pays, entering in the *Withholder Payer Number*, nominating the default superannuation fund and the employer's bank's details);
4. Creating employees' records (cards) with all their personal details and payroll information such as default entitlements (standard pay) and bank details;
5. Adding or editing an existing **Wages** category. Wages categories are used to establish the rates of pay (for example, an overtime wage category may be paid at 1.5 times the normal pay rate), to select the employees who will be entitled to receive a wage category, and to establish whether a particular category is or is not exempt from tax or deductions;
6. Adding or editing (modifying) existing **Entitlements** categories;
7. Adding or editing the default **Deductions** that may be applied to an employee;
8. Setting up the employer **Expense** categories (for example, the employer may be required to contribute to an industry superannuation scheme based on the employee's normal salary).

How to load tax tables for an existing business

Step	Instruction
1	Select the *Setup* pull-down menu at the top of the screen.
2	Select the *Load Payroll Tax Tables*.
3	Click on the *Load Tax Tables* button.

Example 8.1—Loading a tax table

1. Start *MYOB AccountRight Plus*.
2. Open an existing file called dem81.myo. Throughout this chapter you should sign on as the "Administrator" without a password.
3. Select the *Setup* pull-down menu.
4. Select the *Load Payroll Tax Tables* menu item. The *Load Tax Tables* window is displayed as shown in Figure 8.3:

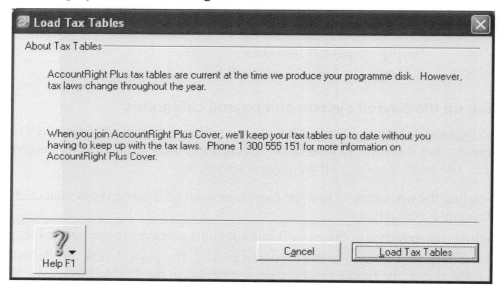

Figure 8.3: The *Load Tax Tables* window

5. Click on the *Load Tax Tables* button.

Video: A video showing you how to load the tax tables is on the DVD

The second task is setting up the payroll linked accounts. This task requires some accounting knowledge. It requires nominating six **default** general ledger accounts to be used by *MYOB AccountRight Plus* to record payroll transactions in the general ledger.

How to set up or edit the payroll linked accounts

Step	Instruction
1	Select the *Setup* pull-down menu at the top of the screen.
2	Select the *Linked Accounts* menu item.
3	Select the *Payroll Accounts* sub-menu item.
4	**If setting up the links**, enter the six <u>*default*</u> general ledger accounts to be linked with payroll to record payroll transactions. **If editing** the linked accounts, modify or change any of the six accounts.
5	Enter or edit the three bank accounts that will be used to record payroll cash payments, cheque payments and electronic payments ↵. **Note:** A bank account can be linked to more than one type of payment.
6	Enter or edit an expense account to record employer expenses (other than wages) such as SGC superannuation and *WorkCover* ↵.
7	Enter or edit a wages expense account to record the gross wages including base salaries and wages, allowances and incentives ↵.
8	Enter or edit a <u>liability</u> account to record the amounts of deductions withheld and payable to third parties ↵.
9	Click the *OK* button.

For the purpose of this exercise the payroll linked accounts are already set up as shown in Figure 8.4 (check these with the file you have and edit any account, as necessary):

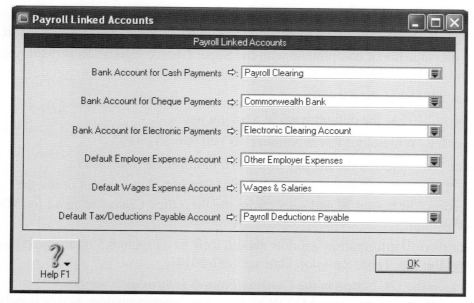

Figure 8.4: *Payroll Linked Accounts* set up in file dem81.myo

Note: If you choose to display accounts <u>by their numbers</u> rather than their names, then the linked account numbers are (from top down): **1-1120, 1-1110, 1-1165, 6-5150, 6-5130** and **2-1410.**

General payroll information

The third task, once the tax table has been loaded and the linked accounts are set up, is to enter the "general payroll information".

How to set up the general payroll information

Step	Instruction
1	Select the *Setup* pull-down menu at the top of the screen.
2	Select the *General Payroll Information* option. (If a message about compliance with the Super Choice legislation is displayed, read it and click the *OK* button.)
3	Enter the year in which the payroll year ends.
4	Enter the default weekly hours to be worked. These hours will also be used to calculate annual salaried employees' pays.
5	Type in the Australian Tax Office *Withholder Payer Number* for the business (if not available leave blank).
6	If pays are to be rounded down to a multiple of cents, enter this amount.
7	Enter the default superannuation fund. (If a message regarding 'MYOB M-Powered' opens, click *Cancel* to continue or *Tell Me More* to read it.)
8	Click the *OK* button. A verification notice will be shown regarding the payroll year-end. Click on the *OK* button to accept.

Example 8.2—Setting up the general payroll information

1. Open the file called dem81.myo if it is not already open.
2. Select the *Setup* pull-down menu and the *General Payroll Information* menu item.
3. If a message about compliance with the Super Choice legislation is displayed, read it and click the *OK* button to continue.
4. Enter "2015" as the payroll year-end ↵.
5. Type in "40" as the default weekly working hours ↵.
6. Enter the 'Withholder Payer Number' as "00 096 341 419" ↵.
7. Enter "10" to round the net pay down to a multiple of 10 cents ↵.
8. The 'Default Superannuation Fund' is "AMP Life". Type this in or use the selection *List* button ▼ and select from the list. Click *Cancel* to an ad for MYOB M-Powered.
9. Your payroll information window should look like Figure 8.5 on the next page **Note**: the Tax Table Revision Date is '1/07/2014'.
10. Click on the *OK* button in the *General Payroll Information* window.
Cancel the message about MYOB M-Powered superannuation, as this is only available for registered users.
11. Accept the verification notice (make sure the current payroll year is 2015). Click the *OK* button otherwise click the *Cancel* button and fix any errors before continuing.

Figure 8.5: The General Payroll Information window

Video: A video showing how to set up payroll general information is on the DVD

Setting up individual employee records (cards) and standard pays

Each employee to be paid needs to have a card. A card in *MYOB AccountRight Plus* is used to record relatively permanent data about customers, suppliers, employees and contacts. Cards have already been used for accounts receivable and accounts payable in previous chapters. For employees, the standard payroll information can also be entered from the *Card File* command centre.

In Example 8.3, following the 'How to …', steps are used to create an employee card for Peter Tomakos. The main payroll and tax information will also be entered:

How to set up or edit employee payroll information

Step	Instruction
1	Select the *Card File* command centre.
2	Select the *Cards List* option.
3	Select the *Employee* tab at the top of the *Cards List* window.
4	Click on the *New* icon button to add a <u>new</u> employee card
	(or click on the detail arrow ⇨ to edit an <u>existing</u> employee card).
5	The *Profile* tab should be the default view.
	(continued on the next page)

Step	Instruction
6	Select "Individual" for the 'Designation' and enter the employee's last name ⏎ and enter first names ⏎ (**refer to the exercise for these details**).
7	Enter 'Card ID' (optional) up to 15 characters as an identifier.
8	Select "Address 1" for 'Location' and enter the employee's address details. **Note**: You can enter up to five addresses. For most employees we usually only need one address. If there is more than one address select "Address 2" through "Address 5" and enter an address for each location. **IMPORTANT:** In the 'Address' field, press *ENTER* to move to the next line of the address field and press *TAB* to exit this field and move to the next.
9	Enter phone (or extension) and fax numbers (if available) ⏎.
10	Enter the employee's internet or intranet email address (if available) ⏎.
11	Enter employee's website address (if available) ⏎.
12	Enter a salutation (optional) for use in form letters or memorandums (for example, if you enter "Jill", the salutation in a letter will read "Dear Jill"). If the salutation field is left blank then the full name on the card will be used in the letter, e.g. "Dear Jill Smith".
13	Select the *Card Details* tab. In this section enter any personal details in the 'Notes:' field, e.g. next of kin, qualifications, employment history, medical problems, general remarks or comments etc. But be aware that the content of this field will be printed on some reports (e.g. Pay Slips!).
14	[Identifiers...] If used, an identifier (A to Z) can be entered for each employee. These are <u>user set</u> identifiers which can be used to group employees according to departments, grades, branches, position or awards etc.
15	Select the *Payment Details* tab. Use the down arrow and select a 'Payment Method' (Cash, Cheque or Electronic). For "Cash" or "Cheque" methods no additional information is necessary. If an employee is to be paid electronically by direct deposit, enter the number of bank accounts to which a pay will be allocated. For *each* bank account, enter the bank details (BSB, Account Number, Account Name, Percentage of net pay or Dollar amount to be deposited in each account and any text to be printed on the employee's statement).
16	Select the *Payroll Details* tab. In this section payroll details can be entered for each employee. There are ten items of payroll details listed on the left-hand side panel. Click on each of these names to select it and complete the information in the fields displayed on the right panel.
17	The first item *Personal Details* should be selected by default. Enter in or select the employee's 'Date of Birth' (the age will be calculated and shown), 'Gender', 'Start Date', 'Employment Basis', 'Employment Category', 'Employment Status' and 'Employment Classification'.

(continued on the next page)

Step	Instruction
18	Click on the second *Payroll Details* item called *Wages*. For the 'Pay Basis' select either "Salary" or "Hourly" and enter the annual salary amount if the employee is paid a salary, otherwise enter an hourly rate and ↵. Accept or change the default 'Pay Frequency' ↵, 'Hours in Weekly Pay Period' ↵ and 'Wages Expense Account'. You can also click (tick) in the left-hand column against any of the "wage categories" that the employee is entitled to.
19	Click on the next *Payroll Details* item called *Superannuation*. If the superannuation fund is not already set, use the *List* button ▼ at the end of the 'Superannuation Fund' field and select the fund (or click on the *New* button and add a fund). TAB twice and type in the 'Employee Membership #'. Click in the left-hand column against the superannuation type that the employee is entitled to or is contributing to.
20	Click on the next *Payroll Details* item called *Entitlements*. Click in the left-hand column against the types of entitlements affecting the employee. Usually, <u>most</u> full-time employees would be entitled to both holiday leave (with or without loading) and sick leave.
21	Click on the next *Payroll Details* item called *Deductions*. Click in the left-hand column against any deductions made from the employee's gross pay.
22	Click on the next *Payroll Details* item called *Employer Expenses*. Click in the left-hand column against the expenses that the employer incurs. This will usually include *WorkCover*, but for particular industries and workplace agreements there may be others.
23	Click on the next *Payroll Details* item called *Taxes*. Click in the 'Tax File Number' field and enter the employee's number ↵. Use the *List* button at the end of the 'Tax Table' field and select the tax table applicable to the employee. In the 'Total Rebates' field enter the dollar value of any rebates claimed by the employee. In the 'Extra Tax' field enter any amount the employee has requested to pay as extra tax. The "PAYG Withholding" tax type should already be selected (ticked in the left-hand column of tax types).
24	Click on the next *Payroll Details* item called *Standard Pay*. Confirm that changes made are correct or click on *Reset to Original Amounts*.
25	Click on the next *Payroll Details* item called *Pay History*. Select a month, quarter or year to date using the drop-down arrow at the end of the 'Show Pay History for' and enter in details for each category. This should be done after all categories have been set up (see later).
26	If the business charges customers on an employee's time basis, click on the *Payroll Details* item called *Time Billing*. Enter the dollar amount to charge a client and the cost per hour for this employee.
27	Click the *OK* button to complete the set up for the employee.

Example 8.3—Setting up employee payroll information

1. Open the file called dem81.myo if it is not already open.

2. Select the *Card File* command centre.

3. Select the *Cards List* option.

4. Select the *Employee* tab at the top of the *Cards List* window.

5. Click on the *New* icon button then select *Individual* for the 'Designation' field.

6. Enter "Tomakos" as the employee's last name, TAB and enter "Peter" as the first name ↵.

7. Enter "E001" in the 'Card ID' field ↵, and leave the 'Location' as 'Address 1' ↵.

8. Type in "46 Masonview Place" as the address and TAB.

9. Enter the city as "BAULKHAM HILLS" ↵, the state as "NSW" ↵ and the postcode as "2153" ↵.

10. Either enter the country as "AUSTRALIA" or leave this field blank ↵.

11. Enter the phone number as "(02) 9680 9999" ↵. Skip the next three fields, as Peter Tomakos has no 'Phone #2', 'Phone #3' or 'Fax' ↵.

12. Enter the email address as "tomo@selltel.com.au". ↵.

13. Skip the 'Website' field in this example ↵.

14. Type in "Peter" for the salutation ↵. Your *Card Information* window under the *Profile* tab should look like Figure 8.6:

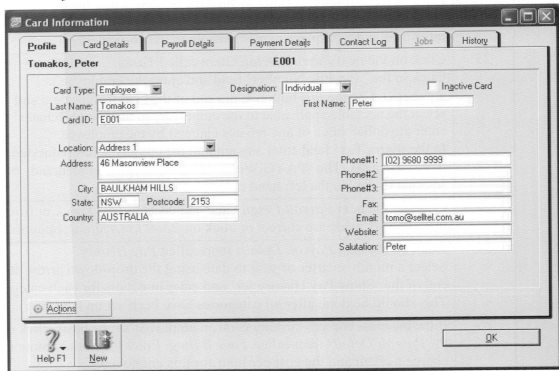

Figure 8.6: Employee card information profile for Peter Tomakos

15. Select the *Card Details* tab and click in the 'Notes' field to enter the employee's next of kin as "N.O.K. Jenny Maria Tomakos (spouse)".

16. This employee is to be paid by direct deposit. Select the *Payment Details* tab.

17. Use the drop down arrow and select "Electronic" as the 'Payment Method'.

18. Leave "1" employee bank account for the 'Electronically distribute net pay among' field.

19. Type in the 'BSB Number' as "222-111" and ↵.

20. Enter "6042182" in the 'Bank Account Number' field and ↵.

21. Type in the 'Bank Acct Name' as "P & J TOMAKOS" ↵.

22. Type in the 'Statement Text' as "SALARY PAYMENT". Your *Card Information* window under the *Payment Details* tab should look like Figure 8.7:

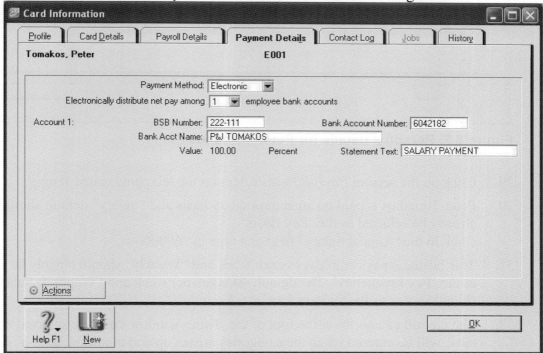

Figure 8.7: Payment details for Peter Tomakos

23. Click on the *Payroll Details* tab at the top of the *Card Information* window.

24. On the left panel of the *Payroll Details* window there is a list of ten sections that may be completed, with the first called *Personal Details* selected.

25. Click in the 'Date of Birth' field and enter "16/11/75" and ↵. The 'Calculated Age' of Peter Tomakos should appear *and this will depend on your system date*.

26. Use the drop down arrow for the 'Gender' field and select "Male" and ↵.

27. Enter the 'Start Date' as "4/5/2015".

28. There is no termination date and the 'Employment Basis' is "Individual". Leave the 'Employment Category' as "Permanent" and 'Employment Status' as "Full Time", and for the 'Employment Classification', use the drop down arrow and select "Salesperson". Leave the 'Pay Slip Email' field blank. The *Personal Payroll Details* window should look like Figure 8.8 on the next page.

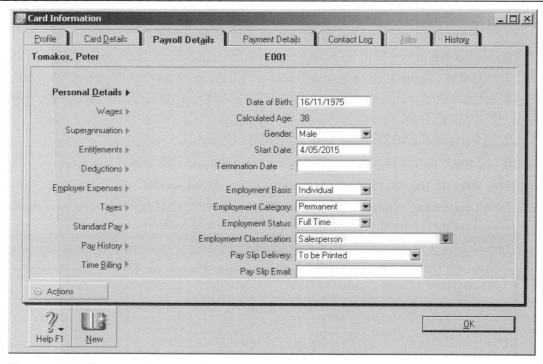

Figure 8.8: Personal details for Peter Tomakos

29. Click on the second *Payroll Details* item on the left panel called *Wages*.

30. Peter Tomakos is paid on an annual salary basis and "Salary" default should already be selected as the 'Pay Basis'.
     Click in the 'Annual Salary' field and type in "60000" ↲.

31. This business pays employees each week and "Weekly" should already be shown as the 'Pay Frequency'. The default 40 hours per week and "Wages & Salaries" should appear as the 'Wages Expense Account'.

32. The payroll categories at the foot of the *Wages* window could be selected now but these will be entered when the categories are set up and modified later. Your *Wages Payroll Details* window should look like Figure 8.9 on the next page.

33. Click on the next *Payroll Details* item on the left panel called *Superannuation*.

34. The 'Superannuation Fund' should be "AMP Life" (as set up earlier as the default) ↲.

35. Type in "ASG345678" as the 'Employee Membership #' for Peter Tomakos.

36. Click in the left-hand column to select "Superannuation Guarantee" as the superannuation category for Peter Tomakos. Your *Superannuation Payroll Details* window should look like Figure 8.10 on the next page.

This example continues on page 8-16

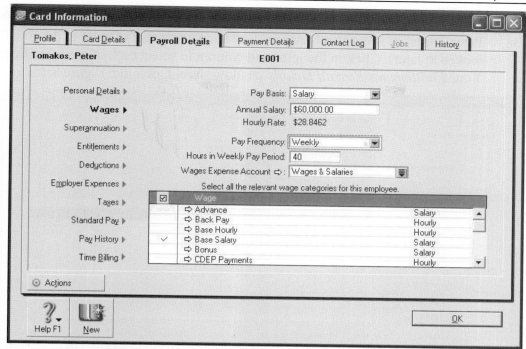

Figure 8.9: Wages payroll details for Peter Tomakos

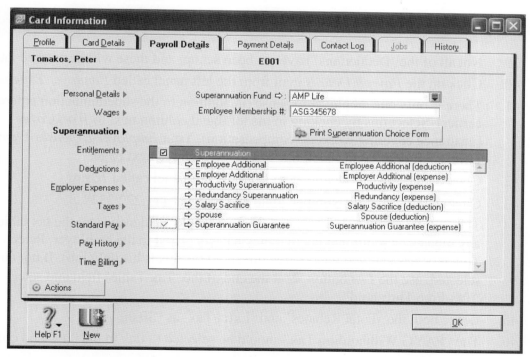

Figure 8.10: Superannuation payroll details for Peter Tomakos

37. Click on the next *Payroll Details* item from the left panel called *Entitlements*.

38. Peter Tomakos is entitled to annual leave and sick leave (details of these will be looked at later). Click in the left-hand column to select both of these entitlements. Your *Entitlements Payroll Details* window should look like Figure 8.11:

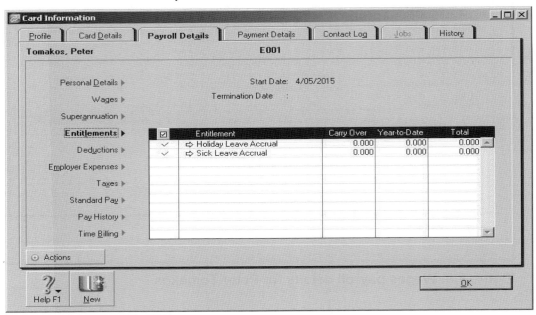

Figure 8.11: Peter Tomakos's entitlements for holiday and sick pay

39. Not all of the 'Deductions' have yet been set up, and these will be entered later.

40. Click on the *Payroll Details* item from the left panel called *Employer Expenses*.

41. There is only one employer expense (in addition to the superannuation entered earlier). Select this by clicking in the left-hand column next to *WorkCover* (insurance covering workers' compensation). Your *Employer Expenses Payroll Details* window should look like Figure 8.12 on the next page.

42. Click on the *Payroll Details* item from the left panel called *Taxes*.

43. Click in the 'Tax File Number' field and type in "111 222 333" ↵.

44. The amount of tax to be deducted from an employee depends on the tax table and any rebates or additional tax that they have declared to the employer. Peter Tomakos has claimed the tax free threshold (as this is his only job). If not already selected, use the *List* button ▼ at the end of the 'Tax Table' field and select "Tax Free Threshold".

45. Leave both the 'Total Rebates' and 'Extra Tax' as "$0.00".

46. The "PAYG Withholding Tax" should be selected (a tick in the left-hand column of the 'Tax' listing).

47. Your *Taxes Payroll Details* window should look like Figure 8.13 on the next page.

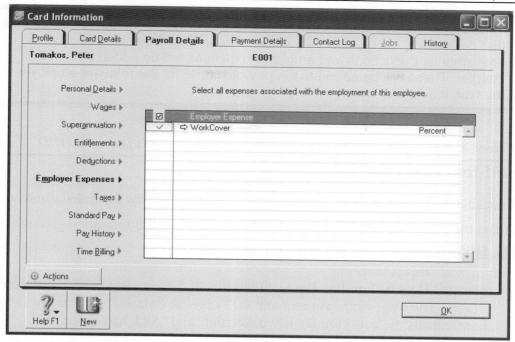

Figure 8.12: The employer expense for *WorkCover* selected

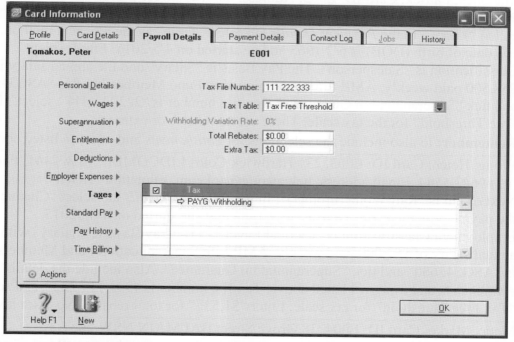

Figure 8.13: Taxes payroll details for Peter Tomakos

48. Click on the *Payroll Details* item called *Standard Pay* to confirm that the base salary is shown as "$1,153.85" for the 40-hour week.

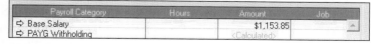

49. The *Pay History* payroll details item will be entered later in this chapter, and *Time Billing* is not used in this example. Click on the *OK* button.

The example above and the following exercise only use the payroll categories that are already set up in *MYOB AccountRight Plus*. Other wage types, entitlements, deductions and employer expenses will be added later in this chapter. These will be added to the payroll details for the relevant employees at the time they are set up.

Video: A video showing you how to create employee cards is on the DVD

Self-test exercise 8.2

If not already open, start *MYOB AccountRight Plus* and open the file called dem81.myo.

Create the following employee cards and enter the payroll information given for each.

The following details are the same for all employees:

In *Payroll Details* tab:
Personal Details: Employ. Bases: "Individual", "Permanent" and "Full Time".
Wages: The wages expense account: is "Wages & Salaries" (number 6-5130).
Entitlements: Select "Holiday leave Accrual" and "Sick leave Accrual".
Employer expenses: Select "WorkCover".

Mahoney, Patrick, Card ID: E002. Address: 34 Way Street BURWOOD NSW 2134. Phone (02) 9378 3344, salutation "Pat". No email address. Next of kin is spouse called "Lizzy". In the *Payment Details* tab select "Cash" as the payment method. His date of birth (DOB) is 6/2/1965 and he started on 4/5/2015. Employment Classification is "Salesperson". The Pay Basis is "Salary" and the annual salary is $58,500 paid weekly. AMP Life Superannuation Fund Membership # is "ASG345679" and tick "Superannuation Guarantee". Tax file number is "222 111 444", select "Tax Free Threshold" for the tax scale. There are no rebates or extra tax.

Remember: to also include the selections for *entitlements* and *expense* listed above.

Wong, Helen, Card ID: E003, 231 Hardwick Court LIDCOMBE NSW 2141. Phone (02) 9643 5544, Email address: helenwong@aol.com, salutation "Helen".
Next of kin is "Ralf Wong (brother)". In the *Payment Details* tab select "Cheque" as the payment method. Her DOB is 30/9/1983 and she started on 4/05/2015. Employment Classification is "Clerical Level 1". The Pay Basis is "Salary" with the annual salary of $52,000 paid weekly. AMP Life Superannuation Fund Membership # is "ASG345680" and tick "Superannuation Guarantee". Also include the details for *entitlements* and *expenses* listed above. Tax file number is "333 111 222", and select "Tax Free Threshold" for tax scale. Enter "$1,535" for total rebates. No extra tax.

Metic, Marko, Card ID: E004, 38 Grove Street BALMAIN NSW 2041.
Phone (02) 9555 1198, Email address: mm@dotel.com.au, salutation "Marko" and next of kin is "Kylie (daughter)". Payment method is "Cash". He started on 4/05/2015 and no date of birth is given. Employment Classification is "Clerical Level 2". His Pay Basis is "Hourly" and the rate is $50 per hour paid weekly. AMP Life Superannuation Fund Membership # is "ASG345681" and tick "Superannuation Guarantee". Also include the details for *entitlements* and *employer expenses* listed above. Tax file number is "444 999 333". Select "Tax Free Threshold" for the tax scale and enter "$1,841" for total rebates. No extra tax.

(continued on the next page)

Self-test exercise 8.2 (continued)

Jamieson, May, Card ID: E005, 67 Forest Road PEAKHURST NSW 2210. Phone (02) 9534 6677. Email address: mjamie@utel.com.au. Salutation "Mrs M Jamieson". Next of kin is "Joan (03) 3588 5456 (sister)". This employee is paid electronically and payment details are: BSB: "310-222", Bank Account Number: "6153215", Bank Account Name "M JAMIESON" and Statement Text "SALARY PAYMENT". Her DOB is 18/3/1982 and she started on 4/05/2015. Employment classification is "Administration". The Pay Basis is "Salary" with Annual Salary of $62,400 paid weekly. AMP Life Superannuation Fund Membership # is "ASG345682" and tick "Superannuation Guarantee". Also include the details for *entitlements* and *expenses* listed on the previous page. Tax file number is "555 666 444" and select "Tax Free Threshold" for the tax scale. No rebates and no extra tax.

Miandad, Javed, Card ID: E006, 321 Wobbly Close CASTLE HILL NSW 2154. Phone (02) 9680 3124. Salutation is "Javed" and next of kin is "Keria (mother)". Javed takes his pay in cash. His DOB is 20/7/1973 and he started on 4/05/2015. Employment Classification is "General Hand Level 1". His Pay Basis is "Hourly" at $18 per hour paid weekly. AMP Superannuation Fund Membership # is "ASG345683" and tick "Superannuation Guarantee". Also include the details for *entitlements* and *expense* listed above. Tax file number is "666 111 222" and select "Tax Free Threshold" for the tax scale. Enter "$1,535" for total rebates and "$5" for extra tax.

Setting up payroll categories

Payroll categories are grouped into:

- *Wages*
- *Superannuation*
- *Entitlements*
- *Deductions*,
- Employer *Expenses* and
- *Taxes*

Once a category is set up, you need to nominate the employees the category will apply to, and select any exemptions for tax or other deductions applicable to the category.

Wages categories

Wages categories define the types of remuneration that can be paid to any employee. Included in this category are the normal base wages, overtime, sick pay, bonuses and annual leave. *MYOB AccountRight Plus* includes a list of the more usual payments made in the payroll. You can use a category item as is, modify it or add a new item. There are two types of wages category – *Salary* or *Hourly*. A wages category can be set up using a rate per hour, otherwise it is paid as a *Salary*, i.e. by a set amount.

How to add, edit or delete a wages payroll category

Step	Instruction
1	Select the *Payroll* command centre.
2	Select the *Payroll Categories* option.
3	Click on the *Wages* tab at the top of the window (if not already selected).
4	To add a new category, click on the *New* button at the bottom of the *Payroll Category List* window, then go to step 5. **OR** To edit an existing wages category: Click on the detail arrow ⇨ next to it and make the necessary changes. To delete a category: Edit it (click on the detail arrow ⇨ next to it) then select *Delete Wage Category* from the *Edit* menu. Go to step 16.
5	Type in wages category name or description.
6	Select either "Salary" or "Hourly" for the type of wages. Any wage category not paid on an hourly or fixed hourly rate basis will be a salary type (e.g. commission based on sales).
7	If an hourly type is selected, enter a multiplier (e.g. 1.5 for overtime) or the fixed hourly rate.
8	If an account **other than** the default wages expense account is to be debited, click on the 'Optional Account:' checkbox and select that account in the 'Override Account:' field.
9	Click on the *Employee* button at the foot of the window.
10	Click in the column headed 'Select' against any employee who is entitled to this wage category. Click on the icon ☑ to select all employees if they are all entitled to this wage category.
11	Click on the *OK* button to close the *Linked Employees* window.
12	Select the *Exempt* button at the foot of the window.
13	Click in the column headed 'Exempt' against any tax or deduction that this wage category is to be exempted from.
14	Click the *OK* button to accept the *Wages Exemptions* window.
15	Click the *OK* button to accept the *Wages Information*.
16	Repeat the above steps for another wage category or click the *Close* button.

Example 8.4—Adding a wages payroll category

1. The file called dem81.myo should be opened.
2. Select the *Payroll* command centre.
3. Select the *Payroll Categories* option.
4. If not already selected, click on the *Wages* tab at the top of the *Payroll Category List* window.
5. Click on the *New* button.
6. Type in "Attendance Bonus" as the wages name ⏎.
7. Leave the type of wages as 'Salary' as it is a set amount per week.
8. The amount paid is to be debited to the <u>default</u> wages expense account (as set up in the 'Payroll Linked Accounts', i.e. 'Wages & Salaries'), so <u>no</u> optional account is required for this wage. Your screen should look like Figure 8.14:

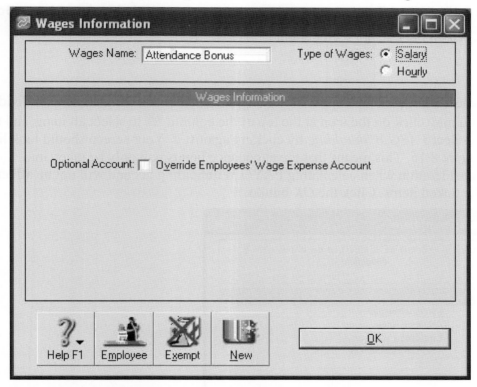

Figure 8.14: *Wages Information* **window for Attendance Bonus**

9. Click on the *Employee* icon button.

10. Click against the employees Metic, Miandad and Wong under the heading 'Select' so that a "tick" appears as shown in Figure 8.15 on the next page. These selected employees are entitled to the attendance bonus.
11. Click the *OK* button.

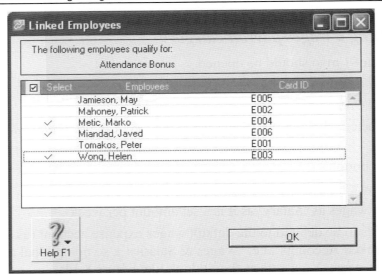

Figure 8.15: *Linked Employees* **window – employees entitled to Attendance Bonus**

12. Click on the *Exempt* icon button.

13. Select all but the "PAYG Withholding". Instead of selecting all items individually, you may click on the icon at the top of the column ☑ to select all items and then deselect *PAYG Withholding* by clicking against it. Your screen should look like Figure 8.16. This means that the attendance bonus will only be taken into consideration when calculating PAYG Withholding tax and will not be affected by the ticked items. Click the *OK* button.

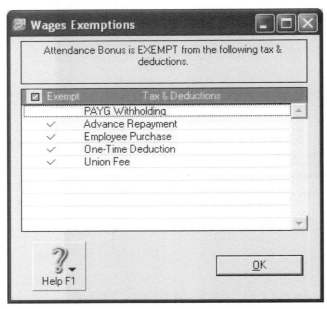

Figure 8.16: Wages exemptions for Attendance Bonus

14. Click the *OK* button to complete the category.

Video: A video showing you how to add a wages category is on the DVD

Self-test exercise 8.3

If not already open, the file called dem81.myo should be opened.

Create a *new* wages category for "Efficiency Bonus", a salary type. The default salaries account is to be debited. All employees are entitled to this bonus (click on the icon at the top of the 'Select' column), and it is subject to income tax (i.e. do not exempt the "PAYG Withholding") – exempt all other deductions.

Edit the *existing* wage category "Commission" so that the amount paid is debited to "Commission on Sales" account (click on the 'Optional Account' tick box and enter the account "Commission on Sales" number "6-1200"). Employees entitled to this commission are Mahoney and Tomakos. Commission is EXEMPT from all deductions except "PAYG Withholding" as it is subject to income tax.

Select all employees for these *existing* wage types: holiday leave loading, holiday pay, both overtime wages categories (1.5x and 2x which represent time-and-a-half and double-time) and sick pay. After selecting each wage category and the *Employee* icon button, use the ☑ icon at the top of the *Select* column and select all employees. There are no exemptions for these wage categories.

Superannuation

Superannuation can either be an employ**er** **expense** or an employ**ee** **deduction**. A superannuation **deduction** is deducted from the employee's gross pay, but the superannuation **expense**, on the other hand, is paid by the employer on behalf of the employee (but NOT to the employee). For example, the Superannuation Guarantee is an employer expense paid by the employer for the benefit of the employee to a superannuation fund.

How to add, edit or delete a superannuation category

Step	Instruction
1	Select the *Payroll* command centre.
2	Select the *Payroll Categories* option.
3	Click on the *Superannuation* tab at the top of the *Payroll Category List* window.
4	To add a new superannuation type, click on the *New* button at the bottom of the *Payroll Category List* window. **OR** To edit an existing superannuation type: Click on the detail arrow ⇨ next to it and make the necessary changes. To delete a superannuation type: Edit it (click on the detail arrow ⇨ next to it) then select *Delete Superannuation* from the *Edit* menu.
5	Type in 'Superannuation Name' and ↵.

(continued on the next page)

Step	Instruction
6	Use the *List* button ≣ and select a 'Contribution Type' from the list. That will determine if the superannuation is an **expense** or a **deduction** type.
7	Type in or use the *List* button ≣ and select the expense account to be debited in the 'Linked Expense Account' field. This field is only used for **expense** type superannuation, not for deduction type.
8	Type in or use the *List* button ≣ and select the liability account to be credited in the 'Linked Payable Account' field.
9	Tick the box next to 'Pay Advice', if the details of this superannuation are required to be printed on the employee's pay advice.
10	Enter in the details for the 'Calculation Basis' and any limits to the amount of expense or deduction as well as the 'Threshold' (if any).
11	Click on the *Employee* button at the foot of the *Superannuation Information* window. Employee
12	Click in the column headed 'Select' against any employee who is involved with this superannuation type. Click on the icon ☑ to select all employees if they are all involved.
13	Click on the *OK* button to close the *Linked Employees* window.
14	Click on the *Exempt* button at the foot of the Superannuation Information window. (Only available if the calculations are on percentage basis.) Exempt
15	Click in the column headed 'Exempt' against any "wages" category that is not included when calculating the percentage amount.
16	Click the *OK* button to accept the *Superannuation Exemptions* window.
17	Click the *OK* button to accept the *Superannuation Information*.
18	Repeat the above steps for another superannuation type or click the *Close* button.

Example 8.5—Adding a Superannuation category

1. If not already open, the file called dem81.myo should be opened.
2. Select the *Payroll* command centre.
3. Select the *Payroll Categories* option.
4. Click on the *Superannuation* tab at the top of the *Payroll Category List* window.
5. Click on the *New* button.

6. Type in "Executive Life" as the 'Superannuation Name' ↵.

7. Use the down arrow at the end of the 'Contribution Type' field and select "Employer Additional (expense)".

8. Change the default 'Linked Expense Account'. Type in or use the *List* button ▼ and select the account "Superannuation" (account number 6-5120) as the expense account to debit.

9. In the 'Linked Payable Account' field, select "AMP Superannuation" (account number 2-1480). Type in or use the *List* button ▼ and select.

10. Click the option to print 'Pay Advice' to select it.

11. The percentage *Equals* option button will be selected by default. Type in "2%" as the rate to apply as a percentage of "Gross Wages".

12. No limits apply to this calculation. Your *Superannuation Information* window should look like Figure 8.17:

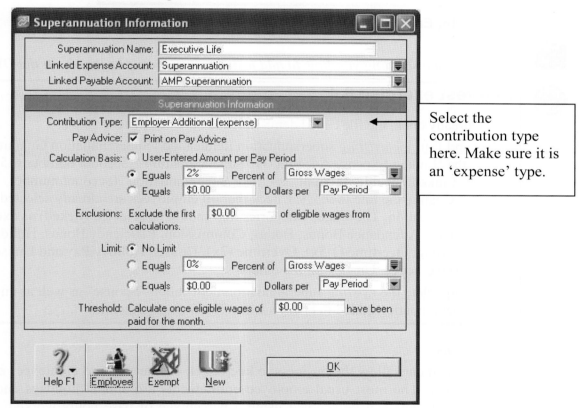

Figure 8.17: New superannuation category

13. Click on the *Employee* button at the bottom of the *Superannuation Information* window. Click in the left-hand column to select Jamieson, May as the person to receive this superannuation benefit. Click the *OK* button **if** your *Linked Employees* window looks like Figure 8.18 on the next page.

14. There are no exemptions for this example superannuation fund (the 2% will be applied to all wages categories). Click the *OK* button to complete the set-up for this superannuation category.

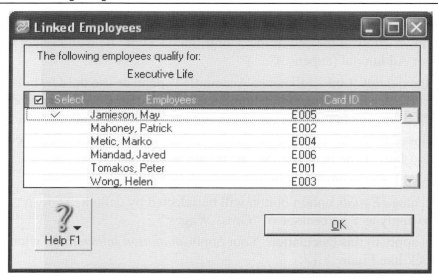

Figure 8.18: Employee linked to Executive Life superannuation

Video: A video showing you how to add a superannuation category is on the DVD

Self-test exercise 8.4

If not already open, the file called dem81.myo should be opened.

Select and Edit the *existing* superannuation item called "Superannuation Guarantee" so that the 'Linked Expense Account' is "Superannuation" (account number 6-5120) and the 'Linked Payable Account' is "AMP Superannuation" (account number 2-1480). Change the rate to 9.5%. Check that **all** employees are already selected for this superannuation. The wages categories that should be selected (ticked) as exempt are: Advance, Attendance Bonus, Bonus, Commission, Efficiency Bonus, Holiday Leave Loading, Overtime (1.5x), Overtime (2x), Unused Holiday Pay and Unused Long Service Leave. Un-tick all the others.

Select and delete the *existing* superannuation item called "Spouse" as well as any other superannuation added in error (such as 'New Superannuation').

Entitlements

These entitlements allow the business to keep track of hours due to employees earned during a year. The most usual employee entitlements are annual holidays and sick leave. Entitlements can be accrued using a percentage of base hours worked, or by adding a set amount each pay period.

How to add, edit or delete an entitlement category

Step	Instruction
1	Select the *Payroll Categories* option from the *Payroll* command centre.
2	Click on the *Entitlements* tab at the top of the *Payroll Category List* window.

(continued on the next page)

Step	Instruction
3	To add a new entitlement, click on the *New* button at the bottom of the *Payroll Category List* window. New
4	To edit an existing entitlement, click on the detail arrow ⇨ next to the item and make the necessary corrections. To delete an entitlement, click on the detail arrow then select "Delete Entitlement" from the *Edit* menu.
5	Type in an entitlement name if it is a new entitlement.
6	Click on the option button ⦿ to select a calculation basis and enter a rate or amount. Click in the field and select from a list the period or hours.
7	If the entitlement is to appear on the pay advice (pay slip), click in the checkbox 'Print on Pay Advice' to select it.
8	If the entitlement can be carried over at the end of one payroll year to the next, tick in the 'Payroll Year End' checkbox to select it.
9	Click on the list box and select a linked wages category that will reduce the accrual when paid.
10	Click on the *Employee* button and select the employees entitled to this category by clicking next to their names. Click the *OK* button when complete.
11	Click on the *Exempt* button and select those wages categories that should be excluded before calculating the entitlement. Click the *OK* button to exit the *Entitlements Exemptions* window.
12	Click the *OK* button to exit the *Entitlements Information* window.

Example 8.6—Editing an entitlement category

1. The file called dem81.myo should be opened.
2. Select the *Payroll* command centre.
3. Select the *Payroll Categories* option.
4. Click on the *Entitlements* tab at the top of the *Payroll Category List* window.
5. Select "Holiday Leave Accrued" by clicking on the detail arrow ⇨.
6. Click on the box showing a percentage and type in "8.3333%" or "4/48*100=" (4 weeks holiday into 48 weeks, i.e. 4/48 = 0.083333 or 8.3333%).

   Note: 48 weeks excludes 4 weeks holiday hence you need to exempt <u>holiday pay</u>.
 <u>Alternatively</u>, if you calculate the entitlement based on 52 weeks (i.e. 4/52 = 7.6923%) then <u>you would NOT</u> exempt the *holiday pay*.

7. Click on the tick-boxes so that the entitlement will appear on pay advices, and will be carried forward into the following payroll year.

8. Check that the 'Linked Wages Category' is "Holiday Pay". Your *Entitlements Information* window should look like Figure 8.19:

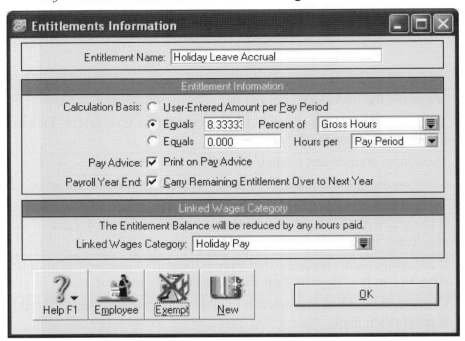

Figure 8.19: Entitlements information window for Holiday Leave Accrual

9. Click on the *Employee* button and make sure that all employees are selected and then click the *OK* button.

10. Click on the *Exempt* button and select all wages categories **except** 'Base Hourly' and 'Sick Pay' as in Figure 8.20. These two categories should add up to 48 weeks.

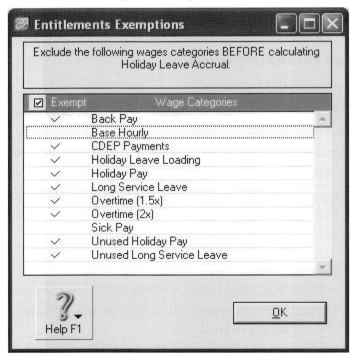

Figure 8.20: Wage categories excluded in calculating leave entitlement

11. Click the *OK* button to leave the *Entitlements Exemptions* window, and click the *OK* button to close the *Entitlements Information* window.

Video: A video showing you how to edit an entitlement category is on the DVD

Self-test exercise 8.5

The file called dem81.myo should be opened.

Edit the *Sick Leave Accrual* entitlement to show 0.769 hours per pay period or you can type "40/52=" in the 'Equals 40/52= Hours per Pay Period' box (i.e. 40 hours sick leave entitlement p.a. over 52 weekly pay periods). The entitlement is not to be shown on pay advices but the entitlement for any unused sick leave can be carried over to the next year.

Make sure this entitlement is linked to the "Sick Pay" wage category.

All employees are entitled to "Sick Leave Accrual".

Note: The *Exempt* button should be inactive as this entitlement is based on a pay period and does not depend on other wage types paid.

Deductions category

Deductions are amounts withheld from an employee's wages. Deductions are *usually* requested by the employee and payable to third parties – e.g. union fees, medical benefit fund contributions and credit union collections. Additional superannuation deductions are set up under the Superannuation categories looked at earlier. These must be paid over to the third parties, usually in the month following the deduction. Other deductions may be "internal" – for example, the repayment of a staff loan, contribution to a social club fund etc. Some deduction types are already set up in *MYOB AccountRight Plus*. Again you may edit, delete or add new deductions.

How to add, edit or delete a deduction

Step	Instruction
1	Select the *Payroll* command centre.
2	Select the *Payroll Categories* option.
3	Click on the *Deductions* tab at the top of the window.
4	To add a new deduction category, click on the *New* button at the bottom of the *Payroll Category List* window.
5	To edit an existing deduction category, click on the detail arrow ⇨ next to the item and modify as necessary. Click the *OK* button and then the *Close* button. To delete a deduction category, open the category for editing then click on the *Edit* menu and select "Delete Deduction". (**Note:** It might be necessary to de-select all employees first before deleting.)
6	If it is a new deduction, type in a deduction name.

(continued on the next page)

Step	Instruction
7	In the 'Linked Payable Account' field, enter the account that will be credited with the amount of the deduction if this is different from the default (*usually* a current liability account). Do <u>NOT</u> use the tax liability account ("PAYG Withholding") as this should be left for that deduction only.
8	Click on the option button  to select the type of deduction: "User-Entered ..." allows you to enter an amount at time of payment. "Equals x%" sets a deduction as a percentage of wages. "Equals $x" sets a dollar amount as a deduction per pay period.
9	If the deduction is to be a percentage of wages, enter the percentage to be used and select the wages category, e.g. percentage of "Gross Wages".
10	If the deduction is to be a fixed amount per pay period enter the amount and period, e.g. per "Pay Period".
11	Limits may be set on the amount to be deducted: There may be no limit set for the deduction or to limit the deduction to either a maximum percentage of a wage or a maximum amount per period. **Note**: If you set the deduction <u>type</u> as *User-Entered Amount per Pay Period* then *MYOB AccountRight Plus* ignores any deduction <u>limits</u> you set here.
12	Click on the *Employee* icon button at the foot of the deduction information window to list employees. Employee
13	Select those employees who are to have the deduction made against them by clicking in the 'Select' column. Click the *OK* button.
14	If the deduction is to be made <u>after</u> calculating the tax, <u>do not</u> exempt the income tax. However, if the deduction is to be made <u>before</u> calculating the tax then select the *Exempt* button and tick next to "PAYG Withholding" to exempt it. Exempt **Note**: If the tax is <u>exempted</u> (ticked) that means the deduction is tax deductible. The deduction is taken off the income first and then the tax is calculated on the reduced income balance and thus the employee pays <u>less</u> tax.
15	Click the *OK* button.

Is it exempt or is it not exempt? That is the question. Ho-hum.

Example 8.7—Adding a deduction category

1. The file called dem81.myo should be opened.
2. Select the *Payroll* command centre.
3. Select the *Payroll Categories* option.
4. Select the *Deductions* tab at the top of the *Payroll Category List* window.
5. Click on the *New* icon button.
6. Type in "ABC Credit Union" as the deduction name.
7. Change the 'Linked Payable Account' to "ABC Credit Union" (account number 2-1450). Type this in or use the *List* button ▼ and select from the list.
8. Enter the amount as $50 per pay period.
9. The deduction 'Limit' is "No Limit".
10. The *Deduction Information* window should look like Figure 8.21:

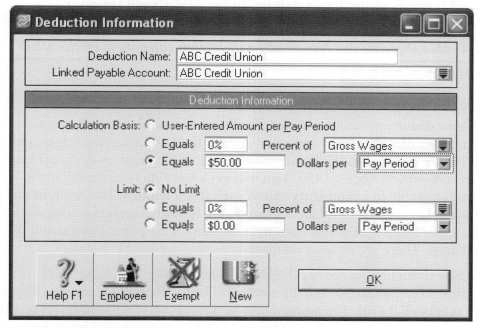

Figure 8.21: Deduction for ABC Credit Union

11. Click on the *Employee* icon and select Helen Wong as the employee, as shown in Figure 8.22 on the next page.
12. Click the *OK* button.
    Note: This deduction is after calculating tax (not tax exempted), so no exemption is made.

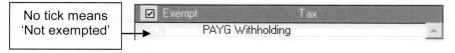

13. Click the *OK* button to close the *Deduction Information* window.

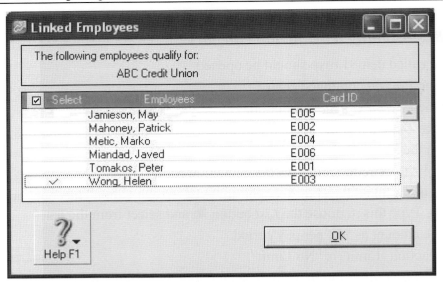

Figure 8.22: Helen Wong has a deduction for ABC Credit Union

Video: A video showing you how to add a deduction category is on the DVD

Self-test exercise 8.6

The file called dem81.myo should be opened.

Create a new deduction category called "Staff Loans – Jamieson": This is a repayment from May Jamieson and is to be equal to 2% of her gross wages with a limit of $40 per pay period. This staff loan account is a current asset: "Staff Loans – Jamieson" account number 1-1450. You will get a warning because usually a deduction is payable to a third party and as such it is a liability. However, in this case the deduction is a repayment of an amount owing to the business, i.e. a repayment of an asset – click *OK* to ignore the warning. Click on the *Employee* button and select May Jamieson. There are no tax exemptions.

Create a new deduction category called "Garnishee Order – Miandad". This is a court order against Javed Miandad, and the credit will be to "Payroll Deductions Payable" (account number 2-1410). The amount is to be $100 per pay period subject to a limit of 50% of each week's wages. Link Miandad to this deduction. No tax exemption.

Click on the detail arrow ⇨ and select the "Union Fee" deduction category. Change the name to "Miscellaneous Staff Union". The 'Linked Payable Account' will be "Miscellaneous Staff Union" (account number 2-1470). Link the employees Metic, Miandad and Tomakos, each of whom wish to contribute $5.00 per pay period into this union. Make sure *No Limit* is selected and there is no tax exemption.

Employer expenses category

In addition to the Superannuation Guarantee employer expense looked at earlier in this chapter, an employer may incur other expenses related to employees. A major employer expense is *WorkCover* insurance. An employer expense does not affect an individual employee's net pay. The amount is debited to an expense account and credited to a liability account pending payment to third parties.

How to add, edit or delete an employer expense

Step	Instruction
1	Select the *Payroll* command centre.
2	Select the *Payroll Categories* option.
3	Click on the *Expenses* tab at the top of the window.
4	To <u>add a new</u> employer expense, click on the *New* button at the bottom of the *Payroll Category List* window.
5	To <u>edit an expense</u> category, click on the detail arrow ⇨ next to the item. To <u>delete an expense</u> category click on the detail arrow and then select "Delete Employer Expense" from the *Edit* menu. (It might be necessary to de-select all employees first before deleting the category.)
6	If adding a new category, type in a name for the employer expense.
7	Enter the expense account (name or number) in the 'Linked Expense Account' field.
8	Enter the 'Linked Payable Account' (name or number) – <u>usually</u> a liability for the amount to be paid in due course to third parties (e.g. insurance company).
9	Select the checkbox 'Print on Pay Advice' if required.
10	Select the expense basis – a percentage or a dollar amount.
11	Select the wages category to use in a percentage calculation or the per pay period for a dollar amount.
12	Set any expense limits (a percentage or an amount) and the minimum wage threshold below which the expense will not be paid.
13	Click on the *Employee* icon button and select those employees who qualify for this expense.
14	Click the *OK* button.
15	Select the *Exempt* icon button and select those wages categories that will not be included in the percentage calculation. **Note:** This button will be greyed if the *Calculation Basis* is <u>not</u> a percentage.
16	Click the *OK* button and then click the *Close* button.

Example 8.8—Adding an employer expense category

1.   The file called dem81.myo should be opened.
2.   Select the *Payroll* command centre.
3.   Select the *Payroll Categories* option.
4.   Select the *Expenses* tab at the top of the *Payroll Category List* window.
5.   Click on the *New* icon button.
6.   Type in "Uniforms and Laundry" as the expense name.
7.   In the 'Linked Expense Account' field, type in or use the *List* button 🔽 and select the expense account "Uniforms and Laundry" (account number 6-2670) to be debited.
8.   In the 'Linked Payable Account' field, type in or use the *List* button 🔽 and select the account "Accounts Payable" (account number 2-1200) for the account to be credited.
9.   The checkbox for 'Print on Pay Advice' should not be selected (not ticked).
10.   Enter the amount per pay period as "$15". There is no expense limit. Your *Employer Expense Information* window should look like Figure 8.23:

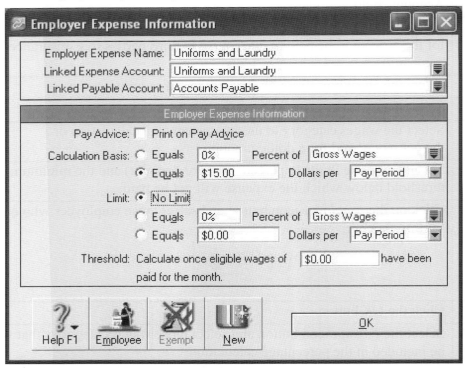

Figure 8.23: Employer expense information for uniforms and laundry

11.   Select the *Employee* button. Select Metic, Miandad and Tomakos as employees who are entitled to this expense category and click the *OK* button.
12.   Click the *OK* button again and then the *Close* button.

Video: A video showing you how to add an employer expense category is on the DVD

Self-test exercise 8.7

The file called dem81.myo should be opened.

Select the expense payroll category "WorkCover". Change the 'Linked Expense Account' to "Insurance" (account number 6-0525). The credit is to be made to a current asset account called "Prepaid WorkCover Insurance" (account number 1-1410). Did you receive a warning notice? Why?

Enter the rate as 2% of gross wages without a limit.

All employees should be selected for this expense. All wage categories are included in calculating this expense, so there are no exemptions.

Set the tax liability account number

The demonstration file dem81.myo has the *Default Tax/Deductions Payable* linked account set as "Payroll Deductions Payable" (account number 2-1410), which is appropriate for most of the payroll deductions. However, it is advisable that the income tax deducted from employees is not credited to this account, but credited to its own account – the "PAYG Withholding" liability account (number 2-1420). This will make it easier to reconcile the *Payment Summaries* (Group Certificates) at the end of the year (see later in this chapter).

How to set the PAYG tax deductions liability linked account

Step	Instruction
1	Select the *Payroll* command centre.
2	Select the *Payroll Categories* option.
3	Click on the *Taxes* tab at the top of the window.
4	Click on the detail arrow ⇨ next to *PAYG Withholding* to edit it.
5	Enter the 'Linked Payables Account' as the tax liability account. Type in the account name (or number), or use the *List* button ▦ and select from the list.
6	You can examine the various tax scales by selecting the tax scale using the drop-down menu in this window. No Tax Free Thre ▼

Example 8.9—Setting the PAYG tax deductions liability linked account

1. The file called dem81.myo should be opened.
2. Select the *Payroll* command centre and then the *Payroll Categories* option.
3. Select the *Taxes* tab at the top of the *Payroll Category List* window.
4. Click on the detail arrow ⇨ next to *PAYG Withholding* to edit it.
5. Select the account "PAYG Withholding Payable" (account number 2-1420) as the 'Linked Payables Account'. If your *Tax Table Information* window looks like Figure 8.24 on the next page click *OK* then *Close*:

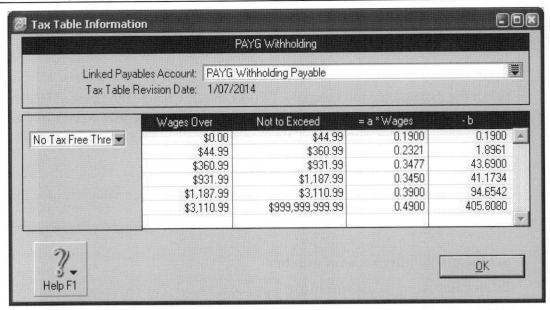

Figure 8.24: 'Linked Payables Account' set to PAYG Withholding Payable

Using the *Easy Setup Assistant*

The payroll setup shown in the preceding pages can also be entered using the *Easy Setup Assistant* as an alternative method. You have the choice of entering information as shown above or in the assistant. Use the following 'How to …' instructions (in conjunction with previous instructions) to set up the payroll using the *Assistant*. You may use either method when doing the assessment material at the end of the chapter, but you will have to read through the whole exercise to note where all the information is contained.

The following instructions can be used for setting up a new payroll in assessment exercises. **Do not complete** this for the file dem81.myo as the payroll is already set up. Skip the next 'How to …' and continue with the topic 'Paying employees each pay period', on the next page.

How to use Easy Setup Assistant for payroll

Step	Instruction
1	Select the *Setup* pull-down menu.
2	Select the *Easy Setup Assistant* menu item.
3	Click on the *Payroll* button.
	(continued on the next page)

Step	Instruction
4	Read the message on the *Welcome to the Payroll Easy Setup Assistant* window. **Note:** At each window of the Setup, you may click on the *Next* button to move forward through the Setup, the *Back* button to return to a previous window and the *Close* button to cancel the set up or to exit if finished. You can also click on the table of contents on the left of the window to jump to any window in this process.
5	Read the message about tax tables and click on the *Load Tax Tables* to load them. If you are not sure about the currency of the tax tables on your program, click on *Check for Updates* to have the most current tables. This requires internet access and to be a subscriber to *MYOB Cover Plan*. For the purpose of completing the exercises ignore the update option.
6	If the payroll year is not set, enter the current payroll year and confirm that the year is correct.
7	Enter the number of hours in a full-time workweek.
8	Enter the 'Withholder Payer Number' (if available) and net pay rounding.
9	Accept or modify the linked payroll accounts (these will be the default accounts and can be changed if necessary).
10	Select *Wages* Category in the '*Select Category Type*' box (if not already selected). Click on the appropriate button to add (*New*), edit or delete payroll wages categories as necessary.
11	Change the category type to *Superannuation*. Add, edit or delete superannuation types.
12	Change the category type to *Entitlements*. Add, edit or delete entitlements.
13	Change the category type to *Deductions*. Add, edit or delete deductions.
14	Change the category type to *Expenses*. Add, edit or delete employer expenses.
15	Change the category type to *Taxes* and edit the PAYG Withholding to change the linked payable account (if necessary).
16	Build the employees list (Employee Cards): Add (*new*), edit or delete employee cards. For each card (new or edited), follow the instructions shown on pages 8-9 to 8-11 earlier in this chapter.
17	At the "Congratulations" message click *Close*. Click *Close* again to exit the *Easy Setup Assistance* Window.

Paying employees each pay period

Having completed the payroll setup as well as creating the employee cards and setting the standard pays for each employee, employees can now be paid.

The **standard pay** for an employee is the normal pay as set up for him or her <u>without any modifications</u>. A standard pay can be modified to include payments for overtime, sick pay, holiday pays and incentive payments such as commission. These modifications to the standard pays will be covered starting from the third pay week.

Paying the *Net Pay* Amounts to employees on payday

Employees are paid using the option *Process Payroll* in the *Payroll* command centre. The *Process Payroll* option allows you to pay individual employees or all employees for a particular pay period. The following are three methods of paying the employees their net pays using *MYOB AccountRight Plus*:

1. Issue a separate cheque to each employee for the amount of his or her net pay from the business bank account.

2. Group the employees that are paid from the business bank account directly to their bank accounts. This can be done through *Process Electronic Payments*.

3. Group the net pays of all the employees to be paid by cash, and issue **<u>one</u>** cheque for the total net pays. This cheque is then cashed at the bank and the cash is distributed among the relevant employees.

The employees in this exercise are to be paid for the weeks ending on 10/5/2015, 17/5/2015, 24/5/2015 and 31/5/2015 (four pays).

For the payrolls paid on 10 and 17 May, all employees will be paid the standard pay – i.e. without any changes to their standard pays. However, for the payrolls paid on 24 and 31 May, there will be modifications to the standard pays.

- Helen Wong will be paid her net pay by a cheque from the business bank account.

- Peter Tomakos and May Jamieson are paid their net pays directly to each of their bank accounts using an electronic file that is saved and sent to the bank.

- Patrick Mahoney, Marko Metic and Javed Miandad are paid in cash. This is achieved in three steps. The first step is processing their pays in the *Process Payroll* option which will 'group' their net pays by crediting "Payroll Clearing" account instead of the business bank account. The second step is to use the *Spend Money* button in the *Process Payments* section of the *Process Payroll* option which will create one cash cheque – this will debit "Payroll Clearing" account and credit the business bank with the total of the three net pays. This cheque is then cashed at the bank to pay these employees their net pays in cash.

How to process a weekly payroll

Step	Instruction
1	Select the *Payroll* command centre.
2	Select the *Process Payroll* option.
3	In the first window for *Select Pay Period*, select the option to pay all employees for a particular pay period (e.g. weekly) or an individual for a particular payment date. If holiday pay is to be paid in advance (usual), select the tick box for this. Enter the payment date, the pay period start and end dates and click on the *Next* button.
4	In the *Select & Edit Employee's Pay* window, select or de-select the employees to be paid by clicking in the first column. To edit a standard pay, click on the detail arrow ⇨ next to the employee's name.

(continued on the next page)

Step	Instruction
5	If the employee's pay is edited, enter the details in the *Pay Employee* window. Make any changes necessary to the standard pay amounts.
6	Click on the *Record* button to record pays for all of the selected employees. Accept any message by clicking on the *Continue* button. Click *OK* when you receive a message that the paycheques have been recorded successfully.
7	In the *Process Payments* window: For employees paid by cheque: **only** if the cheques need to be printed, click on the *Print Paycheques* to print the paycheques. For Employees to be paid directly to their banks or financial institutions: you can click on the *Prepare Electronic Payments* button to process their pays. For employees paid in cash: you need to select *Spend Money* to create a transaction to create a single cash cheque.
8	For employees who are paid in cash, click the *Spend Money* button, then click on the *Record* button in the *Spend Money* window.
9	For an electronic payment, click on the *Prepare Electronic Payments* button. In the *Prepare Electronic Payments* window, select the employees to be paid by clicking on the right-hand column. **Do not** click on *Record* button unless you have an internet connection and an arrangement made with the business bank. As this is not the case in these exercises you need to create a file, instead, which can be sent to the bank to process the pays. Therefore, click on the *Bank File* button at the foot of the window and an "ABA" file will be created for the bank for electronic payments. Click on the *OK* button to record this electronic payment and then click on *Save* to save the resulting ABA file to a suitable location. Click on the *Cancel* button to return.
10	In the *Process Payments* window click on the *Next* button.
11	In the *Print Employee Pay Slips* window, click on the *Print or Email Pay Slips* button, if pay slips are required.
12	In the *Review Pay Slips Before Delivery* window select either the tab 'To Be Printed' or 'To Be Emailed'. Select (tick) next to the employees whose pay slips need to be printed or emailed. Click on the *Advance Filter* button and enter dates from/to and click on the *OK* button to return. Click on the *Print* or *Send Email* button to print or email the pay slips.
13	Back in the *Process Payroll*, click on the *Finish* button.

Example 8.10—Pay standard pays to employees

1. If not already open, the file called dem81.myo should be opened.
2. Select the *Process Payroll* option from the *Payroll* command centre.
3. In the *Process Payroll* window select "Weekly" for 'Process all employees paid:'.

4. You need to enter three dates – the payment date and two dates for the pay period. Enter the 'Payment date' as "10/5/2015". Enter the 'Pay period start' as "4/5/2015" and the 'Pay period end' as "10/5/2015" (ignore any date warning). If your screen looks like Figure 8.25, click on the *Next* button.

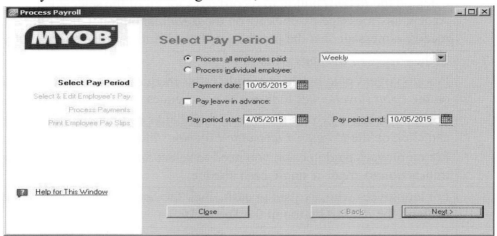

Figure 8.25: *Select Pay Period* **window in the 'Process Payroll' option**

5. In the *Select & Edit Employee's Pay* window, all employees should be selected. If there are any discrepancies click on the ⇨ next to an employee's name and make any necessary adjustments. However, if your window looks like Figure 8.26 and there are no adjustments to the standard pays, click on the *Record* button. Read the message, and click on the *Continue* button.

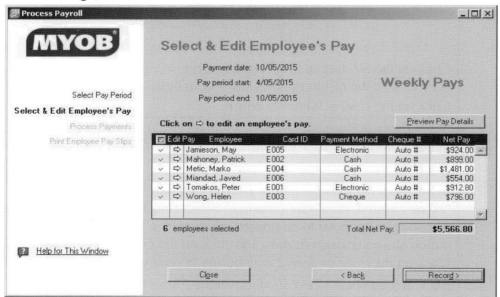

Figure 8.26: *Select & Edit Employee's Pay* **window for all weekly pays**

6. Click the *OK* button when you receive a message that the paycheques have been recorded successfully.

7. Your *Process Payments* window should look like Figure 8.27 on the next page.

8. Click on the *Prepare Electronic Payments* button.

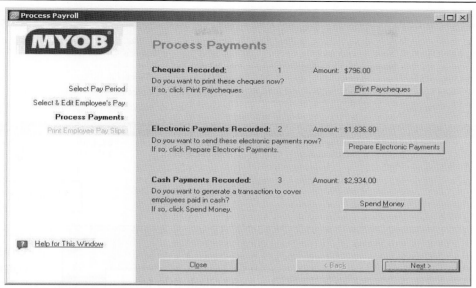

Figure 8.27: The *Process Payments* window in the 'Process Payroll' option

9. In the *Prepare Electronic Payments* window, select both of the employees to be paid by clicking in the right-hand column. The 'Bank Processing Date:' should be "10/5/2015". If your *Prepare Electronic Payments* window looks like Figure 8.28 on the next page click on the *Bank File* button at the foot of the window (**do NOT** click on *Record*.) An "ABA" file will be created to be sent to the bank for these electronic payments. Click on the *OK* button to record this electronic payment and save the resulting file as "CBA.ABA" to a suitable location (ignore any date warnings – you are either paying <u>before</u> the system date or <u>after</u> that date).

10. Click on the *Cancel* button to close the *Prepare Electronic Payments* window.

11. Click on the *Spend Money* button [Spend Money] to draw a cash cheque for the employees to be paid in cash. In the *Spend Money* window, the date should be 10/5/2015. Type "Cash" in the 'Payee' box. If your *Spend Money* window looks like Figure 8.29 on the next page, click the *Record* button to record and return.

> **Warning:** If you repeat the above recording a second transaction will be recorded. If that happens, you need to go to the *Disbursement* tab in the 'Transaction Journal' and delete the extra transaction.

12. Back in the *Process Payment* window click on the *Next* button. In the *Print Employee Pay Slips* window click on the *Print or Email Pay Slips* button.

13. In the *Review Pay Slips Before Delivery* window, select the 'To Be Printed' tab and click on the *Advance Filters* button, tick the box for the payment dates and enter the dates as from 4/5/2015 to 10/5/2015. Click the *OK* button to return.

14. Tick the pay slips <u>to be printed</u> in the *Review Pay Slips Before Delivery* window. Tick **all** employees for the 10/05/2015 then click on the *Print* button.

15. Back in the *Print Employee Pay Slips* window, click on the *Finish* button.

IMPORTANT: Where an employee is paid by cheque, no further processing is required. The entry in the accounts will be completed by processing the payroll. If the business uses pre-printed cheque forms, the *Print Paycheques* button in the *Process Payments* window needs to be clicked to print the cheques.

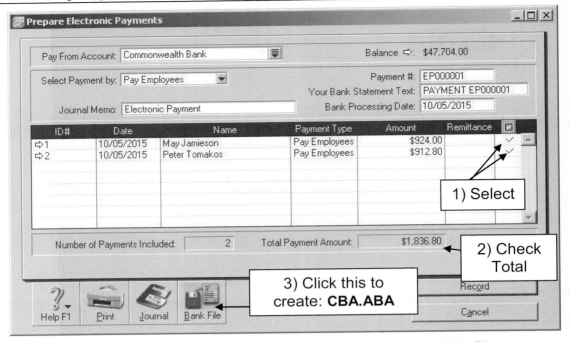

Figure 8.28: Electronic payments to be sent to the bank in an ABA file

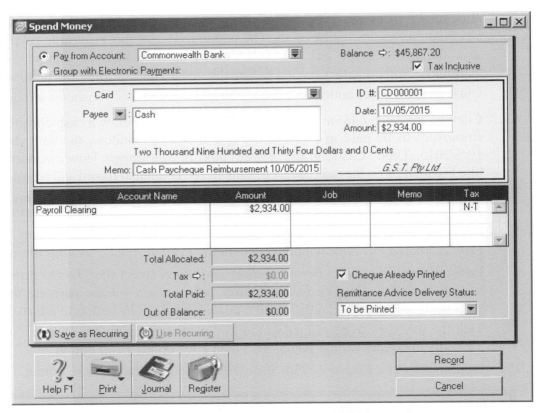

Figure 8.29: Cash cheque for net wages to be paid in cash

Video: A video showing you how to pay standard pays is on the DVD

Self-test exercise 8.8

Process the payroll on 17/05/2015 for the week 11/5/2015 to 17/05/2015. No changes are necessary to the standard pay. Pay Tomakos and Jamieson electronically using a *Bank File* (save it as CBA2.ABA) and draw a cash cheque for the wages paid in cash.

As the 'Pay Slips' are not to be printed for this pay, click on *Finish*. Print the "Payroll Advice" report instead. Click on the *Reports* button below the command centre and select *Payroll*. Select the *Payroll Advice* option. *Customise* to enter the dates from 11/5/2015 to 17/05/2015 and in the *Finishing* tab make sure the option *Separate Pages* is **not** selected.

Automatically adjust base pay amount when employees take days off

A *Wages* category can be set up so that when an employee is paid for that category the base hourly or the base salary amount will automatically be adjusted. For example, if an employee is paid for sick pay, the hours entered in the 'Sick Pay' field will automatically be taken off the base hours (or the base salary amount). Similarly when an employee is paid for holiday pay, the base hours or the base salary amount will be reduced accordingly when processing the pay.

In order to use this feature you need to edit both these *Wages* categories. Refer to the 'How to add, edit or delete a wages payroll category' on page 8-20 to complete the next example.

Example 8.11—Automatically adjust base pay amount when leave is taken

1. The file called dem81.myo should be opened.
2. Select the *Payroll Categories* option from the *Payroll* command centre.
3. If not already selected, click on the *Wages* tab at the top of the *Payroll Category List* window.
4. Click on the detail arrow ⇨ next to the wage category "Holiday Pay" to edit it.
5. Tick the option box: 'Automatically Adjust Base Hourly or Base Salary Details'.
6. Your screen should look like Figure 8.30. Click on the *OK* button.

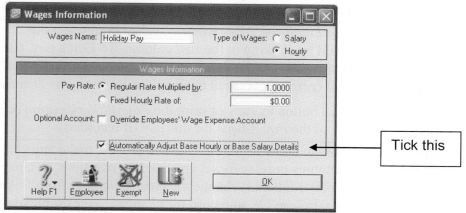

Figure 8.30: Holiday pay edited to automatically adjust base pays

Video: A video showing you how to automatically adjust base pay is on the DVD

Self-test exercise 8.9

Have the data file dem81.myo open.
Edit the existing *Wages* category "Sick Pay" so that the hours taken (or the amount paid) for that category is automatically reduced off the base hourly or the base salary.

Adjustments to the standard pay

The payroll information entered on employee cards is the expected <u>norm</u> for each pay period (the standard pay). In the previous examples and self-test exercises, no changes were made to these standard pays. Changes to the standard pay information set up will occur in situations where an employee becomes entitled (for the current pay period only) to receive overtime pay, sick pay, holiday pay, commissions, bonuses or any other allowances as well as any changes to the normal deductions in the standard pay.

Changes to the standard pay are made in the *Select & Edit an Employee's Pay* window in *Process Payroll*. An employee is selected by clicking on the detail arrow. Each change is then made by clicking on the relevant field in the *Pay Employee* window and entering the new data. **These changes will only affect that particular pay and do <u>not</u> change the underlying standard payroll information**.

<u>Permanent</u> changes to the standard pay can be made either by modifying the *Payroll Categories* or by modifying the *Employee's Payroll Information* on the employee's card.

No permanent change to the standard pay is required for this exercise.

How to process a pay with adjustments to the standard setup

Step	Instruction
1	Select the *Process Payroll* option from the *Payroll* command centre.
2	In the first window for *Select Pay Period*, select the option to pay employees for a particular pay period (e.g. weekly) or an individual for a particular payment date. If holiday pay is to be paid in advance (usual), select the tick box for this and enter the necessary details. Enter the payment date, the pay period (start and end dates) and click on the *Next* button.
3	In the *Select & Edit Employee's Pay* window, select or deselect the employees to be paid by clicking in the first column. To Edit a pay, click on the detail (zoom) arrow ⇨ next to the employee's name. To verify that the changes are entered correctly, you can click on the *Preview Pay Details* Preview Pay Details button to view or print the *Payroll Verification* report which is a preview of the *Pay Advice* for this pay (if recorded).
4	In the *Pay Employee* window for the selected employee, make any changes necessary to the amounts previously set up – such as overtime, sick pay and commission. You may (optional) change the cheque number from '#Auto' to the actual number. Click on *OK* to record the changes to the employee's pay.
5	Click on *Record* and then *Continue* to process the paycheques for this period.

Example 8.12—Process a payroll with adjustments to the standard pays

1. Have the file called dem81.myo open.

2. Select the *Process Payroll* option from the *Payroll* command centre.

3. In the *Select Pay Period* window, select the option to process all employees with a weekly pay period. Enter the payment date as "24/5/2015". Enter the pay period dates as "18/5/2015" to "24/5/2015". Click on the *Next* button.

4. Click on the detail arrow next to the employee: Metic, Marko.

5. Marko Metic is to be paid one day's sick pay (8 hours).
    This business works a normal 40-hour 5-day week hence 1 day = 40/5 = 8 hours.

    Click in the 'Hours' column next to "Sick Pay" and enter "8" and ↵.
    The hours for the "Base hourly" should automatically display 32 now. This is only possible if the "Sick Pay" wages category has been set up to do this in self-test exercise 8.9 on the previous page.

6. Marko works 4 hours overtime at 'time and a half'. Click in the 'Hours' column next to Overtime (1.5x) and enter "4" and ↵.

7. The pay for Marko Metic should be as per Figure 8.31. Scroll down if you cannot check the whole window.

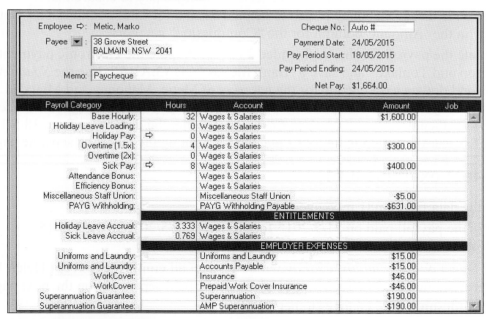

Figure 8.31: Marko Metic's pay with 1 day's sick pay and 4 hours overtime

8. Click on the *OK* button to record the changes for this pay to Marko Metic's wages.

<u>Continue changing standard pays by completing self-test exercise 8.10 on the next page.</u>

IMPORTANT: Check your answers as you go with those at the end of this chapter.

Video: A video showing you how to process payroll with adjustments to the standard pays is on the DVD

Self-test exercise 8.10

Have the data file dem81.myo open. This exercise continues on with the payroll for the week ended 24/5/2015 started in Example 8.12 on the previous page.
Adjust the standard pays if necessary for the following:

Helen Wong is to be paid 2 days sick leave. Click next to "Sick Pay" in the 'Hours' column and enter 16 hours and $400 should display in the 'Amount' column. Check that the "Base Salary" is reduced by $400 automatically, to display $600.

Peter Tomakos and **May Jamieson** have no changes to their standard pays.

Javed Miandad is to be paid 3 hours overtime at time-and-a-half (1.5x) plus 2 hours overtime at double-time (2x).

Patrick Mahoney has purchased a motor vehicle from the business. This has been recorded as a staff loan and he is to repay $40 per pay period starting this pay. This deduction needs to be set up first *before* changing the standard pay for Mahoney. Minimise the *Process Payroll* window so that you can see the *Payroll* command centre. Set up a new payroll deduction category called "Staff Loans – Mahoney" and link it to an account with the same name (Acc. # 1-1460). Enter the amount per period as $40 and No Limit. Make sure to select "Mahoney" as the employee. Click *OK*. Restore *Process Payroll* window and check Mahoney's pay to ensure that this deduction is listed. Mahoney is also to be paid $1,286 for sales commissions. Enter "1286" in the 'Amount' column for the "Commission" category.

Complete the payroll for the week ended 24/5/15. Prepare the electronic payments for Jamieson and Tomakos and save a 'Bank file' as "CBA3.ABA". Use the *Spend Money* button and draw a cash cheque for the net pays of Metic, Mahoney and Miandad. Print the "Payroll Advice" report instead of the Pay Slips. To select *Payroll Advice* click on *Reports* then the *Payroll* tab. Use *Customise* to enter the date range from 18/5/15 to 24/5/15. Clear the option in the *Finishing* tab for printing the report on separate pages.

Self-test exercise 8.11

Have the data file dem81.myo open.
Process the payroll paid on 31/5/2015 for the week 25/5/2015 to 31/5/2015.
The following details relate to this pay period:

In the *Select & Edit Employee's Pay* window select all employees **except** Helen Wong (i.e. clear the tick next to her name). Helen will be paid separately on the next page.

May Jamieson has no changes to her standard pay.

Javed Miandad is to be paid 2 hours overtime at time-and-a-half (1.5x) and 8 hours of sick leave. Check that the "Base Hours" has changed to 32 hrs (40 less 8 hours sick pay).

Patrick Mahoney is to be paid commission of $1,127.00.

Peter Tomakos is to be paid commission of $1,486.00.

Prepare the electronic payments for Tomakos and Jamieson and save a 'Bank file' as "CBA4.ABA". Use the *Spend Money* button and draw a cash cheque on the Commonwealth Bank for the net pays of Metic, Mahoney and Miandad.

Print the *Payroll Advice* report instead of the Pay Slips. Use *Customise* to enter date range as 25/5/2015 to 31/5/2015 and not to print on separate pages.

Self-test exercise 8.12

Process the payroll for **Helen Wong**, who will be paid for two weeks – a week of standard pay and a week's holiday pay <u>in advance</u> plus holiday leave loading:

In the *Select Pay Period* window enter the following details:

Select *Process individual employee*: option.

Click on the *List* button and select **Helen Wong** for this pay.

Payment date "31/5/2015", Pay period start "25/5/2015" and Pay period end "7/6/2015" (ignore any dates error). Tick to select the option 'Pay leave in advance'.

In the *Leave in Advance* window enter "1" for 'Weeks of standard pay',
press TAB (don't press ENTER) and enter "1" for the 'Weeks for leave in advance' and press TAB again. 'Total weeks in this pay' should display "2". Click *OK*.

Click on the *Next* button. In the *Select & Edit Employee's Pay* window click on the detail arrow ⇨ next to Helen Wong to modify her pay details as follows:

> Enter 40 hours for Holiday Leave Loading and 40 hours for Holiday Pay.

> The "Base Salary" amount should automatically change from $2,000 to $1,000.

The 'Number of Pay Periods:' should display "2" at the bottom of the form.
Click *OK*. Back in *Select & Edit Employee's Pay* click *Record* then *Continue*.

In the *Process Payments* window click on *Next*. In the *Print Employee Pay Slips* window click on the *Print or Email Pay Slips* button.

In the *Review Pay Slips Before Delivery* window, click on the *Advance Filters* button first to select "Wong, Helen" as the employee and to enter the 'payment date' as From: "31/5/2015" to "31/5/2015" (same date) and click the *OK* button to return to the *Review Pay Slips Before Delivery* window.

Tick next to her pay slip for the payment date 31/05/2015 and click on *Print*.

Using timesheets for recording hours worked

In the above examples and self-test exercises the total hours worked by the employees were entered from written worksheets recording and summarising the daily hours worked by each employee. *MYOB AccountRight Plus* has an *optional* feature that allows entries of hours worked by 'hourly' employees (i.e. not for salary employees).

You can use timesheets to record information either for payroll only or payroll and time-billing. Before using this feature, it is necessary to set it up. In the *Setup/Preferences* menu option under the *System* tab, make your selection, as well as nominating the day of the week the pay week starts (e.g. Thursdays).

If this option is used, it is important to remember that the hours entered using the *Enter Timesheet* option from the *Payroll* command centre will be added to the hours entered on the employee's card in the *Standard Pay* option of the *Payroll Details* window. Therefore, a decision has to be made whether this option will be used to enter *additional* hours worked, such as overtime, or to enter *all* the hours worked including standard hours. If the latter is the case, it will be necessary, then, to change the standard pay hours to "0" on the employee's card.

As the majority of the employees in the above exercise are not on "hourly" pay and the ones paid on an hourly basis work a fixed number of hours per week and they are not paid for any time-billing activities, there was no need to use this feature.

How to print a payroll report

Step	Instruction
1	Select the *Payroll* command centre.
2	Click on the *Reports* button located at the bottom of the command centre. Reports ▼
3	Scroll down the *Name* panel and click on the report required.
4	Click on the *Customise* button and make selections from the resulting *Report Customisation* window – for example: items to report, report period, range, etc.
5	Click the *Display* button to review the report on screen. Check for all possible errors (this is important to avoid unnecessary printing of incorrect reports).
6	Click on the *Print* icon at the bottom of the window to obtain a printout.

Example 8.13—Printing the payroll journal

1. Have the file called dem81.myo open.
2. Select the *Payroll* command centre.
3. Click on the *Reports* button.
4. Select the report called "Payroll Journal" as shown on Figure 8.32 (scroll down if necessary):

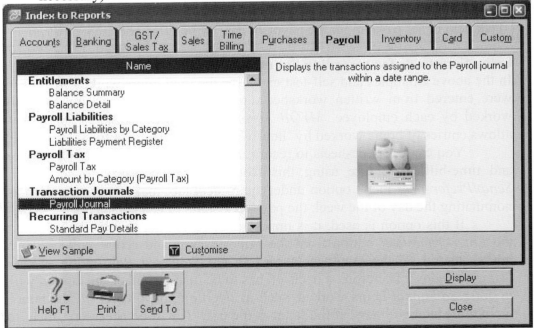

Figure 8.32: "Payroll Journal" report selected

5. Click on the *Customise* button and select "All" for the 'Employees:' field. The period is from 31/5/2015 to 31/5/2015 (only the last pay period will be printed to save paper).

6. Click on the *Display* button to review the report.

7. Click on the *Print* button if a hard copy is required.

Example 8.14—Print a Payroll Register [Summary] report

1. Have the data file dem81.myo open.

2. Select the *Payroll* command centre.

3. Click on the arrow on the *Reports* button and select "Payroll".

4. Click on the "Register Summary" report.

5. Click on the *Customise* button and select the month of "May" as the period and check that "All" has been selected for 'Employees' (top of the screen).

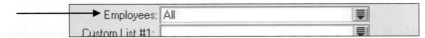

6. Click on the *Display* button and examine the report on screen (if necessary use the maximise button and the horizontal scroll bar to see the whole report, or select "Screen Report" at the top of the *Report Display* window). If your *Report Display* window looks like Figure 8.33, click on the *Print* button.

Payroll Register [Summary]

May 2015

Page 1

Employee		Wages	Deductions	Taxes	Net Pay	Expenses
Jamieson, May		$4,800.00	$96.00	$1,008.00	$3,696.00	$648.00
Mahoney, Patrick		$6,913.00	$80.00	$1,808.00	$5,025.00	$565.76
Metic, Marko		$8,300.00	$20.00	$2,173.00	$6,107.00	$986.00
Miandad, Javed		$3,087.00	$420.00	$316.00	$2,351.00	$395.34
Tornakos, Peter		$6,101.40	$20.00	$1,506.20	$4,575.20	$620.49
Wong, Helen		$5,175.00	$250.00	$830.00	$4,095.00	$578.50
	Total:	$34,376.40	$886.00	$7,641.20	$25,849.20	$3,794.09

Figure 8.33: Payroll Register [Summary] report

Video: A video showing you how to print payroll reports is on the DVD

Self-test exercise 8.13

Have the file dem81.myo open.

Print a "Payroll Activity [Summary]" report (all employees) for the weekly pay ended 31/5/2015.

Hint: Select "Activity Summary" report under the 'Employees' heading at the top then customise the report before printing. Enter date 'From' **and** 'To' as 31/5/2015.

Payroll category inquiry

As well as reports, details of each payroll category can be displayed and/or printed. This can be done using the *Find Transactions* button then selecting *Payroll Category*.

How to make a payroll category inquiry

Step	Instruction
1	Select the *Payroll* command centre.
2	Click on the *Find Transactions* button and *Payroll Category* tab (if not already selected) and search by *Pay Category*.
3	Enter the payroll category required. Use the *ENTER* key or click on the *List* button ▣ to bring up a selection list.
4	Change the 'From' and 'To' dates if necessary.
5	Click on the *Print* button if a printout is required.

Example 8.15—Make an inquiry on sick pay paid in a period

1. Have the data file called dem81.myo open.

2. Click on the *Find Transactions* button (located at the bottom of the command centres) and select *Payroll Category* tab (if not already selected).

3. Search by "Pay Category" and select "Sick Pay" as the "Payroll Category". Enter the period as "1/05/2015" to "31/05/2015".

4. If your screen looks like Figure 8.34, you can click on the *Print* button to print the details for this category.

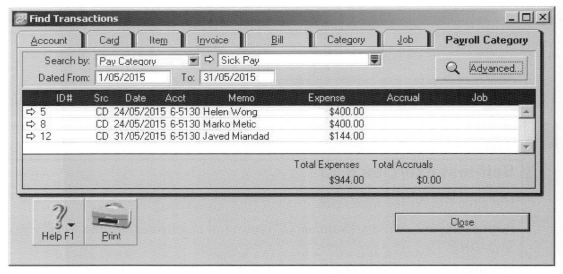

Figure 8.34: *Find Transactions* **window for 'Sick Pay' payroll category**

Video: A video showing you how to make payroll inquiry is on the DVD

Payments of amounts withheld – deductions and employer expenses

Deductions (including PAYG taxes) and employer expenses held in liability accounts need to be disbursed to third parties monthly or when they are due for payment.

How to make payments of liability amounts withheld from payroll

Step	Instruction
1	Click on the *Pay Liabilities* option from the *Payroll* command centre.
2	Check the bank and change it, if necessary, in the 'Pay from Account' field at the top of the *Pay Liabilities* window.
3	In the 'Supplier' field select the supplier if there is a card already made up for this supplier. Alternatively, leave this field blank and enter supplier's details (name and address) in the 'Payee' box.
4	In the 'Cheque No:' change the cheque number, if necessary.
5	Enter the 'Payment Date:' and ↵.
6	Change the 'Memo' if necessary.
7	Click on the down arrow next to 'Liability Type:' and make a selection. ✔ Deductions Expenses Superannuation Taxes
8	Click on the *List* button ▼ next to 'Payroll Categories:' to select the category or categories to be paid to the above supplier.
9	Enter the date range in 'Dated From:' and 'Dated To:'.
10	A list of expenses or deductions will be displayed. Click ☑ in the right column against the amounts to be paid to the supplier selected above.
11	Click on the *Record* button.

Example 8.16—Pay a liability amount withheld as a deduction

1. Have the file called dem81.myo open.
2. Select the *Pay Liabilities* option from the *Payroll* command centre.
3. Change the 'Payment Date:' to "31/05/2015".
4. Leave the 'Supplier' field blank as there is no card for this supplier.
5. In the 'Payee' field enter: "ABC Credit Union".
6. In the 'Memo' field enter: "Helen Wong account".
7. Select "Deductions" for the 'Liability Type'.
8. Click on the *List* button next to 'Payroll Categories', de-select all and tick next to "ABC Credit Union" to select it. Click on the *OK* button.
9. Set the 'Dated From:' as "1/05/2015" and 'Dated To:' as "31/05/2015".
10. Tick next to the amount $250.00 ☑.
 Make sure the 'Total Payment' shows "$250.00".
11. If your screen looks like Figure 8.35 on the next page, click on the *Record* button.

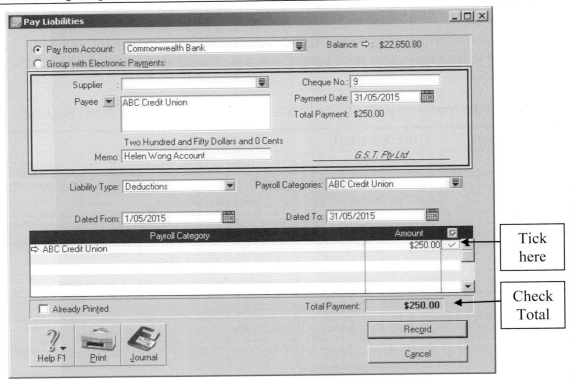

Figure 8.35: Helen Wong's deduction paid to ABC Credit Union

Video: A video showing you how to pay a payroll liability is on the DVD

Self-test exercise 8.14

Have the file dem81.myo open.

Pay the following payroll deduction liability <u>for the month of May 2015</u>:

Using the *Pay Liabilities* option from the *Payroll* command centre:
  Issue a cheque dated 31/05/2015 to "Burwood Court" for $400.00.
  Change the 'Memo' to "Garnishee Order – Javed Miandad".
  Set the 'Liability Type:' to "Deductions".
  Select "Garnishee order" from the 'Payroll Categories' list and set the 'Dated From:' as "1/05/2015" and 'Dated To:' as "31/05/2015".
  Tick next to the amount $400.00 ☑ and click on the *Record* button.

Note: Payments of other deductions and expenses are either not yet due for payment or have been prepaid. For example, *WorkCover* insurance is prepaid and PAYG deductions (for this business) are paid every three months (quarterly) and are due for payment 28 days after the June 2015 quarter.

That is the end of the exercises on the data file dem81.myo. Exit this file. **A new file dem82.myo will be used in the following examples and exercises**.

Carrying out payroll end of year functions

In *MYOB AccountRight Plus* you can have up to two End of Year functions – the normal financial End of Year and payroll End of Year. A business might have its financial year-end on 31 December while the payroll year ends on 30 June. For most businesses, however, the end of payroll year coincides with the end of the financial year at 30 June. In any event, there are two End of Year procedures – one for the financial year (which you would have performed in Chapter 3) and one for the payroll year.

The steps that need to be performed for the payroll End of Year procedure are:

1. Enter all transactions, pay all payroll liabilities that are due, print reports and make any necessary amendments.
2. Make a backup of your data file.
3. Prepare *Payment Summaries* using the *Print Payment Summaries.*
4. Make a final backup of your data file.
    (**Note**: use a different backup file name to that used in step 2.)
5. Start a New Payroll Year.

Notice that there are two backups mentioned in the above steps. The first backup is created *before* you start preparing and issuing the *Payment Summaries* and the other is just *before* you start a New Payroll Year. This is important because you will then be able to go back to any step you wish to re-do.

The existing data file called dem82.myo will be used, which should be copied to your working disk/folder. This file is in fact a continuation of the same business used in the file dem81.myo, but the June weekly pays have been entered, as well as the payment of any payroll liabilities due.

Video: A video showing you how to back up data files is on the DVD

Self-test exercise 8.15

Start *MYOB AccountRight Plus* and open an existing file **dem82.myo.**

Change the business address to "(your name) – dem82.myo".

Back up this data file. You may refer to the 'How to …' in Chapter 1 to assist you with this function. Make sure that you select the option button:

    ⊙   Backup Company File and M-Powered Services only

Save the backup file as: dem82.zip and place it in C:\Temp or any other appropriate folder. (You may copy this .zip file to your working disk after you exit. Remember, the MYOB program will not save a backup file to the same location if the original file is saved on a removable disk such as a floppy or a USB disk.)

How to use the Payment Summary Assistant

Step	Instruction
1	Select the *Payroll* command centre.
2	Click on the *Print Payment Summaries* option. Print Payment Summaries
3	In the first window of the assistant you need to select either 'Individual non-business ...' or 'Labour hire and other specified payments'. For employees/workers employed (not hired) select the first option. ⊙ Individual non-business (NAT 72710B) and Employment termination payment (NAT 70868) Click on the *Next >* button. **Note:** At each window of the setup, you may click on the *Next* button to move forward through the setup, the *Back* button to return to a previous window, the *Close* button to exit or you may go to a particular page by selecting it from the list on the left pane of the *Payment Summary Assistant* window.
4	The second window of the assistant is the *Company Information* page. Enter the company details as well as the contact details – (for example: contact name, phone, email, the ABN, and the authorised signatory).
5	Click *Next*. The third window is the *Payment Summary Fields* page. A table with columns is used to list the 'Payment Summary Field', the 'Description' and the 'Select Payroll Categories':

Payment Summary Fields

Link each payment summary field with the relevant payroll categories.

To link a field, select it in the Payment Summary Field column, type the description that you want to appear on the payment summary (if required) and then select the payroll categories that relate to that field.

Payment Summary Field	Description	Select Payroll Categories
Gross Payments		Advance
Allowance 1		Attendance Bonus
Allowance 2		Back Pay
Allowance 3		Base Hourly
Allowance 4		Base Salary
Allowance 5		Bonus
Allowance 6		CDEP Payments
Allowance 7		Commission
Allowance 8		Efficiency Bonus
Allowance 9		Holiday Leave Loading
Lump Sum Payments A	Termination	Holiday Pay
Lump Sum Payments A	Redundancy	Long Service Leave
Lump Sum Payments B		Other Income
Lump Sum Payments D		Overtime (1.5x)
Lump Sum Payments E	Accrued in 2013-2014	Overtime (2x)
Lump Sum Payments E	Accrued in 2012-2013	Sick Pay
Lump Sum Payments E	Accrued prior to 1/7/2012	Unused Holiday Pay
Work Place Giving 1		Unused Long Service Leave
Work Place Giving 2		ABC Credit Union

	For each 'Payment Summary Field' (in the left column) select the payroll categories (if any) that will be linked to it and reported against it. **Note:** The categories that you select here **cannot** be selected for any other 'Payment Summary Field'. An error message will be displayed if you do. The description column is used to give the field a more appropriate label.
6	Repeat the above for other 'Payment Summary Fields' required.
	(continued on the next page)

Step	Instruction
7	Scroll up or down the left panel to select any field that is relevant and should be included in the payroll summary. For each of these fields, select the payroll categories listed in the last column that need to be linked to it by ticking in the 'Select' column next to the category.
8	Scroll down on the left panel to the "Total Tax Withheld" field and make sure the "PAYG Withholding" is selected on the right panel before proceeding to the next step. (You need to scroll down both lists – left and right.)
9	Click *Next* to go to the *Reportable Employer Super* window and *Next* again to *Reportable Fringe Benefit* window. If there are any reportable employer super or fringe benefits, these amounts need to be calculated and entered in these two windows. You need to check with the ATO for more information.
9	Click *Next* to go to the *Review the Payment Summaries* window. Only the employees that have a mark (tick) in the left-hand column will be issued with a payment summary. Print the "Payment Summaries" and have them checked for accuracy. Click on the *Print Payment Summaries* button. Verify the prints and if there are any errors you can click on the zoom arrow next to the employee's name and do the necessary changes (such as the tax file number, the address etc.) or you can *Close* to exit and fix the errors first. Click on the *Save Payment Summaries* to save the payment summaries. This will create separate PDF files for each employee's "Payment Summary".
10	Click *Next* to go to the *Verify your Payroll Information* window. You can click on the *Preview Verification Report* button at the bottom to get a printout that you can use if you are **manually** completing the payment summary form. However, if you are lodging the forms electronically with the ATO you need to create a file known as the "EMPDUPE File". This file can <u>also</u> be saved to a CD, DVD, floppy disk or USB flash drive and sent to the ATO. Click *Next*.
11	In the '*Create EMPDUPE File*' window you can create the EMPUDE file by clicking on the first button `Create EMPDUPE File`. You will need to nominate the file name and location. The file ***must*** be named "EMPDUPE.A01" (A – zero – one). The saved file can be sent to the ATO accompanied by a form called "Magnetic Media Form" which can be printed by clicking the second button `Print Magnetic Media Form`. **Note:** If you are submitting more than one EMPDUPE file on the same disk, then the second file should have an extension .A02 and so on up to "EMPDUPE.A99". Each file represents a different employer. You will also need a different magnetic form, i.e. "Magnetic Media – Multiple Files" form. This can be obtained from ATO.
12	Click *Next* to go to the last window *Make a Backup*. Click on the *Backup* button to create a backup file.
13	Click on the *Finish* button. You are ready now to roll over your payroll and start a new payroll year.

Example 8.17—Print employees' payment summaries using plain paper

1. Start *MYOB AccountRight Plus* and open the existing file called dem82.myo.

2. Select the *Payroll* command centre.

3. Select the *Print Payment Summaries* option.

4. In the first window select the first option:

   ⊙ Individual non-business (NAT 72710B) and Employment termination payment (NAT 70868)   Then click *Next*.

5. In the *Company Information* page enter the details as shown in Figure 8.36:

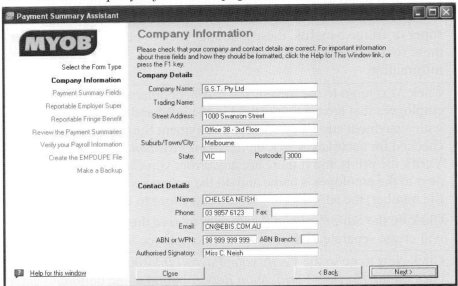

Figure 8.36: *Company Information* window

6. Click on *Next* to the *Payment Summary Fields* page. Select "Gross Payments" field from the left panel then select the following payroll categories on the right panel to be linked to it: Base Hourly, Base Salary, Commission, Holiday Pay, Overtime (1.5x) and (2x), and Sick Pay as per Figure 8.37 on the next page.

   VERY IMPORTANT: Once you link a 'Payroll Category' (from the right panel) for a 'Payment Summary Field' (on the left panel), you CANNOT link the same category to another field. **An error message will be displayed if you do.**

7. Scroll down and select 'Deduction 1' from the left panel, type "Union fees etc" in the description column and select (tick) the 'Miscellaneous Staff Union' payroll category on the right panel.

8. Scroll down and select 'Total Tax Withheld' from the left panel. Scroll down the list on the right panel and check that the category 'PAYG Withholding' is selected (ticked). Click on the *Next* button.

9. There was no Reportable Employer Super or Reportable Fringe Benefit paid, so click on the *Next* button twice to the *Review the Payment Summaries* page.

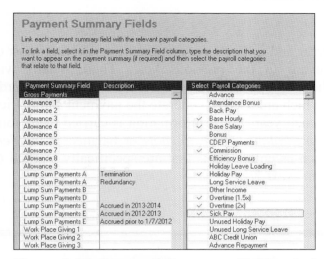

Figure 8.37: Payment Summary Fields window

10. All employees should be ticked (selected) in the first column to have their payment summaries produced. Print the payroll summaries for all the employees by clicking on the button: ⟨ Print Payment Summaries ⟩.

11. Save the Payment Summaries – click on the button ⟨ Save Payment Summaries ⟩. Change the location in the 'Save in:' field and click *Save*. A separate PDF file will be created and saved for <u>each</u> of the Payment Summaries – one for each employee.

12. Click on *Next* to go to the *Verify your Payroll Information* page. You can print a "Preview Verification Report" that will list all the amounts that need to be reported on the employees' payment summaries. That will create a hard copy that can be used for reference or if the form to the ATO is to be filled in manually. Click on the button: ⟨ Preview Verification Report ⟩ View the report and click on *Print* (if a print is required) and *Close*.

13. Click on *Next* to go to the *Create the EMPDUPE File* window. If the payment summaries details are to be sent electronically or by mail or courier to the ATO an EMPDUPE file needs to be created for that purpose. This file will contain exactly the same information as in the report printed on the previous step.

Click on the button: ⟨ Create EMPDUPE File ⟩ and accept the name "EMPDUPE.A01". Change the file location if necessary and click on *Save*. If a message to also print the "Magnetic Media Form" appears, click on *Yes*. Alternatively, you can click on the button: ⟨ Print Magnetic Media Form ⟩

14. Click on *Next* to go to the *Make a Backup* window. Click on the *Backup* button to save a second backup of the data file. Save it as "dem82FIN.zip" onto the hard disk in an appropriate folder such as C:\TEMP, C:\STUDENT or your own USB disk or folder.

15. Click on the *Finish* button.

16. Exit from *MYOB AccountRight Plus*. (You may copy the backup file to your working disk or folder and start a new payroll year.)

Video: A video showing you how to print Payment Summaries is on the DVD

Starting a new payroll year

This process ends one payroll year and rolls it over into the next, clearing most of the payroll details that were relevant to the previous year. These details will be permanently lost except on the backup file. This process is essential in order to maintain <u>*annual*</u> payroll totals, which are used to generate the payment summaries and need to be zeroed at the end of each year. Some information is carried over from one year to the next, including *history balances* and *accruals* or balance of *entitlements* that spread beyond one year, such as entitlements that are specifically marked *Carry Remaining Entitlement Over to the Next Year*.

> **IMPORTANT:**
> Unlike the financial year, in payroll you **cannot** start paying employees in the new payroll year before closing out the current payroll year.

How to start a new payroll year

Step	Instruction
1	Click on the *File* pull-down menu.
2	Select 'Start a New Year' menu item and point and click on "Start a New Payroll Year".
3	A warning is displayed. Read it carefully and make a backup (if you have not already made one), by clicking on the *Backup* button before continuing. You can cancel this process and exit by clicking on *Cancel*, otherwise click on *Continue* to start a new payroll year.
4	Another message regarding the deletion of all payroll history records relevant to the year just ended and a reminder about having a backup copy or copies secured in a safe place. Read this important message and when ready click on *Continue* (or *Cancel* to exit).
,5	In the next step you are required to enter the new payroll year. Check the year entered by *MYOB AccountRight Plus* and if correct click on *Continue*. **Note:** The payroll year must always end on 30 June.
6	Yet another *final* warning and reminder. If everything is in order, click on *Start a New Payroll Year* button.
7	That is the end of this process. To check the payroll year click on the *General Payroll Information* item from the *Setup* menu. **Note:** It is a good idea to update your Tax Table at this stage. You can download the tax tables from MYOB if you are a subscriber to *MYOB Cover*.

Example 8.18—Start a new payroll year

1. Start *MYOB AccountRight Plus* and open the existing file called dem82.myo.
2. Click on the *File* pull-down menu.
3. Click on 'Start a New Year' item and select "Start a New Payroll Year".
4. As a backup was already made in Example 8.17, click on the *Continue* button.
5. Read the warning message and click on the *Continue* button.
6. Make sure the new payroll year is "2016". Click on the *Continue* button.
7. Click on the *Start a New Payroll Year* button.

Select "General Payroll Information" option from the *Setup* drop down menu and check that the payroll year is 2016.

Video: *A video showing you how to start a new payroll year is on the DVD*

That is the end of the exercises on the data file dem82.myo. Exit this file. **A <u>new file</u> dem83.myo will be used in the following examples and exercises**.  **NEW FILE**

Starting a payroll during a payroll year

The business in the previous examples and exercises started paying employees from the date it started using *MYOB AccountRight Plus* payroll. There will be situations where a business has already been operating during a payroll year, and has been paying employees before it introduced *MYOB AccountRight Plus* payroll. The payroll details from the start of the payroll year up to the introduction of *MYOB AccountRight Plus* payroll will need to be entered as historical data.

The example that follows is for a small engineering consultancy business that has been operating for some years and using *MYOB AccountRight Plus* for its accounting functions. On 2 January 2015 it decided to use the payroll module for paying salaries to the three engineers in the business. These employees are paid monthly and their year-to-date payroll historical details for the period 1 July 2014 to 31 December 2014 are to be entered into the records.

> You cannot enter historical pay details if your computer's <u>system date</u> is set to a date that is <u>before</u> the historical month being entered.
> Basically, you cannot nominate a date <u>in the future</u> to enter *historical* data! For example, if your computer system date is set to a date in February, you will not be able to enter *historical* data past January. However, you will not have any problem if you select 'Year to Date' instead of a specific month or period.

How to enter historical payroll data

Step	Instruction
1	Select the *Card File* command centre.
2	Select the *Cards List* option.
3	Click on the detail arrow ⇨ next to an employee's name.
4	Click on the *Payroll Details* tab at the top of the *Card Information* window.
5	Select the *Pay History* item on the left-hand side panel of the *Pay Details* window. Pay History ▶
6	Use the drop-down arrow and select a **month**, **quarter**, or **year-to-date** for entering (or showing) historical details. Show Pay History for: 1st Quarter ▼
7	To enter the historical balances, click on the current balance (usually $0.00) in the 'Activity' column for every category and expense and type in the amount for that category for that period (e.g. month, quarter, year-to-date).
8	You can click on the next cell or use the down-arrow key on your keyboard to move down a column to the next category.

The 'Year-To-Date' historical data for the period 1 July to 31 December 2014 has been prepared on a spreadsheet shown on the next page in Figure 8.38.

Example 8.19—Entering historical payroll data

1. Start *MYOB AccountRight Plus* and open the existing file called dem83.myo.
2. Select the *Card File* command centre.
3. Select the *Cards List* option.
4. Click on the *Employee* tab at the top of the *Cards List* window.
5. Select the employee called Jan Kruger by clicking on the detail ("zoom") arrow ⇨ next to the name.
6. Click on the *Payroll Details* tab at the top of the *Card Information* window.
7. Select the *Pay History* item in the bottom of the left-hand side panel of the window.
8. Click on the down arrow of the 'Show Pay History for' selection box and select the option "Year-To-Date" from the drop-down list.

NEW FILE

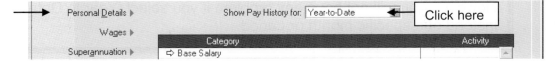

9. Click in the 'Activity' column against the pay category "Base Salary" and type in "37,083.33" – this is the year to date (YTD) total for the base salary figure for Jan Kruger shown in Figure 8.38.

Pay History

for the 'Year to Date'	*Activity*

Kruger, Jan

Base Salary		$37,083.33
Bonus		$5,000.00
PAYG Deductions		$10,398.00

Workcover		$1,262.52
Superannuation		$3,522.91

Tan, Tina

Sick Leave		$538.46
Base Salary		$34,461.52
Bonus		$5,000.00
PAYG Deductions		$9,594.00

Workcover		$1,200.00
Superannuation		$3,325.00

Wilson, Brian

Sick Leave		$307.69
Base Salary		$39,692.33
Bonus		$5,000.00
PAYG Deductions		$11,544.00

Workcover		$1,350.00
Superannuation		$3,800.00

> Historical data 'Year to date' totals for the period July to December for the employees to be entered onto their cards

Figure 8.38: Pay history details for the YTD July to December 2014

10. Use the down arrow or click in the 'Activity' column against the pay category "Bonus" and enter "5000.00".

11. Use the down arrow or click in the 'Activity' column against the pay category "PAYG Withholding" and type in "10,398.00".

12. Click in the 'Activity' column against the Employer Expense "WorkCover" and type in "1,262.52".

13. Use the down arrow or click in the 'Activity' column against the Employer Expense "Superannuation Guarantee" and type in "3,522.91" and ↵.
    If your *Pay History* in the *Payroll Details* window looks like Figure 8.39 on the next page, click *OK*.

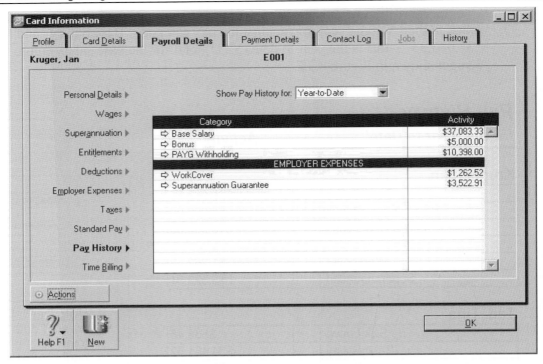

Figure 8.39: Year-to-Date (July to December) pay history for Jan Kruger

Self-test exercise 8.16

Use the existing file **dem83.myo**.

Use the data in Figure 8.38 on the previous page and enter in the pay history data ('Year To Date' balances) for **Tina Tan** and **Brian Wilson**.

I got my PAY !!

Competency checklist

	I can now complete the following assessment criteria:	√
1	Switch the computer and screen on and start *MYOB AccountRight Plus* program	
2	Open or create new *MYOB AccountRight Plus* data files	
3	Adjust chair and equipment to suit ergonomic requirements and use rest periods and appropriate exercises regularly	
4	Access information from manuals and/or on-line help	
5	Solve operational problems	
6	Set up payroll linked accounts	
7	Set up payroll information and payroll categories for employees' payroll	
8	Set up employees' records (cards) and set up their standard pays and maintain payroll information	
9	Enter Historical Opening Balances for Employees' activities	
10	Enter adjustments from time records by setting up and using the optional *timesheets* facility	
11	Process a payroll for a period and print reports for the pay period	
12	Modify periodical standard pays to account for overtime, sick pay and holiday pay as well any other adjustments to the standard pay	
13	Pay to third parties (such as unions, health funds and ATO) Payroll Liabilities for amounts withheld from payroll as deductions	
14	Pay to third parties for employer liabilities regarding expenses such as Superannuation Guarantee and *WorkCover*	
15	Print periodical reports such as Pay Advice and Pay Slips	
16	Print monthly and end of year reports such as "Payroll Summaries", "Payroll Journals" and "Payroll Registers"	
17	Prepare and print employees' "Payment Summaries"	
18	Do regular backups to avoid loss of data and carry out proper backups before major events such as preparing for the *Payment Summaries* and starting a new Payroll Year	
19	Start a new Payroll Year	
20	Find and display or print payroll category enquiries	

Chapter 8: Assessment exercises

Note: Throughout the following practical exercises you should continually observe relevant Occupational Health and Safety practices and apply recycling techniques to minimise paper wastage. In addition, you should use the on-line help facilities (the F1 key and/or Windows Help menu) and the notes to solve any problems you encounter.

The 'Tax Table Revision Date' for ALL the following exercises is 1/07/2014

8.1 *Payroll setup and weekly payrolls*

Fate Pty Ltd is commencing business on 30 January 2015. It wants to start the computerised payroll using *MYOB AccountRight Plus* at that date, with weekly payroll periods ending each Monday starting 6/2/2015.

Start *MYOB AccountRight Plus* and open the file ass81.myo.

Modify the 'Company Information' (from the *Setup* menu) as follows:
Edit the address field to include your full name and student number on the first line of the address.

If you use the *Easy Setup Assistant* for this exercise you will need to read parts (a), (b) and (c) before commencing so that you know where the information for the set up is located.

(a)   General Payroll Information

Use the SETUP menu and **load the tax table**

Check and <u>modify</u> if necessary the following payroll default linked accounts:
Bank Account for Cash Payments: 1-1120 Payroll Clearing
Bank Account for Cheque Payments: 1-1110 ANZ Bank
Bank Account for Electronic Payments: 1-1190 Electronic Clearing
Default Employer Expense Account: 6-5120 Superannuation
Default Wages Expense Account: 6-5110 Salaries and wages
Default Tax/Deductions Payable Account: 2-1410 Payroll deductions
                                         payable

Enter the following **General Payroll Information**
Payroll year ends on 30 June **2015**
No of hours in a full-time week = **40** hours
The Withholding Payer Number is **00 123 654 778**
Tax Table Rev. Date: 1/07/2014
Round pays to the nearest **100** cents
Default Superannuation Fund is **AMP Life**

(b)   Create **Employee cards**:
Individual details of the three staff are set out on the next page. **All employees**:
Start working for this company on **31 January 2015**;
Are paid weekly for 40 hours per week;
Are entitled to holiday and sick pay, and are covered by *WorkCover* insurance;
Have Superannuation Guarantee contributions paid to AMP Life.

Last Name	**Dennis**	**McRae**	**Lee**
First Name	Warren	Moira	Eileen
Card ID	001EMP	002EMP	003EMP
Address	27 Adamson Ave, Thornleigh NSW 2120	133 Aztec Ave, Boorowa NSW 2447	4/67 West Street, Darlinghurst NSW 2010
Phone	02 9419 2265	02 9436 7733	02 9244 5113
Email	wd@fate.com	mm@fate.com	el@fate.com
Salutation	Mr W Dennis	Moira	Eileen
Card Details Notes	N.O.K Elizabeth	N.O.K Derek	N.O.K Patrick
Date of Birth	20/12/1961	30/9/83	20/7/1973
Gender	Male	Female	Female
EMPL. Category	Permanent	Permanent	Permanent
EMPL. Status	Full Time	Full Time	Full Time
EMPL. Classification	Manager	Clerical Level 1	Salesperson
Pay basis	Salary	Hourly	Hourly
Salary or Hourly Rate	$62,400	$95.00	$80.00
SG Superannuation Empl. Membership #	5678943	5678944	5678945
Tax File Number	333 222 666	284 286 120	201 777 444
Tax Table	Tax free threshold	Tax free threshold	Tax free threshold
Rebates	$1,240	$1,100	$0
Payment Method	Electronic	Cheque	Cash
BSB Number	345-678	NA	NA
Bank account number	654789	NA	NA
Bank account name	W & E DENNIS	NA	NA
Statement Text	SALARY	NA	NA

(c)   Add or edit the following Payroll Categories:

Wages categories:

Add a *new* wages category called "Productivity Bonus". The type of wages is "Salary". Any bonus paid will be debited to the *default* 'Wages Expense Account' (No. 6-5110). **All employees** will be entitled to this bonus and it is subject to PAYG Withholding tax but exempt from all other deductions. (That is, **do not tick** next to 'PAYG Withholding tax' but tick all the others.)

Modify the *existing* 'Commission' wage category: Change the 'Employees' Wage Expense account' and select account number 6-2800 "Sales Commission" instead of the default. Only **Eileen Lee** is entitled to commission and it is subject to PAYG Withholding tax but is exempt from all other deductions.

Modify *existing* 'Holiday Pay' and 'Sick Pay' wages categories: Tick the option to 'Automatically Adjust Base Hourly or Base Salary Details' and select all employees for these wages.

Select all employees for the 'Holiday Leave Loading' wages category.

Modify *existing* 'Overtime (1.5x)' and 'Overtime (2x)' wages categories: Only **McRae** and **Lee** will be entitled to any overtime pay.

Deductions category:

All deductions in this exercise are <u>after</u> calculating PAYG tax, i.e. they <u>are not exempted</u> from tax. All deduction amounts are per 'pay period' with no deduction limits:

Modify the *existing* 'Union Fee' wages category. The linked payable account for this deduction is: 'Misc. Workers Union' (2-1440). **McRae** and **Lee** are to have $9.00 each per pay period deducted as union fees.

McRae is to have $48.50 per pay period deducted for 'Hospital & Medical Benefits' payable to Caledonian HS. The linked payable account for this deduction is: 'Caledonian HS' (2-1430).

Superannuation category:

Check (and modify if necessary) the superannuation expense 'Superannuation Guarantee'. The rate is 9.5% on 'Gross Wages', with no limits and the minimum monthly threshold is $450. The expense account to be debited is 'Superannuation' (6-5120) and the linked payable is 'Superannuation Fund' (2-1460). For the superannuation exemptions ***do not exempt*** Base Hourly, Base Salary, Back Pay, Holiday Pay, Long Service Leave and Sick Pay but ***do exempt*** all other wage categories. Print on 'Pay Advice'. **All employees** qualify for this expense.

Warren Dennis will have $150 per week deducted as 'Employee Additional', payable to the MLC Society Ltd. Create a new superannuation deduction and name it "Dennis Additional Super". Change the linked payable account for this superannuation deduction to "MLC Society Ltd" (2-1450). No limit for this deduction. Make sure this deduction is printed on 'Pay Advice'.

Employer Expense category:

Set up a <u>new</u> employer expense for "Uniforms". The expense amount is at a rate of $28 per pay period. **McRae** and **Lee** are the employees involved. The expense account to debit is "Uniforms" (6-5140), and "Accounts Payable" (2-1200) is the payables account. Print on 'Pay Advice'.

Set the rate for *WorkCover* at 3% of gross wages. This expense is paid for **all employees**. The linked expense account is "Workers Compensation" (6-5150) and the linked payable account is "Prepaid WorkCover Insurance" (1-1410).

Taxes category:
Change the default liability account for PAYG Withholding to:
"PAYG Withholding Payable" (2-1420).

(d)   Process the weekly payroll for all three employees on 6/2/2015 for the period 31/1/2015 to 6/2/2015. (No variation to standard pay.)
Save the *Bank File* for the electronic payment as "ANZ1.ABA" and use the *Spend Money* button in the process payroll to draw a cheque for the wages paid by cash.
Do not print the 'Pay Slips'.

(e)   Process the weekly payroll for all three employees on 13/2/2015 for the period 7/2/2015 to 13/2/2015.
McRae is to be paid 3 hours at time and a half and productivity bonus $350.
Lee is to be paid one day's sick leave (8 hours) and 2 hours at double time for Saturday morning work, as well as a productivity bonus $175.
Save the *Bank File* for the electronic payment as "ANZ2.ABA" and use the *Spend Money* button in the process payroll to draw a cheque for the wages paid by cash.
Do not print the 'Pay Slips'.

(f)   Process, in **two** steps, the weekly payroll for all three employees as follows:
Dennis & Lee are paid on 20/2/2015 for the period 14/2/2015 to 20/2/2015.
De-select McRae who will be paid separately next.
Dennis is to receive a productivity bonus of $445.
Lee is to be paid 2 hours at double time for Saturday morning work, plus $854.20 for January's commission on sales.
Save the *Bank File* for the electronic payment as "ANZ3.ABA" and use the *Spend Money* button in the process payroll to draw a cheque for the wages paid by cash.

Process McRae's pay **separately** on 20/2/2015 for the period 14/2/2015 to 27/2/2015:
Pay McRae 1 week standard pay and 1 week leave in advance. Edit her pay and enter 40 hours holiday pay and 40 hours holiday leave loading.
In addition to her standard pay she is also to be paid 4 hours at time and half.
Do not print the 'Pay Slips'.

(g)   Process the payroll for <u>two</u> employees on 27/2/2015 for weekly period 21/2/2015 to 27/2/2015.
Note that McRae has already been paid in advance for this week (click in the left-hand column in the *Select & Edit Employee's Pay* window to de-select McRae from this payroll).
(No variation to the standard pay for Dennis and Lee this week.)
Save the *Bank File* for the electronic payment as "ANZ4.ABA" and use the *Spend Money* button in the process payroll to draw a cheque for the wages paid by cash.
Do not print the 'Pay Slips'.

(h)   Print the following "Payroll" Reports for February 2015:
Date range for the following reports is: 1/02/2015 to 28/02/2015.
        Print a "Payroll Summary"
        Print a "Payroll Journal"
        Print a "Register Summary"

8.2 *Payroll set-up and weekly payrolls*

Hayjude Pty Ltd is to start a computerised payroll using *MYOB AccountRight Plus*. The payroll is to commence in February 2015.

Start *MYOB AccountRight Plus* and open the file **ass82.myo**.

Edit the address for this business to add your name.

If you use the *Easy Setup Assistant* for this exercise you will need to read all parts of this exercise before commencing so that you know where the information is for the set up.

(a)   General Payroll Information

Use the SETUP pull down menu and:

Load the tax table

Check and modify if necessary the following default linked account numbers:

Bank Account for Cash Payments:	1-1120 Payroll Clearing
Bank Account for Cheque Payments:	1-1110 ANZ Bank
Bank Account for Electronic Payments:	1-1190 Electronic Clearing
Default Employer Expense Account:	6-5120 Superannuation
Default Wages Expense Account:	6-5110 Salaries and wages
Default Tax/Deductions Payable Account	2-1410 Payroll deductions payable

Enter the following **General Payroll Information**

Payroll year ends on June 30, **2015**
No of hours in a full-time week = **40** hours
The Withholding Payer Number is **00 448 564 885**
Round pays to the nearest **10** cents
Default Superannuation Fund is **AMP Life**

(b)   Staff – **create cards**:

Individual details of the three staff are set out below and on the next page.
All employees:

Start working for this company on 31 January 2015;
Are paid weekly for 40 hours per week;
Are entitled to holiday and sick pay, and are covered by *WorkCover* insurance;
Have Superannuation Guarantee contributions paid to AMP Life.

Last Name	**Epstein**	**Star**	**McCartney**
First Name	Brian	Ringo	Pauline
Card ID	001	002	003
Address	325 Abbey Road, Chatswood NSW 2067	1 Pepper Drive, Beetleswood NSW 2687	48 Penny Lane, Norwegian Wood NSW 2010

(continued on the next page)

Continued from previous page	Epstein	Star	McCartney
Phone	02 9413 1916	02 9587 5558	02 9784 3341
Salutation	Brian	Ringo	Pauline
Card Details Notes	Manager N.O.K Gail	Bookkeeper N.O.K Rita	Salesperson N.O.K Eleanor Rigby
Date of Birth	16/11/1945	6/2/1950	18/3/1982
Gender	Male	Male	Female
Classification	Administration	Clerical Level 1	Salesperson
Pay basis	Salary	Hourly	Hourly
Salary/Rate	$170,000	$35.00	$75.00
SG Superannuation Empl. Membership #	1456781	1456782	1456783
Tax File Number	211 656 552	234 879 654	221 025 650
Tax Table	Tax free threshold	Tax free threshold	Tax free threshold
Rebates	$1,100	$1,200	$0
Payment Method	Electronic	Cheque	Cash
BSB Number	345-999	NA	NA
Bank account number	12345678	NA	NA
Bank account name	B EPSTEIN	NA	NA
Statement Text	SALARY	NA	NA

(c)   Add or edit the following Payroll Categories:

Wages categories:

Add a **new** wages category called "Monthly Bonus". This a "Salary" type wage. **All employees** will be entitled to this bonus and it will be exempt from tax and deductions other than PAYG tax. The default wages expense account will be debited with payments.

Change the expense account for the **existing** "Commission" from the default employees wage expense account to "Sales Commission" (6-2800) expense account. **Pauline McCartney** is the only employee entitled to commission. It is subject to PAYG tax but exempt from other deductions.

All employees will be entitled to holiday pay, holiday leave loading and sick pay. **Only for** 'Holiday Pay' and 'Sick Pay' wages, tick the option to 'Automatically Adjust Base Hourly or Base Salary Details'.

Star and **McCartney** may be paid overtime at time and a half and at double time, i.e. wages categories: Overtime (1.5x) and Overtime (2x).

Superannuation category:

Check (and modify if necessary) the superannuation expense 'Superannuation Guarantee'. The rate is 9.5% on 'Gross Wages', with no limits and the minimum monthly threshold is $450. The expense account to be debited is "6-5120 Superannuation" and the linked payable is 'Superannuation Fund' (2-1460). *Exempt* all wage categories but **do not exempt** Base Hourly, Base Salary, Back Pay, Holiday Pay, Long Service Leave and Sick Pay. **All employees** qualify for these expenses. Print on 'Pay Advice'.

Epstein will have $63.50 per week deducted for 'Employee Additional'. Name this **new** superannuation deduction: "Epstein Additional Super". Change the linked payable account for this deduction to 'Superannuation Fund' (2-1460). Print on 'Pay Advice'.

Entitlements category:

All employees are entitled to the "Holiday Leave Accrual" and the "Sick Leave Accrual" entitlement categories. Link the Wages categories to "Holiday Pay" and "Sick Pay". Print on 'Pay Advice' and carry any remaining entitlement over to the following year for both entitlements.

Deductions category:

All deductions in this exercise are after calculating PAYG tax, i.e. they are not exempted from tax. All deduction amounts are per 'pay period'.

Before commencing, a new account needs to be created. In the *Accounts* command centre create a current liability account No. 2-1455 and call it "Dedicated Workers Union".

Modify the existing 'Union Fee' deduction: **Star** and **McCartney** are to have $10.00 each deducted for 'Union Fee'. Change the liability account to the account created above.

Create a new deduction and name it "Hospital and Medical Benefits". Change the liability account to "Caledonia HS" (2-1430). **Star** is to have $18.70 deducted per pay period – with no limits.

Expenses category:

Set up a new Employer Expense for "Laundry" at a rate of $10 per week. The expense account is "Uniforms" (6-5140) and the payable account is "Payroll Deduction Payable" (2-1410). The employees are **Star** and **McCartney**. No exemptions.

Set the rate for *WorkCover* at 2% of gross wages. This expense is paid for **all employees**. The linked expense account is "Workers' Compensation" (6-5150) and the linked payable account is "Prepaid WorkCover Insurance" (1-1410).

Taxes category:

Change the default liability account for PAYG Withholding to: "PAYG Withholding Payable" (2-1420).

(d)   Process the weekly payroll for all three employees for the period 31/1/2015 to 6/2/2015. There are no variations to the standard pays. The net pays are paid on 6/2/2015. Save the *Bank File* for the electronic payment as "ANZ5.ABA" and use the *Spend Money* button in the process payroll to draw a cheque for the wages paid by cash.
No pay slips need to be printed.

(e)   Process the weekly payroll for all three employees for the period 7/2/2015 to 13/2/2015. The net pays are paid on 13/2/2015.
Star is to be paid 4 hours at time and a half. McCartney is to be paid 3 hours at double time for Saturday morning work and two days sick leave (16 hours). No changes to Epstein's standard pay.
Save the *Bank File* for the electronic payment as "ANZ6.ABA" and use the *Spend Money* button in the process payroll to draw a cheque for the wages paid by cash.
No pay slips need to be printed.

(f)   Process, in **two** steps, the weekly payroll for all three employees as follows:
Process Star's payroll <u>separately</u> on 20/2/2015 for period 14/2/2015 to 27/2/2015:
Pay Star 1 week standard pay and 1 week leave in advance. Edit his pay and enter 40 hours holiday pay and 40 hours holiday leave loading.
No pay slips need to be printed.

Process McCartney and Epstein together:
They are paid on 20/2/2015 for the period 14/2/2015 to 20/2/2015.
McCartney is to be paid 3 hours at double time for Saturday morning work.
No changes to Epstein's standard pay.
In the *Select & Edit Employee's Pay* window de-select Star from this pay (click in the left-hand column next to his name to clear it).
Save the *Bank File* for the electronic payment as "ANZ7.ABA" and use the *Spend Money* button in the process payroll to draw a cheque for the wages paid by cash.
No pay slips need to be printed.

(g)   Process the weekly payroll for **only two employees** paid on 27/2/2015 for the period 21/2/2015 to 27/2/2015. <u>Star is on holiday and has already been paid</u> in advance for this week. De-select him in the *Select & Edit Employee's Pay* window.
McCartney is to be paid one day sick leave (8 hours) and 3 hours at time and a half for overtime on Monday.
No changes to Epstein's standard pay.
Save the *Bank File* for the electronic payment as "ANZ8.ABA" and use the *Spend Money* button in the process payroll to draw a cheque for the wages paid by cash.
No pay slips need to be printed.

(h)   Print the following Payroll Reports:
Date range for the following reports is February 2015
(i.e. 1/02/2015 to 28/02/2015):
            Print a "Payroll Summary"
            Print a "Payroll Journal"
            Print a "Register Summary"

8.3   *Payroll set-up and fortnightly payrolls*

Alfred Chopin started a small wholesale firm on 4 January 2015, packing and distributing musical items. The business uses a computer accounting package for operations. From 1 February 2015 the payroll option is to be used. You have been engaged to set up the payroll system using *MYOB AccountRight Plus* and to run the payrolls.

Start *MYOB AccountRight Plus* and open the file **ass83.myo**.

Edit the address for this business to add your full name and student ID number.

(a)   General setup – load tax tables, linked accounts and general payroll information:

1. **Load the tax table**
2. **Check and modify if necessary the following default linked accounts:**
   Bank Account for Cash Payments: 1-1120 Payroll Clearing
   Bank Account for Cheque Payments: 1-1110 ANZ Bank
   Bank Account for Electronic Payments: 1-1190 Electronic Clearing
   Default Employer Expense Account: 6-5120 Superannuation
   Default Wages Expense Account: 6-5110 Salaries and wages
   Default Tax/Deductions Payable Acc: 2-1410 Payroll deductions payable

3. The **general payroll information** for this business is:
   Payroll year ends on 30 June, **2015**
   Number of hours worked per week is **40**
   The Withholding Payer Number is **00 448 564 885**
   Round pays to the nearest **100** cents
   Default Superannuation Fund is **AMP Life**

(b)   **Create** the following **employee cards**. Select (tick) for **all employees** the Holiday and Sick Leave *Entitlements* and the *WorkCover Employer Expenses*.

> **Dvorak**, Albert (Card ID EMP_01), 212 Princes Highway, Kogarah NSW 2217. Phone 02 9301 2265. Salutation "Albert". N.O.K. (next of kin) is "Tess Dvorak" (wife). Identifier is "S". Albert is a male with date of birth 3/01/1955. He started on 5/01/2015. Employment classification is "Sales Person". Base annual salary: $85,000 paid fortnightly. AMP Life Superannuation Guarantee Fund Employee Membership # is 3456781. T.F.N. (Tax File Number) is: 111 444 555. Tax scale is "No Tax Free Threshold" with no rebates claimed. Dvorak is paid by cheque.

> **Mahler**, Gustav (Card ID EMP_02), 106 Parramatta Road, Lidcombe NSW 2141. Phone 02 9643 8042. Salutation "Guss". Identifier is "S" and N.O.K. is "Heidi Mahler (mother)". Gustav is a male with date of birth 29/4/1976. He started on 4/1/2015. Employment classification is "Sales Person". Base annual salary is $48,000 paid fortnightly. AMP Life Superannuation Guarantee Fund Employee Membership # is 3456782. T.F.N. is 222 111 777. Tax scale is "Tax Free Threshold" with total rebates of $1,241. Mahler is paid by cheque.

(continued on the next page)

Bach, Stephanie (Card ID EMP_03), 55 Symphony Place, Peakhurst NSW 2210. Phone 02 9534 3314, Mobile 0499 123 532, Fax 02 9934 1419 salutation "Stephie". Identifier: "A" and N.O.K. is "Sebastian Bach" (husband). Stephanie is female with date of birth 2/6/1975. She started on 4/1/2015. Employment classification is "Clerical Level 1". Base annual salary is $52,000 paid fortnightly. AMP Life Superannuation Guarantee Fund Employee Membership # is 3456783. T.F.N. is 666 701 584. Tax scale is "Tax Free Threshold" and no rebates are claimed. Bach is paid electronically (BSB 443-678, account number 5672341, account name S BACH and statement text is SALARY).

Haydn, Joseph (Card ID EMP_04), 49 Surprise Crescent, Castle Hill NSW 2154. Phone 02 9680 3312. Salutation "Joseph". Identifier: "C" and N.O.K. is "Maria Haydn (sister) Mobile 0411 221 199". Joseph is male with date of birth 19/8/1952. He started on 4/1/2015. Employment classification is "Clerical level 2". Base hourly rate is $50 paid fortnightly. AMP Life Superannuation Guarantee Fund Employee Membership # is 3456784. T.F.N. is 666 111 222. Tax scale is "Tax Free Threshold" with $1,165 total rebate. Haydn is paid net wages in cash.

Handel, George (Card ID EMP_05), 66 Water Dance Avenue, Rooty Hill NSW 2766. Phone 02 9675 884. Salutation is "George". Identifier is "L" and N.O.K. is "Frederica Carr (sister)". George is male with date of birth 21/9/1981. He started on 4/1/2015. Employment classification is "General Hand Level 1". Base hourly rate is $35 paid fortnightly. AMP Life Superannuation Guarantee Fund Employee Membership # is 3456785. T.F.N. is 220 111 405. Tax scale is "Tax Free Threshold" with no rebate. Handel pays extra tax of "$10.00", and is paid net wages in cash.

(c)   Add or edit the following payroll categories:

(i)   Create a <u>new</u> wages category called "Productivity Bonus". Employees who may be eligible for this bonus are **Bach, Haydn** and **Handel**. Do not exempt any taxes or deductions.

(ii)   Edit the <u>existing</u> "Commission" wages category so that the correct expense account is debited 'Sales Commission' (6-2800). Only the two salespersons, **Dvorak** and **Mahler**, are entitled to this commission. Do not exempt any taxes or deductions.

(iii)   Edit each of the following existing wages categories: Holiday Pay, Holiday Leave Loading, Overtime (both 1.5x and 2x) and Sick Pay to include **all employees**. **Only for** 'Holiday Pay' and 'Sick Pay' wages tick the option to 'Automatically Adjust Base Hourly or Base Salary Details'. Do not exempt any taxes or deductions.

(iv)   Create a *new* deduction called "Salvation Army Christmas Appeal". The deduction is 1% of 'Gross Wages', <u>with a limit</u> of $20 per 'Pay period'. Create a new *liability* account "Salvation Army Donations" (2-1470) and use this new account as the linked payable account for this deduction. **All employees** participate in this appeal. This deduction is tax deductible – that is, you have to **exempt** the PAYG Tax for this deduction.

(v) Create the following general ledger accounts to be used as the two linked accounts in the following employer expense:

6-5135 "Staff Training"
2-1455 "Prov'n for Staff Training"

Create a new employer expense category for "Training Fees".
This is to be debited to: "6-5135 Staff Training"
and credited to: "2-1455 Prov'n for Staff Training".
The amount to accrue per pay period is $150 per employee, and the employees concerned are **Dvorak** and **Bach**. Print on 'Pay Advice'.

(vi) Check (and modify if necessary) the superannuation expense 'Superannuation Guarantee' that the rate is 9.5% on 'Gross Wages', with no limits and the minimum monthly threshold is $450. The expense account to be debited is "Superannuation" (6-5120) and the linked payable is "Superannuation Fund" (2-1460). Exempt all wage categories but do not exempt Back Pay, Base Hourly, Base Salary, Holiday Pay, Long Service Leave and Sick Pay. All employees qualify for these expenses. Print on 'Pay Advice'.

(vii) Edit the **existing** employer expense for "WorkCover" to show as the expense account: 'Insurance' (6-0525) and the linked payable account: "Prepaid WorkCover Insurance" (1-1410). The rate is to be 8% of 'Gross Wages' per pay period with no limits. This expense is paid on **all employees**. No exemptions. Print on 'Pay Advice'.

(viii) Change the **Taxes** liability account to: 'PAYG Withg. Payable' (2-1420).

(d) Enter the following 'Year-to-Date' historical pay data for January 2015:

Category	Bach	Dvorak	Handel	Haydn	Mahler
Overtime (1.5x)	102.00				
Base Salary/ Hourly	4,000.00	6,538.46	5,040.00	7,200.00	3,692.30
Sick Pay				800.00	
Commission		1,095.60			2,480.00
Productivity Bonus	250.00		195.00	300.00	
Salvation Army	20.00	20.00	20.00	20.00	20.00
PAYG	1,248.00	3,210.00	1,885.00	3,085.00	2,040.00
Training Fees	300.00	300.00			
WorkCover	348.00	610.68	403.20	664.00	493.78
Superannuation Guarantee	360.00	588.46	504.00	702.00	332.31

(e)   Run the payroll for the <u>fortnight</u> ended 14 February 2015.
Payment date is **14/02/2015** for period **1/02/2015** to **14/02/2015**.

There are no changes in this fortnight from standard payroll setup.

Save the ABA *Bank File* as "ANZ140215.ABA" for the electronic payment to a suitable location and use the *Spend Money* button in the process payroll to draw a cheque for the wages paid by cash.

Print the pay slips for all employees. First, you need to use the *Advanced Filters* button in the *Review Pay Slips Before Delivery* window to select 'All Employees' and to set the 'Payment date:' as from "14/02/2015" to "14/02/2015". Click on the *OK* button.
Tick the pays to be printed and then click on the *Print* button.

(f)   Do a payroll run for the <u>fortnight</u> ended 28 February 2015
Payment date is **28/02/2015** for period is **15/02/2015** to **28/02/2015**.

Changes to the standard pays are:

- Stephanie Bach to receive $375 "Productivity Bonus" and 3 hours overtime at 1.5 times plus 2 hours at double time.
- George Handel is sick for two days and is to be paid 16 hours sick pay. George is also to receive $250 "Productivity Bonus".
- Joseph Haydn is to be paid 4 hours overtime at time and a half. He is also to receive $450 "Productivity Bonus".
- Sales commission is to be paid to:
    Albert Dvorak $1,285 and
    Gustav Mahler $3,002

Save the ABA *Bank File* as "ANZ280215.ABA" for the electronic payment to a suitable location and use the *Spend Money* button in the process payroll to draw a cheque for the wages paid by cash.

No Pay Slips need to be printed for this pay.

(g)   Print the following reports:

Use the reports **Customise** button to customise each report

(i)   A "Payroll Journal" for the period 1/2/2015 to 28/2/2015.

(ii)   "Payroll Summary" [for All Categories – Period: **February 2015**]

(iii) "Register Summary" [for All Employees – Period: **February 2015**]

(h)   Print an enquiry result:

Use '*Find Transactions*' to do an inquiry on the payroll category '*Commission*' for the month of February 2015 and print it.

Chapter 8: Answers to self-test exercises

8.1   Refer to Chapter 1 if you need help to open a file and change the company information.

8.2   The employee card profile for Patrick Mahoney – other cards will be similar:

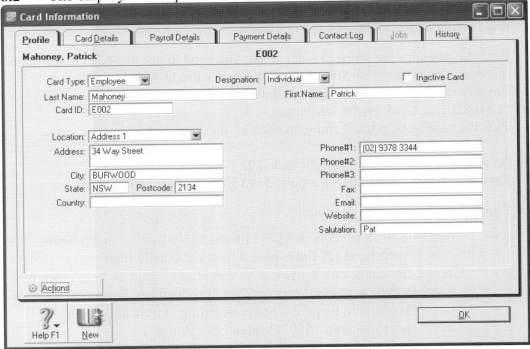

The following window shows the Personal Details for Patrick Mahoney. Other employees' personal details will be similar:

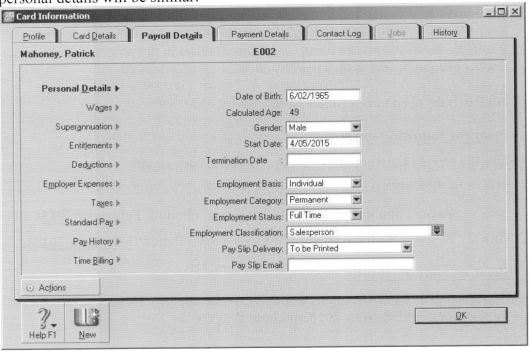

8.2 *(continued)*

The next window shows the Wages item in the Payroll Details for Patrick Mahoney who is paid on an annual salary basis:

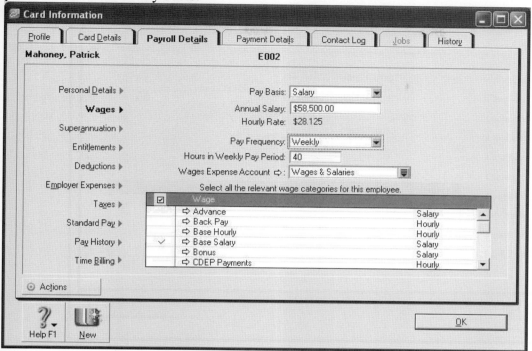

The Superannuation payroll details for Patrick Mahoney:

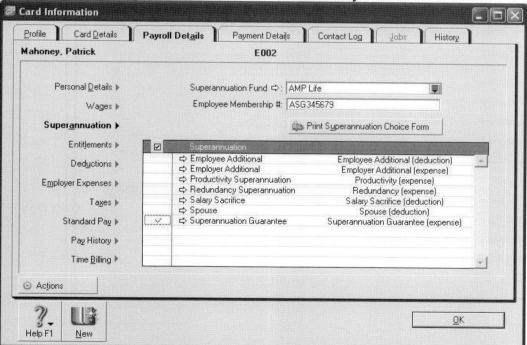

8.2 *(continued)*
Taxes payroll details for Patrick Mahoney:

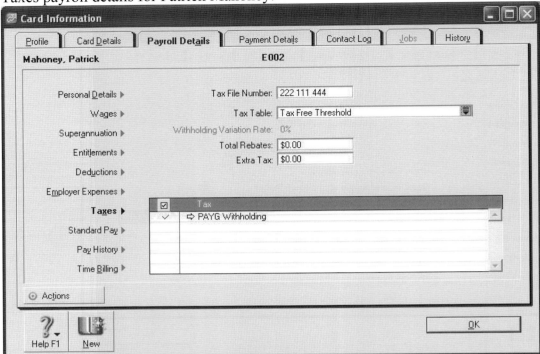

An example of Hourly salary basis – Wages details for Marko Metic:

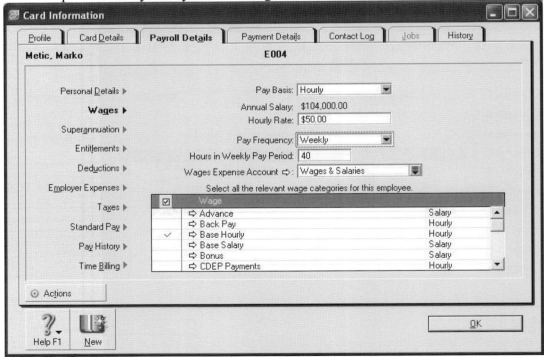

8.2 *(continued)*

Payment details for electronic payment to May Jamieson:

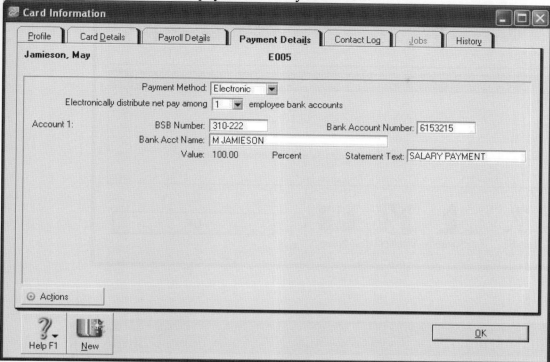

Example of Taxes payroll details showing rebates and extra tax for Javed Miandad:

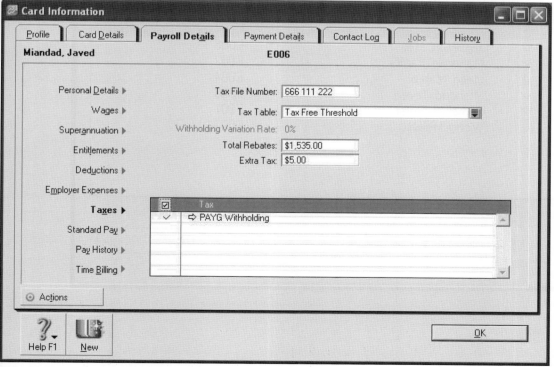

8.3

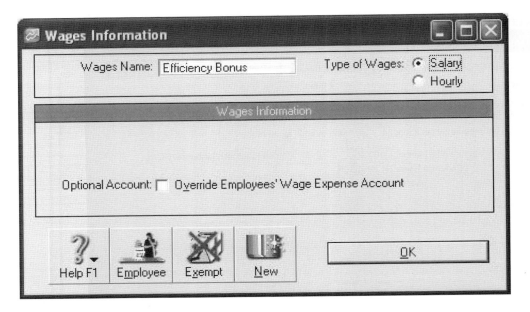

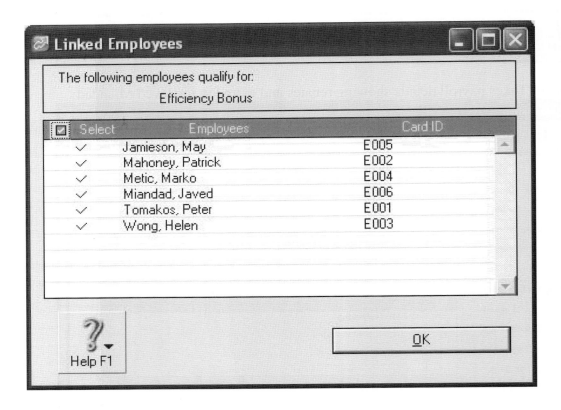

8.3 *(continued)*

An example of a wage category 'Commission' with an optional account selected:

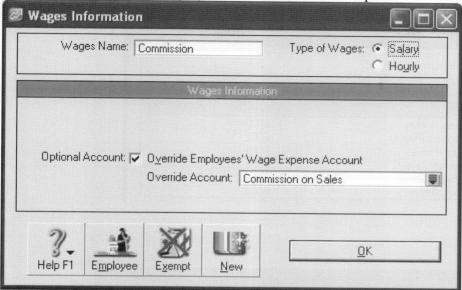

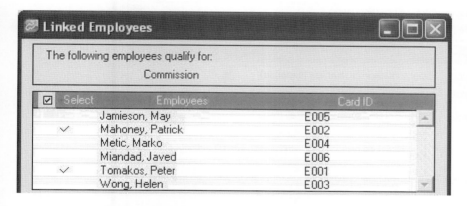

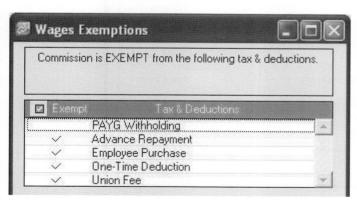

8.3 *(continued)*

The *Linked Employees* window for holiday pay, sick pay and both overtime wages categories will look similar to this:

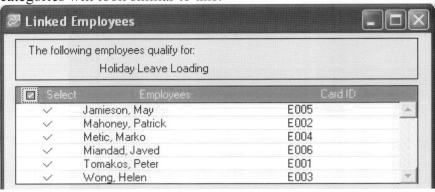

8.4

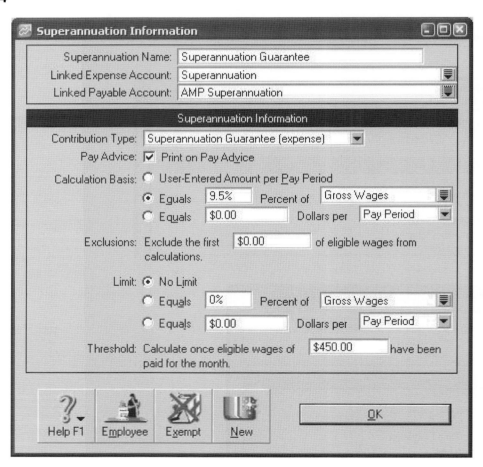

8.4 *(continued)*

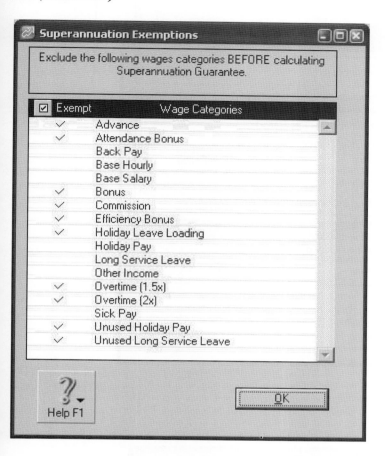

Superannuation payroll categories after addition and deletion:

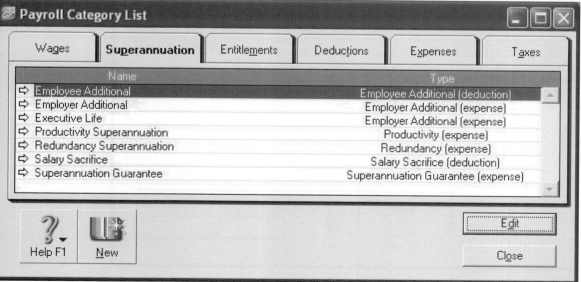

8.5

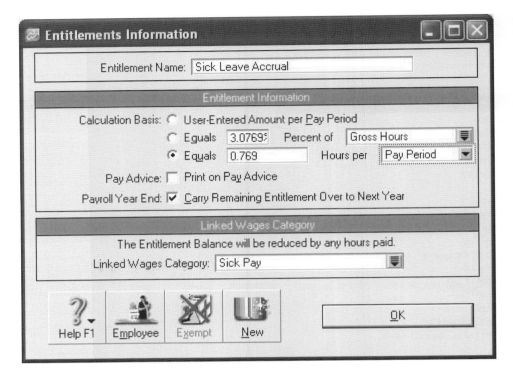

8.6

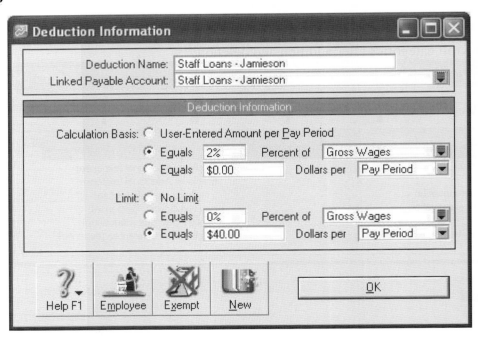

8.6 *(continued)*

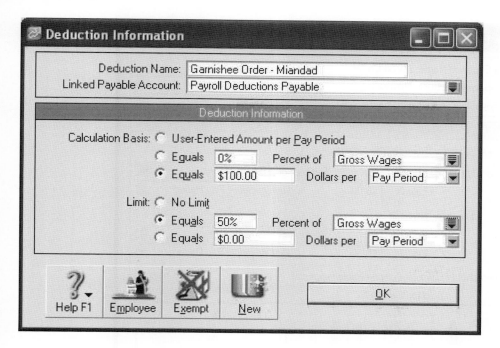

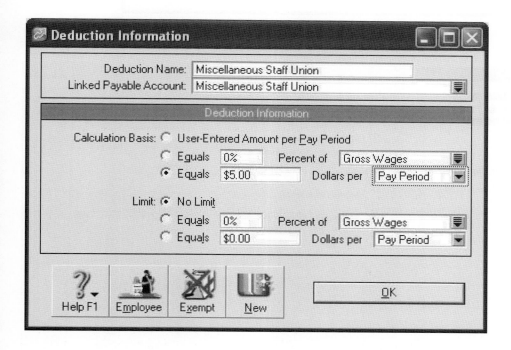

8.7

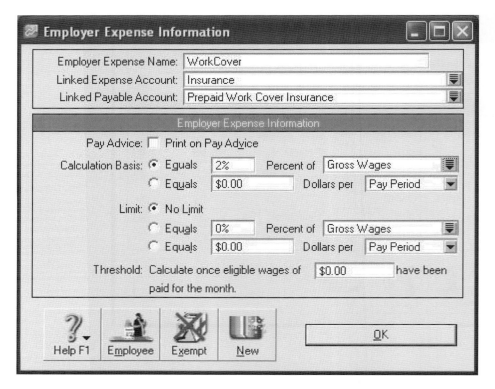

8.8

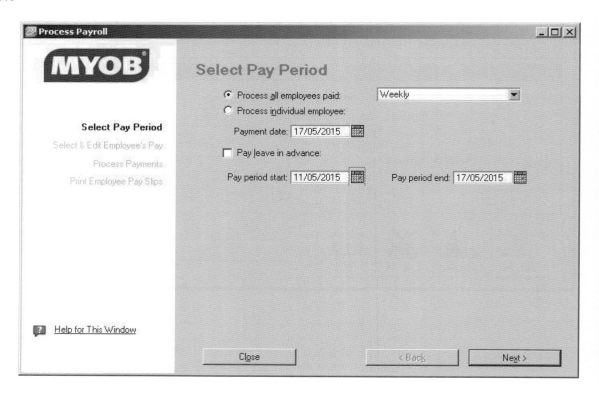

8.8 *(continued)*

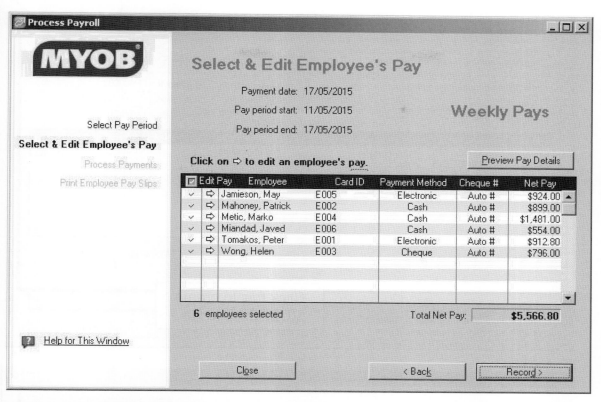

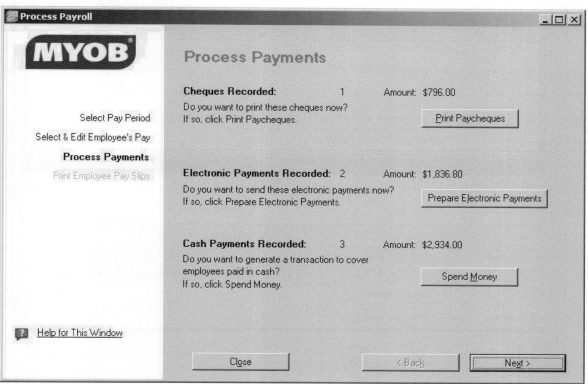

8.8 *(continued)*

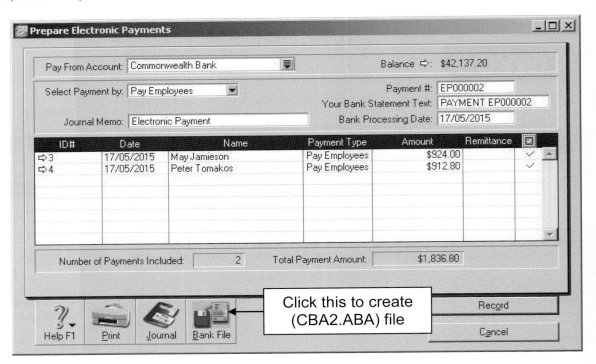

Click this to create
(CBA2.ABA) file

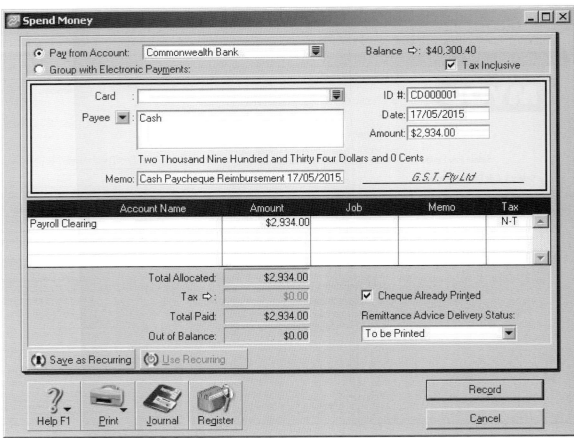

8.8 *(continued)*

Payroll Advice

11/05/2015 To 17/05/2015

G.S.T. Pty Ltd
A.B.N.:   98 999 999 999

Cheque No: 3
Payment Date: 17/05/2015

May Jamieson
Pay Frequency: Weekly
Pay Period: 11/05/2015 To 17/05/2015
Annual Salary: $62,400.00
Hourly Rate: $30.00
Employment Classification: Administration
Superannuation Fund: AMP Life
N.O.K. Joan (03) 3588 5456 (sister)

Gross Pay: $1,200.00
Net Pay: $924.00

Description	Hours	Calc. Rate	Amount	YTD	Type
Base Salary			$1,200.00	$2,400.00	Wages
Staff Loans - Jamieson			-$24.00	-$48.00	Deductions
PAYG Withholding			-$252.00	-$504.00	Tax
Executive Life			$24.00	$48.00	Superannuation Expenses
Superannuation Guarantee			$114.00	$228.00	Superannuation Expenses

---

G.S.T. Pty Ltd
A.B.N.:   98 999 999 999

Cheque No: 4
Payment Date: 17/05/2015

Patrick Mahoney
Pay Frequency: Weekly
Pay Period: 11/05/2015 To 17/05/2015
Annual Salary: $58,500.00
Hourly Rate: $28.125
Employment Classification: Salesperson
Superannuation Fund: AMP Life
N.O.K. Lizzy Mahoney (Spouse)

Gross Pay: $1,125.00
Net Pay: $899.00

Description	Hours	Calc. Rate	Amount	YTD	Type
Base Salary			$1,125.00	$2,250.00	Wages
PAYG Withholding			-$226.00	-$452.00	Tax
Superannuation Guarantee			$106.87	$213.75	Superannuation Expenses

---

G.S.T. Pty Ltd
A.B.N.:   98 999 999 999

Cheque No: 5
Payment Date: 17/05/2015

Marko Metic
Pay Frequency: Weekly
Pay Period: 11/05/2015 To 17/05/2015
Annual Salary: $104,000.00
Hourly Rate: $50.00
Employment Classification: Clerical Level 2
Superannuation Fund: AMP Life
N.O.K. Kylie (daughter)

Gross Pay: $2,000.00
Net Pay: $1,481.00

Description	Hours	Calc. Rate	Amount	YTD	Type
Base Hourly	40	$50.00	$2,000.00	$4,000.00	Wages
Miscellaneous Staff Union			-$5.00	-$10.00	Deductions
PAYG Withholding			-$514.00	-$1,028.00	Tax
Holiday Leave Accrual	3.333			6.67	Entitlements
Superannuation Guarantee			$190.00	$380.00	Superannuation Expenses

8.8 *(continued)*

G.S.T. Pty Ltd
A.B.N.:   98 999 999 999

Cheque No: 6
Payment Date: 17/05/2015

Javed Miandad
Pay Frequency: Weekly
Pay Period: 11/05/2015 To 17/05/2015
Annual Salary: $37,440.00
Hourly Rate: $18.00
Employment Classification: General Hand level 1
Superannuation Fund: AMP Life
N.O.K. Keria (mother)

Gross Pay: $720.00
Net Pay: $554.00

Description	Hours	Calc. Rate	Amount	YTD	Type
Base Hourly	40	$18.00	$720.00	$1,440.00	Wages
Garnishee Order - Miandad			-$100.00	-$200.00	Deductions
Miscellaneous Staff Union			-$5.00	-$10.00	Deductions
PAYG Withholding			-$61.00	-$122.00	Tax
Holiday Leave Accrual	3.333			6.67	Entitlements
Superannuation Guarantee			$68.40	$136.80	Superannuation Expenses

G.S.T. Pty Ltd
A.B.N.:   98 999 999 999

Cheque No: 4
Payment Date: 17/05/2015

Peter Tomakos
Pay Frequency: Weekly
Pay Period: 11/05/2015 To 17/05/2015
Annual Salary: $60,000.00
Hourly Rate: $28.8462
Employment Classification: Salesperson
Superannuation Fund: AMP Life
N.O.K. Jenny Maria Tomakos (spouse)

Gross Pay: $1,153.85
Net Pay: $912.80

Description	Hours	Calc. Rate	Amount	YTD	Type
Base Salary			$1,153.85	$2,307.70	Wages
Miscellaneous Staff Union			-$5.00	-$10.00	Deductions
PAYG Withholding			-$236.05	-$472.10	Tax
Superannuation Guarantee			$109.61	$219.23	Superannuation Expenses

G.S.T. Pty Ltd
A.B.N.:   98 999 999 999

Cheque No: 3
Payment Date: 17/05/2015

Helen Wong
Pay Frequency: Weekly
Pay Period: 11/05/2015 To 17/05/2015
Annual Salary: $52,000.00
Hourly Rate: $25.00
Employment Classification: Clerical Level 1
Superannuation Fund: AMP Life
N.O.K. Ralf Wong (Brother)

Gross Pay: $1,000.00
Net Pay: $796.00

Description	Hours	Calc. Rate	Amount	YTD	Type
Base Salary			$1,000.00	$2,000.00	Wages
ABC Credit Union			-$50.00	-$100.00	Deductions
PAYG Withholding			-$154.00	-$308.00	Tax
Superannuation Guarantee			$95.00	$190.00	Superannuation Expenses

8.9

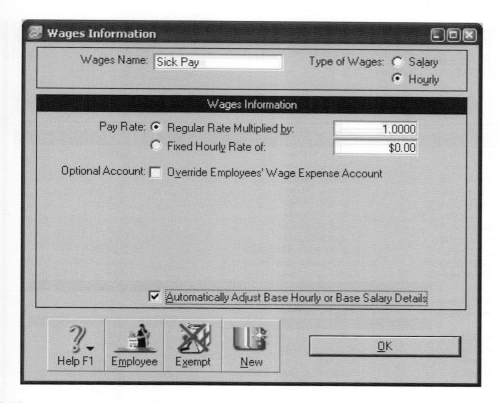

8.10

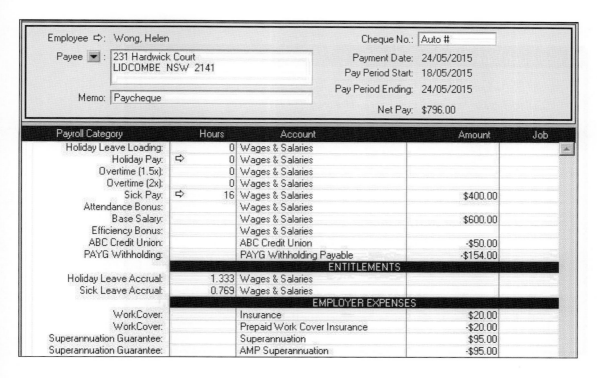

8.10 *(continued)*

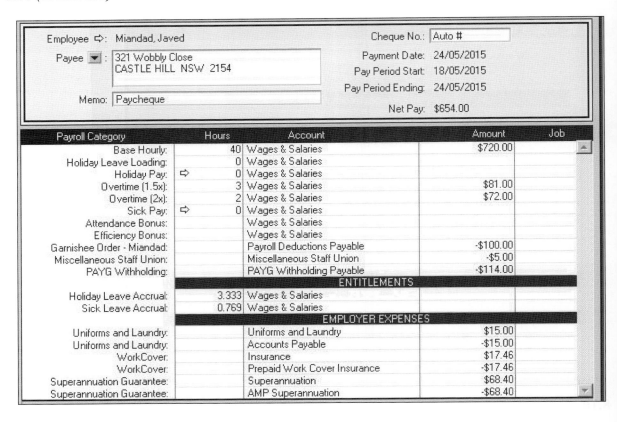

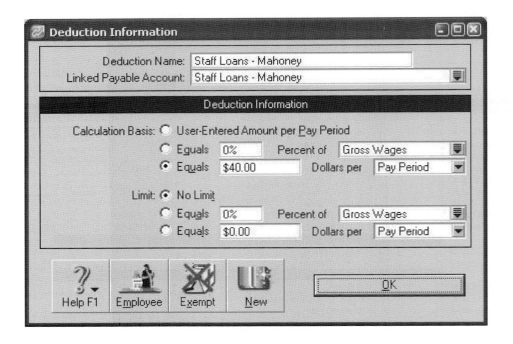

8.10 *(continued)*

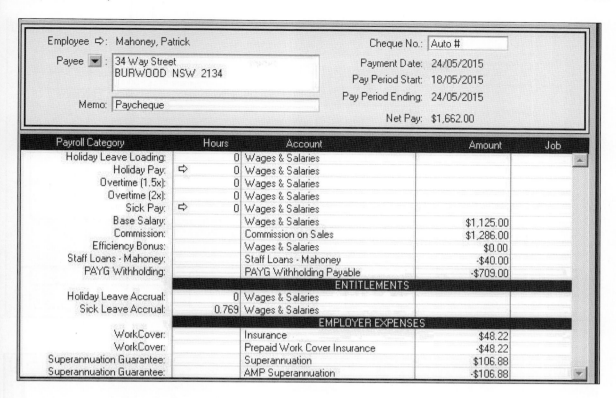

Payroll Category	Hours	Account	Amount	Job
Holiday Leave Loading:	0	Wages & Salaries		
Holiday Pay: ⇨	0	Wages & Salaries		
Overtime (1.5x):	0	Wages & Salaries		
Overtime (2x):	0	Wages & Salaries		
Sick Pay: ⇨	0	Wages & Salaries		
Base Salary:		Wages & Salaries	$1,125.00	
Commission:		Commission on Sales	$1,286.00	
Efficiency Bonus:		Wages & Salaries	$0.00	
Staff Loans - Mahoney:		Staff Loans - Mahoney	-$40.00	
PAYG Withholding:		PAYG Withholding Payable	-$709.00	
ENTITLEMENTS				
Holiday Leave Accrual:	0	Wages & Salaries		
Sick Leave Accrual:	0.769	Wages & Salaries		
EMPLOYER EXPENSES				
WorkCover:		Insurance	$48.22	
WorkCover:		Prepaid Work Cover Insurance	-$48.22	
Superannuation Guarantee:		Superannuation	$106.88	
Superannuation Guarantee:		AMP Superannuation	-$106.88	

Employee ⇨: Mahoney, Patrick
Payee ▼: 34 Way Street BURWOOD NSW 2134
Memo: Paycheque
Cheque No.: Auto #
Payment Date: 24/05/2015
Pay Period Start: 18/05/2015
Pay Period Ending: 24/05/2015
Net Pay: $1,662.00

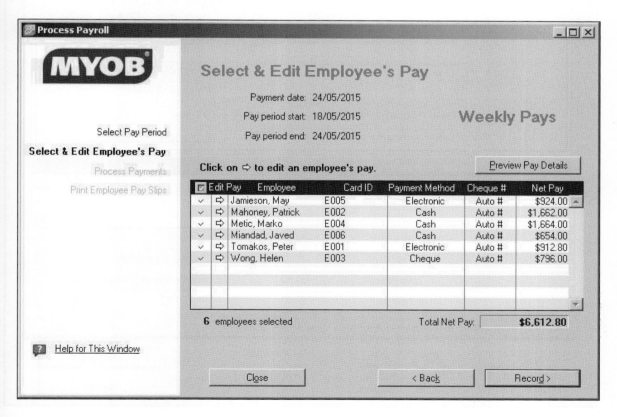

8.10 *(continued)*

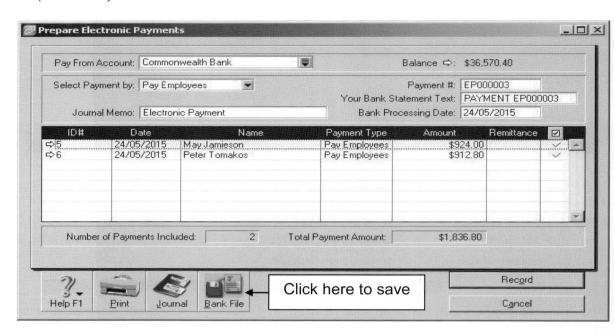

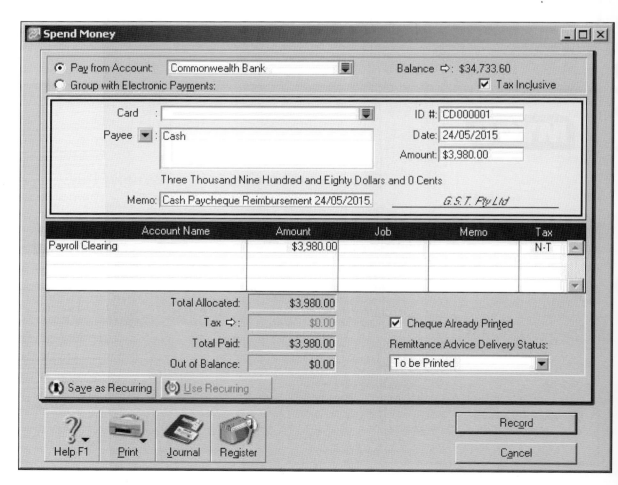

8.10 *(continued)*

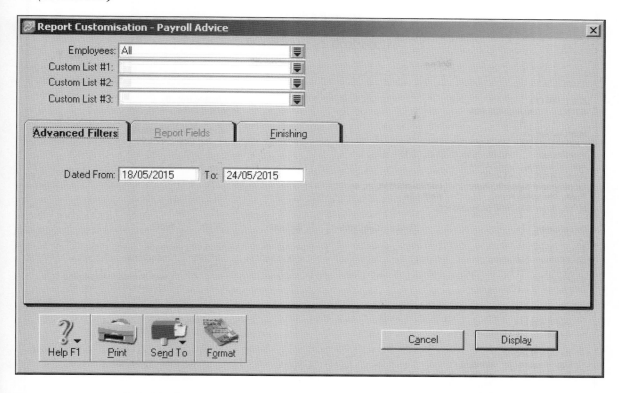

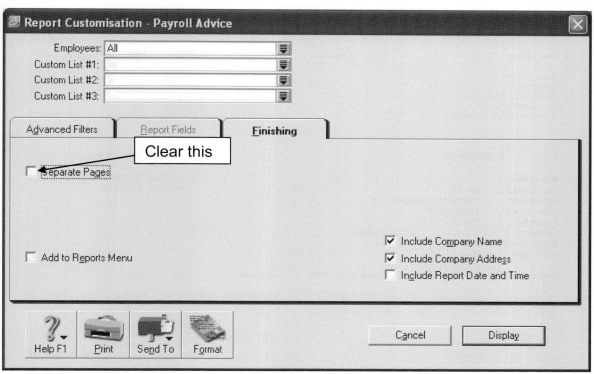

8.10 *(continued)*

Payroll Advice

18/05/2015 To 24/05/2015

G.S.T. Pty Ltd   Cheque No: 5
A.B.N.:   98 999 999 999   Payment Date: 24/05/2015

May Jamieson   Gross Pay: $1,200.00
Pay Frequency: Weekly   Net Pay: $924.00
Pay Period: 18/05/2015 To 24/05/2015
Annual Salary: $62,400.00
Hourly Rate: $30.00
Employment Classification: Administration
Superannuation Fund: AMP Life
N.O.K. Joan (03) 3588 5456 (sister)

Description	Hours	Calc. Rate	Amount	YTD	Type
Base Salary			$1,200.00	$3,600.00	Wages
Staff Loans - Jamieson			-$24.00	-$72.00	Deductions
PAYG Withholding			-$252.00	-$756.00	Tax
Executive Life			$24.00	$72.00	Superannuation Expenses
Superannuation Guarantee			$114.00	$342.00	Superannuation Expenses

---

G.S.T. Pty Ltd   Cheque No: 7
A.B.N.:   98 999 999 999   Payment Date: 24/05/2015

Patrick Mahoney   Gross Pay: $2,411.00
Pay Frequency: Weekly   Net Pay: $1,662.00
Pay Period: 18/05/2015 To 24/05/2015
Annual Salary: $58,500.00
Hourly Rate: $28.125
Employment Classification: Salesperson
Superannuation Fund: AMP Life
N.O.K. Lizzy Mahoney (Spouse)

Description	Hours	Calc. Rate	Amount	YTD	Type
Base Salary			$1,125.00	$3,375.00	Wages
Commission			$1,286.00	$1,286.00	Wages
Staff Loans - Mahoney			-$40.00	-$40.00	Deductions
PAYG Withholding			-$709.00	-$1,161.00	Tax
Superannuation Guarantee			$106.88	$320.63	Superannuation Expenses

---

G.S.T. Pty Ltd   Cheque No: 8
A.B.N.:   98 999 999 999   Payment Date: 24/05/2015

Marko Metic   Gross Pay: $2,300.00
Pay Frequency: Weekly   Net Pay: $1,664.00
Pay Period: 18/05/2015 To 24/05/2015
Annual Salary: $104,000.00
Hourly Rate: $50.00
Employment Classification: Clerical Level 2
Superannuation Fund: AMP Life
N.O.K. Kylie (daughter)

Description	Hours	Calc. Rate	Amount	YTD	Type
Base Hourly	32	$50.00	$1,600.00	$5,600.00	Wages
Overtime (1.5x)	4	$75.00	$300.00	$300.00	Wages
Sick Pay	8	$50.00	$400.00	$400.00	Wages
Miscellaneous Staff Union			-$5.00	-$15.00	Deductions
PAYG Withholding			-$631.00	-$1,659.00	Tax
Holiday Leave Accrual	3.333			10.00	Entitlements
Superannuation Guarantee			$190.00	$570.00	Superannuation Expenses

8.10 *(continued)*

Payroll Advice

18/05/2015 To 24/05/2015

Page 2

G.S.T. Pty Ltd
A.B.N.:   98 999 999 999

Cheque No: 9
Payment Date: 24/05/2015

Javed Miandad
Pay Frequency: Weekly
Pay Period: 18/05/2015 To 24/05/2015
Annual Salary: $37,440.00
Hourly Rate: $18.00
Employment Classification: General Hand level 1
Superannuation Fund: AMP Life
N.O.K. Keria (mother)

Gross Pay: $873.00
Net Pay: $654.00

Description	Hours	Calc. Rate	Amount	YTD	Type
Base Hourly	40	$18.00	$720.00	$2,160.00	Wages
Overtime (1.5x)	3	$27.00	$81.00	$81.00	Wages
Overtime (2x)	2	$36.00	$72.00	$72.00	Wages
Garnishee Order - Miandad			-$100.00	-$300.00	Deductions
Miscellaneous Staff Union			-$5.00	-$15.00	Deductions
PAYG Withholding			-$114.00	-$236.00	Tax
Holiday Leave Accrual	3.333			10.00	Entitlements
Superannuation Guarantee			$68.40	$205.20	Superannuation Expenses

G.S.T. Pty Ltd
A.B.N.:   98 999 999 999

Cheque No: 6
Payment Date: 24/05/2015

Peter Tomakos
Pay Frequency: Weekly
Pay Period: 18/05/2015 To 24/05/2015
Annual Salary: $60,000.00
Hourly Rate: $28.8462
Employment Classification: Salesperson
Superannuation Fund: AMP Life
N.O.K. Jenny Maria Tomakos (spouse)

Gross Pay: $1,153.85
Net Pay: $912.80

Description	Hours	Calc. Rate	Amount	YTD	Type
Base Salary			$1,153.85	$3,461.55	Wages
Miscellaneous Staff Union			-$5.00	-$15.00	Deductions
PAYG Withholding			-$236.05	-$708.15	Tax
Superannuation Guarantee			$109.62	$328.85	Superannuation Expenses

G.S.T. Pty Ltd
A.B.N.:   98 999 999 999

Cheque No: 5
Payment Date: 24/05/2015

Helen Wong
Pay Frequency: Weekly
Pay Period: 18/05/2015 To 24/05/2015
Annual Salary: $52,000.00
Hourly Rate: $25.00
Employment Classification: Clerical Level 1
Superannuation Fund: AMP Life
N.O.K. Ralf Wong (Brother)

Gross Pay: $1,000.00
Net Pay: $796.00

Description	Hours	Calc. Rate	Amount	YTD	Type
Sick Pay	16	$25.00	$400.00	$400.00	Wages
Base Salary			$600.00	$2,600.00	Wages
ABC Credit Union			-$50.00	-$150.00	Deductions
PAYG Withholding			-$154.00	-$462.00	Tax
Holiday Leave Accrual	1.333			1.33	Entitlements
Superannuation Guarantee			$95.00	$285.00	Superannuation Expenses

8.11

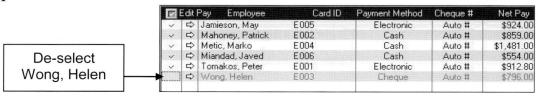

		Edit Pay	Employee	Card ID	Payment Method	Cheque #	Net Pay
✓	⇨		Jamieson, May	E005	Electronic	Auto #	$924.00
✓	⇨		Mahoney, Patrick	E002	Cash	Auto #	$859.00
✓	⇨		Metic, Marko	E004	Cash	Auto #	$1,481.00
✓	⇨		Miandad, Javed	E006	Cash	Auto #	$554.00
✓	⇨		Tomakos, Peter	E001	Electronic	Auto #	$912.80
	⇨		Wong, Helen	E003	Cheque	Auto #	$796.00

De-select Wong, Helen

Payroll Advice

25/05/2015 To 31/05/2015

Page 1

G.S.T. Pty Ltd
A.B.N.: 98 999 999 999

Cheque No: 7
Payment Date: 31/05/2015

May Jamieson
Pay Frequency: Weekly
Pay Period: 25/05/2015 To 31/05/2015
Annual Salary: $62,400.00
Hourly Rate: $30.00
Employment Classification: Administration
Superannuation Fund: AMP Life
N.O.K. Joan (03) 3588 5456 (sister)

Gross Pay: $1,200.00
Net Pay: $924.00

Description	Hours	Calc. Rate	Amount	YTD	Type
Base Salary			$1,200.00	$4,800.00	Wages
Staff Loans - Jamieson			-$24.00	-$96.00	Deductions
PAYG Withholding			-$252.00	-$1,008.00	Tax
Executive Life			$24.00	$96.00	Superannuation Expenses
Superannuation Guarantee			$114.00	$456.00	Superannuation Expenses

G.S.T. Pty Ltd
A.B.N.: 98 999 999 999

Cheque No: 10
Payment Date: 31/05/2015

Patrick Mahoney
Pay Frequency: Weekly
Pay Period: 25/05/2015 To 31/05/2015
Annual Salary: $58,500.00
Hourly Rate: $28.125
Employment Classification: Salesperson
Superannuation Fund: AMP Life
N.O.K. Lizzy Mahoney (Spouse)

Gross Pay: $2,252.00
Net Pay: $1,565.00

Description	Hours	Calc. Rate	Amount	YTD	Type
Base Salary			$1,125.00	$4,500.00	Wages
Commission			$1,127.00	$2,413.00	Wages
Staff Loans - Mahoney			-$40.00	-$80.00	Deductions
PAYG Withholding			-$647.00	-$1,808.00	Tax
Superannuation Guarantee			$106.87	$427.50	Superannuation Expenses

G.S.T. Pty Ltd
A.B.N.: 98 999 999 999

Cheque No: 11
Payment Date: 31/05/2015

Marko Metic
Pay Frequency: Weekly
Pay Period: 25/05/2015 To 31/05/2015
Annual Salary: $104,000.00
Hourly Rate: $50.00
Employment Classification: Clerical Level 2
Superannuation Fund: AMP Life
N.O.K. Kylie (daughter)

Gross Pay: $2,000.00
Net Pay: $1,481.00

Description	Hours	Calc. Rate	Amount	YTD	Type
Base Hourly	40	$50.00	$2,000.00	$7,600.00	Wages
Miscellaneous Staff Union			-$5.00	-$20.00	Deductions
PAYG Withholding			-$514.00	-$2,173.00	Tax
Holiday Leave Accrual	3.333			13.33	Entitlements
Superannuation Guarantee			$190.00	$760.00	Superannuation Expenses
Overtime (1.5x)				$300.00	Wages
Sick Pay				$400.00	Wages

8.11 *(continued)*

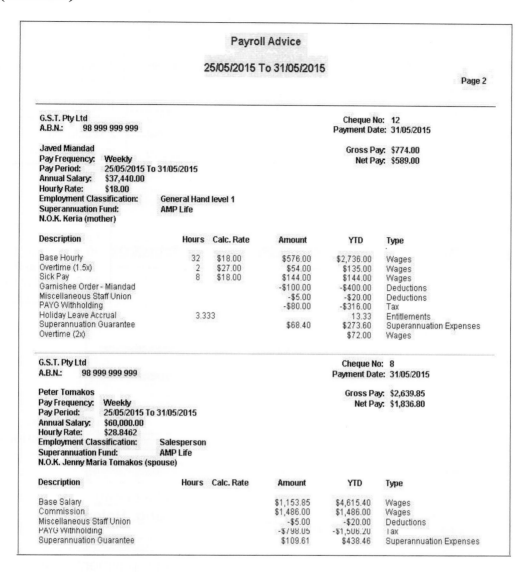

Payroll Advice

25/05/2015 To 31/05/2015

Page 2

G.S.T. Pty Ltd					
A.B.N.: 98 999 999 999				Cheque No: 12	
				Payment Date: 31/05/2015	

Javed Miandad		Gross Pay: $774.00
Pay Frequency: Weekly		Net Pay: $589.00
Pay Period: 25/05/2015 To 31/05/2015		
Annual Salary: $37,440.00		
Hourly Rate: $18.00		
Employment Classification: General Hand level 1		
Superannuation Fund: AMP Life		
N.O.K. Keria (mother)		

Description	Hours	Calc. Rate	Amount	YTD	Type
Base Hourly	32	$18.00	$576.00	$2,736.00	Wages
Overtime (1.5x)	2	$27.00	$54.00	$135.00	Wages
Sick Pay	8	$18.00	$144.00	$144.00	Wages
Garnishee Order - Miandad			-$100.00	-$400.00	Deductions
Miscellaneous Staff Union			-$5.00	-$20.00	Deductions
PAYG Withholding			-$80.00	-$316.00	Tax
Holiday Leave Accrual	3.333			13.33	Entitlements
Superannuation Guarantee			$68.40	$273.60	Superannuation Expenses
Overtime (2x)				$72.00	Wages

G.S.T. Pty Ltd					
A.B.N.: 98 999 999 999				Cheque No: 8	
				Payment Date: 31/05/2015	

Peter Tomakos		Gross Pay: $2,639.85
Pay Frequency: Weekly		Net Pay: $1,836.80
Pay Period: 25/05/2015 To 31/05/2015		
Annual Salary: $60,000.00		
Hourly Rate: $28.8462		
Employment Classification: Salesperson		
Superannuation Fund: AMP Life		
N.O.K. Jenny Maria Tomakos (spouse)		

Description	Hours	Calc. Rate	Amount	YTD	Type
Base Salary			$1,153.85	$4,615.40	Wages
Commission			$1,486.00	$1,486.00	Wages
Miscellaneous Staff Union			-$5.00	-$20.00	Deductions
PAYG Withholding			-$798.05	-$1,506.20	Tax
Superannuation Guarantee			$109.61	$438.46	Superannuation Expenses

8.12

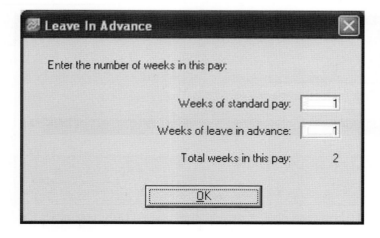

Leave In Advance

Enter the number of weeks in this pay:

Weeks of standard pay: 1

Weeks of leave in advance: 1

Total weeks in this pay: 2

OK

8.12 *(continued)*

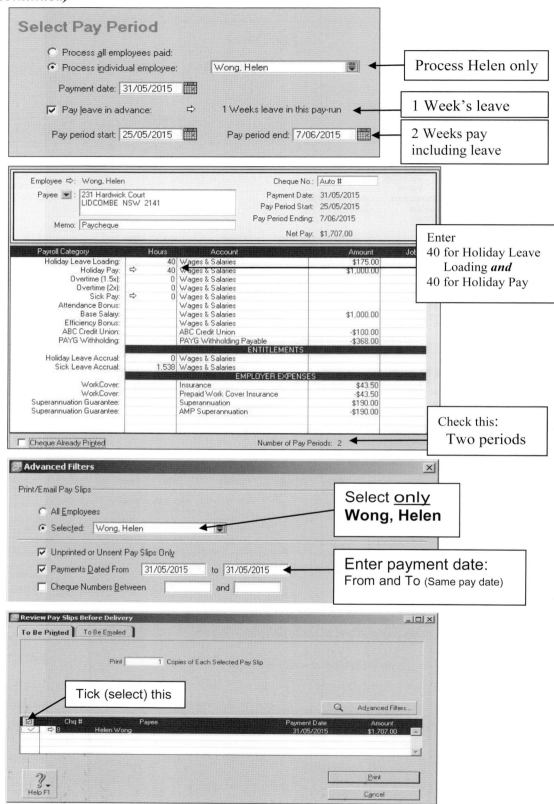

8.12 (*continued*)

G.S.T. Pty Ltd

A.B.N. 98 999 999 999

Pay Slip For: Helen Wong   Cheque No: 8

Classification: Clerical Level 1   Payment Date: 31/05/2015

Annual Salary:	$52,000.00
Hourly Rate:	$25.00
Pay Period From:	25/05/2015 To: 7/06/2015 GROSS PAY: $2,175.00
Superannuation Fund:	AMP Life NET PAY: $1,707.00

DESCRIPTION	HOURS	CALC. RATE	AMOUNT	YTD	TYPE
Holiday Leave Loading	40	$4.37	$175.00	$175.00	Wages
Holiday Pay	40	$25.00	$1,000.00	$1,000.00	Wages
Sick Pay				$400.00	Wages
Base Salary			$1,000.00	$3,600.00	Wages
ABC Credit Union			-$100.00	-$250.00	Deductions
PAYG Withholding			-$368.00	-$830.00	Tax
Holiday Leave Accrual				-38.67	Entitlements
Superannuation			$190.00	$475.00	Superannuation Expenses

8.13

Payroll Activity [Summary]

31/05/2015 To 31/05/2015

Page 1

Employee	Wages	Deductions	Taxes	Net Pay	Expenses
Jamieson, May	$1,200.00	$24.00	$252.00	$924.00	$162.00
Mahoney, Patrick	$2,252.00	$40.00	$647.00	$1,565.00	$151.91
Metic, Marko	$2,000.00	$5.00	$514.00	$1,481.00	$245.00
Miandad, Javed	$774.00	$105.00	$80.00	$589.00	$98.88
Tomakos, Peter	$2,639.85	$5.00	$798.05	$1,836.80	$177.41
Wong, Helen	$2,175.00	$100.00	$368.00	$1,707.00	$233.50
Total:	$11,040.85	$279.00	$2,659.05	$8,102.80	$1,068.70

8.14

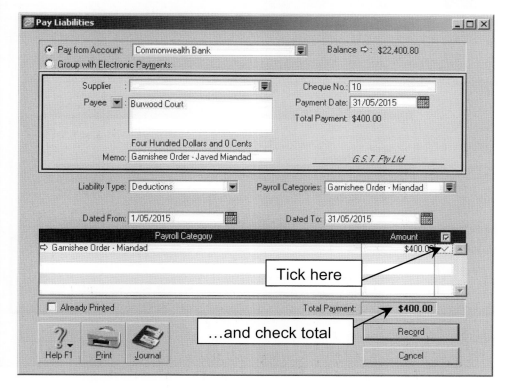

8.15 Check that the backup file **does exist** in the selected folder.

8.16

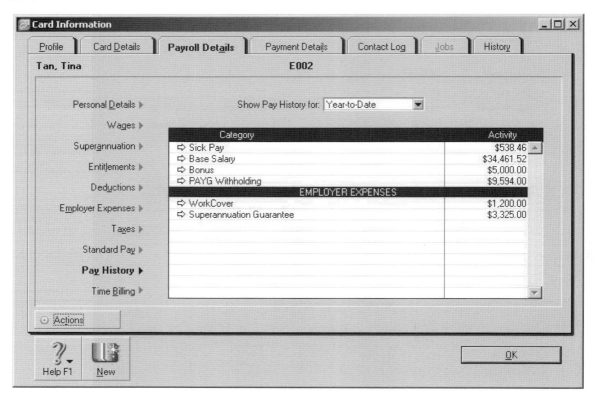

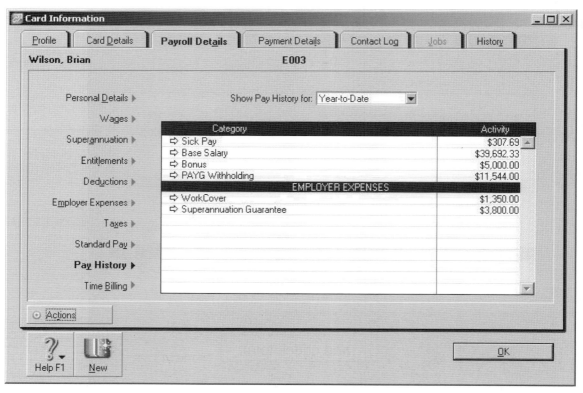

Categories and jobs 9

Classifying transactions by categories and/or jobs and entering budget information.

After completing this chapter you will be able to:

1 Design reports using accounts, categories and jobs.

2 Create categories and set up jobs.

3 Enter budgets for jobs.

4 Record transactions that will include category and job data.

5 Prepare and print profit reports for jobs.

6 Prepare and print reports by category.

Introduction

Normal bookkeeping and accounting processes classify income and expense by using general ledger accounts. At the account level, some classification can be made by using headers for particular classes of income and expense. Where a business would like to know the results for different segments of the business (departments, divisions or other profit centres), income and expense could be <u>categorised</u> for this purpose. At a lower level, a business may want to keep track of income and expense for particular <u>jobs</u> carried out.

The main purpose of this chapter is to demonstrate categories and jobs. It is an extension of previous chapters.

> This chapter is an extension of basic transaction processing. As such, it will be assumed that you have completed Chapters 1 to 7 and are able to record everyday transactions.

Information design

In Chapter 3 the *Accounts List* was set up with "Header" and "Detail" accounts. In this way, the *Sales*, *Cost of Sales* and *Expenses* could be classified under broad headings. A food service business could, for example classify sales and cost of sales into say catering, retail, wholesale and home delivery. A car dealer could classify income and cost of sales into car sales and services, with the car sales further classified into new cars and second-hand cars. The standard profit and loss as printed in Chapter 3 would indicate the income and cost of sales for these accounts.

To obtain a more detailed profit report for each segment of a business, categories can be set up and all transactions are coded with the relevant category. The food services business may set up categories for each of its main business "departments" and all income and expense will be placed into one of the categories. So, for example, the *Accounts List* might have a single "Salaries and Wages" account, but payments for salaries and wages may be categorised into retail, catering etc.

Where the business would like even more detailed information, a Job ID can be given to a particular service provided to a customer and this Job ID would be used for all transactions related to that service. For example, the food service provider may want to know the profit or loss on all major catering jobs – such as catering for a specific wedding, a business conference or any other specific function.

It can be seen that there is a hierarchy of information requirements. A single transaction can be classified a number of ways depending on the level of detail required from final reports.

Self-test exercise 9.1

List the possible categories for the following business types: printers, publishers, builders and electricians. Give some examples of Jobs that might be involved.

Account levels

The accounts in a general ledger can be set up so that a profit statement will show the overall performance of a business. Adding and editing accounts to the *Accounts List*, including "Header" and "Detail" accounts, is demonstrated in Chapter 3 of this book. The instructions in that chapter are not repeated here. "Income" and "Cost of Sales" accounts can be detailed under a heading, as shown in that chapter.

Self-test exercise 9.2

Open the file dem91.myo. Sign on as the Administrator without a password.

The business is in the food services industry. It wants to keep detailed records of the costs of catering operations.

Using the instructions in Chapter 3 (use the 'How to ...' index at the front of the book to find instructions), change the *Cost of Sales* section in the *Accounts List* to show:

Account Number and Name	Type	Tax Code
5-0000 Cost of Sales	**Header**	
5-1000 Food Purchases	**Header**	
5-1010 Food – Meat	Detail	FRE
5-1020 Food – Vegetables	Detail	FRE
5-1030 Food – Other	Detail	FRE
5-2000 Beverage Purchases	**Header**	
5-2010 Beverages – Alcohol	**Header**	
5-2011 Beverages – Beer	Detail	GST
5-2012 Beverages – Wine	Detail	GST
5-2020 Beverages – Other	Detail	GST
5-3000 Other Purchases	Detail	GST
5-5000 Freight	Detail	GST
5-9000 Administration Overhead	Detail	N-T

Hint: As the *Accounts List* already shows account 5-2000 as "Freight", change the account number for "Freight" to 5-5000 <u>first</u>.

Check your answer with the suggested answer at the end of this chapter.

Adding categories

Categories are set up to keep track of financial information for major segments of your business. These segments may be divisions, departments or major functional areas. When transactions for spending money, receiving money, invoicing sales to customers or recording bills from suppliers are entered, the category to which they relate will be nominated. Obviously, when you assign an invoice or a bill to a category, you cannot also assign a category when the payments for these invoices and bills are later recorded.

Setting up categories

Before categories can be used, they need to be set up. If categories are not set up, they will not appear on the transaction forms. Categories are initiated through the *Preferences* item in the *Setup* pull-down menu at the top of the screen.

How to set up category preferences

Step	Instruction
1	Select the *Setup* menu at the top of the screen.
2	Select the *Preferences* menu item.
3	Click on the *System* tab if not already selected.
4	Click on the checkbox for 'Turn on Category Tracking'. ☑ Turn on Category Tracking: Categories are [Not Required ▼] on All Transactions [System-wide]
5	If categories MUST be used for ALL transactions that are capable of having a category, use the drop arrow and change the "Not Required" to "Required". ☑ Turn on Category Tracking: Categories are [Required ▼] on All Transactions [System-wide]
6	Click on the *OK* button to close the *Preferences* window.

Example 9.1—Changing the preferences for categories

1. Start the file dem91.myo. You should sign on as the "Administrator" without a password.
2. Select the *Setup* menu and the *Preferences* menu item.
3. Click on the *System* tab in the *Preferences* window.
4. Select the checkbox for 'Turn on Category Tracking' and use the drop arrow to make this mandatory (that is, required).
5. Check that your *Preferences* window looks like Figure 9.1 on the next page and click the OK button.

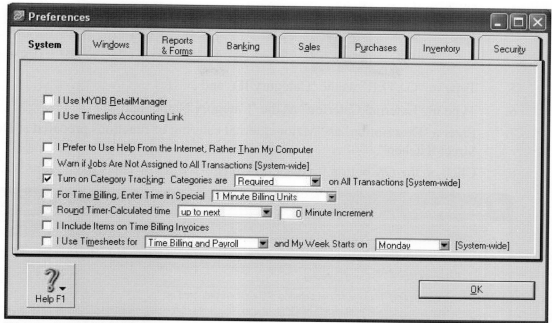

Figure 9.1: Category preference turned on and mandatory

Creating categories

The individual categories are entered using the *Categories* item in the *Lists* menu at the top of the screen.

How to add or edit categories

Step	Instruction
1	Select the *Lists* menu at the top of the screen.
2	Select the *Categories* menu item.
3	To add a new category, click on the *New* button. New
4	Type in a 'Category ID' that will uniquely identify the category and ↵.
5	Type in the 'Category Name' and ↵.
6	Enter a description or notes about the category.
7	Click on the *OK* button to complete the entry.

Example 9.2—Creating a new category

1. Use the file dem91.myo and sign on as the "Administrator".
2. Select the *Lists* menu at the top of the screen.
3. Select the *Categories* menu item.

4. Click on the *New* button.

5. Type in "CATER" as the 'Category ID' and ↵.

6. Type in "External Catering" as the 'Category Name' and ↵.

7. Enter a 'Description' as "Major external catering of functions prepared at Dowling Street Kitchen".

8. Click on the *OK* button if your *Edit Category* window looks like Figure 9.2:

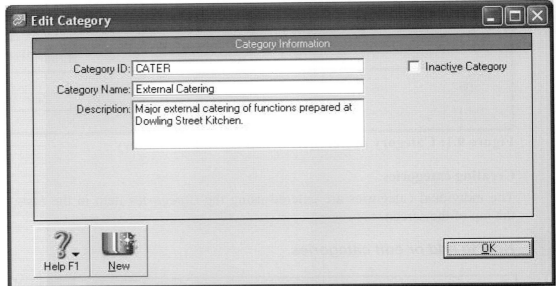

Figure 9.2: The *Edit Category* window with new category created

If categories are required (as set up in this file earlier), you will need to make sure that your categories will cover ALL income and expense transactions. Using a "Sundry" or "Other" category as in the next self-test exercise will ensure this happens.

Self-test exercise 9.3

Enter in the following categories:

Category ID:	Category Name:	Description
WSALE	Wholesale	Wholesale supplied from Penrith premises.
SHOP	Shop Sales	Sales outlet at Mary Anne Street.
OTHER	Other	Unclassified income or expense.

Adding jobs

A Job is a detailed record of a particular task or event. In *MYOB AccountRight Plus*, a Job record can be more than just a list of income and expense for a particular task – budgets can be set up, reimbursable expenses can be tracked, and profit (or loss) can be thoroughly analysed.

Creating jobs

Jobs are created using the *Jobs* menu item from the *Lists* pull-down menu. Jobs can be set up on a hierarchical basis – a main Job linked to a customer with several jobs underneath this main job. For example, a sub-contractor might do several jobs for a single contractor. Where this occurs, a Header Job is set up first and sub-jobs are added to this header.

How to add or edit a header job

Step	Instruction
1	Select the *Lists* menu at the top of the screen.
2	Select the *Jobs* menu item.
3	To add a new category, click on the *New* button.
4	Click on the *Header* selection button. ⦿ Header Job ○ Detail Job
5	Type in a 'Job Number' that will uniquely identify the job and ↵.
6	If this job is subsidiary of a larger job, enter or select that job in the field 'Sub-job of' and ↵.
7	Enter a name for the job and ↵.
8	Type a description of the job. This is a multi-line field so use TAB to go to the 'Contact' field.
9	Enter a contact name for the job and ↵.
10	Enter the commencement date in the 'Start Date:' field and ↵. (Note that you can use the space bar and select the date from the pop-up calendar.)
11	Enter the finish date if there will not be any more jobs under this header.
12	Type in the name of the manager (the person in charge and responsible for looking after the job) and ↵.
13	Click on the *OK* button to complete the entry.

Example 9.3—Creating a new header job

1.   Use the file dem91.myo and sign on as the "Administrator".

2.   Select the *Lists* menu at the top of the screen.

3.   Select the *Jobs* menu item.

4.   Click on the *New* button.

5.   Select the *Header Job* option at the top of the *New Job* window.

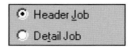

6.   Type in "J100" as the 'Job Number' and ↵.

7.   Leave the 'Sub-job of' field blank and TAB to the 'Job Name' field.

8.   Type in "David James Catering" as the 'Job Name' and ↵.

9.   In the 'Description:' field, type in "Sub-contracting functions for David James Pty Ltd" and use the TAB key when finished.

10.   Type in the 'Contact' as "Sebastian Hargraves" and ↵.

11.   Type the date as "1/7/2011" (or use the space bar and select the date) and ↵.

12.   Leave the 'Finish Date:' field blank and ↵.

13.   The manager for this job is "Wanina Gilbert". Type this name in the 'Manager:' field and ↵.

14.   If your *Edit Job* window looks like Figure 9.3 on the next page, click on the *OK* button.

Self-test exercise 9.4

Enter in the following Header Job in the file dem91.myo:

Job Number F100 with name "Foodrama Catering". The customer, Foodrama Pty Ltd, sub-contracts functions. Helen Marsh is the contact person at Foodrama Pty Ltd. This job started on 1 July 2011 and William Bard is the manager.

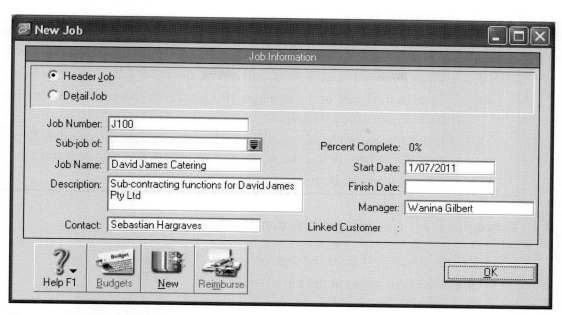

Figure 9.3: The *Edit Job* window with a new header job created

How to add or edit a detail job

Step	Instruction
1	Select the *Lists* menu at the top of the screen.
2	Select the *Jobs* menu item.
3	To add a new category, click on the *New* button.
4	Click on the *Detail* selection button if necessary (it should be the default).
5	If expenses may be reimbursed, click on the checkbox for 'Track Reimbursables'.
6	Type in a 'Job Number' that will uniquely identify the job and ↵.
7	If this job is a sub-job under a Header Job, type in the Job number under which this job comes, or use the *List* button and select the job.
8	TAB through and enter a name for the job and ↵.
9	Type a description of the job. This is a multi-line field so use TAB when finished to exit the text field.
10	Enter a contact name for the job and ↵.
11	The 'Percent Complete' field can be used to keep track of the job's progress.

(continued on the next page)

Step	Instruction
12	Enter the commencement date in the 'Start Date:' field and ↵. (Note that you can use the space bar and select the date from the pop-up calendar.)
13	Enter the finish date if there will not be any more jobs under this header.
14	Type in the name of the manager (the person in charge and responsible for looking after the job) and ↵.
15	If this job has no header, enter the name of any linked customer. Type in the first few letters, or use the selection *List* button and select from the list.
16	Click on the *OK* button to complete the entry.

Example 9.4—Creating a new detail job

1. Use the file dem91.myo and sign on as the "Administrator".
2. Select the *Lists* menu at the top of the screen.
3. Select the *Jobs* menu item.
4. Click on the *New* button.

5. Select the *Detail Job* option at the top of the *New Job* window.

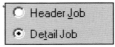

6. Type in "J101" as the 'Job Number' and ↵.
7. In the 'Sub-job of' field, type in or use the selection *List* button to select job. number "J100" as the header job number for this job and ↵.
8. Enter "Newline Ball" as the 'Job Name' and ↵.
9. In the 'Description:' field, type in "Catering for Newline Cricket Club annual ball at Ryde Community Centre" and use the TAB key when finished.
10. Type in the 'Contact' as "Bill Deutrom" and ↵.
11. This is a new job so leave the 'Percent Complete:' field as 0% and ↵.
12. Use the space bar and select "5/7/2011" as the date (or type this in) and ↵.
13. The job should be finished on 10 July 2011. Type this in the 'Finish Date:' field.
14. The manager for this job is "Wanina Gilbert". Enter this in the 'Manager:' field and ↵.
15. In the 'Linked Customer:' field, enter the customer's name as "David James Ltd". You can type the first few letters e.g. "Dav" and ↵ or use the selection *List* button to select the customer from the displayed list.
16. If your *Edit Job* window looks like Figure 9.4 on the next page, click *OK*.

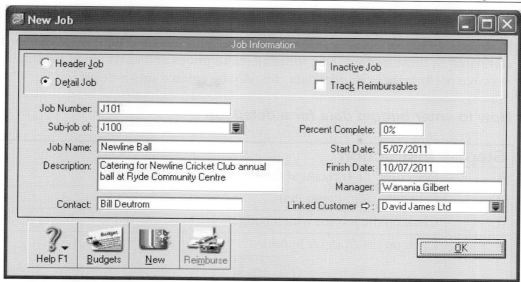

Figure 9.4: The *Edit Job* window with a new header job created

17.	The *Jobs List* window should now look like Figure 9.5. Notice that header jobs are in bold type and detail jobs are indented under the related header.

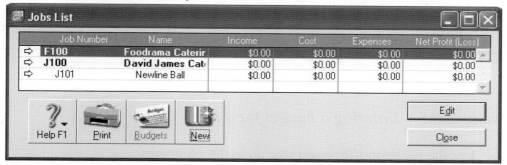

Figure 9.5: The *Jobs List* window with headers and a detail job entered

Self-test exercise 9.5

Enter in the following **Detail** Jobs:

Job Number J102 with name "TWA Awards". This job is a sub-job of Job J100 and is carried out as a sub-contractor for the customer David James Ltd with Wanina Gilbert as the David James function manager. The job requires catering for the Technical Writers Association awards night at the Oatlands Reception Centre. The contact person is Luigi Lambretta and the job is started on 7 July 2011. Reimbursables are to be tracked, the percentage complete should be left as 0% and the function will be completed on 10 July 2011.

Job Number F101 with name "Wedding". The job is a sub-job of Job F100 to supply food, drinks and service for a wedding organised by the customer Foodrama Pty Ltd. The contact person is Helen Marsh and the job is started on 5 July 2011. Reimbursables are to be tracked, the percentage complete should be left as 0% and the function will be completed on 10 July 2011. The Manager is William Bard.

Video: A video on adding detail jobs is on the DVD

Job budgets

A useful feature of Jobs is to be able to set up budgets. Actual results can then be compared to these budgets and adjustments to prices and costs made for future jobs to improve performance. Budget data can only be entered into a detail job.

How to enter budget data for a detail job

Step	Instruction
1	Select the *Lists* menu at the top of the screen.
2	Select the *Jobs* menu item.
3	Click on the job for which budgets are to be entered to highlight it.
4	Click on the *Budgets* button.
5	Click in the 'Budgets' column against the income or expense concerned and type in the amount. Use the down and up arrows to move down and up the 'Budgets' column, or click on an item to enter or edit the amount.
6	Click on the *OK* button when the budget has been entered.

Example 9.5—Entering a budget for a job

1. Use the file dem91.myo and sign on as the "Administrator".
2. Select the *Lists* menu at the top of the screen.
3. Select the *Jobs* menu item.
4. Click on Job F101 "Wedding" to highlight it (do NOT click on the detail arrow).
5. Click on the *Budgets* button.

6. Click in the 'Budgets' column on the line for account 4-3000 "Catering Fees" and type in "6600" (or " 220 * 30 = ") and ↵.   This is 220 guests @ $30 per guest. The amount should show as $6,600.00.
7. Use the down arrow key to move down to account 5-1010 "Food – Meat" and type in "770" and ↵.

Continue entering the following budgeted costs for Job F101:

5-1020 Food – Vegetables	$198.00
5-1030 Food Other	$440.00
5-2011 Beverages – Beer	$900.00
5-2012 Beverages – Wine	$660.00
5-2020 Beverages – Other	$300.00
5-3000 Other Purchases	$100.00
5-9000 Administration Overhead	$440.00
6-1150 Breakages & Replacements	$200.00
6-1500 Employees' Meals	$64.00
6-1800 Laundry and Cleaning	$440.00
6-2300 Kitchen Supplies	$100.00
6-2430 Wages & Salaries	$1,760.00

8.   The top part of your *Job Budgets by Account* window should look like Figure 9.6:

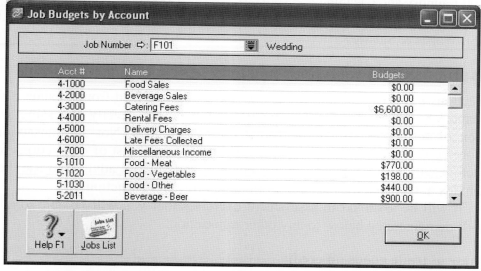

Figure 9.6: Part of the *Job Budgets by Account* window for Job F101

9.   Click on the *OK* button to finish entering the budget for the job.

A budget can be entered for every expense. However, it would be very difficult to estimate some administrative costs, and how much of each actual invoice that is paid goes to each job. A method used by many businesses is to charge an estimated amount to cover expenses that cannot be directly related to particular jobs. In this demonstration, only costs that can be directly related to a job are budgeted. The administration overhead is estimated at 25% of Wages & Salaries and is shown in account 5-9000 in the budget.

Video: A video on entering budget data for jobs is on the DVD

Self-test exercise 9.6

Enter in the following budgets for Jobs:

General Ledger Account	Job J101 $	Job J102 $
4-3000 Catering Fees	15,000.00	19,200.00
5-1010 Food – Meat	1,400.00	2,000.00
5-1020 Food – Vegetables	500.00	650.00
5-1030 Food Other	500.00	540.00
5-2011 Beverages – Beer	1,750.00	1,500.00
5-2012 Beverages – Wine	2,000.00	3,000.00
5-2020 Beverages – Other	1,000.00	780.00
5-3000 Other Purchases	250.00	280.00
5-9000 Administration Overhead	880.00	960.00
6-1150 Breakages & Replacements	250.00	250.00
6-1500 Employees' Meals	80.00	96.00
6-1800 Laundry and Cleaning	1,000.00	1,200.00
6-2300 Kitchen Supplies	150.00	180.00
6-2430 Wages & Salaries	3,520.00	3,840.00

Transactions using categories and jobs

Transactions in *MYOB AccountRight Plus* have been covered from Chapter 3 through to Chapter 8. The transactions demonstrated here are exactly the same with the addition of further classification by categories and jobs. Not all transactions will therefore be covered within this chapter. The 'How to ...' list of instructions for each transaction will not be repeated in this chapter, and you are advised to use the 'How to ...' index at the front of this book to find the relevant instructions.

It will be assumed in assessment exercises that you will be able to adapt the methods demonstrated below to any other transaction.

Purchase of trade goods on credit

The purchase of goods using service invoices was covered in Chapter 6.
The following example extends that coverage with categories and jobs.

Example 9.6—Entering a purchase from Meatworks Pty Ltd

Enter the following purchase from Meatworks Pty Ltd on 7 July 2011. The purchase is for meat delivered to the Dowling Street Kitchens for catering jobs.

1. Have the file dem91.myo open and be signed on as the "Administrator".
2. Select the *Purchases* command centre.
3. Select the *Enter Purchases* option.
4. The supplier is Meatworks Pty Ltd. Remember that you may type in the first few letters (say "Me"), hit enter and select from a list, or use the *List* button ▼.

5. Make sure the purchase layout is *Purchases - New Service*.
If the layout is not 'Service', click on the *Layout* button and change it to 'Service'

 ← Click

and click on the button next to *Service* layout.

6. Check that the default BILL is selected in this exercise.

7. TAB to the 'Purchase #' field so that the 'Ship to:' address remains. Enter "1234" as the purchase number ⏎.

8. Enter the date as "7/7/2011". Remember that if the system date is set to July 2011 or if the date in this field is a date in July 2011, you only have to type '7' ⏎ (alternatively, press the spacebar and select the date from the calendar).

9. The supplier's invoice number (#) is "W338" ⏎.

10. Enter the first description line as "100 kilograms sirloin beef @ $7.20 per kilo" and TAB to the next field.

11. The account to be debited is "Food – Meat" which has an account # of 5-1010. Enter this and TAB to amount field.

12. The amount to enter is $720.00. You can either type "100 * 7.20 =" or "720" and TAB.

13. The Job is "F101" – you may type in "F" and ⏎ or use the selection list arrow, select F101 from the *Jobs List* and ⏎.

14. The 'Tax' column should show a tax code of "FRE" (the default code set up for this account).

15. Enter another line for "160 kilograms of various lamb cuts @ $5.80 per kilo". This is debited to the account 5-1010 "Food – Meat", and is for Job J101.
Enter amount either as "928" or "160 * 5.80 =".

16. Enter a third line as "180 kilograms Scotch Fillet @ $9.80 per kilo". This is debited to the account 5-1010 "Food – Meat" and is for Job J102.
Enter amount either as "1764" or "180 * 9.80 =".

17. Towards the bottom right-hand side of the form (before the buttons) there is a field called 'Category:' with a drop-down selection *List* button. Select "CATER" as the category, as this is the Category ID for catering.

18. Leave the rest of the purchase as is.
The form should look like Figure 9.7 on the next page.

19. To correct any errors, click on the field concerned and overtype or edit.

20. Click on the *Record* button to record the purchase.

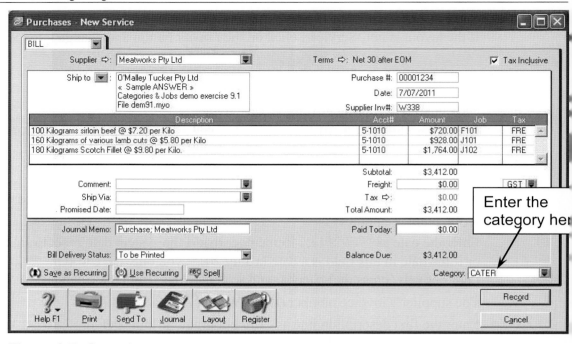

Figure 9.7: Completed purchase with jobs and category

Self-test exercise 9.7

Enter in the following Bills for purchases on credit:

Date	Details	Job
8/7/2011	Purchase # 1235: Groceries for the shop purchased from Davis Foods Pty Ltd on their Invoice D1098. Debit the amount of $3,480.90 (including the GST) to account "Food – Other" 5-1030. The category is "SHOP", the tax code is "GST" and there is no Job number.	NA

8/7/2011	Purchase # 1236: Purchased poultry from Meatworks Pty Ltd on their Invoice W341:
	    85 kilograms chicken breast @ $4.40 per kilogram
	    120 kilograms chicken legs @ $2.60 per kilogram
	The account to debit is "Food – Meat" 5-1010, the Category is "CATER" and the tax code is "FRE".
		
		J101
		J102

9/7/2011	Purchase # 1237: Purchased potatoes from Natural Foods Pty Ltd on their Invoice 3016:
	    75 kilograms Pontiac Potatoes @ $0.80 per kilogram
	    125 kilograms Tassie Chips @ $1.20 per kilogram
	    160 kilograms Tassie Chips @ $1.20 per kilogram
	The account to debit is "Food – Vegetables" 5-1020, the Category is "CATER" and the tax code is "FRE".
		
		F101
		J101
		J102

(continued on the next page)

Chapter 9: Categories and jobs

Self-test exercise 9.7 (continued)

9/7/2011	Purchase # 1238: Purchased mixed vegetables in 5 kg cartons from Natural Foods Pty Ltd on their Invoice 3017:
	    20 cartons mixed prepared vegetables @ $8.00 per carton
	    35 cartons mixed prepared vegetables @ $8.00 per carton
	    42 cartons mixed prepared vegetables @ $8.00 per carton
	The account to debit is "Food – Vegetables" 5-1020, the Category is "CATER" and the tax code is "FRE".
		
		F101
		J101
		J102

9/7/2011	Purchase # 1239: Purchased cartons of assorted uncooked pasta from PastaFizouli Pty Ltd on their Invoice 118:
	    25 cartons assorted pasta @ $14.00 per carton
	    35 cartons assorted pasta @ $14.00 per carton
	    40 cartons assorted pasta @ $14.00 per carton
	The account to debit is "Food – Other" 5-1030, the Category is "CATER" and the tax code is "FRE".
		
		F101
		J101
		J102

9/7/2011	Purchase # 1240: Purchased carcasses from Meatworks Pty Ltd for Penrith wholesale outlet on their Invoice M489:
	    905 kilograms beef @ $3.08 per kilogram
	    426 kilograms lamb @ $2.96 per kilogram
	The account to debit is "Food – Meat" 5-1010, the Category is "WSALE" and the tax code is "FRE".
		NA

9/7/2011	Purchase # 1241: Purchased beer from Antropy Pty Ltd on their Invoice 6612:
	    45 cartons assorted beers @ $20.90 per carton
	    95 cartons assorted beers @ $20.90 per carton
	    80 cartons assorted beers @ $20.90 per carton
	The price per carton shown above includes GST. The account to debit is "Beverages – Beer" 5-2011, the Category is "CATER" and the tax code is "GST".
		
		F101
		J101
		J102

9/7/2011	Purchase # 1242: Purchased wine from Antropy Pty Ltd on their Invoice 6613:
	    110 bottles assorted wines @ $6.60 per bottle
	    250 bottles assorted wines @ $8.80 per bottle
	    300 bottles assorted wines @ $11.00 per bottle
	The price per bottle shown above includes GST (ignore any Wine Equalisation Tax). The account to debit is "Beverages – Wine" 5-2012, the Category is "CATER" and the tax code is "GST".
		
		F101
		J101
		J102

(continued on the next page)

Self-test exercise 9.7 *(continued)*

9/7/2011	Purchase # 1243: Purchased non-alcoholic drinks from Omega Alpha Pty Ltd on their Invoice 44/120:	
	Assorted cans and bottles as per Invoice $330.00	F101
	Assorted cans and bottles as per Invoice $1,100.00	J101
	Assorted cans and bottles as per Invoice $858.00	J102
	The prices above include the GST. The account to debit is "Beverages – Other" 5-2020, the Category is "CATER" and the tax code is "GST".	

Sales invoices

Recording sales invoices is covered in Chapters 5 and 7. The following example extends that coverage with categories and jobs.

Example 9.7—Entering a tax-inclusive invoice for catering fees

Enter the following invoice to David James Ltd for the Newline Cricket Club Job 101. The invoice is to show tax-inclusive amounts.

1. Have the file dem91.myo open and be signed on as the "Administrator".
2. Select the *Sales* command centre.
3. Select the *Enter Sales* option.
4. Check that "INVOICE" is selected.

5. Check that the invoice amounts are to be printed as tax-inclusive.

6. The customer is David James Ltd. Remember that you may type in the first few letters (say "dav"), hit ↵ and select from a list, or use the *List* button ▼.
7. Make sure that the invoice type is *Sales – New Service.*
8. TAB through to the Invoice number field so that the 'Ship to:' address remains (i.e. do <u>not</u> press *Enter* in the 'Ship to:' field). Enter "1001" as the invoice number ↵.
9. Enter the date as 12/7/2011. Remember that if the system date is set to July 2011, you only have to type "12" ↵.
10. The customer's purchase order number (#) is C1123. Type this in and ↵.
11. Enter the description as "Catering for Newline Cricket Club annual ball at Ryde Community Centre" and TAB to the next field.
12. The account to be credited is "Catering Fees" which has an account # of 4-3000. Enter this (or use the *List* button ▼ and select from the accounts list) and TAB to the amount field.

13. The amount to enter is $16,500.00 (this is the GST-inclusive amount for this line of the invoice).

14. TAB and enter the Job as "J101". You may type this in or select from the list by using the *List* button ⬇.

15. The 'Tax' column should show a GST code of "GST".

16. In the 'Salesperson' field select "Gilbert, Wanina" as the salesperson. You may type this in or select from the list by using the *List* button ⬇.

17. Click on the *List* button ⬇ for the 'Comment' field and select "We appreciate your business".

18. On the right-hand side of the form towards the bottom (before the buttons) there is a field called 'Category:' with a drop-down selection list button.
Select "CATER" as the category, as this is the Category ID for catering.

19. Leave the rest of the invoice as is. The invoice should look like Figure 9.8. To correct any errors, click on the field concerned and overtype or edit.

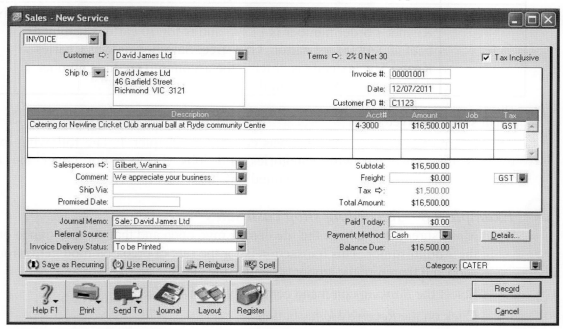

Figure 9.8: Completed service invoice to David James Ltd for Job 101

20. Select the *Record* button to complete this invoice.

Video: A video on entering Invoices is on the DVD

Self-test exercise 9.8

Enter in the following Sales using service invoices:

Date	Details	Job
13/7/2011	Invoice # 1002 to Foodrama Pty Ltd for Food and drinks supplied for wedding on their Order F54. The tax-inclusive fee for this was $7,260.00 and the salesperson was William Bard. The tax code is "GST" and the account to credit is number 4-3000 "Catering Fees". The category is "CATER".	F101
13/7/2011	Invoice # 1003 to David James Ltd for catering at the Technical Writers Association awards night at Oatlands Reception Centre. Their order number was C1125. The tax-inclusive fee for this was $21,120.00 and the salesperson was Wanina Gilbert. The tax code is "GST" and the account to credit is number 4-3000 "Catering Fees". The category is "CATER".	J102
14/7/2011	Invoice # 1004 to Kismet Pty Ltd for meat sold at wholesale. Kismet's order number is 11245 and is for 70 cartons trimmed beef @ $42.00 per carton, GST-free. Salesperson was Charles Keats. The tax code is "FRE", the account to credit is number 4-1000 "Food Sales" and the category is "WSALE".	NA

Cash sales received

The receipt of cash for cash sales was covered in Chapter 4. The following example extends that coverage with categories and jobs. It does not cover the use of *Undeposited Funds* that is also explained in Chapter 4.

Example 9.8—Recording shop cash sales

1.   Make sure that you have the file dem91.myo open and that you are signed on as the Administrator. This transaction is for the sale of prepared food items from a shop and therefore the amounts include the GST.

2.   Select the *Banking* command centre.

3.   Click on the *Receive Money* button.

4.   At the top left-hand corner of the *Receive Money* window the option button for *Deposit to Account* should be active with "Jupiter Bank" selected.

5.   Check that the tick-box for 'Tax Inclusive' at the top of the *Receive Money* window is on.

6.   Leave the ID # as CR000001. This is a computer-generated number to identify the receipt (or in this case a deposit).

7.   Enter the date as 5/07/2011 ⏎.

8.   The "Payor" field is used to enter the name of the person or business making the payment. In *MYOB AccountRight Plus* "cards" can be created for names, addresses and other permanent information for customers, suppliers (vendors), employees and contacts. The information on a card can be entered into various forms by

selecting the card from a card file, and this saves a great deal of typing. Type in "D" and select "Daily Deposit" ↵ ↵.

9. Enter the total amount of the deposit as "3520" and ↵ (note that the dollar sign, the comma separating thousands, the decimal point and zero decimals are not required, and the resulting figure will be shown as $3,520.00).

10. This payment is made in cash. Type "Cash" in the 'Payment Method' field or use the *List* button and select "Cash" from the list. There are no details required for cash.

11. TAB to the 'Memo' field and type in "Daily Deposit of shop sales" and ↵.

12. The account to credit is "Food Sales", account number 4-1000. If you are using account names, type in the first few letters "Sa" and TAB twice. If you are using account numbers, type in the account number as 4-1000 and use TAB. Remember that a slower method is to hit Enter (↵), search for the account and use it. If the account number is known, it is far quicker to type in the known account number.

13. The amount $3,520.00 should be showing in the 'Amount' column (the GST-inclusive amount). TAB through to the 'Memo' column, leaving the 'Job' column blank.

14. Type in additional information about this line item in the 'Memo' column – enter "Prepared food" as the line 'Memo' and TAB.

15. Change the tax code to "GST" (this account has been set up with a default tax code of "FRE" that needs to be changed for the shop sales of prepared food).

16. Towards the bottom right-hand side of the form (before the buttons) there is a field called 'Category:' with a drop-down selection *List* button. Select "SHOP" as the category, as this is the Category ID for the shop.

17. Your *Receive Money* window should look like Figure 9.9 on the next page.

18. If there are any errors click in the incorrect field and edit it.

19. Click on the *Record* button to complete this transaction.

Video: A video showing you how to record and deposit a receipt is on the DVD

Self-test exercise 9.9

Record, for the rest of the week, **five** cash deposits for sales of prepared food at the business shop.

For all the following deposits: the account number is 4-1000 "Food Sales", there is no job number, all amounts are <u>tax inclusive</u> and the tax code is "GST".

The category is "SHOP":

6 July:	$1,690.80	including GST
7 July:	$2,244.00	including GST
8 July:	$1,125.85	including GST
9 July:	$979.99	including GST
10 July:	$3,135.44	including GST

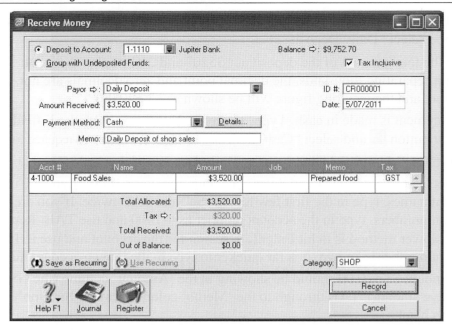

Figure 9.9: Money banked for shop cash sales

Recording cheques paid

The payment of cheques, other than to accounts payable, is covered in Chapter 4. The following example extends that coverage with categories and jobs. It does not cover using the *Payroll* command centre to process payroll payments.

Example 9.9—Spending money

1. Have the file dem91.myo open and be signed on as the "Administrator".
    This transaction is for the wages paid for the catering staff and casuals for the week ended 12 July 2011. This business does not use the *Payroll* command centre to process employees' pays. The wages are calculated manually and the net pays are paid using *Spend Money* option in the *Banking* command centre.

2. Select the *Banking* command centre.

3. Select the *Spend Money* option.

4. Salaries and wages are not reportable for GST purposes and the tax code will be "N-T" for all detail lines. It does not matter, therefore, whether the 'Tax Inclusive' checkbox is ticked or not.

5. The cheque number should be "101002". This will automatically increment by 1 for each cheque.

6. Set the date to "12/7/2011" ↵.

7. Enter the amount as "$7,071.70" ↵.

8. Ignore the 'Card' field – click in the 'Payee' field and enter "Cash". (Alternatively, you can TAB or use the ENTER key a few times to go to the 'Payee' field.)

9. TAB through to the 'Memo' field (do not press ENTER) and type in "Catering Wages paid for week ended 12/07/2011" and ↵.

10. Enter the first account number as 6-2430 "Wages and Salaries" and TAB through to the 'Amount' column.

11. Enter "$1,728.85" in the 'Amount' column and TAB to the 'Job' column.

12. The Job Number is "F101". Type this in or use the *List* 🔽 button and select from the list.

13. No additional detail line memo is required and the tax code should be the correct "N-T" so ↵ to go to the next line of entry.

14. Enter the following wages on Jobs in the same way:
    $3,621.70 for wages and salaries on Job J101 ↵
    $3,715.65 for wages and salaries on Job J102 ↵.

15. Enter the account "PAYG Withholding Payable", account number 2-1420 (type this in or use the List 🔽 button and select from the list of accounts). TAB through to the 'Amount' column.

16. The PAYG Withholding is income tax deducted from employees' gross wages. The amount is therefore entered as a negative so that it will be credited to a liability account (amount owed to the Australian Taxation Office).
    Enter minus "– $1,994.50" (no job number) and ↵.

17. Towards the bottom right-hand side of the *Spend Money* window (before the buttons) there is a field called 'Category:' with a drop-down selection list button. Select "CATER" as the category, as this is Category ID for catering.

18. Make sure that your *Spend Money* window looks like Figure 9.10 on the next page. **Note:** Depending on your computer system setup, the **negative** amount may appear with a minus sign **–$1,994.50** or in brackets **($1,994.50)**.

19. Edit any fields that have errors and click the *Record* button to complete the transaction.

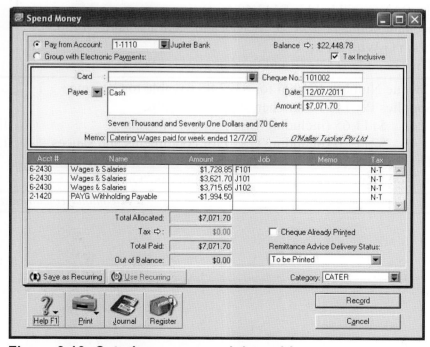

Figure 9.10: Catering wages on jobs paid

Video: A video on making payments using Spend Money is on the DVD

Self-test exercise 9.10

Enter in the following cheques using the *Spend Money* option in the *Banking* command centre:

Date	Details	Job
12/7/2011	Cheque Number 101003 for $1,207.14 payable to Party Supplies Pty Ltd for party food supplied to jobs in week ended 10 July 2011. (**Note**: Use Party Supplies P/L card in the 'Card' field) $227.70 (including GST) for chips, nuts etc $460.35 (including GST) for chips, nuts etc $519.09 (including GST) for chips, nuts etc **Make sure** to change the tax code to "GST". The account to debit is number 5-1030 "Food – Other". The category is "CATER".	 F101 J101 J102
13/7/2011	Cheque Number 101004 for $1,080.40 cash for shop wages. The gross amount is $1,480.00 and the PAYG withheld is $399.60. **Remember** to enter the PAYG amount as **negative**. Use account numbers 6-2430 "Wages and Salaries" and 2-1420 "PAYG Withh. Payable". The tax code is "N-T" and the category is "SHOP".	NA
13/7/2011	Cheque Number 101005 for $2,416.60 cash for wages at the Penrith wholesale premises. The gross amount is $2,860.00 and the PAYG withheld is $443.40 (enter it as negative). Use account numbers 6-2430 "Wages and Salaries" and 2-1420 "PAYG Withh. Pay." The tax code is "N-T" and the category is "WSALE".	NA
13/7/2011	Cheque Number 101006 for $322.85 payable to Catering Supplies Pty Ltd for kitchen supplies on jobs. $111.65 (including GST) for condiments $211.20 (including GST) for condiments and sauces The tax code is "GST" and the account to debit is number 6-2300 "Kitchen Supplies". The category is "CATER".	 J101 J102
	(continued on the next page)	

Date	Details	Job
	Self-test exercise 9.10 (continued)	
15/7/2011	Cheque Number 101007 for $667.26 payable to Mister Fixall Pty Ltd for repairs to furniture and equipment on Jobs. 　$209.00 (including GST) for repairs to furniture 　$221.10 (including GST) for repairs to furniture 　$237.16 (including GST) for repairs to equipment The tax code is "GST" and the account is number 6-1150 "Breakages & Replacements". The category is "CATER".	F101 J101 J102
16/7/2011	Cheque Number 101008 for $192.39 payable to Chips n Cracks Pty Ltd for crockery replacements on jobs. 　$35.20 (including GST) for crockery 　$84.04 (including GST) for crockery and cutlery 　$73.15 (including GST) for crockery The tax code is "GST" and the account is number 6-1150 "Breakages & Replacements". The category is "CATER".	F101 J101 J102
16/7/2011	Cheque Number 101009 for $272.80 cash reimbursing employees for meals. 　$79.20 (including GST) for meals　Tax code "GST" 　$96.80 (including GST) for meals　Tax code "GST" 　$96.80 (including GST) for meals　Tax code "GST" The account to debit is number 6-1500 "Employees' Meals". The category is "CATER".	F101 J101 J102
17/7/2011	Cheque Number 101010 for $2,420.00 paid to Jimmy Choo's Quality Laundry for uniform and linen laundry. 　$484.00 (including GST) for laundry 　$990.00 (including GST) for laundry 　$946.00 (including GST) for laundry The tax code is "GST" and the account is number 6-1800 "Laundry and Cleaning". The category is "CATER".	F101 J101 J102

Recording general journal entries with jobs and categories

General journal entries are extensively covered in Chapter 3. The journal entry form also allows for allocation to jobs and to categories.

Example 9.10—Recording a journal entry

1. Have the file dem91.myo open and be signed on as the "Administrator". This journal entry allocates general administration costs to completed jobs at a predetermined rate of 25% based on gross wages.
2. Select the *Accounts* command centre.
3. Select the *Record Journal Entry* option.

4. As this transaction does not involve any tax, it doesn't matter whether the tax inclusive tick box is ticked or not. The transaction does not involve any sale or purchase, therefore you may select either the "Sales" or "Purchases" BAS report for the GST at the top of the screen

5. Enter the date as "16/07/2011" and ↵.

6. Type in the 'Memo' as "Administration overhead applied to jobs" and ↵.

7. Enter the account as number 5-9000 "Administration Overhead", and TAB to the 'Debit' column.

8. The first amount is 25% of wages on Job F101 of $1,728.85, which is $432.21. Type this in or enter "1728.85 * 0.25 =".

9. TAB to the 'Job' column and select Job F101. Type this in or use the *List* button ⊞ and select from the list. The tax code should be "N-T" so ↵.

10. Repeat the first line: for Jobs J101 the amount is (25% of $3,621.70) and for Job J102 the amount is (25% of $3,715.65).

11. The last account to enter is the "expense" account recording the credit. Enter account number 6-9000 "Allocated to Jobs".
    TAB to the 'Credit' column and enter the amount as $2,266.55 (being the total administration overhead allocated, or applied, to the jobs).

12. Towards the bottom right-hand side of the *Record Journal Entry* window (before the buttons) there is a field called 'Category:' with a drop-down selection *List* button. Select "CATER" as the category, as this is the Category ID for catering.

13. Your *Record Journal Entry* window should look like Figure 9.11 on the next page.

14. Make sure the 'Out of Balance' is $0.00. If not, recalculate the above amounts. Edit any fields that have errors and click the *Record* button to complete the transaction.

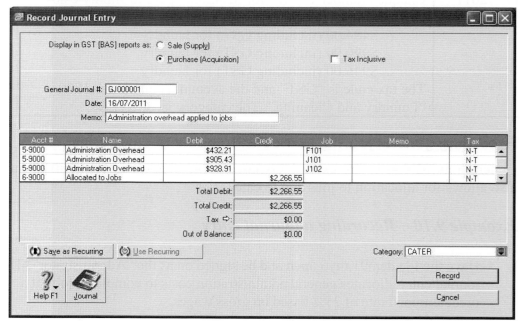

Figure 9.11: Administration overhead allocated to jobs

Changing completion percentage

Before printing reports, especially the "Budget Analysis" report, the percentage to which a job is complete can be edited in the Job details. This is important if the job is not 100% complete, as the budget figures entered are for a complete job and the actual figures will not be final. In our example, the jobs are all 100% complete and this should be shown on the reports.

Example 9.11—Changing completion percentage

1.   Have the file dem91.myo open and be signed on as the "Administrator".
2.   Select the *Lists* menu at the top of the screen.
3.   Select the *Jobs* menu item.
4.   Click on the detail (or zoom) arrow ⇨ next to detail Job F101 (**NOT** the 'header').
5.   Click on the 'Percent Complete:' field and type in "100%" and ↵.
      Your *Edit Job* window should look like Figure 9.12 on the next page.
6.   Click on the *OK* button to complete the edit.

Self-test exercise 9.11

Make the 'Percent Complete:' field "100%" for both Jobs J101 and J102.

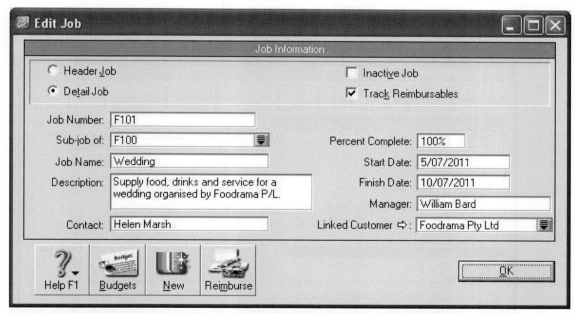

Figure 9.12: *Edit Job* window with 100% percent completion

Printing reports

Most of the previous chapters have covered the printing of reports. Chapter 3 in particular shows how to print reports from the general ledger (*Accounts* command centre).

Example 9.12—Printing a job budget analysis report

1. Have the file dem91.myo open and be signed on as the Administrator.
    This report will compare actual costs with budgets entered earlier. The differences between actual and budget are shown in dollars and as a percentage variation.

2. Select the *Accounts* command centre.

3. Click on the *Reports* button.

4. Scroll down the names of reports under the *Accounts* tab until the section headed **Jobs** is located (note the different reports on Jobs that can be printed!). Click on the report called "Budget Analysis" as shown in Figure 9.13 on the next page.

5. Click on the *Customise* button. In this exercise, only Job F101 is to be reported on. At the top of the *Report Customisation – Budget Analysis* window, select Job F101 – type this in or use the *List* button ▼ and clear all ticks from the list except job F101).

6. Click on the *Display* button. You can use the selection at the top of the *Report Display* window to see a "Print Preview" of the report:

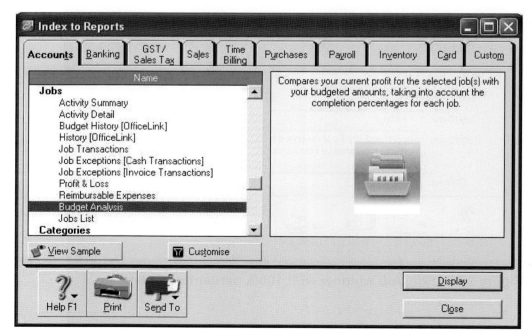

Figure 9.13: Selecting *Job Budget Analysis* report from list of *Accounts* reports

7.　Your screen should look like Figure 9.14:

8.　Click on the *Print* button if you want a hard copy and click *Close* to exit.

O'Malley Tucker Pty Ltd
« Sample ANSWER dem91.myo »

Jobs (Budget Analysis)

Page 1

Account	Budget	Adjusted Budget	Actual	Difference	% Difference
F101 Wedding				**Percent Complete:**	**100.00%**
Income					
Catering Fees	$6,600.00	$6,600.00	$6,600.00	$0.00	0.0%
Total Income	$6,600.00	$6,600.00	$6,600.00	$0.00	0.0%
Cost of Sales					
Food - Meat	$770.00	$770.00	$720.00	-$50.00	(6.5%)
Food - Vegetables	$198.00	$198.00	$220.00	$22.00	11.1%
Food - Other	$440.00	$440.00	$557.00	$117.00	26.6%
Beverages - Beer	$900.00	$900.00	$855.00	-$45.00	(5.0%)
Beverages - Wine	$660.00	$660.00	$660.00	$0.00	0.0%
Beverages - Other	$300.00	$300.00	$300.00	$0.00	0.0%
Other Purchases	$100.00	$100.00	$0.00	-$100.00	(100.0%)
Administration Overhead	$440.00	$440.00	$432.21	-$7.79	(1.8%)
Total Cost of Sales	$3,808.00	$3,808.00	$3,744.21	-$63.79	(1.7%)
Expense					
Breakages & Replacements	$200.00	$200.00	$222.00	$22.00	11.0%
Employees' Meals	$64.00	$64.00	$72.00	$8.00	12.5%
Laundry and Cleaning	$440.00	$440.00	$440.00	$0.00	0.0%
Kitchen Supplies	$100.00	$100.00	$0.00	-$100.00	(100.0%)
Wages & Salaries	$1,760.00	$1,760.00	$1,728.85	-$31.15	(1.8%)
Total Expense	$2,564.00	$2,564.00	$2,462.85	-$101.15	(3.9%)
Net Profit (Loss)	$228.00	$228.00	$392.94	$164.94	72.3%

Figure 9.14: Budget Analysis Report for Job F101

Self-test exercise 9.12

Using the file dem91.myo, print the following reports:

A **Job** "Budget Analysis" report for each of Jobs J101 and J102.

A **Job** "Profit & Loss" report for <u>All</u> jobs for the month of July (that is, a single report for the three jobs).

A **Categories** *Profit & Loss* for <u>All</u> categories in July and in whole dollars (click on the Finishing tab in the *Report Customisation* window to select the whole dollar checkbox).

Competency checklist

	I can now do the following:	✓
1	Design reports using accounts, categories and jobs	
2	Create categories for departments and other business segments	
3	Create Header Job records	
4	Create Detail Job Records	
5	Enter a budget for a Job	
6	Record transactions that will include category and job data	
7	Prepare, display and print profit reports for jobs	
8	Prepare, display and print reports by category	

Graduation is in the category of a job well done!

Chapter 9: Assessment exercises

9.1

Helen Richards, trading as Vacuo-Clean Company, has a franchise business distributing and servicing commercial and industrial vacuum cleaners. *MYOB AccountRight Plus* has been used for a number of years, but from 1 July 2011 management wants to incorporate categories and gross profit on jobs reporting. The business is also converting from a periodic inventory system to a perpetual inventory system (see Chapter 1 for an explanation of this).

Open the file ass91.myo and sign on as the "Administrator" without a password. Select the *Company Information* item from the *Setup* menu at the top of the screen and type your name in the address field.

The month for this exercise is July 2011, the start of a new financial year. **Only a few jobs are to be set up as a trial for fully implementing a full job system in the future.**

(a) Edit the Cost of Sales section in the *Accounts List* to change the accounts so that the new perpetual inventory system can be used and with more detailed levels. The accounts in this section should be:

5-0000	**Cost of Sales**		**Header**
5-1000		**Cost of Cleaners Sold**	**Header**
	5-1010	COGS – Retail	Detail
	5-1020	COGS – Industrial	Detail
	5-1030	COGS – Government	Detail
	5-1200	Purchases	Detail
5-2000	**Cost of Services**		**Header**
	5-2010	**Servicing – Retail**	**Header**
	5-2011	Servicing Retail – Parts	Detail
	5-2012	Servicing Retail – Labour	Detail
	5-2020	**Servicing – Industrial**	**Header**
	5-2021	Servicing Indus. – Parts	Detail
	5-2022	Servicing Indus. – Labour	Detail
	5-2030	**Servicing – Government**	**Header**
	5-2031	Servicing Govt. – Parts	Detail
	5-2032	Servicing Govt. – Labour	Detail

(b) Edit each of the items in inventory to show the correct "Cost of Sales" account. The present Cost of Sales account is currently "Purchases" – account number 5-1200 and needs to be changed to those shown here:

Item Number	Expense Account
E100	5-1020 COGS – Industrial
E200	5-1030 COGS – Government
G1000	5-1030 COGS – Government

(continued on the next page)

G200	5-1030 COGS – Government
IND100	5-1020 COGS – Industrial
IND200	5-1020 COGS – Industrial
Item Number	**Expense Account**
P100	5-2011 Servicing Retail – Parts
PG100	5-2031 Servicing Govt. – Parts
PG200	5-2031 Servicing Govt. – Parts
PIND100	5-2021 Servicing Indus. – Parts
PIND200	5-2021 Servicing Indus. – Parts
PS100	5-2011 Servicing Retail – Parts
PS200	5-2011 Servicing Retail – Parts
R100	5-1010 COGS – Retail
R200	5-1010 COGS – Retail
S100	5-1010 COGS – Retail
S200	5-1010 COGS – Retail

(c)   Use the *Setup* menu, *Preferences* item and under the *System* tab <u>turn on</u> the Category Tracking. However, categories are "Not Required" on all transactions.

(d)   Create the following Categories.

Category ID	Category Name	Description
RETAIL	Retail Sales & Service	Sales of vacuum cleaners and service under warranty for major retail customers.
INDUS	Industrial Sales & Service	Sales of vacuum cleaners, emission controls and service under warranty for major non-government industrial customers.
GOVT	Government Customers	Sales of vacuum cleaners, emission controls and service under warranty for State & Commonwealth government customers.

(e)   In order to examine the usefulness of using Jobs, create the following trial Job records for contracts with the Department of Education as at 1 July 2011:

Header Job Number G1000 with name "DepEd". This Job is a contract to supply certain schools for Department of Education with vacuum cleaners and chemical gas extractors. It also requires service of these for a period of 1 year. Gordon Boyd is the contact person at the department's head office. This contract started on 1 July 2011 and Gustav Mahler is the manager.

Detail Job Number G1010 "DepEd VACS" for the supply of vacuum cleaners and extractors to Department of Education (linked customer) schools. This is a sub-job of job G1000. Gordon Boyd is the contact person at the department's head office. This contract started on 1 July 2011 and Gustav Mahler is the manager. Reimbursables are not tracked.

Detail Job Number G1020 "DepEd SERVICE" for the service of vacuum equipment at the Department of Education (linked customer) schools. This is a sub-job of job G1000. Gordon Boyd is the contact person at the department's head office. This contract started on 1 July 2011 and Gustav Mahler is the manager. Reimbursables are not tracked.

(f) ***Record the following purchases on credit in July 2011 (use Item purchases)***

If necessary, change the layout to **Item** purchases.

First Purchase number is "3148". All prices are GST-inclusive.

Tick the [✔ Tax Inclusive] checkbox ***before*** entering amounts.

No Jobs or Categories are involved in these transactions:

2/7 Davis Manufacturing Pty Ltd – Purchase # 3148. Supplier Invoice # is 18003.
All prices include the GST. Bill:
10 of Item # IND100 "Dust-Miser 100" @ $462.00 each, and
5 of Item # IND200 "Dust-Miser 200" @ $541.20 each.
Delivered (Shipped) by "Best Way".

5/7 Davis Manufacturing Pty Ltd – Purchase # 3149. Supplier Invoice # is 18006.
All prices include the GST. Bill:
10 of Item # G1000 "Dust-Miser 1000" @ $1,100.00 each.
Delivered (Shipped) by "Best Way".

9/7 Spartacus Cleaners Pty Ltd – Purchase # 3150. Supplier Invoice # is 1234.
Bill: 30 of Item # PIND100 "Bags & Hoses IND100" @ $44.55 each (incl. GST). Delivered by "International".

15/7 Vacuum Bliss – Purchase # 3151. Supplier Invoice # is 847.
Bill: 20 of Item # R100 "Turbo A Vac. Cleaner" @ $303.60 each (incl. GST) and 20 of Item # S100 "SuperVac Small" @ $184.80 each (inc. GST). Delivered by "International".

22/7 Suckers & Seers Pty Ltd – Purchase # 3152. Supplier Invoice # is 4430.
Bill: 4 of Item # E100 "Gas Extractor & Cleaner" @ $1,848.00 (incl. GST), and 4 of Item # E200 "Gas Extractor (Gov. Spec)" @ $1,716.00 (incl. GST). Delivered by "Best Way".

(g) ***Record the following sales on credit in July 2011 (use Item sales)***

If necessary, change the layout to **Item** Sales.

First Invoice number is "238". All prices are GST-inclusive.

Tick the [✔ Tax Inclusive] checkbox ***before*** entering amounts.

Only enter Jobs or Categories where indicated in a transaction:

5/7 Department of Education – Invoice # is 238. Customer PO # is WT321Z2.
Shipped:
3 of Item # E200 "Gas Extractor & Cleaner", Job is G1010, and
4 of Item # G200 "Dust-Miser 200 (Govt. Spec)", Job is G1010.
Salesperson is Gustav Mahler. Hills Transport delivered the goods.
The Category is "GOVT".

9/7 Jeffrey's Appliances – Invoice # is 239. Customer PO # is 848. Shipped:
10 packs of Item # P100 "Bags & Rings Turbo vacs". No Job Number.
Salesperson was Albert Dvorak and International delivers the goods.
The Category is "RETAIL".

13/7 MITES LTD – Invoice # is 240. Customer PO # is 3311. Shipped:
2 of Item # IND100 "Dust-Miser 100", no Job Number, and
6 of Item # IND200 "Dust-Miser200", no Job Number
Salesperson is Stephanie Bach and the goods are delivered by Hills
Transport. The Category is "INDUS".

19/7 Department of Education – Invoice # is 241. Customer PO # is WT411Q3.
Shipped:
8 of Item # G1000 "Dust-Miser 1000 (Govt Spec)" Job: G1010, and
6 packs of Item # PG100 "Bags & Hoses IND100 (Govt), Job: G1010.
Salesperson is Gustav Mahler. Hills Transport delivered the goods.
The Category is "GOVT".

20/7 Mad Discounts – Invoice # is 242. Customer PO # is D4431. Shipped:
10 of Item # R100 "Turbo A Vacuum Cleaner", no Job Number.
Salesperson was Richard Wagner and International delivered the goods.
The Category is "RETAIL".

22/7 Hot Shot Appliances – Invoice # is 243. Customer PO # is 2189. Shipped:
10 of Item # R100 "Turbo A Vacuum Cleaner", no Job Number.
Salesperson was Richard Wagner and International delivered the goods.
The Category is "RETAIL".

26/7 Department of Education – Invoice # is 244. Customer PO # is WT418Q3.
Shipped:
15 of Item # PIND100 "Bags & Hoses IND100", Job: G1020. Also charge:
20 hours of Item # SER100 "Standard Service Charge", Job: G1020.
Salesperson is Gustav Mahler. Hills Transport delivered the goods.
The Category is "GOVT".

28/7 MITES LTD – Invoice # is 245. Customer PO # is 3324. Shipped:
6 of Item # E100 "Gas Extractor & Cleaner", no Job Number, and
8 of Item # IND100 "Dust-Miser100", no Job Number.
Salesperson is Stephanie Bach and the goods are delivered by Hills
Transport. The Category is "INDUS".

(h) ***Record cheques received from Accounts Receivable in July 2011***
Note: Deposit each receipt to bank account 1-1110 "National Bank"
and ignore customer cheque details.
Use *Receive Payments* option from the *Sales* command centre for these:

2/7 Received from Hot Shot Appliances (Inv 234) $3,890.70

9/7 Received from Mad Discounts (Inv 235) 4,180.00

16/7 Received from Taylor Square Whitegoods (Inv 236) .. 3,286.80

20/7 Received from Taylor Square Whitegoods (Inv 237) .. 4,752.66

30/7 Received from MITES LTD (Inv 240) 6,952.00

Received from Department of Education (Inv 238) .. 11,748.00

(i) *Record cheques drawn in July 2011 –*

Note: First cheque number should be "123563".

Use *Spend Money* option from the *Banking* command centre for these:

1/7   Paid Emerald Press Pty Ltd $753.50 (including GST) for special stationery for the Department of Education servicing contract. The Job Number is G1020 and the Category is "GOVT".

7/7   Cash cheque of $3,744.00 paid for monthly wages in the retail section of the business. Gross pay is $4,800.00 less PAYG Withholding $1,056.00. Category is "RETAIL". (Remember to enter the PAYG amount as negative.)

Cash cheque of $2,778.50 for monthly wages in the industry section of the business. Gross pay is $3,495.00 less PAYG Withholding $716.50. Category is "INDUS".

14/7   Paid Loden Motors Pty Ltd $55,000 (which includes GST) for a Ford station wagon. Tax code is "CAP".

15/7   Petty Cash re-imbursement – cash cheque for $419.65

Postage .... $81.95 (including the GST)

Travel (JOB G1020)...............$173.80 (including the GST)

Staff Amenities......................$163.90 (including the GST)

22/7   Paid Hogans Ad Agency $2,418.68 (including the GST) for advertising in "Cleaning Industry" journal. The Category is INDUS.

25/7   Paid General Spares $1,237.50 (including GST) for special parts required in services carried out on Job G1020.
Debit account: "5-2031 Servicing Gov – Parts". The Category is "GOVT".

(j) *Record cheques paid to Suppliers (Accounts Payable) in July 2011*

Use *Pay Bills* option from the *Purchases* command centre for these:

25/7 Paid to Davis Manufacturing Pty Ltd (PO #3144)...... $3,031.45

26/7 Paid to Omega Manufacturing Pty Ltd (PO #3145) 3,423.75

28/7 Paid to Spartacus Cleaners Pty Ltd (PO #3146) 4,286.15

29/7 Paid to Vacuum Bliss Pty Ltd (PO #3147) 2,085.16

31/7 Paid to Davis Manufacturing Pty Ltd (PO #3148)........ 7,326.00

(k) *Print the following Reports for the month of July 2011 –*

(i)   Profit & Loss [Accrual] – [Period: 1/7/2011 to 31/7/2011]

(ii)   Jobs Profit & Loss [All Jobs] – [Period: 1/7/2011 to 31/7/2011]

(iii)   Categories Profit and Loss [All Categories] – [Period: 1/7/2011 to 31/7/2011]

Chapter 9: Answers to self-test exercises (where applicable)

9.1

There are of course many different ways in which any one business may categorise. These are just some possibilities – it really depends on the usefulness of the results!

Printer: Books, Magazines, Brochures/Leaflets, Other. Jobs – printing invoices, booklets

Publisher: Schools, TAFE, Universities. Jobs – printed books, electronic media

Builders: Spec Homes, Contracts, Government. Jobs – spec home, flats

Electricians: Contracting, Subcontracting, Home Repairs. Jobs – all contracts, house repairs

9.2

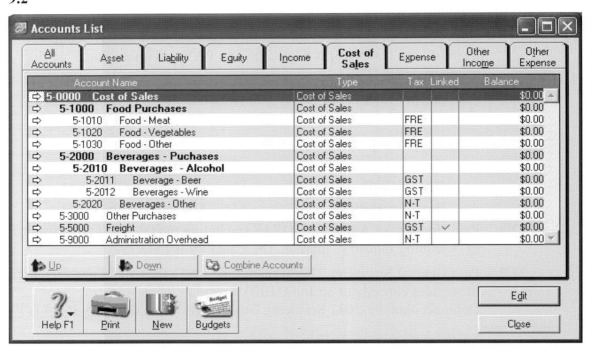

9.3

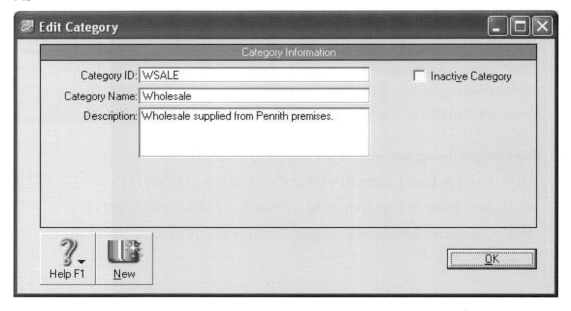

9.3 *(continued)*

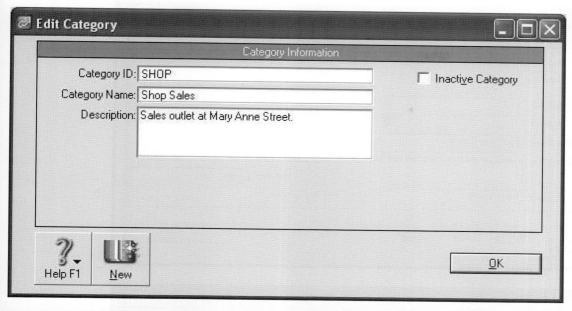

Category List with four categories now added

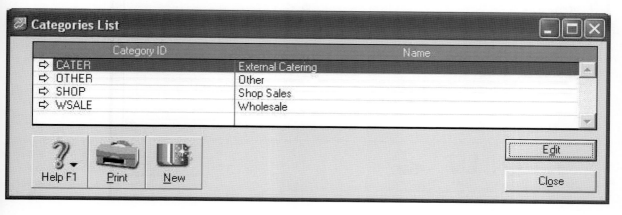

9.4

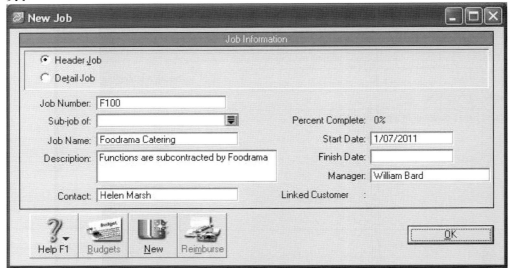

9.5

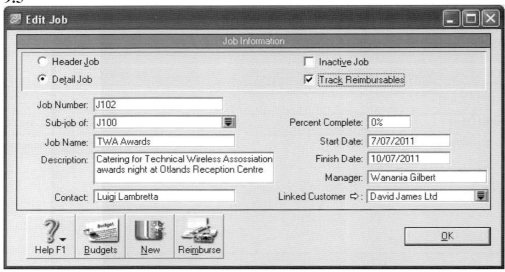

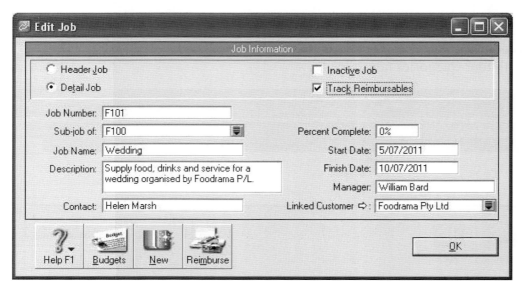

9.5 *(continued)*

The Jobs List after two header and three detail jobs have been created

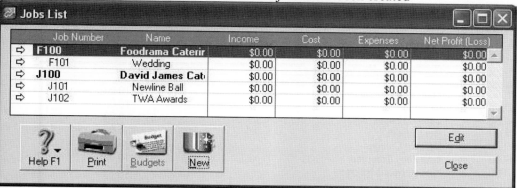

9.6

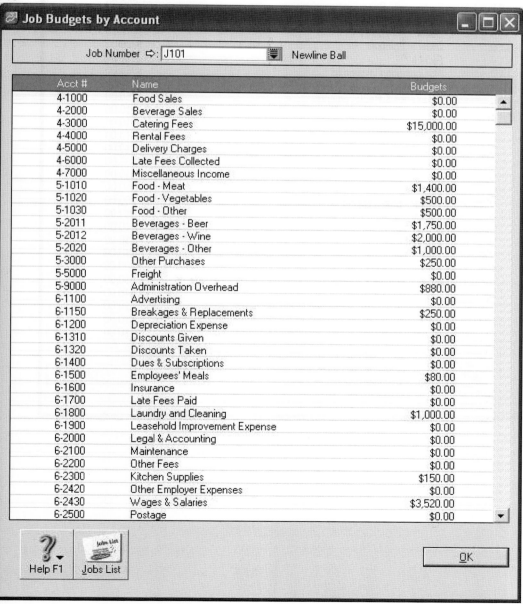

9.6 *(continued)*

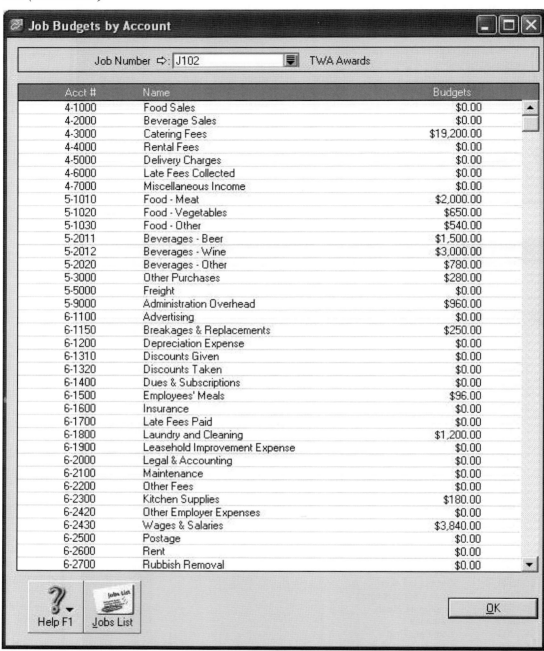

9.7 Only the first five purchases are shown – the other purchases will be similar.

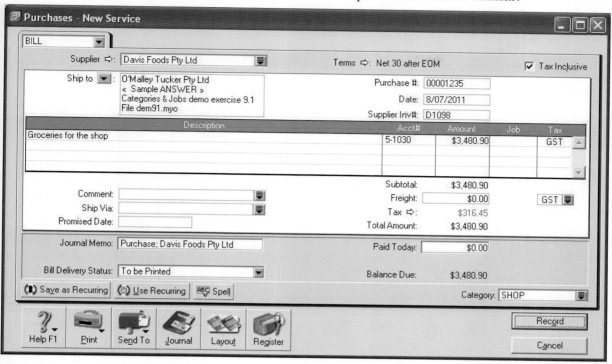

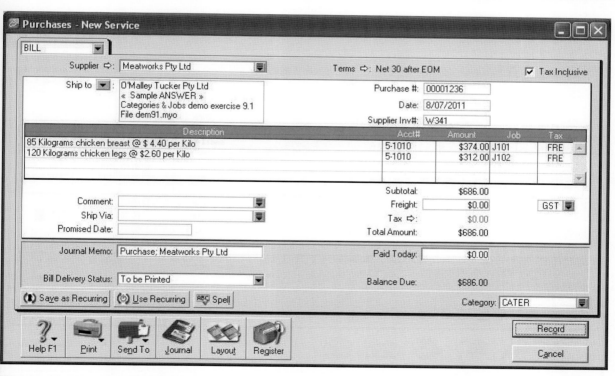

9.7 *(continued)*

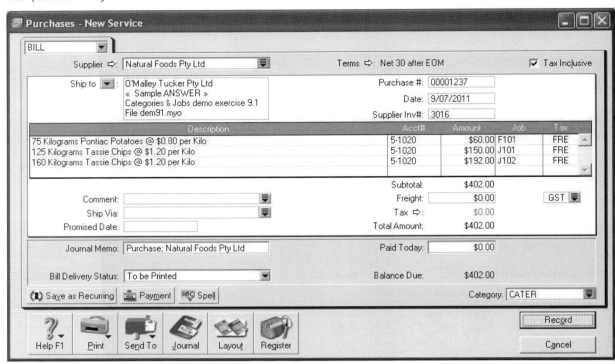

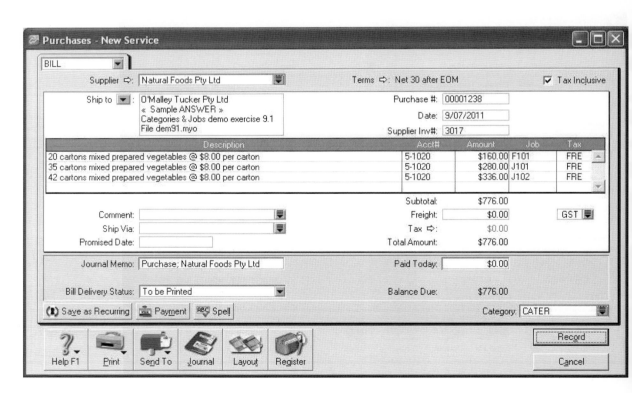

9.7 *(continued)*

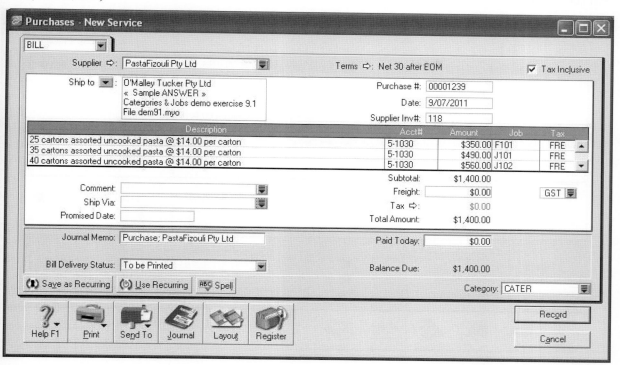

9.8

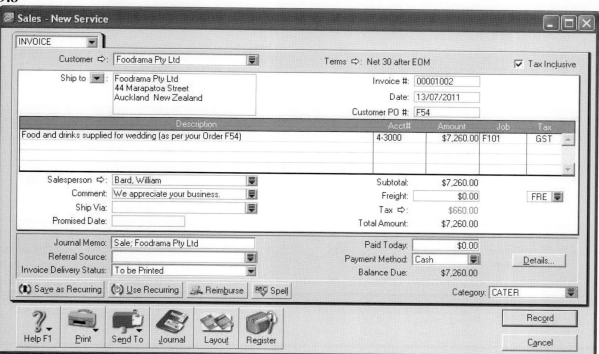

9.8 *(continued)*

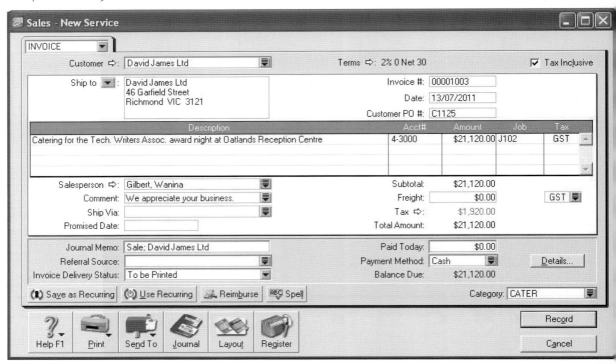

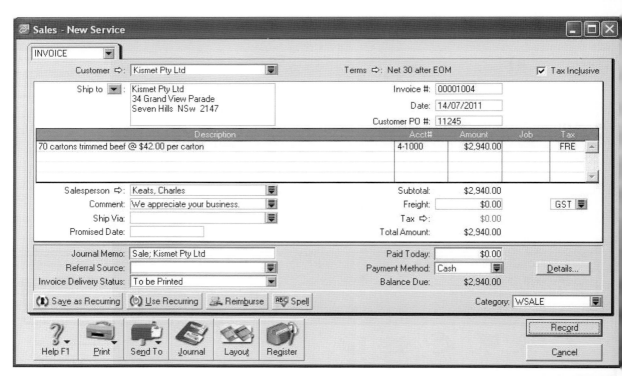

9.9 Only the first cash sale is shown here – the rest are similar.

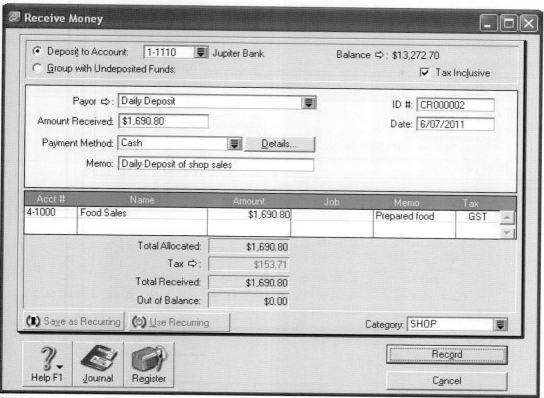

9.10

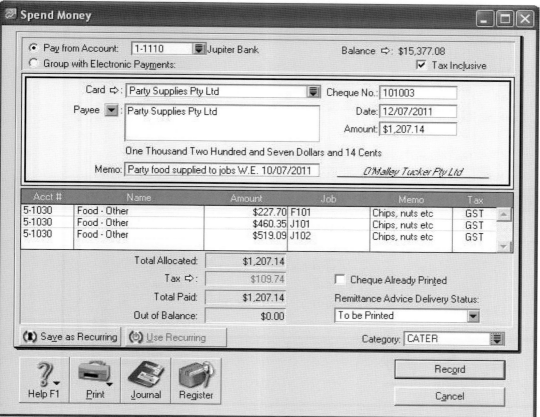

9.10 *(continued)*

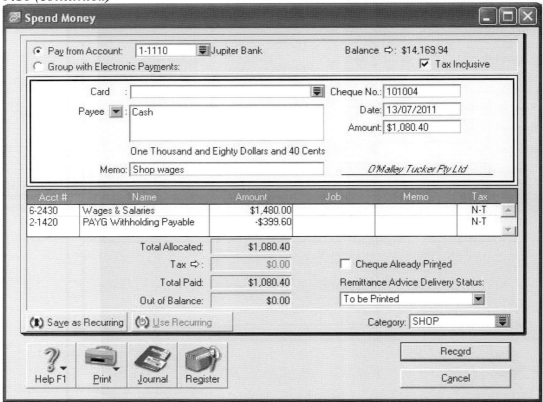

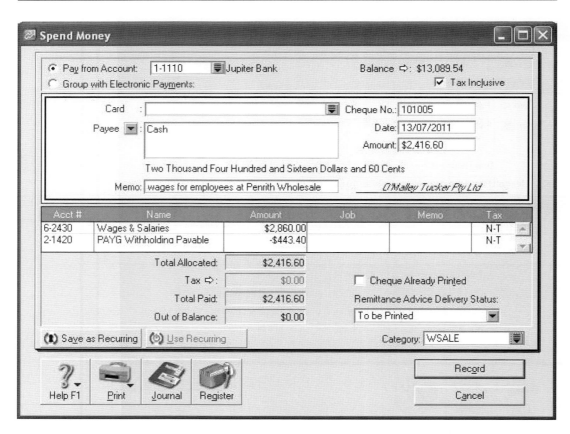

9.10 *(continued)*

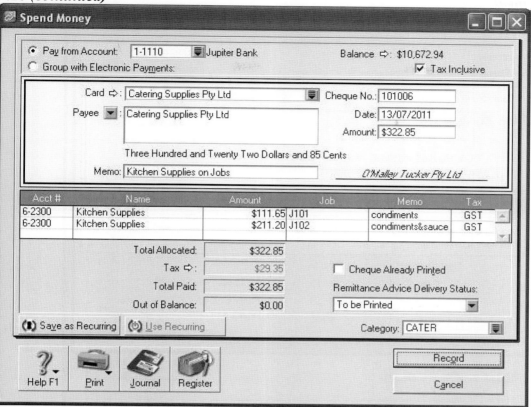

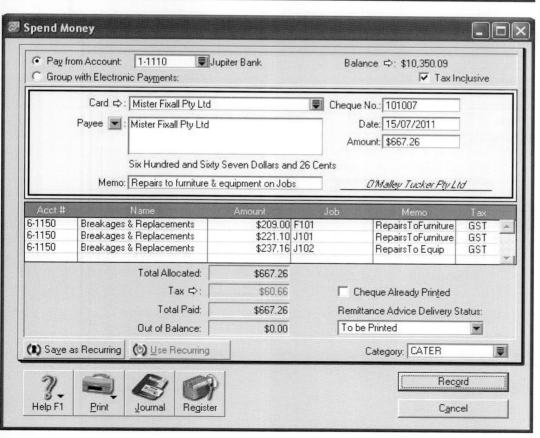

9.10 *(continued)*

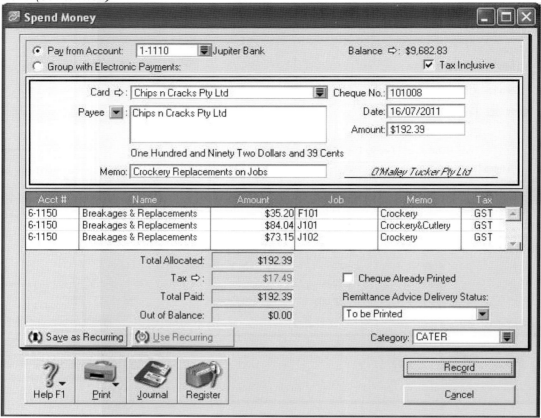

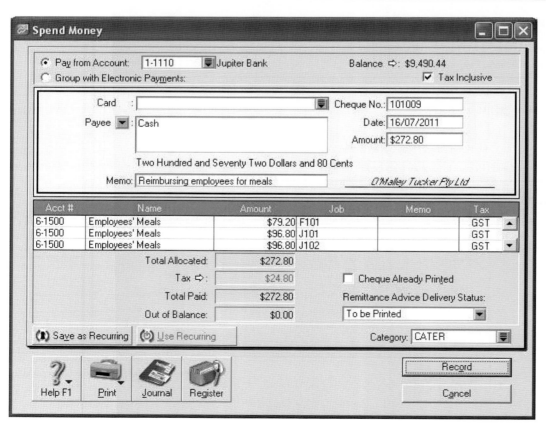

9.10 *(continued)*

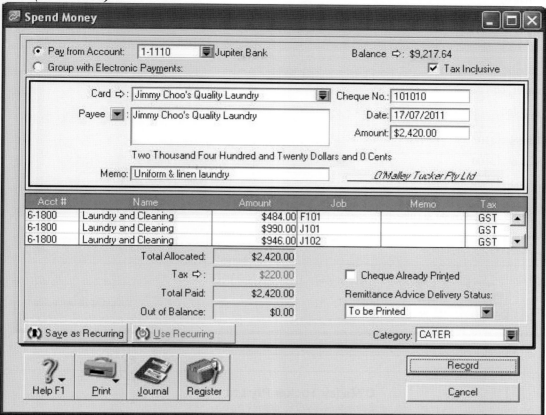

9.11

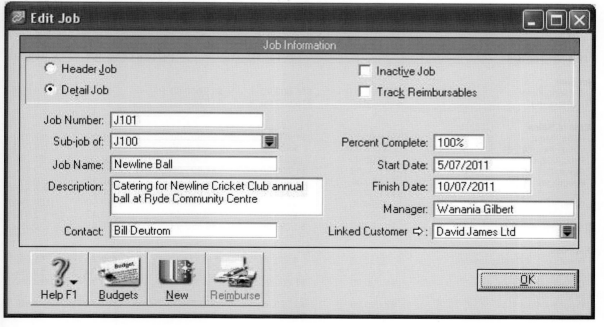

9.11 *(continued)*

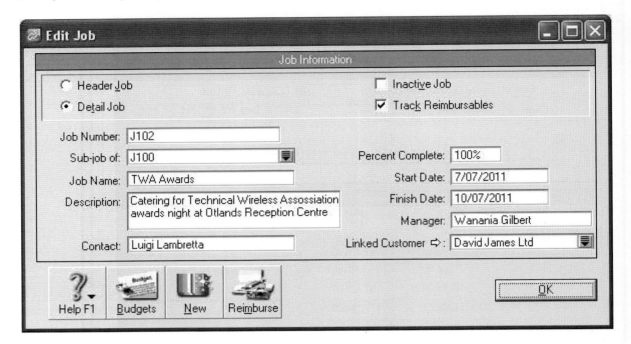

9.12

O'Malley Tucker Pty Ltd

« Sample ANSWER dem91.myo »

Jobs (Budget Analysis)

Page 1

Account	Budget	Adjusted Budget	Actual	Difference	% Difference
J101 Newline Ball				Percent Complete:	100.00%
Income					
Catering Fees	$15,000.00	$15,000.00	$15,000.00	$0.00	0.0%
Total Income	$15,000.00	$15,000.00	$15,000.00	$0.00	0.0%
Cost of Sales					
Food - Meat	$1,400.00	$1,400.00	$1,302.00	-$98.00	(7.0%)
Food - Vegetables	$500.00	$500.00	$430.00	-$70.00	(14.0%)
Food - Other	$500.00	$500.00	$908.50	$408.50	81.7%
Beverages - Beer	$1,750.00	$1,750.00	$1,805.00	$55.00	3.1%
Beverages - Wine	$2,000.00	$2,000.00	$2,000.00	$0.00	0.0%
Beverages - Other	$1,000.00	$1,000.00	$1,000.00	$0.00	0.0%
Other Purchases	$250.00	$250.00	$0.00	-$250.00	(100.0%)
Administration Overhead	$880.00	$880.00	$905.43	$25.43	2.9%
Total Cost of Sales	$8,280.00	$8,280.00	$8,350.93	$70.93	0.9%
Expense					
Breakages & Replacements	$250.00	$250.00	$277.40	$27.40	11.0%
Employees' Meals	$80.00	$80.00	$88.00	$8.00	10.0%
Laundry and Cleaning	$1,000.00	$1,000.00	$900.00	-$100.00	(10.0%)
Kitchen Supplies	$150.00	$150.00	$101.50	-$48.50	(32.3%)
Wages & Salaries	$3,520.00	$3,520.00	$3,621.70	$101.70	2.9%
Total Expense	$5,000.00	$5,000.00	$4,988.60	-$11.40	(0.2%)
Net Profit (Loss)	$1,720.00	$1,720.00	$1,660.47	-$59.53	(3.5%)

9.12 *(continued)*

O'Malley Tucker Pty Ltd
« Sample ANSWER dem91.myo »

Jobs (Budget Analysis)

Account	Budget	Adjusted Budget	Actual	Difference	% Difference
J102 TWA Awards				**Percent Complete:**	**100.00%**
Income					
Catering Fees	$19,200.00	$19,200.00	$19,200.00	$0.00	0.0%
Total Income	$19,200.00	$19,200.00	$19,200.00	$0.00	0.0%
Cost of Sales					
Food - Meat	$2,000.00	$2,000.00	$2,076.00	$76.00	3.8%
Food - Vegetables	$650.00	$650.00	$528.00	-$122.00	(18.8%)
Food - Other	$540.00	$540.00	$1,031.90	$491.90	91.1%
Beverages - Beer	$1,500.00	$1,500.00	$1,520.00	$20.00	1.3%
Beverages - Wine	$3,000.00	$3,000.00	$3,000.00	$0.00	0.0%
Beverages - Other	$780.00	$780.00	$780.00	$0.00	0.0%
Other Purchases	$280.00	$280.00	$0.00	-$280.00	(100.0%)
Freight	$0.00	$0.00	$0.00	$0.00	NA
Administration Overhead	$960.00	$960.00	$928.91	-$31.09	(3.2%)
Total Cost of Sales	$9,710.00	$9,710.00	$9,864.81	$154.81	1.6%
Expense					
Breakages & Replacements	$250.00	$250.00	$282.10	$32.10	12.8%
Employees' Meals	$96.00	$96.00	$88.00	-$8.00	(8.3%)
Laundry and Cleaning	$1,200.00	$1,200.00	$860.00	-$340.00	(28.3%)
Kitchen Supplies	$180.00	$180.00	$192.00	$12.00	6.7%
Wages & Salaries	$3,840.00	$3,840.00	$3,715.65	-$124.35	(3.2%)
Total Expense	$5,566.00	$5,566.00	$5,137.75	-$428.25	(7.7%)
Net Profit (Loss)	$3,924.00	$3,924.00	$4,197.44	$273.44	7.0%

9.12 *(continued)*

Job Profit & Loss Statement

July 2011

Page 1

Account Name	Selected Period	Year to Date
F101 **Wedding**		
Income		
Catering Fees	$6,600.00	$6,600.00
Total Income	$6,600.00	$6,600.00
Cost of Sales		
Food - Meat	$720.00	$720.00
Food - Vegetables	$220.00	$220.00
Food - Other	$557.00	$557.00
Beverages - Beer	$855.00	$855.00
Beverages - Wine	$660.00	$660.00
Beverages - Other	$300.00	$300.00
Administration Overhead	$432.21	$432.21
Total Cost of Sales	$3,744.21	$3,744.21
Expense		
Breakages & Replacements	$222.00	$222.00
Employees' Meals	$72.00	$72.00
Laundry and Cleaning	$440.00	$440.00
Wages & Salaries	$1,728.85	$1,728.85
Total Expense	$2,462.85	$2,462.85
Net Profit (Loss)	$392.94	$392.94
J101 **Newline Ball**		
Income		
Catering Fees	$15,000.00	$15,000.00
Total Income	$15,000.00	$15,000.00
Cost of Sales		
Food - Meat	$1,302.00	$1,302.00
Food - Vegetables	$430.00	$430.00
Food - Other	$908.50	$908.50
Beverages - Beer	$1,805.00	$1,805.00
Beverages - Wine	$2,000.00	$2,000.00
Beverages - Other	$1,000.00	$1,000.00
Administration Overhead	$905.43	$905.43
Total Cost of Sales	$8,350.93	$8,350.93
Expense		
Breakages & Replacements	$277.40	$277.40
Employees' Meals	$88.00	$88.00
Laundry and Cleaning	$900.00	$900.00
Kitchen Supplies	$101.50	$101.50
Wages & Salaries	$3,621.70	$3,621.70
Total Expense	$4,988.60	$4,988.60
Net Profit (Loss)	$1,660.47	$1,660.47

'Job P&L Statement' continued on the next page...

9.12 *(continued)*   Page 2 of Job P&L Statement

J102   **TWA Awards**

Income
Catering Fees	$19,200.00	$19,200.00
Total Income	$19,200.00	$19,200.00

Cost of Sales
Food - Meat	$2,076.00	$2,076.00
Food - Vegetables	$528.00	$528.00
Food - Other	$1,031.90	$1,031.90
Beverages - Beer	$1,520.00	$1,520.00
Beverages - Wine	$3,000.00	$3,000.00
Beverages - Other	$780.00	$780.00
Administration Overhead	$928.91	$928.91
Total Cost of Sales	$9,864.81	$9,864.81

Expense
Breakages & Replacements	$282.10	$282.10
Employees' Meals	$88.00	$88.00
Laundry and Cleaning	$860.00	$860.00
Kitchen Supplies	$192.00	$192.00
Wages & Salaries	$3,715.65	$3,715.65
Total Expense	$5,137.75	$5,137.75

Net Profit (Loss)	$4,197.44	$4,197.44

Category Profit & Loss Statement

July 2011

Page 1

Account Name	**Selected Period**	**Year to Date**

CATER   **External Catering**

Income
Catering Fees	$40,800	$40,800
Total Income	$40,800	$40,800

Cost of Sales
Food - Meat	$4,098	$4,098
Food - Vegetables	$1,178	$1,178
Food - Other	$2,497	$2,497
Beverages - Beer	$4,180	$4,180
Beverages - Wine	$5,660	$5,660
Beverages - Other	$2,080	$2,080
Administration Overhead	$2,267	$2,267
Total Cost of Sales	$21,960	$21,960

Expense
Breakages & Replacements	$782	$782
Employees' Meals	$248	$248
Laundry and Cleaning	$2,200	$2,200
Kitchen Supplies	$294	$294
Wages & Salaries	$9,066	$9,066
Allocated to Jobs	-$2,267	-$2,267
Total Expense	$10,323	$10,323

Net Profit (Loss)	$8,517	$8,517

'Category P&L Statement' continued on the next page…

9.12 *(continued)*

Page 2 of Category P&L Statement

SHOP   **Shop Sales**

Income

Food Sales	$11,542	$11,542
Total Income	$11,542	$11,542

Cost of Sales

Food - Other	$3,164	$3,164
Total Cost of Sales	$3,164	$3,164

Expense

Wages & Salaries	$1,480	$1,480
Total Expense	$1,480	$1,480
Net Profit (Loss)	$6,897	$6,897

WSALE   **Wholesale**

Income

Food Sales	$2,940	$2,940
Total Income	$2,940	$2,940

Cost of Sales

Food - Meat	$4,048	$4,048
Total Cost of Sales	$4,048	$4,048

Expense

Wages & Salaries	$2,860	$2,860
Total Expense	$2,860	$2,860
Net Profit (Loss)	-$3,968	-$3,968

APPENDIX A: Help

Please also refer to Chapter 11 on the accompanying DVD for the unabridged version of this topic.

MYOB AccountRight Plus offers numerous ways to access their help topics. The quickest method is to access the *MYOB Help* from the *Help* menu or press the function key *F1*. Alternatively, in any window, you can

- click the '*Help F1*' button usually located at the bottom of the window, and select "Help for This Window" from the shortcut menu

- right-click in a window and select *Help for This Window* option *or*
- click the question mark in the upper right corner of any command centre.

MYOB Help

MYOB Help demonstrates a very useful facility available at your fingertips. The *Help* pull-down menu is the right-most menu on the *menu bar*.

How to use the *MYOB Help*

When you activate *MYOB Help* from within any window, *MYOB AccountRight Plus* will display the help window, which consists of two panes. On the left pane is a list of available topics and on the right pane the help information relating to the item selected from the left pane.

The first item on the list is usually the 'Welcome' option, which will display an overview or an introduction on the open window or form. In addition, it will usually display a list of links to other related topics.

A 'help screen' or window contains many objects: text, diagrams, drawings and graphics, as well as icons and buttons. Some of these objects are linked to other help screens.

There are different types of text on the help screen. The normal text appears usually in black and the other types are usually displayed in blue or green and sometimes underlined. The coloured text (words or phrases) are mixed in with the normal text and they provide further help screens when you click on them. Similarly, some graphics and icons also provide further information on the relevant topics that they represent. When you move the mouse cursor over any of these objects it (the cursor) changes to a hand with a finger pointing at a topic. That indicates that they are **linked**. Linked objects, e.g. the coloured text and the graphic objects, are called *jumps* or *hyperlinks*. They cause other help screens to be displayed, and thus provide further help, if required.

Search help option:

A *Search MYOB Help* screen will be activated when you use the *Search* button at the t[...] left corner of the help screen. If you are familiar with search engines you will find this very similar, and if you are a first time user you will find this feature very *user friendl[...]* The trick is to fine tune your search outcome by being more specific in the terms of t[...] search.

Type the text to search here

Then click here

You can start a simple search by typing in the text, words or terms you wish to se[...] help on, and then click on the *Search* button. The result of the search will then eith[...] display <u>only</u> the help files that contain <u>all</u> the search words *or* <u>all</u> the files that contain a[...] <u>one</u> of these words.

Here are some 'Advanced Search' techniques:

If you enter more than one word, separate them with spaces. The text can be in upper [...] lower case – it is not case sensitive. Characters that can be entered include all letters a to[...] or A to Z in any combination and numbers 0 to 9. You may also enter dollar sign[...] commas, full stops, percentage and apostrophe characters, as well as asterisks and questic[...] marks (known as *wild cards*). The wild card (?) will substitute one character and the wi[...] card (*) will substitute any number of characters. For example, CH* will search for a[...] word that starts with "CH" such as: <u>Ch</u>apter, <u>Ch</u>ange and <u>Ch</u>aracter. The (?) in L?S[...] substitutes *any* one letter: e.g. L<u>I</u>ST, L<u>A</u>ST and L<u>O</u>ST etc.

You may specify that a word *<u>must</u>* be included in the find result, by placing a "[...] character before it such as: "Suppliers +Purchases". In this case the word "Purchase[...] must be in the find to be displayed. You can do the opposite and make sure a certain wo[...] is *<u>not</u>* included in the find by placing a 'minus' before it. For exampl[...] "Suppliers - Purchases". This will display all finds as long as they do not contain the wo[...] "Purchases".

To activate the 'Index' help window click on the *Index* option from the left par[...] (last option). At the top of the screen an A to Z index links to various topics will [...] displayed:

<u>A</u>|<u>B</u>|<u>C</u>|<u>D</u>|<u>E</u>|<u>F</u>|<u>G</u>|<u>H</u>|<u>I</u>|<u>J</u>|<u>K</u>|<u>L</u>|<u>M</u>|<u>N</u>|<u>O</u>|<u>P</u>|<u>Q</u>|<u>R</u>|<u>S</u>|<u>T</u>|<u>U</u>|<u>V</u>|<u>W</u>|<u>X</u>|<u>Y</u>|<u>Z</u>

When you click on a letter all the topics starting with that letter will be displayed [...] links. Clicking on any of these topics will activate the relative help screen.

Printing help topics

Printing any of the help screens to obtain a hard copy for future reference can be achieve[...] at any time by clicking on the 'Print' option from the File drop down menu.

APPENDIX B:
Ergonomics and OH&S

Please also refer to Chapter 10 on the accompanying DVD for the unabridged version of this topic.

Ergonomics is the study of the *relationship* between the workers, the work they perform, the working environment and the equipment they use. Its purpose is to make the work environment <u>both safe and efficient</u>. In order to maintain that balance between safety and efficiency with emphasis on the *wellness* of the worker, the ergonomist's aim is:

1. To improve the equipment used by the workers, by improving the design and quality of equipment in terms of ease of use and safety.

2. To improve the work environment by improving the safety factor. This minimises occupational hazards such as injury and in so doing you are also maximising job productivity, optimising job satisfaction and efficiency.

3. To help workers practice a better work routine. This includes: (a) adopting safer work practices, (b) recognising and avoiding work hazards, (c) better working posture, (d) rotating tasks, (e) exercising and (f) taking proper breaks.

Good posture

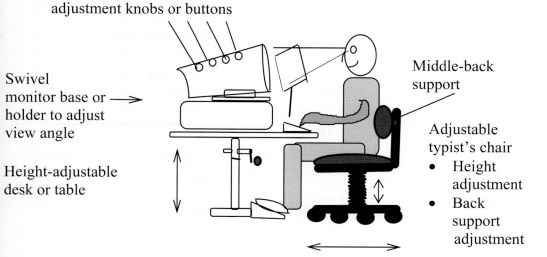

Chair on five castors for better support and stability.
Castors are necessary for horizontal adjustments.

INDEX

R

S

T

U

V

W

Z